D1591746

where the land is greener
case studies and analysis of soil and water conservation initiatives worldwide

*This book is dedicated to those women and men
who take good care of the land –
whose individual and collective efforts go, so often,
unacknowledged.*

where the land is greener

case studies and analysis of soil and water conservation initiatives worldwide

Editors
Hanspeter Liniger and William Critchley

Associate editors
Mats Gurtner
Gudrun Schwilch
Rima Mekdaschi Studer

WOCAT – World Overview of Conservation Approaches and Technologies

WOCAT 2007

Co-published by   CTA, FAO, UNEP and CDE
                       on behalf of the World Overview of Conservation Approaches and Technologies (WOCAT)

Financed by   Swiss Agency for Development and Cooperation (SDC), Bern
                       United Nations Environment Programme (UNEP), Nairobi
                       Food and Agriculture Organisation of the United Nations (FAO), Rome
                       Danish International Development Assistance (DANIDA), Copenhagen
                       Syngenta Foundation for Sustainable Agriculture, Basel
                       Technical Centre for Agricultural and Rural Cooperation ACP-EU (CTA), Wageningen

Editors   Hanspeter Liniger and William Critchley
Associate editors   Mats Gurtner, Gudrun Schwilch and Rima Mekdaschi Studer
Technical drawings   Mats Gurtner
Charts and maps   Gudrun Schwilch and Simone Kummer
Language editing   William Critchley and Theodore Wachs
Layout   Urs Amiet
Printed by   Stämpfli AG, Bern

Citation   WOCAT 2007: where the land is greener – case studies and analysis of soil and water conservation initiatives worldwide.
                       Editors: Hanspeter Liniger and William Critchley.

Copyright   WOCAT 2007

ISBN 978-92-9081-339-2

Cover photo   'where the land is greener' – a protected plot on a degraded hillside in the Varzob Valley, Tajikistan. (Hanspeter Liniger)

Co-publishers' information and disclaimers

CTA	FAO	UNEP	CDE
Postbus 380	Viale delle Terme di Caracalla	PO Box 30552	Steigerhubelstrasse 3
6700 AJ Wageningen	00100 Roma	Nairobi	3008 Bern
The Netherlands	Italy	Kenya	Switzerland
www.cta.int	www.fao.org	www.unep.org	www.cde.unibe.ch

The Technical Centre for Agricultural and Rural Cooperation (CTA) was established in 1983 under the Lomé Convention between the ACP (African, Caribbean and Pacific) Group of States and the European Union Member States. Since 2000, it has operated within the framework of the ACP-EC Cotonou Agreement. CTA's tasks are to develop and provide services that improve access to information for agricultural and rural development, and to strengthen the capacity of ACP countries to produce, acquire, exchange and utilise information in this area. CTA's programmes are designed to: provide a wide range of information products and services and enhance awareness of relevant information sources; promote the integrated use of appropriate communication channels and intensify contacts and information exchange (particularly intra-ACP); and develop ACP capacity to generate and manage agricultural information and to formulate ICM strategies, including those relevant to science and technology. CTA's work incorporates new developments in methodologies and cross-cutting issues such as gender and social capital.

Disclaimer FAO: 'The designations employed and the presentation of material in this information product do not imply the expression of any opinion whatsoever on the part of the Food and Agriculture Organisation of the United Nations concerning the legal or development or boundaries'.

FSC **Mix**
Products containing wood from responsibly
managed forests and recycled wood or fibre
www.fsc.org Cert. No. SQS-COC-23903
© 1996 Forest Stewardship Council

FEB 1 9 2007

Table of contents

Forewords

'where the land is greener' is a powerful title for a book on soil and water management. It conjures up images of where things are better – and the direction farming families want to go, literally or metaphorically. Those millions of people who make their living from soil and water, out of plants and animals, depend quite simply on vegetation. For them 'greener land' means better livelihoods; it means more food, more income – more of everything. These people need that security, since over 800 million of them are amongst the poorest on the globe.

Historically, migrating to greener land has been one of the fundamental survival strategies of farmers. However, while many may look for better land elsewhere – for 'greener pastures' – others go about 'greening' the land they already have. How do they achieve this? It is through an extraordinary deployment of physical, intellectual, social and cultural skills. They test new technologies – some invented, some copied from what they've observed elsewhere. Family traditions have been reshaped in the process. Women have talked their men into investing more time in land and less in leisure, and many women have become the intellectual masterminds of new ways to farm. These families are the true champions of sustainable, productive agricultural systems. Some have benefited from support of their governments, sometimes combined with international funding through projects. Yet the central and decisive element remains the continued effort of the families themselves.

'where the land is greener' is unique in depicting a broad range of important ways in which farming families have achieved these goals, and the contribution of support units to this process. While farmers may often be a cause of land degradation, this book deepens our understanding of how solutions cannot be arrived at without the full commitment – and creativity – of those same farmers. It helps us to understand the mechanics of this process. There is a detailed account of technologies used, the implications on family labour, soil and water use efficiency, and many other criteria. This information is crucial for professionals in their efforts to assist other farmers in 'making their land greener' and sustaining it in that condition. In an overpopulated world this may be the only realistic strategy for poor, rural families.

Martin Sommer, Head of Division Natural Resources and Environment **SDC,** Bern, Switzerland

Farming remains the dominant occupational sector in the global economy. Over one billion people are engaged in agriculture, and about 40% of the world's population – over 2.5 billion women, men and children – live in agricultural households. According to a recent international assessment, small-scale farming is the means of living for the majority of these people, and their livelihoods are intimately linked to the land they use for farming, livestock rearing and forestry. Sustainable management of the land, in economic, social and ecological terms, is thus a prerequisite for equity among those land users. This book ultimately addresses this group of land users, by providing a large sample of positive case studies from different contexts world-wide, and an analysis of why successes can be achieved by some land users, although unfortunately not by all.

'where the land is greener' is a stimulus to apply sustainable land management on all farmland, pastoral areas and forest land. It proposes appropriate technologies and approaches for areas where the land is not yet 'green enough'. But the task lies not just with the land users. A major share of food, feed, fibre and fuel is consumed by non-farming people. And what is more, this other sector of the world's population also has a major impact on natural resources. Fertile lands are being converted from agriculture to build houses, roads and factories. Biodiversity of natural and cultural plants and animals is greatly reduced by industrial development. Climate change and the degradation of the land's resources are mutually linked. 'where the land is greener' provides answers to some of these issues. Fertile soils have higher productivity and biodiversity, and better potential to absorb additional carbon. The global community at large profits from multiple agro-ecosystem services, and thus it is our responsibility to make sure that land users are empowered and enabled to invest more into their land.

WOCAT, the international programme behind the book, has been focusing on sustainable land management for many years. As chair of the World Association of Soil and Water Conservation (WASWC), I initiated WOCAT in 1992 as a new concept to link its members so that they could work together towards a common goal. Thanks to the continuous support and involvement by SDC, and many other institutions and individuals since its inception, the programme has developed and will hopefully continue to grow as a learning and sharing network that responds and adapts to evolving local and global needs.

Hans Hurni, Director **CDE,** University of Bern, Switzerland

The Land and Water Development Division of the Food and Agriculture Organization of the United Nations (FAO) has supported and collaborated with WOCAT for over ten years. Several joint efforts have contributed to the global dissemination of best practice in soil conservation. This book demonstrates that sustainable agricultural technologies are real options that contribute directly to food security and to improve living conditions of people in the rural areas.
Clemencia Licona Manzur, Soil Reclamation and Development Officer, Land and Plant Nutrition Management Service, **FAO,** Rome, Italy.

In 2006, the international community observed the International Year of Deserts and Desertification. This book follows that up, appropriately, by providing a menu of suitable technologies and approaches, that if scaled up, could generate global environmental benefits in terms of enhanced ecosystem functioning and services in drylands and other environments affected by land and water degradation.
Anna Tengberg, Senior Programme Officer Land Degradation, UNEP, Division of **GEF** Coordination, Nairobi, Kenya

This book is very timely in view of current environmental concerns. The successful technologies and approaches, collected from different ecological zones and landscapes around the world, hold potential for replication in other environments with similar characteristics. Most importantly, responding to the MDGs on poverty reduction and environmental protection, the analytical section sheds light on policy options for implementation.
Elizabeth Migongo-Bake, Environment Affairs Officer, **UNEP,** Nairobi, Kenya

WOCAT's mission is very important and we believe that this product is timely: by focusing on success stories and providing a summary of policy points this book will help us – and more broadly TerrAfrica – in our efforts to scale up sustainable land management practices throughout Sub-Saharan Africa.
Christophe Crepin, Africa Regional Coordinator, **World Bank,** Washington, USA

The 'Bright Spots' project shares common ground with WOCAT in its efforts to identify, and build on, successes in conservation of natural resources and sustainable land management. We welcome this book – which provides yet more evidence that there are ways and means of overcoming land degradation and simultaneously addressing poverty.
Deborah Bossio, Theme Leader and Principal Soil Scientist, Land, Water and Livelihoods, **IWMI** Colombo, Sri Lanka

It is a pleasure to welcome the book 'where the land is greener' which has been elaborated under a positive and stimulating approach. This volume represents an outstanding contribution towards combating land degradation. It has a global scope: sharing both scientific knowledge and invaluable practical references. The book shows how old and modern approaches could be used – with the common denominator of a more eco-efficient and more sensible use of the land.
José L. Rubio, President **ESSC,** Valencia, Spain

In agriculture, it is as important to conserve the knowledge of millions of farming families about soil and water management as it is to conserve natural resources. That is what makes WOCAT so important.
Willi Graf, Senior Advisor Natural Resources and Environment, **SDC,** Bern, Switzerland

Sustainable land management is an important prerequisite for meeting the Millennium Development Goals, and in particular those on hunger and environmental sustainability. Moreover, it is also important to mitigate climate change. We see this book as an important landmark in highlighting the possibilities of maintaining land in a productive state and making positive changes to degraded land. Denmark has actively supported WOCAT since 1999 and believes this publication is timely in giving a valuable contribution by presenting lessons learnt and making them readily available for all relevant actors.
Carsten Staur, Ambassador State Secretary, **Danida,** Ministry of Foreign Affairs, Copenhagen, Denmark

The pressure on landscapes to deliver a full range of ecosystem services to meet the growing demands of society makes the efficient sharing of knowledge and experience on better soil and water management ever more important and urgent. This is why we support WOCAT.
Andrew Bennett, Executive Director **Syngenta Foundation** for Sustainable Agriculture, Basel, Switzerland

Land degradation and related environmental catastrophes – essentially caused by man and worsened by climate change – are being felt more than ever. And now, the long awaited WOCAT global overview book is ready, documenting technologies and approaches that can help prevent or at least mitigate their effects. A timely coincidence indeed!
Samran Sombatpanit, Acting Director **WASWC,** Bangkok, Thailand

ISRIC has actively participated in the WOCAT programme since its initiation in 1992. This product is a testimony to the unique collection of SWC case studies compiled over these years. ISRIC is proud to have contributed to this important book - which helps demonstrate the importance of proper documentation and evaluation of lessons learned.
David Dent, Director **ISRIC,** Wageningen, The Netherlands

The Centre for International Cooperation of the Vrije Universiteit Amsterdam has an association with WOCAT that goes back over 10 years. This relationship fits well within our outreach mandate. And we are particularly happy to have been integral in the formulation of this book which promotes sustainable land management as a means to reduce poverty in developing countries – a goal we share.
Kees van Dongen, Director **CIS,** Vrije Universiteit Amsterdam, The Netherlands

Preface

'where the land is greener' had its origins around the turn of the new century. At that time WOCAT had been busy for just over five years with data collection and the creation of a digital database. But there was a promise in WOCAT brochures that there would be written products. It was surely time to collect and collate the 'best' case studies and analyse them – and then illustrate with some of the most striking photographs from that database. Work eventually started in 2002, but the one-year completion target finally stretched out to five. What were the reasons? Basically 'The Book', as it became familiarly known to us, developed into a sub-programme in itself. It evolved from the original proposal of compiling some 15 or so well documented and interesting technologies and approaches from the WOCAT database, to strategically seeking additional case studies to cover different conservation practices, geographical regions, land uses and production systems. The number of technologies ended up at 42. Throughout the preparation of the book, there has been a highly interactive process between the editing team and the contributors – who are scattered all over the world. There is trade–off between stakeholder consultation and timeliness.

This lengthy process, however, proved a blessing in disguise. Not only did it assist in making the book more comprehensive and ensuring quality, but it has helped WOCAT to focus on gaps in information – whether these were technologies (for example the spontaneous spread of Grevillea robusta trees in East Africa or 'Forest catchment treatment' in India) or geographical locations (for example Australia, Tajikistan and China). And has also allowed us to keep abreast of new developments: five years ago 'conservation agriculture' was a relatively little known concept outside of the Americas. Now it is spreading rapidly and we have captured examples from Australia, Kenya, Morocco, and the United Kingdom. And of course the international environmental conventions – those covering desertification, biodiversity and climate change in particular – have begun to have a marked impact on land management policy and practice. Furthermore the concepts of ecosystem services, fair trade production and 'agro-ecotourism' have grown in prominence. The Millennium Development Goals are now having an impact on development and related research. It has been possible to track these developments and integrate them into the analyses and the policy points.

It's been a long road, and there have been frustrations, but above all it has been rewarding. And, let's admit it, fun. Our editorial meetings – from Rome to Marrakech; from a chalet in the Swiss Alps to 'Room 119' in the University of Bern where it all finally came together – didn't just consist of arid soil and water conversations, but were enlivened by discovering all sorts of humorous mistakes and quirks of language: 'howlers' as we termed them. *'Toothless worms which produce flavourless manure'* was one, *'substance farmers'* another and – presumably in honour of the 2006 football World Cup – we had 'off-side impacts of SWC'. That last one nearly caused an own goal.

So many people have contributed that this is the result of a whole WOCAT community effort. Our privilege has been to coordinate and shape the final product: and we of course are ultimately responsible for any mistakes and errors. Finally, many thanks to all those who have put so much effort and time into a book we are proud of. Above all we hope that it will contribute to enlightened policy formulation, and thereby help to achieve WOCAT's goal of spreading the message of sustainable land management worldwide: a goal that we believe can, and must, be achieved.

Hanspeter Liniger and William Critchley

Acknowledgements

First of all we would like to thank the land users behind these case studies for sharing their most valuable experiences with a worldwide audience.

We are immensely grateful to the 93 contributors and contact persons of the case studies – listed on page XI – for their original descriptions and datasets, and for their tolerance in answering our multiple queries. Thanks also to the participants of the WOCAT workshops and steering meetings for reviewing the case studies.

We acknowledge the unwavering support of WOCAT's main funders – the Swiss Development Cooperation (SDC), who have confirmed their faith in WOCAT through continuous commitment that has lasted now for well over a decade. The Food and Agriculture Organisation of the United Nations (FAO) has encouraged and worked with WOCAT all along, not least in this production. Gratitude is due also to the United Nations Environment Programme (UNEP) for financial assistance and support – right at the beginning of this endeavour. DANIDA and Syngenta Foundation have also been long-term sponsors of WOCAT. World Soil Information (ISRIC) in The Netherlands is a long term partner. Thanks to all of these. A special mention should be made to Technical Centre for Agricultural and Rural Cooperation (CTA) for their very generous contribution towards printing and publication. Naturally we also thank our own institutions – the Centre for Development and Environment (CDE) of the University of Bern and the Centre for International Cooperation (CIS) of the Vrije Universiteit Amsterdam. And a special word of gratitude is due to all WOCAT's partner institutions – in particular those represented by the contributors.

All of us are indebted to Hans Hurni, who first came up with the concept of WOCAT and has been a constant source of support and inspiration over these years – not least during the compilation of this book.

Finally, we would like to acknowledge our review team by name: these are all people with a connection to WOCAT who gave us extremely valuable feedback on the analysis, conclusions and policy points in particular. So here's to Andrew Bennett, Charles Bielders, Malcolm Douglas, Markus Giger, Willi Graf, Karl Herweg, Udo Höggel, Hans Hurni, Clemencia Licona-Manzur, Godert van Lynden, Samran Sombatpanit, and Francis Turkelboom.

Contributors of the case studies and associated contact persons

Adamou, Oudou Noufou (Niger)
Agrawal, VK (India)
Akramov, U (Tajikistan)
Asanaliev, Abdybek (Kyrgyzstan)
Ash, Andrew (Australia)
Bai, Zhangou (People's Republic of China)
Barac, Anuschka (South Africa)
Bhattarai, Ramanand (Nepal)
Bhuchar, Sanjeev (Nepal)
Bielders, Charles (Belgium)
Boturov, U (Tajikistan)
Bruggeman, Adriana (Syria)
Budaychiev, Dair (Kyrgyzstan)
Caceres, Ramón (Nicaragua)
Caicedo, Eduardo (Colombia)
Critchley, William (The Netherlands)
Cuervo, Jairo (Colombia)
Danano, Daniel (Ethiopia)
Datta, Sumana (India)
Douglas, Malcolm (United Kingdom)
Ergashev, Murod (Tajikistan)
Gandhi, David (India)
Gitonga, Jeremiah Njeru Lewis (Kenya)
Gómez Martínez, Julio César (Nicaragua)
Grimshaw, Dick (USA)
Güdel, Nicole (Switzerland)
Gurtner, Mats (Switzerland)
Hai, Chunxing (People's Republic of China)
He, Yu (People's Republic of China)
Heim, Georg (Switzerland)
Jones, Ceris (United Kingdom)
Karna, Dileep K (Nepal)
Kihara, Frederick (Kenya)
Kiteme, Boniface (Kenya)
Kumar, Chetan (India)
La Rovere, Roberto (Syria)
Leake, Alastair R (United Kingdom)
Ledermann, Thomas (Switzerland)
Liniger, Hanspeter (Switzerland)
Liu, Baoyuan (People's Republic of China)
Liu, Zhengming (People's Republic of China)
Lougue, Maria (Burkina Faso)
Mahamadkarimova, S (Tajikistan)
Mahood, Kirsten (South Africa)
Malla, Indra Bahadur (Nepal)
Marquina, Rodolfo (Peru)
Masri, Zuhair (Syria)

Maxime, Robert (South Africa)
Mburu, Joseph (Kenya)
McGarry, Des (Australia)
Mejia Marcacuzco, Aquilino P (Peru)
Mekdaschi Studer, Rima (Switzerland)
Mercado, Agustin Jr (Philippines)
van der Merwe, Rinda (South Africa)
Miiro, Henry Dan (Uganda)
Mongalo, Reinerio (Nicaragua)
Moussa, Bonzi (Burkina Faso)
Mrabet, Rachid (Morocco)
Mutunga, Kithinji (Kenya)
Mwaniki, John Munene (Kenya)
Nayak, T (India)
Nekushoeva, G (Tajikistan)
Nie, Bijuan (People's Republic of China)
Njuki, James (Kenya)
Ouedraogo, Elisée (Burkina Faso)
de Pury, Jean Pascal Etienne (France)
Quiros Madrigal, Olman (Costa Rica)
Rodriguez, Roger (Nicaragua)
Rondal, Jose (Philippines)
Rozanov, Andrei (South Africa)
Sadangi, Amitabha (India)
Sanginov, Sanginboy (Tajikistan)
Schwilch, Gudrun (Switzerland)
Sharif, Aliev and family (Tajikistan)
Sombatpanit, Samran (Thailand)
Suksom, Prason (Thailand)
Sydykbaev, Talant (Kyrgyzstan)
Tabarov, Abdugaffor (Tajikistan)
Thomas, Donald (Kenya)
Tielkes, Eric (Germany)
Tubeileh, Ashraf (Syria)
Turkelboom, Francis (Syria)
Ulloa Mercado, Eneida (Nicaragua)
Vargas, Ivan (Bolivia)
Varghese, Paul (India)
Verma, Shilp (India)
Wang, Dongmei (People's Republic of China)
Wang, Yaoling (People's Republic of China)
Webster, Anthony (Australia)
Wen, Meili (People's Republic of China)
Wolfgramm, Bettina (Switzerland)
Yang, Xuezhen (People's Republic of China)
Zöbisch, Michael (Germany)

WOCAT ■ where the land is greener

Policy points – *guiding the process*

As a summary of the book's main messages we present a consolidated list of policy points. These are reproduced from chapter 4 where they are supported by conclusions. The conclusions in turn are drawn from analysis of the 42 worldwide case studies presented in this book – and further informed by WOCAT's broader database. Some of the policy points that follow are new; others reconfirm what is already known but deserves re-emphasising. These guidelines have clear implications for planners and decision-makers in governments and development agencies. Realigning soil and water conservation policy is crucial in addressing land degradation: this is a prerequisite for achieving sustainable land management and improving livelihoods.

Knowledge management – the basis for decision support

■ Concerted efforts to standardise documentation and evaluation of SWC technologies and approaches are needed and fully justified, especially in the light of the billions of dollars spent annually on implementation.

■ To assure the quality and usefulness of information, scattered knowledge about SWC needs to be identified, documented and assessed through a thorough and interactive review process that involves the joint efforts of land users, technical specialists and researchers.

■ Once documented, experiences with SWC need to be made widely available and accessible in a form that allows land users, advisors and planners to review a 'basket' of alternative options, setting out the advantages and disadvantages of each, thereby enabling them to make informed choices rather than following set prescriptions of 'what to do'.

■ The implementation of new SWC efforts should build on existing knowledge from within a location itself or, alternatively, from similar conditions and environments elsewhere.

■ There is need for a standardised methodology – like the WOCAT tools – to facilitate comprehensive data collection, knowledge management and dissemination.

Monitoring and evaluation – *a prerequisite to improve SWC and justify investments*

■ Monitoring and evaluation in SWC projects/ programmes must be improved. It needs to do more than just monitor the timely delivery of project outputs; it should also evaluate whether the expected environmental and development benefits have been realised in a cost-effective manner.

■ Rigorous impact assessment, involving the evaluation of strengths and how to sustain them, as well as evaluation of weaknesses and how to overcome them, is a must.

■ Land users have to be involved as key actors in monitoring and evaluation activities: their judgement of the pros and cons of SWC interventions is crucial.

■ There is a need to develop mechanisms to monitor and evaluate local conservation practices, land management innovations and traditional land use systems.

■ More investment in training and capacity building is needed for objective and unbiased monitoring and evaluation, for impact assessment, and to improve skills in knowledge management including the dissemination and use of information.

■ Mapping of conservation coverage is essential, in order to visualise the extent and effectiveness of human achievements.

left: Rainfed terraces in the Anti Atlas mountain range of Morocco. (Hanspeter Liniger)

right: An international group taking a keen interest in a Nepalese farmer who is enjoying explaining improvements she has made to her land. (Hanspeter Liniger)

Complexity and knowledge gaps – *the role of research*

- There are no simple 'silver bullet' solutions to the complex problems of land degradation. It is therefore important to understand the ecological, social and economic causes of, and processes behind, degradation, to analyse what works and why, and how to modify and adapt particular technologies and approaches to locally specific circumstances and opportunities.

- Technologies and associated approaches need to be flexible and responsive to changing complex ecological and socio-economic environments.

- An urgent and specific area for further investigations and research is quantification and valuation of the ecological, social and economic impacts of SWC, both on-site and off-site, including the development of methods for the valuation of ecosystem services.

- SWC research should seek to incorporate land users, scientists from different disciplines and decision-makers. A continuous feedback mechanism is needed to ensure active participation of these stakeholders.

- Researchers need to take a more active role in further development of tools and methods for knowledge exchange and improved decision support.

Soil and water conservation technologies – *measures and their impacts*

- Given limited financial and human resources, more attention should be focused on the prevention and mitigation of degradation before investing in areas that require costly rehabilitation, even though the achievements may not be so visible.

- Promotion of SWC technologies that lead to improved management of natural resources - soil, water and vegetation - has the potential not only to reduce land degradation but also to address simultaneously global concerns of water scarcity, land use conflicts, climate change (through carbon sequestration), biodiversity conservation, and poverty alleviation.

- Continued, sustained investments in optimising and adapting technologies to their specific environments as well as recognising innovative improvements are needed.

- In dry areas, investments in water harvesting and improved water use efficiency, combined with improved soil fertility management, should be emphasised to increase production, reduce the risk of crop failure, and lower the demand for irrigation water.

- In humid areas, long-term investments are required to maintain soil fertility and minimise on-site and off-site damage caused by soil erosion, as the impacts on production and conservation may only accrue in the medium and long term.

- Agronomic and vegetative measures should be given priority as they are cheaper than structures, often result in rapid increases in yield, and provide additional benefits such as soil cover, soil structure and soil fertility improvements.

- Structural measures should be promoted primarily for extra support where other measures are not sufficient on their own.

- Management measures are especially important on grazing land, where they should be considered as the initial intervention to achieve the major aim of SWC: namely to increase ground cover, and to improve species composition and productivity.

- Combined SWC measures – overlapping, or spaced over a catchment/ landscape, or over time - tend to be the most versatile and the most effective in difficult situations: they are worthy of more emphasis.

Land use types – *cropland, mixed land, grazing land and forest*

- There is a need for continued SWC investments in cropland and mixed land, because of intensification and farming expanding into more marginal and vulnerable areas. Special attention needs to be given to rainfed farming, without neglecting irrigated cropland.

- Grazing land – and especially communally used areas in dry degradation-prone environments – is a priority for attention with regard to its neglected potential for increased production, and provision of on-site and off-site ecosystem services.

- Agroforestry and improved forest management need to be further recognised and promoted due to their multi-purpose functions, which go well beyond conservation – including biodiversity, provision of fuel/construction wood and other forest products.

Soil and water conservation approaches –
supporting and stimulating implementation

- More attention and support should be given to local innovation as well as to traditional systems, rather than focussing solely on project-based SWC implementation of standard technologies.

- Further efforts are needed to identify appropriate SWC technologies that assist small-scale and subsistence farmers to improve their livelihoods and escape from the poverty trap.

- Project/ programme interventions need to break out of the typical three-year project cycle and commit to a minimum of five years, and preferably ten or more. SWC requires long-term commitment from national and international implementation and research institutions. A clear strategy is needed to sustain results beyond the project life-time.

- Partnership alliances need to be developed between different agencies – with their various SWC initiatives and interventions – for synergy of efforts and cost-effectiveness.

Profitability and enabling environment –
motivating the land users

- SWC needs to be stimulated by further emphasising improved production (of plants and animals) and reduced costs, which are the primary interest of land users, and have direct consequences on livelihoods in small-scale subsistence farming.

- Accurate assessment of costs and benefits (in monetary and non-monetary terms) – using participatory and trans-disciplinary methods – is urgently needed to evaluate SWC technologies in terms of their short- and long-term gains: without this, land users and development agencies cannot make informed decisions about which technologies and approaches are the most viable options.

- To help prevent off-site damage, further on-site investment in SWC is required: this is usually cheaper and more effective than dealing with the downstream consequences.

- An enabling environment should be nurtured for SWC to thrive best, building on people's and nature's capacity. Indirect measures such as credit, market opportunities or legislation to stimulate conservation activities must not be overlooked.

- Security of land use rights is important in conservation: policies to improve the rights of individual land users and/or rural communities to use their local land resources on a secure and long-term basis must be recognised as an important means of supporting SWC.

- Opportunities need to be seized that connect SWC with emerging environmental priorities – especially carbon sequestration (by increasing soil organic matter), biodiversity (above and below ground), water and ecosystem service provision. Ways of recognition and payment for these services need to be further explored to justify SWC investments.

- The benefits of improved land management for water quantity and quality must be further stressed and used as a motivation for SWC, especially in areas of water scarcity and water-related conflicts.

- Access to local and international markets has to be improved to enable producers to make SWC investments in their land. Fair prices, certification, and labelling schemes for products can further stimulate conservation.

Subsidising SWC –
the delicate issue of direct incentives

- SWC may require heavy investment costs that exceed the capacity of local land users and thus need to be covered by national and international initiatives. But direct material incentives should – in principle – only be considered where there is a need to overcome initial investment constraints and subsequent maintenance does not require continued support. This may be needed where the environmental improvements and social benefits are likely to be realised only in the long term.

left: Terraces in Machakos District, Kenya: significant soil and water conservation investment for crop production in a semi-arid area. (Hanspeter Liniger)

centre: Improving pasture and grazing management needs further attention as degradation rates remain high: marginal mountains areas, eg Tien Shan, Kyrgyzstan, not only secure livelihoods for people by directly providing resources, but also help protect the lowlands. (Hanspeter Liniger)

right: The value of agroforestry systems for production and protection of land needs to be further recognised. Here, together with local farmers, students are documenting an agroforestry technology developed during Soviet times in Central Asia – but recently modified and adapted by land users. (Peter Niederer)

- Before considering the use of direct incentives, alternative approaches should be explored, such as the adaptation of technologies, or the identification of cheaper technologies. The possibilities of removing some of the root causes of land degradation (related to, for example, land policy framework, land tenure security and market access) also need to be assessed.

- Rural areas may need and deserve compensation from urban/ industrial zones for the environmental and aesthetic/ recreational services they provide. And downstream beneficiaries of the environmental protection provided by upstream communities if possible should be prepared to pay compensation for these services.

- The value of the ecosystem services needs to be determined and agreed upon between users and providers. The establishment of compensation schemes may require support and guidance from policy level and external actors.

- Provision of microcredit at concessionary rates for better land management/ SWC requires serious consideration, as an alternative to handouts and payments, where farmers have financial constraints.

Extension, training and adoption –
building capacity and spreading the message

- On the basis of standardised tools and methods, training in proper documentation, evaluation and dissemination of SWC knowledge, as well as its use for and improved decision-making, needs to be strengthened.

- Investment in training and extension to support the capacity of land users and other local and national stakeholders must be a priority to adapt better to changing environmental, social and economic conditions, and to stimulate innovation.

- Local innovation and farmer-to-farmer extension should be promoted as effective and appropriate strategies.

Overall policy –
investing in soil and water conservation for ecosystems, society and the economy

- Investment in rural areas and SWC is a local concern, a national interest, and a global obligation. Thus it must be given priority:
  - at the local level: to increase income, improve food security, and sustain natural resources – thus helping to alleviate poverty in areas where the livelihoods of the majority depend on agricultural production;
  - at the global and national level: to safeguard natural resources and ecosystem services and in many cases to preserve cultural heritage.

- Investments in SWC must be carefully assessed and planned on the basis of properly documented experiences and evaluated impacts and benefits: concerted efforts are needed and sufficient resources must be mobilised to tap the wealth of knowledge and learn from SWC successes. These investments will give 'value for money' in economic, ecological and social terms.

left: Heavy storms without good soil protection can trigger landslides, as in the Varzob Valley of Tajikistan, blocking and damaging roads, and causing damage to houses. The impacts of such events are multiple, from on-site damage to the land, to destruction of public infrastructure, pollution of rivers and sedimentation of reservoirs. (Hanspeter Liniger)

centre: Enhancing the capacity for the documentation and evaluation of SWC knowledge during a training workshop in Tanzania: specialists are working with land users to enter knowledge into a database. The next step is to utilise this information for decision support. (Hanspeter Liniger)

right: Monitoring of land use change and the spread of soil and water conservation are rarely carried out efficiently: this is an exception from Bolivia. (Georg Heim)

Part 1

Grass emerging through crusted soil in Morocco – regreening is possible even in seemingly hopeless situations. (Hanspeter Liniger)

Analysis and policy implications

1 Introduction – *from hotspots to green spots*

Where the land is greener – *land users showing the way*

All over the world there are examples of winners in the struggle against land degradation. They are to be found on the gentle green hills of south-west Uganda and in the heat and aridity of Madhya Pradesh in India; they are present on the coastal sugar cane belt of far north Queensland, Australia and within the mountainous heights of Colca in Peru. Whether laying down 'trash lines' across the slope, digging water harvesting pits in dry stream beds, carpeting the ground with green cane mulch or rehabilitating thousand-year-old terraces, there is a common denominator: the land users leading the way in making the land greener. However, these positive soil and water conservation efforts – spontaneous or project-based – are hidden away and local achievements are not recorded, let alone documented and disseminated in a systematic way. There are lessons 'out there' that deserve recognition, and can help guide others to conserve or rehabilitate their land, raise production, and

improve rural livelihoods. That is the rationale for the World Overview of Conservation Approaches and Technologies (WOCAT) at large – and this book in particular. 'where the land is greener' presents case studies, encompassing both technologies and their supporting approaches with analyses of these, and provides conclusions and associated policy points for action.

Land degradation and success stories – *the context of the book*

A word about land degradation is required to set the context for this book – and WOCAT in general. At the end of the 1980s the GLASOD (Global Assessment of Soil Degradation) map was produced depicting the extent of soil degradation worldwide (see box below). Based on 'expert opinion' it never claimed absolute accuracy, but what it achieved was to put the scale of the problem in the public arena. It was then used as evidence to support the creation of the UN

Global Assessment of Soil Degradation (GLASOD)

The GLASOD project set out to map global soil degradation. The assessment was based on 'expert opinion' – the perception of experts on the status of soil degradation in the country or region they were familiar with. Resultant statistics were based on continental trends and revealed that erosion by water is the most prominent degradation feature worldwide. Various forms of 'chemical deterioration', such as soil fertility decline and soil pollution, and 'physical deterioration', such as compaction and waterlogging, account for smaller areas. The GLASOD study was the first comprehensive soil degradation overview at the global scale. It raised awareness of various further needs, namely:
- the need for an assessment of measures to control degradation;
- the need for a more objective/quantitative approach (especially for more detailed scales);
- the need for data validation and updating.

Human-induced soil degradation in the world (million hectares)

Type	Light		Moderate		Strong		Extreme		Total	
Water erosion	343.2		526.7		217.2		6.6		1093.7	(55.6%)
Wind erosion	268.6		253.6		24.3		1.9		548.3	(27.9%)
Chemical deterioration	93.0		103.3		41.9		0.8		239.1	(12.2%)
Physical deterioration	44.2		26.8		12.3		–		83.3	(4.2%)
Totals	749.0	(38%)	910.4	(46%)	295.7	(15%)	9.3	(1%)	1964.4	(100%)

Source: (Oldeman et al, 1991)

left: A protected plot of land in the Varzob Valley, close to Dushanbe, Tajikistan, surrounded by degraded grazing land on an eroded hillside. This productive 'green spot' is planted with fruit trees and grass for haymaking. It went previously unnoticed and unappreciated until documented by WOCAT. (Hanspeter Liniger)

right: Another example of a 'green spot' from Colombia: an integrated agroforestry system where several soil and water conservation measures have been combined to rehabilitate formerly degraded land and bring it back into production. (Mats Gurtner)

WOCAT

The World Overview of Conservation Approaches and Technologies (WOCAT) is a **global network** of soil and water conservation specialists which was initiated in 1992. WOCAT is organised as a consortium of national and international institutions and operates in a decentralised manner, through initiatives at regional and national levels, with back-stopping from a management group.

WOCAT's **vision** is that existing knowledge of sustainable land management is shared and used globally to improve livelihoods and the environment.

WOCAT's **mission** is to support decision-making and innovation in sustainable land management by:
- connecting stakeholders
- enhancing capacity
- developing and applying standardised tools for the documentation, evaluation, monitoring and exchange of soil and water conservation knowledge

The **target group** comprises soil and water conservation (SWC) specialists, planners and decision-makers at the field and planning levels.

WOCAT's **tools** include three comprehensive questionnaires and a database system which cover all relevant aspects of SWC technologies and approaches, including area coverage.
WOCAT's **database** currently comprises datasets on 350 technologies and 225 approaches, of which a subset of 135 technologies and 75 approaches are quality assured. The WOCAT knowledge base is in the public domain. Results and outputs are accessible in digital form, either via the internet (www.wocat.net) or on CD-ROM. 'where the land is greener' is the first book compiled by WOCAT at the global level.

Definitions used by WOCAT

Sustainable Land Management (SLM): 'the use of land resources, including soils, water, animals and plants, for the production of goods to meet changing human needs, while simultaneously ensuring the long-term productive potential of these resources and ensuring their environmental functions'.
Soil and Water Conservation (SWC): 'activities at the local level which maintain or enhance the productive capacity of the land in areas affected by, or prone to, degradation'.
SWC Technologies: 'agronomic, vegetative, structural and/or management measures that prevent and control land degradation and enhance productivity in the field'.
SWC Approaches: 'ways and means of support that help introduce, implement, adapt and apply SWC technologies on the ground'.

Convention to Combat Desertification at the Rio Conference of 1992 – desertification being defined under that convention as land degradation in arid, semi-arid and dry subhumid areas. But simultaneously GLASOD lent support to the dominant environmental discourse – that of a downward spiral of land degradation which was perceived as being widespread and pervasive, particularly in the developing world.

WOCAT was originally conceived as an exercise to redress the balance towards achievements. A network was then established to document conservation efforts and to help spread the positive messages of how land can be managed sustainably. WOCAT is, furthermore, a tool to help in monitoring and evaluation of soil and water conservation efforts (see box WOCAT). With respect to new developments in monitoring land degradation, the Food and Agriculture Organisation of the United Nations (FAO), the United Nations Environment Programme (UNEP) and other partners – including WOCAT – are working towards a more comprehensive and scientifically based global assessment of land degradation through the Land Degradation Assessment in Drylands (LADA) project. LADA is funded by the Global Environment Facility (GEF). Among other objectives LADA aims to identify 'hot spots' (problem areas) and 'bright spots' (conservation successes). It is in the 'bright spots' context that WOCAT will feed into the LADA process. The WOCAT network, its database, CD-ROMs and now this book, provide multiple examples of these 'bright spots' or 'green spots'. WOCAT's next challenge is to produce a map which is, so to speak, a mirror image of GLASOD and a complement to the LADA project: in other words a global assessment of conservation and sustainable land management practices.

This book is based on case studies. But even the 42 presented here cannot give a comprehensive overview of SWC worldwide. Nevertheless, they do show a very wide variety of possibilities, complementing other documented success stories, amongst which the WOCAT database is unmatched elsewhere in the field of soil and water conservation. This book essentially presents a sample of that database. Table 1 (page 11) compares some other initiatives which have, similarly, collected success stories.

Compilation of case studies – *the methodology used*

'where the land is greener' represents the result of a process based on selection of case studies, documentation of these and a quality assurance procedure. First, criteria were

Table 1: Success stories and best practices: some recent examples

	Title/ Organisation	Date/ Duration	Region	Technical Focus	Database/ product	Number of cases	Comment
1	'Success Stories' UNEP	1994–02	Global	Success against desertification	'BSGN' database and book	24 (in book)	Based on submissions from the field
2	'Bright Spots' IWMI	2001–04	Global	Sustainable agriculture	Database/ book	286	Mainly secondary data + brief questionnaire
3	'Success Stories in Africa's Drylands' GM-CCD	2003	Africa	Agriculture/rural development in drylands	Documented in report	15	Analysis of projects and interventions from existing data
4	NRM Tracker/Frame USAid	1998–04	Africa	Community-based natural resource management	Database with documents and web resources	185	Based on NRM Tracker questionnaire, now included in FRAMEweb
5	'Building on Successes in African Agriculture' IFPRI	2003–04	Africa	Agricultural systems	Documented in report	08	Syntheses of detailed existing case studies
6	'Ecoagriculture' (McNeely & Scherr, 2003)	N/a	Global	Sustainable ecosystems	Case studies in book	36 (in book)	Analysis based on mainly secondary information
7	Global database of Conservation Approaches and Technologies WOCAT	1992 ongoing	Global	Soil and water conservation/ Sustainable land management	Internet database/ CD-ROM/ book	350 in database (135 quality controlled)	Detailed database from questionnaires at 3 different levels
8	'where the land is greener' WOCAT	2007	Global	Soil and water conservation/ Sustainable land management	Case studies and analysis in book	42 (with 28 associated approaches)	Selected from the overall WOCAT database

Note: see end of chapter for references

defined to select successes: examples of 'where the land is greener'. The intention was to collect case studies where:
- datasets were complete;
- cases were representative of main land use types;
- major degradation types were covered;
- a wide variety of soil and water conservation technologies could be shown;
- the geographical spread was broad; and
- project-based, traditional and spontaneous practices were all represented.

Data were collected by using the standardised WOCAT questionnaires, which were filled in by local contributors. A total of 92 women and men were involved in providing the data for the case studies. They are, for the most part, specialists in the field of soil and water conservation. Some are grassroots development workers/ field technicians (from non-governmental and government organisations alike); others are researchers. They are from both 'developing' and 'devel-

oped' countries. Typically these are the people with first-hand knowledge of a land management system, and people who want to 'tell their story'. When project personnel provide the information, they are in a privileged position with respect to data access, but inevitably there may be some 'wishful thinking' or a degree of self-interest involved in some of the answers given. An outsider describing a non-project related technology has a more difficult task, but s/he may be free of the bias that is sometimes associated with an 'inside job'.

The information compiled through the WOCAT questionnaires was put into an attractive four-page summary format. Quality was assured through a long review process: knowledge gaps, inconsistencies and contradictions were dealt with through an interactive process with the contributors to the book. This constituted a learning process for all involved and was an enriching and stimulating process. A final note on challenges faced when preparing the case studies is that,

left: Documenting information about terraces on the Loess Plateau, Gansu Province, PR China: a land user sharing his field expertise with specialists. (Hanspeter Liniger)

centre: Documentation of an agroforestry system in the field using WOCAT questionnaires: Two SWC specialists interview a Kyrgyz farmer. (Hanspeter Liniger)

right: Compiling and entering knowledge from the field into the database in Syria: quality is assured through querying data. (Hanspeter Liniger)

in some cases, projects have proven to be 'moving targets', changing and developing so rapidly that information quickly became out-of-date. Thus many of the case studies bear two dates: the date of original data collection and an 'update' when final information was contributed.

Objectives and target groups –
defining the focus

The main aim of the book is to highlight and analyse cases of sustainable land management from various parts of the world. It seeks to demonstrate that there *are* possibilities of maintaining land in a productive state, improving conditions where there has been degradation, and rehabilitating badly degraded land. Links are drawn to the Millennium Development Goals, to the various global environmental conventions – on desertification, climate change and biodiversity – and to the pervasive issue of poverty, and particularly rural poverty. It should be noted that the book is not intended to be a manual on SWC. The case studies are a collation of real-life examples from the field.

A secondary aim is to provide and promote a prototype for documentation of knowledge at national and regional levels. WOCAT has long supported and encouraged data collection, and attempted to stimulate interest in documentation, evaluation and dissemination of knowledge as a means for monitoring the success of land management practices. We hope that this book will encourage the compilation of national and regional soil and water conservation achievements and experiences, and the production of overviews. The four-page formats for the presentation of case studies, which are based on the WOCAT basic questionnaires, can act as a basis for further systematic compilation to maintain consistency and aid comparison. The consequent inventories and analyses will provide a reliable basis for decision-making – at local, national and regional levels.

The target audience of 'where the land is greener' comprises all those concerned with sustainable land management and rural development in general. The case studies are accessible to a very wide range of stakeholders: rural development and SWC specialists, field extension workers, and land users themselves. The analyses will be most relevant to academics, researchers and students as well as SWC specialists. The policy points are specifically formulated for planners and decision-makers in governments and development agencies.

Structure and content –
from case studies to policy points

'where the land is greener' has resulted from the challenge of presenting the evidence in an accessible way. This evolved into the collation of representative, positive experiences in a standardised and attractive format – a four-page summary for each technology, and for each approach. Graphics and photographs are used to illustrate the cases. Before the presentation of the case studies in Part 2 of the book, an analysis brings out the main messages and is the basis for the conclusions and policy points.

Case studies

The case studies each describe a technical intervention in conjunction with a specific approach for a given situation, by an on-the-ground specialist. In total we present 42 technologies, and 28 of these are completed by corresponding approaches. Where a technology has been promoted under a project or programme, the approach has been relatively easy to describe. However, where the technology is a tradition or a local innovation that has spontaneously spread, the approach description is not straightforward. That is one of the reasons why some contributors have described a technology without its corresponding approach.

Six continents and twenty-three countries are represented. There are examples from arid plains as well as humid mountains; from poor and from rich areas. Technologies range from ancient and durable traditions to cutting-edge innovation. Furthermore, there is a span of degradation types such as soil erosion, desertification, compaction, fertility decline, water and vegetation degradation. The technologies to deal with them represent a wide array, encompassing agronomic, vegetative, structural and management measures. Some technologies are relatively well known and established, others little known and emerging.

Technologies – as explained in the analytical chapter – have been clustered into groups that are familiar to specialists and land users alike: 'Agroforestry', 'Conservation agriculture', 'Terraces', 'Manuring/ composting', 'Water harvesting', 'Vegetative strips/ cover', 'Gully rehabilitation', 'Grazing land management', and 'Other technologies'. These are described on page 20 and 21. On the other hand, each approach described is unique and we have therefore not attempted to group them. The examples range from top-down to participatory and spontaneous approaches.

Analysis

The analysis of the case studies has been divided into (a) technologies and (b) approaches. In each case the analysis follows (as far as possible) the sequence within the case studies. We have used charts and tables to illustrate several of the quantifiable indicators, and have interpreted the data to bring out important points. The analyses of the case studies have been enriched with knowledge of additional technologies and approaches worldwide – from the WOCAT database, and from that collected during WOCAT training workshops. It is important to stress that the case studies analysed do not represent a 'random sample' from which statistical significance can be drawn. What the analyses do provide, however, is an insight into common denominators of what are (for the great majority) successful and/or widespread examples of natural resource management. The intention was to avoid the temptation of merely presenting 'good-news narratives' in the form of case studies but to provide a balanced critique of these examples leading to solid conclusions and practical policy guidance. What is unique about such analyses of approaches and technologies is that they draw on a very wide range of examples, and are not restricted to one region of the world, to a single land use system – or just to projects that are dedicated exclusively to SWC. The analyses are as comprehensive as possible given the data available.

Conclusions and policy points

While the case studies form the foundation of the book and the analyses help in understanding the various parameters, the conclusions distil the most important issues. Not all of these conclusions are novel. Many are not surprising: some are merely reinforcements of what has been known for a long time. Others, however, are new. From the conclusions, and supported by them, emerge the policy points. We believe these associated policy points are worthy of urgent attention. After fifteen years of working with practitioners and specialists from all over the world, this is now an opportunity for WOCAT to offer pointers on better policy in the field of soil and water conservation – in order to help answer the question: *how best should money be spent to achieve sustainable land management and environmental protection – while improving the livelihoods of people in rural areas?*

References in Table 1

(1) United Nations Environment Programme (2002). *Success stories in the struggle against desertification.* UNEP, Nairobi, Kenya

(2) www.iwmi.cgiar.org/brightspots

(3) Reij C and Steeds D (2003). *Success stories in Africa's drylands: supporting advocates and answering critics.* Global Mechanism of the Convention to Combat Desertification

(4) Page K and Ramamonjisoa N (2002). *NRM Tracker Review: Examples of Local-Level Initiatives from Sub-Saharan Africa.* IRG, Washington, USA. www.frameweb.org

(5) Haggblade S (editor) (2004). *Building on successes in African agriculture.* Focus 12, Brief 1 of 10, IFPRI. www.ifpri.org

(6) McNeely JA and Scherr SJ (2003). *Ecoagriculture.* Island Press, Washington, D.C., USA

(7) www.wocat.net

Other References:

LADA: http://lada.virtualcentre.org
Oldeman LR, Hakkeling RTA and Sombroek WG (1991). *World Map of the Status of Human-Induced Soil Degradation.* An Explanatory Note. Global Assessment of Soil Degradation (GLASOD), October 1991. Second Revised Edition. Wageningen: International Soil Reference and Information Centre (ISRIC) und United Nations Environment Programme (UNEP)

left: Traditional stone bunds in the Anti Atlas mountains of Morocco: there are many lessons to be learned from traditions of soil and water conservation. (Hanspeter Liniger)

centre: Vineyards in Switzerland that are planted up and down the slope to facilitate access with machines: despite this the soil is well protected due to permanent green cover between the vines. (Hanspeter Liniger)

right: Hillside terraces in the Philippines are a 'living tradition'. Note that in the top left corner the terrace wall is being extended with stones carried up from the riverbed in the valley below. (William Critchley)

WOCAT ■ where the land is greener

2 Analysis of technologies – *what works where, and why*

Introduction – *definitions and overview*

According to WOCAT, SWC technologies are defined as 'agronomic, vegetative, structural and/or management measures that prevent and control land degradation and enhance productivity in the field'. In this chapter, the technologies presented in the case studies are analysed and evaluated. It is important to reiterate that the 42 case studies are neither a random sample, nor strictly representative of SWC activities worldwide. Selection was based on other criteria, as explained in the introduction. The case studies span a broad range of successful experience representing different production systems, land use types, climatic conditions and geographical zones. Some of the technologies are widespread; others are innovative and isolated. While the overall WOCAT database has been used to support our arguments, the figures presented are constructed from the case study data alone.

The sequence adopted basically follows that used in the case studies. After an explanation of the grouping of technologies and their constituent measures through an overview table, we continue with sections on land use and forms of land degradation addressed. There is then a description of the main soil and water conservation technologies and measures involved, with their various functions and impacts. This is followed by a section on the environmental context – both natural and human – and concludes with an assessment of impacts, both economic and ecological.

Measures, Technologies, Case Studies and Groups (as defined by WOCAT)

SWC **measures** fall into 4 categories: agronomic (eg mulching), vegetative (eg contour grass strips), structural (eg check dams) or management measures (eg resting of land).

Measures are components of SWC **technologies**. For instance, a terracing system is a technology which typically comprises structural measures – the terrace riser, bed and a drainage ditch – combined with other measures, such as grass on the risers for stabilisation and fodder (a vegetative measure), or contour ploughing (an agronomic measure).

The 42 **case studies** in this book comprise technologies, the majority with related approaches. The technologies are built up from (in most cases – but not all) various measures.

For the purposes of the book: the technologies are clustered into nine **groups** – 'Water harvesting', 'Agroforestry' etc – which are common names, familiar to most SWC and rural development specialists.

The nine technology groups basically cover all the main types of soil and water conservation systems – though there are certain exceptions, such as shifting cultivation/ fallow systems which would form a group of their own but have not been described in our case studies. The 42 case studies are listed in Table 2, by group.

left: Traditional irrigated paddy rice terraces in Bali, Indonesia, make steep and vulnerable slopes productive – they are simultaneously a tourist attraction. (Hanspeter Liniger)

right: Sustainable land management: a productive and well conserved mixed farm growing tea, coffee, bananas, fodder, grass and grevillea trees in Embu District, Kenya. (William Critchley)

Table 2: Case studies/ technologies by group

Group / Case study/ technology	Country	Climatic zone				Land use type						Degradation type						Conservation measure				Intervention type		
		arid	semi-arid	subhumid	humid	annual crops	perennial crops	grazing land	forest	mixed	other[1]	water erosion	wind erosion	chemical deterioration	physical deterioration	vegetation degrad.	water degradation	agronomic	vegetative	structural	management	prevention	mitigation	rehabilitation
1 Conservation agriculture																								
No-till technology	Morocco																							
Conservation agriculture	UK																							
Small-scale conservation tillage	Kenya																							
No-till with controlled traffic	Australia																							
Green cane trash blanket	Australia																							
2 Manuring/ composting																								
Vermiculture	Nicaragua																							
Composting/ planting pits	Burkina Faso																							
Improved trash lines	Uganda																							
3 Vegetative strips/ cover																								
Natural vegetative strips	Philippines																							
Green cover in vineyards	Switzerland																							
Vetiver grass lines	South Africa																							
4 Agroforestry																								
Shelterbelts	P.R. China																							
Grevillea agroforestry system	Kenya																							
Poplar trees for bio-drainage	Kyrgyzstan																							
Multi-storey cropping	Philippines																							
Intensive agroforestry system	Colombia																							
Shade-grown coffee	Costa Rica																							
Conversion of grazing land	Tajikistan																							
Orchard-based agroforestry	Tajikistan																							
5 Water harvesting																								
Sunken streambed structure	India																							
Planting pits and stone lines	Niger																							
Furrow-enhanced runoff harvesting	Syria																							
6 Gully rehabilitation																								
Check dams from stem cuttings	Nicaragua																							
Gully control and catchment protection	Bolivia																							
Landslip and stream bank stabilisation	Nepal																							
7 Terraces																								
Stone wall bench terraces	Syria																							
Rehabilitation of ancient terraces	Peru																							
Traditional stone wall terraces	South Africa																							
Fanya juu terraces	Kenya																							
Small level bench terraces	Thailand																							
Orchard terraces with bahia grass cover	PR China																							
Zhuanglang loess terraces	PR China																							
Rainfed paddy rice terraces	Philippines																							
Traditional irrigated rice terraces	Nepal																							
8 Grazing land management																								
Ecograze	Australia																							
Restoration of degraded rangeland	South Africa																							
Improved grazing land management	Ethiopia																							
Area closure for rehabilitation	Ethiopia																							
9 Other technologies																								
Pepsee micro-irrigation system	India																							
Sand dune stabilisation	Niger																							
Forest catchment treatment	India																							
Strip mine rehabilitation	South Africa																							

[1] other land use types: eg wasteland, degraded land

Land use type   ■ before SWC technology was implemented   ▨ after SWC technology was implemented
Degradation type   ■ main degradation type addressed   ▨ minor degradation type addressed
Conservation measure   ■ main conservation measure   ▨ supportive / optional SWC measure

WOCAT ■ where the land is greener

Land use – *before and after*

Land use is often affected by soil and water conservation measures. Sometimes the technology itself has the effect of bringing land under a different use (eg terrace construction to create cropland on hillsides), and sometimes the SWC technology effectively defines a different land use (eg agroforestry = mixed land by definition). In the case of traditional systems that have long-established conservation/ land management practices, we have not assumed a land use change, even though one took place many centuries ago. About 60% of the case studies are on cropland, with little change after implementation of recent SWC (Figure 1). However mixed land demonstrates a dramatic, four-fold increase at the expense of grazing land, wasteland and mining land. The mixed land category implies a more intensive

form of land use – after conversion into agroforestry systems in particular. This in itself is interesting: successful SWC often leads to more trees within the landscape, intensification of land use, and less pressure on surrounding natural ecosystems. Good forest management and agroforestry systems are often not perceived as SWC and are thus less frequently documented as such. Although the forest/woodland category has diminished as a result of conservation, this is because in two cases it has been transformed into agroforestry, and terraced cropland, respectively. This should not be seen negatively as 'deforestation' but as conversion to other productive uses under sound conservation practices. Even if SWC is applied only on a specific land use type, it is interrelated with other, adjacent land uses. For example, cropland management is affected by, and affects, grazing management: animals may destroy terraces or on the other hand, residues that are used for mulch or compost are then not available for animal feed. Land use needs to be seen in relation to degradation and conservation. Thus more detailed analysis is presented under 'degradation' and 'SWC measures'.

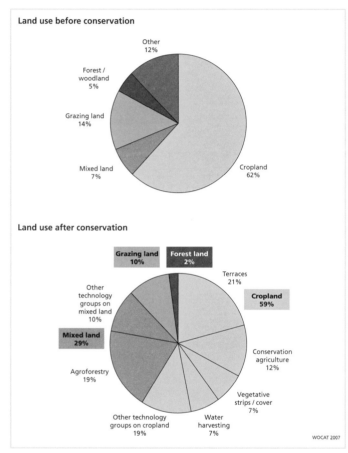

Figure 1: Land use types before (above) and after (below) implementation of SWC, showing dominant SWC groups within the land use types

Degradation – *facing the problem*

Types of degradation – *not just soil erosion*
In only three of the 42 analysed cases was it stated that a single type of land degradation was addressed. All the others gave combinations of at least two degradation types. Frequent combinations were: water erosion and fertility decline in 17 of the 42 cases (17/42); water erosion and water degradation (aridification) (8/42); water erosion and compaction (6/42).

Water erosion (ie soil erosion by water) was the predominant degradation factor mentioned (in almost all cases – 37/42). The few exceptions were those technologies specifically targeted at intensifying production through, for example, manuring/ composting and establishing agroforestry systems. In these cases erosion by water was not mentioned as a specific problem. There were 16 mentions of gully erosion and six of mass movement and offsite degradation (Figure 2).

Wind erosion (ie soil erosion by wind) – and specifically the problem of topsoil loss – was mentioned in over a quarter of the cases (10/42). Various conservation measures address, among others, wind erosion, with windbreaks being the most obvious example.

Rill erosion below a maize crop on a steep hillside in Mexico. Such slopes should not be cultivated without protection from erosive rainfall – through a combination of agronomic and vegetative measures. (William Critchley)

Land degradation

Degraded land is defined as land that, due to natural processes or human activity, is no longer able to sustain properly an economic function and/or the original ecological function. There are a number of interrelated land degradation components, all of which may contribute to a decline in agricultural production and other ecosystem services. The most important are:

Soil degradation – decline in the productive capacity of the soil as a result of soil erosion and changes in the hydrological, biological, chemical and physical functions of the soil. The major types include water erosion (such as inter-rill erosion, gully erosion, mass movement, off-site sedimentation), wind erosion, chemical deterioration (such as fertility decline, reduced organic matter, acidification, salinisation, soil pollution) and physical deterioration (such as soil compaction, surface sealing and crusting, waterlogging)

Vegetation degradation – decline in the quantity and/or quality (species composition, diversity, etc) of the natural biomass and decrease in the vegetative ground cover.

Water degradation – decline in the quantity and/or quality of both surface and groundwater resources (such as aridification and soil moisture problem).

Climate deterioration – changes in the micro- and macro-climatic conditions that increase the risk of crop failure.

Losses to urban/ industrial development – decline in the total area of land used, or with potential for agricultural production as a result of arable land being converted to urban, industrial and infrastructure uses. It needs to be stressed that there are many interactions and interdependencies between these components, and measures to combat land degradation and promote sustainable land management will commonly address more than one at a time.

Source: www.fao.org/ag/agl/agll/lada/seldefs.stm

Physical deterioration was mentioned in nine of the 42 cases. This mainly relates to deterioration of soil structure through compaction. Interestingly, surface sealing and crusting, which are commonly observed problems, were only mentioned once – in the case of ecograze from Australia.

Vegetation degradation was a feature of seven cases – several of these on grazing land, which included reduced cover, deterioration of species richness or proliferation of exotic/ invasive species. Off-site degradation was mentioned six times with respect to erosion by water – related to flooding, increased sediment loads and/or reduced dry season river flow – and once in connection with wind erosion, where cultivated land had been covered by sand.

Water degradation was mentioned in 13 of the 42 cases. These all relate to aridification and soil moisture problems. In dry areas, aridification resulting from the loss of water by evaporation and runoff is naturally a major concern.

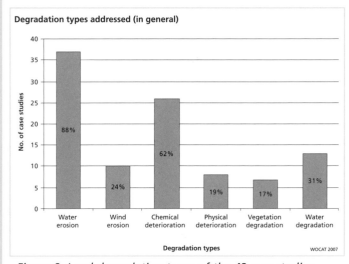

Figure 2: Land degradation types of the 42 case studies

Where **chemical deterioration** was noted, this was usually in relation to soil fertility and organic matter decline. There were 26 cases in which it was mentioned (62% of cases). It occurs over the full range of land use types and is also addressed by a variety of technologies – but especially by manuring/ composting and implementation of agroforestry systems. Only one case addressed salinity (biodrainage in Kyrgyzstan) and one mentioned soil pollution (vineyards in Switzerland).

Degradation by land use type – *deterioration before implementation*

Degradation on cropland (26 case studies): Topsoil erosion by water was the most commonly mentioned problem on cropland – in 20 of the 26 cases (77%), followed by gully erosion in 12 cases (46%), fertility decline in 14 cases (54%), water degradation (aridification) in 10 cases (38%), and compaction in three situations (12%) (note: more than one problem was cited in several cases). The main issues on crop-

land were inappropriate agricultural practices related to reduction of vegetation cover, removal of residues, destruction of soil structure (eg through ploughing), and exposure of topsoil to intensive rain and winds. These problems are commonly exacerbated by spill-over of populations into more and more marginal areas – onto increasingly steep slopes or into drier zones, or into areas characterised by unsuitable and vulnerable soils.

Degradation on mixed land (3 case studies): Of the three cases where degradation has taken place on mixed land, two of these are from the West African Sahel where the problem is attributed mainly to overgrazing and loss of vegetative cover. In the third case, there has been overuse of agroforestry resources in Costa Rica, leading again to loss of vegetation and resultant land degradation.

Degradation on grazing land (6 case studies): Worldwide, degradation problems are common and widespread on grazing land, especially in semi-arid areas. However, only six cases presented in this book deal with degradation on grazing land: this was despite deliberate efforts by the editors to encourage documentation of more grazing land examples. All cases on grazing land have multiple degradation types combined: most commonly vegetation degradation, erosion by water, and fertility decline. Compared to cropland, grazing zones are commonly located in the more marginal areas in terms of climate, soils, topography, fertility and accessibility. Another characteristic – of extensive grazing areas in particular – is the lack of clarity with respect to land use rights. Common property regimes encompass a very wide range of tenure systems, which are difficult to untangle or characterise. Due to periodic (or continuous) high grazing pressure, sparse cover and trampling, the soil is often bare, compacted and crusted. This accelerates water runoff and soil loss, and can initiate a vicious cycle of degradation.

Degradation on forest land (2 case studies): Only two of the case studies are associated with forest land, where topsoil erosion and water loss are the main issues cited. These cases focus on forest that has become degraded. Natural forest maintained in good condition confers excellent protection through its canopy and its 'floor' (ground cover). Where the canopy cover is reduced and the forest floor disturbed and impoverished, this can lead to serious soil erosion problems and loss of 'forest function' – especially in terms of hydrology and biodiversity.

Degradation on other land (5 case studies): Wasteland is often the result of pervasive erosion by water, leading to severe fertility decline. In each of the five cases documented here, SWC interventions had the effect of restoring biological functions in such wastelands, bringing them back into productive use: three of these were turned into agroforestry systems, one into cropland, and one into grazing land.

SWC measures – what they are, and what they do

The stage of intervention – prophylaxis, therapy or 'rehab'?

Depending on what stage of land degradation has been reached when SWC interventions are made, we can differentiate between prevention and mitigation of land degradation or rehabilitation of already degraded land.

Prevention implies employment of SWC measures that maintain natural resources and their environmental and productive function on land that may be prone to degradation. The implication is that good land management practice is already in place: it is effectively the antithesis of human-induced land degradation.

Mitigation is intervention intended to reduce ongoing degradation. This comes in at a stage when degradation has already begun. The main aim here is to halt further degradation and to start improving resources and their functions. Mitigation impacts tend to be noticeable in the short to medium term: this then provides a strong incentive for further efforts. The word 'mitigation' is also sometimes used to describe reducing the impacts of degradation.

Rehabilitation is required when the land is already degraded to such an extent that the original use is no longer possible, and land has become practically unproductive. Here longer-term and more costly investments are needed to show any impact.

Inputs and achievements depend very much on the stage of degradation at which SWC interventions are made. The best input-benefit ratio will normally be achieved through measures for prevention, followed by mitigation, and then rehabilitation. While the impacts of (and measures involved in) rehabilitation efforts can be highly visible, the related achievements need to be critically considered in terms of the cost and associated benefits. Of the 42 case studies analysed here, seven were classified as prevention of degradation (including the three traditional agroforestry systems of

left: Multiple forms of degradation in a single location in Niger: water erosion (gully), wind erosion, physical degradation (crusting and compaction) and chemical degradation (fertility loss). (Hanspeter Liniger)

centre: Salinisation in cotton fields due to a rising water table resulting from over-irrigation and inefficient drainage. This example from Tajikistan demonstrates a common problem that renders investment in irrigation useless. (Hanspeter Liniger)

right: the technology groups
1 Conservation agriculture in Switzerland: this is an example of no-till and direct seeding in a highly mechanised farming system. (Hanspeter Liniger)
2 Manuring/ composting improves soil fertility, soil structure, and infiltration, and helps to reduce soil and water loss. It is especially important in dry zones – as here in Orissa, India where both water availability and soil fertility need to be enhanced. (Hanspeter Liniger)

multi-storey cropping in the Philippines, shade-grown coffee in Costa Rica and grevillea in Kenya). Twenty-two were presented as mitigation of damage to the land (including all the cases of 'Conservation agriculture', 'Manuring/ composting', and 'Vegetative strips/ cover') and the remaining 13 were described as rehabilitation (including check dams in Nicaragua and conversion of grazing land in Tajikistan: see Figure 3).

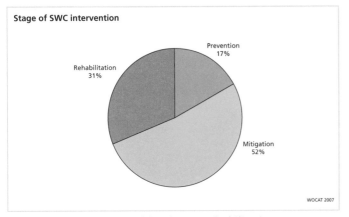

Figure 3: Prevention, mitigation or rehabilitation of land degradation

Ironically, the least spectacular yet most cost-effective category – preventing degradation – is often not perceived as a conservation achievement in itself. An analogy can be drawn to human health, where prophylaxis (preventing malaria, for example) often goes unnoticed, while therapy (curing a malarial fever) is dramatic. And thus in soil and water conservation, systems that maintain the soil and its fertility in place are commonly overlooked, and money instead poured into mitigating damage and rehabilitating badly degraded land. The fact that over 80% of the cases analysed here are mitigation or rehabilitation efforts gives some indication of where the money is going, and where the focus of attention is. Nevertheless, where land needs to be rehabilitated and this can be justified (eg for downstream protection), there may be no alternative. The overall message is: use limited funds to achieve their greatest impact.

Technology groups – *a typology*

The common groups, with familiar names, that have been used to cluster the technologies can be briefly described as follows:

Conservation agriculture (mainly agronomic measures; 5 case studies): this group is characterised by systems incorporating three basic principles: minimum soil disturbance, a degree of permanent soil cover, and crop rotation.

Manuring/ composting (mainly agronomic measures; 3 case studies): organic manures and composts are intended to improve soil fertility, and simultaneously enhance soil structure (against compaction and crusting) and improve water infiltration and percolation.

Vegetative strips/ cover (mainly vegetative measures; 3 case studies): in this group, grasses or trees are used in various ways. In the case of strips, these often lead to the formation of bunds and terraces due to 'tillage erosion' – the downslope movement of soil during cultivation. In the other cases, the effect of dispersed vegetation cover is multiple, including increasing ground cover, improving soil structure, and infiltration, as well as decreasing erosion by water and wind.

Agroforestry (mainly vegetative, combined with agronomic; 8 case studies): agroforestry describes land use systems where trees are grown in association with agricultural crops, pastures or livestock – and there are usually both ecological and economic interactions between components of the system. There is a wide range covered here: from shelterbelts, to trees with coffee, to multi-storey cropping.

Water harvesting (structural, but also combined; 3 case studies): water harvesting is the collection and concentration of rainfall runoff for crop production – or for improving the performance of grass and trees – in dry areas where moisture deficit is the primary limiting factor.

Gully control (structural combined with vegetative; 3 case studies): gully control encompasses a set of measures that address this specific and severe type of erosion, where land rehabilitation is required. There is a whole range of different and complementary measures, though structural barriers dominate – often stabilised with permanent vegetation. Commonly, such technologies are applied over a whole catchment.

Terraces (structural, but often combined with vegetative and agronomic measures; 9 case studies): this is perhaps the best-known and most spectacular group of SWC technologies. There is a wide variety of different terrace types, from forward-sloping terraces to level or backward-sloping bench terraces, with or without drainage systems. Irrigated ter-

WOCAT ■ where the land is greener

races (usually for paddy rice) are a special case in terms of water management and its implications for terrace design.

Grazing land management (management practices with associated vegetative and agronomic measures; 4 case studies): improved management of grazing land relates to changing control and regulation of grazing pressure. It is associated with an initial reduction of the grazing intensity through fencing, followed either by rotational grazing, or 'cut-and-carry' of fodder, and vegetation improvement and management change.

Other technologies (various; 4 case studies): this group embraces a mixed bag of case study technologies, namely the use of drip irrigation to increase water use efficiency, sand dune stabilisation, forest treatment, and the rehabilitation of mining lands.

Conservation measures – *constituents of technologies*

Each case study comprises a technology, made up of management, agronomic, vegetative, or structural measures or, very commonly, combinations of these. Not surprisingly, the technologies within a particular group all have similar compositions in terms of their component measures. WOCAT disaggregates technologies into specific measures in order to help understand how these technologies function.

Agronomic measures are related to soil management, soil cover, and crop mixtures and rotations. Typically, they are relatively cheap, requiring low inputs, can be very effective, and are often related to fertility management such as compost/ manuring and thus to productivity. They are usually integrated into farming activities and often not considered as SWC by the land users or specialists: these measures achieve conservation as a side-effect of good land management. Agronomic measures have, in recent years, received much more attention. Perhaps the most notable example is 'Conservation agriculture', represented here by five case studies. Conservation agriculture rose to prominence when it was recognised by land users, rather than specialists, that with reduced tillage and lower costs erosion could be minimised, water used much more efficiently, and soil organic matter and biodiversity enhanced. The other group here that is agronomic in nature is 'Manuring/ composting'.

Vegetative measures: The most common and widespread types of vegetative measures amongst our cases are the 'Vegetative strips/ cover' group and the 'Agroforestry' systems. Agroforestry (comprising mainly vegetative measures, but with some agronomic components) is particularly common in humid, tropical conditions where, often, no structural measures are needed due to the ground protection provided by the vegetation – except on the steepest slopes. In drier conditions where wind erosion increases water stress, vegetative measures also have very positive impacts through reducing wind speed – for example the shelterbelts described in China. Vegetative measures can compete with crops for moisture – especially in drier areas – and special management is required to reduce this competition. Thus

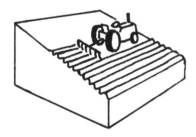

Agronomic measures such as conservation agriculture, manuring/ composting, mixed cropping, contour cultivation, mulching, etc
- are usually associated with annual crops
- are repeated routinely each season or in a rotational sequence
- are of short duration and not permanent
- are often not zoned
- do not lead to changes in slope profile
- are normally independent of slope

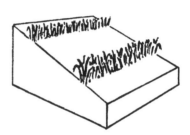

Vegetative measures such as grass strips, hedge barriers, windbreaks, or agroforestry, etc
- involve the use of perennial grasses, shrubs or trees
- are of long duration
- often lead to a change in slope profile
- are often aligned along the contour or against the wind
- are often spaced according to slope

from left to right: the technology groups (continued)
3 Vegetative strips/ cover: fodder grass combined with grevillea trees in Kenya. Terraces form over time. (Hanspeter Liniger)
4 Agroforestry: here a highly productive and protective system from Papua New Guinea, based on vanilla vines growing up palm and gliricidia trees. (William Critchley)
5 Water harvesting through *demi-lune* ('half moon') microcatchments in an arid zone of Niger, collecting water and nutrients from an unproductive area. (Hanspeter Liniger)
6 Gully control through stone check dams showing its effect in slowing down water flow and trapping sediments – in southern Ethiopia. (Hanspeter Liniger)
7 Terraces for traditional cultivation of paddy rice under extreme conditions in Bali: very steep slopes and high rainfall intensities. (Hanspeter Liniger)
8 Grazing land management through regulating grazing pressure on sand dunes in Niger: the impact (right) after 3 years. (Hanspeter Liniger)

negative and positive impacts need to be assessed and weighed against each other. Vegetative measures are often overlooked in regard to their SWC function, especially under traditional land use systems where erosion has been prevented.

Structural measures are usually considered to be the centerpiece of SWC: in the recent past, most SWC campaigns have been based on the implementation of physical barriers to prevent movement of eroded soil. Amongst our groups, terraces stand out clearly as being structural, though they are often combined with other supplementary measures, such as grasses to stabilise risers. There are many traditional and even ancient terrace systems, which are still in use today: some of the older structures now require rehabilitation. Other technologies presented here that are basically structural include water harvesting systems, palisades against wind erosion, and check dams in gullies.

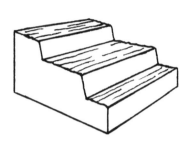

Structural measures such as terraces, banks, bunds, constructions, palisades, etc
- often lead to a change in slope profile
- are of long duration or permanent
- are carried out primarily to control runoff, wind velocity and erosion
- often require substantial inputs of labour or money when first installed
- are often aligned along the contour or against the wind
- are often spaced according to slope
- involve major earth movements and/or construction with wood, stone, concrete, etc

Management measures are often applied to grazing land in situations where uncontrolled use has led to degradation and where other measures simply do not work without a fundamental change in land management. Examples presented here are systems involving enclosures – thus protection from grazing – to allow regeneration of vegetation cover. Such measures are often essential for the rehabilita-

tion of badly degraded areas where technical measures and other interventions are not adequate on their own (but can act in a supplementary way). But there are also examples of intensification of grazing land use where fodder crops are planted and used for cut-and-carry feeding of livestock. One of the major advantages of management measures is that they often do not involve very high investments of money or labour. On the other hand, taking land out of use can lead to increased pressure on neighbouring land – which may also be in poor condition and vulnerable to further degradation. Another disadvantage is that management measures are often not clear-cut; they require great flexibility and responsiveness, not only initially, but over the years that follow. However, there are often implications for land tenure that can complicate decision-making and may sour relationships between neighbours.

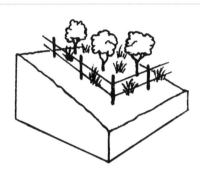

Management measures such as land use change, area closure, rotational grazing, etc
- involve a fundamental change in land use
- involve no agronomic and structural measures
- often result in improved vegetative cover
- often reduce the intensity of use

Combinations: Frequently, measures have been implemented together, combining different functions and creating synergies. Amongst the nine groups of technologies described in this book, 'Agroforestry', 'Terraces' and 'Grazing land management' are each made up of various measures: they are not simply vegetative (agroforestry) or structural (terraces) or management (grazing land). Additional measures involved play a supplementary, but crucial role in conserving the soil and water.

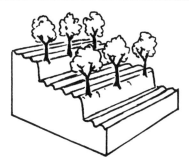

Combinations in conditions where different measures are complementary and thus enhance each other's effectiveness.

Any combination of the above measures is possible, eg:
- **structural**: terrace
- **vegetative**: grass and trees
- **agronomic**: mulching
- **management**: fencing off

To take specific examples, at first glance, check dams built from wooden stakes in Nicaragua appeared to be structural measures. However, not just dead branches are used, but green stakes are planted – which then 'strike' and begin to grow. This constitutes a vegetative measure. In fact, this living component is more effective (and more durable) in controlling rapid water flow in a gully. In the case of the traditional stonewall terracing in South Africa, contour ploughing was also applied; in the vetiver grass example, also from South Africa, mulching and minimum tillage are crucial to its functioning. Combinations of measures within a technology are much more common and important than had first been thought when WOCAT was designed. Overall, 23 of the 42 cases represent combinations (see Table 2). These are either (a) superimposed on the same plot of land, or (b) dispersed over a catchment (eg cut-off drains and afforestation in the upper catchment and check dams in gullies), or (c) phased over time (eg through a rotation system). Combinations support each other and often address multiple degradation types.

Various technologies are spaced in different locations within a catchment depending on the situation and degradation processes. They address specific on-site conditions but they also depend on upstream, and interact with downstream, SWC technologies. Thus their function is not just local but they also play a role in the whole catchment or landscape. Impacts as well as costs and benefits need to be seen at both levels: at the local, as well as at the catchment/ landscape scale. Several examples illustrate this: eg the case from

Bolivia; 'Forest catchment treatment' in India; 'Area closure for rehabilitation' in Ethiopia. In the example of the terraces on the loess plateau in China, a landscape approach is followed: here the ridge tops are protected usually by afforestation, the terraces (described in the case study) conserve the slopes and various gully control and water harvesting technologies (eg small dams) are applied in the valleys.

Looking at the SWC technology groups, in respect to the terrace cases, for example, only three of the nine examples are purely structural; all the other cases are combinations with agronomic and vegetative measures. On the other hand, only one of the five conservation agriculture cases combines measures: the other four are purely agronomic. Agroforestry systems, however, typically combine measures: only two of the eight are purely vegetative (see Table 2). This illustrates the complexity of the case study examples, making it difficult to disentangle the various measures and their functioning within the technologies. This, however, is attempted in the following section.

Technical functions and impacts of SWC – *what is targeted, what is achieved*

Figure 4 shows the technical functions/ impacts of the SWC technologies in combating different forms of land degradation, as presented in the case studies. It is clear from Figure 4 that combinations of different functions and impacts are very common.

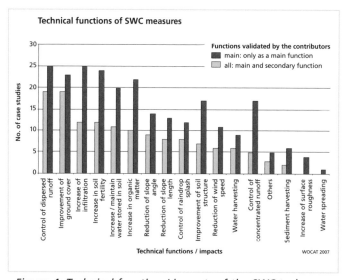

Figure 4: Technical functions/ impacts of the SWC technologies in combating different forms of land degradation

from left to right: Categorisation of SWC measures
Agronomic measures: conservation agriculture in Australia comprising no-till combined with direct seeding – replacing centuries of farming with the plough. (Hanspeter Liniger)

Vegetative measures: grass strips planted on the contour, leading to terrace development over time in Kenya. Hedges around cropland/ agroforestry system constitute another vegetative measure – as seen in upper right part of the photo. (Hanspeter Liniger)

Structural measures: terraces on the Loess Plateau in China cover 80,000km² and are one of the world's wonders – most of them have been built manually. (Hanspeter Liniger)

Soil erosion by water is the most frequently addressed degradation type, and the following conservation principles can be differentiated:
- diverting/ draining runoff and run-on;
- impeding runoff;
- retaining runoff/ preventing runoff; and
- collecting and trapping runoff (harvest runoff/ run-on).

Soil erosion is most commonly a water-related problem and the solution lies in better management of rainwater, whether through infiltration into the soil or other ways of managing surface runoff. Although in the case studies SWC specialists have indicated how the different measures function, the lack of supporting data shows that the efficiency, effectiveness and impacts are inadequately monitored or evaluated.

Taking the groups of SWC technologies:
- The first two groups, 'Conservation agriculture' and 'Manuring/ composting' have similar functions. These are mostly related to improvement of soil structure, and increase of organic matter and soil fertility. There is an increase in infiltration and water stored, and as a result of all these functions, runoff is also controlled – as is mentioned in around half of the cases. In conservation agriculture, ground cover improvement is an additional major factor that underlies its functioning.
- 'Vegetative strips/ cover' and 'Agroforestry' work in relation to controlling runoff and increasing ground cover, infiltration, organic matter, soil fertility, and water storage in the soil.
- 'Water harvesting' systems function through the collection of runoff from a catchment area, and the concentration and increase of water stored in the soil where production is located. While there is reduced infiltration in the area from which the runoff is harvested, this is compensated by enhanced infiltration where the water is accumulated and stored.
- 'Gully rehabilitaion' mainly addresses the problem of concentrated runoff; 'Terracing' deals with dispersed runoff down a hillside. Otherwise, what these two groups have in common is the reduction of the slope angle and slope length. Terraces often aim more for increased water storage in the soil (while providing for drainage in areas of rainfall excess), whereas gully control works through ground cover improvement and infiltration increase brought about by this vegetation, and through the physical effect of check dams.
- Technologies on grazing land function through control of dispersed runoff, improvement of ground cover, and improving soil fertility. In about two-thirds of the cases,

control of concentrated runoff, increase of infiltration, and improvement of soil structure are indicated as the main ways these systems function.

Environment – *the natural and human setting*

Natural environment – *how nature influences the technologies*

Climatic zones: With respect to climate there is a reasonable balance between the 42 technologies documented, with 19 in arid to semi-arid and 23 in subhumid to humid zones (Figure 5). Looking now at the groups, some differentiation can be noted regarding their location. The 'Vegetative strips / cover' examples from our 42 case studies are all from the sub-humid/ humid areas, where vegetation prospers and there is relatively little competition for water compared with drier areas. Six agroforestry systems out of eight reported here are in subhumid/ humid areas, while all of the 'Water harvesting' technologies – not surprisingly – are located in semi-arid conditions. We need to differentiate between two basic types of terraces: (a) rainfed terraces of which about half are in semi-arid and subhumid areas; and (b) irrigated terraces (mainly paddy rice terraces), which in the case studies are all from subhumid or humid zones. The grazing land cases are mainly located in subhumid environments (three-quarters), with the remainder from semi-arid regions. This is perhaps a surprising selection, as semi-arid

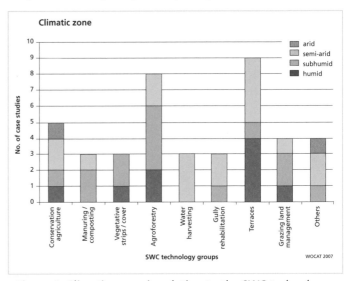

Figure 5: Climatic zones in relation to the SWC technology groups

grazing lands often have the most pronounced and widespread degradation problems. One would have expected more examples from these regions. The examples from the subhumid areas, however, illustrate that the success rate can be high, as the land can produce good fodder for 'cut-and-carry' systems (for example in Ethiopia). More rapid and sustained processes of rehabilitation based on vegetative recovery can, naturally, occur in the more humid areas.

Elevation: Two main elevation zones cover the 42 case studies. These are (a) below 500 m and (b) between 1,000 and 2,000 m. In the tropics and subtropics, the zone between 1,000 and 2,000 m often has favourable conditions for agriculture: it tends not to be too hot and benefits from favourable rainfall. Nevertheless, this is an area where SWC is a priority, and both agronomic and vegetative measures can work well through combining conservation with production. The agroforestry and also manuring/ composting cases are mainly drawn from this zone. Above 2,000 m conditions become more marginal for agriculture, and at this altitude only gully, terraces and grazing land management cases are represented here. With increasing elevation, the potential effects of land degradation on downstream areas increase, and SWC can have considerable off-site/ downstream impacts.

Slope: Terraces are (naturally) found on sloping land: a third of those in this book are on slopes steeper than 30%. On these slopes, production is difficult without terraces and

their beds that effectively provide cultivation platforms. On the contrary, agroforestry systems are more or less independent of slope; there are examples here from the gentlest to (almost) the steepest. Vegetative strips/ cover tend to be located on sloping land between 8 and 30%: these have emerged as a cheaper alternative to terrace construction in this situation. Conservation agriculture is mainly implemented on gentle slopes – below 8% (see Figure 6).

Soil fertility and organic matter: None of the case studies are characterised by soils with very high fertility (before intervention with SWC). Around half, however, are located on very low, to low fertility soils and the other half on soils with medium (including two on 'high') fertility. This shows the concentration of efforts on soils where degradation (and also nutrient mining) has probably already reduced soil fertility.

Soil organic matter (SOM) is closely related to soil fertility and has an impact on physical, chemical and biological properties. Not surprisingly, we see that in around half of the cases the SOM was initially low, while almost all the remainder are on soils with medium levels of SOM (see Figure 7). Because most soils where SWC has been applied contain a rather low level of SOM, they correspondingly have the potential to increase that proportion and by doing so, to increase nutrient holding capacity and simultaneously sequester carbon in the degraded soil. This is an important characteristic of conservation agriculture systems, and here

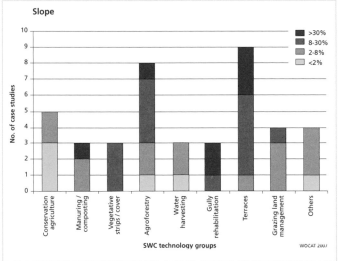

Figure 6: Slope categories in relation to the SWC technology groups

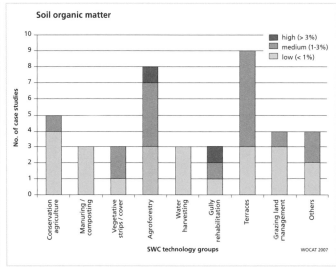

Figure 7: Level of soil organic matter in relation to the SWC technology groups

from left to right: **Categorisation of SWC measures** (continued)
Management measures: improved management can lead to better conservation and increased output, for example by turning open access grazing into cut-and-carry fodder production systems (Iran). (William Critchley)

Combinations of measures: in this case from Nepal, terraces (structural) with molasses grass *(Melinis minutiflora)* on their risers for fodder and stability (vegetative) and manure to enrich the soil (agronomic) for sesame production. (Hanspeter Liniger)

Combinations of measures: a 'landscape approach' in the Uluguru Mountains, Tanzania, where various measures interact both within, and between plots. This includes terracing for irrigation (foreground), intercropping of annual and perennial crops, and agroforestry systems (background). (Hanspeter Liniger)

lies a potential for vast amounts of carbon to be fixed. In the global debate about climate change, the potential for carbon sequestration in the soil is crucial. Given the extensive areas of degraded land and the potential of SWC to increase soil organic matter in the topsoil, SWC offers a substantial and potentially long-lasting sink for carbon. And this is a win-win/ local-global benefit combination. However, once soils are rehabilitated and have reached their climax in terms of SOM, no additional carbon can be sequestered.

Human environment – *livelihood conditions*

Production orientation: With respect to the type of production orientation (from subsistence to commercial), the cases presented are relatively well distributed: subsistence accounts for 31% (13/42), mixed (subsistence and commercial) for 40% (17/42), and purely commercial represent the remaining 29% (12/42) (see Figure 8). Looking at some of the technology groups, 'Gully rehabilitation' is only reported under subsistence conditions. This supports the common observation that gullies are a major problem in poorer areas and on common land. Investments are needed to stop this degradation. While under our case studies three-quarters of the agroforestry and terrace systems occurred under mixed or commercial systems, they can also be found in subsistence farming situations. Under 'Terraces, market orientation is well represented, indicating that the high investments made (both in maintenance and establishment) must be affordable – and can be paid for – through farming on terraced

hillsides. None of the 'Manuring/ composting' or 'Water harvesting' systems examples fall under commercial farming regimes. These cases are drawn from either the drier or poorer areas or both.

Size of land holding: The range of land sizes across different case studies is very considerable (see Figure 9). 'Terrace systems', 'Manuring/ composting' systems, and 'Gully rehabilitation' are all implemented in the context of smallholder farms with less than two hectares per farmer. Water harvesting is found on farms up to five hectares in size. It is only when we look at agroforestry systems that the plot sizes increase towards 15 hectares. 'Conservation agriculture' has a very wide distribution, covering a broad range from less than one hectare to over 1,000 ha. 'Grazing land management' also varies enormously: from small 'cut-and-carry' fodder-based plots (Ethiopia) to very large holdings of land (Australia). However, what is striking is that two-thirds of the case studies focus on land holdings of less than two hectares in size on average. This helps to support the theory that there is a significant and underestimated investment, worldwide, in conservation within the smallholder farming sector.

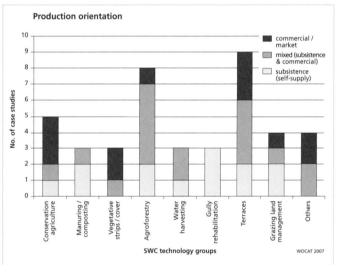

Figure 8: Production orientation in relation to the SWC technology groups

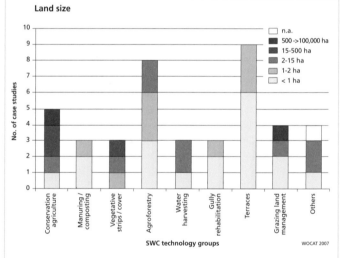

Figure 9: Land size in relation to the SWC technology groups

Socio-economic impacts – *weighing the costs and benefits*

Costs and investments – *crucial inputs*

In compiling the cost of a technology, it is often difficult to separate normal agricultural inputs from additional expenses for the technology. In some cases (for example, conservation agriculture) the costs are actually less than for the normal or conventional practice. Thus it is relatively difficult to determine the incremental (or alternative) costs (and benefits) for SWC. This is especially the case when the production system changes, for example in agroforestry systems (eg shade-grown coffee in Costa Rica), in conservation agriculture, or when changing a grazing land management system. An additional difficulty occurs if there are multipurpose uses of the system. The question here is how relevant it is to weigh and compare financial advantages of one system over another, when there may be various other economic benefits that are not so easy to quantify. It is still a considerable challenge to account for costs and benefits – ecological and social gains – that cannot simply be expressed in monetary terms. Increased investment costs are rarely accounted for in terms of improved ecosystem services – for example raised groundwater levels, maintained biodiversity or reduced off-site/ downstream damage. There are also other considerations to be taken into account, such as social status, and emotional, aesthetic, ideological, and cultural values.

All costs are country- and site-specific. In order to analyse the differences among the case studies, it is important not to forget the different situations regarding daily wages. There is a huge difference between the costs of labour in 'developing' and 'developed' countries.

Establishment costs are defined as those specific one-off, initial costs which are incurred during the setting up of a SWC technology. These investments are made over a period that generally lasts from a few weeks to two or three years. Typically included are extra labour, hire of machinery, purchase of equipment such as tools, fencing materials, and tree seedlings. There is generally no establishment phase involved in agronomic measures. However, in the group of case studies on conservation agriculture – which is based on agronomic measures – whereas in four out of five cases there are almost no extra costs recorded for the establishment phase, there has to be a change to new machinery at some stage. These costs, however, may be 'hidden' as part of general farm investments in equipment.

The highest establishment costs were associated with terrace construction (Figure 10). Only two of them were below US$ 500/ha (the *'Fanya juu* terraces' from Kenya, and 'Small level bench terraces' in Thailand). Five of them recorded figures of US$ 500 to 2,000/ha and the remaining two were both above US$ 2,000/ha. These two were the traditional Nepal and Philippine paddy rice terraces, estimated on the basis of 'if constructed today'. 'Agroforestry' also shows a wide range of investment costs, depending much on the cost of trees and labour required to plant them. Establishment costs for the agroforestry systems presented ranged from US$ 160 to 2,700/ha. As most of the grazing land examples are from the subhumid areas with quite good production potential, considerable investments were made, ranging from a few hundred to slightly over a thousand dollars per hectare. Establishment of vegetative strips and cover is generally also cheap, except for the Swiss case study where labour costs are very high – compared with the Philippines, for example.

There are a number of cases where input is needed to lift ancient systems out of current deterioration, and revitalise them and bring them back into productivity. These include the Roman terraces in Syria, and those of the Inca terraces in Peru. Investments required now to restore such systems to a functional level are too high to be met by the land users in the short term. Thus, in these cases support to the land users may be justified, as a one-off investment by governments and/or international donors. However, once these investments are made, the recurrent maintenance costs should be low enough to be covered by the local land users with minimal additional support. Otherwise, there is a danger once again of degradation. The relevant case studies here are too recent to provide information about the post-reconstruction period.

Maintenance (recurrent) costs are those that relate to keeping a system functional. They are incurred regularly – and costed on an annual basis. They are generally made up of labour, equipment, and agricultural inputs. In the current analysis, there were very low maintenance costs for a number of the technologies under the nine groups: for 'Manuring/ composting', for 'Water harvesting', for 'Gully rehabilitation', and also for 'Vegetative strips/ cover' (except for the Swiss example, where labour costs are very high). In contrast, the (absolute) maintenance costs for 'Conservation agriculture' are, surprisingly, quite high (Figure 10). But this can partially be explained by the fact that, of the five examples, two are from commercial farming systems in Australia and one from the United Kingdom. In fact, when the main-

left: Land use and land use change: left – large-scale conservation farming of barley with contour bunds; right – small-scale encroachment into previously forested zone of Mount Kenya where farmers are starting to conserve land with grass strips. (Hanspeter Liniger)
centre left: Manual construction of terraces: heavy labour inputs and financial investments are sometimes needed to bring degraded land into productivity as on China's Loess Plateau.
(Ministry of Agriculture, PR China)
centre right: Unterraced, steep slopes in the Uluguru Mountains, Tanzania – yet no sign of degradation due to good soil cover management, combinations of measures in the same fields and low erodibility of the soil. This combines low cost with high benefits– and is attractive to the eye as well. (Hanspeter Liniger)
right: A steep hillside in Kabale, Uganda, being cleared for cultivation: an erosion hazard in this area with its erodible soils. A solution here is to lay trash lines across the contour and allow grass to grow through them, providing strips of protection after three or four years. (William Critchley)

Table 3: A comparison of inputs involved in terrace establishment and maintenance

Technology	Country	Slope	Rainfed/ irrigated	Establishment			Maintenance		
				Person-days/ha	Total costs/ha US $	% met by land users	Person-days/ ha/year	Total costs/ha/ year US $	% met by land users
Orchard terraces with bahia grass cover	China	16–30%	Rainfed	350	1,840	70	60	376	100
Loess plateau terraces	China	16–30%	Rainfed	600	1,200	95	12	25	95
Fanya juu terraces	Kenya	5–8%	Rainfed	90	320	100	10	38	100
Rainfed paddy rice terraces	Philipp.	30–60%	Rainfed	800	2,700	100	10	40	100
Traditional stone wall terraces	Syria	16–30%	Rainfed	375	1,270	100	50	160	100
Small level bench terraces	Thailand	8–16%	Rainfed	125	275	100	20	45	100
Stone wall bench terraces	S. Africa	16–30%	Rainfed	420	1,460	100	5	20	100
Traditional irrigated rice terraces[1]	Nepal	30–60%	Irrigated	unknown	unknown	100	125	840	100
Rehabilitation of ancient terraces[2]	Peru	30–60%	Irrigated	130	1,400	35	6	126	100

[1] no information on labour input in contraction of these ancient terraces
[2] refers to rehabilitation of ancient systems, not original establishment

tenance activities of the conservation agriculture systems are compared with the conventional cultivation activities, the costs of the former are lower. The implication is that by changing to conservation agriculture there are cost savings in terms of annual field operations, even though there might be new inputs needed – especially herbicides. The reduced recurrent costs are one of the attractive aspects of the system to farmers.

Table 3 compares and contrasts the labour input and costs involved in construction and maintenance of the terrace sys-

tems described in the case studies. Generally speaking terraces are labour-intensive and expensive options for SWC. There are two exceptions though: (a) the *fanja juu* system from Kenya, where only the bund is constructed and the terrace bed levels out over time, and (b) the small step terraces from Thailand. Significantly, also, these are both located on moderate slopes. A general rule in terracing is that the steeper the slope the more soil needs to be moved and the higher the cost. This is confirmed here. With the exception of the orchard terraces from China, the major cost in all cases is associated with labour. However, the relationship

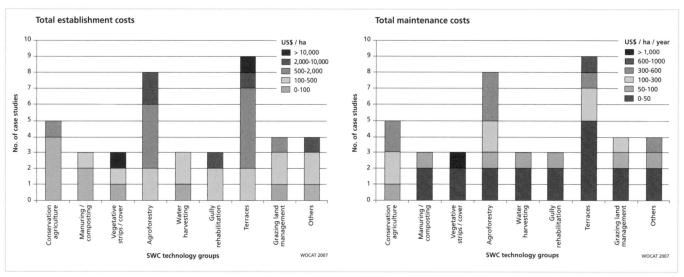

Figures 10: Establishment and maintenance costs in relation to the SWC technology groups

between person-days and costs is complicated because of the different rates calculated for daily labour, the cost of labour itself varies among countries. Allowance has been made for the historical change in costs; labour and other inputs have been calculated on the basis of 'what it would have cost in 2006'.

Costs and benefits (on-site) – *profitability of SWC*

The most convincing argument for land users to invest in SWC is an increase in land productivity and the associated economic returns. However, compiling relevant and reliable information for a rigorous cost-benefit analysis presents a major challenge to land users and soil and water conservation specialists alike. This analysis of the 42 case studies reveals that there are marked differences in land productivity and in economic returns between the various technologies. The whole basket of investments made, and the benefits accruing, need to be considered together in order to make informed decisions on selection and combination of measures.

Cost and benefits are extremely difficult to assess, but are obviously a crucial factor in justifying SWC interventions. The basic problem is the lack of hard and reliable data. In the absence of such data, WOCAT has had to rely on 'perceived benefits'. This, however, is not just a poor substitute for data – it is intrinsically important in itself: without a positive perception of benefits, land users (or outside donors) are unlikely to invest. Figure 11 shows the perceived benefits of the SWC technologies with respect to establishment (investments needed during the first three years) and maintenance (costs that are incurred annually). These were assessed by asking the land users to rank the benefits on a scale ranging from 'very negative' to 'very positive'. Three caveats are required here. First, it should be noted that these ratings are rarely supported by hard data – but based on experience and perceptions. Second, the assessment of the returns and benefits might give a too rosy picture due to contributors 'talking-up' their cases. Thirdly, the answers are derived from those land users active on-site. Thus benefits perceived by those off-site (or global benefits, for that matter) are not reflected.

Establishment cost and benefits over the short-term:
With the exception of 'Terraces', there are examples in each group of cases where there are positive returns within a short period of time. Terraces are a case in point: in only three of the nine cases were 'neutral to slightly positive' benefits recorded in the short term; the other five were

classed as 'slightly negative' (two) or 'very negative' (three). This reflects high investment costs and, probably, some initial reduction of the production level due to exposure and disturbance of subsoil during terrace bed levelling, or surface area loss due to the space taken up by terrace structures. In some cases the initially unproductive establishment phase of fruit trees means some years without any significant returns. However, the irrigated paddy rice terraces, as well as the newly established terraces in Tajikistan and on the Loess Plateau of China, pay back after a few years, since in these cases terracing leads to much higher, sustained productivity. In the latter case badly degraded hillsides have been converted into good farmland.

Establishment cost and benefits over the long-term:
Thirty three cases (of the 35 where establishment costs were incurred) indicate that establishment costs were not only covered but gave a 'positive to very positive' return, except for one example – the stabilisation of the sand dunes in Niger. Here, compared to the high investment costs, the on-site benefits were low. However, the assessment does not take the possible off-site benefits into account: it is more difficult to assess what it would mean in terms of benefits if dunes threaten a village or an oasis with associated irrigated land.

Maintenance cost and benefits over the short term and the long term:
Regarding maintenance, the extra benefits compared with returns to recurrent annual costs within the first years were already perceived to be 'positive' in around two-thirds of the cases. Only in the agroforestry examples, where new systems were established and degraded land was upgraded to agroforestry, did short-term maintenance fail to pay back quickly. Examples were in Costa Rica with shade-grown coffee, and the conversion from degraded rangeland to fruit orchards in Tajikistan. In the long term, the maintenance inputs gave positive returns in all case studies except for, once again, the fixation of the sand dunes in Niger (Figure 11d).

left: A mulched vegetable plot in the Solomon Islands of the South Pacific – demonstrating a low external input, simple technology that conserves the land and leads directly to productive impact. (William Critchley)

centre: The initial costs of this high technology conservation agriculture system from Queensland, Australia are considerable – including equipment for precision, satellite guided direct seeding/ fertilizing. But over time this proves cheaper than regular conventional tillage, and furthermore fertilizer requirement is reduced substantially making wheat production economic under dryland conditions. (Hanspeter Liniger)

right: Bringing home the harvest of fodder: this productive cut-and-carry system in Colombia protects the land from being overgrazed. (Mats Gurtner)

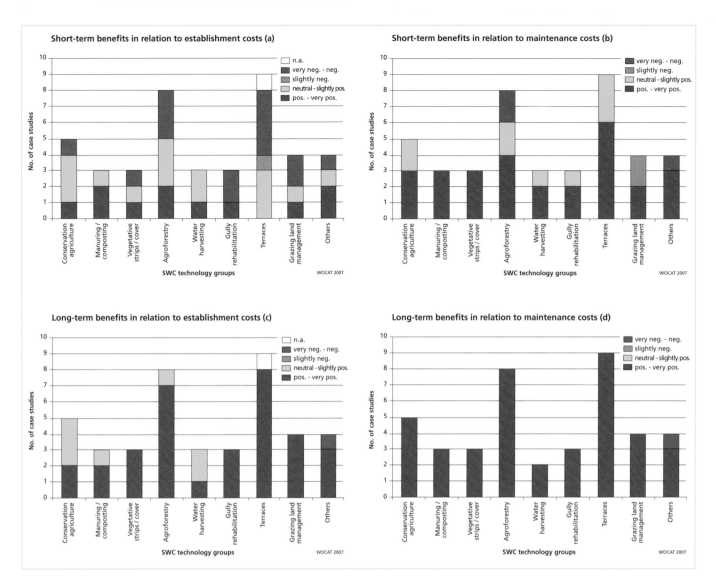

Figures 11: Perceived benefits of SWC technologies: short-term benefits in relation (a) to establishment costs and (b) to maintenance costs, and long-term benefits in relation (c) to establishment costs and (d) to maintenance costs

Establishment and maintenance cost and benefits over the short-term: Another look at the short-term costs and benefits is illustrated in Figure 12. Those cases that have rapid pay-back are worthwhile for every land user to invest in, as the increased returns are immediate. Those with short-term negative returns in relation to establishment, but positive returns in relation to maintenance, often require some support by projects, by the government, or the communities for a 'kick-start'. However, those with negative returns both from investment and maintenance (six examples) are unlikely to be taken up by small-scale subsistence farmers, unless they are awarded incentives. These technologies would inevitably require long-term external support if they are to be promoted – and could only be justified for other reasons, such as off-site benefits.

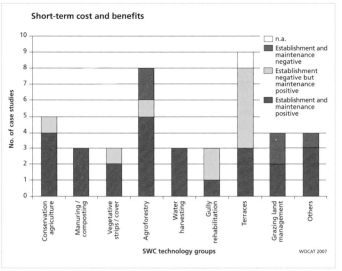

Short-term cost and benefits

No. of case studies

SWC technology groups

- n.a.
- Establishment and maintenance negative
- Establishment negative but maintenance positive
- Establishment and maintenance positive

WOCAT 2007

Figure 12: Establishment and maintenance cost and benefits over the short-term

Improving livelihoods and production – *more output for better lives*

Livelihoods: For each technology, the land users' judgment and perceptions were used with respect to the benefits of the technology – in both the short and the long term. SWC technologies with low investment and maintenance costs and rapid, as well as long-term benefits, help all farmers, and are especially useful in assisting small-scale subsistence land users to climb out of poverty. Several technologies – mainly those based on agronomic and vegetative measures – fulfil these criteria. Increase in farm income generated from improved land use through SWC was recorded in two-thirds of the cases.

Production: Figure 13 demonstrates how increases in pro-duction – across the nine groups – are often high (or at least medium) for crops, fodder and/or wood production. The first and most important point here is that SWC technologies increase primary production. This may be directly connected to the agronomic and vegetative components of many tech-nologies, and associated with increases in soil fertility, or improved availability of water in the drier areas. Under 'Conservation agriculture', for example, crop yield increase is high in three of the five cases, and this is basically related

Figures 13: Increase/ decrease in crops, fodder and/or wood production across the SWC technology groups

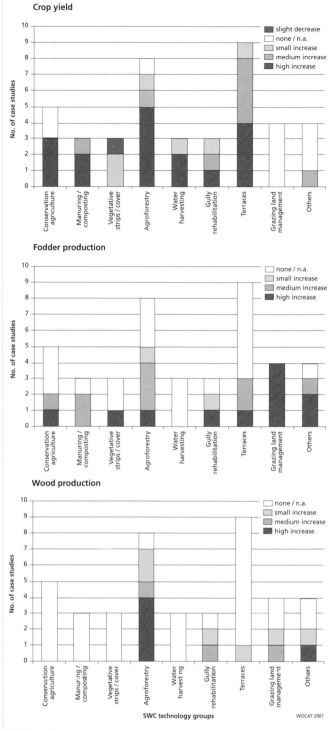

Crop yield

No. of case studies

- slight decrease
- none / n.a.
- small increase
- medium increase
- high increase

Fodder production

No. of case studies

- none / n.a.
- small increase
- medium increase
- high increase

Wood production

No. of case studies

- none / n.a.
- small increase
- medium increase
- high increase

SWC technology groups

WOCAT 2007

left: Forward-sloping terraces in Uganda demonstrating a water and nutrient 'gradient': relatively higher yields behind the barrier due to an accumulation of sediment and moisture. (William Critchley)

centre: In the highlands of Eritrea huge investment is needed for the establishment of hillside terraces/ microbasins associated with tree planting on a very large scale – but it takes time to pay back: how can that gap be bridged? (Mats Gurtner)

right: Maize production under conventional ploughing in dryland areas, such as here in Kenya, carries a high risk of crop failure (left): but in this case the neighbour (right) – with his conservation agriculture system – had a harvest and furthermore, at reduced cost. (Hanspeter Liniger)

to improved water conservation. 'Agroforestry' systems are, not surprisingly, reported as providing consistent production increases (generally medium and high) in terms of crops, fodder and wood. 'Terraces' also generally provide medium to high production increases for crops. An important by-product is increased fodder production from grass planted on the risers. A word of caution is required: as yields and impacts are seldom measured, they have generally been estimated by the contributors and land users, and thus there may have been a temptation to overstate the benefits.

The 'island effect': a word of caution

The 'island effect' refers to a specific (and relatively rare) situation under SWC interventions where benefits accrue to an isolated individual/activity precisely because of that isolation. The case study from Kyrgyzstan illustrates the point. The planting of poplar trees provides locally beneficial 'bio-drainage' and simultaneously supplies wood for a hungry market. An expansion of the system, however, could lower the water table excessively – and flood the market with wood at the same time. The broader lesson here is that calculations of benefits, based on extrapolation from local success, should be done with caution, and that planning by local institutions to avoid oversupply of the market, and accordingly adapt technologies to local conditions, is crucial.

Ecological impacts –
improving ecosystem functions

Water and the land

By definition, all SWC technologies function in relation to water – usually in relation to control of runoff and increase of infiltration, and as a result, an increase in water stored in the soil. Even control of wind erosion improves soil moisture. Some technologies are more explicitly related to drainage, and some specifically harvest water. Nearly all (88%) of the SWC technology cases indicated an increase in soil moisture (Figure 14). In 71% of all cases, improvement was rated as 'medium' or 'high'. A second water-related issue is that in one-third of the cases drainage was said to have improved. Reduced water loss through runoff and increased water infiltration and storage in the soil were strongly perceived as leading to greater water availability. Cases from dryland areas report seasonal water loss in the order of 15–20% due to surface runoff. Additionally, the potential of reducing evaporation from the soil, especially in drier environments, where 40–70% of the rainfall can be lost, has been described clearly in examples of conservation agriculture. The com-

bined water loss through runoff and evaporation often leaves less than half of the rainfall – or irrigated water – available for crops or other vegetation. This clearly demonstrates the need for, and potential of, SWC. Terraces, rainfed as well as irrigated, also have a profound impact on water. Rainfed terraces generally provide for storage of rainfall through a raised 'lip' and are often designed to discharge excess runoff through a drainage system. Examples of this are the 'Rainfed paddy rice terraces' in the Philippines and the 'Zhuanglang loess terraces' in China.

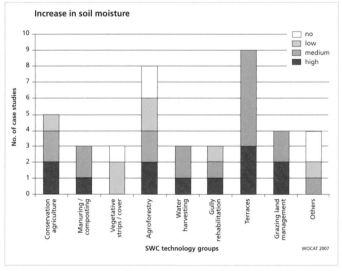

Figure 14: Increase of soil moisture within the SWC technology groups

Improved soil resources – *where roots can thrive*

Soil loss reduction: Generally all the groups of technologies are reported to have achieved a 'high' soil loss reduction – especially 'Terraces' (8 out of 9), 'Agroforestry' (5 out of 8), 'Conservation agriculture' (4 out of 5) and all 'Gully rehabilitation' and 'Vegetative strips/ cover'. The exceptions are 'Manuring/ composting' and 'Water harvesting' where the technologies are more concerned with fertility improvement and increasing water availability, respectively (Figure 15).

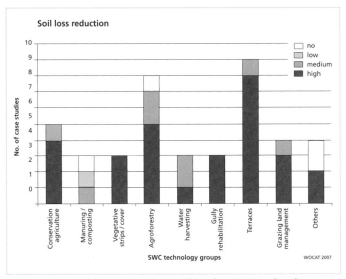

Figure 15: Soil loss reduction within the SWC technology groups

Soil cover improvement: The major achievers in terms of cover improvement are the cases under 'Grazing land management' (more grass; increased tree canopies), 'Conservation agriculture' (mulch) and 'Agroforestry' (multistorey canopies and improved undercover) (Figure 16). Terraces score poorly in this respect: most are still cultivated through inversion tillage (ploughs drawn by tractors or by oxen/ donkeys, tillage by hand hoes) and kept weed-free.

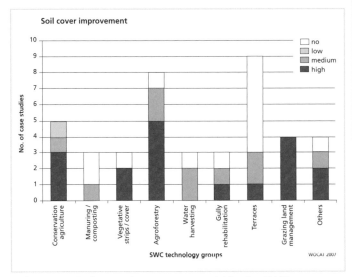

Figure 16: Soil cover improvement within the SWC technology groups

Manure and composts are usually incorporated into the soil rather than being used as mulch. Where water harvesting is practised, the catchment areas need to be kept relatively bare of cover to encourage runoff. This then comprises a system with a built-in self-contradiction: runoff and (to a lesser extent) surface erosion are actively encouraged in parts of the system to feed other parts.

Increase in soil fertility: The greatest increase in soil fertility recorded amongst the case study groups, not surprisingly, was under 'Manuring/ composting', as this was the primary objective of this group (see Figure 17). Nevertheless, 'Agroforestry' also scores well; two of the cases noting a 'high' increase and the remaining six all recording 'medium'. The 'Gully rehabilitation' and 'Water harvesting' cases are not primarily concerned with soil fertility management – though this may be achieved as a spin-off from sediment (and organic matter) harvesting behind physical barriers. Indeed more than half of the technologies (22 of 42) led to increased soil organic matter.

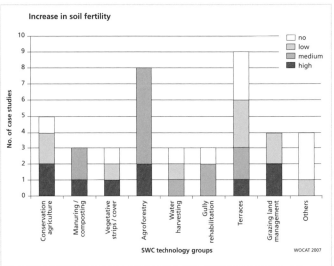

Figure 17: Increase in soil fertility within the SWC technology groups

On-site disadvantages – *drawbacks to in-field conservation*

Disadvantages mentioned by the contributors were presented as either 'high' 'medium' or 'low' in terms of their severity. The most commonly cited disadvantages were increased labour constraints (mentioned in around half the case studies for establishment; just less than half for maintenance),

left and centre left: Given declining availability of water for irrigation and domestic supplies, as well as growing incidence of water conflicts, the impact of SWC on river flow is crucial. This river in the Varzob valley of Tajikistan drains a degraded catchment: before heavy rain (left) and afterwards. (Hanspeter Liniger)

centre right: In Switzerland, with no conservation there can be serious on-site erosion, and consequent off-site impacts: roads covered with soil; drainage systems clogged. (Hanspeter Liniger)

right: In contrast, the neighbouring field with good soil cover and direct seeding – no damage at all after the same rainfall event. (Hanspeter Liniger)

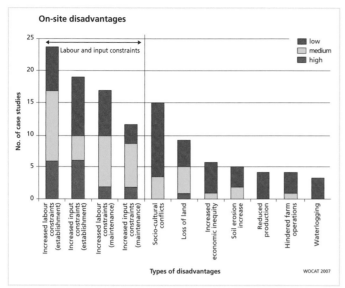

Figure 18: Perceived on-site disadvantages

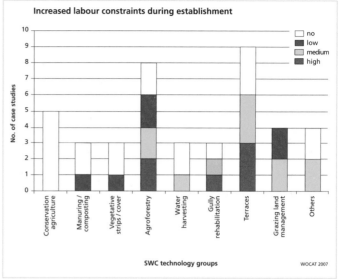

Figure 19: Perceived labour constraints during the initial phase of implementation in relation to SWC technology groups

and increased input costs (Figure 18). The only other two significant categories are loss of land (a common problem under terrace construction where land is 'lost' to the bunds and risers) and 'socio-economic conflicts,' which is a mixed bag of problems including, for example, the conversion of grazing areas to cropland, and thus some conflict between pastoralists and agriculturalists.

Additional disadvantages mentioned include a few cases where those who invest in SWC do not receive the benefits, which instead accrue to others – typically downstream – creating inequity. In other cases, erosion initially increases and production is also reduced before the measures begin to have impact. Others mention an alteration in the division of labour between men and women, and a change of values and norms regarding land use practices. All these factors need studied attention as they affect the acceptance, spread and adoption of SWC. It also needs pointing out that perceptions can change fast, and what was believed to be unlikely or even impossible, can sometimes, suddenly become accepted norms and practices.

Figure 19 demonstrates that the most frequently mentioned labour constraints are clearly related to those SWC groups that require the largest inputs. These are terraces and gully control, which comprise structural measures. Agroforestry also requires initial investment for the establishment of the tree component. Interestingly, water harvesting which generally depends on structural measures was not perceived as

a burden in the case studies: this is probably due to the immediate improvement in plant production from water harvested in dry areas. Increased labour constraints were not noted in association with conservation agriculture, nor the adoption of manure/ compost, nor systems involving vegetative strip and cover.

Off-site impacts – *the great unknown*

Figure 20 presents a summary of the perceived off-site (generally 'downstream') advantages and disadvantages of the technologies described in the case studies. The most striking water-related off-site benefit is the reduced downstream flooding and siltation reported in three-quarters of the case studies. Around half indicated a high to medium impact. Just less than half (43%) indicated reduced river pollution, and about one-third noted increased river/ stream flow in the dry season. However, the information – derived from SWC specialists working with land users – has seldom been quantified. One exception is the case of Australia's 'Green cane trash blanket', where research is currently assessing impacts on rivers and on the Barrier Reef. In the absence of such impact assessments, the question arises whether this high rating of off-site impacts is more wishful thinking than proven fact. However, there are also a few off-site disadvantages mentioned; reduced overall river flow was reported in four cases, though the impact was assessed as 'low' in three

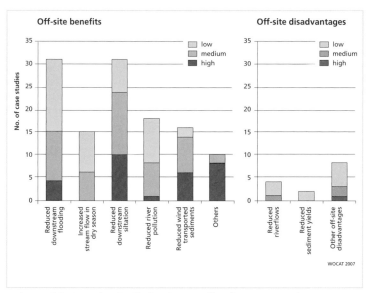

Figure 20: Perceived off-site (generally 'downstream') advantages/ benefits and disadvantages of the technologies described in the case studies.

cases. These cases referred to situations where terracing, and additional irrigation and water harvesting structures, reduced flows to downstream zones.

left: Agroforestry on steep slopes of the humid topics and subtropics have evolved into traditional systems - as here in the Kilimanjaro area of Tanzania. They are highly productive, have a positive impact on soil fertility, and provide crops, fodder, timber and fuelwood. (Hanspeter Liniger)

centre: An example of changing and adapting SWC practices over time in Kenya: in this situation earth bunds are being removed after 30 years of conservation service. The change in cultivation practice from deep to minimum tillage combined with mulching has resulted in greatly reduced runoff and soil erosion – even after heavy storms – and the protective soil bunds have become redundant. (Hanspeter Liniger)

right: Land use not only has on-site impacts, but it also affects people and settlements downstream. Originally, this settlement was built in a favourable location on a river fan from a mountain valley in Syria, where people depend directly on the water resources provided. If the mountains above are overused, floods will become a threat. (Hanspeter Liniger)

WOCAT ■ where the land is greener

3 Analysis of approaches –
putting the practices into place

Introduction – *definitions and overview*

According to WOCAT, a SWC approach constitutes 'the ways and means of support that help introduce, implement, adapt and apply SWC technologies on the ground'. This definition fits most comfortably within a project or programme framework where particular technologies are encouraged. It is also applicable to a technology that has spread spontaneously, although some issues such as 'extension' and 'use of incentives' are not relevant in these cases. This spread may have occurred either recently or through the ages as a tradition. Here the 'approach' is/was basically through transfer of knowledge within a community and through generations. An overall concept that best describes both situations (project promotion and spontaneous spread) is an 'enabling environment' within which conservation thrives. This analysis of approaches, we believe, sheds light on how SWC technologies can spread, and shows where investments can be made to 'make the land greener'.

This chapter reviews and analyses the 28 case studies of approaches presented in Part 2. The analysis broadly follows the various sections in the case studies: thus we look at names, objectives and emphases, followed by strengths and weaknesses and then the use of incentives and subsidies. Governance and decision-making issues are followed by a section on extension, training and adoption. Experience with land use rights is examined and this leads to monitoring, evaluation and responsiveness. A section on research completes the analysis.

The approaches documented in this book range from examples of self-mobilisation to those characterised by heavy subsidies and strong external technical support. However, it is not a simple matter of comparing these and saying one approach is necessarily 'better' than another: it all depends on the given situation. Allowance has to be made for the very great differences in circumstances: these include climatic zones, production systems, SWC technologies, wealth categories and development 'norms' concerning social goals and use of incentives and subsidies. Nevertheless we look for common threads, while trying to explain the differences.

A few words are necessary about the sample of approaches, and some basic differences between them. As discussed above, because the concept of an 'approach' is more readily applicable to a project or programme, this is where the datasets are most comprehensive and the data easiest to analyse. Where the questionnaire has been completed to describe a tradition (for example stone terracing in South Africa – the only tradition in this book where an approach is documented) a number of the questions are difficult to answer or irrelevant. In these cases (for example paddy rice terraces in Nepal and in the Philippines; stone terraces in Syria) the technology case studies stand alone. Only dedicated research could help unravel the circumstances leading to the evolution of these traditional technologies. Of the 28 approaches presented in the book, 20 are basically allied to projects/ programmes, and the other eight are descriptive of how spontaneous spread has occurred outside a structured campaign. One of these eight describes a tradition – the remaining seven refer to recent developments (Table 4).

There are 14 technology cases described in this book that are not matched one-to-one by approaches. In five situations the technologies comprise traditions where, as noted, we do not have information to reconstruct their origins. In a further two examples – from Ethiopia and Niger – a single approach in each case is 'shared' by two technologies. And in two further cases (from Kyrgyzstan and Australia, respectively) a single farmer has developed a conservation system outside a project framework. In the remaining five cases the specialist contributors have concentrated on the technologies, and not supplied the required information regarding the approach that led to the technological developments.

Without exception the sample here constitutes approaches that are viewed as being positive or at least 'promising'. Thus the analysis opens a window on denominators of success. Some of these denominators are common to many approaches, others are situation-specific. Within the sample there is a bias towards those approaches that have underpinned relatively successful technologies, and particularly technologies which are remedial (through mitigation or rehabilitation of erosion problems) rather than preventive (helping maintain sustainable systems). There is also, in-

left: A village discussion in Burkina Faso about the effects of degradation and solutions involving different stakeholders: while participatory, there are important questions to consider such as: who has a say? and who is marginalised? (Hanspeter Liniger)

right: Awareness raising in an indigenous reserve within Colombia where people are urged to cooperate: 'let's protect the natural resources; avoid slash-and-burn practices; do not remove earth'. (Mats Gurtner)

Table 4: Approaches analysed, titles, types, origin and lead actors/ agencies

Type/ name of approach	Country	Lead actor/ agency
Local initiative (tradition)		
Community tradition	South Africa	Local land users
Local initiative (recent)		
The 'triple bottom line' (TBL)	Australia	Local land users
Spontaneous spread	Kenya	Local land users
Transition from centralised regime to local initiative	Tajikistan	Local land users
Self-help group approach	Kenya	Local land users; with external support
Farmer initiative within enabling environment	Switzerland	Local land users; with external support
Self-teaching	South Africa	Individual initiative
Farmer innovation and self-help groups	Tajikistan	Individual initiative
Project/ programme		
Development and promotion of Ecograze	Australia	NGO
Incentive-based catchment treatment	Bolivia	NGO
Zabré women's agroecological programme	Burkina Faso	NGO
Integrated rural community development	Colombia	NGO
Soil management initiative (SMI)	United Kingdom	NGO
Market support and branding for input quality	India	NGO
Productive development and food security programme	Nicaragua	NGO
Participatory catchment rehabilitation	Peru	NGO
Joint forest management (JFM)	India	NGO/Government
Promoting farmer innovation (PFI)	Uganda	NGO/Government
Terrace approach	China	Government
Agroforestry extension	Costa Rica	Government
Local level participatory planning approach	Ethiopia	Government
Comprehensive watershed development	India	Government
Catchment approach	Kenya	Government
Applied research and knowledge transfer	Morocco	Government
Integrated watershed management	Nepal	Government
Participatory land rehabilitation	Niger	Government
Landcare	Philippines	Government
Participatory technology development (PTD)	Syria	Government

evitably, a focus on project/ programme-related initiatives, as these are the most conspicuous and best-known SWC interventions.

Titles, objectives and emphases –
what's in a name?

The language of development – *justified jargon?*

The current thinking in rural development – including soil and water conservation – emphasises the importance of participation of land users in all aspects of the project cycle, and is reflected in new terminology. These changes reflect the 'new approach' that emerged at the end of the 20th century. That approach was a reaction to shortcomings in top-down policies and practices in the past. Several of the approaches reported here have the word 'participation' either specified in their titles or mentioned in their brief description, yet only one has it highlighted under objectives. While the names and objectives of many projects genuinely try to reflect the end-of-century new approach, it may well be that some are using terminology because it is 'developmentally correct' or even necessary to attract funding.

Apart from participation, other common terms in titles amongst the approaches documented here – and within the WOCAT database at large – are 'integrated', 'innovation'/

'initiative', 'community'/ 'group' and 'catchment'/ 'watershed'. These are mainstream concepts in the vocabulary of the new approach. Not many projects appear to have deliberately sought catchy descriptive titles, or simple acronyms, to set them clearly apart. Exceptions are 'Joint forest management' (JFM, from India) 'Promoting farmer innovation' (PFI, from East Africa) 'Landcare' (from the Philippines, originally from Australia) and 'Development and promotion of Ecograze' (from Australia). The name 'Catchment approach' from Kenya's highlands is actually misleading. That is because it basically comprises an approach based on communities or administrative units rather than a hydrological catchment. Naturally, descriptive names for approaches have had to be created in this book for most of the traditional and contemporary spontaneous technologies – where there was no specific project support. Thus we have suggested titles such as 'Farmer initiative within enabling environment' (from Switzerland) and 'The triple bottom line' (from Australia).

Objectives – *taking aim*

A search through the objectives of the various approaches brings up an interesting array of aims – several of which are broader than just targeting better soil and water conservation. Commonly, the contributors to the case studies mistakenly cite the objectives of the technology supported by the approach, rather than the objectives of the approach itself. Thus 'environmental impacts' may be put forward rather than, for example, 'institution strengthening'. In most cases we have reworded these and then returned to the contributors for approval.

Many of the case studies involve SWC as just one element – a subset – of a wider rural development programme. However, a common general pattern emerges regarding objectives, actions and implementation arrangements. This can be represented as follows:
- *goals:* environmental improvement and poverty alleviation
- *through:* improved plant and livestock production, requiring conservation of specific resources
- *based on:* raised awareness, a sense of ownership, gender equality and improved governance
- *combining:* joint efforts of various actors with strengthened institutions

Few sets of objectives are defined as explicitly as this but many, if not most, combine one or more of these elements. It is very common to see, for example, social and environmental goals expressed simultaneously. Some projects take particular and specific angles: in Costa Rica the agroforestry extension initiative deliberately seeks to harmonise different approaches within the country. 'Promoting farmer innovation' (from East Africa) sees the stimulation of local innovation as a key objective. Food security is explicit in a number of cases (eg in Burkina Faso, PR China and Nicaragua) and in Bolivia the paid-for gully control measures are aimed firstly at achieving downstream benefits for the city of Cochabamba. Four research-based initiatives ('Participatory technology development' from Syria, 'Development and promotion of Ecograze' from Australia, the 'Soil management initiative' from the UK and applied research and technology transfer from Morocco) all set out, deliberately, to refine and spread technologies through land users. The two non-project, spontaneous developments from Tajikistan have implicit objectives of restoring control of land and production from the state to individual farmers.

A new focus – *alternatives for financing SWC*

Looking at the most recent trends, we can see a new set of objectives emerging in SWC interventions. These new objectives address rapidly emerging global environmental concerns, particularly those of mitigating climate change (hence carbon sequestration through biomass and increased soil organic matter levels), above and below ground biodiversity, and water (hence ecosystem functioning as well as water use efficiency under rainfed and irrigated agriculture). There are some indicators of future trends in the cases analysed. It is likely that increasing attention will be paid to addressing SWC concerns through new marketing opportunities – of which fair trade coffee from Costa Rica and 'Vinatura' environmentally friendly wine from Switzerland are examples from our current analysis. It is reported that the community development project from Colombia has now branched out into production of various organic products. There are also wide-ranging possibilities of accreditation/ labelling schemes to command market premiums. These may even go beyond fair trade and eco-labels and eventually into the realms of 'SWC-friendly products'. Pilot schemes promoting payment/ compensation for ecosystem services are almost certainly forerunners for a new breed of programme. These, typically, comprise compensation to land users in upland areas for maintaining vegetation in catchment areas, from industries, dwellers in towns or farmers downstream, to ensure water supply and mitigate damage from floods and landslides. The rate of compensation should be based on estimated values of these services. The case study from Bolivia is an example of where this type of

left: World heritage sites include agricultural land: a signboard announcing the famous terraced landscape of Ifugao in the Philippines where local and international agro-ecotourism is growing in importance. (William Critchley)

centre: The terraces foothills of Annapurna in Nepal add to the touristic value of the area. Here land users benefit from directly from improved production on their terraces – and have off-farm income opportunities from tourism. (Hanspeter Liniger)

right: 'Max Havelaar' coffee and 'Vinatura' wine: labelling of products helps promote ecological production and fair wages – as well as opening new market niches. (www.vitiswiss.ch)

approach could be developed. Ecotourism is already popular in parts of the world and agro-ecotourism is following cautiously in its environmental footsteps. In the case of the Ifugao terraces in the Philippines, agro-ecotourism helps, indirectly, to pay for their upkeep. Agro-ecotourism is currently on the agenda as a possibility to capitalise on the spectacular terraces of the Loess Plateau in China.

Strengths and weaknesses – *what works well and where challenges remain*

Strong points – *successes to learn from*

It is revealing to look through the strengths of the various approaches, as recorded by SWC specialists closely associated with the related project (where the approach is project-based). While the strengths are supposed to be a combination of the specialist's and the land users' views, it is probable that the specialist's voice is the more prominent. What tends to be reiterated in these 'strengths' are several of the objectives stated earlier. Thus we have institution building for specific aspects of natural resource management (UK, Peru, Kenya's self-help groups and landcare in the Philippines), ownership and involvement of the land users and indigenous knowledge (Syria, Nepal, Kenya's catchment approach and the example from Ethiopia) and changed attitudes (Peru and Bolivia). However, there are some less expected strengths highlighted in other cases. These include the impact of 'local promoters' in Colombia, the challenge to entrenched gender roles in Burkina Faso, and institutionalisation of the approach in Costa Rica.

Shortcomings – *weaknesses to address*

The documented weaknesses of the approaches are at least as important to this analysis as their strengths. These include:
- the period of intervention and funding needing to be of significant duration, but often too short to achieve lasting impact (many examples of this)
- the problem of participatory approaches being very demanding on human resources (Nicaragua; East Africa)
- the need for more training (Australia) and material incentives given to land users having the effect of being temporary 'bribes' and getting in the way of voluntary work afterwards (several examples)
- other less expected and location-specific weaknesses were: problems associated with over-supplied markets (for coffee in Costa Rica; for forest products in India), with land conflicts in Niger (once conservation invest-

ments had raised the value of land), and power struggles between various stakeholders in Burkina Faso, the Philippines and Tajikistan.

On the other hand, where the 'approach' describes a tradition or spontaneous spread of a technology, the weaknesses usually highlight the lack of support or recognition from outside.

Incentives – *helping hands or addictive stimulants?*

Incentives and participation – *hand-outs and taking part*

Genuine 'participation' is related to the level of input (labour, materials and intellectual) provided voluntarily by the land users/ beneficiaries. In other words, the lower the degree of outside subsidy, incentive or other support, the greater the level of genuine land user participation. Thus, one key aspect of any approach is the extent to which the approach includes subsidies and support for existing/ local efforts and resources to implement SWC technologies, and how far this might then influence further, and future, spread. If a high level of material subsidy is given, spontaneous uptake will be unlikely, as people will expect to receive continued support. The majority of direct or 'external' incentives provided by projects take the form of minor material inputs, such as seeds, tools and fertilizer, and payment for labour. However, in 15 out of the 20 project/ programme-based approaches there were low or negligible levels of inputs. In fact, 5 of these 15 cases provided no material incentives to land users at all, implying full cost borne – and thus full commitment – by land users. Examples are promoting farmer innovation (Uganda), market support (India) and participatory technology development (Syria).

Food-for-work – *earning a meal*

The use of food-for-work (labour paid through food rather than cash), especially when associated with acute food shortages, was commonplace in the late 20th century. But it has become largely discredited due to logistical complications, misadministration, and a growing awareness by donors of the 'dependency syndrome' that can so quickly result. The only such example we see here is from Ethiopia. In the agroforestry system from Colombia (integrated rural community development) food-for-work is mentioned as having been phased out. Nevertheless in this latter case, the cost of implementation was so high and the subsidy so large

that (regardless of the nature of the subsidy) one wonders indeed whether the technology can ever expand spontaneously outside the immediate surroundings of the project. One alternative to food-for-work is support given to institutions in terms of materials, training and infrastructure. This is becoming increasingly common, and is said to be a strong feature in 12 of the 20 project/ programme approaches. Another alternative form of support, a specific credit facility for farmers to tap into, is provided in only four cases. This could be a promising avenue for the future.

Support for labour – rewards for work

There are arguments in favour of subsidies under specific circumstances, such as the rehabilitation of the ancient stone bench terraces in Peru. The original, historic, investment in terracing will be lost unless the poverty-stricken local people are assisted in a one-off rehabilitation process to re-establish dilapidated terraces. Another consideration is the different norms and standards from country to country. Thus in India, under joint forest management, participation of the community is considered a cornerstone of the approach. Indeed, unless the community acts together in 'social fencing', meaning collective agreement to protect an area from livestock and other uses, the concept collapses. The long-term commitment of the government and donors to broaden the cover of this initiative, combined with the poverty of the people, means that spread will continue to occur despite the very high level of subsidy. Here the national norm for paid labour is 85–95% of the local cost of a daily wage. In most parts of Africa, under most SWC initiatives, this relatively high level of subsidy would certainly not be considered to constitute 'true' participation.

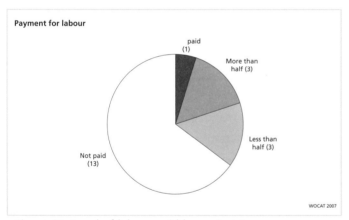

Payment for labour

paid (1)

More than half (3)

Less than half (3)

Not paid (13)

WOCAT 2007

Figure 21: Level of labour paid by projects/ programme under reported approaches

Voluntary labour is provided by land users in 13 of the 20 cases (Figure 21). It is fully paid by the project in only one situation documented here: the exceptional case of Bolivia where the primary beneficiaries are not those involved in the gully control treatments, but city dwellers, downstream. In over half of the project/ programme-based approaches it is believed that there will be at least a 'moderately negative' impact of current material incentives on the land users in years to come. The 'negative impact' here implies a perceived constraint on voluntary uptake or maintenance in the future, after apparent enthusiasm proves later to be 'pseudo-interest' in SWC. Nevertheless, initial, highly subsidised investment in SWC – as in Ethiopia during the 1970s – may in some cases leave a framework that persists several decades after, and forms the basis for future, participatory soil and water conservation.

The discussion about incentives is central in project/programme-based initiatives. Locally originated approaches appear to be fully participatory, as there is/ was no outside agency providing inputs. The main incentive at play in those cases is/ was evidently that of improved production resulting from conservation efforts. This is essentially an 'internal' incentive. Most traditions – take stone terracing in South Africa, for example – have not arisen through projects or programmes, and labour has been voluntary (though perhaps coercive under some ancient civilisations?), from original construction through maintenance by successive generations. Thus incentives should not exclusively be seen as payments, but the stimulus that a land user experiences through higher production, or through saving time and money.

Uptake of technologies and incentives – *stimulating adoption*

In three of the technology groups more than 50% of the current uptake is attributable to incentive schemes: these are (a) grazing land management, (b) gully rehabilitation and (c) water harvesting measures. One common denominator that connects these three groups of technologies is the high initial labour requirement – and this partially explains why they are so often subsidised. One would have expected terraces also to fit into this category with their high labour requirement. The reason why only half of the terrace-related technologies are supported by incentives is because several of the cases are ancient traditions that are no longer under construction: incentives are simply not required when they didn't exist (presumably) during construction. Few incentives are used in the terrace approach from China. But it is an exception in a number of ways. Not only is this the

largest, most closely organised implementation programme analysed here, but the achievements are remarkable, considering the low level of material support to land users. The key here is the conversion of eroded slopes to highly productive farmland. This production stimulus also underpins those groups of technologies that have the highest rates of adoption without incentives. These are the three groups of (a) vegetative strips/ cover, (b) conservation agriculture, and (c) manure/ composting systems. It is no coincidence that these are the technologies that give the quickest returns to land users, at the lowest investment cost.

Subsidies and markets – *manipulating the economy*

The cases from the 'developed' countries in Europe – Switzerland and the UK – stand apart. Here there are heavy government subsidies in general for agriculture, though the current tendency is to decouple these from production and link farm level support instead to environmental protection and 'stewardship'. However, the triple bottom line case from Australia does not benefit from subsidies for sugar cane, which is not protected from world market prices: environmental protection has been achieved despite the relatively low prices and lack of external support. These same global market prices can have a direct influence on land management in other situations. In Kenya, the high price of coffee in the 1970s stimulated and helped pay for construction of terracing systems amongst small-scale producers. Most have been kept up, despite the slump in prices soon afterwards. In Costa Rica, however, the international drop in coffee prices over the last two decades has had a negative impact on spontaneous uptake of the Café arbolado system.

While conservation agriculture does not attract a direct subsidy in the UK case presented here, it does form part of an environmental package that helps the farmer qualify for benefits. This transition towards environmental protection is the shape of things to come in 'developed' countries, where food production has become a secondary concern in the countryside. Aesthetic, recreational and cultural considerations, ecosystem services, and food quality concerns have taken over. And there is the need to keep some farmers on the land as 'stewards' of the countryside. In these situations there is, effectively, an urban-rural flow of tax money, dedicated to keeping the countryside from degenerating. Payments for ecosystem services are a promising policy and management approach with two options:
- payment or tax concessions by the government for ecosystem services rendered (eg through subsidies, as in Europe)

- payment or compensations directly by users of an ecosystem service to those who ensure that service (eg as suggested in the Bolivia case study – namely payments from city inhabitants to the farmers in the catchments above). The idea is that this type of payment/compensation could be sustainable, and would economically underpin investment in SWC.

Ecosystem services

Ecosystem services are the benefits people obtain from ecosystems. These include provisioning services: the products obtained from ecosystems, including food, fibre, medicine; regulating services: including air quality regulation, climate regulation (carbon sequestration), water regulation; cultural services: the nonmaterial benefits people obtain from ecosystems through spiritual enrichment, cognitive development, reflection, recreation, and aesthetic experiences etc; supporting services: those that are necessary for the production of all other ecosystem services, including soil formation, photosynthesis, nutrient cycling, water cycling, etc [note: the term 'Environmental services' is commonly used as an alternative].

Source: summarised from Millennium Ecosystem Assessment, 2005. Ecosystems and Human well-being Synthesis. Island Press, Washington, DC.

Funding, governance and decision-making – *who calls the tune?*

Taking all the 20 project-based case studies together, it is striking that – calculating the average proportions of fund-

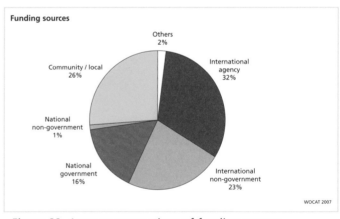

Figure 22: Average proportions of funding sources in reported approaches

ing sources – a quarter of the contributions are from local communities and nearly one-sixth from national governments (Figure 22). The international community provides, on average, just over half, namely 55%. Outside donors are important investors in these successful examples of SWC interventions – but not at such a high level as might have been expected. The level of community/ individual contributions and their 'buy-in' to the initiatives is generally impressive, considering that many of the projects cover very poor areas.

'Participation' does not just mean providing labour, materials or ideas. There is a governance dimension to it also. The ultimate form of participation, namely 'self-mobilisation', is applicable de facto to all the spontaneous approaches. Under the project/ programme approaches, the great majority are 'interactive' or 'self-mobilised' during most of the phases of the initiatives (initiation, planning, implementation, monitoring/ evaluation and research; Figure 23), implying that there is strong local initiative as well as two-way communication between outsiders (who naturally benefit also through salaries) and local beneficiaries. This is a firm indicator of self-governance, and is clearly a trademark of the new approach to participatory development that characterises most of the cases analysed.

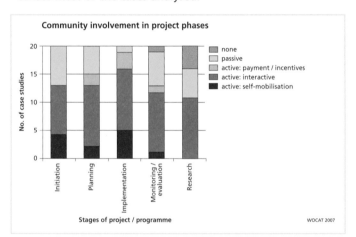

Figure 23: Community involvement in different stages for project-based case studies

Strong community involvement is highlighted further by the fact that nearly half of the projects/ programmes claim that the choice of technology was principally the choice of the land users (either alone or supported in their choice by SWC specialists; Figure 24). The final piece of evidence regarding ownership of the process is that the actual design of the

approach shows significant international 'expert' input in less than half of the project/ programme approaches. The others were designed by national and local experts.

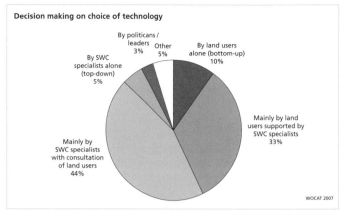

Figure 24: Decision making on choice of technology for project-based case studies

While the question pertaining to the difference in participation between men and women was asked at a very basic level, gender as an issue in SWC (as with many other rural activities) was highlighted in the results. There is a marked division of tasks in SWC responsibilities and activities: there is a 'moderate or great' difference in the roles of men and women related to SWC, in nearly two-thirds of the cases. However, this should not be interpreted automatically as proof of bias or discrimination. Some SWC tasks are traditionally divided between men and women: in a number of cases, for example, it is said that the heavy construction work of terrace bunds is left to the men. On the other hand, although there are not enough data to support the proposition definitively, the in-field agronomic measures that contribute so much to conservation (and are often 'unseen' as SWC) are very much the preserve of women in developing countries. Women's conservation activities may not always be conspicuous, but they are often vital.

Extension, training and adoption – *spreading and accepting the word*

Methods used – *the means towards the end*

The answers given to the various questions on extension and training tend to mix and match these two aspects to the extent that it is difficult to disaggregate them. To most respondents, training (in skills) and extension (spreading the

left and centre: Participatory approaches involve land users and specialists reviewing problems and solutions together. They require sensitivity and mutual respect, but can generate lasting solutions through considering priorities of all stakeholders. Examples here from India (Hanspeter Liniger), Syria (Francis Turkelboom) and Burkina Faso (Hanspeter Liniger)

centre right: Gender sensitivity is essential in understanding and documenting good land management practices – women often feel freer to express themselves to other women, as here in Iran. (William Critchley)

right: Father to son transfer was the traditional way of passing on knowledge: now this needs to be supplemented by documentation (Nicaragua). (Mats Gurtner)

message) go hand-in-hand. In all of these areas there has been a switch to more participation, devolution of powers, and less authoritarianism. There is, for example, a common view about the need for empowerment of beneficiaries, a shared concern that marginalised people in society should receive more attention, and a joint recognition of the need for accountability and openness. In the case from Nicaragua, this common ground is clear: the conservation approach documented under WOCAT is described as being part of a much wider programme of 'popular education'.

Broadly speaking, there are three forms of extension and training:
- First, that which could be termed the 'multiple strategy'. This is what is adopted by the majority of the project/ programme-based approaches. It includes several or all of the following: awareness-raising ('sensitisation' is a term often used, artificially constructed from French and Spanish equivalents), training workshops and seminars around specific themes, exposure visits, hands-on training, and the use of demonstration plots.
- The second main form is based on informal farmer-to-farmer extension and exchange of ideas. Here projects assist through facilitating exchange between farmers: for example by enabling farmers to visit each other for mutual learning.
- The third is centred on the use of trained 'local promoters'. These are basically local farmers who are trained to become facilitators/ extension workers under a project.

None of these are mutually exclusive, and all are forward-thinking methods. Spontaneous spread of technologies has almost exclusively occurred through farmer-to-farmer exchange of information, including visitors from afar, not just neighbours. Farmer-to-farmer transmission was the only form of 'extension' for thousands of years, and not only has it not died out, but it is being rejuvenated through progressive projects. The recent cases of spontaneous spread of specific technologies (eg grevillea in Kenya; green cover in Switzerland; green cane trash blanket in Australia) may have been helped by the media (radio, television, the press, internet, etc), though this does not come across clearly in the case studies. The spread of conservation agriculture in the UK is an exception, however, being the only explicit example of internet-supported extension. Even in this case the internet is secondary, behind face-to-face learning and written material.

WOCAT's philosophy is that specialists, and literate land users as well, learn from what is written (or available on CD-ROM or the internet). The self-taught implementation of vetiver grass barriers in South Africa is the only case amongst those 28 analysed here where the written or digital media are explicitly cited as the *main* source of inspiration and guidance. However, as noted above, this might have happened to some extent in some other examples. Correspondingly, there is very little mention in the case studies of producing or using extension materials. Not surprisingly, there is no mention of internet-based learning in developing countries. Perhaps this will change as digital barriers are increasingly broken down and the internet (and even more so, the mobile phone) infiltrates into rural areas.

Adoption – *uptake and spread*

So, what of adoption rates being stimulated by extension and training programmes? How far has the message been spread? Information is limited to the case study areas – and it should be recalled that the WOCAT case study approach presents information from limited areas, rather than an assessment of the spread of technologies or approaches countrywide or internationally. Amongst the approaches presented here, adoption runs into the thousands of people, with respect to compost pits in Burkina Faso and rehabilitation of terraces in Peru; with respect to the 'Green cane trash blanket' system for sugar cane in Australia; and with people managing forest land under 'Joint forest management' in India. The *fanya juu* terrace under Kenya's catchment approach has also spread widely. But it may have become a victim of its own success, being implemented sometimes where cheaper agronomic (or vegetative) remedies may have been more appropriate. The most widely spread technology documented here is that of conservation agriculture in the UK, which covers approximately 40% of arable land in England. In other examples the spread is either less in absolute terms (eg conservation agriculture in Morocco, which is in an experimental stage, or the single farmer examples from Tajikistan and South Africa), or the case study covers only a sample area and, as a result, the coverage appears to be less than it actually is. Examples of this latter situation are green cover within the vineyards of Switzerland, which is actually widespread throughout the vine growing regions, and terracing on the Loess Plateau of China, where again only a small area was considered for the case study.

Land use rights – *a sense of security*

Whether land use rights affect the spread of SWC technologies – and if so, in what way – is one of the most interesting issues here. A common assumption is that private ownership

of land equals security, thus giving the owner an incentive to invest. This is confirmed by at least two case studies reviewed – examples from Nicaragua and Kenya. However, the issue here seems to be security of tenure rather than titled ownership, the former providing as great an incentive as the latter. Thus, where there is security even if actual ownership is absent, this can give the same degree of confidence to carry out SWC measures. This is highlighted in the cases from Burkina Faso, Nepal and China, and the lack of security of tenure is given as a hindrance in Ethiopia. Confirming this point, building structures or planting trees on land may help make an imprint of rights to the land, effectively 'staking a claim'. This can be witnessed through the case of traditional terracing in South Africa, and in a slightly different way in the case of the innovative farmer and his fruit garden in Tajikistan. The farm boundary planting of grevillea trees in Kenya works in much the same way. A variation on this is in Niger, where a land market has opened up, as fields have been brought back into production and reacquired value, bringing with it problems of claims to ancient lands. In India, the success of the joint forest management approach is based on the transfer of usufruct rights of degraded forest land from the state to villagers. A new challenge emerges from countries in the former Soviet block, and from China, where land use rights, previously held by the state, are now being transferred to villages and sometimes individuals. Figure 25 illustrates the importance of individual land use rights in relation to technologies. Three-quarters of the technology case studies (31 out of 42) originate from individually controlled land. Of the others, three are on leased land, three on common land with regulations, and a further three on common land which is subject to open access (without regulations). One of the remaining two is situated on land granted under a mining concession, and in the last case the land use rights are unclear.

The most difficult situations are open access regimes. Such tenure systems are represented in this book under gully rehabilitation, grazing land management, and riverbank stabilisation. There is a need to try to identify and evaluate more successful examples on land with open access – especially on grazing land, where there is very little evidence of recent successes. Under open access regimes (or common property situations with weak regulatory mechanisms), there is the double dilemma of nobody accepting responsibility and no-one being prepared to invest in the land. The potential for 'tragedy of the commons' situations is an active and present danger. That scenario, which depicts a free-for-all descent into land degradation, needs to be countenanced.

Monitoring, evaluation and research – *counting the costs, assessing the consequences*

Monitoring and evaluation – *weighing the evidence*

The majority of projects are involved in monitoring and evaluation (M&E). However, this mainly refers to the basic requirements imposed by governments or funding agencies: financial indicators, and recording physical targets of dubious value (eg 'running kilometres' of conservation structures built; number of tree seedlings raised in nurseries). There is little or no mention of truly 'participatory' M&E, with only five of the 20 project-based cases being 'self-mobilised' to carry out monitoring. Apparently, even the most forward-thinking projects have not ventured so far into the realms of participation that they open up that complex set of issues, which involve such questions as: What is meaningful to whom to measure? Who measures what? Who records the results? Who interprets the results and uses them?

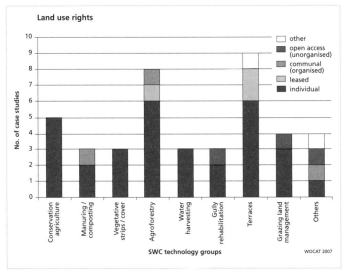

Figure 25: Land use rights with respect to SWC technology groups (see Analysis of Technologies for descriptions of these groups)

The most interesting aspects of M&E reported are the reactions of projects to findings derived from M&E. Figure 26 demonstrates that 17 out of 19 projects/ programmes have responded by modifying the approach or some of the activ-

left: Insecure land user rights limits the acceptance and maintenance of labour-intensive SWC measures. Runoff after heavy rainfall in Afdeyu, Eritrea indicates clearly where maintenance needs to be improved. (Mats Gurtner)

centre: Farmer-to-farmer learning is becoming increasingly recognised as a vital part of knowledge sharing. It is a component of many successful SWC initiatives (Uganda). (William Critchley)

right: Photo-monitoring of an upper catchment where farmers are encouraged to implement SWC measures to protect their own resources and to avoid off-site effects of degradation in the city of Cochabamba, Bolivia. (Georg Heim)

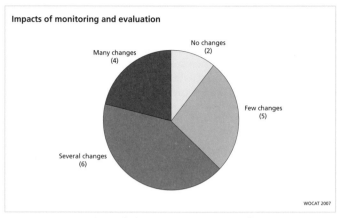

Figure 26: Number of changes – either modifications to technologies or to approach (or both) – as a result of M&E under project-based case studies

Impacts of monitoring and evaluation

Many changes (4)
No changes (2)
Few changes (5)
Several changes (6)

WOCAT 2007

ities to a certain extent (note: in the case from Morocco it is said to be 'too early to know' as M&E is ongoing – thus Morocco is not included in the figure).

In specific cases there are notable changes in activities and even in the approach design itself. A steady evolution has taken place in many (if not most) of the longer-term interventions, as would be expected. Thus we see changes over the years reported in the cases from Colombia, Nicaragua and Niger. In the case of the 'Catchment approach' in Kenya, the contributing SWC specialist warns that it is changing continuously, and each time an update is asked for, the data will differ. Here the project is a true 'moving target' for a questionnaire. Two projects reported major changes: in Nepal this was the result of an external evaluation, and in Costa Rica, the project was struggling to make headway with its top-down methodology. It turned this on its head, making it 'bottom up', and the participatory approach that emerged was eventually institutionalised in the ministry. Adaptation, in order to remain relevant to land users and changing conditions, is vital. 'Development and promotion of Ecograze' (Australia) notes that it needs to adapt to each given situation and individual rancher. In the UK, the 'Soil management initiative' 'is constantly refining its advice on the basis of results monitored in the field'. A final comment is the scarcity of written information regarding the approaches presented here. With notable exceptions (the 'Soil management initiative' from the UK, 'Development and promotion of Ecograze' from Australia, and the 'Catchment approach' from Kenya, for example) for most contributors, this WOCAT-related exercise is the first time their methodol-

ogy and experience have been documented, proving that very point.

Research – *the need to enhance knowledge*

A number of the technologies reported here were designed through a strong research initiative; this is true of 'Ecograze' in Australia, and conservation agriculture both in the UK and in Morocco. However, while 16 of the 20 project-based approaches claim a significant research component, this is rarely comprehensive, and usually concentrates on specific aspects of the project or the associated technology. In the UK, the 'Soil management initiative' looks at various specific problems such as slugs and grass weeds; under 'Joint forest management' in India, various elements of the programme have been studied, including socio-economic aspects; in Costa Rica, research has been limited to on-farm trials. However, the knowledge gaps in the data – as well as various contradictions – bear testimony to the fact that we need a broader contribution from research. How otherwise is it possible to assess technical, ecological, social and economic impact? Naturally, research must be transdisciplinary: scientists simply have to work together with land users to achieve optimal impact.

A further researchable area concerns preconceived notions of success or impacts. What is 'right and beneficial' for the environment can evolve into an unchallenged belief system. Examples are in India where the amount of groundwater recharge seems to be overestimated, given the small recharge area; in Kenya, where the *fanja juu* terrace is sometimes applied in areas where it is actually unnecessary; and tree-planting everywhere being perceived as unquestionably 'good'. There is a need for objective research, to look at things in context, and to avoid the danger of extrapolation and generalisation: 'good' or 'bad' depends on the context. A clear opportunity exists for research to engage in long-term monitoring, both on-site and off-site. We need to know impacts on the land – soil, water and vegetation – and the three should not be dissociated.

left: Monitoring the impacts of different land use and conservation efforts is an identified weakness where research needs to take a more active role (Switzerland). (Hanspeter Liniger)

centre: Training specialists to document and evaluate SWC in PR China: joint efforts are needed to close the gap in knowledge management. (Xin Shen)

right: Documenting and evaluating SWC as a team is a learning process between stakeholders: here a local farmer, an SWC specialist and a researcher working together in Nepal. (Hanspeter Liniger)

4 Conclusions and policy points – *support for descision makers*

The following comprises the consolidated conclusions from analysis of the case studies – 42 technologies and 28 approaches – which cover a wide range of soil and water conservation from all over the world. These conclusions are further informed and influenced by WOCAT's broader database, and have been developed through discussions amongst the WOCAT network partners. Some of the conclusions are new; others reconfirm what is already known but deserves repeating. They are presented under the following headings: 'Knowledge management', 'SWC technologies', 'SWC approaches' and 'Overall conclusions'.

In reviewing the conclusions, it has been possible to identify a number of related points that have clear policy implications for planners and decision-makers in governments and development agencies. These are presented in boxes following each of the sets of conclusions. Given that they are based on a global-level analysis, they may require fine-tuning and more explicit formulation to reflect specific national and regional situations. These policy points reflect, furthermore, 'what' needs to be done rather than 'how' it can be achieved. Once again the particular circumstances must be taken into account to define specific strategies and the activities that are appropriate in each case. This global overview provides a 'model' that could be used for the comprehensive documentation and analysis of experience leading to refined policy guidelines at the national and regional levels.

Knowledge management– *capitalising on scattered experiences*

Documentation – *the basis for decision support*

Worldwide, there are numerous positive experiences derived from investments in soil and water conservation (SWC) that contribute to sustainable land management (SLM). These counter the prevailing and pessimistic view that land and environmental degradation is inevitable and continuous: 42 of the 350 cases in the WOCAT database are presented in this book.

Apart from the cases documented through WOCAT (and elsewhere), the vast body of knowledge and wealth of experience in SWC remains scattered and localised. There is still a rich untapped SWC diversity which is not readily available to land users, those who advise them, or planners and decision-makers. Thus the basis for sound decision making is lacking, mistakes are being repeated, and 'the wheel is being reinvented'.

The WOCAT tools provide a unique standardised method for the comprehensive documentation, evaluation and dissemination of SWC knowledge from various sources (including land users, SWC specialists and researchers from different disciplines). This has been lacking so far: with few exceptions – 'Ecograze' from Australia; '*Fanya juu* terraces' from Kenya; 'Forest catchment treatment' from India – the experiences presented in the book have not been reported comprehensively elsewhere.

Land users and SWC specialists are usually happy and willing to discuss their work, and they welcome interest and recognition from outsiders. Occasionally, however, there is a reluctance to report weaknesses in government or donor-sponsored programmes. This challenges the documentation process, and affects the comprehensiveness and quality of the data.

Knowledge gaps, inconsistencies, and contradictions within the case studies have been uncovered while compiling them, and data quality has been considerably improved through an intensive review process.

Policy points: documentation

Concerted efforts to standardise documentation and evaluation of SWC technologies and approaches are needed and fully justified, especially in the light of the billions of dollars spent annually on implementation.

To assure the quality and usefulness of information, scattered knowledge about SWC needs to be identified, documented and assessed through a thorough and interactive review process that involves the joint efforts of land users, technical specialists and researchers.

left: … 'where the land is greener' … there are numerous positive experiences that contribute to sustainable land management – but this wealth of information is not tapped, and often not even recognised. There is an urgent need to make use of this valuable knowledge (Tajikistan). (Hanspeter Liniger)

right: Local knowledge is vital in designing effective and appropriate solutions. It is vital to give local land users a forum to share their knowledge with other farmers and specialists – and more investments are justified under SWC projects to facilitate this process (Syria). (Hanspeter Liniger)

Once documented, experiences with SWC need to be made widely available and accessible in a form that allows land users, advisors and planners to review a 'basket' of alternative options, setting out the advantages and disadvantages of each, thereby enabling them to make informed choices rather than following set prescriptions of 'what to do'.

The implementation of new SWC efforts should build on existing knowledge from within a location itself or, alternatively, from similar conditions and environments elsewhere.

There is need for a standardised methodology - like the WOCAT tools – to facilitate comprehensive data collection, knowledge management and dissemination.

Monitoring and Evaluation – *a prerequisite to improve SWC and to justify investments*

Monitoring and evaluation (M&E), especially of the technical efficiency and cost-effectiveness of SWC technologies and approaches, are weak spots in many, if not most projects. Likewise, traditional land use systems and local land management innovations are rarely documented and assessed for their conservation effectiveness.

All too often 'institutional amnesia' means that governments and donors remain unaware of historical experience in SWC, and fail to learn the lessons from past efforts.

Experience shows that M&E leads to important changes and modifications in approaches and technologies: nearly all (17 of 20) of the project-based approaches presented here reported changes as a result of M&E.

SWC initiatives are constantly evolving: they are 'moving targets'. This is a positive sign; the implication is that they are responding to changing circumstances and opportunities that arise. However, it also means that monitoring of changes and evaluation of impacts must keep track: 'snapshot' data quickly become outdated.

In the evaluation process land users play a central role in the assessment of the specific, as well as the overall, benefits and disadvantages.

In the compilation of SWC knowledge using WOCAT tools, a number of issues are addressed where commonly little or no information is available. Through the case studies in this book a special effort was made to fill gaps regarding the on-

and off-site environmental, social and economic impacts of SWC, including short and long-term costs and benefits.

An additional lack of information concerns the geographic coverage of SWC. This results from inadequate monitoring of the extent and effectiveness of conservation. Although several countries and regions have land degradation maps, mapping of SWC efforts and areas under SLM has been badly neglected. Such mapping can contribute to raising awareness of what has been achieved, as well as justifying further investments and guiding future decision-making.

In the process of compiling the case studies, we noted preconceived notions of what constitutes success and over-optimistic assumptions of impacts. Special efforts were made to reduce biases and misconceptions, unsubstantiated extrapolation, and generalisation.

Policy points: monitoring and evaluation

Monitoring and evaluation in SWC projects/ programmes must be improved. It needs to do more than just monitor the timely delivery of project outputs; it should also evaluate whether the expected environmental and development benefits have been realised in a cost-effective manner.

Rigorous impact assessment, involving the evaluation of strengths and how to sustain them, as well as evaluation of weaknesses and how to overcome them, is a must.

Land users have to be involved as key actors in monitoring and evaluation activities: their judgement of the pros and cons of SWC interventions is crucial.

There is a need to develop mechanisms to monitor and evaluate local conservation practices, land management innovations and traditional land use systems.

More investment in training and capacity building is needed for objective and unbiased monitoring and evaluation, for impact assessment, and to improve skills in knowledge management including the dissemination and use of information.

Mapping of conservation coverage is essential, in order to visualise the extent and effectiveness of human achievements.

Complexity and knowledge gaps –
the role of research

The problems of land degradation are complex and so are the answers. There is a danger of simplification. Blueprint solutions for the implementation of SWC do not take account of this complexity.

Effective SWC depends on both suitable technologies and closely matched approaches for their promotion.

Despite the fact that 16 of the 20 project-based approaches presented here claim a significant research component, information regarding on-site impacts is rarely quantified, and off-site impacts are often completely neglected. The main issues concern short and long-term costs, benefits and impacts, valuation of ecosystem services, area coverage, and the extent and effectiveness of SWC.

There are still important research questions to be addressed with respect to the processes that drive spontaneous spread of technologies and how project approaches can best stimulate these processes: we do not yet fully understand why SWC technologies are spontaneously adopted in some situations, while under other circumstances the same technologies spread very slowly.

The case studies have shown that participatory development of technology – where SWC specialists, researchers and land users act together – yields positive and practical results. Examples from the case studies include those from Syria ('Participatory technology development'), Australia ('The triple bottom line'), Kenya ('Self-help groups') and the Philippines ('Landcare'). The main challenge for research is not to 'invent' new SWC technologies, but rather to identify – together with land users – the most suitable technologies for a given set of conditions.

Policy points: complexity and knowledge gaps

There are no simple 'silver bullet' solutions to the complex problems of land degradation. It is therefore important to understand the ecological, social and economic causes of degradation, to analyse what works and why, and how to modify and adapt particular technologies and approaches to locally specific circumstances and opportunities.

Technologies and associated approaches need to be flexible and responsive to changing complex ecological and socio-economic environments. An urgent and specific area for further investigations and research is quantification and valuation of the ecological, social and economic impacts of SWC, both on-site and off-site, including the development of methods for the valuation of ecosystem services.

SWC research should seek to incorporate land users, scientists from different disciplines and decision-makers. A continuous feedback mechanism is needed to ensure active participation of these stakeholders.

Researchers need to take a more active role in further development of tools and methods for knowledge exchange and improved decision support.

SWC technologies –
measures and their impacts

General

Soil erosion by water is cited as being addressed in almost 90% of the examples. Chemical degradation (typically soil fertility decline) is addressed in 62%, wind erosion and water degradation each in around 30% of the cases, while vegetation degradation is mentioned in only 17%, and physical degradation (mainly compaction) in merely 9%. Frequently, multiple degradation types are stated as being addressed by SWC measures.

The responses indicate the common perception of soil erosion by water as being the main degradation problem, rather than the consequence of other less obvious degradation processes such as declining vegetation cover, soil compaction, etc.

We can differentiate between prevention, mitigation and rehabilitation of land degradation. Of the case studies in the book, 17% fall under prevention, 52% under mitigation and 31% under rehabilitation. Prevention and mitigation usually provide the best pay-back. Rehabilitation may be the most visible form of SWC – but can be very costly.

It is commonly assumed that enough is known about SWC technologies and that it is 'just' a question of applying them. However, modifications to technologies and new combinations of measures are frequently necessary to make them match area-specific social, political, economic and environmental situations.

left: In this example from Ethiopia, introduced terraces have not been accepted by local land users: they are being ploughed under. In situations like this, it is important to know in what circumstances they were established and to understand the reasons why they are not maintained. (Karl Herweg)

right: Documenting and evaluating local knowledge in Nepal: land users and SWC specialists discuss the strengths and weaknesses of traditional irrigated rice terraces and document these through the use of WOCAT tools. (Hanspeter Liniger)

Most conservation technologies can spread widely with incremental on- and off-site benefits. Some, however, are subject to the 'island effect', where the measures thrive *because* they are isolated. An example is water harvesting where the area of concentration (the 'island') benefits from runoff water harvested from a catchment area without conservation measures.

Improved soil cover (mentioned in 55% of the cases), and fertility (57%) are the most prominent factors underpinning increased productivity and minimized land degradation.

Where improvements to the soil are cited, these are manifested in terms of better structure (mentioned in 40% of the cases) improved infiltration (60%), and reduced surface runoff (60%) as well as reduced evaporation loss and increased soil biological activity. Successful technologies support nature to self-restore its functions and services.

In the cases located in humid areas (45%) the main focus is on maintenance of soil fertility, drainage of excess water, and reduction of soil loss. Benefits may only be noted in the long-term – apart from situations where terraces, for example, bring land into production for the first time.

In the cases located in dry areas (55%), the main focus is on water rather than soil conservation. Although water is the main limiting factor, it is wasted without appropriate conservation measures. Seasonal surface runoff in the order of 15–20% and evaporation loss from the soil surface of an additional 40–70% are common, leaving less than half of the rainfall available for crop and fodder production. Significant improvements to infiltration and water storage in the soil as well as reduction of water loss by evaporation have been achieved mainly through mulching, minimum tillage, intercropping and water harvesting – either in-situ or by storage in dams (for example conservation agriculture from Kenya; *doh* from India). There is considerable evidence of increased yields in rainfed agriculture through improved water management, combined with simultaneous attention to soil fertility through better residue management, composting and crop rotation, which counter nutrient depletion.

The importance of land management for water-related benefits is often neglected, even in areas of water scarcity and water conflicts. This is despite the wide range of ecologically and economically promising technologies available that reduce water wastage and pollution.

Around half of the technologies described in the book are applied on soils with low/ very low fertility or low organic matter. Half of these cases report a medium to high increase in soil fertility after treatment with SWC technologies.

Conservation measures leading to increased soil organic matter and thus carbon sequestration represent a win-win scenario: land resources are improved at the local level and at the same time a contribution is made to the mitigation of climate change.

Policy points: SWC technologies – general

Given limited financial and human resources, more attention should be focused on the prevention and mitigation of degradation before investing in areas that require costly rehabilitation, even though the achievements may not be so visible.

Promotion of SWC technologies that lead to improved management of natural resources - soil, water and vegetation - has the potential not only to reduce land degradation but also to address simultaneously global concerns of water scarcity, land use conflicts, climate change (through carbon sequestration), biodiversity conservation, and poverty alleviation. Continued, sustained investments in optimising and adapting technologies to their specific environments as well as recognising innovative improvements are needed.

In dry areas, investments in water harvesting and improved water use efficiency, combined with improved soil fertility management, should be emphasised to increase production, reduce the risk of crop failure, and lower the demand for irrigation water.

In humid areas, long-term investments are required to maintain soil fertility and minimise on-site and off-site damage caused by soil erosion, as the impacts on production and conservation may only accrue in the medium and long term.

Soil and water conservation measures – *the combination challenge*

Agronomic measures

Agronomic measures, such as manuring/ composting and crop rotation, have the advantage that they can be integrated into daily farming activities. They are not perceived as an additional 'conservation' burden, as they require comparatively low inputs and have a direct impact on crop productivity.

'Conservation agriculture', which is expanding rapidly worldwide, combines the benefits of lower input costs, reduced workload, minimised erosion, more efficient water use, and improved soil properties, while maintaining or improving yields.

Whenever measures are combined, the agronomic component is usually prominent. In the case studies, 70% of combined measures have an agronomic component.

Vegetative measures

Many vegetative measures have developed under traditional land use systems: for example agroforestry.

In all the cases presented, vegetative measures are noted as being multipurpose in function. Agroforestry systems, for example, apart from their conservation effect, can be directly useful for production of fodder, fruits, nuts, fuelwood and timber, as well as for nitrogen fixation.

Successful SWC associated with intensive and diverse smallholder agroforestry systems can lead to partial restoration of 'forest function': in some areas 'more people means more trees'.

Some vegetative measures compete with crops for nutrients and water: this is a particular problem where land is scarce and the vegetation is not directly productive itself (eg vetiver grass lines and windbreaks). In these situations, the protective vegetation needs to be carefully managed, eg through pruning of roots and branches.

In many situations – even in severely erosion-prone areas (steep slopes, high rainfall) – vegetative measures such as agroforestry may be adequate alone. Nine of the 11 vegetative measures documented in this book are employed in the humid tropics where they provide protective ground cover and effective maintenance of soil fertility. However, in certain circumstances, supplementary structural measures are required.

Structural measures

Structures are 'attention grabbers' because they are spectacular and conspicuous. However, they are hardly ever adequate on their own. Terraces on steep slopes or barriers within gullies, form physical frameworks which need additional agronomic and vegetative measures to be fully effective.

Structural measures are commonly associated with high investments. There are exceptions; for example V-shaped microcatchments or small contour bunds. Terraces are also low in cost when they gradually evolve through water and tillage erosion, leading to sedimentation behind vegetative strips.

There is always a danger of exacerbating erosion, through concentration of runoff, if structures breach as a result of poor design, construction or maintenance.

There are many traditional and ancient terrace systems, where maintenance and rehabilitation are needed and can further be justified on the basis of cultural heritage, for aesthetic reasons, or even for income-generating 'agro-ecotourism'.

Water harvesting systems rely on structural measures to impound rainfall runoff but are also combined with other measures designed to reduce evaporation – for example mulching. They have great potential for further application in drought-prone areas.

Management measures

Management measures are particularly applicable to land used communally – for example improvement of grazing land, where uncontrolled 'open-access' use has led to degradation. In this situation no interventions work without an initial, fundamental change in management.

These measures often result in improved vegetative cover by initially reducing the intensity of land use. Subsequently, land use intensity can be increased due to natural regeneration – or where climatic conditions allow, through the planting of more productive species. Increased intensity of use cannot be maintained, however, without ensuring continued improved management.

Combined SWC measures

55% of the technologies presented in the book are combinations of various agronomic, vegetative, structural and/or management measures. These are either (a) superimposed on the same plot of land, or (b) dispersed over a catchment (eg cut-off drains and afforestation in the upper catchment and check dams in gullies) or a landscape, or (c) phased over time (eg through a rotation system). Combinations support each other and often address multiple degradation types.

left: The way land is used - and its conservation/ degradation status – has a profound impact on water supplies: here in Kyrgyzstan, as elsewhere, soil erosion causes siltation of reservoirs and affects hydropower generation amongst other off-site impacts. (Hanspeter Liniger)

right: A Colombian farmer demonstrating the establishment of a SWC technology: he was trained by a local NGO programme and works now as a promoter assisting community members in SWC implementation. (Mats Gurtner)

Land use types –
a lack of focus on marginal areas and grazing land

SWC applied on a specific land use type interacts with other, adjacent land with different uses: for example, interventions on cropland can be affected by, and can affect, grazing land nearby.

Most SWC efforts have been made on cropland, and new challenges are emerging as crop cultivation continues to be intensified and expanded into marginal areas.

All but six of the SWC technologies presented in this book are applied under purely rainfed conditions. These illustrate the wide variety of options and the great potential for improving land management in degradation-prone rainfed areas.

On the other hand, irrigated farming systems are of global importance for food production. Poor irrigation practices and associated problems – such as depletion of water resources, salinisation and waterlogging – are widespread (eg the case from Kyrgyzstan). Measures for the sustainable use of irrigated land have not yet been adequately identified and documented.

Only three case studies in this overview book address grazing land. This reflects not just a general neglect of documentation, but insufficient SWC investments in these areas, and the difficulty of identifying viable solutions. This is despite

the fact that the livelihoods of many rural people are primarily based on ranching or pastoral livestock production systems – often located in highly vulnerable dryland and marginal areas. The potential for sustainable production increases and improved ecosystem services in such areas are not being adequately tapped.

Successful combinations of management and vegetative measures on grazing land vary from 'cut-and-carry' of improved fodder species in subhumid or humid areas, to protection (enclosure) for regeneration of natural species in the drier regions.

Improved forest management and agroforestry systems are often not perceived as SWC and are thus less frequently documented as such.

SWC approaches – supporting
and stimulating the implementation

General

The case studies documented span a wide variety of different approaches: about two thirds of the technologies are implemented under a project, while the others are based on local innovation, traditional/ indigenous systems, and individual initiatives.

Two thirds of the case studies relate to small-scale farming systems. 31% are associated with subsistence farming, helping to reduce poverty and improve livelihoods. However, for

mixed (40% of cases) and commercial farming (29%), there are also opportunities for improved SWC and related benefits.

As is the case with technologies, there are no 'one-size fits all' solutions to approaches. But there are common denominators of success, including a focus on production aspects, security of access, long-term commitment and investment, participation of stakeholders, and capacity building. Successful approaches are always built upon human resources: people's knowledge, creativity and initiative.

Many factors such as the level of incentives, type of training, and institutional arrangements are locally specific and need to be tailored to a given situation.

Scattered independent project interventions and approaches cannot achieve the same impact as a coherent and collaborative programme. The Kenyan 'Catchment approach' and Chinese 'Terrace approach' provide positive examples of such collaborative programmes.

Development rhetoric ('participation', 'bottom-up', 'gender balance', 'accountability', etc) permeates through the objectives and titles of SWC approaches. While this serves a useful purpose in defining direction, the practice still often lags behind the rhetoric.

Policy points: soil and water conservation approaches – general

More attention and support should be given to local innovation as well as to traditional systems, rather than focussing solely on project-based SWC implementation of standard technologies.

Further efforts are needed to identify appropriate SWC technologies that assist small-scale and subsistence farmers to improve their livelihoods and escape from the poverty trap.

Project/ programme interventions need to break out of the typical three-year project cycle and commit to a minimum of five years, and preferably ten or more. SWC requires long-term commitment from national and international implementation and research institutions. A clear strategy is needed to sustain results beyond the project life-time.

Partnership alliances need to be developed between different agencies – with their various SWC initiatives and interventions – for synergy of efforts and cost-effectiveness.

Profitability and enabling environment –
motivating the land users

Some drivers of conservation at times have little to do with degradation. Other reasons, especially economic factors, can propel farmers to change, and addressing degradation may be only a spin-off: three quarters of the 'SWC' cases analysed are directly related to increasing productivity and/or farm income, with conservation coming in 'through the back door'.

In areas characterised by subsistence farming and rural poverty, SWC is an opportunity for improving livelihoods or merely ensuring survival. There are several clear cases of this, including those from Niger ('Planting pits and stone lines'), India ('Forest catchment treatment') and the Philippines ('Natural vegetative strips').

Generally, it is assumed that SWC implies high investment, but there are examples of profitable cost- and time-saving technologies, such as conservation agriculture, that provide a strong motivation for further implementation.

The assessment of costs and benefits were difficult for contributors to compile and may not be free of bias. In 62% of the cases, benefits in the short-term in relation to investment costs were noted by land users, thus demonstrating rapid pay-back. However in the remaining cases, more than three years were required before benefits began to outweigh the investment costs.

Off-site damage caused by degradation as well as off-site benefits of conservation – eg protection from flooding, sedimentation or pollution – are mentioned in three quarters of the case studies, and one third mentioned increased river flow during dry seasons. However, the value of these off-site benefits has not yet been assessed, and needs to be, in order to justify investments on that basis.

The establishment of an 'enabling environment' is extremely important in the promotion of SWC, emphasising the 'pull' (motivation), eg better marketing channels or secure access to land, as well as the 'push' (enforcement), eg SWC legislation and national campaigns.

While private ownership tends to stimulate conservation of land, adequate security of access – under private ownership or other tenure regimes – is the key to investing willingly in SWC. There are challenges to overcome, for example in

left: Grazing land has been neglected and viable solutions, especially for drylands, need to be further identified and documented: here is an example from Central Asia. Land use rights is a major issue. (Hanspeter Liniger)

right: Traditional terraces in the foothills of the Himalayas showing the investments made over generations. Such terraces are commonly associated with irrigation, but here – where there is rainfall alone to depend on – land users have found a way to survive by catching water where it falls. (William Critchley)

countries where land was, or is still, held by central authority.

The establishment of effective marketing channels for agricultural products can help stimulate SWC; on the other hand, markets can become saturated or depressed, and discourage conservation initiatives through reduced producer prices.

The current international concern with environment – climate change, loss of (agro-) biodiversity, scarcity of water, and a renewed interest in combating desertification and alleviating rural poverty – presents a new opportunity for product marketing using labels such as 'organic'; 'fair trade'; 'land friendly'; 'sustainably harvested', and perhaps even 'anti-desertification'.

Policy points: profitability and enabling environment

SWC needs to be stimulated by further emphasising improved production (of plants and animals) and reduced costs, which are the primary interest of land users, and have direct consequences on livelihoods in small-scale subsistence farming.

Accurate assessment of costs and benefits (in monetary and non-monetary terms) – using participatory and transdisciplinary methods – is urgently needed to evaluate SWC technologies in terms of their short- and long-term gains: without this, land users and development agencies cannot make informed decisions about which technologies and approaches are the most viable options.

To help prevent off-site damage, further on-site investment in SWC is required: this is usually cheaper and more effective than dealing with the downstream consequences.

An enabling environment should be nurtured for SWC to thrive best, building on people's and nature's capacity. Indirect measures such as credit, market opportunities or legislation to stimulate conservation activities must not be overlooked.

Security of land use rights is important in conservation: policies to improve the rights of individual land users and/or rural communities to use their local land resources on a secure and long-term basis must be recognised as an important means of supporting SWC.

Opportunities need to be seized that connect SWC with emerging environmental priorities – especially carbon sequestration (by increasing soil organic matter), biodiversity (above and below ground), water

and ecosystem service provision. Ways of recognition and payment for these services need to be further explored to justify SWC investments. The benefits of improved land management for water quantity and quality must be further stressed and used as a motivation for SWC, especially in areas of water scarcity and water-related conflicts.

Access to local and international markets has to be improved to enable producers to make SWC investments in their land. Fair prices, certification, and labelling schemes for products can stimulate conservation.

Subsidising SWC –
the delicate issue of direct incentives

While norms regarding incentives differ considerably from country to country, the case studies show that direct material incentives (money, inputs, etc) should be used carefully – in 15 out of the 20 project-based case studies of approaches there were low or negligible levels of direct incentives, illustrating the fact that these did not play a major role. At best they offer a step-up to impoverished farmers, at worst they can distort priorities and do great harm by creating dependency and pseudo-interest in SWC.

High levels of subsidies to agriculture in industrialised countries present a complex and controversial case. The new tendency to support environmental stewardship of the countryside may offer a less controversial form of incentives (see case study from the UK).
Off-site benefits and other ecosystem services are mentioned in over 90% of the case studies, but not valued in monetary terms. This information is required for cost-benefit analysis and as a basis for negotiations between different stakeholders – and is also required under various international conventions.

Where there are substantial off-site benefits but no significant on-site gains, direct payment/ compensation for ecosystem services is an opportunity to promote SWC, providing the lasting advantages that continuous payments can ensure: examples are the case studies from Switzerland and (potentially), Bolivia.

Only four of the documented projects provide or facilitate access to credit. The potential for provision of concessionary credit (below normal market rates), to enable investment in the land, has not been sufficiently exploited.

Policy points: subsidising SWC

SWC may require heavy investment costs that exceed the capacity of local land users and thus need to be covered by national and international initiatives. But direct material incentives should – in principle – only be considered where there is a need to overcome initial investment constraints and subsequent maintenance does not require continued support. This may be needed where the environmental improvements and social benefits are likely to be realised only in the long term.

Before considering the use of direct incentives, alternative approaches should be explored, such as the adaptation of technologies, or the identification of cheaper technologies. The possibilities of removing some of the root causes of land degradation (related, for example, to land policy framework, land tenure security and market access) also need to be assessed.

Rural areas may need and deserve compensation from urban/ industrial zones for the environmental and aesthetic services they provide. And downstream beneficiaries of the environmental protection provided by upstream communities should be prepared to pay compensation for these services.

The value of the ecosystem services needs to be determined and agreed upon between users and providers. The establishment of compensation schemes may require support and guidance from policy level and external actors.

Provision of microcredit at concessionary rates for better land management/ SWC requires serious consideration, as an alternative to handouts and payments, where farmers have financial constraints.

Extension, training and adoption – *building capacity and spreading the message*

Training and extension are key elements of project-based approaches. There has been a general switch to more participation, devolution of powers, and less authoritarianism. But increased empowerment requires enhanced capacity. During the compilation of the case studies, clear shortcomings regarding documentation and evaluation of SWC were identified. However, training in knowledge management is not reported under any of the approaches documented in this book.

More than half the successful projects/ programmes analysed in this book have had little or no international expert input. Clearly local and national initiatives are worth trusting and investing in.

Individual SWC innovations by local land users are also a potential way forward. There are several examples (Tajikistan; East Africa, etc) where local initiative has uncovered promising technologies and methods that are being spread informally: in the current situation of downsized and under-funded extension services, 'do-it-yourself' in terms of research and extension is making a comeback amongst land users.

Population pressure and demographics have complex relationships with the state of the land. Rapid land use change can lead to degradation; but increased population density may drive improved conservation of limited land resources, and close contact with neighbours can stimulate farmer-to-farmer exchange of ideas.

Policy points: extension, training and adoption

On the basis of standardised tools and methods, training in proper documentation, evaluation and dissemination of SWC knowledge, as well as its use for and improved decision-making, needs to be strengthened.

Investment in training and extension to support the capacity of land users and other local and national stakeholders must be a priority to adapt better to changing environmental, social and economic conditions, and to stimulate innovation.

Local innovation and farmer-to-farmer extension should be promoted as effective and appropriate strategies.

Overall conclusions – *investing in SWC for ecosystems, society and the economy*

The cases presented in this book demonstrate the value of investing in rural areas despite recent global trends of neglecting agriculture and focusing on industry and the service sector.

Ecologically, SWC technologies – in all their diversity – effectively combat land degradation. But a majority of agricultural land is still not sufficiently protected, and SWC needs to spread further. The potential ecosystem benefits go far beyond reducing soil erosion and water loss; these include regulation of watershed hydrological function – assuring base flows, reducing floods and purifying water supplies – as well as carbon sequestration, and preservation of above- and below-ground biodiversity.

left: Supporting and stimulating implementation: farmers sharing their SWC knowledge and experience with other farmers – and external specialists also (Kenya). (Hanspeter Liniger)

right: Profitability is the fruit of investment in the land: if measures are maintained and soil fertility built up, a good harvest is the result (Nepal). (Hanspeter Liniger)

Socially, SWC helps secure sustainable livelihoods by maintaining or increasing soil productivity, thus improving food security and reducing poverty, both at household and national levels. It can also support social learning and interaction, build community spirit, preserve cultural heritage, and counterbalance migration to cities.

Economically, SWC pays back investments made by land users, communities or governments. Agricultural production is safeguarded and enhanced for small-scale subsistence and large-scale commercial farmers alike, as well as for livestock keepers. Furthermore, the considerable off-site benefits from SWC can often be an economic justification in themselves.

Policy points: investing in SWC

Investment in rural areas and SWC is a local concern, a national interest, and a global obligation. Thus it must be given priority:
- at the local level: to increase income, improve food security, and sustain natural resources – thus helping to alleviate poverty in areas where the livelihoods of the majority depend on agricultural production;
- at the global and national level: to safeguard natural resources and ecosystem services and in many cases to preserve cultural heritage.

Investments in SWC must be carefully assessed and planned on the basis of properly documented experiences and evaluated impacts and benefits: concerted efforts are needed and sufficient resources must be mobilised to tap the wealth of knowledge and learn from SWC successes. These investments will give 'value for money' in economic, ecological and social terms.

left: Investment in rural areas needs to continue for environmental, social and economic reasons. The justification for stepping up efforts is based on maintaining ecosystem services as well as securing livelihoods (Kenya). (Hanspeter Liniger)

right: Building on local knowledge to document, monitor, evaluate and disseminate SWC: it all adds up to better support for decision making by land users and specialists (Thailand). (Hanspeter Liniger)

Part 2

Women carrying manure to terraces in Nepal for rice and potato
cultivation: maintaining fertility and investing in the future.
(Hanspeter Liniger)

Case studies

where the land is greener

Green cover in
vineyards/
Farmer initiative

Conservation agri-
culture/
Soil manag. initiative

No-till technology/
Applied research and
knowledge transfer

UK

Switz

Morocco

Vermiculture/
Productive develop-
ment programme

Shade-grown coffee/
Agroforestry extension

Sand dune stabilisation

Nicaragua

Costa Rica

Colombia

Check dams from stem
cuttings

Planting pits and stone
lines/
Participatory land rehab.

Peru   Bolivia

Composting and
planting pits/
Zabré women's progr.

Intensive agroforestry/
Integrated rural com-
munity development

Improved trash lines/
Promoting farmer
innovation

Ancient terraces/
Participatory catchment
rehabilitation

Gully control/
Incentive-based catch-
ment treatment

Strip mine
rehabilitation

Restoration
of degraded rangeland

Case studies of soil and water conservation initiatives worldwide

42 technologies and 28 approaches
documented under the WOCAT methodology
by local contributors

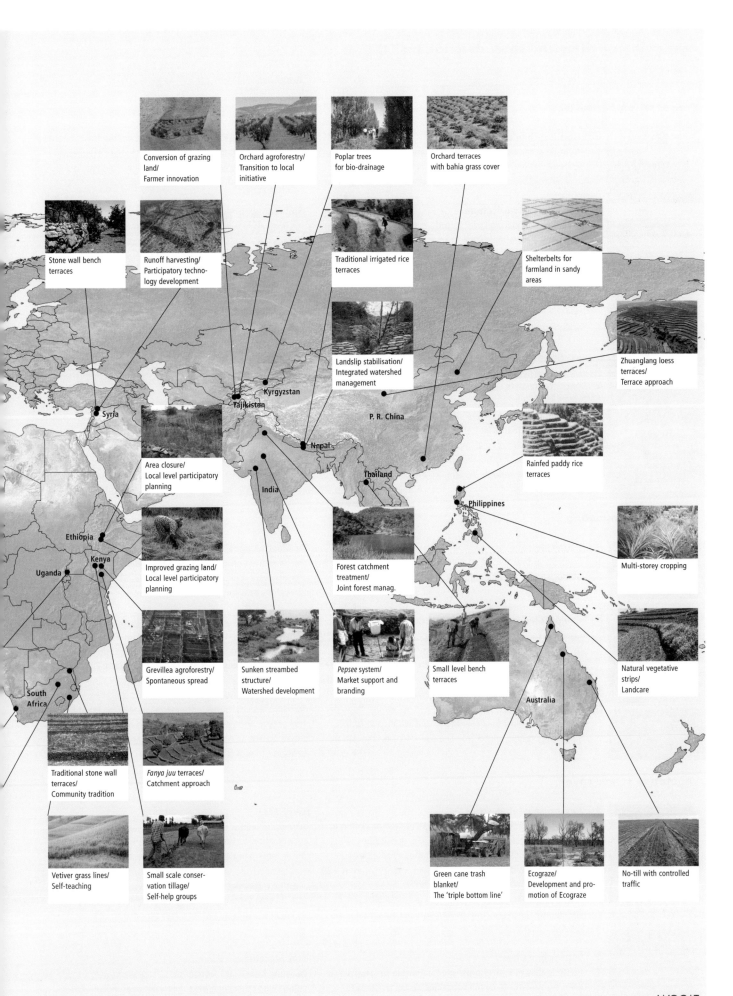

Conversion of grazing land/
Farmer innovation

Orchard agroforestry/
Transition to local initiative

Poplar trees
for bio-drainage

Orchard terraces
with bahia grass cover

Stone wall bench
terraces

Runoff harvesting/
Participatory technology development

Traditional irrigated rice
terraces

Shelterbelts for
farmland in sandy areas

Landslip stabilisation/
Integrated watershed management

Zhuanglang loess
terraces/
Terrace approach

Syria

Kyrgyzstan

Tajikistan

P. R. China

Nepal

Area closure/
Local level participatory planning

India

Thailand

Rainfed paddy rice
terraces

Philippines

Ethiopia

Kenya

Improved grazing land/
Local level participatory planning

Uganda

Forest catchment
treatment/
Joint forest manag.

Multi-storey cropping

Grevillea agroforestry/
Spontaneous spread

Sunken streambed
structure/
Watershed development

Pepsee system/
Market support and branding

Small level bench
terraces

Natural vegetative
strips/
Landcare

South
Africa

Australia

Traditional stone wall
terraces/
Community tradition

Fanya juu terraces/
Catchment approach

Vetiver grass lines/
Self-teaching

Small scale conservation tillage/
Self-help groups

Green cane trash
blanket/
The 'triple bottom line'

Ecograze/
Development and promotion of Ecograze

No-till with controlled
traffic

WOCAT

	Technology	Approach

Conservation agriculture

Morocco

No-till technology
A no-till system with crop residue management for medium-scale wheat and barley farming.

→ p 69

Applied research and knowledge transfer
Innovative, cross-disciplinary community-based approach for development and transfer of no-till technology at the farm level.

→ p 73

UK

Conservation agriculture
Improved soil management based on non-inversion tillage for cost-effective and timely crop establishment.

→ p 77

Soil management initiative
An independent organisation that promotes the adoption of appropriate soil management practices, especially conservation agriculture, within England.

→ p 81

Kenya

Small-scale conservation tillage
Ripping of soil using oxen-drawn implements, to improve water storage capacity and cropland productivity on small-scale farms.

→ p 85

Self-help groups
Small-scale farmers forming self-help groups to provide mutual support for adopting and promoting conservation agriculture.

→ p 89

Australia

No-till with controlled traffic
Large-scale no-till grain production with permanent wheel tracks common to all on-farm equipment.

→ p 93

no approach described

Australia

Green cane trash blanket
Elimination of burning as a pre-harvest treatment of sugar cane, and managing the resultant trash as a protective blanket to give multiple on and off-site benefits.

→ p 97

The 'triple bottom line'
A new expression used by agriculturalists in Australia to explain why farmers change practices: the 'triple bottom line' implies economic, environmental and social concerns.

→ p 101

Manuring/ composting

Nicaragua

Vermiculture
Continuous breeding of earthworms in boxes for production of high quality organic compost.

→ p 105

Productive development and food security programme
An integrated programme-based approach promoting participatory testing and extension of various SWC technologies, as well as providing institutional support.

→ p 109

Burkina Faso

Composting associated with planting pits
Compost production, and its application in planting pits (zai) by farmers on fields near their homes.

→ p 113

Zabré women's agroecological programme
A demand-driven initiative, by women's association, aimed at the promotion of composting through training and extension, using project staff and local facilitators.

→ p 117

Uganda

Improved trash lines
Weeds and crop residues, laid in bands across the slope of annual crop fields, to conserve soil and water, and to incorporate organic matter into the soil after decomposition.

→ p 121

Promoting farmer innovation
Identification of 'farmer innovators' in SWC and water harvesting, and using them as focal points for visits from other farmers to spread the practices and stimulate the process of innovation.

→ p 125

Vegetative strips/ cover

Philippines

Natural vegetative strips
Within individual cropland plots, strips of land marked out on the contour and left unploughed in order to form permanent, cross- slope barriers of naturally established grasses and herbs.

→ p 129

Landcare
Associations that help diffuse, at low cost, soil and water conservation technologies among upland farmers to generate income while conserving natural resources.

→ p 133

Switzerland

Green cover in vineyards
Naturally growing or sown perennial grasses/herbs providing cover between rows in sloping vineyards, where the vines are usually oriented up and down slope.

→ p 137

Farmer initiative within enabling environment
Initiative and innovation of land users, stimulated by government's technical and financial support.

→ p 141

South Africa

Vetiver grass lines
Contour lines of vetiver grass planted within fields of sugar cane, on stream banks and roadsides, to act as 'hedges against erosion'.

→ p 145

Self-teaching
Learning how to use vetiver grass as a vegetative conservation barrier through instructions from a booklet and hands-on, practical experience.

→ p 149

Case studies – titles and short descriptions (2)

	Technology	Approach

Agroforestry

P. R. China
Shelterbelts for farmland in sandy areas
Belts of trees, planted in a rectangular grid pattern within areas of farmland, to act as windbreaks.

→ p 153

no approach described

Kenya
Grevillea agroforestry system
Multipurpose *Grevillea robusta* trees planted along farm boundaries, on terrace risers and occasionally scattered in cropland.

→ p 157

Spontaneous spread
Spontaneous land users' initiative to meet household needs – especially firewood and timber – through planting *Grevillea robusta* trees as part of an agroforestry system.

→ p 161

Kyrgyzstan
Poplar trees for bio-drainage
Poplars planted to lower the ground water table and reduce salinity where irrigation drainage systems have broken down; lucerne cultivated between the tree lines.

→ p 165

no approach described

Philippines
Multi-storey cropping
Cultivating a mixture of crops with different heights (multistorey) and growth characteristics which together optimise the use of soil, moisture and space.

→ p 169

no approach described

Colombia
Intensive agroforestry system
A protective and productive high-input agroforestry system comprising multi-purpose ditches with bunds, grass barriers, contour ridges, annual crops and fruit trees.

→ p 173

Integrated rural community development
Development of an impoverished indigenous reserve – incorporating alternative land use systems – through intensive training provided by a small NGO.

→ p 177

Costa Rica
Shade-grown coffee
An agroforestry system which combines coffee with shade trees – including fruit, timber and leguminous species – in a systematic fashion.

→ p 181

Agroforestry extension
Participatory extension of agroforestry systems, especially of shade-grown coffee, to promote sustainable and productive use of natural resources among small and medium scale farmers.

→ p 185

Tajikistan
Conversion of grazing land to fruit and fodder plots
Fencing-off part of an overgrazed hillside, combined with terracing, manuring and supplementary irrigation for grape, fruit and grass production.

→ p 189

Farmer innovation and self-help group
Overcoming administrative and technical problems, an innovative land user, assisted by a self-help group, has established a fruit garden within degraded communal grazing land.

→ p 193

Tajikistan
Orchard-based agroforestry
An agroforestry system where legumes and cereals are planted in fruit orchards, giving simultaneous production and conservation benefits.

→ p 197

Transition from centralised regime to local initiative
A land use system established during the authoritarian regime of the Soviet Union is being adapted to farmers' needs through their own initiative.

→ p 201

Water harvesting

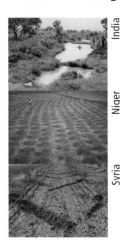

India
Sunken streambed structure
Excavations in streambeds to provide temporary storage of runoff, increasing water yields from shallow wells for supplementary irrigation.

→ p 205

Comprehensive watershed development
Participatory approach that includes a package of measures leading to empowerment of communities to implement and sustain watershed development.

→ p 209

Niger
Planting pits and stone lines
Rehabilitation of degraded land on gentle slopes through manured planting pits, in combination with contour stone lines.

→ p 213

Participatory land rehabilitation
Planning and management of individual and village land, based on land users' participation, with simultaneous promotion of women's activities.

→ p 217

Syria
Furrow-enhanced runoff harvesting for olives
Runoff harvesting through annually constructed V-shaped microcatchments, enhanced by downslope ploughing.

→ p 221

Participatory technology development
Participatory technology development, through close researcher-farmer interaction, for sustainable land management of olive orchards in dry marginal areas.

→ p 225

	Technology	Approach

Gully rehabilitation

Nicaragua

Check dams from stem cuttings
Gully rehabilitation by check dams constructed from stem cuttings of trees which retard concentrated runoff and fill up the gullies gradually with sediment.
→ p 229

no approach described

Bolivia

Gully control and catchment protection
Integrated gully treatment consisting of several simple practices including stone and wooden check dams, cut-off drains and reforestation in sediment traps *(biotrampas)*.
→ p 233

Incentive-based catchment treatment
A project supported, incentive-based approach. Farmers are sensitised about erosion, and involved in gully control and other measures to protect catchments.
→ p 237

Nepal

Landslip and stream bank stabilisation
Integration of vegetative and structural measures for landslip, stream bank and gully stabilisation on hillsides.
→ p 241

Integrated watershed management
Integrated watershed management based on fostering a partnership between community institutions, line agencies, district authorities and consultants.
→ p 245

Terraces

Syria

Stone wall bench terraces
Ancient level bench terraces with stone walls, built to stabilise slopes, retain moisture, and create a suitable environment for horticulture.
→ p 249

no approach described

Peru

Rehabilitation of ancient terraces
Repair of ancient stone wall bench terraces with stone walls, and of an associated irrigation and drainage system.
→ p 253

Participatory catchment rehabilitation
Promoting the rehabilitation of ancient terrace systems based on a systematic watershed management approach.
→ p 257

South Africa

Traditional stone wall terraces
Stone walls built on sloping fields to create terraces for cultivation and conservation: both ancient and contemporary.
→ p 261

Community tradition
Inherited, and still current, tradition of stone terracing – passed down from generation to generation.
→ p 265

Kenya

Fanya juu terraces
Terrace bund in association with a ditch along the contour, or on a gentle lateral gradient. Soil is thrown on the upper side of the ditch to form the bund, which is often stabilised by planting a fodder grass.
→ p 269

Catchment approach
A focused approach to integrated land and water management, including soil and water conservation, where the active participation of the villagers – often organised through common interest groups – is central.
→ p 273

Thailand

Small level bench terraces
Terraces with narrow beds, used for growing tea, coffee, and horticultural crops on hillsides cleared from forests.
→ p 277

no approach described

P. R. China

Orchard terraces with bahia grass cover
Rehabilitation of degraded hillsides through the establishment of fruit trees on slope-separated orchard terraces, with bahia grass planted as protective groundcover.
→ p 281

no approach described

P. R. China

Zhuanglang loess terraces
Level bench terraces on the Loess Plateau, converting erodible, sloping land into a series of steps suitable for cultivation.
→ p 285

Terrace approach
Highly organised campaign to assist land users in creating terraces: support and planning from national down to local level.
→ p 289

Philippines

Rainfed paddy rice terraces
Terraces supporting rainfed paddy rice on steep mountain slopes: these have been in existence for more than a thousand years.
→ p 293

no approach described

	Technology	Approach

Terraces (continued)

Nepal

Traditional irrigated rice terraces
Level bench terraces with risers protected by fodder grasses, used for irrigated production of rice, potatoes and wheat.

→ p 297

no approach described

Grazing land management

Australia

Ecograze
An ecologically sound and practical grazing management system, based on rotation and wet season resting.

→ p 301

Development and promotion of Ecograze
Research-based development and promotion of Ecograze principles and practices through on-farm testing and demonstration.

→ p 305

South Africa

Restoration of degraded rangeland
Eradication of invasive species and revegetation of degraded rangelands by different treatments, including oversowing with grass seed mixture, supplementing with lime, cattle dung, and 'brush packing'. → p 309

no approach described

Ethiopia

Improved grazing land management
Rehabilitation of communal grazing lands, through planting of improved grass and fodder trees and land subdivision, to improve fodder and consequently livestock production.

→ p 313

Local level participatory planning approach
An approach used by field staff to implement conservation activities, involving farmers in all stages of planning, implementation and evaluation.

→ p 321

Ethiopia

Area closure for rehabilitation
Enclosing and protecting an area of degraded land from human use and animal interference, to permit natural rehabilitation, enhanced by additional vegetative and structural conservation measures. → p 317

Local level participatory planning approach
An approach used by field staff to implement conservation activities, involving farmers in all stages of planning, implementation and evaluation.

→ p 321

Other technologies

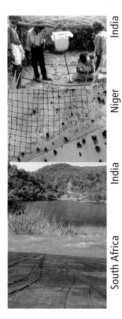

India

Pepsee micro-irrigation system
A grassroots innovation that offers most of the advantages of conventional micro-irrigation at a much lower establishment cost.

→ p 325

Market support and branding for input quality
Market development and support through use of a brand name – *Krishak Bandhu* ('the farmer's friend') – to help ensure quality amongst manufacturers and suppliers of drip irrigation equipment. → p 329

Niger

Sand dune stabilisation
A combination of three measures: area closure, mechanical stabilisation through palisades, and vegetative fixation through natural regeneration as well as planting.

→ p 333

Participatory land rehabilitation
Planning and management of individual and village land, based on land users' participation, with simultaneous promotion of women's activities.

→ p 217

India

Forest catchment treatment
Catchment treatment of degraded forest land including social fencing, infiltration trenches and enrichment planting with trees and grasses for production and dam protection.

→ p 337

Joint forest management
Government and NGO supported community protection of forested catchments, through village-based Hill Resource Management Societies.

→ p 341

South Africa

Strip mine rehabilitation
Rehabilitation of areas degraded by strip mining, through returning stockpiled topsoil and transplanting of indigenous species, to promote revegetation.

→ p 345

no approach described

No-till technology

Morocco – الزراعة بدون فلاحات

A no-till system with crop residue management for medium-scale wheat and barley farming.

This no-till technology (NTT) system, with direct seeding and crop residue management, was designed by the National Institute of Agricultural Research (INRA) in Settat, Morocco. A special no-till drill was developed to simultaneously seed and fertilize annual crops: the drill cuts through residue, opens a 20 cm wide slot which, after seed and N/P-fertilizers are dropped into it, is closed firmly to encourage contact between seed and soil. Seeding is earlier than in the case of conventional tillage – which requires seedbed preparation. Spacing between rows is adjusted according to crop type: 20 cm for wheat or barley, and 40 cm for lentils and chickpeas. Tillage depth is between 5–12 cm depending on soil workability and moisture content.

Crops, planted in rotation with a fallow period, are barley, wheat, legumes (lentils and chickpea) and also fodder species. Application of special herbicides replaces tillage for weed control, and enables the farmer to have an 18-month fallow period (a 'chemical fallow') after two crops have been taken over a 6-month period. Fallowing is essential for water conservation in this semi-arid area. NTT reduces passes with heavy machines to three times per year. Residue management involves maintaining the soil partially covered with stubble and straw. Overall, yields are higher and costs are lower than under conventional tillage. NTT reduces soil erosion and soil compaction while conserving water in the soil. Optimum use of scarce and low rainfall to stabilise/increase crop yields is essential in this area.

The use of the special no-till drill ensures both minimal working of the soils, and precise incorporation of phosphate fertilizer beneath seeds. Depending on the specific site, residue management is adjusted from low residue maintenance (stubble/controlled grazing) to medium surface cover (stubble/straw maintenance, forage crops and exclusion of grazing). Erosion and evaporation suppression/control are the main impacts of the system: runoff and concentrated flow in watersheds are reduced. Chemicals are applied for weed control, but this takes into account the environment, and can be reduced over time. Maintaining crop residues in the fields increases soil organic matter and thus the amount of carbon sequestered, as well as nutrient levels. Hence application of inorganic fertilizers can be reduced.

Location: Settat, Khourigba and Benslimane Provinces, Chaouia Ouardigha Region, Morocco
Technology area: 20 km²
SWC measure: agronomic and management
Land use: cropland
Climate: semi-arid, subhumid
WOCAT database reference: QT MOR10
Related approach: Applied research and knowledge transfer, QA MOR10
Compiled by: Rachid Mrabet, INRA, Settat, Morocco
Date: April 2003, updated June 2004

Editors' comments: No-till technology (NTT) is a promising system, still at an early adoption stage, but spreading gradually in Morocco as well as in Tunisia. Worldwide, conservation agriculture is expanding rapidly: by 2002, there were up to 60 million hectares under these systems. While it is well documented in Latin America, this case is an example from Northern Africa where it is not common.

Classification

Land use problems

Conventional tillage practices are often inappropriate, leading to various problems: disk plough operations make soils more vulnerable to erosion, evaporation, loss of organic matter and nutrients (due to inversion of soil) and thus reduce soil fertility. Furthermore, land preparation often takes place when soils are too dry or too wet. The soils in this area have a weak structure, due to low organic matter content, and are thus susceptible to compaction. Energy input in conventional tillage is much higher than in NTT.

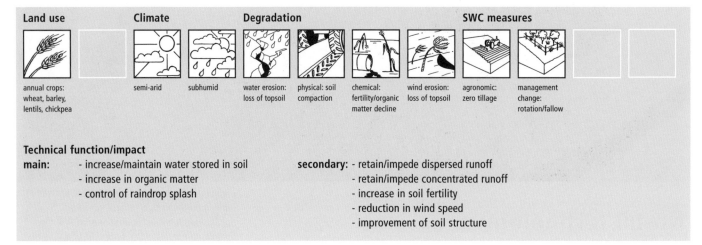

Land use	Climate	Degradation				SWC measures	
annual crops: wheat, barley, lentils, chickpea	semi-arid / subhumid	water erosion: loss of topsoil	physical: soil compaction	chemical: fertility/organic matter decline	wind erosion: loss of topsoil	agronomic: zero tillage	management change: rotation/fallow

Technical function/impact

main:
- increase/maintain water stored in soil
- increase in organic matter
- control of raindrop splash

secondary:
- retain/impede dispersed runoff
- retain/impede concentrated runoff
- increase in soil fertility
- reduction in wind speed
- improvement of soil structure

Environment

Natural environment*

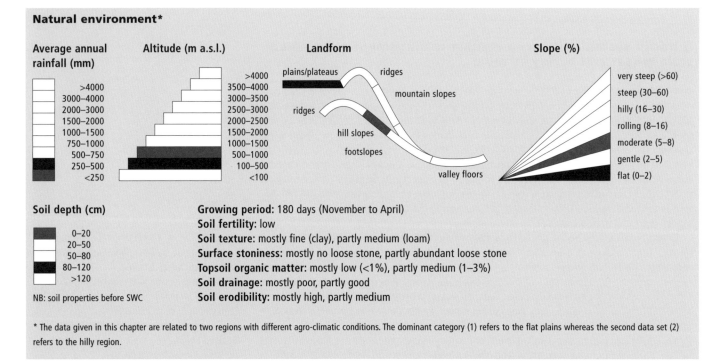

Average annual rainfall (mm)
- >4000
- 3000–4000
- 2000–3000
- 1500–2000
- 1000–1500
- 750–1000
- 500–750
- 250–500
- <250

Altitude (m a.s.l.)
- >4000
- 3500–4000
- 3000–3500
- 2500–3000
- 2000–2500
- 1500–2000
- 1000–1500
- 500–1000
- 100–500
- <100

Landform
- plains/plateaus
- ridges
- mountain slopes
- ridges
- hill slopes
- footslopes
- valley floors

Slope (%)
- very steep (>60)
- steep (30–60)
- hilly (16–30)
- rolling (8–16)
- moderate (5–8)
- gentle (2–5)
- flat (0–2)

Soil depth (cm)
- 0–20
- 20–50
- 50–80
- 80–120
- >120

NB: soil properties before SWC

Growing period: 180 days (November to April)
Soil fertility: low
Soil texture: mostly fine (clay), partly medium (loam)
Surface stoniness: mostly no loose stone, partly abundant loose stone
Topsoil organic matter: mostly low (<1%), partly medium (1–3%)
Soil drainage: mostly poor, partly good
Soil erodibility: mostly high, partly medium

* The data given in this chapter are related to two regions with different agro-climatic conditions. The dominant category (1) refers to the flat plains whereas the second data set (2) refers to the hilly region.

Human environment

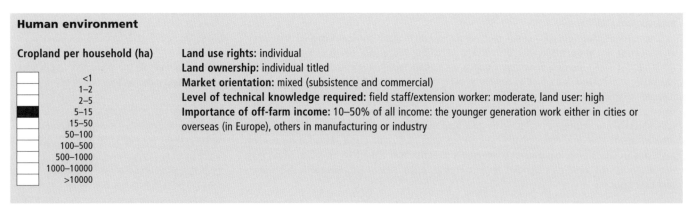

Cropland per household (ha)
- <1
- 1–2
- 2–5
- 5–15
- 15–50
- 50–100
- 100–500
- 500–1000
- 1000–10000
- >10000

Land use rights: individual
Land ownership: individual titled
Market orientation: mixed (subsistence and commercial)
Level of technical knowledge required: field staff/extension worker: moderate, land user: high
Importance of off-farm income: 10–50% of all income: the younger generation work either in cities or overseas (in Europe), others in manufacturing or industry

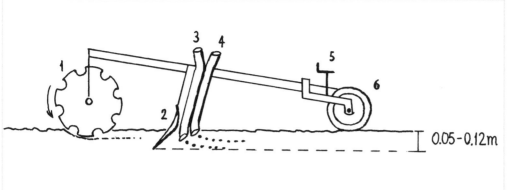

Technical drawing
Schematic view of the specially
designed no-till drill that simultaneously plants and applies
fertilizer.
Note the key components
of the drill:
1 disc/opener
2 hoe
3 fertilizer tube
4 seed tube
5 seeding depth control
6 wheel packer

0.05–0.12m

Implementation activities, inputs and costs

Establishment activities

Usually agronomic measures do not have initial establishment costs,
but in this case a major investment is needed to buy the special drill. An
explanation of the cost calculation is given below (see remarks).
Duration of establishment: not applicable

Establishment inputs and costs per ha

Inputs	Costs (US$)	% met by land user
Equipment		
- No-till drill	600	0%
TOTAL	**600**	**0%**

Maintenance/recurrent activities

1. Stubble maintenance (no grazing, only partial straw removal after harvest).
2. Direct seeding/fertilizer (N/P) banding using no-till drill (early November).
3. Chemical weed control (December/January).
4. Nitrogen fertilization (March).
5. Harvest (May: after 6 months crop period).
6. Leave fields to fallow for 18 months; apply herbicides if needed.

Time of seeding is earlier than in the case of conventional tillage systems
that need seedbed preparation. Depending on rainfall pattern and efficiency of first herbicide application, a second application may be needed.
Activities are carried out by fuel driven machines (no-till seed drill,
sprayer, tractor and combine/harvester) except nitrogen application, some
weeding and other minor activities by hand.

Maintenance/recurrent inputs and costs per ha per year

Inputs	Costs (US$)	% met by land user
Labour (16 person days)	160	100%
Equipment		
- Machines (11 hours)	110	0%
Agricultural		
- Seeds (140 kg)	60	0%
- Fertilizers (130 kg)	30	0%
- Biocides	40	0%
TOTAL	**400**	**40%**

Remarks: Annual recurrent costs are calculated on a two years basis, including a 6-month cropping and 18-month fallow
period, divided by two. The initial cost for the no-till drill is calculated – on a per hectare basis – for an average farm size of
10 ha. In this case a 'pilot' farmer's case is taken, where the drill is supplied free. As with conventional drills, a new no-till
drill costs US$ 6,000 but it is subsidised by up to 50% by the Government. Thus farmers can buy it for US$ 3,000 (though 'pilot'
farmers receive it free of charge – as noted above). They have no extra costs (compared to conventional tillage) and they can
share the price of the drill between them if they wish. The price of certified seeds and fertilizers, energy and equipment are
the main factors affecting the costs of no-till, when subsidies are cut after the pilot phase. However, the costs of NTT are
lower than for conventional farming, even when the cost of the drill is included.

Assessment

Acceptance/adoption

- All the 14 pilot farmers accepted the technology with incentives, receiving all inputs (machinery, seeds, fertilizers and biocides) in the first 3 years.
- These pilot farmers are still in the phase of adoption. Out of the 14 farmers, there are two or three that still resist the
  change. Farmers' attitudes alter slowly and complete acceptance is only reached after several years.

Benefits/costs according to land user

Benefits compared with costs	short-term:	long-term:
establishment	not applicable*	not applicable*
maintenance/recurrent	slightly positive	very positive

* Pilot farmers receive the no-till drill fully financed by the project (thus no benefits under 'investment costs' above). Farmers who purchase the drill on their own (with a 50% subsidy) will recover its cost in less than two years.

Impacts of the technology

Production and socio-economic benefits
+ + + crop yield increase of 1.0 t/ha (wheat)
+ + + fodder production/quality increase
+ + + farm income increase
+ +   reduced labour and energy inputs

Socio-cultural benefits
+ +   national institution strengthening
+ +   improved knowledge SWC/erosion

Ecological benefits
+ + + soil cover improvement (residues, early seeding)
+ + + increase in soil moisture
+ + + increase in soil fertility
+ + + soil loss reduction
+ + + increase in soil organic matter
+ +   biodiversity enhancement

Other benefits
+ + + flexible labour inputs: seeding is independent of rain onset
+ + + timeliness
+ +   costs: fewer tractor passes in field

Off-site benefits
+ + + reduced downstream siltation
+ + + reduced transported sediments
+ + + reduction of wind erosion: improved air quality
+ + + extra carbon sequestration
+ +   reduced downstream flooding
+ +   increased stream flow in dry season

Production and socio-economic disadvantages
– –   initial investment for special drill/tractor
–   increased input constraints
–   increased economic inequity

Socio-cultural disadvantages
– –   stubble grazing by neighbours can cause socio-cultural conflicts (it is no longer allowed)

Ecological disadvantages
–   herbicide use: herbicide persistence/carry over

Other disadvantages
– –   increased skills and technical knowledge (expertise) needed: new system of managing crops/soils, new equipment/herbicides

Off-site disadvantages
none

Concluding statements

Strengths and → how to sustain/improve

Erosion control → Maintaining sufficient soil cover.

Soil quality improvement → Controlled biomass exportation and grazing; on-time seeding.

Efficient use of soil water: increased infiltration, water loss reduced, increased water availability for plants → Fallowing, maintaining sufficient soil cover.

Increased crop production and yield stability → Promote productive and pest-resistant crop varieties and early seeding in order to cover soils and protect them from rainfall impact.

Improved land use and diversified cropping systems with higher yields than in conventional system → Refine the integrated crop management and pest control system.

More flexibility in planting, early land access and easier management of soils → Continue to cover soils with residues at planting/seeding to ensure sufficient soil moisture.

Reduced energy, labour and cost: in NTT the tillage and seedbed preparation operations are eliminated; the no-till drill applies P and N fertilizers with the seed → Stress the use of appropriate equipment and inputs.

Weaknesses and → how to overcome

High level of management is required → Training of land users.

Sensitive to nitrogen level management → Soil tests/apply N according to needs of crops under NTT.

High disease and pest prevalence if crop residues are not well managed → Resistant varieties and early seeding of diverse crops.

Reduced availability of straw (fodder) → Optimise crop/livestock integration: straw production under NTT is higher but farmers have to be convinced to remove only part it; use fodder crops in rotation.

Unforeseen environmental risks: eg soil or ground water contamination with herbicides/phosphate → Training, video presentations etc.

Costly machinery (drills, tractor, sprayer) required → Subsidies, purchase of equipment by groups of farmers.

Weed control in NTT is critical: weed infestation if not well managed; high cost of herbicides → Apply environment-friendly herbicides, crop diversification; hand weeding.

Socio-economic constraints of Moroccan farmers → Technology needs a long-term approach for full acceptance and implementation.

Key reference(s): Mrabet R, Ibno-Namr K, Bessam F and Saber N (2001) Soil chemical quality changes and implications for fertilizer management after 11 years of no-tillage wheat production systems in semi-arid Morocco. *Land Degradation & Development* 12: 505-517 ■ Mrabet R (2002) Wheat yield and water use efficiency under contrasting residue and tillage management systems in a semi-arid area of Morocco. *Experimental Agriculture* 38: 237–248

Contact person(s): Rachid Mrabet, *INRA Institut National de la Recherche Agronomique, Centre Aridoculture*, 26000 Settat, PO Box 589, Morocco; phone ++212 23 729300/01/02/03, fax ++212 23 720927; rachidmrabet@yahoo.co.uk

left: No-till field day in Benahmed region. The sign says: 'trial with barley, direct seeding'. (Ait Lhaj A.)
right: Barley samples from on-farm plots at Khourigba, showing improved growth under no-till technology compared with conventional farming. (Ait Lhaj A.)

Applied research and knowledge transfer

Morocco – البحوث التطبيقية ونقل المعرفة

Innovative, cross-disciplinary community-based approach for development and transfer of no-till technology at the farm level.

After 15 years of on-station research at the National Institute of Agricultural Research (INRA), testing and evaluation of no-till technology (NTT) at farm level started in 1997 with three pilot farmers. Recently two new projects were established to promote the introduction and adoption of NTT, in collaboration with the regional council and extension service of the Ministry of Agriculture (MoA). Fourteen pilot farmers are now involved in NTT.

The overall purpose is to promote no-till technology to restore soils, improve production, mitigate drought, increase wealth and strengthen farmers' organisations. NTT has been shown to be socially, economically and ecologically adapted to the local conditions. The approach has three stages: (1) Initiation: this includes basic research, strategic research and applied research; (2) Consolidation: planning is followed by detailed evaluation of technology adoption on farmers' fields; (3) Maturity: this involves the acceptance/spread of NTT with an increased number of farmers in the future.

INRA carries out research, information dissemination, gives training to technicians and farmers, and provides both technical assistance and monitoring. The regional council was convinced by the technology and now financially supports research activities, drill manufacture and extension of NTT. It also facilitates contacts with decision makers and farmers, and carries out evaluations. MoA development and extension services provide financial support, advice, technical assistance, and logistical support to farmers: they help to make the drills available. NGOs are engaged in the development of local/regional networks and farmers' associations, as well as in funding and providing incentives. Farmers themselves are involved in the implementation, evaluation and dissemination of NTT.

Participation, cross-discipline and bottom-up planning are key elements of the approach. Methods for implementation include long-term community on-farm trials, on-site training and information exchange, participation of stakeholders, information dissemination tools, and multi-directional knowledge flow. These are supplemented by intensive measurement/monitoring schemes, establishment of local/regional networks and farmers' association creation. On-the-job training is also provided.

Location: Settat, Khourigba and Benslimane Provinces Chaouia/Ouardigha, Morocco
Approach area: 16,760 km²
Land use: cropland
Climate: semi-arid, subhumid
WOCAT database reference: QA MOR10
Related technology: No-till technology, QT MOR10
Compiled by: Rachid Mrabet, INRA, Settat, Morocco
Date: April 2003, updated June 2004

Editors' comments: This is a unique approach within Morocco, developed by INRA (National Institute of Agricultural Research) in that it integrates several institutions and stakeholders (research institute, government extension service, manufacturers, NGOs, community and farmers) at different levels. It is specifically designed for the promotion of no-till farming.

Problem, objectives and constraints

Problem
- previous absence of an integrated research and extension programme
- lack of technical options in a harsh and risky environment
- underlying problems of land degradation and drought periods

Objectives
- spread the no-till technology: thereby enhancing soil productivity and reducing susceptibility to land degradation
- develop the production of no-till drill machinery
- generally: to ameliorate the living conditions of rural people through enhancing expertise, capacities and knowledge of farmers in managing their soils and crops

Constraints addressed

Major	Specification	Treatment
Technical	Lack of adapted machinery.	Promotion of no-till drill industry in Morocco.
Institutional	Extension services are not well incorporated in the approach due to lack of knowledge/information on no-till.	Special training programme, changing institutional thinking regarding no-till systems.
Financial	Lack of specific funds, credit, loans for investment in new machinery.	Prioritise funds for no-till development.
Social/cultural/religious	Over-reliance on traditions in soil management; attitudes of farmers towards conventional tillage need challenging through information about alternatives.	Training, video conferences, travelling workshops etc.

Minor	Specification	Treatment
Legal	Lack of SWC-related laws.	Recommendations on laws to cover SWC technologies.
Legal	Small field sizes.	Encouragement of collaboration between farmers to establish 'economies of scale' (per unit input of labour/machinery a larger area can be treated than in conventional farming).

Participation and decision making

Target groups

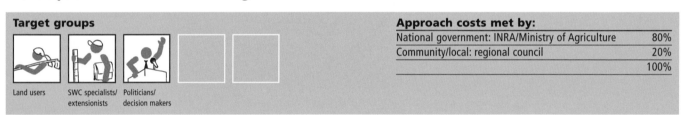

Land users — SWC specialists/extensionists — Politicians/decision makers

Approach costs met by:

National government: INRA/Ministry of Agriculture	80%
Community/local: regional council	20%
	100%

Decisions on choice of the technology: Mainly made by SWC specialists, supported by politicians, with the consultation of land users. Recognition of no-till as an appropriate technology by decision-makers at local, regional and national level is due to research results as well as to the international call to promote this technology.

Decisions on method of implementing the technology: Mainly made by SWC specialists with consultation of land users; no-till technology was under research and on-farm trials (3 farmers) and showed very marked benefits, particularly during drought years.

Approach designed by: National specialists.

Community involvement

Phase	Involvement	Activities
Initiation	passive	open days (public meetings, workshops)
Planning	payments/incentives	public meetings, workshops
Implementation	payments/incentives	responsibility for minor steps, also casual labour
Monitoring/evaluation	payments/incentives	field observations, interviews, measurements, public meetings, workshops
Research	interactive	on-farm demonstration plots

Differences in participation of men and women: There are no differences. Both men and women participate.

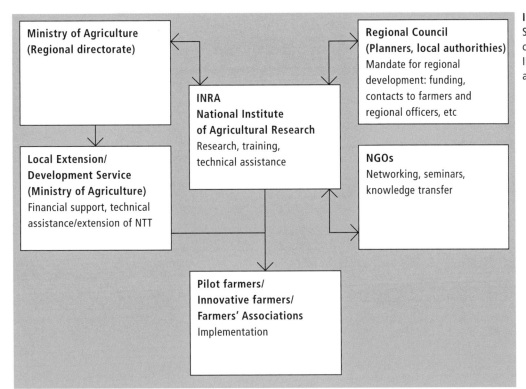

Institutional framework
Stakeholders and their roles:
cross-disciplinary linkages between
INRA, collaborating institutions
and farmers.

Extension and promotion

Training: Training is provided in the no-till system, including weed control, machinery use, cropping systems, and crop varieties. The following methods are used: on-the-job training, demonstration areas, and also public meetings. The effectiveness of training on land users, planners and politicians has been 'good', on trainers/extensionists it is 'excellent'.

Extension: The two key elements are as follows: (1) participation of extension agents and farmers (observations on the crop, weeds, disease, seeding condition, yield components); (2) training/open days (field days) to allow farmers and extension staff to discuss no-till technology. Extension and awareness raising have had a good impact on land users, but extension continuation through government is inadequate as yet. Extension agents need to be further trained.

Research: Research on technology, ecological and agronomic aspects were carried out by INRA in collaboration with pilot farmers. Topics were as follows: crop performance, soil analysis, no-till drill design and evaluation, and socio-economic analysis of NTT. Research is an essential part of the project, and its impact has been, and continues to be, great.

Importance of land use rights: Small field size requires collaboration between farmers for the use of the no-till drill and other equipment. It is important to share the costs of drills.

Incentives

Labour: Labour inputs by the farmers are not reimbursed.

Inputs: Drills, seeds, fertilizers and biocides have been provided and fully financed by the project. The Government (MoA) has purchased drills for pilot farmers in order to encourage implementation of NTT. This is to help farmers to understand the benefits of no-till systems, but also to encourage them to purchase their own no-till drills in the future.

Credit: To promote the acceptance of the technology, farmers receive a 50% subsidy on the purchase price of the no-till drill (as is the general case for all types of drills).

Support to local institutions: Moderate support: both financial and in terms of training.

Long-term impact of incentives: Once no-till is adopted by the farmers the ecological effects of NTT (increase in crop production and soil quality changes) will last and incentives can be reduced. However with direct incentives there is some risk that when these are phased out, some farmers may abandon NTT.

Monitoring and evaluation

Monitored aspects	Methods and indicators
Bio-physical	regular measurements of soil properties, soil water content, weeds, disease, insects, production (straw and grain yield)
Technical	regular measurements of drill performance (seeding depth, plant vigour, fertilizer banding depth, roughness, residue management), energy (fuel consumption, traction needs, speed of seeding), inputs, herbicide application (rate, distribution, amount of water needed, efficacy on weeds, toxicity on crops), harvest (straw and grain yields, stubble, yield components, seed quality, seed health)
Socio-cultural	ad hoc evaluation of farmers' observations and constraints, labour (household/off-farm) and traditional farming (type, tools, crop management skills, soil management knowledge, level of education and technical knowledge)
Economic/production	regular measurements of use of agricultural inputs , energy consumption, yield, labour
Area treated	ad hoc measurements
No. of land users involved	regular assessment
Management of approach	ad hoc observations: during field days and seminars the remarks, comments and suggestions of farmers regarding the no-till system are discussed

Impacts of the approach

Changes as result of monitoring and evaluation: The evaluation is still in process: thus too early to state what changes are likely.

Improved soil and water management: Better use of the rainwater stored in the soil by crops leads to improvement of soil and water management: increase in soil organic matter has multiple benefits.

Adoption of the approach by other projects/land users: This no-till system can now be considered for several different agroecological situations where a similar approach can be applied.

Sustainability: Progress can continue to be made, assuming that training, subsidised drills, and the creation of farmers' organisations all persist.

Concluding statements

Strengths and ➜ how to sustain/improve	Weaknesses and ➜ how to overcome
The NTT project has integrated several institutions -which is unique in Morocco. Now research, extension, community and farmers are working together towards the same objective ➜ Further develop, refine and spread NTT.	The programme's duration is currently too short to overcome resistance (to new technology adoption) and to address economic constraints of farmers ➜ A long term programme is needed to increase acceptance among farmers.
Progressive implementation of a 'bottom-up' approach; integration of farmers' decisions, opinions and criticisms ➜ Further involve farmers and farmers' associations in all stages of the process.	Direct incentives: there is always a risk that when eliminating these incentives, farmers will abandon NTT ➜ Eliminate incentives gradually and replace with loans and credits.
Cross-discipline: involving land users, research and extension agents has helped in building up an approach suitable for the local conditions.	Information availability: up to now information and communication on NTT is scarce ➜ Intensify training.
NGO development: the association of NTT farmers and environmental clubs are important for spreading NTT and for re-enforcing the importance of NTT amongst government officers and decision makers ➜ Encourage special NGOs to respect soils, nature, and the environment.	In some situations (farmers with very low incomes), the need for external inputs such as herbicides, seeds, fertilizers and drills may retard implementation of NTT ➜ Incentives should be maintained for a short period and supplemented by credit systems.
Incentives make it possible for land users to experiment with a new cultivation system ➜ Diversification of incentives: eg reduction in seed prices and herbicides for NTT farmers; award 'NTT best producers'; reduction in interest rates for NTT farmers (for credits or loans); special NTT training courses.	
Adaptability to farmers' needs and constraints ➜ Improve integration of livestock and crops.	

Key reference(s): Segry L, Bousinac S and Pieri C (1991) *An approach to the development of sustainable farming systems*. World Technical Paper N-2. IBSRAM Proceedings 1991 ■ Wall et al (2002) *Institutional aspects of conservation agriculture*. International Workshop on Conservation Agriculture for Sustainable Wheat Production, 14-18, October 2002, Tashkent, Uzbekistan

Contact person(s): Rachid Mrabet, *INRA Institut National de la Recherche Agronomique, Centre Aridoculture*, 26000 Settat, PO Box 589, Morocco; phone ++212 23 729300/01/02/03, fax ++212 23 720927; rachidmrabet@yahoo.co.uk

left: A tractor with the 'Väderstad Rapid Cultivation Drill' in action: a light surface tillage followed by direct seeding. (Soil and Water Protection, SOWAP)
right: The grain crop emerging through a light mulch of straw. (SOWAP)

Conservation agriculture

England, UK

Improved soil management based on non-inversion tillage for cost-effective and timely crop establishment.

Conservation agriculture (CA), involving superficial non-inversion tillage, began to be widely taken up in England following advances in seed drill technology, non-selective herbicides and straw-chopping combine harvesters in the late 1980s. This case focuses on the Game Conservancy Trust's Allerton Project at Loddington, which in 2000 pooled resources with its neighbour to purchase a single set of cultivation equipment, and replaced conventional mouldboard ploughing (with its multiple cultivations) by state-of-the-art CA. Contract services offered by the joint venture means that 1,000 ha are now covered each year. The main winter crops are wheat, oats, and oilseed rape. Beans are sown in the spring. The heavy clay loam is vulnerable to excessive surface moisture, restricting crop establishment 'windows'.

Immediately after harvest the soil is loosened and straw incorporated, and then soil is consolidated (using a 'cultivation train' combining two machines: the 'Simba Solo' and the 'Cultipress'). This encourages up to 60% of the weeds to emerge in a 'stale seedbed'. Spraying then removes all the weeds and volunteer plants of previous crops. This is followed by a light surface tillage, using the 'Väderstad Rapid Cultivator Drill', before sowing into the seedbed created. Equipment comprises implements with tines and/or discs which create a tilth to around 10 cm without inverting the soil. Cambridge rollers are then used to consolidate the sown land. After crop maturity, combine harvesting takes place – with simultaneous chopping of straw/crop residues. A trash rake is used to disperse the chopped straw. This way excessive trash is incorporated rapidly into the soil. Compaction may arise in the transition phase, because of the lack of soil loosening through ploughing: minimising traffic, keeping to tramlines and headlands can all help. In time, increases in soil organic matter content and earthworm biomass make compaction less of a problem. The problem of slugs can be reduced by improving seed-to-soil contact, and by drilling deeper.

The main purpose of conservation agriculture is cost effective, timely and rapid crop establishment, under good soil conditions. High-speed operations are the key. Compared with conventional ploughing, labour is saved and fuel costs lowered. However, an additional application of herbicides represents an extra expenditure. Yields per hectare haven't risen but the key difference is that about four times as many hectares can be prepared in time for autumn planting under conservation tillage, thus improving overall production. Incorporation of crop residues improves soil structure and leads to a more friable, less erodible topsoil.

Location: Leicestershire, England
Technology area: 10 km²
SWC measure: agronomic
Land use: cropland
Climate: subhumid
WOCAT database reference: QT UNK01
Related approach: Soil management initiative, QA UNK01
Compiled by: Alastair Leake, The Allerton Trust, Loddington, Leicestershire, UK
Date: October 2004, updated March 2005

Editors' comments: Conservation agriculture is rapidly catching on throughout the world. While most attention has been focussed on the Americas, a revolution is taking place in Europe also. In England, for example, around 40% of the large scale arable area is now under CA – a rise from just 10% a decade ago. CA helps to minimise costs and reduce local, and global, environmental impacts. This is a case from a leading proponent of CA in England. Comparative case studies are documented from Morocco, Australia and Kenya.

Classification

Land use problems
Traditional inversion tillage is slow and costly. By moving to high speed non-inversion conservation tillage farmers can spread costs over a larger area and maximise the area under winter crops. The speed at which ground can be worked in the autumn is critical: one month earlier planting can mean an extra ton in cereal yield.

Land use	Climate	Degradation				SWC measures			

annual crops: wheat, oats, oilseed rape

subhumid (temperate)

water erosion: loss of topsoil, gully erosion

chemical: decline in organic matter and fertility

agronomic: non-inversion tillage

Technical function/impact
main:
- improvement of ground cover
- improvement of soil structure
- increase in organic matter
- increase in soil fertility
- increase in infiltration

secondary: - none

Environment

Natural environment

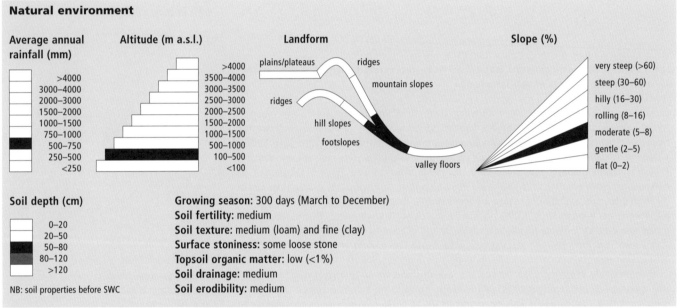

Average annual rainfall (mm)
- >4000
- 3000–4000
- 2000–3000
- 1500–2000
- 1000–1500
- 750–1000
- 500–750
- 250–500
- <250

Altitude (m a.s.l.)
- >4000
- 3500–4000
- 3000–3500
- 2500–3000
- 2000–2500
- 1500–2000
- 1000–1500
- 500–1000
- 100–500
- <100

Landform
plains/plateaus, ridges, mountain slopes, ridges, hill slopes, footslopes, valley floors

Slope (%)
- very steep (>60)
- steep (30–60)
- hilly (16–30)
- rolling (8–16)
- moderate (5–8)
- gentle (2–5)
- flat (0–2)

Soil depth (cm)
- 0–20
- 20–50
- 50–80
- 80–120
- >120

NB: soil properties before SWC

Growing season: 300 days (March to December)
Soil fertility: medium
Soil texture: medium (loam) and fine (clay)
Surface stoniness: some loose stone
Topsoil organic matter: low (<1%)
Soil drainage: medium
Soil erodibility: medium

Human environment

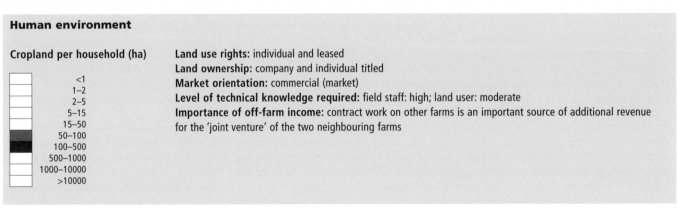

Cropland per household (ha)
- <1
- 1–2
- 2–5
- 5–15
- 15–50
- 50–100
- 100–500
- 500–1000
- 1000–10000
- >10000

Land use rights: individual and leased
Land ownership: company and individual titled
Market orientation: commercial (market)
Level of technical knowledge required: field staff: high; land user: moderate
Importance of off-farm income: contract work on other farms is an important source of additional revenue for the 'joint venture' of the two neighbouring farms

Detailed view of the 'Väderstad Rapid Cultivation Drill' with tines and discs. (Alastair Leake)

Implementation activities, inputs and costs

Establishment activities
not applicable

Establishment inputs and costs per ha

Inputs	Costs (US$)	% met by land user
not applicable		

Maintenance/recurrent activities
1. Loosen the soil and incorporate the straw using the 'Simba Solo'; soil consolidation, using the 'Cultipress' (immediately post-harvest).
2. Spray the stale seedbed to remove all the weeds/volunteer plants of previous crops (mid September).
3. Light surface tillage and sowing into the seedbed; using the 'Väderstad Rapid Cultivator Drill' (usually end September, just after spraying).
4. Consolidation of the sown land (using Cambridge rollers).
5. After crop maturity, combine harvesting – with simultaneous chopping of straw.
6. Disperse the chopped straw, using a trash rake.

Maintenance/recurrent inputs and costs per ha per year

Inputs	Costs (US$)	% met by land user
Equipment		
- various machines	180	100%
TOTAL	180	100%

Remarks: No establishment costs for purchase of special conservation tillage equipment are included here – though this investment is considerable. Tractors of sufficient horsepower and a couple of special machines (see above) are needed. The investment in this case was shared by two neighbouring farms, who implemented conservation agriculture on a joint venture basis. The only costs presented in the table above are total recurrent annual costs for tillage operations. This total, US$ 180, compares with US$ 260 for conventional tillage operations. While drilling is not included in the above conventional tillage calculation, subsequent application of additional herbicides represents an extra cost of conservation tillage of about US$ 80/ha. In balance the costs per hectare are broadly similar. Labour inputs however are reduced considerably as a proportion: the Allerton farm with its 260 ha of arable land is operated by a farm manager and just one farm worker.

Assessment

Acceptance/adoption
- From just 10% in 1995, approximately 40% of arable land in England is currently (2004) under conservation agriculture/ cultivation tillage. The farmers involved have adopted the system without incentives other than those of timeliness, lower cost, speedier crop establishment, reduced soil erosion and benefits to wildlife.
- There is significant growing spontaneous adoption: the extent of adoption depends on farm size, enterprise, and soil type.
- There are government subsidies to farmers for following sound land management practices (see associated approach 'Soil Management Initiative', under 'Inputs').

Benefits/costs according to land user

Benefits compared with costs	short-term:	long-term:
establishment*	negative	positive
maintenance/recurrent	positive	very positive

* change of machinery

Impacts of the technology

Production and socio-economic benefits

+			overall farm income increase

Production and socio-economic disadvantages

−			reduced yields in the early years (due to initial compaction) until the soil restructures

Socio-cultural benefits

+	+		community institution strengthening
+	+		improved knowledge SWC/erosion
+			national institution strengthening

Socio-cultural disadvantages

−			socio-cultural conflicts

Ecological benefits

+	+	+	runoff and soil loss reduced
+	+	+	loss of nutrients (through leaching) reduced
+	+		soil cover improvement
+	+		increase in soil moisture
+	+		biodiversity enhancement (above and below ground)
+	+		improved soil structure
+	+		increase in soil organic matter
+	+		carbon sequestration increased
+			efficiency of excess water drainage
+			increase in soil fertility

Ecological disadvantages

−			organic matter depletion (in certain sandy soils)
−			increased reliance on herbicides

Off-site benefits

+	+		reduced downstream flooding
+	+		reduced downstream siltation
+	+		reduced river pollution
+	+		reduced transported sediments

Off-site disadvantages

Concluding statements

Strengths and → how to sustain/improve

Lowers recurrent soil tillage costs – mainly due to reduction in fuel use (down by about one third) and labour (saving around one person day per hectare) → Spread over greater area to maximise cost reduction.

Increases overall farm yield (and income) by speeding up land preparation in autumn, allowing a larger area to be planted as winter crops → Ditto.

Improves soil structure and physical properties in various ways → Maintain system over time to maximise these benefits.

Reduces runoff (by a half), soil erosion (by two thirds), and leaching of nutrients (by three quarters) thus decreasing movement of phosphates and nitrates to streams and rivers → To improve further, combine with other measures such as adding organic matter or growing green manures and cover crops.

Increases soil buffering capacity against climatic extremes (especially rainfall) through maintaining surface cover and building up soil organic matter → Maintain system over time to maximise these benefits.

Increases soil biota (more than doubling earthworm mass) and bio-diversity generally (nearly doubling the number of different organisms) → Maintain system over time to maximise these benefits.

Weaknesses and → how to overcome

Increased growth of grass weeds and thus greater cost of herbicides → Use 'stale seedbeds' – surface tillage immediately post-harvest to induce weed germination – followed by spraying. Crop rotation, spring cropping, occasional ploughing (every few years as necessary).

Not suitable for all soil types (not appropriate on some sandy soils) → Don't introduce/promote CA indiscriminately.

Excessive surface trash/crop residues → Good chopping, then spreading and incorporation.

Problems with slugs → Drill seed deeper, ensure good seed-to-soil contact.

Surface compaction in the early stages of conversion to conservation agriculture → Appropriate loosening of soil, using tined implement.

Key reference(s): Soil Management Initiative/Department for Environment, Food and Rural Affairs (DEFRA) (undated) *A guide to managing crop establishment*. SMI, UK (www.smi.org.uk) ■ Soil Management Initiative (undated) *Improved soil management for agronomic and environmental gain*. SMI, UK ■ Soil Management Initiative/Väderstad (undated) *Target on establishment: innovation for the future of farming*. SMI, UK
Contact person(s): Dr A R Leake, Chairman UK Soil Management Initiative, Loddington House, Main Street, Loddington, LEICESTERSHIRE LE7 9XE, UK; phone ++44 1572 717220; aleake@gct.org.uk; www.gct.org.uk; www.allertontrust.org.uk

Soil management initiative

England, UK

left: Extension methods include practical and theoretical elements: farmers attending a field day organised by SMI. (Soil and Water Protection – SOWAP)
right: Classroom training sessions on conservation agriculture with presentations from experts (SOWAP).

An independent organisation that promotes the adoption of appropriate soil management practices, especially conservation agriculture, within England.

The zero tillage systems promoted in the UK during the 1970s were radical. Pioneering farmers moved from ploughing to zero tillage using special direct drilling machines and non-selective contact herbicides. However, they encountered serious problems with slugs, persistent grass weeds and straw, and zero tillage was largely abandoned. Pressures to reduce crop establishment costs then led to the intermediate method of 'conservation agriculture' (CA).

The Soil Management Initiative (SMI) has been central to the development and promotion of CA. SMI is an independent non-profit organisation that was established by a small, committed group in 1999. Its aim is to promote the adoption of cultivation systems which improve soil quality, minimise soil erosion and water pollution, and simultaneously maintain or enhance farm economic returns.

SMI brings together organisations with varied expertise and technical abilities, and provides both research results and advice to the large numbers of farmers who are progressively adopting CA. Furthermore, SMI was a founder member of the European Conservation Agriculture Federation (ECAF), under which there are 14 national organisations. Competence within SMI is drawn from research institutes, educational establishments, farmers and landowners, machinery manufacturers, crop protection companies, charitable trusts, and from independent agronomists and advisers.

The EU Life fund provided an initial three-year allocation to support SMI. This ended in 2002. SMI now raises finance from the UK and EU governments, commercial sponsorship (international agrochemical and machinery companies) and fees paid by farmers. In the current climate of privatisation of advisory services, there is no targeted governmental advisory body to carry out such a function. DEFRA (The UK Government's Department for Environment, Food and Rural Affairs) does however provide some support to SMI with both funds and expertise, and is an associate member.

Amongst SMI's methods for spreading the message of improved soil management are field days – where farmers pay to attend – an interactive web-based help-line on 'lo-till' and farmers' magazines. SMI also undertakes extension 'roadshows', visiting specific farms for question and answer sessions. A formal session with presentations from experts precedes a practical outdoor demonstration. SMI gains knowledge and practical experience from the 'joint venture' at Loddington (see associated technology).

Location: England, UK (based at: Loddington, Leicestershire)
Approach area: England
Land use: cropland
Climate: subhumid
WOCAT database reference: QA UNK01
Related technology: Conservation agriculture, QT UNK01
Compiled by: Alastair Leake, The Allerton Trust, Loddington, Leicestershire, UK
Date: October 2004, updated March 2005

Editors' comments: SMI is an example of an independent organisation set up to advise farmers in appropriate cultivation and conservation practices. As government-based advisory services within Europe are reducing in size and scope, farmers are turning to specialised organisations for help.

Problem, objectives and constraints

Problem
- Attempts to apply conservation agriculture by arable farmers in the 1980s and 90s were not matched by an understanding of the whole system. There was a thirst for more knowledge.
- Privatisation of government advisory services has left a gap to be filled – in this case an advisory body in sustainable soil management.

Objectives
- improve technology transfer through extension to farmers
- promote agricultural and environmental policies to support sustainable soil management
- improve information exchange in and amongst the research, policy and practitioner communities and private companies (machinery and agrochemical etc)
- research, develop, evaluate and promote soil management systems to improve crop production and protection of the environment

Constraints addressed

Major	Specification	Treatment
Technical	Farmers lacked adequate knowledge regarding use of new CA implements, and emerging weed and pest control methods.	SMI provides demand-driven technical support services.
Financial	SMI has needed to operate within a tight budget, and this was reduced further in 2002 when the 3-year allocation from the EU Life fund ended.	The remedy has been to depend more on support from private companies (agrochemical and machinery) and payment by farmers for advice/attendance at field days.

Participation and decision making

Target groups

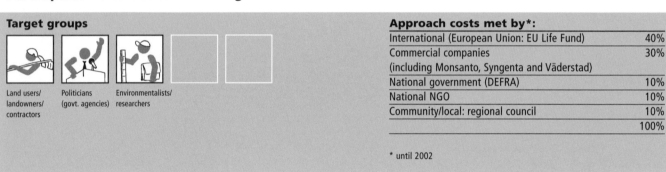

Land users/ landowners/ contractors   Politicians (govt. agencies)   Environmentalists/ researchers

Approach costs met by*:

International (European Union: EU Life Fund)	40%
Commercial companies (including Monsanto, Syngenta and Väderstad)	30%
National government (DEFRA)	10%
National NGO	10%
Community/local: regional council	10%
	100%

* until 2002

Decisions on choice of the technology: Made by land users alone.
Decisions on method of implementing the technology: Made by land users alone (farmers).
Approach designed by: National specialists (SMI's specialists, and especially the executive committee).

Community involvement

Phase	Involvement	Activities
Initiation	passive	setting up SMI
Planning	passive	setting up SMI
Implementation	interactive	advisory services/demand-driven field events
Monitoring/evaluation	passive	M&E of SMI's activities
Research	interactive	on-farm research on conservation agriculture

Differences in participation between men and women: None in principle, though *de facto* most farmers are male, and they constitute the majority at field days.

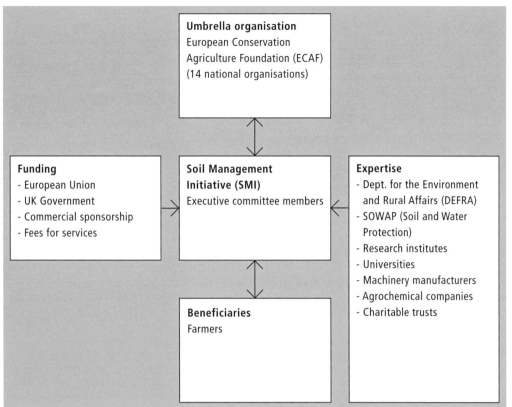

Institutional framework
Linkages between the Soil Management Institute, the European Conservation Agriculture Foundation, funding agencies, research institutions, land users and producers of machinery and agrochemicals.

Umbrella organisation
European Conservation Agriculture Foundation (ECAF) (14 national organisations)

Funding
- European Union
- UK Government
- Commercial sponsorship
- Fees for services

Soil Management Initiative (SMI)
Executive committee members

Expertise
- Dept. for the Environment and Rural Affairs (DEFRA)
- SOWAP (Soil and Water Protection)
- Research institutes
- Universities
- Machinery manufacturers
- Agrochemical companies
- Charitable trusts

Beneficiaries
Farmers

Extension and promotion

Training: Technical demonstrations in the field are the primary means of knowledge transfer. A formal session with presentations from experts precedes a practical outdoor demonstration. Although conservation agriculture is the 'umbrella topic', specific issues – such as herbicide application – are treated on demand.

Extension: SMI undertakes extension 'roadshows', visiting specific farms for question and answer sessions. It also hosts an e-mail/website based 'lo-till' helpline – through the Farmers' Weekly magazine (www.fwi.co.uk). SMI furthermore contributes to frequent press articles as well as producing publications (see key references). These methods have proved to be very effective: this is evidenced by the number of farmers willing to pay for advice, and by the number of hits on the helpline.

Research: Conservation agriculture was initially supported by public funded research. Current research – through SMI but also some research institutes and farmers themselves - is focused on specific issues, including slug control, grass weeds, trash management and soil compaction. Recently, environmental, economic and social concerns arising from the practice of conventional agriculture have been taken up by SOWAP (Soil and Water Protection), a collaborative initiative, supported by the EU Life scheme, between commercial companies, NGOs, academic institutions and farmers.

Importance of land use rights: Ownership and the attitude of the owner towards CA can affect uptake significantly. For example, some landlords do not like tenants to practice conservation agriculture because 'it looks messy' with trash lying on the surface rather than neatly ploughed fields.

Incentives

Labour: Farmers themselves provide labour – though the adoption of conservation agriculture involves a considerable saving on labour inputs compared with conventional agriculture.

Inputs: There are no subsidies specifically connected to CA or sustainable soil management. However, the CA principles fall within UK's new 'cross-compliance' conditions for the Single Farm Payment scheme which effectively constitutes a subsidy to farmers for following sound land management practices. There is also a recently introduced 'Environmental Stewardship Scheme', which embraces environmental concerns. Under this scheme, it is likely that much of the area under conservation agriculture will qualify for, at least, the entry-level category of subsidy, currently set at approx. US$ 60/ha/year: note – this is on top of the single farm payment, which will be considerably greater (for more details see www.defra.gov.uk). Manufacturers of non-inversion tillage equipment provide machines for demonstration. Manufacturers of biocides provided finance and support to specific farmers in the early stages of progressive development.

Credit: None provided.

Support to local institutions: None specifically, though the promotion of conservation agriculture tends to encourage collaborative ventures and sharing between farmers.

Long-term impact of incentives: Not applicable.

Monitoring and evaluation

Monitored aspects	Methods and indicators
Bio-physical	regular observations/measurements by SMI
Technical	regular observations/measurements by SMI
Socio-cultural	ad hoc observations by SMI
Economic/production	regular observations/measurements by SMI
Area treated	ad hoc measurements (survey) by SMI
Management of approach	ad hoc observations by SMI

Impacts of the approach

Changes as result of monitoring and evaluation: SMI is constantly refining its advice on the basis of results monitored from the field.

Improved soil and water management: Considerable: erosion reduced, organic matter built up, nitrate losses reduced etc

Adoption of the approach by other projects/land users: There are other similar service providers in different aspects of farming, though not in soil management.

Sustainability: SMI can continue to support land users with advice as long as they are prepared to continue paying for the services, and sponsorship continues from agencies and commercial companies. Land users can continue to practice CA without external support – but services such as those provided by SMI are extremely valuable.

Concluding statements

Strengths and ➜ how to sustain/improve	Weaknesses and ➜ how to overcome
Has successfully stimulated conservation agriculture, which should in turn ultimately lead to environmentally sound and sustainable land management in England ➜ Continue operations for as long as possible.	SMI has an on-going problem with adequacy of funding ➜ Through top-class services, continue to attract funds and voluntary contributions from a wide range of actors.
SMI has acted effectively as a channel for making results from research, and a wide body of experience, readily available to farmers ➜ Continue to focus on farmers as the main target group and link them with research and private companies.	
SMI has managed to combine the efforts and expertise of a wide range of actors towards a common goal: to provide a unique advisory service in conservation agriculture ➜ Continue to serve as a centre of excellence.	
Improvements in soil management techniques have been documented in an accessible way ➜ Continue to publish simply and clearly as new messages develop.	
Ad hoc advice available via a web-based helpline ➜ Continue.	

Key reference(s): Soil Management Initiative/Department for Environment, Food and Rural Affairs (DEFRA) (undated) *A guide to managing crop establishment.* SMI, UK (www.smi.org.uk) ■ Soil Management Initiative (undated) *Improved soil management for agronomic and environmental gain.* SMI, UK ■ Soil Management Initiative/Väderstad (undated) *Target on establishment: innovation for the future of farming.* SMI, UK
Contact person(s): Dr A R Leake, Chairman UK Soil Management Initiative, Loddington House, Main Street, Loddington, LEICESTERSHIRE LE7 9XE, UK; phone ++44 1572 717220; aleake@gct.org.uk; www.gct.org.uk; www.allertontrust.org.uk

Small-scale conservation tillage
Kenya – *ConTill / Kupiga tindo*

left: Demonstration of conservation tillage through shallow ripping of soil using draught animals: Lines are spaced at 30 cm, reaching a depth between 10 cm and 30 cm, depending on the purpose. (Hanspeter Liniger)
right: 'Victory' plough toolbar with extension to provide extra penetration: deep ripping is practiced every 3–5 years if soil compaction requires this. (Fredrick Kihara)

Ripping of soil using oxen-drawn implements, to improve water storage capacity and cropland productivity on small-scale farms.

Laikipia District in Kenya is characterised by a semi-arid climate, high altitude and rolling terrain. Most of the soil and water loss occurs during a few heavy storms at the beginning of each growing season. More than 90% of families have under two hectares of land, and few have alternative sources of income.

The form of conservation agriculture described in this case study involves the use of ox-drawn ploughs, modified to rip the soil. Ripping is performed in one pass, to a depth of 10 cm, after harvest. Spacing between the rip lines is 30 cm – in the case of wheat. Deep ripping (subsoiling) with the same implement is done, when necessary, to break a plough pan and reaches depths of up to 30 cm. An adaptation to the ordinary plough beam (the common mouldboard 'Victory' plough) makes adjustment to different depths possible and turns it into a ripper for surface and deeper ripping.

The aim of ripping is to increase water infiltration and reduce runoff. In contrast to conventional tillage, the soil is not inverted, thus leaving a certain amount of crop residue on the surface. As a result, the soil is less exposed and not so vulnerable to the impact of splash and sheet erosion, and water loss through evaporation and runoff. In addition, there are savings in terms of energy used for cultivation. In well-ripped fields, rainfall from storms at the onset of the growing season is stored within the rooting zone, and is therefore available to the crop during subsequent drought spells. Ripping the soil during the dry season combined with a mulch cover reduces germination of weeds, leaving fields ready for planting. In case of stubborn weeds, pre-emergence herbicides are used for control. Yields from small-scale conservation tillage can be more than 60% higher than under conventional ploughing. An additional important benefit is that crops mature sooner in conservation agriculture, because they can be planted earlier: under inversion tillage the farmer has to wait for the soil to become moist before ploughing. Earlier crop maturity means access to markets when prices are still high.

There are various supportive technologies in use which can improve the effectiveness of the ripping. These include: (1) use of compost/manure to improve soil structure for better water storage; (2) use of a cover crop (eg *Mucuna pruriens*) planted at the end of the season to prevent erosion, control weeds and improve soil quality; (3) agroforestry: principally *Grevillea robusta* planted on the field boundaries (see also 'Grevillea agroforestry system').

Location: Umande, Daiga, Laikipia District, Kenya
Technology area: 4 km²
SWC measure: agronomic
Land use: cropland
Climate: semi-arid
WOCAT database reference: QT KEN30
Related approach: Self help groups, QA KEN13
Compiled by: Frederick Kihara, Nanyuki, Kenya
Date: June 2003, updated August 2004

Editors' comments: Optimum use of the limited water is crucial for crop production in semi-arid environments. Over the last decade conservation agriculture (including minimum and zero tillage) has spread worldwide. While it was originally adopted by large-scale farmers in the case study area, conservation farming has recently begun to be taken up by small-scale farmers. Other examples of conservation agriculture are presented from Morocco, UK and Australia.

Classification

Land use problems
- loss of rainwater through runoff and direct evaporation from soil surface
- runoff causing surface erosion
- fertility decline due to erosion and nutrient mining

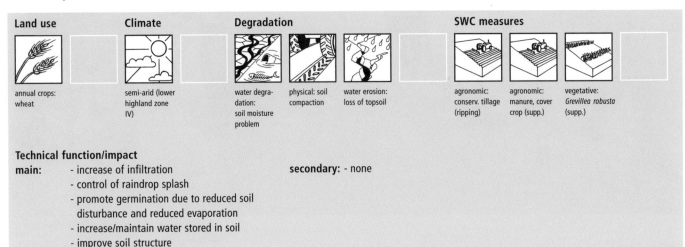

Land use

annual crops: wheat

Climate

semi-arid (lower highland zone IV)

Degradation

water degra-dation: soil moisture problem

physical: soil compaction

water erosion: loss of topsoil

SWC measures

agronomic: conserv. tillage (ripping)

agronomic: manure, cover crop (supp.)

vegetative: *Grevillea robusta* (supp.)

Technical function/impact
main:
- increase of infiltration
- control of raindrop splash
- promote germination due to reduced soil disturbance and reduced evaporation
- increase/maintain water stored in soil
- improve soil structure
- improvement of ground cover

secondary: - none

Environment

Natural environment

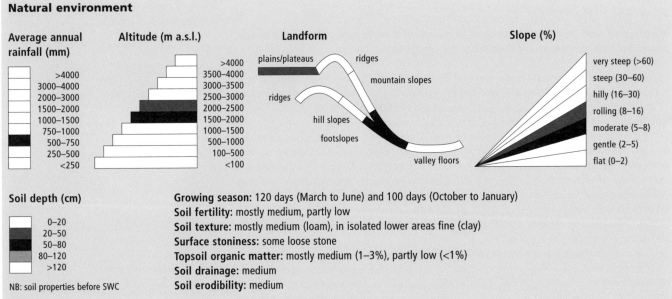

Average annual rainfall (mm)

>4000
3000–4000
2000–3000
1500–2000
1000–1500
750–1000
500–750
250–500
<250

Altitude (m a.s.l.)

>4000
3500–4000
3000–3500
2500–3000
2000–2500
1500–2000
1000–1500
500–1000
100–500
<100

Landform

plains/plateaus, ridges, mountain slopes, ridges, hill slopes, footslopes, valley floors

Slope (%)

very steep (>60)
steep (30–60)
hilly (16–30)
rolling (8–16)
moderate (5–8)
gentle (2–5)
flat (0–2)

Soil depth (cm)

0–20
20–50
50–80
80–120
>120

NB: soil properties before SWC

Growing season: 120 days (March to June) and 100 days (October to January)
Soil fertility: mostly medium, partly low
Soil texture: mostly medium (loam), in isolated lower areas fine (clay)
Surface stoniness: some loose stone
Topsoil organic matter: mostly medium (1–3%), partly low (<1%)
Soil drainage: medium
Soil erodibility: medium

Human environment

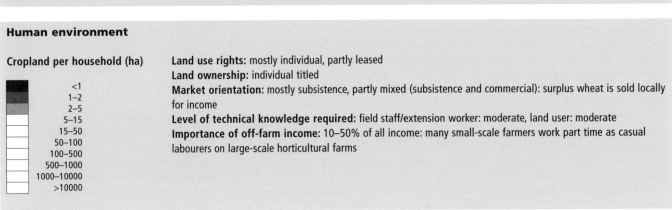

Cropland per household (ha)

<1
1–2
2–5
5–15
15–50
50–100
100–500
500–1000
1000–10000
>10000

Land use rights: mostly individual, partly leased
Land ownership: individual titled
Market orientation: mostly subsistence, partly mixed (subsistence and commercial): surplus wheat is sold locally for income
Level of technical knowledge required: field staff/extension worker: moderate, land user: moderate
Importance of off-farm income: 10–50% of all income: many small-scale farmers work part time as casual labourers on large-scale horticultural farms

left: The ox-drawn ripper used for small-scale conservation tillage. (Hanspeter Liniger)
right: Conservation tillage using a ripper with seeder attached for direct planting. (Hanspeter Liniger)

Implementation activities, inputs and costs

Establishment activities
not applicable

Establishment inputs and costs per ha

Inputs	Costs (US$)	% met by land user
not applicable		

Maintenance/recurrent activities
1. Spreading of crop residue as mulch: up to 3 t/ha (before planting, dry season).
2. Application of compost/household waste: up to 4 t/ha.
3. Ripping of soil with modified plough (dry season).
4. Subsoiling: every 3 years; or as required to break a plough pan.
5. Seeding and application of mineral fertilizer (nitrogen, phosphorus) at the rate of 20 kg/ha, close to seed.
6. Legume interplanting *(Dolichos lablab)* into the cereal crop (supplementary measure): *Dolichos* needs replanting every 3 years.

All activities are carried out using animal traction, mulching done manually.
Equipment/tools: pair of oxen, modified 'Victory' plough beam, plough unit, ripper/chisel (tindo) used for ripping/deep ripping.

Maintenance/recurrent inputs and costs per ha per year

Inputs	Costs (US$)	% met by land user
Labour (3–5 person days)	25	100%
Equipment		
- Animal traction (included in Labour)	0	
- Tools (modified plough)	0	
Agricultural		
- Seeds for wheat (50 kg)	25	100%
- Fertilizers (20 kg)	8	100%
- Compost/manure (4,000 kg)	35	100%
TOTAL	**93**	**100%**

Remarks: Cost calculated charges for hiring equipment, draught animals and operator: these are all rolled up into the 'cost of labour' at US$ 25/ha. Conventional tillage costs US$ 37.5/ha compared with US$ 25/ha for conservation tillage operations: other costs remain more or less the same.

Assessment

Acceptance/adoption
- All the 200 families who accepted the technology did so without incentives.
- Some innovative farmers noticed the practice on large scale farms and decided to test it for themselves. Furthermore, enterprising individuals saw an opportunity to contract their services (oxen, equipment) to neighbouring farms.
- Women did not adopt the practice as technological operations and animal ownership are typically male preserves. But women and youth are being trained and are attending demonstrations to the extent that they are now beginning to participate in field operations.
- There is some growing spontaneous adoption through self-help groups (see corresponding approach 'self-help group').

Benefits/costs according to land user

Benefits compared with costs	short-term:	long-term:
establishment	not applicable	not applicable
maintenance/recurrent	very positive*	positive*

* large increases in yields and reduction in costs after introduction

Impacts of the technology

Production and socio-economic benefits
+ + + crop yield increase (>60%)
+ + fodder production/quality increase
+ + farm income increase
+ + earlier crop maturity

Production and socio-economic disadvantages
none

Socio-cultural benefits
+ + community institution strengthening (farmers' associations formed)
+ + improved knowledge SWC/erosion

Socio-cultural disadvantages
– male-oriented activity (heavy equipment/animals) compared to using the hoe

Ecological benefits
+ + increase in soil moisture; better rainwater harvesting
+ + soil loss reduction
+ + reduction of evaporation
+ soil cover improvement (crop residue)
+ reduced energy consumption

Ecological disadvantages
– waterlogging (contingency plans needed for draining excess water in very wet years – only 1 in 10 – but still important)
– more prone to weeds; may require annual use of pre-emergence herbicides

Other benefits
+ + time-saving
+ timely weeding reduces yield loss

Other disadvantages
none

Off-site benefits
+ + reduced downstream siltation
+ + improved streamflow characteristics (more gradual discharge of groundwater to streams over the season)
+ reduced downstream flooding
+ reduced river pollution (chemical contamination)

Off-site disadvantages
none

Concluding statements

Strengths and ➜ how to sustain/improve

Better soil and water management resulting in (1) reduction of runoff (heavy storm runoff reduced from 75% to 50% and medium storm runoff from 50% to 25%; no runoff from small storms); (2) reduction of evaporation loss (without crop residues 40–60% of the rainwater is lost through direct evaporation from the exposed soil surface)[1]; (3) improved soil moisture (25-60% with better results for high rainfall and heavy storms)[2]; (4) reduced amount of soil inverted: impact is energy saving and organic matter conservation; (5) earlier crop maturity (16% reduction in crop maturity period for wheat: reduced risk of suffering from drought and able to get crops to market early); (6) improved crop production and yield (from 1.5 to 2.7 t/ha/year of wheat)[3] ➜ Access to more appropriate varieties, diversify cropping, better weather predictions to enable farmer to better spread risk.

Large potential for increased income (yield surplus sold) ➜ Continuous encouragement of entrepreneurial skills in farmers; maintain equipment in good order.

Sustainable and stable crop production ➜ Opportunity for expanding marketing capacity for the equipment and technology to raise more income and collective bargaining power for the farmers.

Intensification of production with reduced inputs (a 'win-win' situation): mitigates the problem of declining plot sizes.

Weaknesses and ➜ how to overcome

No clear advantage in extreme climatic conditions ➜ Make farmers aware about this so they do not become discouraged.

As crop residues are often used for feeding animals, there is a conflict between using residues as mulch and as livestock fodder ➜ Greater yields mean a higher income, and savings can be put aside to buy fodder; through water conservation there is more residue production also.

Equipment and animal maintenance cost ➜ Possible loan scheme (microfinance option); build farmer self-help-groups to share costs.

In areas with stubborn weeds pre-emergence herbicides application is necessary ➜ Mulch application reduces negative effects of weeds.

1 Mutunga, 1995; 2 Liniger & Thomas, 1998; 3 Ngigi, 2003

Key reference(s): Kihara FI (1999) *An investigation into the soil loss problem in the Upper Ewaso Ng'iro basin, Kenya.* MSc. Thesis. University of Nairobi, Kenya ∎ Mutunga CN (1995) *The influence of vegetation cover on runoff and soil loss – a study in Mukogodo, Laikipia district Kenya.* MSc Thesis, University of Nairobi, Kenya ∎ Ngigi SN (2003) *Rainwater Harvesting for improved land productivity in the Greater Horn of Africa.* Kenya Rainwater Association, Nairobi ∎ Liniger HP and Thomas DB (1998) GRASS – Ground Cover for Restoration of Arid and Semi-arid Soils. *Advances in GeoEcology* 31, 1167–1178. Catena Verlag, Reiskirchen
Contact person(s): Frederick Kihara, Bonlface Kiteme, CETRAD   Centre for Training and Integrated Research in ASAL Development, PO Box 144, Nanyuki, Kenya; phone ++254-62 31328; b.kiteme@africaonline.co.ke

Self-help groups
Kenya

left: Farmer explaining the difference between conventional tillage (left of picture) and conservation tillage (right of picture). (Hanspeter Liniger)

right: Contractor demonstrating the plough extension for deep ripping to members of the self-help group. (Hanspeter Liniger)

Small-scale farmers forming self-help groups to provide mutual support for adopting and promoting conservation agriculture.

The self-help group approach described here is an initiative which grew from the local land users themselves. Farmers with common interests and goals came together, formed and registered groups and developed constitutions. Conservation agriculture groups started forming in 1997: within two years, five groups had been set up in the study area with over 150 members

The Ministry of Social Services facilitated the registration process. Groups have liased with technology promoters from the Ministry of Agriculture, KENDAT (Kenya Network for Draught Animal Technology), and research and development projects, to gain access to technical knowledge. These organisations have set up research and monitoring projects to assess the impact of conservation agriculture in this area. The groups receive more attention from local development partners than individuals would.

The overall purpose behind the formation of the groups is to improve household food security and raise income. More specific objectives include: (1) mutual adoption of the technology, enabling group members to improve their farm operations and yields, and thereby; (2) creation of opportunities for additional income to help and support each other; (3) sharing knowledge, and conservation tillage equipment.

Groups involve themselves in farmer-to-farmer training. They develop training modules which cover all aspects of conservation agriculture as well as practical training of the animals. Meetings are held once a month to plan group activities. The groups also solicit loans from local development partners for equipment, and they access training on technology from national institutions. Further collaboration with national institutes is planned to facilitate availability of drought-tolerant crop varieties. The members of the self-help groups make various contributions including time, money, animals and some equipment – for joint group activities. Farmers with equipment contract their services to those without, but this is provided at a 20% discount to members.

High adoption levels of conservation agriculture have been achieved through the self-help groups, due to the sharing of resources for technology development and mutual support. The interest in conservation agriculture and demand for equipment is high and growing. Group members are also diversifying their activities into, for example, agroforestry, water harvesting and bee-keeping.

Location: Umande, Daiga, Laikipia District, Kenya
Approach area: 60 km²
Land use: cropland
Climate: semi-arid
WOCAT database reference: QA KEN13
Related technology: Small-scale conservation tillage, QT KEN30
Compiled by: Frederick Kihara, Nanyuki, Kenya
Date: June 2003, updated August 2004

Editors' comments: Self-help groups are common in Kenya, and in parts of the country have been instrumental in the success of SWC campaigns. The formation of such groups, to share knowledge and to give each other practical assistance in conservation agriculture, is a promising approach to promote this new technology, and other SWC measures, amongst smallholders.

Problem, objectives and constraints

Problem
- insufficient individual resources to invest in/or learn about new technology
- underlying problems of (1) food security and (2) insecure water supply for rainfed crop production due to insufficient and poorly distributed rainfall

Objectives
- increase household food security and raise income within the group
- provide mutual support and thereby develop collective bargaining power – an example is the ability to attract technology training from national organisations
- seek possible ways of acquiring equipment for all members of the group, through securing donor support or sponsorship
- all cropland to be under conservation tillage, with all members being fully trained in the technology and having the necessary equipment

Constraints addressed

Major	Specification	Treatment
Technical	Technology was new and initially not well understood.	As organised groups, the members were able to attract technical training from experts (eg KENDAT and Kenya Conservation Tillage Initiative) which was paid by local development partners.
Financial	Equipment is costly and generally cannot be afforded by many.	Ability to hire services from farmers in the group who have equipment.

Minor	Specification	Treatment
Organisational	Group formation and group dynamics.	Two to three enthusiastic, visionary individuals ensure success.
Social/cultural/religious	Use of draught animals seen as backward, non-progressive and gender-biased.	The number of practising farmers providing mutual support neutralises such thinking and the group approach has created an avenue for women to participate.

Participation and decision making

Target groups

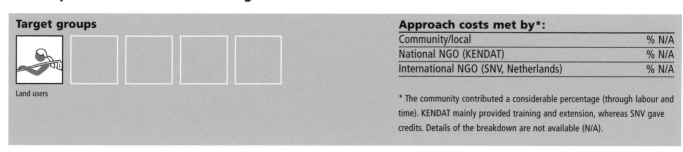

Land users

Approach costs met by*:

Community/local	% N/A
National NGO (KENDAT)	% N/A
International NGO (SNV, Netherlands)	% N/A

* The community contributed a considerable percentage (through labour and time). KENDAT mainly provided training and extension, whereas SNV gave credits. Details of the breakdown are not available (N/A).

Decisions on choice of the technology: Mainly made by land users supported by SWC specialists supported by the National Soil and Water Conservation programme under the Ministry of Agriculture (MoA). SWC specialists created awareness of the technology in the local community, with land users independently deciding to adopt.

Decisions on method of implementing the technology: Made by land users alone (bottom-up). Farmers adopted the technology with modifications so that they could use their animals for draught power. However, there was a degree of follow-up by SWC specialists.

Approach designed by: Land users.

Community involvement

Phase	Involvement	Activities
Initiation	interactive	farmers received information about an innovation that could be beneficial to them; they then mobilised themselves into self-help groups, elected leaders and sought formal registration
Planning	self-mobilisation	the group plans its own agenda in meetings
Implementation	interactive	the group is responsible for procuring equipment and inputs; they train their animals, while training on technology is provided by specialists
Monitoring/evaluation	self-mobilisation	group members keep yield records which are reported and discussed at meetings (without participation of specialists)
Research	interactive	farmers themselves compare cultivation methods; in addition, some research plots by KENDAT, the extension services (MoA) and students have also been set up in farmers' fields

Differences in participation between men and women: Men traditionally own animals and have easier access to investment capital to purchase equipment than women. However, this is changing. In addition, in one group, the treasurer is a woman. The group also trains women how to use the technology. Within the first year, one woman had obtained the whole set of equipment plus a pair of oxen.

left: Farmer-led discussion on conservation tillage equipment with facilitation by extension staff. (Frederick Kihara)
right: Demonstration of improved draught animal technology. (Frederick Kihara)

Extension and promotion

Training: The main element is farmer-to-farmer training within the group on use of appropriate equipment, equipment maintenance, animal health and care. Members attend training courses organised by extension staff and NGOs including KENDAT and Operation Comfort (from Central Kenya). Apart from courses, there are demonstration areas on research sites and group plots, as well as farm visits amongst and between farmers. The overall impact of training on land users is considered to be good.

Extension: Extension is carried out through governmental and non-governmental specialists, equipment sales person and well-informed group members. This is facilitated by the way groups formed and tapped into the extension advice, and also shared information amongst themselves. The impact of extension on land users is good.

Research: On-farm research is carried out by KENDAT, who conduct field trials to investigate the best technological practices. The data is collected in collaboration with participating farmers. Research has been quite effective: results from on-farm trials and NRM3 (Natural Resource Monitoring, Modelling & Management) Research Station at Kalalu have been quickly assimilated and acted upon by farmers. The field research activities have included long-term experiments, demonstration sites and field days.

Importance of land use rights: Small land size can hinder adoption of the technology: the group approach can help to overcome this limitation. Those with small land parcels can access and afford the technology without having to keep animals.

Incentives

Labour: All labour is voluntary.
Inputs: No free inputs are provided except for technical training and back up.
Credit: Two year loans are available from international development partners (SNV). Generally 50% is repaid in the 1st year, 50% in the 2nd year. These loans are used to purchase equipment, with group members acting as guarantors for each other.
Support to local institutions: Local self-help groups were supported by national and local development agencies in group formation and management; loans were given for the purchase of implements; training was provided on the use of implements.
Long-term impact of incentives: No incentives provided, thus the question of impact – negative or positive- does not arise.

Monitoring and evaluation

Monitored aspects	Methods and indicators
Bio-physical	ad hoc observations (informal)
Technical	ad hoc observations of work undertaken
Socio-cultural	regular observations of rate of adoption, attitudinal changes
Economic/production	ad hoc measurements of yield/area with the data from research station being occasionally analysed and results shared out
Area treated	ad hoc measurements of acreage
No. of land users involved	ad hoc observations (members of the group being followed up season after season by extension staff)
Management of approach	regular observations as membership feedback at meetings

Impacts of the approach

Changes as result of monitoring and evaluation: There have been a few changes to the approach itself: the success of the technology – conservation agriculture – has strengthened group collective bargaining power to attract further extension input support, regular visitation and advice on best agronomic practices. There has also been a move to encourage women's uptake of the technology.

Improved soil and water management: Great improvements have been achieved: these include in situ moisture conservation (reduced evaporation and runoff), water harvesting, increased soil fertility and reduced soil loss.

Adoption of the approach by other projects/land users: Many self-help groups have arisen and are addressing their particular problems related to conservation agriculture.

Sustainability: Land users can continue group formation and the associated activities without external support because they can seek technical support for the specific activities.

Concluding statements

Strengths and ➜ how to sustain/improve	Weaknesses and ➜ how to overcome
Easier for extension services to target a group of like-minded farmers than individuals ➜ Encourage further self-help group formation.	Self-help groups are not optimal where some individuals are relatively poor and cannot afford contributions ➜ Modify arrangements to permit higher contributions by more financially able members who then get a greater share of the profits.
Self-help groups are self-sustaining ➜ Ensure continual success by providing refresher courses on technology by extensionists, introduce innovations to keep group interest alive.	Greater time and energy input from the innovative farmers, because they pass on their knowledge without direct reward ➜ Farmers gain confidence and status in the group or area as leaders.
Collective bargaining power is achieved through good accounting and positive group financial status. This tends to attract donor support for further collective activities.	
Sharing of technological knowledge, as well as equipment, within the groups and exchange between groups.	

Key reference(s): Kihara FI (1999) *An investigation into the soil loss problem in the Upper Ewaso Ng'iro basin, Kenya.* MSc. Thesis. University of Nairobi, Kenya ■ Mutunga CN (1995) *The influence of vegetation cover on runoff and soil loss – a study in Mukogodo, Laikipia district Kenya.* MSc Thesis, University of Nairobi, Kenya ■ Ngigi SN (2003) *Rainwater Harvesting for improved land productivity in the Greater Horn of Africa.* Kenya Rainwater Association, Nairobi ■ Liniger HP and Thomas DB (1998) GRASS – Ground Cover for Restoration of Arid and Semi-arid Soils. *Advances in GeoEcology* 31, 1167–1178. Catena Verlag, Reiskirchen

Contact person(s): Frederick Kihara, Boniface Kiteme, CETRAD – Centre for Training and Integrated Research in ASAL Development, PO Box 144, Nanyuki, Kenya; phone ++254-62 31328; b.kiteme@africaonline.co.ke

No-till with controlled traffic

Australia

Large-scale no-till grain production with permanent wheel tracks common to all on-farm equipment.

This controlled traffic, no-till farming system (CT/NT) is practiced on a 1,900 ha farm on the broad, almost flat Jandowae Plains in semi-arid Queensland, Australia. Principal soil types are vertisols, with some poorer areas where the sand content is greater, and these have a tendency to hard-set and crust.

Over the past five years, the farm owner has changed the farming system completely from conventional farming to no-till with controlled traffic. Controlled traffic means permanent uncropped wheel tracks or 'tramlines': all equipment has 2 metre axles. The total farm machinery comprises a tractor, a spray rig and two 11 meter zero-till planter/fertilizer units; one each for wheat and sorghum sowing. The tramlines were laid out two years ago by a contractor using Geographical Positioning System (GPS).

The main technical objective was to eliminate soil compaction. The CT/NT combination ensures the land – between the tramlines – remains in excellent condition. There has been no ploughing or tillage at all in those 5 years. He practices a three year rotation between winter wheat, summer sorghum and fallow, but the system is not fixed: it depends very much on soil moisture status and thus on the rainfall (opportunity cropping). Generally in summer about one third is in summer sorghum and in winter about one third in winter wheat, the rest of the land is under fallow. The one-year fallow is maintained through the use of herbicides sprayed onto the undisturbed residue from the previous crop. The system is designed for rain capture – to build up soil moisture stores in the fallow periods for subsequent crops – and for disease control (to 'spell' the land). During the cropping cycle, the key to his effective weed control system is 'to get in early' and 'actively chase weeds' through judicious spraying. The farm is now free of the locally common persistent weed *Erigeron annuus*. In the five years his sorghum yields have risen from 3 to 7 tons per hectares. Over the last three years the soil has improved, becoming soft, friable and moist between his plant lines. Infiltration has improved a lot and soil structure is now excellent.

Tractor use and overall fuel consumption has decreased to less than one quarter of that under conventional tillage. Correspondingly the workload is hugely reduced: from four men required under the conventional system for an equivalent area, the farmer is the sole operator, very occasionally assisted by his son, and a paid contractor for harvesting. He is so satisfied with the CT/NT system that he is attempting to purchase a nearby property to extend the area that he can farm using his current machinery.

left: A view of a set of tramlines in the previous winter's wheat stubble. Spacing is 2 m between the two permanent wheel tracks and 10 m between two sets of tramlines (visible to the left and right). (Hanspeter Liniger)
right: Two soil profiles (0–30 cm depth): from the sorghum 'bed' with excellent, crumb and small blocky structure, with abundant root growth (top) and – only 50 cm apart – from the wheel track with massive and platy structure (bottom). (Des McGarry)

Location: Jimbour (north of Dalby), Queensland, Australia
Technology area: 19 km²
SWC measure: agronomic
Land use: cropland
Climate: semi-arid
WOCAT database reference: QT AUS02
Related approach: not documented
Compiled by: Des McGarry, Natural Resource Sciences, Queensland, Australia
Date: February 2004; updated May 2005

Editors' comments: No-till with controlled traffic is a specific form of conservation agriculture (CA) – of which there are also examples in this book from Kenya, Morocco and the UK. In Australia, where CA is practiced, random in-field traffic remains the norm, though there is now an estimated one million hectares of arable land (2–3% of the total) under combined no-till and controlled traffic. The controlled traffic system is the special feature of this conservation agriculture case study.

Classification

Land use problems
The farmer's main reason for starting the combination of CT and NT was to rid himself of soil compaction, in order to achieve better utilisation of locally low and unpredictable rainfall amounts while minimising costs and reducing labour and machinery requirements.

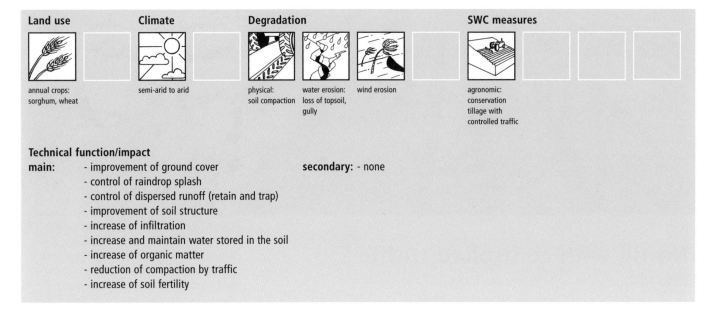

Land use	Climate	Degradation		SWC measures
annual crops: sorghum, wheat	semi-arid to arid	physical: soil compaction	water erosion: loss of topsoil, gully wind erosion	agronomic: conservation tillage with controlled traffic

Technical function/impact
main:
- improvement of ground cover
- control of raindrop splash
- control of dispersed runoff (retain and trap)
- improvement of soil structure
- increase of infiltration
- increase and maintain water stored in the soil
- increase of organic matter
- reduction of compaction by traffic
- increase of soil fertility

secondary: - none

Environment

Natural environment

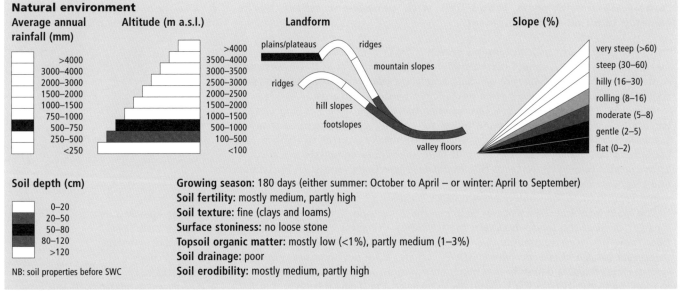

Average annual rainfall (mm)
- >4000
- 3000–4000
- 2000–3000
- 1500–2000
- 1000–1500
- 750–1000
- 500–750
- 250–500
- <250

Altitude (m a.s.l.)
- >4000
- 3500–4000
- 3000–3500
- 2500–3000
- 2000–2500
- 1500–2000
- 1000–1500
- 500–1000
- 100–500
- <100

Landform
- plains/plateaus
- ridges
- mountain slopes
- ridges
- hill slopes
- footslopes
- valley floors

Slope (%)
- very steep (>60)
- steep (30–60)
- hilly (16–30)
- rolling (8–16)
- moderate (5–8)
- gentle (2–5)
- flat (0–2)

Soil depth (cm)
- 0–20
- 20–50
- 50–80
- 80–120
- >120

NB: soil properties before SWC

Growing season: 180 days (either summer: October to April – or winter: April to September)
Soil fertility: mostly medium, partly high
Soil texture: fine (clays and loams)
Surface stoniness: no loose stone
Topsoil organic matter: mostly low (<1%), partly medium (1–3%)
Soil drainage: poor
Soil erodibility: mostly medium, partly high

Human environment

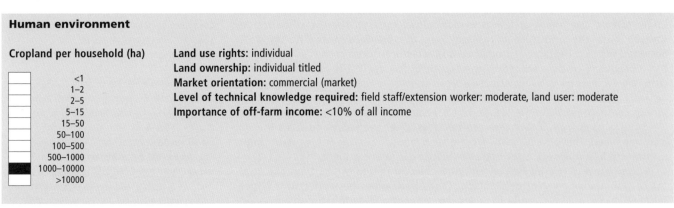

Cropland per household (ha)
- <1
- 1–2
- 2–5
- 5–15
- 15–50
- 50–100
- 100–500
- 500–1000
- 1000–10000
- >10000

Land use rights: individual
Land ownership: individual titled
Market orientation: commercial (market)
Level of technical knowledge required: field staff/extension worker: moderate, land user: moderate
Importance of off-farm income: <10% of all income

left: All equipment has wheels on 2 meter axles to fit the tramlines. The no-till air-seeder (with disk openers and press wheels) is used mainly for sowing wheat: as large rates are applied (40 kg/ha), precision seed placement is not vital; the seed/fertilizer tank is installed in front of the tractor and connected with tubes. For sorghum a seeder with seed boxes mounted on the bar is used: rates of seed applied are very low (1 kg/ha), so precision placement is essential. Both seeders are 11 m wide. The tractor is small size (for a grain producing farm in this area). (Hanspeter Liniger)
right: The Spray-Coupe (rear view) is used for weed control; it is 22 m wide with booms extended, ie double the width of the 'planting footprint', so it travels in every 2nd set of tramlines. (Des McGarry)

Implementation activities, inputs and costs

Establishment activities
1. Layout of the controlled traffic lines (tramlines) using GPS mounted in a 4x4 vehicle. Two days were adequate for the whole farm.

Duration of the establishment: within 1 year

Establishment inputs and costs per ha

Inputs	Costs (US$)	% met by land user
Labour (contracted) and machines	5	100%
TOTAL	**5**	**100%**

Maintenance/recurrent activities
Summer sorghum (650 ha, during 1 season or half a year)
1. Weed control (spray-coupe) with roundup, using 1.25 l Glyphosate/ha
2. Fertilizing, using 200 kg Urea/ha.
3. Sowing: 2 kg seed/ha and simultaneous application of starter fertilizer 25–30 kg/ha (mid-October)
4. Spraying pre-emergent herbicide (3.8 l/ha) to kill summer grasses;
5. Harvest by contractors (early March)
Winter wheat (650 ha, during 1 season or half a year)
6. Weed control (details see above)
7. Fertilizing (Urea, details see above)
8. Sowing: 42 kg seed/ha and simultaneous application of starter fertilizer 25–30 kg/ha (mid-May)
9. In-crop weed spray (5 g broadleaf herbicide/ha)
10. Harvest by contractors (October)
Fallow (1,250 ha, during 2 seasons or totally 1 year)
11. Weed control: 5–6 times per fallow period (combination of roundup mixed with broadleaf herbicide, see above)
To determine soil moisture he uses an iron rod; if he can push it into the heavy clay soil, then the soil is moist. Additionally, he measures rainfall.

Maintenance/recurrent inputs and costs per ha per year

Inputs	Costs (US$)	% met by land user
Labour: 0.02 person days	5	100%
Equipment		
- Machines: 0.2 hours	6	100%
Agricultural		
- Seeds	8	100%
- Fertilizers	53	100%
- Biocides	22	100%
Other		
- Harvesting by contractors	17	100%
TOTAL	**111**	**100%**

Remarks: In average one third of the farm area is in crop and two thirds are fallow. This means that overall farming costs per ha are reduced, since during fallow period activities are limited to spraying herbicides. Labour costs approximately US$ 160 per day. Machinery costs average out at US$ 20 per hour (diesel costs US$ 0.9 per litre). All the data comes from this single farmer. Purchase of equipment is not included in the table above.

Comparison of costs between conventional tillage and no-till farming (CT/NT): (1) Labour costs are 4x less in CT/NT: 4 men used to work on the farm (conventional), now the farmer is alone – (plus contractors for harvesting). (2) Average annual diesel consumption: reduced from 108,333 litres (conventional) to 13,636 litres (no-till) which is 8 times less. (3) Costs of equipment to set up a CT/NT system (US$ 240,000) are 3 times less than that for conventional tillage equipment (US$ 700,000). (4) For biocides he has to invest 5 times more in CT/NT. The conventional values are estimates.

Assessment

Acceptance/adoption
- Approximately 200 farmers have adopted CT/NT in the Queensland grain growing area, and none of them received any subsidies or incentives. Adoption stemmed from farmer observations at field days on adjoining farms – where they saw the potential/real benefits and carried them over to their own farms.
- The farmer of this case study only received a small bank loan to buy the land and equipment, and he as been given a little assistance with fertilizer and spraying strategies from a local agronomist.
- There isn't a strong trend now towards growing spontaneous adoption: uptake has slowed dramatically as many conservative farmers prefer to continue their traditional tillage practices.

Benefits/costs according to land user

Benefits compared with costs	short-term:	long-term:
establishment	very positive	very positive
maintenance/recurrent	very positive	very positive

Impacts of the technology

Production and socio-economic benefits	Production and socio-economic disadvantages
+ + + crop yield increase	none
+ + + farm income increase	

Socio-cultural benefits	Socio-cultural disadvantages
+ + + improved knowledge SWC/erosion	none

Ecological benefits	Ecological disadvantages
+ + + soil cover improvement	none
+ + + increase in soil moisture	
+ + + efficiency of excess water drainage	
+ + + increase in soil organic matter	
+ + + increase in soil fertility	
+ + + soil loss reduction	
+ + + biodiversity enhancement	
+ + + reduced soil compaction	

Off-site benefits	Off-site disadvantages
+ + reduced transported sediments	none
+ increased stream flow in dry season	
+ reduced downstream siltation	
+ reduced river pollution	
+ reduced downstream flooding	

Concluding statements

Strengths and → how to sustain/improve
Land that previously was un-farmable is now under crops. Site inspection shows initially poor land to be now in good condition (after only 5 years). The value of the land has increased → Farmers practising CT/NT can and are buying/leasing more land, which will improve the overall state of the land in Queensland.

Farmers can manage much larger growing areas with less personnel and equipment. A single operator is well able to run a large arable farm on his own → Ditto.

Cereal farming is now less prone to yield losses (and crop failure) in drought years – as there is better rainwater infiltration and water use efficiency with CT/NT → Continue with the system.

He has all weeds under control (without need for tillage).

Weaknesses and → how to overcome
The contract harvester runs on 3 m wide axles, so the wheels run on the beds. However, there has only been one wet harvest in 5 years so the incidence of soil compaction from harvesting is negligible → This is not really seen as a problem. One solution would be to build a dedicated harvester (too expensive) or find a contractor with equipment that fitted the system.

A conservative mentality towards conservation agriculture is constraining the adoption of the system by other farmers → Continue demonstrating and disseminating knowledge about benefits.

Key reference(s): Blackwell P (1998) Customised controlled traffic farming systems, instead of standard recommendations or 'tramlines ain't tramlines'. *In Second national controlled farming conference,* pp. 23–26. Eds JN Tullberg and DF Yule. Gatton College: University of Queensland ▪ Hulme PJ, McKenzie DC, MacLeod DA and Anthony DTW (1996) An evaluation of controlled traffic with reduced tillage for irrigated cotton on a Vertisol. *Soil and Tillage Research* 38:217–237 ▪ McGarry D, Bridge BJ and Radford BJ (2000). Contrasting soil physical properties after zero and traditional tillage of an alluvial soil in the semi-arid tropics. *Soil and Tillage Research* 53:105–115

Contact person(s): Noel Griffith, Jimbour (north of Dalby), Queensland, Australia → *through:* Dr Des McGarry, Natural Resource Sciences, Queensland Government, Block 'B', 80 Meiers Road, Indooroopilly, Queensland, Australia; mcgarrd@nrm.qld.gov.au

Green cane trash blanket
Australia

left: Harvesting of green sugar cane and simultaneous spreading of the separated residues, leaving a dense mulch cover, the so called green cane trash blanket. (Hanspeter Liniger)

right: A 'ratoon': a re-growing sugar cane sprouts through the trash blanket after harvest. (Hanspeter Liniger)

Elimination of burning as a pre-harvest treatment of sugar cane, and managing the resultant trash as a protective blanket to give multiple on and off-site benefits.

Under conventional production systems, sugar cane is burnt before being harvested. This reduces the volume of trash – comprising green leaves, dead leaves and top growth – making harvesting of the cane simpler, and subsequent cultivation of the soil easier. In the humid tropics of Far North Queensland, harvesting of cane used to be carried out by hand – as it still is in many parts of the developing tropics. Burning was necessary to make harvesting possible in a dense stand (and to reduce the danger of snakes). However, with the advent of mechanical harvesters in the 1960s, burning continued to be practiced through habit.

A new system then brought fundamental changes in soil management: The 'green cane trash blanket' (GCTB) technology refers to the practice of harvesting non-burnt cane, and trash blown out behind in rows by the sugar cane harvester. This trash forms a more or less complete blanket over the field. The harvested lines of cane re-grow ('ratoon') through this surface cover, and the next year the cycle is repeated: the cane is once again harvested and more trash accumulates in the inter-rows. Generally the basic cropping cycle is the same, whether cane is burnt or not. This involves planting of new cane stock (cuttings or 'billets') in the first year, harvesting this 'plant crop' in the second year, and then in years three, four, five and six taking successive 'ratoon' harvests. In year six, after harvest, it is still common, even under the GCTB system, to burn the residual trash so that the old cane stools can be more easily ploughed out, and the ground 'worked up' (cultivated) ready for replanting. A minority of planters, however, are doing away with burning altogether, and ploughing in the residual trash before replanting. A further variation is not to plough out and replant after the harvest in year six, but to spray the old cane stock with glysophate (a broad spectrum non-selective systemic herbicide) to kill it, then to plant a legume (typically soy bean) as a green manure crop, and only replant the subsequent year after ploughing-in the legume. Under this latter system, one year of harvest is lost, but there are added benefits to the structure and nutrient content of the soil.

Whatever variation of GCTB is used, there are advantages in terms of increased organic matter, improved soil structure, more biodiversity (especially below ground) and a marked reduction in surface erosion – from over 50 t/ha to around 5 t/ha on average. Less erosion is good for the growers – but is also of crucial importance off-site, as sediment lost from the coastal sugar cane strip is washed out to sea, and damages the growing coral of the Great Barrier Reef.

Location: Far North Queensland, Australia
Technology area: 800 km²
SWC measure: agronomic
Land use: cropland
Climate: humid
WOCAT database reference: QT AUS03
Related approach: The 'triple bottom line', QA AUS03
Compiled by: Anthony Webster, CSIRO, Mossman, Queensland, Australia
Date: September 2005

Editors' comments: Burning of crop residues on large scale farms causes air pollution, and has negative impacts on biodiversity and soil organic matter. In the tropics of far north Queensland burning of sugar cane before harvest has been eliminated, and the increase in trash forms a beneficial 'blanket' giving multiple on-site benefits, as well as reducing pollution, from eroded sediment, of the adjacent Great Barrier Reef.

Classification

Land use problems
Conventional burning of sugar cane before harvest can lead to compaction of top soil and reduced organic matter. There is also, despite the low slopes, a serious problem of sheet/rill erosion that has a negative impact both on the fields, and also off-site on the coral reef.

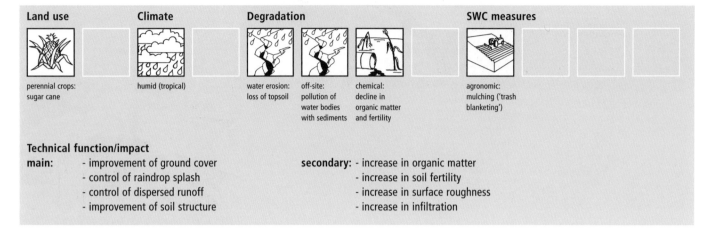

Land use	Climate	Degradation			SWC measures
perennial crops: sugar cane	humid (tropical)	water erosion: loss of topsoil	off-site: pollution of water bodies with sediments	chemical: decline in organic matter and fertility	agronomic: mulching ('trash blanketing')

Technical function/impact
main:
- improvement of ground cover
- control of raindrop splash
- control of dispersed runoff
- improvement of soil structure

secondary:
- increase in organic matter
- increase in soil fertility
- increase in surface roughness
- increase in infiltration

Environment

Natural environment

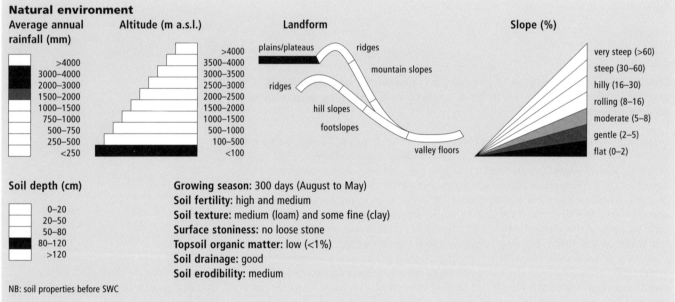

Average annual rainfall (mm)
- >4000
- 3000–4000
- 2000–3000
- 1500–2000
- 1000–1500
- 750–1000
- 500–750
- 250–500
- <250

Altitude (m a.s.l.)
- >4000
- 3500–4000
- 3000–3500
- 2500–3000
- 2000–2500
- 1500–2000
- 1000–1500
- 500–1000
- 100–500
- <100

Landform
- plains/plateaus
- ridges
- ridges
- mountain slopes
- hill slopes
- footslopes
- valley floors

Slope (%)
- very steep (>60)
- steep (30–60)
- hilly (16–30)
- rolling (8–16)
- moderate (5–8)
- gentle (2–5)
- flat (0–2)

Soil depth (cm)
- 0–20
- 20–50
- 50–80
- 80–120
- >120

Growing season: 300 days (August to May)
Soil fertility: high and medium
Soil texture: medium (loam) and some fine (clay)
Surface stoniness: no loose stone
Topsoil organic matter: low (<1%)
Soil drainage: good
Soil erodibility: medium

NB: soil properties before SWC

Human environment

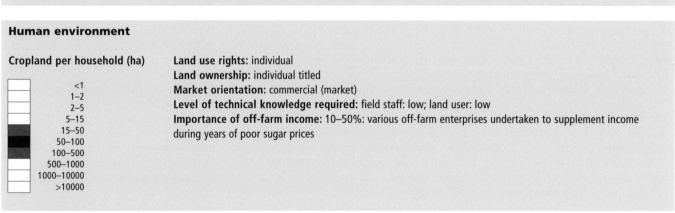

Cropland per household (ha)
- <1
- 1–2
- 2–5
- 5–15
- 15–50
- 50–100
- 100–500
- 500–1000
- 1000–10000
- >10000

Land use rights: individual
Land ownership: individual titled
Market orientation: commercial (market)
Level of technical knowledge required: field staff: low; land user: low
Importance of off-farm income: 10–50%: various off-farm enterprises undertaken to supplement income during years of poor sugar prices

WOCAT ■ where the land is greener

Comparison of conventional sugar cane production (above left) and green cane trash blanket technology (above right): the soil under the trash cover is moist and has a good structure (below right) while the unprotected soil is hard and sealed (below left). (William Critchley)

Implementation activities, inputs and costs

Establishment activities
not applicable

Establishment inputs and costs per ha

Inputs	Costs (US$)	% met by land user
not applicable		

Maintenance/recurrent activities
1. August: harvest green cane through contractor and simultaneous mulching of inter-rows with trash
   [previously: burn cane with associated trash and then harvest]
2. September: no field work
   [previously: cultivate land]
3. October: fertilize cane
   [previously: cultivate and fertilize]
4. November: spray with Amicide (very efficient herbicide, systemic and non-selective)
   [previously: cultivate land]
5. December: no field work
   [previously: cultivate and spray with Diuron, a non-selective contact herbicide]
6. January: Spray with Amicide
   [previously: no field work]

Maintenance/recurrent inputs and costs per ha per year

Inputs	Costs (US$)	% met by land user
Contract harvesting	390	100%
Agricultural		
- Fertilizer	120	100%
- Herbicide	33	100%
TOTAL	**543**	**100%**

Remarks: The year budgeted above is a non-planting year – the costs therefore refer to an established crop which grows throughout the year and is harvested in August. The assumption is a cane yield of 80 t/ha. Each of the three categories of costing groups machinery, labour (at US$12 per hour) and inputs together. The comparative costs for a burnt cane crop system with the same yield are (a) contract harvesting = US$ 378 (b) fertilizer = US$ 120 (c) herbicide = US$ 56, plus (d) cultivation = US$ 30. Note that under the burnt cane system, soil cultivation/tillage is required, but the cost of harvesting is a little cheaper. The total for the burnt crop system is US$ 584 compared with US$ 543 for the GCTB crop, representing a saving of approx. US$ 40 (around 7%) per hectare per year.

Assessment

Acceptance/adoption
- Adoption has spread from a handful of growers in the mid 1970s, to 95% of the (approximately) 1,000 growers today. The growers have adopted the GCTB without any incentives other than those of lower costs, reduced soil erosion and benefits to biodiversity etc.
- It is possible that the few growers who persist in burning will eventually adopt the GCTB system through social and environmental pressure.

Benefits/costs according to land user	Benefits compared with costs	short-term:	long-term:
	establishment	not applicable	not applicable
	maintenance/recurrent	slightly positive	positive

Impacts of the technology

Production and socio-economic benefits	Production and socio-economic disadvantages
+ overall farm income increase	none

Socio-cultural benefits	Socio-cultural disadvantages
+ + improved knowledge SWC/erosion	none
+ + enhanced reputation of sugar cane growers as 'environmentally friendly'	

Ecological benefits	Ecological disadvantages
+ + + runoff and soil loss reduced (from >50 t/ha to 5 t/ha; although the location is relatively flat, soil erosion can be high due to high rainfall)	none
+ + + soil cover improvement	
+ + loss of nutrients reduced	
+ + increase in soil organic matter	
+ + biodiversity enhancement (above and below ground)	
+ + improved soil structure	
+ increase in soil moisture	
+ carbon sequestration increased	
+ efficiency of excess water drainage	
+ increase in soil fertility	

Off-site benefits	Off-site disadvantages
+ + reduced transported sediments	none
+ + reduced downstream siltation	
+ reduced river pollution	
+ reduced downstream flooding	

Concluding statements

Strengths and → how to sustain/improve
GCTB systems offer multiple on-farm environmental benefits → Continue to refine the system, by encouraging (a) non burning of trash in the planting year and (b) planting a one-year green manure fallow when/if necessary.

Increases overall farm income by maintaining yields of sugar cane while reducing costs by 5–10% → Continue to refine the system.

GCTB systems provide protection to the coral reef, through substantially reducing the sediment yield that reaches the lagoon and thence the Great Barrier Reef → Give recognition to the growers for their overall environmental contribution.

Weaknesses and → how to overcome
Some burning still continues through (a) the few farmers who have not yet adopted GCTB and (b) the common practice of burning trash before replanting → Continue to encourage non-burning for multiple reasons.

Key reference(s): Mullins JA, Truong PN and Prove BG (1984) Options for controlling soil loss in canelands – some interim values. *Proc. Aust. Soc. Sugar Cane Technol.,* 6: 95–100 ■ Vallis I, Parton WJ, Keating BA and Wood AW (1996) Simulation of the effects of trash and N fertilizer management on soil organic matter levels and yields of sugarcane. *Soil and Tillage Research.* 38: 115–132 ■ Wood AW (1991) Management of crop residues following green harvesting of sugarcane in north Queensland. *Soil Till. Res.* 20: 69–85
Contact person(s): Anthony Webster, Research Agronomist, CSIRO, Mossman, Queensland, Australia; tony.webster@csiro.au; www.csiro.au

The 'triple bottom line'

Australia

left: Moist soil beneath mulched (trash blanketed) cane. (William Critchley)
right: Automatic monitoring station measuring climatic parameters, runoff and nutrient flows to assess infield effects and downstream impacts on the Great Barrier Reef. (Hanspeter Liniger)

A new expression used by agriculturalists in Australia to explain why farmers change practices: the 'triple bottom line' implies economic, environmental and social concerns.

A fundamental change has occurred in farming practice amongst sugar cane growers in the tropics of far north Queensland. Where it was once standard practice to burn cane before harvest (defoliating green canes for easier harvest), tradition has been turned on its head and now almost no-one burns. Instead a 'green cane trash blanket' system has developed, with multiple benefits and few or no drawbacks.

There has been no official campaign or punitive sanctions imposed, no enticing financial incentives offered or charismatic environmental leadership – just a quiet technological revolution, based on the principles of the 'triple bottom line' (TBL). TBL has recently emerged into common usage amongst agriculturalists in Australia. Rather than attributing farmers' actions as simple responses to economic stimuli ('the bottom line') TBL is a framework that helps explain the complexity of factors that influence farmers to modify their practices. TBL suggests that farmers do indeed respond to money, but also to environmental concerns, and furthermore to social considerations as well. This gives credit to farmers for being responsible stewards of the land.

In this particular case, the transition in technology started in 1974, when sugar cane growers in the far north of Queensland were simply unable to burn their cane prior to harvest because of the exceptionally heavy rains. Instead, they had to harvest wet – and green. The technical implications were first, a slower harvest speed because machinery had to cope with a greater load of biomass, and second, a thick residual blanket of trash that covered the soil. The multiple benefits of mulching were recognised by a few growers, who then continued to harvest green cane. Non-burning spread – a technology now described as the 'green cane trash blanket' – until almost every grower adopted it within one generation. While the extension service has supported the transition, growers themselves took the initiative to change. There are indeed small financial benefits, chiefly in terms of reduced overall input costs, but growers have simultaneously been motivated by social and environmental considerations. Burning has come to be considered anti-social: a dirty practice, carrying the danger of fire spreading outside the targeted fields. Neither is it a pleasant task, requiring help of family and friends, often at inconvenient times. From an environmental perspective, the benefits of trash mulch are tangible in terms of improved soil quality, and reduced erosion rates. And, equally important, the end result is reduced damage to the close-by Great Barrier Reef with its sediment-sensitive living coral.

Location: Far North Queensland, Australia
Approach area: 800 km²
Land use: cropland
Climate: humid
WOCAT database reference: QA AUS03
Related technology: Green cane trash blanket, QT AUS03
Compiled by: Anthony Webster, CSIRO, Mossman, Queensland, Australia
Date: September 2005

Editors' comments: The 'triple bottom line' (TBL) is an expression which has evolved in Australia to help explain why farmers act as they do. Its three components of economics, the environment and social aspects cover the considerations that cause farmers to modify technologies. TBL implicitly gives credit to farmer for being sensitive to multiple external signals. In this case the change in practice is from burning sugar cane to harvesting it green in Far North Queensland. This is a case where emerging conservation-friendly farmer practice and the goals of the environmental lobby have neatly coincided.

Problem, objectives and constraints

Problem
- anti-social farming practice of burning sugar cane which also has negative environmental impacts, both in situ, and off-site in the coral reef
- resistance to change in traditional farming practice

Objectives
- the spread of non-burning practices, specifically the 'green cane trash blanket' technology to promote sustainable and environmentally friendly sugar cane production
- indirectly: to satisfy social concerns associated with burning of sugar cane

Constraints addressed

Major	Specification	Treatment
Technical	Harvesting machines at first were not so well able to cope with the greater biomass to be harvested.	Manufacturers developed higher capacity harvesters.
Financial	Higher costs of harvesting (a small premium charged by contractors per tonne of green cane harvested).	These costs are offset by lower tillage input, no costs associated with burning, and lower inputs of agrochemicals also.

Participation and decision making

Target groups

Growers

Politicians (govt. agencies)

Environment-alists

Approach costs met by*:

State Government (Bureau of Sugar Experiment Stations)	20%
Growers themselves	80%
	100%

* rough estimate

Decisions on choice of the technology: Made by land users alone (sugar cane growers).
Decisions on method of implementing the technology: Made by land users alone.
Approach designed by: Farmers (with limited support from extension and research).

Community involvement

Phase	Involvement	Activities
Initiation	self-mobilisation	starting up the practice of green cane trash blanket (GCTB)
Planning	not applicable	no specific planning involved
Implementation	interactive	growers spreading the word, support by extension services
Monitoring/evaluation	interactive	growers joining hands with research
Research	interactive	ditto

Differences in participation between men and women: None in principle, though *de facto* most growers are male.

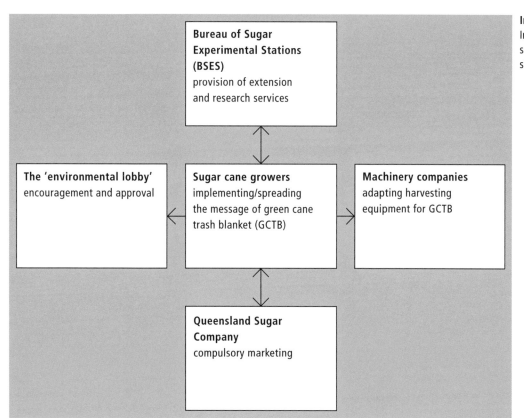

Bureau of Sugar Experimental Stations (BSES)
provision of extension and research services

The 'environmental lobby'
encouragement and approval

Sugar cane growers
implementing/spreading the message of green cane trash blanket (GCTB)

Machinery companies
adapting harvesting equipment for GCTB

Queensland Sugar Company
compulsory marketing

Extension and promotion

Training: There was no specific training involved.
Extension: The Bureau of Sugar Experimental Stations (BSES) provides an extension service to Queensland's growers. The green cane trash blanket (GCTB) system was supported through this extension service, as one component of the general extension message, and a variety of methods were used (visits, field days, publications) to help get the message across. Nevertheless the main form of extension was informal farmer-to-farmer spread.
Research: There has been some ad hoc research carried out on technical parameters by both the BSES as well as CSIRO.
Importance of land use rights: The ownership of the land makes no difference to the uptake of GCTB.

Incentives

Labour: Farmers themselves provide labour – though it should be noted that the adoption of GCTB involves a saving on labour inputs compared with conventional cane burning systems.
Inputs: There are no subsidies connected to GCTB. Australia does not subsidise its sugar cane growers and sugar is sold at the world price.
Credit: None provided.
Support to local institutions: None.

Monitoring and evaluation

Monitored aspects	Methods and indicators
Bio-physical	ad hoc observations/measurements of nutrients/ sediment by BSES & CSIRO
Technical	ad hoc observations/measurements of yield by BSES
Socio-cultural	ad hoc observations by growers
Economic/production	regular measurements by BSES
Area treated	ad hoc observations/calculations by millers
No. of land users involved	ad hoc calculations
Management of approach	not applicable

Impacts of the approach

Changes as result of monitoring and evaluation: Not applicable.

Improved soil and water management: Considerable: nutrient losses reduced, erosion reduced, organic matter built up, etc.

Adoption of the approach by other projects/land users: The 'triple bottom line' is probably active throughout Australia in influencing farmers' decisions.

Sustainability: By definition this is sustainable: it is an internal mechanism amongst farmers.

Concluding statements

Strengths and ➜ how to sustain/improve	Weaknesses and ➜ how to overcome
Has successfully stimulated the spread of the green cane trash blanket system ➜ Outsiders should continue to support farmers' multiple concerns.	The fact that farmers are responsive to environmental and social as well as economic stimuli is covered up by conventional thinking that 'only money matters to them' ➜ Investigation and documentation of the 'triple bottom line' is required.
Farmers take the responsibility of choosing a land management practice that has a positive 'triple bottom line': environmental, economic and social benefits ➜ Support awareness raising and give appreciation to the on-site and off-site benefits; acknowledge sugar produced under this system an environmentally friendly and economic product.	
Sugar cane growing has previously had a bad environmental and social reputation, especially here, close to the Great Barrier Reef, which is a World Heritage Site. This change in practice, resulting from the 'triple bottom line' has changed the reputation of sugar cane growers ➜ Make this public.	

Key reference(s): none

Contact person(s): Anthony Webster, Research Agronomist, CSIRO, Mossman, Queensland, Australia; tony.webster@csiro.au; www.csiro.au

Vermiculture

Nicaragua – *Lombricultura*

left: Boxes for earthworm culture, mounted on poles and covered with dark, thick plastic sheeting (or corrugated iron, see right) to provide shade, maintain an ideal microclimate and give protection from birds. (Mats Gurtner) right: Every three days a new layer of cattle manure is added to feed the worms. (Mats Gurtner).

Continuous breeding of earthworms in boxes for production of high quality organic compost.

Vermiculture is a simple and cheap way to produce a continuous supply of organic compost of high quality. *Eisenia foetida,* the Red Californian earthworm (also called 'the red wiggler') is ideal for vermiculture since it is adapted to a wide range of environmental conditions. Under culture, the worms are kept under shade, in long wooden boxes filled with earth, cattle manure and an absorbent material (eg straw). The box is covered by sheet metal (or wood, thick plastic sheeting, or banana leaves) to protect the worms against UV radiation and birds/ chickens, and also to maintain a favourably humid microclimate. Fresh cattle manure is a perfect food for the worms, but rotten coffee pulp can also be fed. Chopped crop residues (eg cowpeas, leucaena leaves or other legumes) may be added.

The compost produced by the earthworms has a dark colour, no smell and a loose and spongy structure. It is a high value, high quality product which is very rich in nutrients, and in a form that makes them readily available to vegetation. The content of a full box can be harvested every 3–4 months, and is used for crops -mainly coffee and vegetables, but also maize and beans. It is very effective in increasing soil fertility and thus crop production. It also improves soil structure, infiltration and water storage capacity.

The compost can either be applied directly to coffee, mixing it with an equal amount of earth and applying 1 kg to each plant. Alternatively it can be sprayed: for preparation of liquid fertilizer 50 kg compost are mixed with 50 litres of water and left to soak for 5 days. The concentrated solution produced is mixed with water at a ratio of 1 to10 and applied to the crop using a knapsack sprayer. The earthworms reach their reproductive age after three months and live for many years. In perfect conditions an earthworm produces up to 1,500 offspring per year. Thanks to their rapid reproduction, new cultures can easily be established, or earthworm stocks can be sold according to the farmer's needs. A certain amount of earthworm compost is kept back and being used instead of fresh earth to reinitiate the whole process, or to start new cultures.

The area is characterised by humid climate, steep slopes and low soil fertility. Farmers are mainly smallholders with individual properties. Earthworm culture does not depend closely on the external environment, but it is essential to maintain favourable conditions inside the box – namely continuous feeding and wetting. That's why it is usually recommended to keep cultures near the house and the home-garden. Ants, the main enemy of earthworms, can be controlled standing the boxes on poles in cans filled with water.

Location: Pancasán, Matiguas, Matagalpa, Nicaragua
Technology area: approx. 5 km²
SWC measure: agronomic
Land use: cropland
Climate: humid, subhumid
WOCAT database reference: QT NIC01
Related approach: Productive development and food security programme, QA NIC03
Compiled by: Julio Gómez, Ramón Caceres, ADDAC, Matagalpa, Nicaragua
Date: April 2000, updated February 2004

Editors' comments: Earthworms produce compost ('casts') of high quality: however vermiculture for compost production is new in Nicaragua, where it shows promise but is not yet widespread. This case study demonstrates that it can work efficiently. *Lombricultura* has been copied from Cuba where it has been used successfully for over 10 years.

Classification

Land use problems
- low crop yields due to soil fertility decline
- water and wind erosion
- small landholdings

Land use		Climate		Degradation				SWC measures			

annual crops: maize/beans, vegetables	perennial crops: coffee	humid	subhumid	chemical: fertility decline/ reduced organic matter				agronomic: applying compost			

Technical function/impact
main:
- increase in soil fertility
- improvement of soil structure
- increase in organic matter

secondary:
- increase of surface roughness
- increase in infiltration

Environment

Natural environment

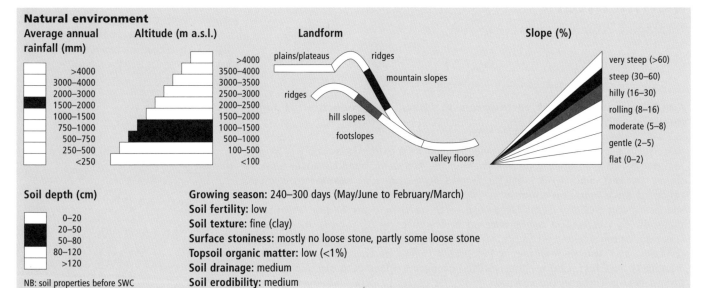

Average annual rainfall (mm)
- >4000
- 3000–4000
- 2000–3000
- 1500–2000
- 1000–1500
- 750–1000
- 500–750
- 250–500
- <250

Altitude (m a.s.l.)
- >4000
- 3500–4000
- 3000–3500
- 2500–3000
- 2000–2500
- 1500–2000
- 1000–1500
- 500–1000
- 100–500
- <100

Landform
plains/plateaus, ridges, mountain slopes, ridges, hill slopes, footslopes, valley floors

Slope (%)
- very steep (>60)
- steep (30–60)
- hilly (16–30)
- rolling (8–16)
- moderate (5–8)
- gentle (2–5)
- flat (0–2)

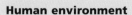

Soil depth (cm)
- 0–20
- 20–50
- 50–80
- 80–120
- >120

NB: soil properties before SWC

Growing season: 240–300 days (May/June to February/March)
Soil fertility: low
Soil texture: fine (clay)
Surface stoniness: mostly no loose stone, partly some loose stone
Topsoil organic matter: low (<1%)
Soil drainage: medium
Soil erodibility: medium

Human environment

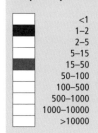

Cropland per household (ha)
- <1
- 1–2
- 2–5
- 5–15
- 15–50
- 50–100
- 100–500
- 500–1000
- 1000–10000
- >10000

Land use rights: mainly individual (95%), some leased (note: holding size is highly polarised: many with small plots, a few with large farms)
Land ownership: mainly individual not titled, some individual titled
Market orientation: subsistence (self-supply) and mixed (subsistence and commercial)
Level of technical knowledge required: field staff/extension worker: moderate, land user: moderate
Importance of off-farm income: <10% of all income: nearly all land users are fully occupied with agricultural activities, very few are involved in commerce or are employed

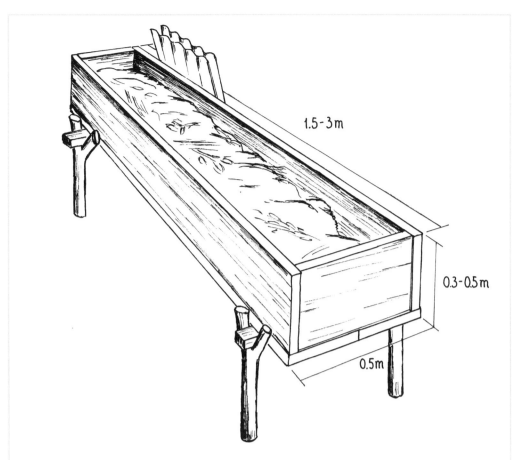

1.5-3 m

0.3-0.5 m

0.5 m

Implementation activities, inputs and costs

Establishment activities

1. Construct 3 wooden boxes (for design see technical drawing); another possibility is to dig pits in the soil, same measurements, with cut-off drain above pit to protect from flooding.
2. Fill with earth and cattle manure (2 kg each per box, not too wet/not too dry).
3. Put in stock of earthworms (1–2 kg per box).
4. Protect from natural enemies (ants, birds, certain snails): roof, set the poles in cans filled with water.

No specific timing (implementation possible at any time).
Tools: hammer, nails, buckets/wheelbarrow, shovel, possibly water hose.
Duration of establishment: 2 days

Establishment inputs and costs per ha

Inputs	Costs (US$)	% met by land user
Labour (3 person days)	6	100%
Materials total		
- Wood (6–10 m³)	50	100%
- Earth (6 kg)	0	
- Sheet metal, plastic	6	100%
Agricultural		
- Cattle manure (6 kg)	0	
- Residues	0	
Others		
- Earthworms (3 kg)	60	0%
TOTAL	**122**	**51%**

Maintenance/recurrent activities

1. Feeding: every 3–5 days add another layer of cattle manure (1 kg earthworms eat 1 kg manure per day).
2. Maintain humidity at 80%, water frequently in dry season, maintain temperature between 15–30°C: do not exceed 42°C.
3. Gather compost every 3–4 months: discontinue feeding and irrigation for 5 days, then put a sieve with fresh manure on top of the compost. The worms migrate into the fresh manure. After 2–3 days take out the sieve and gather the ready, worm free compost.
4. Apply compost to the crops (1 kg/coffee plant, see description).
5. Continue the process.
6. Possible improvement: add lime to raise pH to a optimum level of 7.0.

Tools: buckets/wheelbarrow, shovel, possibly water hose.

Maintenance/recurrent inputs and costs per ha per year

Inputs	Costs (US$)	% met by land user
Labour (30 person days)	60	100%
Agricultural		
- Fresh cattle manure (3,000 kg)	0	
- Residues	0	
TOTAL	**60**	**100%**

Remarks: 60% of the land users have their own cattle, others get manure free from their neighbours. The cattle manure has no commercial price in the region – there is no market for it. The inputs and costs are estimated for the production of approx. 4,000 kg of worm compost, which is enough for one hectare of coffee per year (note figures from India for vermiculture suggest higher input-output ratios: in other words less output for the same amount of input).

Assessment

Acceptance/adoption
By the year 2000, 88 land users had implemented the system supported by incentives; the trend is towards further adoption. The programme provides an initial stock of earthworms as an incentive to the participating farmers. Maintenance is usually good. As ADDAC (the Association for Agricultural Community Development and Diversification) has a permanent and long-term presence in the approach area, most interested farmers are directly involved in the programme activities: this explains the fact that only 5% of the technology users (6 people) took up earthworm culture without incentives (see approach).

Benefits/costs according to land user

Benefits compared with costs	short-term:	long-term:
establishment	positive	very positive
maintenance/recurrent	very positive	very positive

Impacts of the technology

Production and socio-economic benefits	Production and socio-economic disadvantages
+ + + crop yield increase	none
+ + fodder production/quality increase	
+ + farm income increase	

Socio-cultural benefits	Socio-cultural disadvantages
+ + improved knowledge SWC/erosion	none

Ecological benefits	Ecological disadvantages
+ + + increase in soil fertility	– pests: the compost attracts pests like ants, chickens, moles
+ + + stimulation of soil fauna	
+ + increase in soil moisture (through improvement of soil water storage capacity)	
+ + improvement of soil structure	

On-site benefits	Off-site disadvantages
+ + reduced river pollution (lower inputs of chemical fertilizers)	none

Concluding statements

Strengths and → how to sustain/improve	Weaknesses and → how to overcome
Continuous and increasing production of organic and very effective compost with high nutrient content (replacing chemical fertilizers) → Expand the use of worm culture.	Requires permanent access to water → A close fitting and secure box cover, as well as placement of the box in the shade reduces loss of humidity. Roof-top rainwater collection helps to get over dry periods.
Appropriate for different crops (though in different forms – direct application or spraying).	Requires continuous availability of manure to feed worms.
Simple and cheap technology; low labour input → Keep boxes close to the house.	Attracts natural enemies like ants, chickens, moles, flies; needs protection → Improve the construction of the boxes (close holes and cover the box tightly).
Increased crop yields → Expand the use of worm culture.	
Earthworm culture is becoming an integrated part of the production system, especially for land users who have cows.	
Additional economic income through commercialisation of earthworm stocks → Continuous maintenance of technology.	
Health: clean products without chemical treatment.	

Key reference(s): PASOLAC (2000) *Guía Técnica de Conservación de Suelos y Agua*. PASOLAC, Managua ■ Ferruzzi C (1986) *Manual de Lombricultura*. Ediciones Mundi-Prensa. Madrid, Spain ■ Castillo H (1994) *La lombricultura*. in *Altertec. Alternativas de Mejoramiento de Suelos. Proceso de Capacitación para Profesionales. Modulo II*. Altertec, Ciudad de Guatemala

Contact person(s): Julio César Gómez Martínez, De ENITEL 3c al Norte y 75 varas al Este. Calle Santa Ana, Apartado Postal 161, Matagalpa, Nicaragua; addacentral@addac.org; www.addac.org; phone: (505) 0772-7108; fax: (505) 0772-5245

Productive development and food security programme

Nicaragua – *Programa de desarrollo productivo y seguridad alimentaria*

An integrated programme-based approach promoting participatory testing and extension of various SWC technologies, as well as providing institutional support.

The Association for Agricultural Community Development and Diversification (ADDAC) is a non-profit NGO, founded in 1989, whose mission is to improve the living standard of poor rural families engaged in small/medium scale farming in marginal areas to the north of Nicaragua. The main purpose of ADDAC's approach is to develop and strengthen local capacity to analyse problems and find solutions for rural sustainable development. There are five main components: (1) food security and productive development, including technological improvement and diversification within traditional crop cultivation, and extension of alternative agricultural land use practices; (2) support to farmers' organisations; (3) promotion of gender equality; (4) identification of alternatives in marketing; and (5) provision of an alternative credit system for farming. These fields of activities are based on the principles of organic agriculture and a powerful training process – using the methodology of 'popular education', which involves participatory training and extension activities.

ADDAC initiates its work in communities through PRA (Participatory Rural Appraisal) – evaluating problems and potential solutions. These serve as a base for the formulation of project proposals which are then submitted to interested financing organisations. Further steps include participatory planning, and later, evaluation, in collaboration with the land users. For execution of activities ADDAC contracts an interdisciplinary crew of specialists, which stays in the area. Twice a year a participatory reunion is organised to evaluate, and accordingly improve, the activities. Key to the approach is the formation of a grassroots organisation in each community to guarantee local management, build up alternative enterprises and promote community development. These organisations consist of representatives of local support groups, and farmers with a leading role in SWC application and extension. The organisations have various functions during the lifetime of a project: they are the counterparts of the extensionists for project execution, and later they ensure sustainability of activities. Farmers' associations are formed to improve storage and marketing of crops. Networks of local promoters exchange experience between communities and consolidate extension of alternative technologies. Demonstration farms serve as a tool for technology extension, innovation and validation.

left: Training based on the methodology of popular education: two ADDAC specialists presenting and explaining a simple water pump which can be constructed by the land users themselves. (Mathias Gurtner)
right: A farmer proudly showing her vermiculture compost box with the earthworms. The compost is ready to be applied to her coffee plants. (Mats Gurtner)

Location: Matagalpa, Nicaragua
Approach area: approx. 7,500 km²
Land use: cropland
Climate: humid, subhumid
WOCAT database reference: QA NIC03
Related technology: Vermiculture, QT NIC01
Compiled by: Julio Gómez, Eneida Ulloa Mercado, ADDAC, Managua, Nicaragua
Date: April 2000, updated February 2004

Editors' comments: Integrated approaches to development – which include soil and water conservation – based on 'popular education' are becoming increasingly important in Central America. This is an example from northern Nicaragua where it is spreading strongly.

Problems, objectives and constraints

Problem
Lack of organisation and skills to analyse and overcome underlying problems of:
- poverty; lack of financial resources for investments (eg in SWC)
- insufficient food/poor nutrition
- soil degradation/indiscriminate burning of vegetation
- lack of appropriate technologies
- lack of access to public services and markets

Objectives
- support the economical sustainability and food security of land users in the project area through increased production, diversification, soil conservation and environmental protection
- develop feasible production models, aimed at self-sufficiency and the integration of land users into an alternative internal and external market; build up alternative forms of marketing and credit systems
- community development and capacity building: build-up local farmers' organisation

Constraints addressed

Major	Specification	Treatment
Institutional	Lack of collaboration between land users.	Strengthen farmers' organisation.
Social/cultural/religious	Resistance to implement SWC technologies by some land users.	Awareness raising, demonstration plots, convince with facts.
Financial	Poverty, lack of resources for investments into SWC.	Support in the form of credit, basically in kind but also in cash (see credit section).
Minor	**Specification**	**Treatment**
Legal	Lack of land use rights.	Problem cannot be resolved under the project.

Participation and decision making

Target groups

Land users

Approach costs met by:

International NGO	90%
National NGO	10%
	100%

Decisions on choice of the technology: Mainly made by land users supported by SWC specialists.
Decisions on method of implementing the technology: Mainly made by land users supported by SWC specialists.
Approach designed by: National specialists.

Community involvement

Initiation	interactive	participatory rural appraisal (PRA), participatory planning in public meetings
Planning	interactive	public meetings, workshops/seminars: assemblies for municipal planning (elaboration of community action plan)
Implementation	interactive	responsibility for major steps: execution of the action plans where each community decides
Monitoring/evaluation	interactive	particularly public meetings, also measurements/observations and workshops/seminars: a specialist is in charge of the continuation of activities and of the planning process with each community; annual assembly of delegates representing all communities assisted by ADDAC
Research	interactive	on-farm experimentation with interested land users: assessment of different technologies (variety tests, evaluation of ecological effects, etc)

Differences in participation of men and women: The integration of women is a key element of the approach. Nevertheless, there are moderate differences due to cultural factors: men are mainly in charge of agricultural activities, whereas women work in the household.

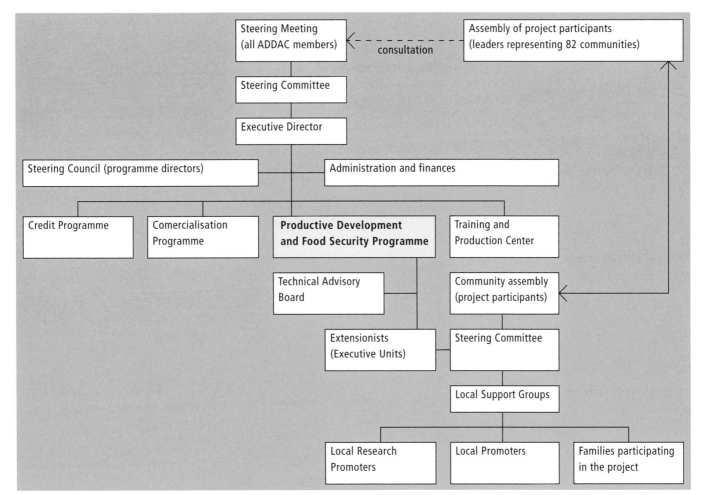

Organogram
'Productive Development and Food Security Programme' – one of the focal development activities of the Association for Agricultural Community Development and Diversification (ADDAC).

Extension and promotion

Training: The form of training promoted by ADDAC is called 'popular education'. It is a continuous and participatory process of mutual learning between farmers and technicians, based on a course of 'action – reassessment – action', with the aim of re-establishing indigenous knowledge, improving local self-esteem and the ability to analyse innovations, and, in the long term, to build up the capacity within the community to independently manage development activities according to their needs. Popular education involves a whole range of different methods of participatory training for poor land users: workshops, field days/trips, farm visits, demonstration areas, public meetings, formation of local support groups, and farmer-to-farmer experience exchange. Main subjects treated include: SWC practices, gender issues, land users' organisation, marketing and accounting. The impact on land users is excellent.
Extension: Key elements are demonstration areas, technical assistance through farm visits, farmer-to-farmer extension, local promoters organised into 'Local Support Groups', and an associated network. The impact is considered to be good.
Research: Research is carried out on demonstration farms through local promoters. Topics include on-farm testing of technologies, and adaptive trials with maize and pea varieties. The impact has been excellent, especially in terms of introduction of new crops and SWC technologies.
Importance of land use rights: Most of the land users have individual properties which facilitates the implementation of the SWC approach activities.

Incentives

Labour: Voluntary: land users works on their own farms at their own cost.
Inputs: Tools were partly financed under the project. For production of manure from earthworms, fresh cattle manure is given as a gift from neighbours to farmers who don't have their own cattle. Earthworms are initially provided by the project, then further stocks are produced by the farmers themselves. Community infrastructure has been fully financed – for example the training and meeting centre.
Credit: Credit was provided through the programme of alternative financing by ADDAC. The 1.5% interest rate (lower than the market rate) is accessible to individuals and organised groups.
Support to local institutions: Institutional capacity building: 3 local farmers' organisations have been built up: Association of Organic Coffee Farmers, Breeders' Association, Association *Banco de granos buena esperanza* (Organisation for Storing and Commercialisation of Grain) and Farmer Support Groups (local promoters) for technology extension.
Long-term impact of incentives: Moderate positive long-term impacts are expected: the incentives have direct effects on the adoption. Soil conservation – stimulated by incentives – often has positive impacts in the long term on production.

Monitoring and evaluation

Monitored aspects	Methods and indicators
Socio-cultural	land users' needs
Economic/production	% of land users achieving nutritional security, cost-benefit ratio, diversification, organic products, certified production; % of land users producing for market
No. of land users	regular measurements
Management of approach	the strategic plan is revised annually; the progress made by the projects is evaluated and reported twice a year
Training	% of land users trained as local promoters (SWC extension)

Impacts of the approach

Changes as result of monitoring and evaluation: There were several changes: at the beginning the approach consisted only of two components: training and research. Then it was broadened to involve extension of SWC technologies and promotion of crop diversification. Later the credit programme and the organisational component became part of the approach. The approach activities are supposed to be a continuously expanded based on the needs of the land users. Evaluation is carried out twice a year. This is part of a constant process of adjustment of policies, methods and concepts of the approach. However there is always emphasis on promotion of organic agriculture, agricultural diversification and organisational development based on participation.

Improved soil and water management: Moderate improvement through the implementation of SWC practices.

Adoption of the approach by other projects/land users: There are 6 more projects assisted by ADDAC, which use the same approach in the north of Nicaragua.

Sustainability: Land users can continue activities without further support

Concluding statements

Strengths and → how to sustain/improve	Weaknesses and → how to overcome
Evaluation of land users' needs and involvement of new approach components according to their needs; continuous mutual learning process between land users and between land users and extensionists/specialists → Continue the present 6-monthly evaluation procedures; implement a system of information, communication, evaluation and monitoring to analyse the impact of the approach activities.	Process takes long and requires high inputs of human resources and materials → In an integrated approach with strong participation of land users this problem is unavoidable; formulation of good project proposals help in finding donors to finance long-term programmes.
Efficient extension method: 86% of involved land users apply more than 3 different SWC technologies promoted by the approach which contributes to sustainable development of the region → Maintain and extend present farmer-to-farmer extension system: continue training of local promoters, network of promoters, local support group.	
Growing active integration of women (25% more contribution to farm income and >25% more participation in decision making in comparison with non-participants) → Keep the gender programme as a component of the approach.	
Farmers' organisations: build up capacity for autonomous management of alternative development activities → Integrate more farmers in the baseline organisations.	
Increasing self-esteem of the people.	

Key reference(s): Rolando Bunch (1990) *Dos Mazorcas de Maíz* ■ Anon (1990) *El pequeño agricultor en Honduras* ■ ADDAC (2002) *Plan estratégico Institucional 2003–2005*

Contact person(s): Julio César Gómez Martínez, De ENITEL 3c al Norte y 75 varas al Este. Calle Santa Ana, Apartado Postal 161, Matagalpa, Nicaragua; addacentral@addac.org; www.addac.org; phone: (505) 0772-7108; fax: (505) 0772-5245

Composting associated with planting pits

Burkina Faso – *Zai avec apport de compost*

Compost production, and its application in planting pits *(zai)* by farmers on fields near their homes.

Compost is produced in shallow pits, approximately 20 cm deep and 1.5 m by 3 m wide. During November and December layers of chopped crop residues, animal dung and ash are heaped, as they become available, up to 1.5 m high and watered. The pile is covered with straw and left to heat up and decompose. After around 15–20 days the compost is turned over into a second pile and watered again. This is repeated up to three times – as long as water is available. Compost heaps are usually located close to the homestead. Alternatively, compost can be produced in pits which are up to one metre deep. Organic material is filled to ground level. The pit captures rain water, which makes this method of composting a valuable option in dry areas.

The compost is either applied immediately to irrigated gardens, or kept in a dry shaded place for the next sorghum seeding. In the latter case one handful of compost is mixed with loose soil in each planting pit *(zai)*. These pits are dug 60 cm by 60 cm apart. Three to four grains of sorghum are planted in each pit. Compost in the pits both conserves water and supplies nutrients. This enables the sorghum plants to establish better, grow faster and reach maturity before the rains finish. As compost is applied locally to the crop, not only is the positive effect maximised, but also the weeds between the pits do not benefit. The water retaining capacity of the compost (absorbing several times its own weight) makes the difference. This is much more important than the additional nutrients, which only become available in subsequent years, and do not anyway completely replace all the nutrients extracted by the crops.

The planting pits also help by harvesting runoff water from the microcatchments between them. Boulgou experiences erratic and variable rainfall with frequent droughts. The poor soils are often crusted and have a low water-retention capacity. Due to a high and increasing population, the land has become exhausted, and fallow periods are no longer sufficient as a consequence. Fertility and yields have declined. Sorghum without compost is more vulnerable to drought and crop failure.

During the dry season, after harvest, fields are grazed by cattle of the nomadic pastoral *Peuhl*, who also herd the agriculturalists' livestock. Interestingly, the *Peuhl* have started to systematically collect the manure for sale, since the increased demand (for composting) has led to doubling of the price. Composting has been applied in Boulgou Province of Burkina Faso since 1988.

left: Compost pits in Bam province with low containing walls: Pit compost requires little or no additional water and is preferable in dry zones. (William Critchley)
right: After her training, this young farmer succeeded in compost making. She is seen holding composted material ready for use: next to her is a heap still decomposing, under its straw cover. (Reynold Chatelain)

Location: Boulgou Province, Burkina Faso
Technology area: 200 km²
SWC measure: agronomic
Land use: mixed: agro-pastoral
Climate: semi-arid
WOCAT database reference: QT BRK10
Related approach: Zabré women's agro-ecological programme, QA BRK10
Compiled by: Jean Pascal Etienne de Pury, CEAS Neuchâtel, Switzerland
Date: August 2002, updated July 2004

Editors' comments: Soil fertility decline is a major problem for much of Africa, and composting provides an opportunity for local mitigation of this. There are many ways of making compost, and this case is a good example of 'aerobic heap compost' from Burkina Faso. Here, the compost is concentrated in planting pits, which additionally harvest water.

Classification

Land use problems
Population increase has led to cultivation of all the available arable land, thus shortening or eliminating fallow periods. Organic matter in the soil is reduced, the water holding capacity of the soil has diminished and consequently yields have fallen. This has been compounded by the droughts of the 1970s and 1980s. Thirty years ago farmers harvested 800 kg/ha each year, but by the 1980s yields had fallen to merely 400 kg/ha on average.

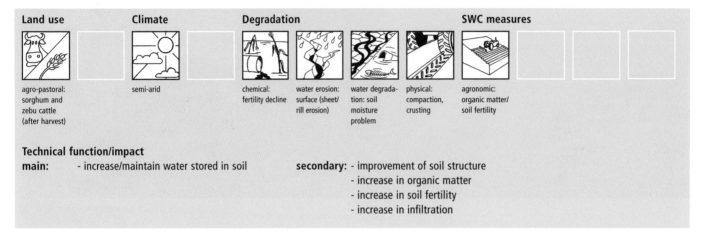

Land use	Climate	Degradation				SWC measures
agro-pastoral: sorghum and zebu cattle (after harvest)	semi-arid	chemical: fertility decline	water erosion: surface (sheet/rill erosion)	water degradation: soil moisture problem	physical: compaction, crusting	agronomic: organic matter/soil fertility

Technical function/impact
main: - increase/maintain water stored in soil

secondary: - improvement of soil structure
- increase in organic matter
- increase in soil fertility
- increase in infiltration

Environment

Natural environment

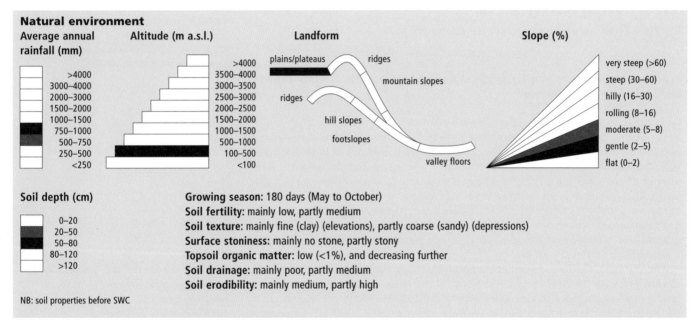

Average annual rainfall (mm)
- >4000
- 3000–4000
- 2000–3000
- 1500–2000
- 1000–1500
- 750–1000
- 500–750
- 250–500
- <250

Altitude (m a.s.l.)
- >4000
- 3500–4000
- 3000–3500
- 2500–3000
- 2000–2500
- 1500–2000
- 1000–1500
- 500–1000
- 100–500
- <100

Landform
- plains/plateaus
- ridges
- mountain slopes
- ridges
- hill slopes
- footslopes
- valley floors

Slope (%)
- very steep (>60)
- steep (30–60)
- hilly (16–30)
- rolling (8–16)
- moderate (5–8)
- gentle (2–5)
- flat (0–2)

Soil depth (cm)
- 0–20
- 20–50
- 50–80
- 80–120
- >120

Growing season: 180 days (May to October)
Soil fertility: mainly low, partly medium
Soil texture: mainly fine (clay) (elevations), partly coarse (sandy) (depressions)
Surface stoniness: mainly no stone, partly stony
Topsoil organic matter: low (<1%), and decreasing further
Soil drainage: mainly poor, partly medium
Soil erodibility: mainly medium, partly high

NB: soil properties before SWC

Human environment

Mixed land per household (ha)
- <1
- 1–2
- 2–5
- 5–15
- 15–50
- 50–100
- 100–500
- 500–1000
- 1000–10000
- >10000

Land use rights: communal (organised)
Land ownership: communal/village
Market orientation: mainly subsistence (self-supply), in good years mixed (subsistence and commercial)
Level of technical knowledge required: field staff/extension worker: moderate, land user: low
Importance of off-farm income: <10% of all income

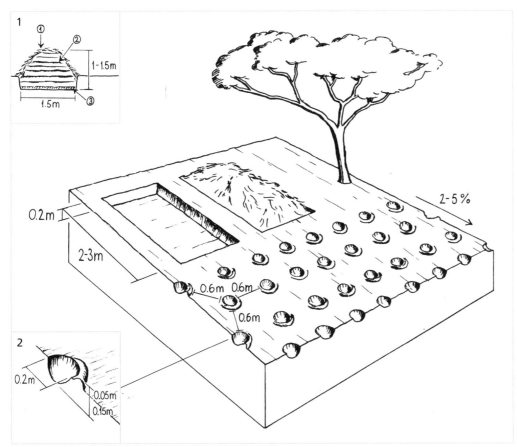

Technical drawing
Overview of compost making and *zai* planting pits within a field. Tree shade helps to conserve moisture in the compost pits.
Insert 1: Cross section of compost pit: protective straw (1); successive layers of compost (2), clay layer at the bottom (3).
Insert 2: Detailed view of *zai* planting pit.

Implementation activities, inputs and costs

Establishment activities

1. Dig two compost pits (3 m by 1.5 m and 20 cm deep) at beginning of the dry season (November).
2. Cover the bottom of each pit with 3 cm clay layer.

Duration of establishment: 1 week

Establishment inputs and costs per ha

Inputs	Costs (US$)	% met by land user
Labour (2 person days)	2	100%
Equipment		
- Tools: hoe, knife, digging stick bucket	10	100%
Materials		
- Clay (0.5 m³)	0	
TOTAL	**12**	**100%**

Maintenance/recurrent activities

1. Put 20 cm layer of chopped crop residues (cereal straw) into the compost pit (water with one bucket) in November.
2. Add 5 cm layer of animal manure.
3. Add 1 cm layer of ash.
4. Repeat steps 1–3 until the compost pile is 1.0–1.5 m high.
5. Cover pile with straw to reduce evaporation, and leave to decompose. Check heating process within the heap by inserting a stick.
6. Turn compost after 15 days into the 2ⁿᵈ pit, then after another 15 days back into the 1ˢᵗ pit. Turning over is done up to 3 times (as long as water is available).
7. Water the pile after each turning with 3 buckets of water.
8. Store ready compost in dry shady place (January).
9. Transport compost to the fields by wheelbarrow or donkey-cart (April).
10. Deepen planting pits *(zai)* with a hoe (to original dimensions of 15 cm deep, 20 cm diameter, and 60 cm apart) and apply a handful of compost mixed with earth, just before planting sorghum (after the first rains).

Maintenance/recurrent inputs and costs per ha per year

Inputs	Costs (US$)	% met by land user
Labour (20 person days)	20	100%
Equipment		
- Wheelbarrow renting	6	100%
Materials		
- Ash	0	
- Wet straw	0	
Agricultural		
- Manure (100 kg)	2	100%
Others		
- Compost transportation	2	100%
TOTAL	**30**	**100%**

Remarks: Costs relate to production and application of one ton of compost per hectare – which a farmer can make in one year and is the product of one full compost pit. The compost is directly applied to each planting pit: since the pits all in all constitute only around 10–15% of the field surface, compost is effectively applied at a concentration of 7–10 t/ha. This rate is equal to actual rates applied in small irrigated gardens (<0.1 ha). If compost is produced in deep pits, production is cheaper because there is less work involved.

Assessment

Acceptance/adoption

All the land users (5,000 families) who accepted the technology have done so without external incentives. Even some pastoralists use it in their gardens. There is a strong trend towards growing spontaneous adoption. Almost everybody, man or woman, rich or poor, wants to imitate his or her trained neighbours – but not everyone had received adequate training by 1997. Demand grew because of the expanded membership of the association.

Benefits/costs according to land user

Benefits compared with costs	short-term:	long-term:
establishment	very positive	very positive
maintenance/recurrent	very positive	very positive

Impacts of the technology

Production and socio-economic benefits
+ + + crop yield increase
+ + + farm income increase (by several times in dry years, compared to no compost use)
+ + fodder production/quality increase

Production and socio-economic disadvantages
– increased labour constraints
– increased input constraints (water for compost making)

Socio-cultural benefits
+ + + community institution strengthening
+ + improved knowledge SWC/erosion
+ + integration of agriculturalists and pastoralists

Socio-cultural disadvantages
none

Ecological benefits
+ + + increase in soil moisture
+ + increase in soil fertility
+ + soil cover improvement
+ + efficiency of excess water drainage
+ soil loss reduction

Ecological disadvantages
none

Off-site benefits
none

Off-site disadvantages
none

Concluding statements

Strengths and → how to sustain/improve

All land users, even the poorest, can learn to make and apply compost. No jealousy amongst land users, which is a prerequisite for its spread/acceptance → Keep going with training and extension.

Possibility of doubling cereal yields in normal years: any surplus production can be sold → Produce enough good compost/manure.

Ensures yields in dry years, giving security against drought and hunger.

Gives high income in dry years due to production increase and double prices on the market for the surplus → However the government is attempting to stabilise prices, so this benefit might not endure.

Requires only locally available resources, and knowledge about compost application is 'owned' by the farmers: nobody can take it away from them.

Weaknesses and → how to overcome

The modest quantity of compost applied is not enough to replace the nutrients extracted by the crops in the long term → Small amounts of nitrogen and phosphorous fertiliser need to be added and crop rotation practiced.

The short/medium term local benefits are not associated with a positive overall, long-term ecological impact because there is a net transfer of organic matter (manure) to the fields from the surroundings → Improve management of the vegetation outside the cropland, avoiding overgrazing etc to increase manure production.

Needs considerable water and thus also extra labour → Pit composting helps to reduce water requirement in drier areas and at the same time reduces labour input.

Key reference(s): Ouedraogo E (1992) *Influence d'un amendement de compost sur sol ferrugineux tropicaux en milieu paysan. Impact sur la production de sorgho à Zabré en 1992*. Mémoire de diplôme. CEAS Neuchâtel, Switzerland ■ Zougmore R, Bonzi M, et Zida Z (2000) *Etalonnage des unités locales de mesures pour le compostage en fosse de type unique étanche durable*. Fiche technique de quantification des matériaux de compostage, 4pp

Contact person(s): Ouedraogo Elisée, Ingénieur agronome, c/o CEAS, 2 rue de la Côte, 2000 Neuchâtel, Switzerland; oelisee@hotmail.com; www.ceas.ch ■ Moussa Bonzi, INERA, B.P. 8645, Ouagadougou 04, Burkina Faso

Zabré women's agroecological programme

Burkina Faso – *Programme agroecologique de l'association des femmes Pag-La-Yiri de Zabré (AFZ)*

A demand-driven initiative, by a women's association, aimed at the promotion of composting through training and extension, using project staff and local facilitators.

Leaders of the women's association of Zabré *(Association des Femme de Zabré, AFZ)* initiated a training programme for their members on compost making, and its application in planting pits *(zai)* after they visited a seminar on the topic in 1987. AFZ actively sought technical and financial help, and found this through the *Centre Ecologique Albert Schweitzer* (CEAS, based in Switzerland). Support began with the establishment of a first demonstration site where five local facilitators (one from each zone), learned about and developed the technology together over a whole year – comparing the results with sorghum fields without compost. In the following year, those five facilitators each trained 20 women in their zones, using the same training methods as they themselves had experienced.

AFZ set up demonstration and training sites in each of the five zones. These demonstration areas were protected by a wire netting fence, contained a well, a cement water tank, and some shade trees for the compost heaps and training sessions. Machines for the wells, hand tools and manure were fully financed, whereas community infrastructure was only partly funded. Each demonstration site had one hectare of cultivated land, with irrigated vegetables in the dry season and sorghum in the rainy season. The facilitators used this land to demonstrate the effect of the compost, and thus to visually convince the trainees. Each of the trainees carried 20 kg of compost home and applied it to their own sorghum fields. During the first 18 months, a CEAS technician visited the zones regularly.

In the following years, the neighbouring villages each sent groups of 20 women to the established demonstration and training sites, each group for one day a week. They carried out the successive phases of composting in the demonstration plots, while simultaneously implementing the practice at home – where they were supervised by the facilitators as far as possible. In this way, 500 women were trained within one year. Although it took a while, men gradually began to take part and assist their wives when they lost their fear of being ridiculed by others. Many more women then put themselves forward for training. While waiting, they tried to imitate their neighbours, but with mixed results. The support of the CEAS project decreased over the years until 1997, after which it was phased out, being no longer necessary. Training has since continued through the five zonal facilitators and the local agriculture extension service.

left: Result of the technology: sorghum yield (25 heads) grown with compost (left) and 25 heads without compost. On-farm trials are used to compare yields between plots with, and without, compost: this helps convince the land users to adopt the technology. (Reynold Chatelain)
right: Heaps of compost in the field prior to planting. (Moussa Bonzi)

Location: Boulgou Province, Burkina Faso
Approach area: 2,000 km²
Land use: mixed: agro-pastoral
Climate: semi-arid
WOCAT database reference: QA BRK10
Related technology: Composting and planting pits, QT BRK10
Compiled by: Jean Pascal Etienne de Pury, CEAS Neuchâtel, Switzerland
Date: August 2002, updated July 2004

Editors' comments: Support for women's groups in rural areas of the developing world became an explicit feature of development aid and investment from the 1970s onwards. This is an example of empowerment of women at political, financial and socio-cultural levels. The approach described takes an example from Burkina Faso, in relation to a simple but effective technology composting, which has found wide acceptance.

Problems, objectives and constraints

Problem
Since the drought and famine periods of 1970–74 and 1981–84, the main concern of the women in Zabré was how to feed their families. This meant trying to raise crop production again to the pre-1970s average of 800 kg/ha from the level of 400 kg/ha to which it had fallen. The soils were deteriorating because of declining organic matter as increased population led to continuous cultivation without fallow periods. The status of women was low, and they found it hard to generate income through other activities.

Objectives
- train 6,000 women members of AFZ (in 1987) in making compost, and applying it to planting pits (*zai*) in order to double yields of sorghum or maize – the eventual target is for all farmers of the two departments to make, and apply compost on their fields
- improve the status of women and their livelihoods
- encourage women's participation in development
- promote training and cooperative action

Constraints addressed

Major	Specification	Treatment
Social/cultural/religious	Men were afraid of being ridiculed in case of failures.	Contrastingly, women don't fear being laughed at. The expectation of increasing the yields encourages them to take risks: eventually men also followed for the same reasons.
Institutional	The existing institution of the women's association of Zabré (AFZ), which has functioned well for 12 years, needed to adapt to the new agroecological programme promoted by CEAS.	The management of the AFZ was motivated to adopt and integrate the technology offered by CEAS.

Minor	Specification	Treatment
Financial	Training of farmers is relatively expensive.	The donors (Fondation pour le Progrès de l'Homme) and CEAS took care of the approach costs.
Technical	One key question was: how best to teach composting to 6,000 women?	AFZ already had an extension structure and the five facilitators served as 'multipliers'.

Participation and decision making

Target groups

Land users

SWC specialists/extensionists

Approach costs met by:

International NGO	80%
Community/local	20%
	100%

Decisions on choice of the technology: Made by the leaders of the women's association of Zabré (AFZ).
Decisions on method of implementing the technology: Made by the leaders of AFZ in consultation with experts from the *Centre Ecologique Albert Schweitzer* (CEAS).
Approach designed by: National and international specialists. CEAS, their engineers at Zabré and the facilitators designed the approach, which fitted well into the existing structure of AFZ.

Community involvement

Phase	Involvement	Activities
Initiation	interactive	discussion of problems in public meetings
Planning	interactive	meetings with those in charge of the groups of women farmers
Implementation	interactive	in exchange for the training received, some land users volunteered themselves as temporary/part-time facilitators
Monitoring/evaluation	interactive	the land users learned to control the quality and the efficiency of their work and voluntarily contributed to monitoring/evaluation which involved measurements/observations, interviews, public meetings – the facilitators were responsible for progress reports
Research	passive	visit of international researchers to the farms

Differences in participation between men and women: There were great differences – in the beginning at least – when AFZ merely asked the men to 'allow' their wives to learn about composting. After two years, men started to participate in the training and eventually as many of them as women began to make and use compost. Another difference was in discussions, when men tended to dominate.

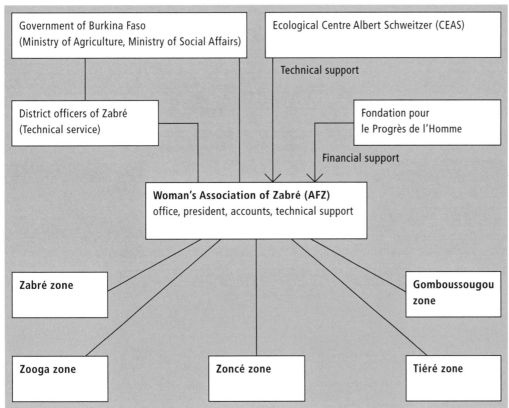

Government of Burkina Faso
(Ministry of Agriculture, Ministry of Social Affairs)

Ecological Centre Albert Schweitzer (CEAS)

Technical support

District officers of Zabré
(Technical service)

Fondation pour
le Progrès de l'Homme

Financial support

Woman's Association of Zabré (AFZ)
office, president, accounts, technical support

Zabré zone

Gomboussougou zone

Zooga zone

Zoncé zone

Tiéré zone

Extension and promotion

Training: Training, as the central focus of the approach, was provided on two levels: project staff trained local facilitators, who then further spread the gained SWC knowledge among the land users. Subjects treated included compost making and application, reforestation, soil protection and anti-erosion measures. This was a mixture of on-farm and demonstration station training. Farm visits, public meetings and courses were also included. The training of facilitators and extension agents was viewed as being excellent, and the further training of land users was good. Not all land users gained the same value from the training provided, however, but all put it into practice.

Extension: Extension basically comprised demonstrations and practical training of of AFZ's members in the five demonstration areas in the respective AFZ zones. As the technology is now practiced by all farmers, women and men, the facilitators only intervene if there is a request. This method has proved to be effective.

Research: Applied research was not part of this approach. However CEAS used previous recommendations from an applied research station in Gorom (Burkina Faso) and thereby adapted the technology to the local situation.

Importance of land use rights: Ownership rights did not affect the implementation of the approach. Even though the land users do not own the land they cultivate (the state officially owns the land, though land use rights are traditional and secure) they receive immediate and full benefits through improved crop yields.

Incentives

Labour: Labour was provided voluntarily by the land users: the hope of increasing yields served as an effective incentive.

Inputs: Beside the free training, there were no inputs provided directly to the land users. However for the five demonstration areas of one hectare each, machines (for the wells), hand tools and manure were fully financed and community infrastructure (see list above) were partly financed by the approach.

Credit: No credit was provided. AFZ does have its own credit scheme, but no credit was needed by the members for composting.

Support to local institutions: There was a great level of support to the Women's Association of Zabré (AFZ): financial, training and equipment.

Long-term impact of incentives: There may be moderate negative long-term impacts of the 'extra yield incentive'. While compost application in planting pits assures increased yields in the short term, continuous application over many years can contribute to soil mining, because it does not replace the nutrients extracted and additional fertilizer and crop rotation will be needed.

Monitoring and evaluation

Monitored aspects	Methods and indicators
Bio-physical	regular observations and measurements of colour, texture and temperature of compost
Technical	regular observations of learning progress and production
Socio-cultural	ad hoc observations of effects on input and product prices
Economic/production	regular measurements of agricultural output
Area treated	regular observations and measurements of fields with compost
No. of land users involved	regular observations and measurements of trained land users and implementers of technology
Management of approach	regular measurements of CEAS' accounting expertise (in 1992, Fondation pour le Progrès de l'Homme funded a general evaluation of the AFZ agroecological programme and of CEAS' technical support)

Impacts of the approach

Changes as result of monitoring and evaluation: There were no major changes to the approach.

Improved soil and water management: The compost making and its application has helped to improve soil and water management, as the compost returns humus to the soil and increases its water retention capacity and thus improves ground cover.

Adoption of the approach by other projects/land users: Many women's groups from other regions throughout the country invite delegations from AFZ to teach them compost making. The AFZ delegates are provided with food, accommodation, travel costs and presents in exchange for training. This is much cheaper than the 'official' compost training provided by the Association for Agroecological Technology Development (ADTAE).

Sustainability: The land users are continuing activities and can do so in future, assuming no new problems arise.

Concluding statements

Strengths and ➜ how to sustain/improve	Weaknesses and ➜ how to overcome
Training of local trainers/facilitators ➜ Positive feedback from the farmers will stimulate the facilitators to continue their work.	Internal conflicts within the association may cause problems and there is a danger of CEAS specialists becoming involved in these AFZ rivalries ➜ CEAS should be aware of AFZ power struggles and not get involved. CEAS must stick to its technical role – which is related to knowledge only and not to power.
AFZ represents female land users, it is local and not 'created' by CEAS and is thus an ideal structure ➜ CEAS has the knowledge, but AFZ has the power. AFZ needs to learn to use its power to access CEAS' knowledge bank.	
AFZ was convinced about the necessity of compost before they knew about CEAS. They searched for a technical collaborator for training and financial support ➜ This preliminary motivation is an asset and the technical partner has to fulfil neither less, nor more, than what AFZ expects.	
Land users have confidence in their organisation (AFZ) and learn while working in the fields and discussing with the facilitators ➜ The facilitators know to nurture this confidence until the land users get profit from the compost (which in turn reinforces that confidence).	

Key reference(s): UNEP (2002) Enriching soils naturally. In: *Success stories in the struggle against desertification* pp 5–8

Contact person(s): Jean Pascal Etienne de Pury, ancien directeur du Centre Ecologique Albert Schweitzer, 2 rue de la Côte, CH-2000 Neuchâtel, Switzerland; ceas.ne@bluewin.ch, ceas-rb@fasonet.bf; www.ceas-ong.net/burkina1.html, www.ceas.ch ■ Maria Lougue, Association des femmes Pag-La-Yiri de Zabré (AFZ), O9 B.P. 335 Ouagadougou 09, Burkina Faso; http: www.ccaeburkina.org/afz.html

Improved trash lines

Uganda – *Emikikizo*

left: Extension agent with trash lines – newly formed from cereal residues. (William Critchley)
right: An improved trash line, laid out along the contour, in a field of beans. (William Critchley)

Weeds and crop residues laid in bands across the slope of annual crop fields to conserve soil and water, and to incorporate organic matter into the soil after decomposition.

Trash lines of organic material across the slope constitute a traditional land husbandry practice in south-west Uganda. These traditional, 'unimproved', trash lines are beneficial, but even better is an improved version designed through Participatory Technology Development (PTD). Improved trash lines are smaller, closer spaced, and of longer duration than the traditional type. They are more effective in controlling runoff and maintaining soil fertility.

All trash lines (improved and traditional) are composed of cereal stover (straw) and weeds that are collected during primary cultivation (hand hoeing), and heaped in strips along the approximate contour. Creeping grasses should not be used in trash lines: they can alternatively be decomposed in bundles, and then used as mulch in nearby banana plantations. Trash lines are used in hillside fields where annual crops, including sorghum, finger millet, beans and peas, are grown. The recommended spacing between the improved trash lines is 5–10 m, depending on the slope: the steeper the closer. The amount of material available determines the cross section of each trash line (typically ±0.5 m wide and ±0.3 m high). Improved trash lines are left in place for four seasons (there are two seasons a year in Kabale) before they are dug into the soil. Much of the material used has, by this time, decomposed or been eaten by termites. Through incorporation into the topsoil, they improve soil fertility acting effectively as 'mobile compost strips'. New trash lines are then established between the sites of the former lines. Upkeep comprises removal of weeds that sprout within the lines – before they set seed – and the addition of more trash during each new cultivation and weeding cycle.

Improved trash lines are multipurpose in retarding dispersed runoff while, as discussed, maintaining soil fertility. They are a low-cost option for soil and water conservation. However, they need to be complemented by other measures on the steeper slopes. The climate in this part of Uganda is subhumid, with a bimodal rainfall regime, and average annual rainfall of around 800 mm. Hill tops are used for grazing, the lower slopes are cultivated with annual crops (where the trash lines are found) and the valleys are dedicated to bananas and other cash crops. Families are large: 8–10 persons, and the population density is high, at nearly 200 persons/km².

Location: Kamwezi, Kabale District, Uganda
Technology area: 0.25 km²
SWC measure: agronomic
Land use: cropland
Climate: subhumid
WOCAT database reference: QT UGA04
Related approach: Promoting farmer innovation, QA UGA04*
Compiled by: Henry Dan Miiro, Entebbe, Uganda
Date: 1998, updated June 2004

Editors' comments: Cross-slope trash lines of weeds and crop residues are a well-known practice in East Africa and elsewhere in the tropics. In some situations these are the basis of permanent structures. In this case study of improved trash lines – developed through a participatory process – they are temporary, acting effectively as 'mobile compost strips'.

* note: not the precise approach used in this area, but many common elements

Classification

Land use problems
Continuous cultivation of annual crops on slopes prone to erosion, with little or no restitution of fertility through manures or fertilizers.

Land use	Climate	Degradation			SWC measures			
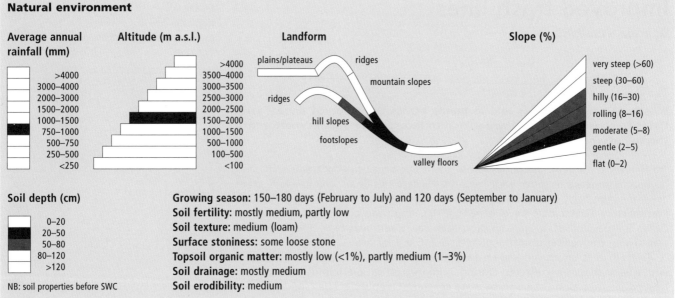								
annual crops: sorghum, finger millet, beans and peas	subhumid	chemical: fertility decline	water erosion: loss of topsoil	water degradation: soil moisture deficit	agronomic: trash lines			

Technical function/impact
main: - increase in soil fertility   **secondary:** - none
           - retard dispersed runoff
           - increase of infiltration

Environment

Natural environment

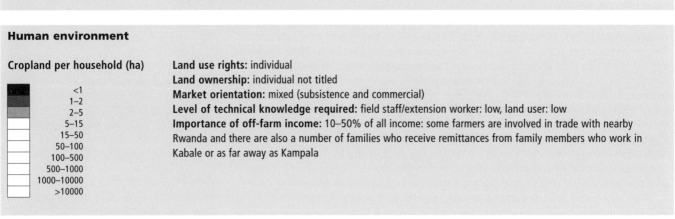

Average annual rainfall (mm)
>4000
3000–4000
2000–3000
1500–2000
1000–1500
750–1000
500–750
250–500
<250

Altitude (m a.s.l.)
>4000
3500–4000
3000–3500
2500–3000
2000–2500
1500–2000
1000–1500
500–1000
100–500
<100

Landform
plains/plateaus
ridges
mountain slopes
ridges
hill slopes
footslopes
valley floors

Slope (%)
very steep (>60)
steep (30–60)
hilly (16–30)
rolling (8–16)
moderate (5–8)
gentle (2–5)
flat (0–2)

Soil depth (cm)
0–20
20–50
50–80
80–120
>120

NB: soil properties before SWC

Growing season: 150–180 days (February to July) and 120 days (September to January)
Soil fertility: mostly medium, partly low
Soil texture: medium (loam)
Surface stoniness: some loose stone
Topsoil organic matter: mostly low (<1%), partly medium (1–3%)
Soil drainage: mostly medium
Soil erodibility: medium

Human environment

Cropland per household (ha)
<1
1–2
2–5
5–15
15–50
50–100
100–500
500–1000
1000–10000
>10000

Land use rights: individual
Land ownership: individual not titled
Market orientation: mixed (subsistence and commercial)
Level of technical knowledge required: field staff/extension worker: low, land user: low
Importance of off-farm income: 10–50% of all income: some farmers are involved in trade with nearby Rwanda and there are also a number of families who receive remittances from family members who work in Kabale or as far away as Kampala

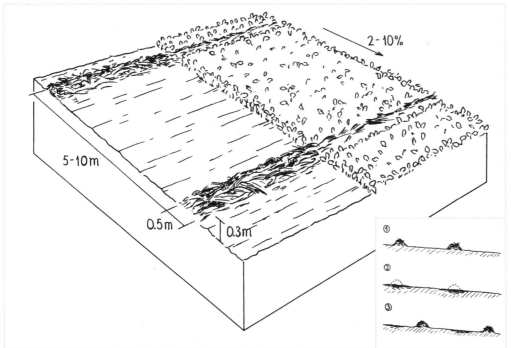

Technical drawing
Trash lines without crops (left) and with crops (beans; right). The insert shows the stages of the technology: regularly spaced trash lines are kept place for four seasons (1); then decompose over time and are incorporated into the soil (2); and finally new trash lines are placed between the previous strips (3).

Implementation activities, inputs and costs

Establishment activities
not applicable

Establishment inputs and costs per ha

Inputs	Costs (US$)	% met by land user
not applicable		

Maintenance/recurrent activities

First season:
1. During land cultivation by hand hoe, existing (old) trash lines are dug into the soil.
2. New trash lines are then created exactly between the (cross-slope) locations of the old lines using weeds and crop residues.
3. The size of the trash lines depends on the amount of trash available, but typically they are ±0.5 m wide and ±0.3 m high. Spacing between lines depends on slope (and amount of trash) but is between 5 and 10 metres – the steeper, the closer.

Second season:
4. Weeds are added to the trash lines, and, in preparation for the second season, trash lines are built up again during land cultivation by hand hoe.

Third and fourth seasons:
5. Trash lines are kept free of growing weeds and built up with more trash.

Full cycle for improved trash lines: 4 seasons (2 years)

Maintenance/recurrent inputs and costs per ha per year

Inputs	Costs (US$)	% met by land user
Labour (25 person days)	25	100%
Equipment		
- Tools (hand hoes)	5	100%
Materials		
- Organic material/weeds	0	
TOTAL	**30**	**100%**

Remarks: These figures are approximate, representing a typical situation with 1,500 running metres of improved trash lines, per hectare, at a spacing of 7 m apart on a 10% slope. The 1st year (first and second seasons) involves more work than the 2nd year (third and fourth seasons): the figure given is an annual average of all work associated with trash lines. The costs of the traditional, larger and wider spaced trash lines are about 50% more than these given above – because trash has to be carried further.

Assessment

Acceptance/adoption
- All families (around 30 families in the locality) who took up the improved trash line technology did so without incentives: they saw the benefits on the farms where the system was developed.
- There is some evidence of growing spontaneous adoption.

Benefits/costs according to land user	Benefits compared with costs	short-term:	long-term:
	establishment	not applicable	not applicable
	maintenance/recurrent	positive	very positive

Impacts of the technology

Production and socio-economic benefits	Production and socio-economic disadvantages
+ + crop yield increase	– – less material for mulching bananas in valleys
+ farm income increase	

Socio-cultural benefits	Socio-cultural disadvantages
none	none

Ecological benefits	Ecological disadvantages
+ + increase in soil fertility	none
+ + increase in soil moisture	
+ + soil loss reduction	

Off-site benefits	Off-site disadvantages
none	none

Concluding statements

Strengths and ➜ how to sustain/improve	Weaknesses and ➜ how to overcome
The technology is very simple and uses locally available material. It is easy to understand, being a modification of an existing tradition ➜ Continue with farmer-to-farmer visits for first hand learning.	The trash lines are not enough on their own to control erosion on the steeper slopes ➜ Introduce/promote supplementary structural remedies such as earth bunds.
Multiple ecological and SWC benefits: improves soil fertility, reduces erosion, increases infiltration etc ➜ Continue to encourage adoption of (and further farmer experimentation with) the improved trash lines.	Competition for crop residues which have an alternative use as livestock fodder and, especially, mulch in banana plantations ➜ Grow hedgerows of shrubs/grasses to increase availability of material for fodder, trash lines and mulching.
Improved trash lines have small but significant advantages over the traditional trash lines (which are beneficial themselves) in terms of (a) less labour (b) improved crop performance ➜ Continue with farmer-to-farmer visits for this to be explained.	Source of weeds ➜ Pull out weeds before they set seed and don't use stoloniferous or rhizome-forming (creeping) grasses in trash lines (see picture).

Key reference(s): Briggs SR et al (1998) *Livelihoods in Kamwezi, Kabale District, Uganda.* Silsoe Research Institute, UK ■ Mutunga K and Critchley W (2001) *Farmer's initiatives in land husbandry* Technical Report No 27, Regional Land Management Unit, Nairobi, Kenya ■ Critchley W and Mutunga K (2003) Local innovation in a global context: documenting farmer initiatives in land husbandry through WOCAT *Land Degradation and Development* (14) pp 143–162

Contact person(s): Henry Dan Miiro, Ministry of Agriculture, Animal Industry and Fisheries, Entebbe, Uganda; entebbe@ulamp.co.ug

Promoting farmer innovation

Uganda

Identification of 'farmer innovators' in SWC and water harvesting, and using them as focal points for visits from other farmers to spread the practices and stimulate the process of innovation.

The 'Promoting Farmer Innovation' (PFI) approach seeks to build on technical initiatives – 'innovations' in the local context - developed by farmers themselves in dry/marginal areas where the conventional approach of 'transfer of technology' from research to extension agents, and then on to farmers, has so often failed.

The approach basically comprises identifying, validating and documenting local innovations/initiatives. Simple monitoring and evaluation systems are set up amongst those innovative farmers who are willing to co-operate. Through contact with researchers, extra value is added to these techniques where possible. Farmer innovators are brought together to share ideas. Finally, 'best-bet' technologies, in other words those that are considered to be good enough to be shared, are disseminated through farmer-to-farmer extension. This takes two forms. First, farmers are brought to visit the innovators in their farms. Secondly farmer innovators are used as teachers/trainers to visit groups of farmers – including FAO's 'farmer field schools' in some cases. Only in this second form of extension is an allowance payable to the innovator. A ten-step field activity methodology has been developed.

At programme level, there is capacity building of in-line extension and research staff, who are the main outside actors in the programme. In each of the countries the project has been implemented through a government ministry, which partners various NGOs in the field. The principle, and practice, is not to create separate project enclaves, but to work through existing personnel, sharing buildings and vehicles that are already operational in the area. A 'programme development process' methodological framework shows how the ultimate goal of institutionalisation can be achieved. PFI's first phase, completed in 2000, was financed by the Government of The Netherlands, through UNDP, and was active in Kenya, Tanzania and Uganda.

Location: East Africa (parts of Kenya, Tanzania and Uganda)
Approach area: 15,000 km²
Land use: cropland
Climate: semi-arid, subhumid
WOCAT database reference: QA UGA02
Related technology: Improved trash lines, QT UGA04
Compiled by: Kithinji Mutunga & William Critchley (Ministry of Agriculture, Kenya & Vrije Universiteit Amsterdam, Netherlands)
Date: 2000, updated July 2004

Editors' comments: 'Promoting Farmer Innovation' is one amongst several new, related approaches to participatory research and development. The starting point is acknowledging the skills and creativity of land users to develop appropriate technologies, and their capacity to spread their ideas to others. Farmers, researchers and extensionists work together in this new methodology.

Problem, objectives and constraints

Problem
- poor supply of relevant recommendations from research for small scale farmers in marginal areas
- poor delivery of SWC technologies (where they exist) to farmers
- lack of motivation of research and extension staff
- isolation of promising 'innovative' SWC/water harvesting ideas which address low crop yields, land degradation and poverty
- lack of exchange of this knowledge

Objectives
Improve rural livelihoods through an increase in the rate of diffusion of appropriate SWC/water harvesting technologies based on farmer innovation, and through farmer-to-farmer exchange visits. At a higher level: to demonstrate the effectiveness of such an approach so that it can be institutionalised.

Constraints addressed

Major	Specification	Treatment
Social	'Favoured farmer syndrome' – where too much attention is given to particular innovative farmers and jealousy is aroused in others.	1. Avoid working with innovators who are so exceptional that they are 'outside society' and others cannot relate to them. 2.'Rotate' the farmers who are used as learning points: in other words once another farmer has adopted the technology, use him or her as the focal point.
Financial	Danger of identifying innovations that are good technically but too expensive for ordinary farmers to implement.	Linked to point (1) above: beware of farmers who are too exceptional/too rich.
Cultural	Gender imbalance in identification of innovators: women overlooked.	Gender sensitisation and training: bring together the 'identifiers' (usually extension staff) with the farmers – male and female.

Minor	Specification	Treatment
Legal	Who gets the credit for the particular innovation?	Important to make sure that an innovation is traced back – within the locality – to its roots, identifying the 'owner'. Especially important when a name is attached to an innovation.

Participation and decision making

Target groups

Land users   SWC specialists/   Planners   Politicians/
              extensionists   decision makers

Approach costs met by:

International agency	60%
National government	20%
Community/local	20%
	100%

Decisions on choice of the technology: 'Best –bet' technologies chosen by extension agents/researchers based on the selection of innovative farmers' technologies identified in the field – but the farmers choose (develop) which technology to implement.
Decisions on method of implementing the technology: Made by land users alone.
Approach designed by: International specialists interacting with national specialists.

Community involvement

Phase	Involvement	Activities
Initiation	passive/interactive	interviews/Participatory Rural Appraisals etc
Planning	passive/interactive	interviews/Participatory Rural Appraisals etc
Implementation	interactive	farmer-to-farmer exchange
Monitoring/evaluation	interactive	monitoring, using forms designed mainly by specialists
Research	interactive	on-farm

Differences in participation between men and women: Moderate difference: men have tended to 'volunteer' themselves as innovators and to ignore their wives. This led to (1) gender studies within the project in each country and (2) gender sensitisation and training workshops for extension staff and farmers alike which helped to overcome the problem (see 'constraints addressed' section).

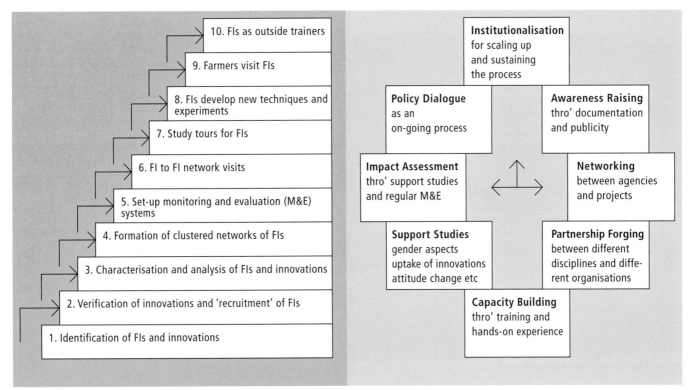

Farmer innovation methodology
left: Field activities: the ten steps– from identification through to using innovators as trainers. (Critchley, 2000)
right: Programme development processes: the framework of a farmer innovation programme. (Critchley, 2000)
FI: Farmer Innovator, M&E: Monitoring and Evaluation

Extension and promotion

Training: Staff seconded from Ministries of Agriculture/NGOs provide: (1) methodology training for participating staff (2) presentational skill training for farmer innovators and (3) training in gender aspects. Training has proved very effective – partially because it was provided on a 'response to need' basis and not predetermined.
Extension: There are new roles for government/NGO extension staff under this methodology - as trainers and facilitators. Substantive extension work is carried out by the innovators themselves, through (a) other farmers visiting their plots/homes (b) the innovators going outside to act as trainers themselves, either to individual farmers or to train groups as happens under PFI Kenya, through FAO supported 'farmer field schools'. Farmer-to-farmer extension has been a main strength of the programme.
Research: Theoretically, researchers should respond to the farmers' research agenda, though this has proved difficult to achieve in practice. Apart from process monitoring of the methodology, which has led to improvements, technical research into the innovations has been relatively weak.
Importance of land user rights: Farmers will only invest time and effort in innovation when they have secure land use rights (though not necessarily ownership), which is the case in all the areas where PFI has been operational.

Incentives

Labour: All labour involved in the implementation of innovations is voluntary – done by the farmers themselves.
Inputs: Meals are provided during field days/exchange visits, and farmers often are given or collecting themselves planting materials from the locations they visit.
Credit: None is provided under this approach.
Support to local institutions: Support to institutions has been moderate: it has mainly taken the form of transporting existing groups (for example women's groups/church groups) to learn from farmer innovators.
Long-term impact of incentives: There are expected to be none because no incentives have been used, apart from small allowances given when farmers are on outside study tours.

Monitoring and evaluation

Monitored aspects	Methods and indicators
Bio-physical	regular observations by farmers and some measurements by researchers (soils, moisture etc)
Technical	regular observations by farmers and some measurements by researchers (inputs etc)
Socio-cultural	ad hoc measurements (eg number of men/women participating)
Economic/production	regular observations by farmers and some measurements by researchers (yields)
Area treated	ad hoc estimations
No. of land users involved	ad hoc impact assessment exercises
Management of approach	none

Changes as result of monitoring and evaluation: Some changes, for example (a) increased numbers of women identified as innovators in response to gender sensitisation/training and (b) 'rotation' of farmer innovators used for training – that is not using the same farmers all the time, as this can create envy.

Improved soil and water management: Considerable local adoption of innovative SWC/land husbandry measures, all of which lead to improved production and conservation.

Adoption of the approach by other projects/land users: There are examples in each of the three countries of Government and NGOs adopting at least certain elements of the approach: for example it is cited in the project document for Kenya's National Agricultural and Livestock Extension Programme (NALEP). UNDP has joined hands with FAO in Kenya to set up a joint 'PFI-Farmer Field School' project.

Sustainability: There are examples of spontaneous voluntary continuation of farmer innovator groups in all three countries – but on a reduced level after initial project support ended.

Concluding statements

Strengths and → how to sustain/improve	Weaknesses and → how to overcome
Builds on local ideas → Continue the approach and institutionalise.	Dependent on individual commitment and flexibility → Training in skills and methodologies.
Revitalises the extension service → Train and make use of existing Government extension agents.	Does not follow the conventional institutional chain of command → Considerable training in skills and methodologies required.
Is attractive to stakeholders at all levels → Involve and inform stakeholders at all levels of plans and progress.	Sometime confers too much prestige on a particular group of 'favoured farmers' → 'Rotate' farmers who are the focus of attention.
Gives land users more confidence in their own abilities → Continue to prioritise farmers and keep them at centre of activities.	Researchers reluctant to respond to farmers' agenda → Effort needed to convince research staff of the need for, and potential benefits from, joint research with farmers.
Offers new locally tested ideas/technologies which work → Keep the focus on the farmers' initiatives and use participatory technology development processes to improve these technologies.	

Key reference(s): Critchley WRS (2000) Inquiry, Initiatives and Inventiveness: Farmer Innovators in East Africa. *Phs Chem Earth (B),* Vol 25, no 3, pp 285–288 ■ Mutunga K and Critchley W (2001) *Farmers' initiatives in land husbandry.* Regional Land Management Unit, Nairobi, Kenya ■ Critchley W and Mutunga K (2003) Local innovation in a global context: documenting farmer initiatives in land husbandry through WOCAT. *Land Degradation and Development* (14) pp 143–162

Contact person(s): Kithinji Mutunga, Ministry of Agriculture, Nairobi, Kenya; Kithinji.Mutunga@fao.org

Natural vegetative strips

Philippines

Within individual cropland plots, strips of land are marked out on the contour and left unploughed in order to form permanent, cross-slope barriers of naturally established grasses and herbs.

Natural vegetative strips (NVS) are narrow live barriers comprising naturally occurring grasses and herbs. Contour lines are laid out with an A-frame or through the 'cow's back method' (a cow is used to walk across the slope: it tends to follow the contour and this is confirmed when its back is seen to be level). The contours are then pegged to serve as an initial guide to ploughing. The 0.3–0.5 m wide strips are left unploughed to allow vegetation to establish. Runoff flowing down the slope during intense rain is slowed, and infiltrates when it reaches the vegetative strips. Eroded soil collects on and above the strips and natural terraces form over time. This levelling is assisted by ploughing along the contour between the NVS – through 'tillage erosion' – which also moves soil downslope.

The vegetation on the established NVS needs to be cut back to a height of 5–10 cm: once before planting a crop, and once or twice during the cropping period. The cut material can be incorporated during land preparation, applied to the cropping area as mulch, or used as fodder. This depends on whether the farmer has livestock or not, on personal preference, and on the time of cutting. If the grass is applied as mulch or incorporated, the technology can be considered to be an agronomic, as well as a vegetative, measure.

NVS constitutes a low-cost technique because no planting material is required and only minimal labour is necessary for establishment and maintenance. Some farmers had already practiced the technology for several years before the intervention of the ICRAF (The World Agroforestry Centre) in 1993. ICRAF came to realise that farmers here preferred NVS to the recommended 'contour barrier hedgerows' of multipurpose trees – which land users viewed as being too labour intensive. When farmers became organised into 'Landcare' groups, NVS began to gain wide acceptance.

Land users appreciate the technique because it effectively controls soil erosion and prevents loss (through surface runoff) of fertilizers applied to the crop. As an option, some farmers plant fruit and timber trees, bananas or pineapples on or above the NVS. This may be during establishment of the contour lines, or later. The trees and other cash perennials provide an additional source of income, at the cost of some shading of the adjacent annual crops.

Location: Misamis Oriental and Bukidnon, Philippines
Technology area: 110 km²
SWC measure: vegetative
Land use: cropland
Climate: humid
WOCAT database reference: QT PHI03
Related approach: Landcare, QA PHI04
Compiled by: Jose Rondal, Quezon City, Philippines & Agustin Mercado, Jr, Claveria, Misamis Oriental, Philippines
Date: October 1999, updated June 2004

Editors' comments: Contour grass strips within cropland can be found worldwide: the difference in this example is that the grass/herb mixture isn't planted – hence the name. Natural vegetative strips are also preferred here to 'contour barrier hedgerows' of densely planted multipurpose trees – a research recommendation that farmers view as too labour demanding.

Classification

Land use problems
Loss of topsoil through sheet erosion and rills, leading to rapid soil fertility decline. In turn soil fertility decline results in the need for increasing levels of fertilizer inputs to maintain crop yield. However, these fertilizers are often washed away by surface runoff – a vicious circle.

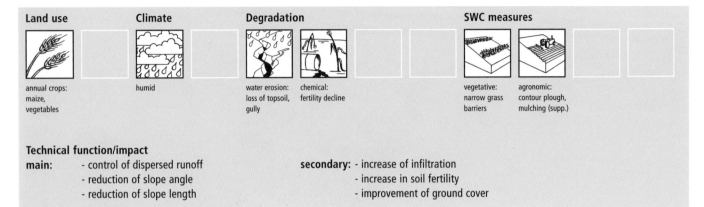

Land use	Climate	Degradation		SWC measures	
annual crops: maize, vegetables	humid	water erosion: loss of topsoil, gully	chemical: fertility decline	vegetative: narrow grass barriers	agronomic: contour plough, mulching (supp.)

Technical function/impact

main:
- control of dispersed runoff
- reduction of slope angle
- reduction of slope length

secondary:
- increase of infiltration
- increase in soil fertility
- improvement of ground cover

Environment

Natural environment

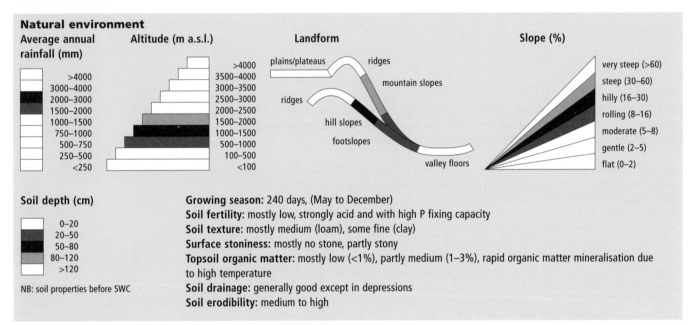

Average annual rainfall (mm)
>4000
3000–4000
2000–3000
1500–2000
1000–1500
750–1000
500–750
250–500
<250

Altitude (m a.s.l.)
>4000
3500–4000
3000–3500
2500–3000
2000–2500
1500–2000
1000–1500
500–1000
100–500
<100

Landform: plains/plateaus, ridges, mountain slopes, ridges, hill slopes, footslopes, valley floors

Slope (%)
very steep (>60)
steep (30–60)
hilly (16–30)
rolling (8–16)
moderate (5–8)
gentle (2–5)
flat (0–2)

Soil depth (cm)
0–20
20–50
50–80
80–120
>120

NB: soil properties before SWC

Growing season: 240 days, (May to December)
Soil fertility: mostly low, strongly acid and with high P fixing capacity
Soil texture: mostly medium (loam), some fine (clay)
Surface stoniness: mostly no stone, partly stony
Topsoil organic matter: mostly low (<1%), partly medium (1–3%), rapid organic matter mineralisation due to high temperature
Soil drainage: generally good except in depressions
Soil erodibility: medium to high

Human environment

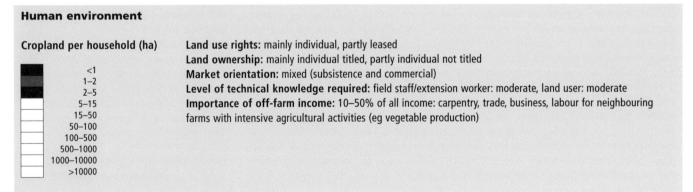

Cropland per household (ha)
<1
1–2
2–5
5–15
15–50
50–100
100–500
500–1000
1000–10000
>10000

Land use rights: mainly individual, partly leased
Land ownership: mainly individual titled, partly individual not titled
Market orientation: mixed (subsistence and commercial)
Level of technical knowledge required: field staff/extension worker: moderate, land user: moderate
Importance of off-farm income: 10–50% of all income: carpentry, trade, business, labour for neighbouring farms with intensive agricultural activities (eg vegetable production)

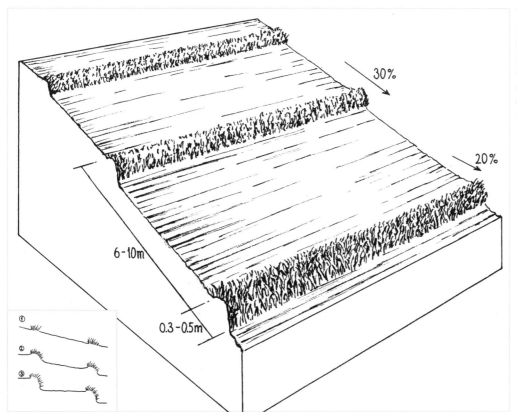

Implementation activities, inputs and costs

Establishment activities
1. Layout of contours with the use of an A-frame (or cow's back method: see description) during the dry season before land preparation, placing wooden pegs along the contours.
2. Initial ploughing along the contour: leaving unploughed strips.

Duration of establishment: 1 year

Establishment inputs and costs per ha

Inputs	Costs (US$)	% met by land user
Labour (5 person days)	15	100%
Equipment		
- Animal traction (32 hours)	40	100%
- Tools (2): Plough and harrow	25	100%
- Stakes (pegs)	4	100%
TOTAL	**84**	**100%**

Maintenance/recurrent activities
1. Slashing grass by manual labour using machete (twice per cropping season; two cropping seasons per year).
2. Spreading the cut materials evenly in the alleys (between strips) as mulch and/or use as fodder for livestock.
3. Ploughing mulch into the soil during normal land cultivation.

Maintenance/recurrent inputs and costs per ha per year

Inputs	Costs (US$)	% met by land user
Labour (12 person days)	36	100%
TOTAL	**36**	**100%**

Remarks: Costs of establishing contours and maintenance by slashing are calculated by total length of NVS. This example is from a typical field with an 18% slope: at an NVS spacing of 5 m, the approximate total linear distance for one hectare is 2,000 m. In this example, the farmer has paid for everything him/herself (see section on acceptance/adoption). Note that the establishment cost is more or less equivalent to the cost of standard land preparation by ploughing. When 'enrichment planting' of the strips is carried out, extra cost for seedlings (of fruit trees for example) and associated labour for planting are incurred.

Assessment

Acceptance/adoption:
50% of the land users (2,000 families out of 4,000) who implemented the technology did so without incentives. The other 50% (a further 2,000) received free crop seeds, breeding animals (eg heifers or just simply technical assistance (eg laying out of contours). All are marginal farmers, who adopted NVS because of its cheapness, ease of maintenance and for environmental protection. A factor that helped was the formation of Landcare associations which have benefited their members in various ways. Non-landowners have not implemented the technology due to insecurity of tenure. There is a strong trend towards spontaneous adoption, especially where Landcare associations are in operation.

Benefits/costs according to land user

Benefits compared with costs	short-term:	long-term:
establishment	positive	very positive
maintenance/recurrent	positive	very positive

Impacts of the technology

Production and socio-economic benefits
+ + +	fodder production/quality increase (or biomass as mulch)
+ + +	very low inputs required
+ +	farm income increase
+	crop yield increase

Production and socio-economic disadvantages
−	pest sanctuary
−	crop area loss, before NVS can evolve to fodder grasses
−	hinders some farm operations

Socio-cultural benefits
+ + +	improved knowledge SWC/erosion
+ +	community institution strengthening
+ +	national institution strengthening (government line agencies and educational institutions)

Socio-cultural disadvantages
none

Ecological benefits
+ + +	soil cover improvement
+ + +	soil loss reduction
+ + +	soil structure improvement
+	increase in soil moisture
+	increase in soil fertility
+	biodiversity enhancement

Ecological disadvantages
− − −	weed infestation due to seed dispersion and grass roots spreading from the NVS to nearby areas (especially with *cogon* grass: *Imperata cylindrica*)

Off-site benefits
+ +	reduced river pollution
+	reduced downstream flooding
+	increased stream flow in dry season

Off-site disadvantages
none

Concluding statements

Strengths and ➜ **how to sustain/improve**
Easy to establish and maintain ➜ Strengthen farmers associations. Intensify information and education campaign.
Little competition with crops for space, sunlight, moisture and nutrient ➜ Ensure continued regular trimming of vegetative strips and use of these as fodder or mulch.
Low requirement of labour and external inputs ➜ Use only naturally growing grass species.
Effective in reducing soil erosion (by up to 90%) ➜ Adopt other supportive technologies like mulching, zero tillage/minimum tillage, etc.

Weaknesses and ➜ **how to overcome**
Effect on yield and income is not readily felt, since reduced erosion is not easily translated into increased income or yield ➜ Farmers should have supplementary sources of income (eg livestock). Education about what long-term sustainability means.
Reduction of productive area by approx 10% ➜ Optimum fertilization to offset production loss. Nutrients are conserved under NVS and this will result in the reduction of fertilizer requirement after some years.
Creation of a fertility gradient within the alley (soil is lost from the top of the alley and accumulates above the NVS where fertility then concentrates) ➜ Increased application of fertilizer on the upper part of alley.
Overall increase of production value is low ➜ Land users could ask for subsidy/assistance from Government: eg for fertilizers, establishment of nurseries, free seedlings (for higher value fruit trees).

Key reference(s): Garrity DP, Stark M and Mercado Jr A (2004) Natural Vegetative Strips: a bioengineering innovation to help transform smallholder conservation. pp 263–270 in Barker DH, Watson AJ, Sombatpanit S, Northcutt B and Maglinao AR *Ground and Water Bioengineering for Erosion Control and Slope Stabilisation*. Science Publishers inc. Enfield, USA ■ Stark M, Itumay J and Nulla S (2003) *Assessment of Natural Vegetative Contour Strips for Soil Conservation on Shallow Calcareous Soil in the Central Philippines*. World Agroforestry Centre (ICRAF), Nairobi, Kenya
Contact person(s): Jose Rondal, Bureau of Soils and Water Management, Diliman, Quezon City, Philippines, joserondal@yahoo.com ■ Agustin Mercado, Jr, ICRAF – Claveria Research Site, MOSCAT Campus 9004, Claveria, Misamis Oriental, Philippines, agustin9146@yahoo.com, ICRAF-Philippines@cgiar.org

Landcare

Philippines – *Claveria Landcare Association (CLCA)*

left: Farmer sharing the technology with his fellow land users. (Agustin Mercado, Jr)
right: Cutting the natural vegetative strips during maintenance. The cut material may be spread as mulch before being ploughed under to enhance soil organic matter. (Agustin Mercado, Jr)

Associations that help diffuse, at low cost, soil and water conservation technologies among upland farmers to generate income while conserving natural resources.

In parts of the Philippines, farmers who are interested in learning and sharing knowledge about sustainable land management and new SWC measures organise themselves into the so-called 'Landcare' associations. These self-help groups are a vehicle for knowledge exchange, training and dissemination of SWC technologies. A main objective is the empowerment of farmers' groups in their efforts to improve their livelihoods as well as the environment.

Landcare has three components and aims at strengthening collaboration between those: (1) grassroot farmers' organisations (Landcare organisations); (2) technical facilitators, for example the World Agroforestry Centre (formerly the International Centre for Research in Agroforestry: ICRAF) and government and academic agencies and (3) Local Government Units (LGUs).

The Landcare associations are structured as municipal groups, village groups *(barangay* level or affiliate peoples' organisations), and village sub-groups *(sitio* or *purok level).* This ensures effective dissemination of technologies from the municipal level down to the smallest village. To give the associations a legal status, they are registered with the Securities and Exchange Commission (SEC). Landcare associations conduct regular monthly meetings to promote exchange of information, ideas, and experience, thus promoting spread of SWC technologies. Extension service is carried out through the Local Government Units, which allocate 20% of their development funds for Landcare related activities such as meetings, training and visits, and nursery establishment. Farmers organised in Landcare groups have better access to technical and financial support for SWC activities from LGUs and other technical facilitators.

LGUs also enact local laws to encourage adoption of SWC technologies, such as giving tax incentives, and Landcare members are given priority access to programmes and financial assistance. Landcare acts as a guarantor against loans. The facilitating agencies provide technical assistance, and also help create an environment of dynamism among Landcare groups. A link is created between Landcare associations and these service providers.

Landcare enhances sharing of labour, builds camaraderie, and encourages group decisions on matters relating to SWC. The approach is spreading rapidly: from the original one association with 25 members in 1996, this increased to 45 groups with over 4,000 members by 1999.

Location: Misamis Oriental and Bukidnon, Philippines
Approach area: 140 km²
Land use: cropland
Climate: humid
WOCAT database reference: QA PHI04
Related technology: Natural vegetative strips (NVS), QT PHI03
Compiled by: Agustin Mercado, Jr, Claveria, Misamis Oriental, Philippines
Date: October.1999, updated June 2004

Editors' comments: The 'Landcare' concept originates from Australia where groups of farmers came together in the 1980s to jointly conserve land for their mutual benefit. Landcare has been modified to the Philippines, and elsewhere, with the same basic principles. This is a case study of how land users within a watershed can organise themselves into self-help groups.

Problem, objectives and constraints

Problem
- lack of appropriate local organisations and institutions
- low adoption of SWC technologies
- financial problems
- food/nutritional insecurity

Objectives
- organise farmers with common concerns, problems, needs and aspirations into self help groups
- establish farmers' groups as conduits for financial and other support for SWC technologies
- empower farmers' groups in their efforts to improve their livelihoods as well as the environment
- strengthen working linkages between farmers and the LGU, NGOs and technical facilitators
- promote sharing of new technologies, information, ideas and experiences about sustainable agriculture and natural resources management among Landcare groups and members
- facilitate collective efforts in activities – which cannot be carried out at household level (eg communal nurseries)
- assist in the marketing of agroforestry-derived products of the members, and to develop links to studies on agroforestry-based farming

Constraints addressed

Major	Specification	Treatment
Legal	Insecurity of land tenure – since some land is classified as forest land and belongs to the government.	Speed up the land reclassification and land registration program of the Department of Environment and Natural Resources (DENR).
Financial	Insufficient capital.	Members of Landcare are recommended to lending institutions for production loans.

Minor	Specification	Treatment
Technical	Insufficient knowledge by farmers about land and animal husbandry.	Farmer training and cross visits to nearby farmers.

Participation and decision making

Target groups

Land users   SWC specialists/ extensionists   Planners

Approach costs met by:

International NGOs	20%
Community/local	80%
	100%

Decisions on choice of the technology: Made by land users supported by SWC specialists.
Decisions on method of implementing the technology: Made by land users supported by SWC specialists through the Landcare associations.
Approach designed by: National specialists, international specialists and land users. ICRAF facilitated the organisation of farmers. Specialists established the linkage between Landcare and LGUs/NGOs.

Community involvement

Initiation	self-mobilisation, interactive	public meetings, rapid/participatory rural appraisal, workshops/seminars
Planning	interactive	public meetings, rapid/participatory rural appraisal, workshops/seminars
Implementation	self-mobilisation	organisation of major and minor activities: coordination of casual labour
Monitoring/evaluation	interactive	measurements/observations, public meetings, interviews/questionnaires
Research	interactive	on-farm research (supported by LGU, academics, ICRAF)

Differences in participation between men and women: Men attend public meetings and make the major decisions regarding field activities. Women carry out home-related/domestic tasks.

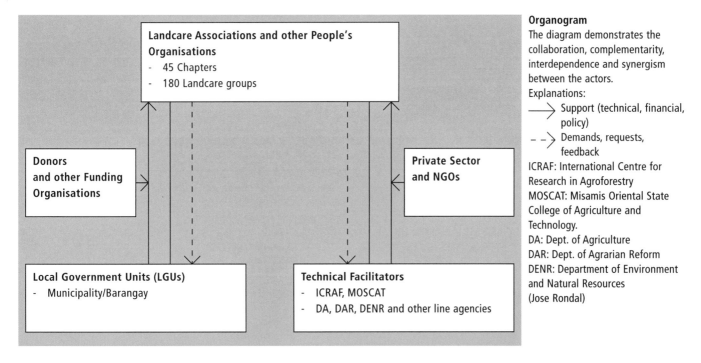

Organogram

The diagram demonstrates the collaboration, complementarity, interdependence and synergism between the actors.
Explanations:
⟶ Support (technical, financial, policy)
- -> Demands, requests, feedback
ICRAF: International Centre for Research in Agroforestry
MOSCAT: Misamis Oriental State College of Agriculture and Technology.
DA: Dept. of Agriculture
DAR: Dept. of Agrarian Reform
DENR: Department of Environment and Natural Resources
(Jose Rondal)

Landcare Associations and other People's Organisations
- 45 Chapters
- 180 Landcare groups

Donors and other Funding Organisations

Private Sector and NGOs

Local Government Units (LGUs)
- Municipality/Barangay

Technical Facilitators
- ICRAF, MOSCAT
- DA, DAR, DENR and other line agencies

Extension and promotion

Training: Training (by LGU, ICRAF, academics) is given to land users, extension workers/trainers, and SWC specialists (at different levels) in tree nursery establishment and seeding, soil sampling and soil fertility assessment, layout of contours for natural vegetative strips, and pest and disease control in the farm. This has been through on-the-job training, while also using farm visits and specific demonstration areas. The training has generally been effective; in the case of SWC specialists it has been 'excellent'.

Extension: The key elements of extension are 'training and visit', formation of Landcare groups and technical backstopping to these groups. Some farmers are trained and used as extension agents, especially for layout of contour lines. The extension service of the government is now carried out through the LGUs. Its functioning is adequate, but most of the staff tend to be poorly motivated and are lacking in direction. Planning is still 'top-down' from national/regional level. Activities and projects are target driven and set by the national/regional office. The effectiveness of extension on farm management, however, is good.

Research: On-farm research on sociology and technology is an important part of the overall approach. ICRAF has been conducting research in the area on SWC for more than ten years. This includes understanding the biophysical and socio-economic factors that influence adoption or non-adoption of SWC technologies. The effectiveness of the applied research is considerable. Research results are fed back to the Landcare groups to meet their needs. Farmers accept or reject technologies on the basis of joint evaluation.

Importance of land use rights: Ownership rights have helped implementation of the approach. Land tenure is still an important factor in adoption of SWC technology.

Incentives

Labour: There has been no payment for the labour involved in SWC activities under the approach. Voluntary labour by land users includes that for land preparation, laying out contours and maintenance of contour strips.

Inputs: Coffee and tree seedlings, seeds and fertilizers and breeding animals have been provided to some farmers.

Credit: There has been no credit provided directly for SWC activities (some land users may have obtained credit but not directly for SWC activities, although SWC practitioners were given preference for loans for fertilizers, seeds – see comment below).

Support to local institutions: Landcare is very supportive to local institutions, and to SWC activities in general. The local government enacts laws to support SWC implementation. Among the incentives are endorsement to lending institutions for production loans, tax credit and, in some cases, the provision of seeds, fertilizer and breeding animals to the land users.

Long-term impact of incentives: The impact of incentives has still to be reviewed and evaluated. Although incentives certainly hasten the adoption of SWC technologies, in some cases interest is not sustained once these incentives are discontinued. There should perhaps be some system of preferential assistance to those who adopt technologies without incentives.

Monitoring and evaluation

Monitored aspects	Methods and indicators
Bio-physical	regular observations of improvement in crop yield
No. of land users involved	regular measurements of numbers of groups and farmers under Landcare

Impacts of the approach

Changes as result of monitoring and evaluation: There have been no significant changes in the approach itself due to monitoring and evaluation.

Improved soil and water management: The approach has greatly helped land users in the implementation of soil and water management technologies. Farmers now adopt 'natural vegetative strips' (NVS). Large farms (> 3 ha) have generally evolved into commercial production of tree crops (coffee) and trees (timber).

Adoption of the approach by other projects/land users: Many other NGOs, local government units (LGUs) and line agencies have adopted – and further adapted – the Landcare approach in their respective areas. The approach has been proven effective and it is now being looked upon as a model for the implementation of SWC and other related activities, particularly in Mindanao.

Sustainability: Landcare has become an integral part of civil organisation. It is characterised by a triangular relationship between grass-roots organisations (farmers), local government units (LGUs), and technical facilitators. The financial resources required for this approach are embedded in the regular budget of the municipality or *barangay*. The LGUs (politicians) consider Landcare groups as political voting blocks: if they are to stay in politics, they are obliged to sustain Landcare. The Landcare groups have learnt to demand technical backstopping, financial support and policy support from line agencies such as the Department of Agriculture, Department of Environment and Natural Resources – and LGUs.

Concluding statements

Strengths and → how to sustain/improve	Weaknesses and → how to overcome
Promotes rapid adoption of SWC technologies. Provides easy and fast access/implementation of SWC technologies → Encourage meetings and cross-visits between Landcare groups to share knowledge, ideas and experience. Encourage Landcare members to participate in information and education campaigns.	Over-emphasis of political patronage by some LGUs alienates people of different orientation/background → Encourage more transparent government at LGU and particularly at barangay level.
Encourages farmers to gain access to services and financial support from LGU, technical facilitators and service providers → Promote strong leadership among Landcare groups. Encourage Landcare groups to be very open in requesting financial and technical assistance.	Some farmers join Landcare expecting handouts or grants → Project objectives and strategies should be explicitly explained to farmers.
Provides a vehicle for participatory research and technical interventions and ensures that newly-developed technologies are appropriate → Encourage expression of needs by different Landcare groups.	Lack of leadership and organisation skills of some Landcare leaders, who are unable to guide groups into cohesive, dynamic organisation. It takes time to get consensus and to make them work together → Landcare group leaders need to be better trained in leadership skills group facilitation and participation.
Makes extension activities cost-effective → Encourage farmer-to-farmer transfer of technology. LGUs to share the cost of technology transfer.	Over-reliance on ICRAF for technical innovation → Encourage farmers to conduct farmer level experimentation.
Ensures sustainability of actions → Continue to strengthen Landcare groups. Develop leadership skills.	Participation entails time away from farm work → Meetings and discussions should be scheduled during evenings or holidays.
Promotes social integration and addresses other social issues which are beyond individual household capacity to solve (burials, weddings, etc) → Encourage regular meeting and conduct activities to enhance social integration.	Individual problems not easily addressed, as few members are frank and open → Encourage everybody to share their problems and concerns.
Makes farm work easier → Encourage workgroups.	

Key reference(s): Mercado Jr A, Patindol M and Garrity DP (2001) The Landcare experience in the Philippines: technical and institutional innovations for conservation farming. *Development in Practice*, Vol. 11, No. 4

Contact person(s): Agustin Mercado, Jr, ICRAF – Claveria Research Site, MOSCAT Campus 9004, Claveria, Misamis Oriental, Philippines, agustin9146@yahoo.com, ICRAF-Philippines@cgiar.org

Green cover in vineyards

Switzerland – *Begrünung auf Rebflächen*

left: Green cover in a vineyard with rows oriented up and down the slope, Twann, Lake Biel, Switzerland. (Nicole Güdel)
right: Details of a vineyard: every second row freshly ripped, leaving rich plant diversity in the rows between – which supplies pollen for beneficial insects. May, Twann, Lake Biel, Switzerland. (Nicole Güdel)

Naturally growing or sown perennial grasses/herbs providing cover between rows in sloping vineyards, where the vines are usually oriented up and down slope.

The area around Lake Biel has a strong wine growing tradition dating back several centuries. The vineyards are, for micro-climatic reasons, sited on the south-west facing slope close to the lake. Annual rainfall is about 1,000 mm, with at least one erosive storm per year, and the soils are highly erodible. In conventional viniculture all weeds are controlled chemically. The 'green cover technology' comprises sown, or naturally occurring, perennial grasses and herbs which form a biodiverse green cover – a 'living mulch' – over the soil surface between vine rows. In this region, rows are generally oriented up and down the slope for ease of machine operation. Green cover may also be applied where vines are grown on narrow bench terraces. The purpose is the prevention of soil degradation, especially soil erosion by water. Secondary purposes include protection of the soil surface from compaction when using mechanised equipment, and promotion of biodiversity.

Green cover is generally established naturally – except on contour-planted terraced vineyards, where cover is planted for immediate stabilisation of the terraces. To avoid competition, a 10–40 cm diameter zone around the freshly planted vines is kept free from vegetation: during the three year establishment period it is removed by hoe, later it is controlled with herbicides (either as a strip along vine rows or around individual vines). The topsoil between the vine rows is ripped every few years with an implement pulled by a small caterpillar tractor. The green cover vegetation is cut, chopped and left as mulch several times using special mulching machines. These operations are not carried out over the whole field at once: alternate rows are left untouched to ensure that some vegetation remains to maintain biodiversity. When these rows redevelop their green cover, the others are then treated. This is effectively a minimum tillage system, building up organic matter in the soil. Cutting and mulching, in addition to ripping, serves to circulate nutrients. Mineral fertilizer and herbicides are applied once a year around the vines. Experiments with the technology started in the 1970s, but green cover has now become standard practice.

Supportive measures include not removing crop residues (from vineyards) which are chopped later – simultaneously with the cover crop (grass) – to protect the soil surface, and irrigation in dry years.

Location: Region around Lake Biel, Canton of Berne, Switzerland
Technology area: 2 km²
SWC measure: vegetative and agronomic
Land use: cropland
Climate: subhumid
WOCAT database reference: QT SWI01
Related approach: Farmer initiative within enabling environment, QA SWI01
Compiled by: Nicole Güdel, Berne, Switzerland
Date: October 2003, updated September 2004

Editors' comments: Green cover is very widespread in Swiss vineyards, covering approximately 60% of the total 15,000 ha. Such green cover of grasses and herbs is common also in Germany, France and Italy – except in dry regions. Biodiversity is enhanced, amongst other environmental benefits. This is a case study from a single village, where it started in the 1970s and is now the accepted practice.

Classification

Land use problems
The main problem was decreasing soil fertility, especially through soil erosion by water, caused by lack of soil cover and intensive cultivation. There were associated negative offsite effects including sand/sediment deposition and contamination of groundwater by nutrients. This became a serious problem from the 1960s when the traditional labour-intensive methods were superseded by a mechanised-industrial agricultural system.

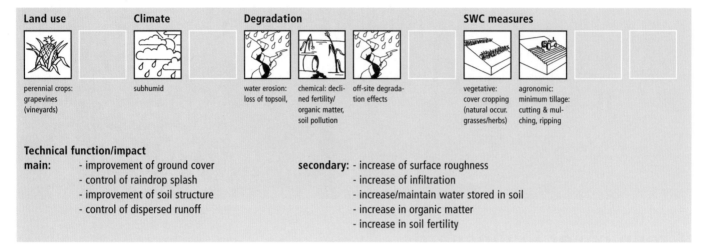

Land use

perennial crops: grapevines (vineyards)

Climate

subhumid

Degradation

water erosion: loss of topsoil,

chemical: declined fertility/ organic matter, soil pollution

off-site degradation effects

SWC measures

vegetative: cover cropping (natural occur. grasses/herbs)

agronomic: minimum tillage: cutting & mulching, ripping

Technical function/impact
main:
- improvement of ground cover
- control of raindrop splash
- improvement of soil structure
- control of dispersed runoff

secondary:
- increase of surface roughness
- increase of infiltration
- increase/maintain water stored in soil
- increase in organic matter
- increase in soil fertility

Environment

Natural environment

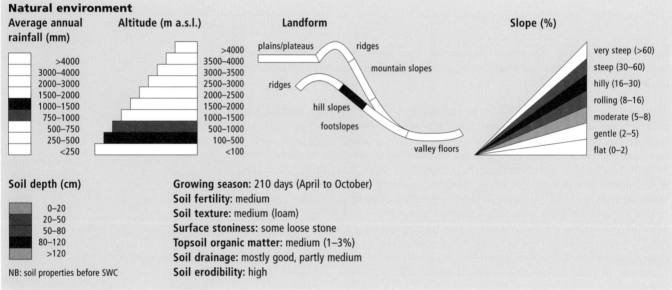

Average annual rainfall (mm)
- >4000
- 3000–4000
- 2000–3000
- 1500–2000
- 1000–1500
- 750–1000
- 500–750
- 250–500
- <250

Altitude (m a.s.l.)
- >4000
- 3500–4000
- 3000–3500
- 2500–3000
- 2000–2500
- 1500–2000
- 1000–1500
- 500–1000
- 100–500
- <100

Landform

plains/plateaus, ridges, mountain slopes, ridges, hill slopes, footslopes, valley floors

Slope (%)
- very steep (>60)
- steep (30–60)
- hilly (16–30)
- rolling (8–16)
- moderate (5–8)
- gentle (2–5)
- flat (0–2)

Soil depth (cm)
- 0–20
- 20–50
- 50–80
- 80–120
- >120

NB: soil properties before SWC

Growing season: 210 days (April to October)
Soil fertility: medium
Soil texture: medium (loam)
Surface stoniness: some loose stone
Topsoil organic matter: medium (1–3%)
Soil drainage: mostly good, partly medium
Soil erodibility: high

Human environment

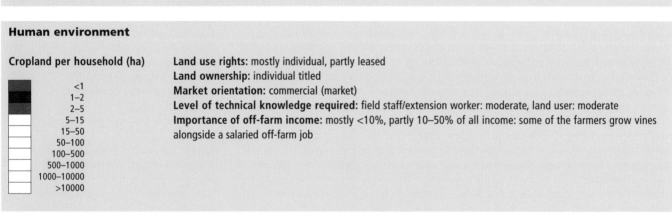

Cropland per household (ha)
- <1
- 1–2
- 2–5
- 5–15
- 15–50
- 50–100
- 100–500
- 500–1000
- 1000–10000
- >10000

Land use rights: mostly individual, partly leased
Land ownership: individual titled
Market orientation: commercial (market)
Level of technical knowledge required: field staff/extension worker: moderate, land user: moderate
Importance of off-farm income: mostly <10%, partly 10–50% of all income: some of the farmers grow vines alongside a salaried off-farm job

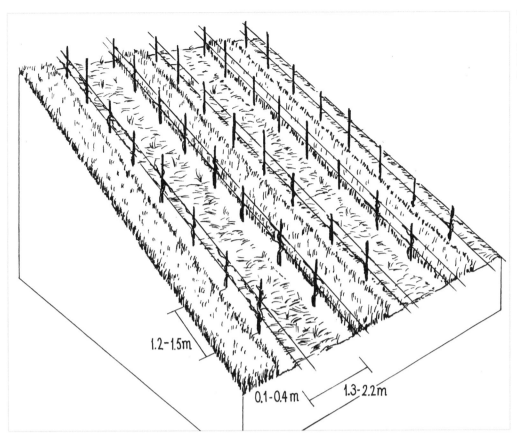

1.2–1.5m

0.1–0.4 m

1.3–2.2m

Implementation activities, inputs and costs

Establishment activities

1. Allow natural cover to establish.
2. Weeding around base of vines to reduce competition, 2–4 times during growing season. Done manually, using a hoe, since young grapes are sensitive to chemicals.
3. Apply mineral fertilizer to the vines (particularly K, N, P, Mg) by hand at the beginning of the growing season (April, May).
4. Cut cover vegetation with a portable motor scythe or mower with tracked vehicle and leave in situ as mulch during growing season: 2–4 times.

Duration of establishment: 3 years (steps 2 to 4 are repeated each year; the total establishment costs thus represent the sum of the average annual costs in the first 3 years)

Establishment inputs and costs per ha

Inputs	Costs (US$)	% met by land user
Labour	13,800	100%
Equipment		
- Machine hours	1000	100%
- Tools	n/a	100%
Agricultural		
- Fertilizers	200	100%
- Biocides	0	
- Naturally occuring seeds of cover vegetation	0	
TOTAL	**15,000**	**100%**

Maintenance/recurrent activities

1. Minimum tillage (rip topsoil) of alternating inter-rows with machine in May/early June. Each inter-row is treated every few years.
2. Cut/mulch cover vegetation with machine during season 2–4 times. Cut/chop vine leaves and wood for mulching.
3. Apply mineral fertilizer to the vines (particularly K, N, P, Mg) by hand in April/May: once a year.
4. Apply herbicides (Glyphosate) around vines. Either done manually (knapsack sprayer) or by machine (biocide tank transported by tracked vehicle). Applied once beginning of season (May), and if necessary a second time in August/September.

Maintenance/recurrent inputs and costs per ha per year

Inputs	Costs (US$)	% met by land user
Labour (8.5 person days)	1,500	100%
Equipment		
- Machine hours	650	100%
Agricultural		
- Fertilizers (70–120 kg)	60	100%
- Biocides	90	100%
TOTAL	**2,300**	**100%**

Remarks: Costs are calculated on the basis of vine rows being oriented up and down the slope, a distance between rows of 1.3–2.2 m and 6,500 vines per ha on a slope of <60%. Establishment costs have been estimated and are representative of the situation when green cover is encouraged to establish at the same time as new vines are planted (normal practice). This means that the estimated costs include all the annual agronomic and vegetative inputs within the first 3 years during the establishment phase. If green cover is implemented more than 3 years after planting new vines, establishment costs are much reduced, because the vines are bigger, competition with the green cover is less, and the vines are not so sensitive to herbicides, which permits the replacement of labour intensive manual weeding by application of herbicides. Maintenance costs are based on one typical winegrower in the region. Initial investments in machinery and costs directly attributable to 'plant capital' (the vines) are not included. Labour is the major cost component, since wage levels are very high in Switzerland.

Assessment

Acceptance/adoption
Nearly all of the land users have adopted green cover independently of the direct incentives received for growing vines. The spontaneous spread of green cover occurred before these incentives were tied to 'ecological production'. Note: Swiss agriculture in general is highly subsidised (see approach).

Benefits/costs according to land user

Benefits compared with costs	short-term:	long-term:
establishment	negative	positive
maintenance/recurrent	positive	positive

Impacts of the technology

Production and socio-economic benefits	Production and socio-economic disadvantages
+ + farm income increase (indirectly due to less erosion damage in the long-term – also due to subsidies related to green cover, marketing under the label of 'ecological agricultural production', and other criteria)	– – increased input constraints: (special machines required). – reduced maximum production capacity (10–20% due to competition for water/nutrients) – increased labour constraints (weeding, cutting, ripping)

Socio-cultural benefits	Socio-cultural disadvantages
+ + green cover/sustainable viniculture as personal satisfaction + improved knowledge on SWC/erosion + community institution strengthening + national institution strengthening (research stations) + healthier due to less application of biocides	– socio-cultural conflicts between generations or between farmers applying green cover and others; traditionally every 'plant-out-of-place' was seen as a weed and fought with a hoe – change of landscape and appearance of vineyard – again, different norms of 'how a vineyard should look'

Ecological benefits	Ecological disadvantages
+ + + soil cover improvement + + + soil loss reduction + + + increase in soil fertility + + + biodiversity enhancement + + + improved biological pest control through beneficial animals + less compaction of soil + increase in soil moisture + reduced wind erosion	– competition for water and nutrients (in drier regions and years) – undesirable plant species – undesirable animal species, especially mice – higher susceptibility to fungal decay – danger of frost in spring due to transpiration of green cover, especially in plains and depressions

Off-site benefits	Off-site disadvantages
+ + + reduced downstream siltation + + + reduced transported sediments + reduced river pollution (and groundwater) + reduced downstream flooding	– transport of seeds (grasses, weeds, etc) to neighbouring areas where it might not be desired)

Concluding statements

Strengths and → how to sustain/improve	Weaknesses and → how to overcome
Prevention of erosion → Maintain green cover.	General competition of water and nutrients depending on climate, soil depth and species of cover vegetation → Eliminate/reduce competitive effect of cover vegetation by cutting/mulching vegetation or ripping/ploughing soil.
Improvement of soil quality (fertility, organic matter, moisture retention, soil structure) → Ensure that cover vegetation doesn't compete with the vines; improve soil properties by applying mentioned agronomic measures.	Application of herbicides around vines because of undesirable vegetation in proximity of vine → Find alternative solutions, or minimise application of herbicides.
Contribution to a better balanced and more stable ecosystem (with living space for a wider range of organisms) → Specific management of cover crops (alternating treatment of inter-rows; find solutions to replace application of herbicide).	
In the long-term economically beneficial because of cutting costs of restoration of soils and fertility loss after heavy erosion events.	
Possibilities of farm income increase through marketing wine under the 'vinatura' label, certifying ecologically produced wine.	
Personal satisfaction/challenge for ecologically and economically sustainable viniculture → Promote ecologically sustainable agriculture.	
Increased exchange of knowledge and contacts in winegrowers' associations → Sustain/strengthen farmers' institutions.	
Improved knowledge/awareness regarding SWC/erosion: among winegrowers, but perhaps also to some extent among consumers (through ecological marketing) or walkers passing by.	

Key reference(s): Güdel N (2003) *Boden- und Wasserkonservierung in Schweizer Rebbergen. Ein Beispiel im Rahmen von WOCAT.* Unpublished diploma thesis. Centre for Development and Environment (CDE), University of Berne
Contact person(s)/institution(s): Nicole Güdel, CDE, University of Berne, 3008 Berne, Switzerland, nguedel@gmx.ch ▪ FAW (Federal Research Station for fruit-growing, viniculture and horticulture) www.faw.ch ▪ RAC (Federal Research Station for fruit-growing, viniculture and horticulture) www.agroscope.admin.ch/inde.html

Farmer initiative within enabling environment

Switzerland

left: Typical vineyards around Lake Biel: traditional small-scale plots with terraces (upper right) and 'improved' plots, with terraces removed for ease of mechanisation (bottom and left). (Nicole Güdel)
right: Winegrower cutting green cover with a portable motor scythe, Ligerz, Lake Biel, Switzerland. (Laila Teutsch)

Initiative and innovation of land users, stimulated by government's technical and financial support.

The application of green cover (a 'living mulch' between vine rows) in viniculture within the case study area has been developed and spread, primarily, by experimentation and exchange of knowledge between winegrowers. Individual initiatives and personal contacts have been the most important elements. Other channels are: (1) higher education and specific training courses (the majority of winegrowers have undergone at least 3 years of agricultural college, including both applied and theoretical training); (2) participation in conferences and meetings; (3) self-teaching using the internet and national and international journals or books; and (4) extension services. Disseminated results from national research institutions also play an important role – over and above individual knowledge and experimentation.

The approach is thus characterised by responsiveness of winegrowers to the various information sources listed above. This should be seen in the context of national agricultural policy which provides an 'enabling environment' including payments to farmers: the production quotas of the 1950s were replaced in 2001 by direct grants (subsidies) based on area grown and/or other specific criteria, eg ecological services such as green cover. However, the technology of green cover spread spontaneously before direct incentives were tied to 'ecological production'. Government policy supports agriculture as a weak sector of the national economy, and guarantees, through subsidies, a high percentage of the overall national production. Subsidies in Swiss agriculture are amongst the highest in the world. These subsidies effectively keep wine production going. Vineyards are seen as an important part of the rural cultural heritage and as a characteristic feature of the landscape.

Recently, with this type of production system, there has emerged a further opportunity – to market wine under a label of controlled ecological production ('vinatura'). A step further is the label of 'organic production' which, in addition to green cover, requires a range of other criteria to be strictly fulfilled (eg no use of chemical fertilizers/biocides). Customers are increasingly willing to pay a premium for such products. This is an example of a win-win situation: the environment is protected and simultaneously farmers are rewarded with a higher value for their output.

Within the framework of subsidies to farmers and information availability, the 'approach' to improved viniculture can therefore be viewed as an enabling environment for land users to take initiatives themselves. The diffusion of innovative technologies is also largely left to the land users.

Location: Swiss viniculture area, Switzerland
Approach area: 150 km²
Land use: cropland
Climate: subhumid
WOCAT database reference: QA SWI01
Related technology: Green cover in vineyards, QT SWI01
Compiled by: Nicole Güdel, Berne, Switzerland
Date: October 2003, updated September 2004

Editors' comments: Many developments in Swiss agriculture, ancient and modern, have originated from the initiative and innovation of farmers themselves - and have been spread by them also. This has been facilitated by an 'enabling environment' put in place by national policies. Subsidies are employed deliberately to maintain the aesthetic quality of the countryside.

Constraints and objectives

Problem
- initial technical problem of soil degradation within vineyards: no 'off the shelf' solutions
- slow spread of technical solutions (such as 'green cover' which requires fundamental changes in land users' attitudes)

Objectives
The overall objective of national policy is, within a framework of subsidies, to allow farmers to develop and spread solutions themselves through access to sources of knowledge and information. The objectives of the farmers themselves are to improve their production systems through ecologically sound conservation.

Constraints addressed

Major	Specification	Treatment
Technical	The optimal implementation of green cover strongly depends on specific farm or field situations (infrastructure/equipment/age of vines, planting system etc).	Individual consultation with extension service where specific advice required.
Natural environment	Climatic (drought, frost) and pedological (soil depth) factors can hamper the effectiveness of green cover.	Information provided by the various sources mentioned above: many technical variations of the green cover treatment possible.

Minor	Specification	Treatment
Socio-cultural	In a community of winegrowers who are used to either clean tillage (the traditional method) or chemical weeding, green cover implies a change of values and priorities. This can cause conflicts especially between neighbours and within families.	First, raising awareness of advantages and possible disadvantages of green cover by (further) education, literature, meetings/conferences and internet by research institutions and extension services. The second step is conflict resolution on a one-to-one basis.

Participation and decision making

Target groups

Land users   SWC specialists/ extensionists   Politicians/ decision makers   Teachers/school children/students

Approach costs met by:

National government	70%
Community/local	30%
	100%

Decisions on choice of the technology: Made by land users alone (land user driven, bottom-up).
Decisions on method of implementing the technology: Made by land users alone (land user driven, bottom-up).
Approach designed by: Arose spontaneously through land users' initiatives within the national 'enabling environment'.

Community involvement

Initiation	self-mobilisation	spread of ideas between innovative winegrowers who probably had seen green cover (or other technical developments) elsewhere – or had heard/read about it
Planning	interactive	the basic idea was further enhanced by planning based on available information from various sources
Implementation	self-mobilisation	responsibility of winegrowers for all steps of technology implementation
Monitoring/evaluation	mostly self-mobilisation, partly interactive	observation by land users; some indicators are monitored and evaluated by extension services or research institutions
Research	interactive	both on-farm and on-station

Differences in participation of men and women: The integration of women is a key element of the approach. Nevertheless, there are moderate differences due to cultural factors: men are mainly in charge of agricultural activities, whereas women work in the household.

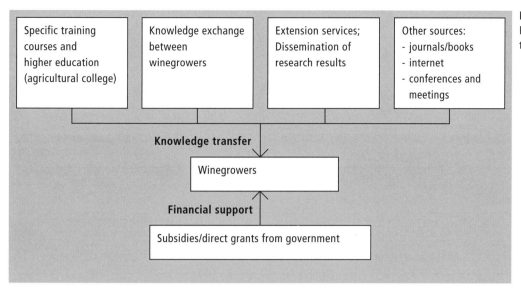

Enabling environment
Factors facilitating winegrowers to implement green cover.

Extension and promotion

Training: There are various possibilities which include green cover as one of several topics: (1) agricultural college (three years, including both practical and theoretical knowledge); (2) further education (full time or short courses) at agricultural universities; (3) attendance at regional, national or international meetings/conferences, organised by research institutions, extension services, or regional associations; (4) workshops or farm visits.

Extension: Extension of ideas including green cover in vineyards was/is essentially a function of the winegrowers themselves. It comprises informal contact, discussions and observations of different systems under personal trials. In the region of Lake Biel winegrowers often own many small plots scattered over the hills: travelling between them gives the growers the opportunity to get an impression of different winegrowing practices and discuss techniques with neighbours. There is also a government extension service which can be consulted if necessary.

Research: Research is an important part of this approach. The topics related to green cover are primarily focused on the management of the vegetative cover. These include aspects such as competition between the cover and the vines, and providing living conditions for animals (especially insects) beneficial to grape production – for example promoting predators for biological pest control.

Importance of land use rights: On the one hand it could be said that fragmentation of holdings (owning several small plots) enhances the possibility of learning through observations and discussions while travelling between the holdings (see 'extension' above). On the other hand, the presence of some large parcels allows various trial options such as using different mechanised equipment.

Incentives

Labour: Labour is a substantial input and exclusively carried out voluntarily by land users – though the overall agricultural system is subsidised (see below).

Inputs: There are no specific inputs – apart from general financial subsidies to Swiss winegrowers. Since 1992 these incentives in agriculture have been tied to a certain standard of ecological management in the vineyards, including green cover. But in the area of the case study, green cover was established mainly before this date, and can therefore hardly be attributed directly to these financial incentives. The list below shows the different financial incentives in Swiss viniculture, all of them requiring green cover as one component.

Type of direct payment	Specification	US$/ha/year
Direct payments independent of slope		1,200
Additional direct payments for sloping vineyards (one option of the three)	slopes 30–50%	1,125
	slopes >50%	2,250
	vineyards on stone terraces	3,750
Special additional direct payments for certified organic production		900

Credit: None specifically provided.
Support to local institutions: Negligible.
Long-term impact of incentives: It should be noted that even though the financial incentives are linked to green cover, in most cases, it would be applied anyway. The adoption should therefore be seen as spontaneous. A positive long-term impact of the general incentives to winegrowers is that, in the long term, green cover is not more expensive – and may be even cheaper – than conventional system or other alternatives. Therefore from an ecological perspective the general incentives lead to a more sustainable use of natural resources (in particular a significant reduction of soil erosion, and improvement in soil fertility). It is clear that Swiss viniculture (as is the case for Swiss agriculture as a whole) would be threatened without subsidies – at least under marginal environmental and economic conditions. Also, the national winegrowing training, extension and research system supports the principle of green cover.

Monitoring and evaluation

Monitored aspects	Methods and indicators
Bio-physical	ad hoc observations (by land users and research stations) and measurements (by research stations); indicators: rate of erosion, organic matter content, soil moisture, water potential in vine leaves (to measure water competition), compaction, soil structure, soil temperature, biodiversity, chemical analysis of wine, nutrient elements (especially nitrogen) in soil and vines
Technical	ad hoc observations (by land users and research stations)
Socio-cultural	ad hoc observations (by land users and research stations); indicators: change of attitude towards green cover, knowledge about SWC and awareness of natural environment, change of appearance of man-made landscape
Economic/production	ad hoc and regular observations (by land users) and measurements (by extension service with data from land users); indicators: costs (per ha), production (kg/ha; l/m³), quality, manual labour, machine hours etc – often data are not specifically gathered for green cover; but total establishment and annual recurrent costs for different winegrowing systems (of which green cover is part) can give some insight into the economic status of green cover
Area treated	ad hoc observations; indicators: diffusion of green cover (visual impression of the current status, time-series photos, descriptions from past)
No. of land users involved	ad hoc observations and measurements (by Swiss Agency for Statistics); indicators: number of households involved (with a questionnaire, personal estimations, visual impressions): number of farmers receiving direct payments

Impacts of the approach

Changes as result of monitoring and evaluation: Few changes to the technology or the approach have resulted directly from formal monitoring and evaluation.
Improved soil and water management: The approach (with all its elements) has led to greatly improved soil and water management.
Adoption of the approach by other projects/land users: As described before the 'enabling environment' for land user innovation and dissemination is typical of Swiss agriculture as a whole.
Sustainability: Within the framework of the existing national policies the approach is sustainable.

Concluding statements

Strengths and ➜ how to sustain/improve	Weaknesses and ➜ how to overcome
Very bottom-up oriented. The interest, the own initiative and the generation of own experience and knowledge is the dominant motor ➜ Maintain the enabling environment put in place by the government which is the framework for this approach.	Winegrowing as a whole is highly dependent on financial incentives. Without direct payments, continuation of Swiss winegrowing and therefore green cover would be threatened – at least under marginal conditions ➜ Continue the incentive policy (though this may conflict with international efforts to reduce farm subsidies worldwide).
Many information sources and ways of receiving information are available and used frequently.	

Key reference(s): Güdel N (2003) *Boden- und Wasserkonservierung in Schweizer Rebbergen. Ein Beispiel im Rahmen von WOCAT.* Unpublished diploma thesis. Centre for Development and Environment, University of Berne
Contact person(s)/institution(s): Nicole Güdel, Centre for Development and Environment (CDE), University of Berne, Steigerhubelstrasse 3, 3008 Berne, Switzerland, nguedel@gmx.ch ■ SVBL (Swiss Association for Agricultural Extension): www.lbl.ch/svbl/wer.htm ■ FAW (Federal Research Station for fruit-growing, viniculture and horticulture in Wädenswil) www.faw.ch ■ RAC (Federal Research Station for fruit-growing, viniculture and horticulture in Changins) www.sar.admin.ch/scripts/get.pl?rac+index_e.html+0+90010

Vetiver grass lines

South Africa

left: Mature vetiver barriers protect fields of sugar cane, forming 'hedges against erosion'. Terraces develop over time. (Hanspeter Liniger)
right: The effectiveness of vetiver depends on maintaining a gap-free barrier: here a space that should have been filled. (William Critchley)

Contour lines of vetiver grass planted within fields of sugar cane, on stream banks and roadsides, to act as 'hedges against erosion'.

This example of vetiver grass barriers comes from a commercial farm in Kwa-Zulu Natal, South Africa, where sugar cane is grown on a large scale under a rainfall regime of around 1,000 mm per year. Vetiver grass *(Vetiveria zizanioides)*, which had been growing naturally on the farm for years in isolated clumps, began to be used in 1989 to form vegetative hedges along the contour.

The purpose of these hedges is to protect the land from surface erosion by creating semi-permeable barriers, allowing excess runoff to filter through but holding back sediment. Infiltration is thus increased and moisture conserved in-situ. Although sugar cane in itself protects the soil quite well when the canopy is closed, after harvest on the moderate to steep slopes (10% to >30%) and erodible soils of the north coast of Kwa-Zulu Natal, extra protection is required. The vetiver system is supplemented by other soil conservation measures such as strip cropping, terraces, mulching and minimum tillage – all of which are used to some extent on this farm. Vetiver also helps by permanently marking the contour line, which then guides land preparation. In common with other vegetative barriers, vetiver lines lead to the formation of terraces over time, through the effect of tillage and water erosion between the strips.

Vetiver clumps are dug up and separated into slips (tillers), cut to a length of 10 cm and then planted 10–15 cm apart along the contour, also by stream banks, and by roadsides, just before the rains. This ensures good establishment. Single lines are used in this farm, though double lines are more effective at creating a hedge, and are the normal recommendation. Work starts at the top of the slope, and continues downwards. The cross-slope grass hedges are sited at 5 m vertical intervals on slopes of more than 10%, in lines about 200 m long. The cost of vetiver grass planting depends very much on slope (and thus the number of lines to be planted), availability of materials and labour.

Maintenance is very important, as vetiver often requires 'gapping-up' to keep the barrier dense, and it needs also to be cut back before the dry season to prevent it burning. The cut material can be used for mulching. Vetiver is poorly palatable, and therefore not useful as fodder. The maximum height of a vetiver hedge is kept down to approximately 50 cm. This minimises shading and competition, keeps the fire risk low, increases tillering (for production of vegetative splits) and ensures adequate density.

Location: Lower Tugela District, Kwa-Zulu Natal Province, South Africa
Technology area: 8 km²
SWC measure: vegetative
Land use: cropland
Climate: subhumid
WOCAT database reference: QT RSA04
Related approach: Self-teaching, QA RSA04
Compiled by: Robert Maxime, Vallonia Estate, KZN, South Africa
Date: September 1999, updated February 2004

Editors' comments: Vetiver grass has been strongly promoted worldwide by the World Bank as a vegetative hedge against erosion – but it has often proved unpopular with small-scale farmers, mainly because it does not simultaneously provide fodder for livestock, in contrast to other grass barriers. However it has found an appropriate niche in certain places, as in this case study.

Classification

Land use problems
- erodible soils on slopes under sugar cane
- need for cheap supplementary SWC options to support other technologies, including mulching, terracing, minimum tillage and strip cropping

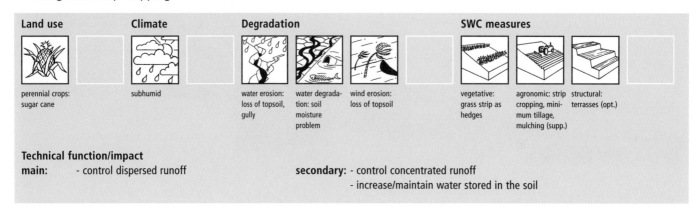

Land use	Climate	Degradation			SWC measures		
perennial crops: sugar cane	subhumid	water erosion: loss of topsoil, gully	water degradation: soil moisture problem	wind erosion: loss of topsoil	vegetative: grass strip as hedges	agronomic: strip cropping, minimum tillage, mulching (supp.)	structural: terrasses (opt.)

Technical function/impact
main: - control dispersed runoff

secondary: - control concentrated runoff
           - increase/maintain water stored in the soil

Environment

Natural environment

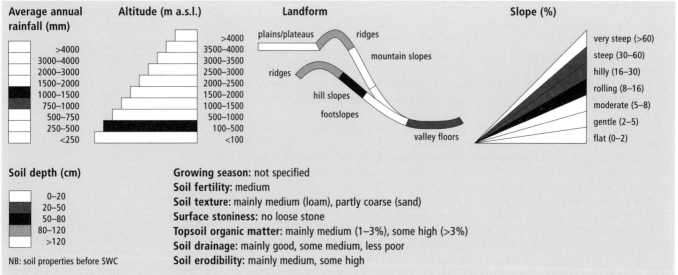

Average annual rainfall (mm): >4000, 3000–4000, 2000–3000, 1500–2000, 1000–1500, 750–1000, 500–750, 250–500, <250

Altitude (m a.s.l.): >4000, 3500–4000, 3000–3500, 2500–3000, 2000–2500, 1500–2000, 1000–1500, 500–1000, 100–500, <100

Landform: plains/plateaus, ridges, mountain slopes, ridges, hill slopes, footslopes, valley floors

Slope (%): very steep (>60), steep (30–60), hilly (16–30), rolling (8–16), moderate (5–8), gentle (2–5), flat (0–2)

Soil depth (cm): 0–20, 20–50, 50–80, 80–120, >120

NB: soil properties before SWC

Growing season: not specified
Soil fertility: medium
Soil texture: mainly medium (loam), partly coarse (sand)
Surface stoniness: no loose stone
Topsoil organic matter: mainly medium (1–3%), some high (>3%)
Soil drainage: mainly good, some medium, less poor
Soil erodibility: mainly medium, some high

Human environment

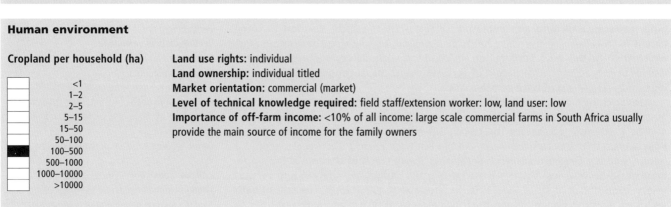

Cropland per household (ha): <1, 1–2, 2–5, 5–15, 15–50, 50–100, 100–500, 500–1000, 1000–10000, >10000

Land use rights: individual
Land ownership: individual titled
Market orientation: commercial (market)
Level of technical knowledge required: field staff/extension worker: low, land user: low
Importance of off-farm income: <10% of all income: large scale commercial farms in South Africa usually provide the main source of income for the family owners

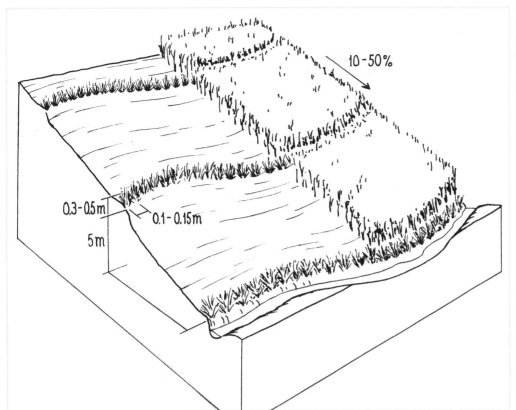

Implementation activities, inputs and costs

Establishment activities

1. Mature vetiver clumps growing on the farm are dug up and split to provide planting material before the rains.
2. These slips are trimmed, and planted using hand tools, with fertilizer, and watered for improved establishment (during summer rains: December/January).
4. The lines are weeded and gaps filled with new young splits during the summer growing season.
5. The plants are cut back (after the growing season) to promote tillering and prevent burning.

Duration of establishment: approx. one year to plant 2.5 hectares – though it takes three years for the hedge to reach a width of approx 50 cm and full effectiveness

Establishment inputs and costs per ha

Inputs	Costs (US$)	% met by land user
Labour (15 person days)	30	100%
Equipment		
- Tools (hoe)	4	100%
Agricultural		
- Slips (approx. 5,000)	66	100%
- Fertilizers (200 kg)	40	100%
TOTAL	**140**	**100%**

Maintenance/recurrent activities

1. Repairs to the fence are carried out every year.
2. Vines and trees that fail are replaced.
3. Irrigation of new seedlings.
4. Grapes and trees pruned every year.
5. Harvesting of fruits and fodder: transport of the yield to the house by donkey.
6. Manuring, when replacing grapes or trees that had died: manure is transported from summer pastures to the village by cars and to the plot by donkeys (every year).

Maintenance/recurrent inputs and costs per ha per year

Inputs	Costs (US$)	% met by land user
Labour (5 person days)	10	100%
Equipment		
- Tools (hoe)	4	100%
Agricultural		
- Slips (small amount)	6	100%
- Biocides	5	100%
TOTAL	**25**	**100%**

Remarks: In this single case study, taking the large vertical interval (VI) of 5 m (the normal recommendation is a VI of 2 m), and thus a wide spacing between lines – of 25 metres on a 20% slope – and single lines of vetiver slips rather than double (which is normally recommended), costs are relatively cheap. Costs differ very much from situation to situation depending on conditions including: (1) price of labour; (2) slope of land; (3) availability of planting material; (4) single or double lines.

Assessment

Acceptance/adoption

- three local land users (commercial farmers) in the neighbourhood have taken up vetiver barriers (without incentives) because they perceive soil moisture, and other, benefits
- there is evidence that other farmers are adopting/likely to adopt spontaneously

Benefits/costs according to land user	Benefits compared with costs	short-term:	long-term:
	establishment	nautral/balanced	positive
	maintenance/recurrent	positive	very positive

Impacts of the technology

Production and socio-economic benefits	Production and socio-economic disadvantages
+ crop yield increase	− loss of land
Socio-cultural benefits	**Socio-cultural disadvantages**
none	none
Ecological benefits	**Ecological disadvantages**
+ + + efficiency of excess water drainage (slowing flows) because of their semi-permeability	− − − fire hazard
+ + + soil loss reduction	
+ + reduction of wind velocity	
Other benefits	**Other disadvantages**
+ + + demarcates the contour	none
Off-site benefits	**Off-site disadvantages**
+ + + reduced downstream siltation	none

Concluding statements

Strengths and ➜ how to sustain/improve

When planted correctly, vetiver forms a dense, permanent hedge which retains soil and water so increases crop yield ➜ Make sure there are no gaps between slips in order to maintain a dense vegetative barrier.

It has a strong fibrous root system that penetrates and binds the soil to a depth of up to 3 meters and can withstand the effects of tunnelling and cracking.

Vetiver grass seed is sterile so it doesn't spread.

Not very competitive to crops growing alongside.

The cut material can be used for mulching and has multiple secondary uses (thatching, basket making, etc).

Once established it can withstand periods of drought and waterlogging. It is also resistant to grazing and to most pests and diseases.

Adaptability: can be planted in various environments and grows well in most soil types.

Depending on the availability of planting materials and the spacing adopted, can be relatively cheap and easy to establish and – once well established – vetiver requires minimal maintenance.

Weaknesses and ➜ how to overcome

Burns easily when mature ➜ Strategic/controlled burning at end of growing season or trimming back.

Susceptible to certain chemicals used in sugar cane ➜ Keep chemicals off vetiver.

Planting material expensive to buy: therefore costs increase considerably unless farmer has own nursery ➜ Establish own nursery.

Takes time to plant a large area (in this case 2.5 ha per year).

Key reference(s): World Bank (1990) *Vetiver Grass: The Hedge against Erosion.* World Bank, Washington DC, USA ■ South Africa Vetiver Network (undated: c 2001) *Utshani I-Vetiver: Vetiver Grass.* Institute of Natural Resources, Scottsville, South Africa

Contact person(s): Rinda van der Merwe, Institute for Soil, Climate and Water, P/Bag x79, 0001 Pretoria, South Africa; rinda@arc.agric.za ■ Dick Grimshaw; dickgrimshaw@vetiver.org

Self-teaching

South Africa

left: Slips of vetiver grass are planted according to instructions in the booklet. (William Critchley)

right: Spacing between slips is 10–15 cm apart at the time of planting. This should form a dense barrier but 'gapping-up' may be necessary in subsequent seasons. (William Critchley)

Learning how to use vetiver grass as a vegetative conservation barrier through instructions from a booklet and hands-on, practical experience.

The manager of the farm from which this case study is taken was given a booklet on vetiver grass produced by the World Bank. His objective was to teach himself to improve his conservation system. Already he had a number of conservation strategies, including terracing, minimum tillage, mulching and strip cropping, but he felt there was a need to better his system. Through self-teaching he gave himself an opportunity to do so.

There had been some vetiver plants on the farm for 40 years, and the vetiver visibly held the soil in place where it grew. These plants had grown into huge clumps comprising multiple tillers or 'slips'. The practical handbook, disseminated very widely throughout erosion-prone countries by the World Bank, demonstrated how vetiver could be dug up, split and planted to form a continuous barrier hedge for soil and water conservation (World Bank, 1990: see references). In other words, in this situation, the booklet offered the possibility of improving what was already there.

The 'approach' therefore comprised taking ideas from a book, testing those ideas and seeing how they worked in practice. The approach has developed further by the farmer spreading his message to neighbours, some of whom have copied the system after visiting his farm and seeing the results for themselves. While the original handbook had been aimed especially at Indian farmers, subsequent to the successful experience of this particular farmer, a locally focussed handbook has been recently prepared in English and Zulu by the South African Vetiver Network (see references).

Location: Lower Tugela District, Kwa-Zulu Natal South Africa
Approach area: 8 km²
Land use: cropland
Climate: subhumid
WOCAT database reference: QA RSA04
Related technology: Vetiver grass lines, QT RSA04
Compiled by: Robert Maxime, Vallonia Estate, Lower Tugela District, KZN, South Africa
Date: June 1999, updated February 2004

Editors' comments: Using documents (or the internet, or the media in general) is not a common way to learn about and initiate a soil and water conservation system, but is an approach that should be encouraged. It fits perfectly with the WOCAT philosophy of learning from other people's experience through information exchange.

Problems, objectives and constraints

Problem
- lack of knowledge about alternative conservation technologies
- need for a new and cheap supplement to existing forms of soil and water conservation within sugar cane, that could be tested and tried by the farmer himself without need for outside advice

Objectives
- 'test and try' a new method by self-teaching and gaining hands-on experience

Constraints addressed

	Specification	Treatment
Financial	Need to find a cheap supplement to existing SWC in sugar cane.	Discovery of vetiver grass barrier hedge technology described in a booklet.

Participation and decision making

Target groups

Land users (large scale individual farmers)

Approach costs met by*:

Individual farmers	100%
	100%

*does not include the costs of developing/distributing the booklet

Decisions on choice of the technology: Made by land user.
Decisions on method of implementing the technology: Made by land user.
Approach designed by: The land user (by using the handbook).

Community involvement

Phase	Involvement	Activities
Initiation	self mobilisation	looking for ideas
Planning	self mobilisation	reading and thinking through the possibilities
Implementation	self mobilisation	paying farm labourers to plant the grass
Monitoring/evaluation	self mobilisation	observations
Research	not applicable	not applicable

Differences in participation between men and women: No difference in theory: but mainly men participating in practice.

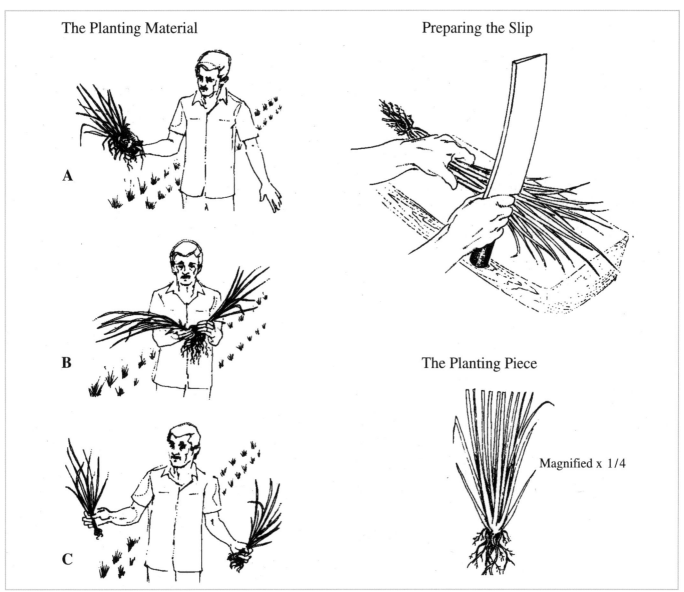

The Planting Material

Preparing the Slip

The Planting Piece

Magnified x 1/4

Establishing vetiver hedges: instructions on preparation for planting in the vetiver handbook. (World Bank, 1990)

Extension and promotion

Training: Self-taught through use of World Bank's vetiver handbook (see references); hands-on experience.
Extension: Nothing formalised: merely informal farmer-to-farmer visits (by the farmer's neighbours to learn from his experience).
Research: No formal research: the farmer relies on observation and comparison with neighbours.
Importance of land use rights: Owning the land was a great help because the farmer-owner can do as he pleases in terms of conservation.

Incentives

Labour: Implemented at own cost.
Inputs: Conservation material bought/grown by the farmer himself – though the promotional material (booklet) was provided free of charge.
Credit: None.
Support to local institutions: None.
Long-term impact of incentives: Not relevant as no incentives are provided.

Monitoring and evaluation

Monitored aspects	Methods and indicators
Bio-physical	regular observations of vetiver performance by the farmer
Technical	ad hoc observations by the farmer
Economic/production	ad hoc observations by the farmer
Area treated	measurements carried out each year by the farmer
No. of land users involved	ad hoc observations by the farmer

Impacts of the approach

Changes as result of monitoring and evaluation: No information given.

Improved soil and water management: There was a great improvement noted by the farmer.

Adoption of the approach by other projects/land users: Three neighbouring farmers have adopted the technology through their observations (not necessarily directly influenced by the publication, but by visiting/talking to the innovative farmer).

Sustainability: Land users can continue without support and at least a modest spontaneous expansion of adoption is expected.

Concluding statements

Strengths and → how to sustain/improve	Weaknesses and → how to overcome
A technical system devised from a handbook and experience rather than needing a project or intensive visits from extension agents → Make sure such handbooks are spread and available in local languages.	Not everyone has access to such teaching material – or is literate → Spread literature and information more widely and in local languages – both in written form and on the radio.
Neighbours can easily see and copy → Farmer-to-farmer visits could be promoted through self-help groups and associations.	
A very cheap method of extension/ knowledge transfer → Produce and disseminate booklets (and information on the internet) more widely.	

Key reference(s): World Bank (1990) *Vetiver Grass: The Hedge against Erosion*. World Bank, Washington DC ■ South Africa Vetiver Network (undated) *Utshani I-Vetiver: Vetiver Grass*. Institute of Natural Resources, Scottsville, South Africa

Contact person(s): Rinda van der Merwe, Institute for Soil, Climate and Water, P/Bag x79, 0001 Pretoria, South Africa; rinda@arc.agric.za ■ Dick Grimshaw; dickgrimshaw@vetiver.org

Shelterbelts for farmland in sandy areas

China – 沙区农田防护林

left: Bird's-eye view of the rectangular grid of shelterbelts established over wide expanses of cropland to reduce natural hazards and protect crops. (Liingqin Meng)
right: Detailed view of a shelterbelt established in the early 1960s. A road and an irrigation channel run between the tree rows. (Anonymous)

Belts of trees, planted in a rectangular grid pattern or in strips within, and on the periphery of, farmland to act as windbreaks.

Shelterbelts to protect cropland are a specific type of agroforestry system comprising certain tall growing tree species. Such shelterbelts around farmland help reduce natural hazards including sandstorms, wind erosion, shifting sand, droughts and frost. They also improve the microclimate (reduced temperature, wind speed, soil water loss and excessive wind-induced transpiration) and create more favourable conditions for crop production. Thus the establishment of shelterbelts plays a crucial role in the sandy drylands that are affected by wind and resultant desertification especially during winter and spring. Where there is irrigation, the shelterbelts protect the infrastructure from silting-up with wind-borne sediment.

Strips of tall growing species (15–25 m) of poplar *(Populus spp.)* or willow *(Salix spp.)* were originally (from 1960s onwards) planted in a 400 by 600 m rectangular grid pattern within extensive areas of cropland, with an extra belt of windbreaks on the windward side (against the prevailing wind). Generally, the distance effectively protected is 15–25 times the tree height. Strips are of variable width, consisting of 2–5 tree lines (1–3 m apart) with trees planted every 1–2 m within the lines. Selective felling is used to maintain adequate growing space and the protective effect of the trees.

The impact of the shelterbelts depends on the planting pattern of the trees (the format of strips and grids), the orientation of the shelterbelts in relation to the wind, the spacing between, and the width of each strip and the type of trees planted. The specific design is primarily based on preventing the negative effects of wind, but depends also on local conditions such as the layout of the land, the location of the roads, farm boundaries and irrigation canals. Ideally the tree strips are perpendicular to the prevailing wind direction, and the angle between the strip and the prevailing wind is never less than 45 degrees. The structure of the strips determines the way the wind is controlled, ranging from blocking the wind to letting it diffuse through semi-permeable shelterbelts. The best effect is achieved if the wind is not blocked entirely, as this can cause turbulence.

The ownership of the land and the shelterbelts still rests with the state, but management has been more and more transferred to individual households. On condition that the impact of the shelterbelt is not affected, the local forestry agencies now allow some felling of mature trees – on a rotational and selective basis, for timber and firewood. Pine trees *(Pinus sylvestris var. mongolica* and *P. tabulaeformis),* which command high value as timber for construction, and fruit (and cash) trees like the apricot tree *(Prunus armeniace)* are increasingly used.

Location: Inner Mongolia Autonomous Region, People's Republic of China
Technology area: 500 km²
SWC measure: vegetative
Land use: cropland (before), mixed: agroforestry (after)
Climate: semi-arid
WOCAT database reference: QT CHN48
Related approach: not documented
Compiled by: Hai Chunxing, Wang Dongmei, Wang Yaolin, PR China
Date: May 2002, updated October 2006

Editors' comments: In China, a total of 1.84 million km² suffer from desertification related to sand storms, shifting sands and wind erosion, making up 19% of the total land area. In those dry and desertified zones, farmland is barely productive, even with irrigation. The construction of shelterbelts in this northeastern part of China has had multiple benefits that outweigh the loss of cropland. However, maintenance has become an important issue with the changes in China's land use laws. This is one of two examples of windbreaks amongst the case studies in this book.

Classification

Land use problems
Strong winds in the winter and spring result in serious natural hazards including sand storms, sand encroachment and wind erosion, while dry and hot winds in the summer increase transpiration leading to plant stress and reduced crop yields.

Land use	Climate	Degradation	SWC measures

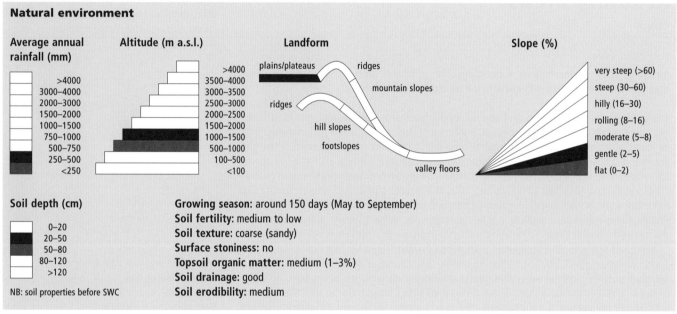

Land use:
annual crops: maize/wheat, suppl. irrig. (before)
agroforestry, suppl. irrig. (after)

Climate:
semi-arid

Degradation:
wind erosion: loss of topsoil, deflation/ deposition
water: reduced soil moisture

SWC measures:
vegetative: aligned trees (windbreaks)

Technical function/impact
main:
- reduction in wind speed
- protection from wind erosion
- protection from sand encroachment
- protection of crops from mechanical damage
- reduction in evaporation loss
- soil moisture conservation

secondary:
- mitigation of sand storms
- preventing siltation of irrigation canals
- maintenance of organic matter

Environment

Natural environment

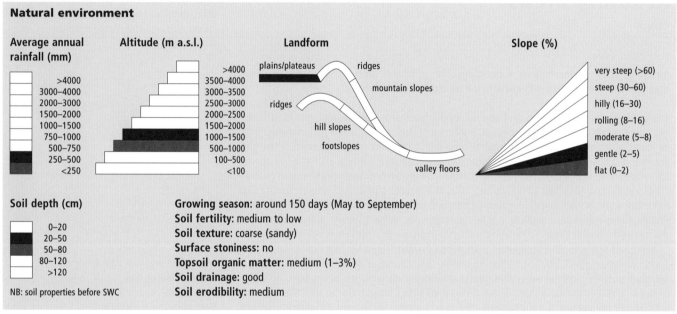

Average annual rainfall (mm)
>4000
3000–4000
2000–3000
1500–2000
1000–1500
750–1000
500–750
250–500
<250

Altitude (m a.s.l.)
>4000
3500–4000
3000–3500
2500–3000
2000–2500
1500–2000
1000–1500
500–1000
100–500
<100

Landform
plains/plateaus, ridges, mountain slopes, ridges, hill slopes, footslopes, valley floors

Slope (%)
very steep (>60)
steep (30–60)
hilly (16–30)
rolling (8–16)
moderate (5–8)
gentle (2–5)
flat (0–2)

Soil depth (cm)
0–20
20–50
50–80
80–120
>120

NB: soil properties before SWC

Growing season: around 150 days (May to September)
Soil fertility: medium to low
Soil texture: coarse (sandy)
Surface stoniness: no
Topsoil organic matter: medium (1–3%)
Soil drainage: good
Soil erodibility: medium

Human environment

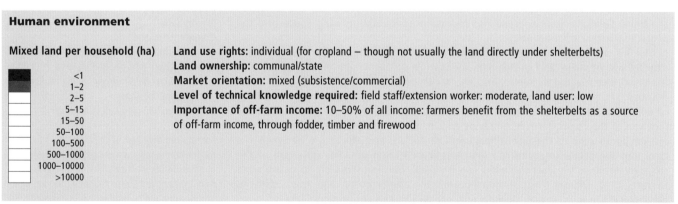

Mixed land per household (ha)
<1
1–2
2–5
5–15
15–50
50–100
100–500
500–1000
1000–10000
>10000

Land use rights: individual (for cropland – though not usually the land directly under shelterbelts)
Land ownership: communal/state
Market orientation: mixed (subsistence/commercial)
Level of technical knowledge required: field staff/extension worker: moderate, land user: low
Importance of off-farm income: 10–50% of all income: farmers benefit from the shelterbelts as a source of off-farm income, through fodder, timber and firewood

Remark: In the 1960s, all land ownership and land use rights in China were communal and cropland was farmed collectively by village communes. After reform and open policy was put into practice in 1978, land use rights were transferred to the villages, to groups and individuals. Land itself and the shelterbelts however still belonged to the state. Nowadays the rights to cultivate specific parcels of land, within protected blocks, are generally granted to individual farm households. In some cases, in recent years, the shelterbelts too have been redistributed to individuals to look after. Inevitably maintenance has become an issue. But most of the shelterbelts are managed well.

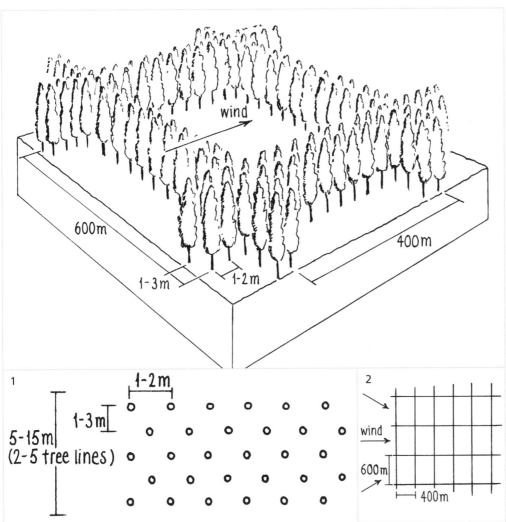

Technical drawing
Overview of the shelterbelt layout.
Insert 1: Planting scheme: shelterbelts comprise 2–5 tree lines
forming the windbreak about
5–15 m wide and 15–25 m high.
Insert 2: Rectangle grid layout
of shelterbelts. Spacing of the rows
is denser against the prevailing
wind.

Implementation activities, inputs and costs

Establishment activities

1 Planning/designing of shelterbelt.
2 Selection and collection of trees seedlings.
3 Clearing and preparing land for planting of shelterbelt in late spring and autumn.
4 Pits for planting the seedlings are dug by hand using shovels and pickaxes in late autumn and spring.
5 Tree seedlings are planted in late spring.
6 After planting each seedling is watered by hand for up to two years.
Duration of establishment: 2–3 years

Establishment inputs and costs per ha

Inputs	Costs (US$)	% met by land user
Labour (25 person days)	95	0%
Equipment		
- Tools (shovel, pickaxe, bowser)	5	100%
Agricultural		
- Tree seedlings (104)	25	0%
TOTAL	**125**	**4%**

Maintenance/recurrent activities

Pruning of trees.
Pest and disease control within shelterbelt.
Intermediate/ selective tree felling.
Once established the shelterbelt requires minimal maintenance.
Replanting is carried out after felling of single lines of mature trees.

Maintenance/recurrent inputs and costs per ha per year

Inputs	Costs (US$)	% met by land user
Labour (2 person days)	8	100%
Agricultural		
- Seedlings (10)	3	100%
TOTAL	**11**	**100%**

Remarks: The costs are calculated according to current standards/costs. The original planting is paid for by the state: re-planting and maintenance are the responsibility of the land user. If pines are the species of choice for re-planting, the cost is considerably more than that shown above (which relates to poplar and willow).
Assuming: shelterbelts of 600 m by 400 m; each strip has 5 lines of trees (3 m apart), 2 m between trees within lines: resulting in 104 trees/ha, including the cropland between the strips (density within strips is 1666 trees/ha).
Labour for establishment (104 trees): Land preparation, planting 10 days and 15 days for watering, weeding, etc (for first 3 years).

Assessment

Acceptance/adoption
Shelterbelts and irrigation canals were established through a government project in which the large majority of the costs were met by the state. The technology has not spontaneously spread beyond the areas developed through government intervention.

Benefits/costs according to land user

Benefits compared with costs	short-term:	long-term:
establishment	not specified	not specified
maintenance/recurrent	slightly positive*	very positive*

* If farmer cuts mature timber (for example a 40 year-old poplar), he/she can sell it for US$ 20–25 per tree. With maturity of shelterbelts, the timber production increases, which brings increasing economic benefits; meanwhile, the effect of protection from wind erosion also improves.

Impacts of the technology

Production and socio-economic benefits
+ + + wood production increase
+ + crop yield increase
+ + farm income increase
+ + off-farm income increase (extra timber and firewood)

Production and socio-economic disadvantages
− − loss of land (width of the shelterbelt)
− − competition with crops for solar radiation, fertilizer, and water

Socio-cultural benefits
+ improved knowledge SWC/erosion

Socio-cultural disadvantages
− − shelterbelts of trees are not a direct source of food – this leads to a negative attitude amongst some farmers

Ecological benefits
+ + + soil cover improvement
+ + + increase in soil moisture
+ + + soil loss reduction
+ + + reduction of wind velocity
+ + + reduction of sand encroachment
+ + + improving microclimate for crops: regulating temperature, increasing humidity
+ + conservation/maintenance of soil fertility

Ecological disadvantages
− water consumption by trees

Off-site benefits
+ + + reduced effects of sand storms (encroachment)
+ + + improved microclimate around protected cropland areas

Off-site disadvantages
none

Concluding statements

Strengths and → how to sustain/improve
Reduced wind speed and trapped wind-blown sand particle → Combine deciduous and evergreen trees to maintain shelterbelt's protective function throughout the year.

Increased crop yield → Extend shelterbelt technology to unprotected croplands.

Increased cash income → Improve rotational felling regimes that maximise quantity and quality of tree products (timber; fruit etc) without reducing the shelterbelt's protective function. In Inner Mongolia apricot (Prunus armeniaca) and sea buckthorn (Hippophae rhamnoides) and in Gansu Province the Chinese dates (Ziziphus jujuba) are incresingly used.

Apart from their effect on the wind, the overall benefits of the shelterbelts – for timber, firewood, fruits and fodder for animals – outweigh the loss of cropland occupied by the trees → Experience over 40 years has demonstrated that narrower trees strips and smaller grid size (100 by 200 m) would increase ecological efficiency, but due to higher costs and potential competition with crops, the spacing of the shelterbelts has mostly remained as it was originally.

From 1960 onwards, approximately 22 million hectares – of vulnerable cropland have been protected in eastern Inner Mongolia.

Weaknesses and → how to overcome
Loss of land due to area used for the shelterbelts → In this wind-prone part of Inner Mongolia, overall gains from the protected zones compensate for the reduced area under crops, especially if economically valuable species are planted in the shelterbelt, such as Caragana korshinskii, which can be used as forage, for 'green fertilizer' through leaf mulch and for firewood.

Competition for sunshine, fertilizer and water → Pruning of branches and digging of ditches to prevent roots penetrating the adjacent cropland

Farmers lost the right to crop the tree-occupied land (since the shelterbelts belonged to the state). Originally, farmers were not allowed to fell trees → Nowadays the local forestry department permits farmers to occasionally cut trees, which is a source of income. If land users were allowed to cut trees on a more systematic basis, it would help them to better appreciate the benefits.

High cost (labour and money) for establishment → Government support required.

Shelterbelts comprised of single tree species are less resistant to pests and diseases → Combine trees and shrubs/ different species, which improves both resistance and also the protective effect.

Shelterbelts consume more water → But they also help in drainage (where this is a problem) through lowering the ground water table and simultaneously reducing salinity. Appropriate tree species need to be selected and bred.

Key reference(s): Compilation Committee of Inner Mongolia Forest (1989) *Inner Mongolia Forest,* Beijing: China Forestry Publishing House, 1989, 299–319
Contact person(s): Hai Chunxing, College of Geographical Sciences, Inner Mongolia Normal University, No. 295 Zhaowuda Road, Hohhot, Inner Mongolia 010022, People's Republic of China ■ Wang Yaolin, Gansu GEF/OP12 Project Office, Lanzhou, PR China

Grevillea agroforestry system

Kenya – *Mukima / Mubariti*

left: Boundary planting in drier areas of the Mount Kenya region: grevillea provides a variety of ecological and economic benefits and is adapted to different agro-ecological zones. (Hanspeter Liniger)
right: Scattered grevillea trees associated with annual crops protecting slopes by a stream. (Hanspeter Liniger)
For a picture of grevillea lines on terrace risers ('alley cropping'), see page 20.

Multipurpose *Grevillea robusta* trees planted along farm boundaries, on terrace risers and occasionally scattered in cropland.

While *Grevillea robusta* (the 'silky oak', an Australian native tree) was originally introduced from India to East Africa as a shade tree for tea and coffee estates, it is now more commonly associated with small-scale farming areas. There are three main forms of grevillea agroforestry systems: (1) most commonly trees are planted along farm boundaries, initially at a close spacing (0.75–1 m), then later thinned to 1.5–3 m, giving approximately 400 plants/ha; (2) scattered grevillea trees associated with annual or perennial crops: resembling open forests with multi-storey layers; (3) grevillea is sometimes grown in a form of 'alley cropping' on terraces, with 4–8 m interval between the rows and a spacing of 3–5 m within the rows.

Grevillea is primarily used in combination with annual (maize/beans) and perennial crops (coffee). It can be easily propagated and established and is relatively free of pests and diseases. Trees are managed through periodic pollarding – the pruning of side branches (for use) while maintaining the trunk. This gives the visual impression of 'telegraph poles', but competition with crops (which is little, in any case) is reduced and pruned branches rapidly regrow. An additional measure for avoiding competition with crops is to dig a small trench around the trees, thus cutting the superficial roots.

Grevillea is planted for a number of purposes. These include marking property boundaries, supplying fuelwood and building materials, providing shade and for ornamental value. Simultaneously it can control raindrop splash (when an understorey of litter builds up beneath), increases organic matter, and provides mulching materials to improve ground cover in the farm. Grevillea reduces wind speed, and encourages nutrient recycling due to its deep rooting.

While the climate in the case study area is subhumid, and the slopes moderate to steep with soils of medium erodibility, grevillea can be planted over a wide range of agroecological zones – from semi-arid to humid zones, and from sea level up to 2,000 metres and higher. It is ideally suited to intensive areas of small-scale mixed farming, where grevillea is valued primarily for the supply of products (fuel and construction wood in particular) to meet various household needs: it is not mainly targeted at soil erosion control though this is achieved in various ways as explained above. To effectively combat soil erosion problems on slopes, grevillea planting must be combined with additional measures such as *fanya juu* and bench terraces, grass strips and other vegetative and agronomic forms of conservation.

Location: Kiawanja catchment, Nembure division, Embu, Kenya
Technology area: 1.5 km²
SWC measure: vegetative
Land use: cropland (before), mixed: agroforestry (after)
Climate: subhumid
WOCAT database reference: QT KEN16
Related approach: Spontaneous spread, QA KEN08
Compiled by: John Munene Mwaniki, Embu, Kenya/updated by Ceris Jones, Agronomica, UK
Date: September 2002, updated June 2004

Editors' comments: *Grevillea robusta* originates from Australia. It was used in India for shade, and as a windbreak, in tea and coffee estates. Then, during the early 20th century, it was introduced to East Africa for the same purpose. It has gained increasing popularity amongst local farmers since the 1970s, and is now the most common multipurpose agroforestry tree in small-scale farms in the region.

Classification

Land use problems
- land degradation, mainly by water erosion
- soil fertility decline due to continuous cropping and few inputs
- lack of fuelwood, building materials, and other tree related products

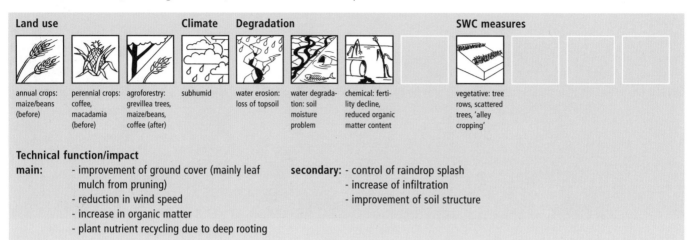

Land use

annual crops: maize/beans (before)

perennial crops: coffee, macadamia (before)

agroforestry: grevillea trees, maize/beans, coffee (after)

Climate

subhumid

Degradation

water erosion: loss of topsoil

water degradation: soil moisture problem

chemical: fertility decline, reduced organic matter content

SWC measures

vegetative: tree rows, scattered trees, 'alley cropping'

Technical function/impact

main:
- improvement of ground cover (mainly leaf mulch from pruning)
- reduction in wind speed
- increase in organic matter
- plant nutrient recycling due to deep rooting

secondary:
- control of raindrop splash
- increase of infiltration
- improvement of soil structure

Environment

Natural environment

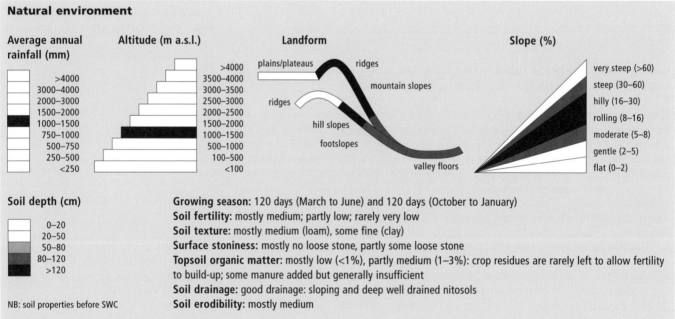

Average annual rainfall (mm)

>4000
3000–4000
2000–3000
1500–2000
1000–1500
750–1000
500–750
250–500
<250

Altitude (m a.s.l.)

>4000
3500–4000
3000–3500
2500–3000
2000–2500
1500–2000
1000–1500
500–1000
100–500
<100

Landform

plains/plateaus, ridges, mountain slopes, ridges, hill slopes, footslopes, valley floors

Slope (%)

very steep (>60)
steep (30–60)
hilly (16–30)
rolling (8–16)
moderate (5–8)
gentle (2–5)
flat (0–2)

Soil depth (cm)

0–20
20–50
50–80
80–120
>120

NB: soil properties before SWC

Growing season: 120 days (March to June) and 120 days (October to January)

Soil fertility: mostly medium; partly low; rarely very low

Soil texture: mostly medium (loam), some fine (clay)

Surface stoniness: mostly no loose stone, partly some loose stone

Topsoil organic matter: mostly low (<1%), partly medium (1–3%): crop residues are rarely left to allow fertility to build-up; some manure added but generally insufficient

Soil drainage: good drainage: sloping and deep well drained nitosols

Soil erodibility: mostly medium

Human environment

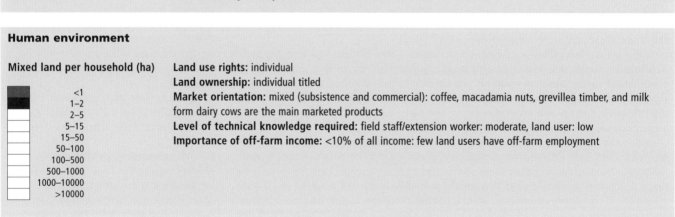

Mixed land per household (ha)

<1
1–2
2–5
5–15
15–50
50–100
100–500
500–1000
1000–10000
>10000

Land use rights: individual

Land ownership: individual titled

Market orientation: mixed (subsistence and commercial): coffee, macadamia nuts, grevillea timber, and milk form dairy cows are the main marketed products

Level of technical knowledge required: field staff/extension worker: moderate, land user: low

Importance of off-farm income: <10% of all income: few land users have off-farm employment

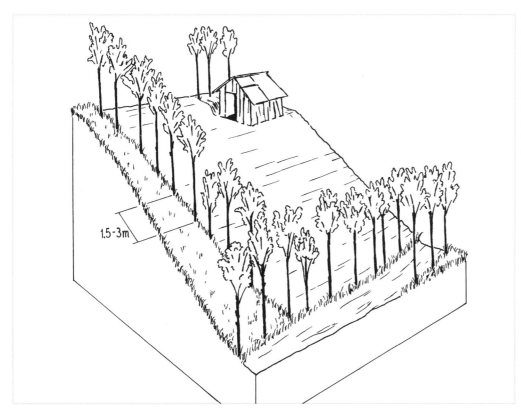

1.5–3m

Implementation activities, inputs and costs

Establishment activities
1. Dig planting pits (before rainy seasons).
2. Purchase seedlings from nurseries/collection of wildings (naturally regenerated seedlings) at onset of rains.
3. Transplant (at onset of rains).

All activities carried out by manual labour using *pangas* (machetes) and hand hoes.

Duration of establishment: 1–2 years

Establishment inputs and costs per ha

Inputs	Costs (US$)	% met by land user
Labour (20 person days)	25	100%
Equipment		
- Tools	10	100%
Agricultural		
- Seedlings of grevillea (1,000)	125	100%
TOTAL	**160**	**100%**

Maintenance/recurrent activities
1. Weeding around seedlings when necessary (rainy season).
2. Pruning as necessary (pruned branches are dried and used for fuelwood): annually.
3. Pollarding (pruning of side branches; ensures large and straight tree trunks): annually, after crop harvest.
4. Root pruning: dig a trench (60 cm from tree, 25 cm deep) and cut the shallow roots to reduced competition with annual crops every four years.
5. Felling some trees to reduce density as they grow bigger (during dry season).
6. Replanting if/when trees are harvested for timber.

All activities carried out by manual labour using machetes *(panga)*, hoes and handsaws.

Maintenance/recurrent inputs and costs per ha per year

Inputs	Costs (US$)	% met by land user
Labour (50 person days)	65	100%
Equipment		
- Tools	25	100%
TOTAL	**90**	**100%**

Remarks: Basis of costing: boundary planting (assuming average plot size of 25 m x 25 m (0.16 ha) and an average spacing of 1 m between trees = 1,000 trees/ha. 1 person plants 50 trees in one day. The labour required for management (pruning and pollarding) of established trees is high. Seedling purchase price is also high, but this can be reduced by collecting 'wildings' (seedlings growing in the wild) as well as establishment of personal or group nurseries.

Assessment

Acceptance/adoption
- 100% of land users (all 120 families in the area) accepted the technology without incentives. Adoption was spontaneous. Men and women are both involved with grevillea: men focus on timber for construction and sale, while women are more concerned with fuelwood.
- There is no longer a trend towards 'growing spontaneous adoption' because all land users in the catchment plant grevillea.

Benefits/costs according to land user	Benefits compared with costs	short-term:	long-term:
	establishment	slightly positive	very positive
	maintenance/recurrent	slightly positive	very positive

Impacts of the technology

Production and socio-economic benefits

+ + +   wood production increase (for timber and fuelwood)

+ +   farm income increase

+   fodder production (leaves provide limited fodder during dry periods)

+   crop yield increase (through mulching and nutrient pumping)

Socio-cultural benefits

+ +   improved knowledge on SWC/erosion (interaction with other stakeholders)

Ecological benefits

+ + +   reduction of wind velocity (windbreaks for crops and homesteads)

+ +   soil cover improvement (mulch and canopy cover)

+ +   microclimate improvement

+ +   increase in soil fertility (leaf litter and nutrient recycling)

+ +   soil loss reduction

+   increase in soil moisture (encouraging infiltration through mulching)

+   biodiversity enhancement (bees, birds, etc)

Other benefits

+ +   improved housing (more timber available)

+   ornamental value

Off-site benefits

+ + +   reduced deforestation (alternative source of fuel and timber)

+ +   creation of employment (through tree management and harvesting)

+   reduced downstream siltation (reduced soil erosion)

+   reduced river pollution (reduced sediment load in the streams)

+   reduced downstream flooding (infiltration encouraged)

+   increased stream flow in dry season

Production and socio-economic disadvantages

– –   increased labour constraints (labour for tree establishment and maintenance can conflict with other activities)

–   reduced production (only where tree management is poor)

–   loss of land (occupies part of cropland) – but compensated by tree products

Socio-cultural disadvantages

–   boundary conflicts (potential for shading neighbours' crops)

Ecological disadvantages

Other disadvantages

– –   growing reliance on single exotic, replacing other local tree species; potential problem of reduced biodiversity

Off-site disadvantages

Concluding statements

Strengths and ➜ how to sustain/improve

Multipurpose tree, meeting various socio-economic needs: provision of fuelwood (for household energy needs) and timber, boundary marking, ornamental function; leaves provide fodder during severe drought ➜ Self-sustaining (no action needed).

Ease of propagation with minimal technical skill ➜ Self-sustaining (no action needed).

Income generation opportunities (eg selling tree products) ➜ Improvement in rural access roads to facilitate transport of tree products and other farm produce to market; encourage diversification: eg furniture making.

Microclimate improvement.

Crop yields are boosted by the tree nutrient recycling, fallen leaves add organic matter on decomposition.

Reduction of runoff and hence soil erosion can be significant. The tree canopy associated with an understorey of litter reduces raindrop impact while the roots hold soil in place.

Weaknesses and ➜ how to overcome

Seedlings and wildings not always readily available ➜ Encourage local seed collection and setting up of group tree nurseries.

Timber susceptibility to pests attack ➜ Timber treatment with appropriate chemicals; breeding of more pest tolerant varieties – particularly against weevils.

Livestock sometimes damage the young seedlings ➜ Protection by fencing.

Dry periods result in low seedling survival rates: planting not possible in dry areas ➜ With water harvesting and moisture management techniques, the technology could spread to lower rainfall areas.

Key reference(s): ICRAF (1992) *A selection of useful trees and shrubs in Kenya.* ICRAF, Nairobi ■ Guto et al (1998) *PRA report, Kiawanja catchment, Nembure division, Embu District-Kenya.* Ministry of Agriculture, Nembure division, Embu ■ Harwood CE (1989) *Grevillea robusta: an annotated bibliography:* ICRAF, Nairobi ■ Rocheleau D, Weber F and Field-Juma A (1988): *Agroforestry in dryland Africa:* ICRAF, Nairobi
http://www.winrock.org/forestry/factpub/factsh/grevillea.htm ■ http://www.ces.uga.edu/pubcd/b949-w.html
Contact person(s): John Munene Mwaniki, Ministry of Agriculture & Rural Development, Box 4, Embu, Kenya; phone ++254-722383771; mwanikijm2002@yahoo.com ■ Ceris Jones, Agronomica, UK; ceris.a.jones@btopenworld.com

Spontaneous spread

Kenya

left: Discussing the relative merits of grevillea planting among farmers and extension agents. (Ceris Jones)
right: Detailed view of a dense grevillea tree row planted along a farm boundary. (Ceris Jones)

Spontaneous land users' initiative to meet household needs – especially firewood and timber – through planting *Grevillea robusta* trees as part of an agroforestry system.

Grevillea robusta is a well-known shade tree, used in coffee and tea plantations in East Africa since the early part of the 20th century. While it originates from Australia, it was brought over from India and Sri Lanka by European settlers. Smallholder farmers in the highlands of Kenya noted that there was little or no competition between grevillea and neighbouring crops. Indeed this is one of the reasons it was so successful as a shade tree amongst plantation crops. Responding to the local lack of timber and firewood, due to the expansion of farmland into previously forested areas, smallholders took to planting grevillea, especially as a boundary tree, from the 1970s onwards. While the immediate effect of grevillea planting was to satisfy those needs for wood, the tree also helps in various ways to conserve land and improve the soil. This too was probably a reason for its spontaneous spread.

Because planting of grevillea requires few resources other than tools, even poor land users can readily adopt the technology. Although seedlings can be bought from local Government, NGO or private nurseries, it is also possible to collect 'wildings' (naturally generated seedlings) and plant these at minimal cost. The management of grevillea trees, once established, is important to their performance in the field, but the skills of thinning, and pollarding (pruning side branches for use) can be easily learned from neighbours. The success of the spontaneous spread of grevillea, basically through farmer-to-farmer exchange of knowledge, demonstrates that tree planting is not something that has always to be 'pushed' by outside agencies. Where smallholders perceive a need for trees and tree products – and an appropriate species is available – they will respond positively. However there is still an important 'pulling' role to be played by the Ministry of Agriculture's extension agents and NGOs, especially through support for tree nurseries and for training to establish private tree nurseries.

Location: Kiawanja catchment, Nembure district, Embu, Kenya
Approach area: 1.5 km²
Land use: cropland (before), mixed: agroforestry (after)
Climate: subhumid
WOCAT database reference: QA KEN08
Related technology: Grevillea agroforestry system, QT KEN16
Compiled by: John Munene Mwaniki, MoA, Embu, Kenya; update by Ceris Jones, Agronomica, UK
Date: May 1999, updated June 2004

Editors' comments: There are few recent examples of the spontaneous spread of sustainable land management practices that have occurred without any significant outside push. The planting by smallholders of *Grevillea robusta* in East Africa, as part of an agroforestry system, is one. In the case study area almost all farmers now plant the multi-purpose grevillea tree.

Problem, objectives and constraints

Problem
- shortage of fuelwood and building materials, environmental degradation
- need for farm boundary marking
- lack of simple, widely applicable agroforestry recommendations

Objectives
- improve availability of tree products (fuelwood and wood for construction)
- demarcate own land easily and cheaply (after land registration)
- reduce land degradation
- increase land productivity
- improve household income

Constraints addressed

Major	Specification	Treatment
Technical/financial	Shortage of tree seedlings and sourced from long distance.	Setting up of individual on-farm tree nurseries and collection of wildlings.
Social/cultural/religious	Boundary planting disagreements.	Agreement between neighbours on planting trees 6 m from their mutual boundaries.

Minor	Specification	Treatment
Social/cultural/religious	Gender bias – women not expected to plant trees.	Although not directly related to this approach, various campaigns were conducted by government and NGOs to encourage gender balance with respect to tree planting.

Participation and decision making

Target groups

Land users

Approach costs met by:

National government	10%
Individual land user	90%
	100%

Decisions on choice of the technology: Made by land users alone (land user-driven initiative by shortages/problems).
Decisions on method of implementing the technology: Made by land users alone (the land user decided on when and how to plant the trees).
Approach designed by: Land users.

Community involvement

Initiation	self-mobilisation	innovative individuals planting grevillea
Planning	self-mobilisation	informal, individual plans
Implementation	self-mobilisation	some support by government
Monitoring/evaluation	passive	ad hoc observations by MoA
Research	none	no activities

Difference in participation between men and women: It was traditionally the role of adult men to purchase, collect and plant trees. This is however changing: other groups – women and youth – are now planting trees as well.

Farmers and extension agents monitoring grevillea tree rows in the field (left). The advantages of the trees are manifold: economically, the most important benefits are production of timber (centre) and firewood (usually through pruning of side branches – 'pollarding' – right). (Hanspeter Linger)

Extension and promotion

Training: Some demonstrations of benefits of tree planting by Government at provincial agricultural shows.
Extension: Informal farmer-to-farmer exchange of ideas and skills. Additionally, on national tree planting days, the government has provided some free seedlings. Grevillea planting has been encouraged during national campaigns (involving the Ministry of Agriculture, the Ministry of Environment and Natural Resources, and NGOs) to encourage soil and water conservation. There is also some collaboration between the Government extension service and KARI (Kenya Agricultural Research Institute) to further promote the technology.
Research: Research has not been part of this approach.
Importance of land use rights: Private land ownership has given farmers confidence to invest the land, and has also been a direct stimulus through the need to mark plot boundaries.

Incentives

Labour: All labour has been provided voluntarily by individual land users.
Inputs: No inputs – apart from some seedlings on national tree planting days – provided.
Credit: No credit has been provided, nor has it been necessary.
Support to local institutions: No support provided.
Long-term impact of incentives: No incentives provided.

Monitoring and evaluation

Monitored aspects	Methods and indicators
Technical	ad hoc observations of management methods by Ministry of Agriculture (MoA) extension staff
Economic/production	ad hoc observations of better housing, and fuelwood supply by MoA extension staff
Area treated	ad hoc observations of tree density by MoA extension staff

Impacts of the approach

Changes as result of monitoring and evaluation: There were no changes.

Improved soil and water management: Moderate improvements through planting of grevillea trees: better soil and water management, increase in soil organic matter levels, nutrient pumping and reduced soil erosion.

Adoption of the approach by other projects/land users: Some other extension programmes are utilising individual initiatives as an entry point.

Sustainability: As land users developed this approach they can continue activities without support.

Concluding statements

Strengths and ➔ how to sustain/improve	Weaknesses and ➔ how to overcome
Self-driven initiative ➔ MoA extension staff and land users to encourage other farmers to be self-reliant.	Adoption rates under such approaches depend on the number and efforts of innovators to stimulate others ➔ SWC extensionists (Ministry and NGOs) to undertake more community mobilisation and awareness raising.
Very low inputs (resources) required. However there is still an important 'pulling' role to be played by the Ministry of Agriculture's extension agents and NGOs ➔ More support for individual and government tree nurseries.	Approach is dependent on social cohesiveness for dissemination ➔ Promote more farmer interaction at community level.
Incentives not necessary.	Poor collaboration and institutional linkages ➔ Encourage and create forums where stakeholders can share experiences and inform land users about where to seek additional information and assistance.
Adaptability, flexibility and simplicity since it is user driven.	
Strong land user 'ownership' of the approach.	
Valuable lessons from a farmer-driven success for development agencies that promote tree planting and agroforestry systems.	

Key reference(s): Njiru NN et al (1998) *Participatory Rural Appraisal report of Kiawanja catchment.* Nembure District, Eastern Province ▪
See 'Grevillea agroforestry system' case study for technical references
Contact person(s): JM Mwaniki, Ministry of Agriculture/Soil and Water Conservation Branch, Embu, Kenya; mwanikijm2002@yahoo.com ▪
Ceris Jones, Agronomica, UK; ceris.a.jones@btopenworld.com

Poplar trees for bio-drainage

Kyrgyzstan - *Выращивание тополя на заболоченных и сильно засоленных почвах*

left: Lines of hybrid poplar trees, 15 years old. Soil around the poplars is much drier: at a distance of around 20 m the soil is moist and covered by reeds. (Hanspeter Liniger)
right: Training in the field: a researcher explains the impact of the poplar system on the groundwater level to a group of students. (Hanspeter Liniger)

Poplars planted to lower the ground water table and reduce salinity where irrigation drainage systems have broken down; lucerne cultivated between the tree lines.

In irrigated areas of Central Asia, the drainage system introduced during soviet times has broken down due to lack of maintenance. As a result, water tables have been rising and soil salinity increasing. In the Chui Valley, which is the main crop production area in Kyrgyzstan, approximately 90% of the cultivated land is irrigated for wheat, maize, sugar beet, lucerne and vegetables. Of this, approximately one third (ca. 320,000 ha) is degraded due to loss of fertility, salinisation and waterlogging.

The individual initiative described here – poplar planting – has been applied on a degraded plain (about 400 m a.s.l.), under semi-arid conditions on a plot of 5 hectares. Though initially planted for timber, an important side effect was noted by the farmer in question. Poplar trees, well known for their tolerance to waterlogging and salinity, provide 'bio-drainage'. Excess water is rapidly taken up by the root system and transpired through the dense foliage. Within the plantation the humidity level of the lower layers of air is increased, thus reducing the influence of the dry, hot winds. A more favourable microclimate for plant growth is thus created. Simultaneously the original purpose of planting – to obtain cheap timber and firewood – is achieved through the rapid growth of the trees: there is a severe shortage of wood locally.

The varieties used include the local *Populus alba* and *Populus nigra* as well as a hybrid from Kazakhstan, *P. pyramidalis*. The trees are planted in rows about 5 metres wide, separated by 10–15 metre strips planted with *Medicago sativa* (lucerne) and *Bromus inermis* (a grass), both of which are grown for hay (see technical drawing). Around 3,000 saplings are needed per hectare. The young poplars require irrigating during the first year before their roots can reach the water table. The trees are weeded and their lower branches pruned to encourage straight and fast growth. They are thinned twice before they are 14 years old: these thinnings can be sold. The poplars then remain until they are 20–25 years old and suitable for felling. The output of commercial timber of a poplar plantation is 3,000 m² per hectare (1 m² per mature tree). Slow-growing/sick trees, as well as pruned branches, are used as firewood - which can amount to 20–30 m³ per hectare. The cycle begins again after approximately 10 years, when new saplings are planted between the existing, thinned, lines of poplars. Desalinisation of the soil takes 10 years or a little longer, when it again becomes suitable for irrigated cereal cropping.

Location: Besh-Terek, Chui valley, Kyrgyzstan
Technology area: 0.05 km²
SWC measure: vegetative and agronomic
Land use: wasteland (before), mixed: agroforestry (after)
Climate: semi-arid (harsh continental)
WOCAT database reference: QT KYR01
Related approach: not documented
Compiled by: Budaychiev Dayr, Asanaliev Abdybek, Sydykbaev Talant, Bishkek, Kyrgyzstan
Date: January 2004, updated May 2004

Editors' comments: Some trees are known to drain ground water and lower water tables. Eucalyptus is perhaps the best-known example. This case study shows how one farmer in Kyrgyzstan originally planted poplar trees for wood. The effect of lowering the water table and reducing salinity was only realised later on. It shows great potential where groundwater tables have risen due to failures in maintaining conventional drainage systems.

Classification

Land use problems

Irrigation drainage systems have deteriorated (silted up, choked with weeds and reeds) due to lack of maintenance. This has led to a raised water table, waterlogging and increased salinity, thus seriously affecting productivity and making cultivation of some crops impossible. Farmers' incomes have significantly reduced as a result.

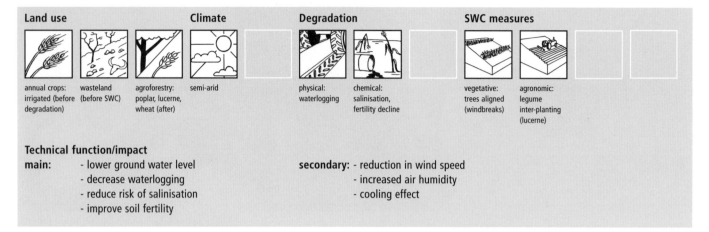

Land use

annual crops: irrigated (before degradation)

wasteland (before SWC)

agroforestry: poplar, lucerne, wheat (after)

Climate

semi-arid

Degradation

physical: waterlogging

chemical: salinisation, fertility decline

SWC measures

vegetative: trees aligned (windbreaks)

agronomic: legume inter-planting (lucerne)

Technical function/impact

main:
- lower ground water level
- decrease waterlogging
- reduce risk of salinisation
- improve soil fertility

secondary:
- reduction in wind speed
- increased air humidity
- cooling effect

Environment

Natural environment

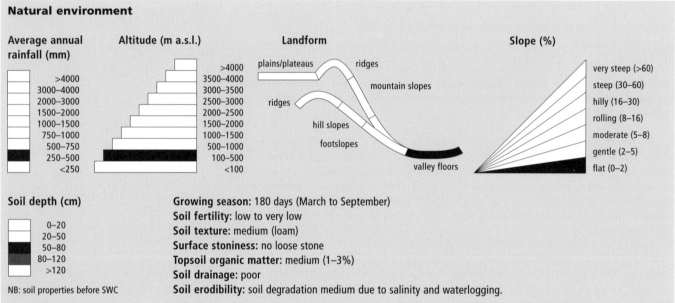

Average annual rainfall (mm)

>4000
3000–4000
2000–3000
1500–2000
1000–1500
750–1000
500–750
250–500
<250

Altitude (m a.s.l.)

>4000
3500–4000
3000–3500
2500–3000
2000–2500
1500–2000
1000–1500
500–1000
100–500
<100

Landform

plains/plateaus, ridges, mountain slopes, ridges, hill slopes, footslopes, valley floors

Slope (%)

very steep (>60)
steep (30–60)
hilly (16–30)
rolling (8–16)
moderate (5–8)
gentle (2–5)
flat (0–2)

Soil depth (cm)

0–20
20–50
50–80
80–120
>120

NB: soil properties before SWC

Growing season: 180 days (March to September)
Soil fertility: low to very low
Soil texture: medium (loam)
Surface stoniness: no loose stone
Topsoil organic matter: medium (1–3%)
Soil drainage: poor
Soil erodibility: soil degradation medium due to salinity and waterlogging.

Human environment

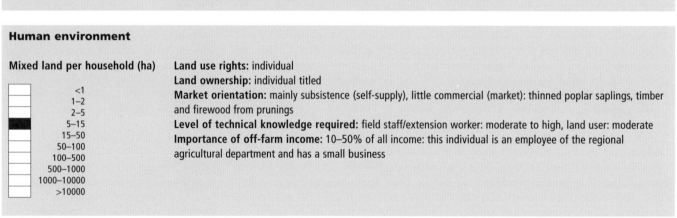

Mixed land per household (ha)

<1
1–2
2–5
5–15
15–50
50–100
100–500
500–1000
1000–10000
>10000

Land use rights: individual
Land ownership: individual titled
Market orientation: mainly subsistence (self-supply), little commercial (market): thinned poplar saplings, timber and firewood from prunings
Level of technical knowledge required: field staff/extension worker: moderate to high, land user: moderate
Importance of off-farm income: 10–50% of all income: this individual is an employee of the regional agricultural department and has a small business

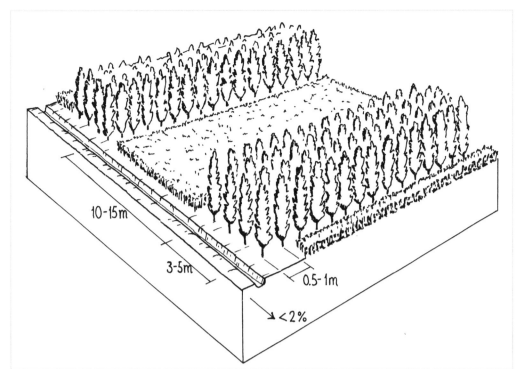

Technical drawing
Alternating strips of poplar trees for bio-drainage, and lucerne for fodder. Drainage channels (left) are spaced at 50 metres apart.

10-15m

3-5m

0.5-1m

<2%

Implementation activities, inputs and costs

Establishment activities

1. Set up tree nursery one year before planting: take cuttings about 25–30 cm long with 3 buds above the ground and plant.
2. Demarcate lines in field.
3. Dig drainage trenches in the marshy area (50 cm deep, 50 cm wide, 50 m apart) with tractor (end of summer, early autumn).
4. Plough where seedlings of the poplars are to be planted.
5. Transplant tree seedlings from the nursery to the field in spring.
6. Irrigate the seedlings by furrow for one year.
7. Protect the area from animals.
8. Plant lucerne (sown by machine in first year after planting of poplars).

Duration of establishment phase: 1–2 years

Establishment inputs and costs per ha

Inputs	Costs (US$)	% met by land user
Labour (150 person days)	350	100%
Equipment		
- Machines (ploughing, drainage: 30 hours)	100	100%
- Animal traction (transportation of seedlings)	5	100%
- Tools: shovel, axe, saw	15	100%
Agricultural		
- Seeds (10 kg)	20	100%
- Seedlings (about 3,000)	350	100%
- Nursery (preparation of land, weed control)	80	100%
TOTAL (rounded)	**920**	**100%**

Maintenance/recurrent activities

1. Prune lower branches of the trees to encourage tall and straight growth.
2. Continue protection of the plot (because of lucerne).
3. Cut lucerne for hay 4 times per year (mechanically).
4. Weed control by hand (main weeds are *Chenopodium album*, *Capsella bursa-pastoris*, and *Agropyron repens*).

Maintenance/recurrent inputs and costs per ha per year

Inputs	Costs (US$)	% met by land user
Labour (10 person days)	25	100%
Equipment		
- Machines (2 hours)	5	100%
- Tools: shovel, axe, saw (already owned by farmer)	0	
TOTAL	**30**	**100%**

Remarks: Labour for establishment and maintenance are provided by the farmer and his family. After 10–15 years trees are thinned for timber and the cycle begins again – with reduced establishment costs: new saplings are planted between the existing, thinned, lines of poplars. On two sides the plot is protected by a drainage ditch and a concrete canal protect the plot respectively. Furthermore, there is an agreement with the neighbours not to let the animals graze the lucerne. However after the last cut of lucerne animals are allowed to graze the plot.

Assessment

Acceptance/adoption

A single farmer has developed this technology. It should be possible to spread the technology among other farmers but financial support (eg interest-free credit) will need to be provided. A recent assessment has showed that there is growing interest in the system by farmers in the region. Additionally, in the lower Yanvan Valley of Tajikistan, a similar bio-drainage system has been described - using poplars and mulberry trees. In that situation wheat is planted in association with the trees.

Benefits/costs according to land user	Benefits compared with costs	short-term:	long-term:
	establishment	negative	very positive
	maintenance/recurrent	positive	very positive

Impacts of the technology

Production and socio-economic benefits	Production and socio-economic disadvantages
+ + + wood production increase	− − main benefit (timber) only after 10–15 years, however, short-term benefit from lucerne as fodder and from firewood through pruning
+ + + increased crop production (after desalinisation of soil)	
+ + fodder production/quality increase (lucerne between tree lines)	− increased input constraints: not all the farmers have enough resources for introduction of this technology (equipment, seedlings)
+ + farm income increase	
+ + reclamation of degraded land	− increased labour constraints for establishment

Socio-cultural benefits	Socio-cultural disadvantages
+ + + improved knowledge SWC/erosion	none

Ecological benefits	Ecological disadvantages
+ + + draining of excess water and thus lowering of water table (1 m) through increased evapotranspiration	− increased danger of fire
+ + increase of soil fertility (due to lucerne: 100–130 kg of N are accumulated per 3 years; soil structure is improved, acidity is lowered, waterlogging and salinity are reduced)	
+ biodiversity enhancement	
+ reduction of wind velocity	
+ increased air humidity (less dry and hot winds)	

Off-site benefits	Off-site disadvantages
+ + reduction in wind velocity	none
+ + general drop of water table	

Concluding statements

Strengths and ➜ how to sustain/improve	Weaknesses and ➜ how to overcome
Positive ecological effect: salinity and area of marshy land can be reduced and waterlogged soils reclaimed ➜ Awareness raising and training of farmers to show the effect of poplar trees on reduction of waterlogging and salinisation.	The implementation of the technology is not possible for all land users due to input and labour constraints ➜ Financial support, better organisation/share of equipment.
Rapid benefit through the production of lucerne and grass. Long-term production of valuable firewood and timber (both are in short supply) ➜ Show the economic benefits of additional lucerne production and timber and firewood; demonstrate marketing opportunities.	Major benefit from timber production comes only after 25 years ➜ Create awareness about additional short-term benefits, especially firewood and fodder, as well as the long-term effects and the sustainability of the system.
	Cannot be replicated by all farmers in the valley at the same density as the market for trees (timber, firewood) will be saturated, and trees can never completely take the place of irrigated food crops: nevertheless the benefits will extend to those growers through the drainage function of the poplars ➜ A new overall production system will have to be worked out for the region.
	The case reported here works in its current design because of its isolated 'island effect': if more farmer grew poplar, the same bio-drainage effect could be achieved over the whole valley at a lower density of trees per unit area, implying a larger proportion of cultivable land.

Key reference(s): Budaychiev D (2002) The prospects for hybrid poplar forest plantations. Resolving problems and the strategy of reforming agrarian science. *News of Kyrgyz Agrarian Academy* Vol. 2, Issue 3, 4.1 Bishkek

Contact person(s): Asanaliev Abdybek and Sydykbaev Talant, Kyrgyz Agrarian University, 68 Mederov St, 720005 Bishkek, Kyrgyzstan; phone ++996(312) 547894; asanaly61@mall.ru, s.talant_n@mall.ru ■ Budaychiev Dair Kyrgyz Agrarian University, 68 Mederov St, 720005 Bishkek, Kyrgyzstan; phone ++996(312) 216279

Multi-storey cropping

Philippines – *Maramihang pagtatanim*

Cultivating a mixture of crops with different heights (multi-storey) and growth characteristics which together optimise the use of soil, moisture and space.

Under the *maramihang pagtatanim* multi-storey cropping system, perennial crops (coconut, banana, coffee, papaya, pineapple) and annuals/biennials (root crops: taro, yam, sweet potato etc) are interplanted to maximise productivity and income. This is most applicable where farms are small and the system needs to be intensive. In this particular area, Cavite, coconuts are usually planted first. When they reach a height of 4.5 meters (after 3–4 years), bananas, coffee and/or papaya are planted underneath. Black pepper may also be part of the system. After sufficient space has developed at ground level in about three to four years, root crops are planted. At full establishment, the system develops different layers: coconut (tallest) followed by banana, coffee, papaya (middle), root crops and pineapple (lowest). In recent years, because of its relatively low productivity and decreasing price, coconut has tended to be replaced in the system with higher value crops like the fruit tree *santol (Sandoricum koetjape)*, papaya and sometimes black pepper. However most multi-storey farms adhere to no specific planting layout.

The multi-storey agroforestry system is intended to make the best use of resources (soil, moisture and space) for increased farm income. It is also very effective against soil erosion. Previously, continuous monocropping of annual crops resulted in erosion and serious soil fertility decline. Even though the land is sloping and rainfall during the monsoon is extremely intensive, multi-storey cropping provides adequate soil cover throughout the year, protecting the land from erosion.

Fertilization, weeding and pruning are necessary elements of maintenance. 'Natural' mulching through fallen leaves from leguminous trees helps restore and maintain soil fertility The system is applied in a volcanic-derived soil with distinct wet and dry periods (6 months wet season, 6 months dry season). There is the risk of a destructive typhoon every 10 years. Farm income is relatively high, but labour and input costs are also high – and the technology is mostly used by relatively wealthy landowners. There is strong spontaneous adoption, as *maramihang pagtatanim* has been proven to be effective and remunerative. This technology has been practiced in Cavite since the 1970s. Implementation is by individual farmers with strong extension support from the Local Government Units (LGUs), NGOs and the Cavite State University.

Location: Cavite, Philippines
Technology area: 40 km²
SWC measure: vegetative and agronomic
Land use: cropland (before); mixed: agroforestry (after)
Climate: humid
WOCAT database reference: QT PHI07
Related approach: not documented
Compiled by: Jose Rondal, Quezon City, Philippines
Date: July 2001, updated July 2004

Editors' comments: Multi-storey cropping occurs in many parts of the world. It is a highly intensive and productive use of cropland, and is most often found in 'home gardens' of the subhumid and humid tropics. The system described here is a case study from Cavite, in the Philippines – with a combination of four or more crops in three main storeys. This system shares elements with the *Café arbolado* reported from Costa Rica.

Classification

Land use problems
Productivity decline, unstable prices of agricultural products and high costs of inputs are the main land use problems. Inputs also have to be increased to maintain the same yield level in annual cropping systems. There is a severe land use competition: a large proportion of the land is being converted to non-agricultural uses, especially residential and industrial areas because of the proximity to the rapidly expanding capital.

Land use		Climate		Degradation			SWC measures	
annual crops: mainly vegetables (before)	agroforestry: various crops and trees (after)	humid		water erosion: loss of topsoil	chemical: fertility decline		vegetative: tree/shrub cover (multi-storey, aligned)	agronomic: better soil cover by vegetation, chem. fertilizer

Technical function/impact
main: - improvement of ground cover
- control of raindrop splash

secondary: - control of dispersed runoff (impede/retard)
- increase in organic matter

Environment

Natural environment

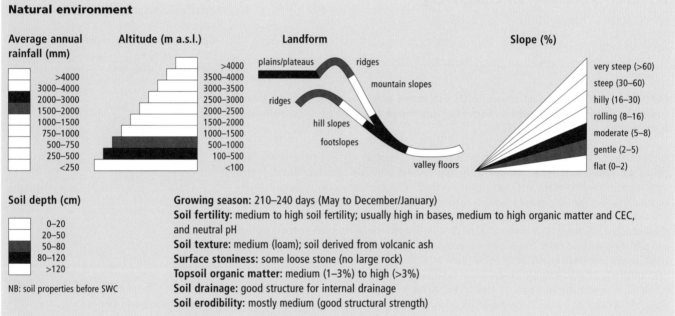

Average annual rainfall (mm)
>4000
3000–4000
2000–3000
1500–2000
1000–1500
750–1000
500–750
250–500
<250

Altitude (m a.s.l.)
>4000
3500–4000
3000–3500
2500–3000
2000–2500
1500–2000
1000–1500
500–1000
100–500
<100

Landform: plains/plateaus, ridges, mountain slopes, ridges, hill slopes, footslopes, valley floors

Slope (%)
very steep (>60)
steep (30–60)
hilly (16–30)
rolling (8–16)
moderate (5–8)
gentle (2–5)
flat (0–2)

Soil depth (cm)
0–20
20–50
50–80
80–120
>120

NB: soil properties before SWC

Growing season: 210–240 days (May to December/January)
Soil fertility: medium to high soil fertility; usually high in bases, medium to high organic matter and CEC, and neutral pH
Soil texture: medium (loam); soil derived from volcanic ash
Surface stoniness: some loose stone (no large rock)
Topsoil organic matter: medium (1–3%) to high (>3%)
Soil drainage: good structure for internal drainage
Soil erodibility: mostly medium (good structural strength)

Human environment

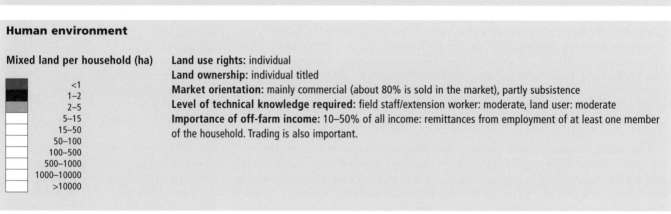

Mixed land per household (ha)
<1
1–2
2–5
5–15
15–50
50–100
100–500
500–1000
1000–10000
>10000

Land use rights: individual
Land ownership: individual titled
Market orientation: mainly commercial (about 80% is sold in the market), partly subsistence
Level of technical knowledge required: field staff/extension worker: moderate, land user: moderate
Importance of off-farm income: 10–50% of all income: remittances from employment of at least one member of the household. Trading is also important.

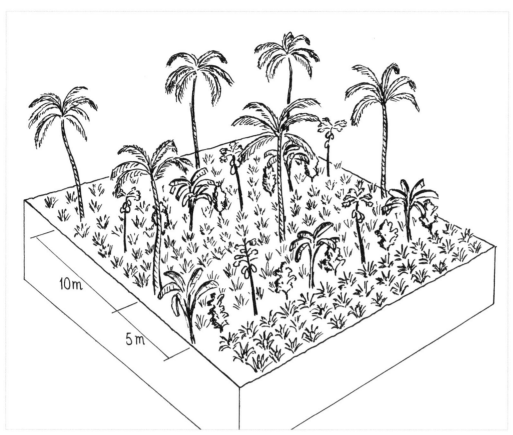

Technical drawing
Multi-storey cropping includes various species interplanted systematically to optimise use of resources: pineapple and other root crops (lowest storey); rows of banana trees, coffee and papaya (middle storey); rows of coconut (highest storey).
Note: in practice farmers adjust this layout to meet their needs.

Implementation activities, inputs and costs

Establishment activities

1. Planting of tallest storey (coconut).
2. Planting of middle storey (coffee and banana).
3. Planting of lowest storey (pineapple).
4. Planting of lowest storey continued (root crops).

All activities are carried out in the early rainy season by manual labour, using animal draft wooden plough, machete, iron bar and spade. Animal ploughing is used for pineapples. 'Natural' mulching through fallen leaves from leguminous trees helps restore and maintain soil fertility.

In some cases, all the crop components are planted at the same time. Coffee and banana are considered permanent (20 years for coffee) while papaya, pineapple and root crops are of shorter duration.

Duration of establishment: 4–5 years

Establishment inputs and costs per ha

Inputs	Costs (US$)	% met by land user
Labour (50 person days) only for land preparation and planting	150	100%
Equipment		
- Animal traction (32 hours)	50	100%
- Tools	40	100%
Agricultural		
- Seedlings	840	100%
- Fertilizers (1,000 kg)	160	100%
- Biocides (5 kg)	30	100%
- Compost/manure (1,000 kg)	120	100%
TOTAL	**1,390**	**100%**

Maintenance/recurrent activities

1. Pruning.
2. Weeding.
3. Harvesting.
4. Spraying.
5. Fertilizing.

Simple tools as machetes, wooden ploughs and harrows are used, as in the establishment phase.

Maintenance/recurrent inputs and costs per ha per year

Inputs	Costs (US$)	% met by land user
Labour (100 person days)	300	100%
Agricultural		
- Fertilizers (1,000 kg)	160	100%
- Biocides (5 kg)	30	100%
TOTAL	**490**	**100%**

Remarks: Cost was calculated assuming a per hectare population of 100 coconuts, 400 coffee plants and 3,000 pineapples. Maintenance activities entail more work than during the establishment phase. Note that the establishment phase usually lasts for 4–5 years, so the labour is spread, unlike during the maintenance phase when all of the components have to be attended to.

Assessment

Acceptance/adoption
All of the land users (1,000 families) who have implemented the technology have done it without incentives. These are land-owners with a high income. There is strong spontaneous adoption as the technology has been proven to be very effective.

Benefits/costs according to land user	Benefits compared with costs	short-term:	long-term:
	establishment	slightly positive	very positive
	maintenance/recurrent	very positive	very positive

Impacts of the technology

Production and socio-economic benefits
+ + + crop yield increase due to high plant population (density)
+ + + farm income increase

Production and socio-economic disadvantages
– – – increased labour constraints during planting/harvesting
– – – increased input constraints (system is capital intensive)

Socio-cultural benefits
+ + + improved knowledge SWC/erosion
+ + community institution strengthening through the formation of cooperatives or farmers organisation
+ + national institution strengthening through the involvement of line agencies and strengthening of research component of research institutions

Socio-cultural disadvantages
none

Ecological benefits
+ + + soil cover improvement (almost 100% soil cover)
+ + + increase in soil fertility (organic matter accumulation)
+ + + soil loss reduction (reduced runoff)
+ biodiversity enhancement
+ reduction of wind velocity

Ecological disadvantages
none

Other benefits
+ + + increase in knowledge of crop production system, especially for small size farms

Other disadvantages
none

Off-site benefits
+ + reduced downstream flooding (reduced runoff)
+ + reduced downstream siltation
+ + reduced river pollution

Off-site disadvantages
none

Concluding statements

Strengths and → how to sustain/improve

Generates high farm income → Continue strong extension service - especially for pest and disease control.

The technology is flexible. It can be modified to suit market condition. Failure of one crop component can be compensated by other components (improved food security) → Try other high value crops as possible component of the system. Diversify further.

It maintains soil fertility through the recycling of nutrients → Incorporate tree legumes in the system (eg gliricidia as support for black pepper).

It is a very effective way of using and conserving water → Establish trash line along farm boundaries to add to this effect.

Strong research and development: because of its importance in the economy, the technology has spawned various research activities → Adequate and sustained government support.

Weaknesses and → how to overcome

High investment cost → Government to provide low interest production loans (seeds, fertilizers).

Highly fluctuating farm prices → Spread out production schedule. Target off-season harvesting of crop (eg pineapple).

Pest and diseases (eg papaya virus, which may have developed because it has been part of the system for a long time) → Intensified research and development.

Prone to typhoon damage → Establishment of windbreaks: Leguminous trees such as Acacias could provide wind protection for lower crops like papaya or coffee.

High labour requirement (eg weeding, harvesting). Weeding may be reduced for some components (eg coffee), but pineapple always requires difficult (due to its thorny leaves) and intensive weeding → (1) Use labour-reducing techniques (eg mulching), (2) spread activities over the growing season.

Key reference(s): FAO and IIRR (1995) *Resource management for upland areas in Southeast Asia.* FARM Field Document 2. Food and Agriculture Organisation of the United Nations, Bangkok, Thailand and International Institute of Rural Reconstruction, Silang, Cavite, Philippines.
Contact person(s): Jose Rondal, Bureau of Soils and Water Management, Diliman, Quezon City, Philippines; joserondal@yahoo.com

Intensive agroforestry system

Colombia – *Silvoagricultura*

A protective and productive high-input agroforestry system comprising multi-purpose ditches with bunds, live barriers of grass, contour ridging, annual crops and fruit trees.

The intensive agroforestry system *(silvoagricultura)* combines traditional and newly developed practices adapted to the area's conditions. The idea is to concentrate cropping on a limited area, a plot of 0.4 ha per household, in a highly integrated, intensive and diversified continuous land use system, thereby integrating soil and water conservation – specifically avoiding traditional slash and burn practices.

Each 'agroforestry plot' comprises four to five 50 cm wide and 40 m long multi-purpose ditches that are excavated along the contour, 6 to 12 m apart, depending on the slope. The ditches retain runoff water which infiltrates the soil, thus reducing erosion and improving soil moisture. They also act as compost ditches for all types of organic residues on the farm. Residues, enriched with manure (from chickens and guinea pigs) are tipped into the ditches, and within 8 to 12 months this decomposes into a fertile medium for the cultivation of vegetables and other crops.

Grass strips are planted on the earth bund on the upper side of the ditch for stabilisation of the structure, retention of runoff and capture of eroded sediment. The grass is cut several times a year to feed guinea pigs, which in turn recycle this into manure. On the lower side of the contour ditches, fruit trees and bananas are planted. Rows of multipurpose trees (mainly indigenous species) are planted around each agroforestry plot as a windbreak and for economic reasons: yielding fruit and timber. Between the structures, annual (and semi-perennial) crops are grown on hand-dug micro-terraces/ridges, again sited along the contour. Some farmers intercrop with legumes. Supportive technologies are protection of wells, afforestation and, where possible, irrigation to enhance production. Production is based on principles of organic farming.

High initial inputs of external manure are subsidised by the project (CISEC; see associated approach). The remainder of each farmer's land is left to natural regeneration, reforested, or where needed, used for conventional cropping. The main purpose is to increase and diversify production, and at the same time to protect natural resources and regenerate degraded areas.

The system is implemented on degraded and often steep slopes in subhumid areas where intensive rainfall and dry periods alternate. The land is officially owned communally (an 'Indigenous Reserve'), but land use rights are individual. The region has a high population density: people are basically of indigenous origin and live in very poor conditions.

left: Combination of structural measures (multi-purpose ditches), vegetative measures (tree lines, grass strips) and agronomic measures (compost production, intercropping). (Mats Gurtner)
right: The highly integrated and diversified land use system is concentrated on a 0.4 ha plot, while adjacent land is left to regenerate naturally. The tree belt around the plot is not yet established. (Mats Gurtner)

Location: Resguardo Indígena Las Canoas, Santander de Quilichao, Cauca, Colombia
Technology area: 1.2 km²
SWC measure: structural, vegetative and agronomic
Land use: wasteland (before), mixed: agroforestry (after)
Climate: subhumid
WOCAT database reference: QT COL02
Related approach: Integrated rural community development, QA COL02
Compiled by: Jairo Cuervo, CISEC, Cali, Colombia
Date: July 1998, updated July 2004

Editors' comments:
This new and promising high-input agroforestry system combines traditional and new elements in relation to Colombia. The emphasis is on protection with production. There are interesting similarities with agroforestry systems reported from Kenya, Costa Rica and the Philippines.

Classification

Land use problems
- soil degradation/reduced soil fertility
- inappropriate soil management: monoculture, slash and burn, no or short fallow periods
- intensive rainfall on steep, unprotected slopes
- drought and wind erosion in dry season
- lack of economic resources
- high population density

Land use		Climate		Degradation				SWC measures			

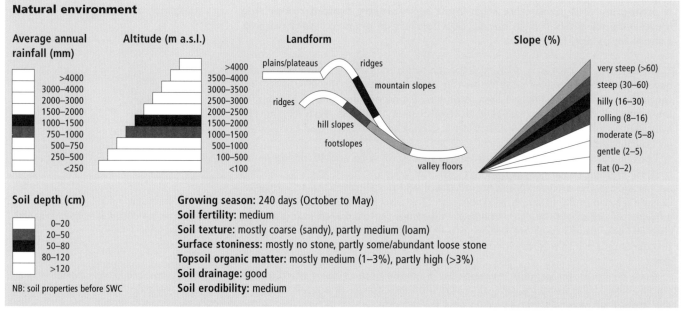

Land use: wasteland: degraded land (before) | agroforestry: fruit trees, bananas, maize, legumes (after)

Climate: subhumid

Degradation: chemical: fertility decline | water erosion: loss of topsoil | wind erosion: loss of topsoil

SWC measures: structural: level bunds/ ditches; micro-terrace | vegetative: aligned trees, grass strips | agronomic: compost, intercropping, manuring

Technical function/impact

main:
- control of dispersed runoff
- increase in organic matter
- reduction of slope length
- increase/maintain water stored in soil
- increase in soil fertility

secondary:
- improvement of ground cover
- control of raindrop splash
- reduction in wind speed
- increase of infiltration
- reduction of slope angle
- sediment harvesting

Environment

Natural environment

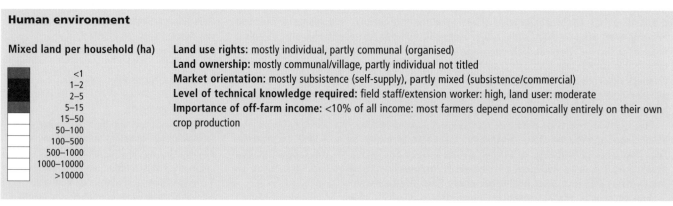

Average annual rainfall (mm): >4000, 3000–4000, 2000–3000, 1500–2000, 1000–1500, 750–1000, 500–750, 250–500, <250

Altitude (m a.s.l.): >4000, 3500–4000, 3000–3500, 2500–3000, 2000–2500, 1500–2000, 1000–1500, 500–1000, 100–500, <100

Landform: plains/plateaus, ridges, mountain slopes, ridges, hill slopes, footslopes, valley floors

Slope (%): very steep (>60), steep (30–60), hilly (16–30), rolling (8–16), moderate (5–8), gentle (2–5), flat (0–2)

Soil depth (cm): 0–20, 20–50, 50–80, 80–120, >120

NB: soil properties before SWC

Growing season: 240 days (October to May)
Soil fertility: medium
Soil texture: mostly coarse (sandy), partly medium (loam)
Surface stoniness: mostly no stone, partly some/abundant loose stone
Topsoil organic matter: mostly medium (1–3%), partly high (>3%)
Soil drainage: good
Soil erodibility: medium

Human environment

Mixed land per household (ha): <1, 1–2, 2–5, 5–15, 15–50, 50–100, 100–500, 500–1000, 1000–10000, >10000

Land use rights: mostly individual, partly communal (organised)
Land ownership: mostly communal/village, partly individual not titled
Market orientation: mostly subsistence (self-supply), partly mixed (subsistence/commercial)
Level of technical knowledge required: field staff/extension worker: high, land user: moderate
Importance of off-farm income: <10% of all income: most farmers depend economically entirely on their own crop production

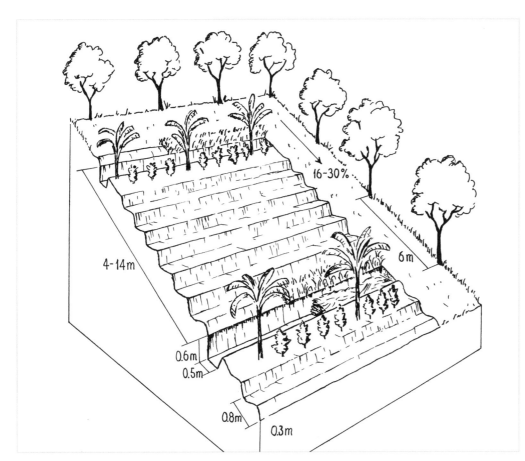

Technical drawing
Detailed overview of the complex and intensive high-input, high-output agroforestry system, usually limited to an area of 64 x 64 metres. The agroforestry plots are bordered by trees of various species. Note the multipurpose ditches that serve as compost pits (lower ditch, right). Associated bunds are covered by grass (right).

Implementation activities, inputs and costs

Establishment activities
During the dry season (June to September):
1. Clear land (only slashing, no burning).
2. Determine contours with A-frame, spacing between structures depends on slope (4 m between ditches on steepest slopes, 14 m on gentle slopes).
3. Dig ditches, build bunds above, and dig holes for tree seedlings.
4. Establish micro-terraces/ridges (earth enriched with manure and residues: all structures along the contour).
5. Fill ditches with organic residues, adding earth mixed with manure.

Beginning of rainy season (April):
6. Plant grass strips on the bund (for stabilisation of structure).
7. Plant fruit/banana trees and legumes below the bunds.
8. Plant fruit and timber trees along the boundaries of the agroforestry plot (life fence/wind break).

Duration of establishment: 1 year

Establishment inputs and costs per plot*

Inputs	Costs (US$)	% met by land user
Labour (44 person days)	220	100%
Equipment		
- Tools: machete, shovel, pickaxes, A-frame, planting stick (chuzo)	0	
Agricultural		
- Seeds (6 kg)	15	5%
- Seedlings (920)	450	5%
- Compost/manure (14 t)	600	5%
TOTAL	**1285**	**21%**

Maintenance/recurrent activities
1. Cut grass (4–6 times/year, grass used to feed guinea pigs).
2. Control weeds (3 times/year).
3. Rebuild/repair structures (dry season).
4. Fill ditches with organic material, residues (after harvest), manure, etc and let it decompose.
5. Plant vegetables on fertile composted earth in ditches (dry season, optional).
6. Dig out compost and spread (beginning of growing season (September).
7. Apply additional fertilizer/manure (3 times/year).
8. Plant various crops: contour cropping, intercropping, integrate green manures (legumes).

Maintenance/recurrent inputs and costs per plot* per year

Inputs	Costs (US$)	% met by land user
Labour (20 person days)	100	100%
Equipment:		
- Tools: machete, shovel, etc	0	
Agricultural		
- Fertilizers (1,000 kg)	45	100%
TOTAL	**145**	**100%**

* plot size is 0.4 ha

Remarks: As an exception in this case study costs are calculated per plot and not per ha, since establishment is strictly limited to an area of 0.4 ha per household. The remaining area is not treated but left for natural regeneration of vegetation or conventional farming (if needed). Labour costs vary according to slope: a typical/average situation is given in the tables above (no further details available). Note that for comparison purposes with other technologies on a per hectare basis these costs would equate to US$ 3,135 for establishment and US$ 355 for maintenance.

Assessment

Acceptance/adoption
- All of the land users who accepted the technology (260 families) did so with incentives.
- The project gives educational assistance, training, technical assistance in the field, manure and seeds/seedlings and the starting capital for a revolving fund that helps in buying the inputs needed to maintain the initiative (this fund is managed by the land users themselves). In exchange the land users have to work on the demonstration areas of the local research plots of the investigation centre (CISEC). They also have to meet the conditions implemented by the project (timing of activities, layout of technology, etc).
- There is a slight growing spontaneous adoption by land users living outside the approach area.

Benefits/costs according to land user		Benefits compared with costs	short-term:	long-term:
		establishment	positive	very positive
		maintenance/recurrent	positive	very positive

Impacts of the technology

Production and socio-economic benefits
+ + + crop yield increase
+ + fodder production/quality increase
+ + improved nutrition (household level)
+ farm income increase
+ wood production increase

Production and socio-economic disadvantages
– – increased labour constraints
– increased economic inequity
– increased input constraints

Socio-cultural benefits
+ + + improved knowledge SWC/erosion
+ + community institution strengthening

Socio-cultural disadvantages
– socio-cultural conflicts (friction between participants and non-participants)

Ecological benefits
+ + + soil loss reduction
+ + + biodiversity enhancement
+ + + increased diversification
+ + soil cover improvement
+ + increase in soil moisture
+ + increase in soil fertility
+ + increase in pest control
+ reduction of wind velocity

Ecological disadvantages
– – increased soil acidity (high content of organic matter)

Off-site benefits
+ reduced transported sediments
+ reduced downstream siltation
+ reduced river pollution

Off-site disadvantages
– reduced river flows (use of water for irrigation)

Concluding statements

Strengths and → how to sustain/improve
Rehabilitation of soil fertility over short term → Continue to use the ditches for compost production.

Increased and permanent production → Constant maintenance.

Increased food security and balanced diet → More diversification.

Reduction of erosion processes → Improve the soil cover through implementation of green manure and cover crops.

Adapted to very heterogeneous climatic and topographic conditions.

Protective-productive system: compromise between land capability class (forest) and cultivation needs → Consistent maintenance of all elements that interact in this agroforestry system: trees, grass strips, earth structures, compost production and green manure.

Weaknesses and → how to overcome
Rigid design of the technology and fixed guidelines for implementation activities (pre-conditions for incentive support by project) → Give more flexibility to the farmers for individual modifications.

High demand for manual labour → Emphasis on group work, implement in dry season (when labour force is available at the household level).

High external inputs at the beginning (makes the technology very expensive) → Manure is needed to restore soil fertility in the short-term, land users pay the inputs in form of labour in the CISEC; revolving funds and composting ensure manure supplies on the long term.

Decreased pH (soil acidity) → Compensate by ecological improvements such as application of lime and ashes.

Key reference(s): CISEC (1998) *Establecimiento de Lotes de Silvoagricultura* ■ Gurtner M (1999) *Bodendegradierung und Bodenkonservierung in den Anden Kolumbiens – Eine Nachhaltigkeitsstudie im Rahmen des WOCAT-Programms,* unpublished MSc Thesis, Science Faculty, University of Berne, Centre for Development and Environment

Contact person(s): Eduardo Caicedo, Calle 4B* 95–82 Barrio Melendez, Cali, Colombia; phone/fax 092-3320067/ 3324640/ 3326779; ecaicedo@emcali.net.co, alternativacomunitaria@telesat.com.co

Integrated rural community development

Colombia – *Desarrollo rural integral comunitario*

Development of an impoverished indigenous reserve – incorporating alternative land use systems – through intensive training provided by a small NGO.

The Foundation for Rural Community Development is a small NGO, working in a 5 km² indigenous reserve – characterised by ecological and economic crises. In this area, the foundation has built up a Centre for Research and Community Services (CISEC – *Centro de Investigacion y Servicios Comunitarios*).

CISEC operates an experimentation and training centre in the reserve, where large demonstration/production areas also exist. For 15 years CISEC has provided training to local promoters in the fields of sustainable land use and health care. Workshops are held, and a team of specialists guarantee continuous supervision and technical assistance for the land users. The specialists plan the approach and the development of the technology. Its design, and the precise implementation steps are clearly prescribed.

The overall purpose of the approach is to raise the living standard of the marginalized indigenous people through alternative development opportunities. This is achieved by focussing on four principle areas: (1) Promoting an alternative land management system ensuring sustained and diversified production based on the principles of organic farming (see related technology: 'intensive agroforestry system'); (2) Improving basic health services, sanitation and promoting balanced nutrition; (3) Training, education and capacity building at three levels: (a) integration of sustainable land management as a topic in the local college – directed by CISEC; (b) basic training on technology implementation, ecological processes and accounting for all participants; (c) special workshops to train local promoters who continue to advise land users after the implementation stage through various means, including development of teaching materials, libraries, workshops, courses, farm visits, and demonstration sites. (4) Economical dimension: a new initiative within the programme focuses on marketing of organic products.

Participating land users have to adhere to specific requirements and fulfil certain conditions. For example, the layout of the agroforestry system has to be done to plan, groups must be organised, and a schedule for implementation developed. Participatory identification of problems and needs takes place in community assemblies, and through individual talks between extensionists and land users. To facilitate the implementation and ensure the continuation of SWC practices, land user groups manage a revolving fund – based on the subsidised provision of manure ('manure-for-work') during the establishment phase of the technology.

left: Local promoters (trainers) participating in a three day workshop at the Centre for Research and Community Services – CISEC. Different topics related to sustainable land use are treated. (Mats Gurtner)
right: The approach area is characterised by severe erosion and fertility decline. The promoted technology limits agricultural production to a small but intensively used area. (Mats Gurtner)

Location: Resguardo Indígena Las Canoas, Santander de Quilichao, Cuaca, Colombia
Approach area: 5 km²
Land use: wasteland (before), mixed: agroforestry (after)
Climate: subhumid
WOCAT database reference: QA COL02
Related technology: Intensive agroforestry system, QT COL02
Compiled by: Jairo Cuervo, CISEC, Cali, Colombia
Date: July 1998, updated July 2004

Editors' comments: In many parts of the world NGOs are taking responsibility for reaching rural indigenous peoples and helping them to help themselves. The first experience was in an indigenious reserve in Southern Columbia. Further extension is being carried out through a network of local NGOs, and there is some spontaneous adoption in nearby areas.

Problem, objectives and constraints

Problem
- high level of unsatisfied basic needs
- land degradation
- lack of technical and social infrastructure
- lack of support from outside

Objectives
- achieve sustainable and efficient use of local resources
- improve the living standard of the indigenous population
- strengthen land users' organisations
- promote land rehabilitation and increase agricultural production
- promote environmental education through training of the community

Constraints addressed

Major	Specification	Treatment
Legal	Land fragmentation leads to small-sized properties; access to water is limited.	Construction of small private water tanks.
Financial	Lack of economic resources.	Land users are provided with subsidised inputs during establishment phase.

Minor	Specification	Treatment
Social/cultural/religious	Slow adoption of technologies at the beginning; reluctance and prejudice towards the white specialists from outside; difficulty in convincing local leaders.	Discussions with interested land users, farmer-to-farmer interaction.

Participation and decision making

Target groups

Land users

Teachers/
students

Approach costs met by:

International NGO: Helvetas (Switzerland)	55%
National NGO	5%
Community/local	40%
	100%

Decisions on choice of the technology: Mainly made by SWC specialists with consultation of land users, through experimentation and development of the technology by CISEC (including traditional elements) and consulting the needs of the land users.

Decisions on method of implementing the technology: Mainly made by SWC specialists with consultation of land users: implementation of the technology according to directives of CISEC (regarding implementation steps and time-schedule). Modifications by land users only regarding the selection of crops.

Approach designed by: National and international specialists.

Community involvement

Phase	Involvement	Activities
Initiation	passive	experimentation and demonstration of the technology on test areas, participatory identification of problems and needs in assemblies and individual discussions
Planning	passive	planning of the approach and technology implementation steps by specialists; for planning of workshops the land users are consulted regarding their needs
Implementation	interactive	the land users implement the technology on their own, organised in groups, supported and assisted by the local promoters and by the CISEC specialists
Monitoring/evaluation	interactive	continued assistance and supervision by the specialists by means of farm visits, evaluations and reports (by CISEC and local promoters); during workshops observations made by land users are evaluated
Research	passive	research activities take place basically on CISEC's plots, some experimentation is carried out on the land users' farms; there is integration of land users' ideas into the investigation process

Differences in participation of men and women: There are moderate differences between the roles of men and women originating from *machismo* – the traditional relationships between (and roles of) men and women. While the difference currently is quite pronounced, the participation of women is increasing.

A local promoter, a land user who was trained by the Research Centre CISEC to extend the agroforestry system within the approach area, demonstrates different steps of technology implementation: demarcation of the contour lines using A-frame, pegs and rope, and digging of an infiltration ditch. His son, who is assisting, will soon learn about, and practice, sustainable land management practices at the rural college, which was established and is managed through the programme. (Mats Gurtner)

Extension and promotion

Training: Training is carried out in agroforestry, livestock management, protection and sustainable use of forests, soils, watershed management, organic weed control (spraying organic liquids), basic accounting, and nutrition. This is done through courses, demonstration areas and farm visits. The training of local promoters has been very effective, and the impact on land users and students is said to be good.

Extension: Workshops and farm visits are the main means of extension. Key element of extension method is the training of local promoters who pick up extension activities in the community after the implementation phase has been completed, thus guaranteeing the continuation of extension services in the long term. So far, the impact of extension on land users and specialists has been good.

Research: Experimental investigation takes place on the demonstration plots of CISEC: there have been variety trials, and testing of SWC measures. The impact of research has been considerable.

Importance of land use rights: Land use rights are secure in the long term, thus no negative impact on approach or technology has been observed.

Incentives

Labour: Labour was mainly voluntary.

Inputs: Initial inputs of seeds, seedlings, manure, biocides and construction material for irrigation infrastructure were subsidised by the project for establishment of the agroforestry system. Farmers pay for those inputs through working for CISEC (on CISEC's production and demonstration areas). A basic stock of manure is provided by the project to establish a revolving fund to ensure the continuation of the SWC activities.

Credit: No credit was provided.

Support of local institutions: Considerable support to local institutions was given in the form of training.

Long-term impact of incentives: A moderate positive long-term impact is expected: through initial incentives land users have begun to notice the changes: this motivates them to continue in the same direction. Moreover, CISEC provides continued support to the land users by providing inputs at low prices. However some land users only participate in order to benefit from initial free manure provision.

Monitoring and evaluation

Monitored aspects	Methods and indicators
Bio-physical	regular qualitative soil assessment
Technical	regular observations of design modifications
Economic/production	regular accounting of costs and benefits
Area treated	ad hoc counts of agroforestry plots
No. of land users involved	regular counts of participants
Management of approach	regular revision of distribution of limited project resources

Impacts of the approach

Changes as result of monitoring and evaluation: There have been several changes: these include schedule of technology implementation, incentives, the integration of animals into the production systems, training on specific topics that have been identified as important (maintenance of particular measures, keeping of accounts, etc).

Improved soil and water management: Soil and water management has improved very much. Land users have implemented the agroforestry system, which combines different measures to control soil erosion, restore soil fertility, and improve soil water holding capacity.

Adoption of the approach by other projects/land users: None.

Sustainability: Land users can continue activities initiated under the approach without further external support. The revolving fund helps them to access the necessary inputs, and technical assistance is available through the trained local promoters. SWC specialists from CISEC also follow up and monitor the implemented SWC practices during frequent farm visits.

Concluding statements

Strengths and ➜ how to sustain/improve	Weaknesses and ➜ how to overcome
Training of land users and of local promoters (human capacity building) ➜ Maintain activities.	There are land users who participate only to receive manure for work (negative impact of incentives) ➜ Put more emphasis on on-farm manure/compost production.
Improve agricultural production through utilisation of local resources ➜ Maintain activities.	Lack of awareness raising and training in some important topics (eg green manuring etc) ➜ Strengthen training.
Strengthen self-sufficiency/independence of the community ➜ Maintain activities.	The design and implementation processes of the technology are rather fixed and static ➜ Allow more possibilities for modification by land users.
'Involvement' of the land users by responding to their needs.	The 'manure-for-work' system is limited to the first year for each participant; afterwards some land users find it difficult to get access to manure.
Sustained and/or increased agricultural production and marketing of 'healthy', organic products.	Very labour intensive technology design (but already overcome by provision of incentives and implementation in organised groups) ➜ Emphasise production increase as an incentive.

Key reference(s): Gurtner M (1999) *Bodendegradierung und Bodenkonservierung in den Anden Kolumbiens – Eine Nachhaltigkeitsstudie im Rahmen des WOCAT-Programms,* unpublished MSc Thesis, Science Faculty, University of Berne, Centre for Development and Environment
Contact person(s): Eduardo Caicedo, Calle 4B* 95–82 Barrio Melendez, Cali, Colombia; phone/fax 092-3320067/ 3324640/ 3326779; ecaicedo@emcali.net.co, alternativacomunitaria@telesat.com.co

Shade-grown coffee

Costa Rica – *Café arbolado*

left: An overview showing variations of the technology with different levels of tree cover and different stages of coffee growth: newly established (upper left) and well-developed coffee (lower right). (Esther Neuenschwander) **right:** Coffee planted along the contour, associated with banana and other fruit trees. Additional measures such as dense strips of lemon grass protect the soil from erosion. (Esther Neuenschwander)

An agroforestry system which combines coffee with shade trees – including fruit, timber and leguminous species – in a systematic fashion.

Shade-grown coffee is a traditional and complex agroforestry system where coffee is associated with various other species in different storeys (or 'levels'). This provides ecologically and economically sustainable use of natural resources. *Café arbolado,* the example promoted by PRODAF (Programme for Agroforestry Development, see related approach: 'Agroforestry Extension') since 1987 is one technical option for shade-grown coffee.

While based on a traditional system the shade-grown coffee technology has a specific layout, and a reduced number of intercropped species. It comprises: (1) Coffee *(Coffea arabica)* planted on the contour at approximately 5,000 plants per hectare; (2) Associated trees: fruits, most commonly oranges (120 trees/ha), cedar *(Cedrela odorata)* or *caoba (Swietenia macrophylla)* for timber (60 trees/ha) and also two legumes, *poró (Erythrina poeppigiana)* and *chalum (Inga sp.)* which act as shade trees and at the same time improve the soil by fixing nitrogen (60 trees/ha). Farmers often include bananas in the system. In some cases, orange trees have partly been substituted by avocado *(Persea americana)*, soursop *(Anona muricata)*, and/or *jocotes (Spondias purpurea)*. The latter two command good market prices and do not compete with labour needed for harvesting and other activities; (3) Supportive soil conservation measures on steep slopes to avoid soil erosion, predominantly strips of lemon grass *(Cymbopogon citratus)* on the contour, retention ditches and soil cover improvement; (4) Fertilizers: both organic and inorganic combined.

Full establishment of a shaded coffee plot can be achieved in two years – after replanting trees which fail to establish. Coffee yields a harvest after two years, but timber from associated trees can be expected after only 25 years. The trees grown in association allow more efficient cycling of nutrients (because of deep rooting and nitrogen fixation) and provide a favourable microclimate for coffee.

This production system is well adapted to the local biophysical and socio-economic conditions, characterised by steep erosion-prone mountain slopes, humid climate and small to medium scale agriculture. Based on *café arbolado* a new, and further developed system of 'sustainable coffee' has evolved. This involves certification of the overall process and is attractive to the growing number of environmentally conscious consumers.

Location: Acosta-Puriscal, San José/Río Parrita, Costa Rica
Technology area: 400 km²
SWC measure: vegetative and agronomic
Land use: mixed: agroforestry
Climate: humid
WOCAT database reference: QT COS02
Related approach: Agroforestry extension, QA COS02
Compiled by: Quiros Madrigal Olman, Puriscal, Costa Rica
Date: August 2001, updated July 2004

Editors' comments: About three quarters of Costa Rica's coffee is grown in association with shade trees. The expanding international market for coffee produced in an environment-friendly way opens further opportunities for shade-grown coffee. This agroforestry system differs from the less systematically managed 'forest coffee' commonly practiced in the region.

Classification

Land use problems
Severe deforestation, inappropriate land management practices (monocultures on steep slopes; lack of conservation measures); resulting in physical (soil erosion) and chemical (fertility decline) degradation of agricultural soils, low productivity and low yields.

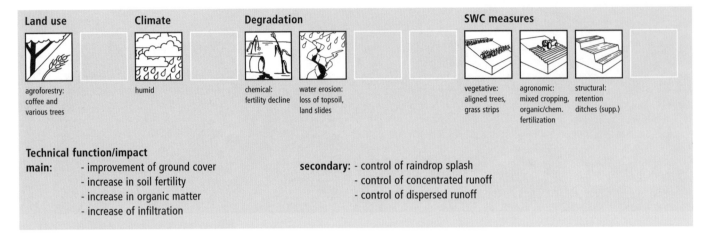

Land use

agroforestry:
coffee and
various trees

Climate

humid

Degradation

chemical:
fertility decline

water erosion:
loss of topsoil,
land slides

SWC measures

vegetative:
aligned trees,
grass strips

agronomic:
mixed cropping,
organic/chem.
fertilization

structural:
retention
ditches (supp.)

Technical function/impact

main:
- improvement of ground cover
- increase in soil fertility
- increase in organic matter
- increase of infiltration

secondary:
- control of raindrop splash
- control of concentrated runoff
- control of dispersed runoff

Environment

Natural environment

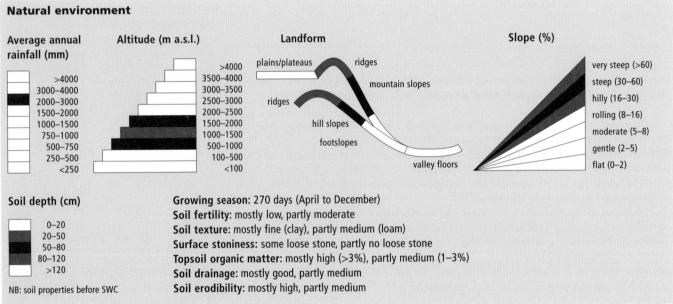

Average annual rainfall (mm)

>4000
3000–4000
2000–3000
1500–2000
1000–1500
750–1000
500–750
250–500
<250

Altitude (m a.s.l.)

>4000
3500–4000
3000–3500
2500–3000
2000–2500
1500–2000
1000–1500
500–1000
100–500
<100

Landform

plains/plateaus   ridges

ridges   mountain slopes

hill slopes

footslopes

valley floors

Slope (%)

very steep (>60)
steep (30–60)
hilly (16–30)
rolling (8–16)
moderate (5–8)
gentle (2–5)
flat (0–2)

Soil depth (cm)

0–20
20–50
50–80
80–120
>120

NB: soil properties before SWC

Growing season: 270 days (April to December)
Soil fertility: mostly low, partly moderate
Soil texture: mostly fine (clay), partly medium (loam)
Surface stoniness: some loose stone, partly no loose stone
Topsoil organic matter: mostly high (>3%), partly medium (1–3%)
Soil drainage: mostly good, partly medium
Soil erodibility: mostly high, partly medium

Human environment

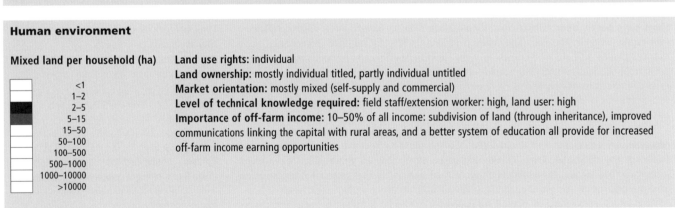

Mixed land per household (ha)

<1
1–2
2–5
5–15
15–50
50–100
100–500
500–1000
1000–10000
>10000

Land use rights: individual
Land ownership: mostly individual titled, partly individual untitled
Market orientation: mostly mixed (self-supply and commercial)
Level of technical knowledge required: field staff/extension worker: high, land user: high
Importance of off-farm income: 10–50% of all income: subdivision of land (through inheritance), improved communications linking the capital with rural areas, and a better system of education all provide for increased off-farm income earning opportunities

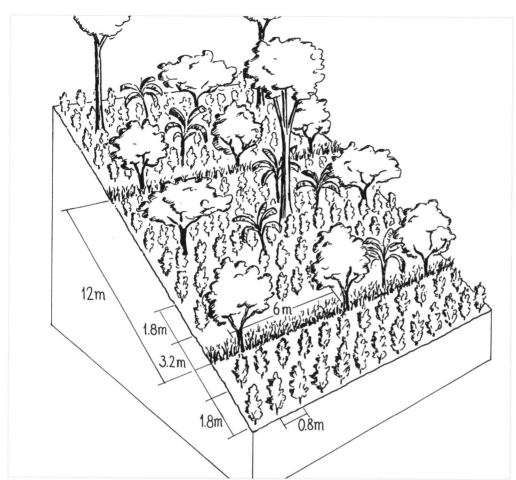

Technical drawing
Example layout of coffee grown below shade trees: various species are used for shade, and each has intrinsic value of its own – orange trees (for fruit) are associated with strips of lemon grass, tall cedars (for timber) are planted in rows alternating with *Erythrina sp.* (for fertility improvement). Optionally, banana trees are interplanted.

Implementation activities, inputs and costs

Establishment activities
1. Clearing of land.
2. Surveying for contour planting of coffee, grass strips, trees etc.
3. Digging holes, fertilizer application.
4. Planting coffee, trees, grass barriers etc along the contour.
5. Replanting coffee that fails to establish in first year.

All activities are carried out at beginning of rainy season (March/April).
Duration of establishment: 2 years

Establishment inputs and costs per ha

Inputs	Costs (US$)	% met by land user
Labour (100 person days)	700	100%
Equipment		
- Tools (shovel, machete)	0	
Agricultural		
- Seedlings: *poró*/cedar (approx. 150)	15	0%
- Seedlings: orange trees (approx. 150)	220	0%
- Seedlings: coffee (5,000 initially + 500 replanted = 5,500)	1240	0%
- Fertilizers (8,000 kg)	350	0%
Others		
- Transport	10	0%
TOTAL	**2535**	**28%**

Maintenance/recurrent activities
1. Weed control (June and August).
2. Pruning coffee (February or March).
3. Fertilization (1–3 times: May, July, November).
4. Pest control (spraying 1–2 times: May, September).
5. Pruning shade trees.
6. Application of lime.

Maintenance/recurrent inputs and costs per ha per year

Inputs	Costs (US$)	% met by land user
Labour (4 person days)	28	100%
Equipment		
- Tools (knapsack, machete)	0	
Agricultural		
- Fertilizers (500 kg)	175	100%
- Biocides (4 kg)	127	100%
TOTAL	**330**	**100%**

Remarks: The costs of planting coffee are included. Shade-grown coffee is an integrated production system, and thus costs for coffee and the agroforestry component cannot be disaggregated.

Assessment

Acceptance/adoption
- All the land users who accepted the technology did so with incentives.
- Those land users received incentives in form of donated seedlings (for coffee, fruit and timber trees) and subsidised agricultural inputs for the establishment of agroforestry plots. Tools were only provided when absolutely necessary.
- There is a slight trend towards growing spontaneous adoption – after the end of the programme. However, the crisis triggered by the big drop in coffee prices has had a negative impact on adoption of the technology. Many coffee farms have been abandoned specially those located under 800–900 m a.s.l. where coffee is of a lower quality due to climatic conditions.

Benefits/costs according to land user

Benefits compared with costs	short-term:	long-term:
establishment	negative*	positive
maintenance/recurrent	positive	very positive

*establishment costs are high, but after 5 years the system becomes very profitable.

Impacts of the technology

Production and socio-economic benefits	Production and socio-economic disadvantages
+ + + crop yield increase (fruits)	– reduced production: coffee, about 10% less than in conventional systems (per ha per year)
+ + + wood production increase (trees)	
+ + improved profitability	– increased labour constraints
Socio-cultural benefits	**Socio-cultural disadvantages**
+ + + improved knowledge SWC/erosion	– – lack of incentives for technology adoption
+ + national institution strengthening	– socio-cultural conflicts
Ecological benefits	**Ecological disadvantages**
+ + + soil loss reduction	none
+ + + soil cover improvement	
+ + increase in soil moisture	
+ + increase in soil fertility	
+ biodiversity enhancement	
+ reduction of wind velocity	
Off-site benefits	**Off-site disadvantages**
+ + reduced downstream flooding	none

Concluding statements

Strengths and ➜ how to sustain/improve	Weaknesses and ➜ how to overcome
Increased overall crop production and diversity: coffee, fruit, timber, legumes ➜ Include other legumes, native species.	Slight decrease in production of coffee per hectare compared to the conventional pure stand ➜ Compensate by additional benefits: wood production, fruit, etc.
Different crops harvested at different periods, gives better distribution of labour (and income) throughout the year; participation of all family members; increased food security and minimal economic risk ➜ Maintain the system well.	Short-term negative cost-benefit ratio in the first 4–5 years: Cost-intensive technology in the establishment phase.
Improved profitability.	Timber harvest only in the long term (after 25 years) ➜ Identify fast growing species or species providing intermediate products.
More efficient use of nutrients, nitrogen fixation, lower inputs of fertilizers.	
Increased pest resistance, lower external inputs of biocides.	
Coffee plants continue to produce over 25 years due to optimal microclimate (only 15 years in conventional system without trees).	
Production system adapted to steep erosion prone slopes, thus a productive alternative to simple afforestation.	
Not labour-intensive compared with structural measures of SWC.	
High commercial potential of environmentally friendly produced coffee due to new market trends.	
Price increase for agricultural inputs has favoured a shift from conventional to shade-grown coffee, the latter being a system with a higher ratio of applied inputs/harvested yields although total production is usually lower than in modern coffee plantations.	

Key reference(s): PRODAF (1994) *Sistema agroforestal – Café arbolado*, Ecología y economía para el progreso, Puriscal, Costa Rica ▪
Neuenschwander E (2002) *Agorforstwirtschaftlicher Kaffeeanbau als Lösungsansatz für eine ökologisch nachhaltige Bodennutzung der Hanglagen in Costa Rica: eine Fallstudie im Rahmen des WOCAT Programms*, unpublished MSc thesis, Science Faculty, University of Berne, Centre for Development and Environment
Contact person(s): Quiros Madrigal Olman, *Ministerio de Agricultura y Ganadería*, Santiago de Puriscal, 85-6000 Puriscal, Costa Rica; phone ++ 506 416 87 35, fax ++ 506 416 87 38; ojquiros@yahoo.com

Agroforestry extension
Costa Rica – *Extensión agroforestal*

Participatory extension of agroforestry systems, especially of shade-grown coffee, to promote sustainable and productive use of natural resources among small and medium scale farmers.

The Programme for Agroforestry Development (PRODAF) pioneered a new type of agroforestry extension in Costa Rica between 1987 and 1994. PRODAF was positioned under two national ministries (the Ministry of Agriculture and Livestock – MAG and the Ministry of Natural Resources, Energy and Mines – MINAE) and was supported by GTZ (German Technical Cooperation).

Agroforestry extension underpinned the following sectors: environmental education, promotion of training and technical assistance in agriculture and forestry, development of programmes for afforestation and agroforestry systems, and promotion/support of farmers' organisations. The approach was based on land users' participation at all stages.

The main purpose of the agroforestry extension approach was the development and promotion of sustainable production systems, which were adapted to the local biophysical and socio-economic conditions. This was to enable environmentally friendly production on steep slopes, while at the same time generating sufficient income for small and medium scale farmers in marginal areas of the Acosta-Puriscal region. In this case study, shade-grown coffee was identified to be a system that fulfilled these conditions. Another important objective was the involvement of all family members – including the younger generation.

In the first years PRODAF operated with a top-down development approach implementing technologies, designed by specialists, without consultation of land users. Local needs and experiences were not considered: as a result both adoption of shade-grown coffee was low, and maintenance was poor, despite initial incentives. The change to a participatory, bottom-up approach, with land users being represented in the steering committee (which during this period was absolutely innovative) increased acceptance among the majority of farmers towards shade-grown coffee. Participation of land users during planning and implementation was rewarded with provision of tools, seeds, fertilizer and biocides (fully financed or subsidised). The technology was evaluated on the test plots within existing coffee plantations together with the land users. PRODAF's legacy has been an institutional change in Government policy towards extension.

left: Discussion between farmers and extensionists during a workshop organised by the Ministry of Agriculture and Livestock. (Esther Neuenschwander)
right: Coffee seedlings ready to be planted. Seedlings for coffee, fruit trees and grass strips are provided free of charge to the land users who implement the agroforestry system. (Esther Neuenschwander)

Location: Acosta-Puriscal, San José/Río Parrita, Costa Rica
Approach area: 400 km²
Land use: mixed: agroforestry
Climate: humid
WOCAT database reference: QA COS02
Related technology: Shade-grown coffee, QT COS02
Compiled by: Quiros Madrigal Olman, Puriscal, Costa Rica
Date: August 2001, updated March 2004

Editors' comments: This is an example where a national programme conducted through a government agency has emerged from the success of a specific project. PRODAF's efforts regarding institutional coordination and participation of land users had a pioneer status within the country. Convinced by the positive results of the project, the national government decided to support elements of such an extension approach with its own funds.

Problem, objectives and constraints

Problem
- various different approaches of forest and agricultural technicians regarding choice and implementation of the technology – which needed harmonising
- lack of incentives for farmers to adopt technology
- lack of participatory technology development

Objectives
Promotion of appropriate management of natural resources and adoption of the shade-grown coffee agroforestry system – *café arbolado* – among small and medium scale farmers.

Constraints addressed

Major	Specification	Treatment
Technical	Lack of technical knowledge, lack of research activities/trials with SWC technologies.	Promotion of alternative production systems and SWC measures had great impact. Technology was tested on-farm. PRODAF did not focus on research activities.

Minor	Specification	Treatment
Institutional	Lack of collaboration and coordination between different institutions.	Innovative incorporation of land users in decision making, which in the meantime has become a common approach.
Financial	Lack of credit for SWC implementation.	Credit has been made available through the 'productive re-conversion programme' and other credit systems for organic/conservation production, eg Fideicomiso (see under credit).
Legal	Subdivision of land hinders adoption of SWC measures.	Not directly treated by the approach. Diverse incentive mechanisms have to be identified to promote SWC activities on small areas.

Participation and decision making

Target groups

Land users | SWC specialists/ extensionists | Politicians/ decision makers

Approach costs met by:

International agency: GTZ	50%
National government: MAG, MINAE	50%
	100%

Decisions on choice of the technology: Mainly made by SWC specialists with consultation of land users.
Decisions on method of implementing the technology: Mainly made by SWC specialists with consultation of land users.
Approach designed by: National and international specialists.

Community involvement

Phase	Involvement	Activities
Initiation	interactive	good participation basically through participative rural appraisal
Planning	interactive/incentives	workshops/seminar; incentives are provided for participating land users
Implementation	interactive/incentives	land users are responsible for major steps; incentives are provided for participating land users
Monitoring/evaluation	interactive	interviews/workshops
Research	interactive	on-farm

Differences in participation of men and women: Mainly men participated: women are not usually expected to carry out field activities for cultural reasons. The coffee harvest is the only activity where men and women work together in the field.

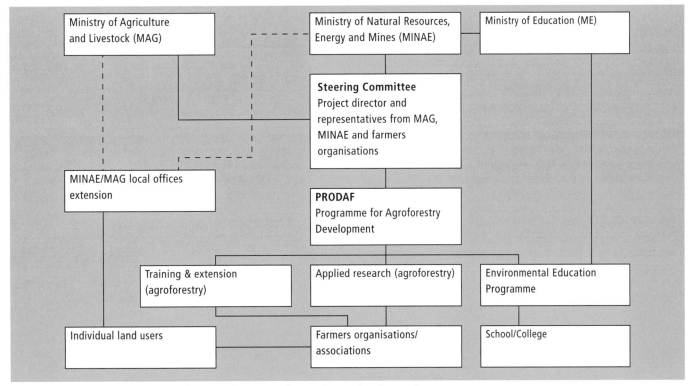

Organogram: Organisational set-up of PRODAF (Programme for Agroforestry Development)

Extension and promotion

Training: Training was provided in the form of demonstration areas, farm visits, field days, workshops, trips to projects in other regions for knowledge exchange, and public meetings. The following subjects were treated: coffee agroforestry system, fruit trees and soil conservation, silvo-pastoralism, soil conservation in general. Beside knowledge transfer, awareness raising and motivation were important aims of training. Training and extension showed good effects on land users, conservation specialists (MAG, GTZ) and extension agents. The environmental education programme was developed as a pilot project in different schools/college in the approach area by MINAE, in coordination with ME. The effectiveness of environmental education programme on students and of training on land users was excellent.

Extension: Extension carried out through extension workers was the key element of the overall approach – and the adequacy of extension for continuation was very good. Different methods were used: on-farm technical assistance; farmer-to-farmer knowledge exchange; demonstration areas and workshops. For the rating of the impact of extension on different target groups – see under 'training'.

Research: Research was included at a low to moderate level as PRODAF was not a research programme, basically in the form of on-farm trials, treating ecological and technological topics. Results were rather meagre, and the effect on the approach was thus moderate. Previous to PRODAF there was a research project conducted by CATIE (Tropical Agricultural Research and Higher Education Centre) in the approach area, but results were not broadly disseminated.

Importance of land use rights: Land fragmentation leads to very small areas per household. This hinders implementation of SWC activities. Land users do not have the resources to invest in initial inputs and activities.

Incentives

Labour: Labour was basically voluntary, although the provision of tools by the project worked as an encouragement.

Inputs: PRODAF provided all seedlings for the tree components in the *café arbolado* system, free of charge. The farmers only needed to present themselves to qualify for the coffee plants. During the implementation phase hand tools, fertilizer and transport costs were partly subsidised by PRODAF.

Credit: Credit was provided through the 'productive re-conversion programme' to support small-scale organic production and soil conservation. Interest rate was lower than the market rate. After PRODAF a larger (national) credit programme to promote agroforestry systems was launched in the approach area, under MAG and National Production Council (CNP). *Fideicomiso* is another national financing programme based on a contract between a bank and development institutions.

Support of local institutions: Moderate support: financial support, training, equipment and construction of buildings.

Long-term impact of incentives: Initial incentives were important to compensate the costs of technology implementation. In combination with the provided training and environmental education, it is assumed that the impact will be positive in the long term.

Monitoring and evaluation

Monitored aspects	Methods and indicators
Bio-physical	ad hoc measurements of yields
Socio-cultural	regular observations of family size
Economic/production	regular measurements of yields and produce marketed
No. of land users involved	regular measurements of land users involved in organisation

Impacts of the approach

Changes as result of monitoring and evaluation: The approach changed completely after evaluation of the first phase, from an initial top down methodology with low technology adoption by land users, to a more participative approach heeding land users' opinions and needs, and improving communication between technicians and land users. This was helped by the development of educational materials.

Improved soil and water management: There was substantial improvement of soil and water management through application of the agroforestry systems.

Adoption of the approach by other projects/land users: Some projects in the region as well as in other parts of the country adopted the approach. Various SWC extension programmes have adopted the extension methods promoted by PRODAF, based on the principles of land users participation. In the Ministry of Agriculture and Livestock it has been taken as a basic principle in the National Programme of Agricultural Extension.

Sustainability: While the approach has been institutionalised (see above) and a national credit programme set up promoting shade-grown coffee and silvo-pastoral systems (see section on credit), continuation of field production activities is uncertain. Farmers' motivation to apply SWC technologies was raised with the Environmental Education Programme, but if market prices for coffee decrease or show high variability, farmers lose the motivation to maintain their plantations.

Concluding statements

Strengths and ➜ how to sustain/improve	Weaknesses and ➜ how to overcome
Institutionalisation of the basic participatory extension approach within the Ministry of Agriculture and Livestock.	No economic security guaranteed in the long term because of price fluctuations ➜ Provide a system of incentives, eg lower taxes for those who apply SWC technologies.
Initial top-down approach replaced by participation with land users ➜ Continue to spread information about the effectiveness of this change in attitude, and the need for responsiveness in projects and programmes.	
Training of land users (knowledge of soil degradation processes and soil and water conservation) ➜ Collaboration with farmers organisations, NGOs and agricultural extension services. Better dissemination of research results.	
Environmental education in schools ➜ Continue support through the Ministry of Education.	

Key reference(s): PRODAF (1992) *Informe de evaluación de las parcelas agroforestales establecidas por PRODAF, Periodo 88–91,* Puriscal, Costa Rica ■ Quiros O (2000) *Nachhaltigkeit von landwirtschaftlichen Produktionsverfahren in bäuerlichen Familienbetrieben in Costa Rica.* Vauk-Kiel KG: *series of: Sozialökonimische Schriften zur Ruralen Entwicklung,* Vol. 20

Contact person(s): Quiros Madrigal Olman, *Ministerio de Agricultura y Ganadería,* Santiago de Puriscal, 85-6000 Puriscal, Costa Rica; phone ++ 506 416 87 35, fax ++ 506 416 87 38; ojquiros@yahoo.com

left: Narrow terraces, each with a water retention ditch, for fruit trees (note grape vine in the foreground). (Bettina Wolfgramm)
right: Agroforestry plot surrounded by overgrazed and heavily, degraded grazing land; note also fenced plot with grass plot for hay making above the plot. (Hanspeter Liniger)

Conversion of grazing land to fruit and fodder plots

Tajikistan – Ивазнамудани замини чарогох ба богот

Fencing part of an overgrazed hillside, combined with terracing, manuring and supplementary irrigation for grape, fruit and grass production.

In the Varzob valley of Tajikistan, slopes of around 30% are used communally, and are heavily overgrazed. This has led to a reduction in vegetation cover, to soil compaction and to severe sheet and rill erosion. In 1982, one innovative land user began to set up half a hectare vineyard/fruit plot with intensive grass/fodder production for cut-and-carry and separate section above for hay making – through his own initiative. By the application of various conservation measures, within five years an area exposed to severe water erosion was converted into sustainable use. Fodder and fruits are now flourishing and the natural resources of soil and water are conserved effectively.

The start of the process was fencing of the plot to keep out animals. Scrap metal and other materials from a machinery depot were used to build a 1.5 m high fence. To harvest and hold runoff water from the hillside for grapes and fruit trees, narrow backsloping terraces were constructed, each with a water retention ditch along the contour. During the initial phase, the terraces did not harvest enough water for establishment of the seedlings. So water for supplementary irrigation was carried to the plot by donkeys in old inner tubes from car tyres. Manure is applied to the plot to improve soil fertility. The manure is collected on the high pastures where the herders graze their animals during summer. The total amount of manure applied to the plot so far amounts to about 3 t/ha over 20 years.

For the innovator, his most valuable fruits are grapes, followed by apricots, almonds and plums. He has also successfully grown mulberry, pomegranate and cherry trees. Not all the seedlings survive: the farmer considers a 40% survival rate of grape vines to be reasonable. The harvest of fruit is mainly used for home consumption. However, in a good year the table grapes and apricots are sold on the market. The hay harvest, from naturally regenerated grasses and fodder plants between the fruits amounts, on average, to 0.2 t/ha/year. The pruned branches from the vines are collected and used as firewood.

The establishment of such a plot is very demanding in terms of manpower. However within 5–6 years the system becomes self-sustaining and the productivity of the land is improved several times over. Following this positive experience, other households in the area have adopted the technology spontaneously, and today about 15 ha of degraded grazing land in the Varzob valley have been converted into productive fruit gardens.

Location: Khagatai, Varzob, Tajikistan
Technology area: 0.15 km²
SWC measure: management, structural, vegetative and agronomic
Land use: grazing land (before), mixed: agro-silvopastoral (after)
Climate: subhumid
WOCAT database reference: QT TAJ04
Related approach: Farmer innovation and self-help group, QA TAJ04
Compiled by: Ergashev M, Nekushoeva G and Wolfgramm B, Soil Science Institute, Dushanbe, Tajikistan
Date: June 2004, updated October 2004

Editors' comments: Where open access communal grazing leads to land degradation, individuals sometimes enclose land for productive purposes. This positive example is from Tajikistan where the initiative began during the period of the soviet regime. Similar initiatives can be seen in western Iran. However, if a significant number of land users follow suit, there will be a reduction in the amount of land available for common use.

Classification

Land use problems
- shortage of cultivable land on the gentle slopes next to the rivers
- low yield of natural pastures due to overgrazing
- heavy erosion taking place near residential areas

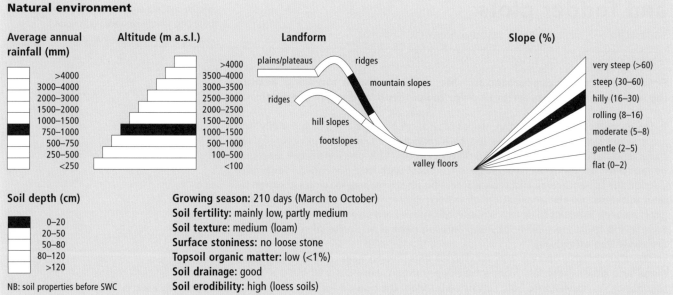

Land use		Climate		Degradation				SWC measures			
extensive grazing (before)	agro-silvopastoral: fruit trees/vines (irrig.), cut-and-carry (after)	subhumid		water erosion: loss of topsoil	physical: compaction	vegetation: reduced cover		management: land use change from grazing land to tree crops	structural: bench terraces (backward sloping)	vegetative: fruit trees/vines aligned	agronomic: manuring

Technical function/impact

main:
- improvement of ground cover
- retain/trap dispersed runoff
- increase in organic matter
- increase in soil fertility

secondary:
- reduction of slope angle
- water harvesting
- retain/trap concentrated runoff (prevention of gully erosion)
- reduction of wind speed

Environment

Natural environment

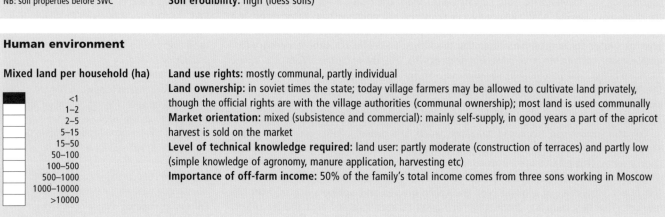

Average annual rainfall (mm)
- >4000
- 3000–4000
- 2000–3000
- 1500–2000
- 1000–1500
- 750–1000
- 500–750
- 250–500
- <250

Altitude (m a.s.l.)
- >4000
- 3500–4000
- 3000–3500
- 2500–3000
- 2000–2500
- 1500–2000
- 1000–1500
- 500–1000
- 100–500
- <100

Landform
- plains/plateaus
- ridges
- mountain slopes
- ridges
- hill slopes
- footslopes
- valley floors

Slope (%)
- very steep (>60)
- steep (30–60)
- hilly (16–30)
- rolling (8–16)
- moderate (5–8)
- gentle (2–5)
- flat (0–2)

Soil depth (cm)
- 0–20
- 20–50
- 50–80
- 80–120
- >120

NB: soil properties before SWC

Growing season: 210 days (March to October)
Soil fertility: mainly low, partly medium
Soil texture: medium (loam)
Surface stoniness: no loose stone
Topsoil organic matter: low (<1%)
Soil drainage: good
Soil erodibility: high (loess soils)

Human environment

Mixed land per household (ha)
- <1
- 1–2
- 2–5
- 5–15
- 15–50
- 50–100
- 100–500
- 500–1000
- 1000–10000
- >10000

Land use rights: mostly communal, partly individual
Land ownership: in soviet times the state; today village farmers may be allowed to cultivate land privately, though the official rights are with the village authorities (communal ownership); most land is used communally
Market orientation: mixed (subsistence and commercial): mainly self-supply, in good years a part of the apricot harvest is sold on the market
Level of technical knowledge required: land user: partly moderate (construction of terraces) and partly low (simple knowledge of agronomy, manure application, harvesting etc)
Importance of off-farm income: 50% of the family's total income comes from three sons working in Moscow

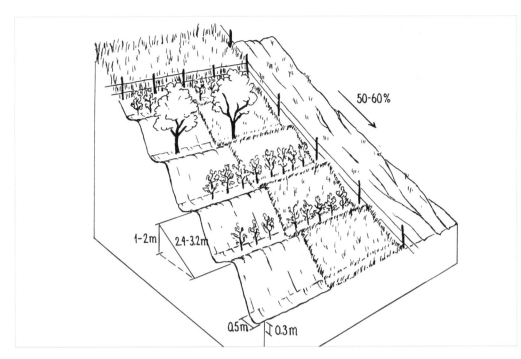

Technical drawing
The fenced-off agroforestry system comprising fruit trees and cereals grown on a steep hillside. Terracing is crucial for water conservation. Grass cover (right) is established for fodder production and simultaneous soil conservation. Note the adjacent plot for haymaking (above) and degraded rangeland outside the protected area (right).

Implementation activities, inputs and costs

Establishment activities
1. Fencing of an area of 0.5 ha using waste material from a machinery depot.
2. Construction of backward sloping bench terraces.
3. Planting of vines and fruit tree seedlings (apricot, plumes, almonds) along the terraces.
4. Irrigation (old inner tubes filled with water carried to the plot by donkeys) during the first 5–6 years after planting. In spring: every 3 weeks. In summer: 5 litres of water per tree, per week.
5. Manuring: applied at first to the newly planted vines/trees only, due to restricted availability. During the second half of the establishment phase also applied elsewhere within the plot.

Duration of establishment: 5–6 years

Establishment inputs and costs per ha

Inputs	Costs (US$)	% met by land user
Labour (around 300 person days)	600	100%
Equipment		
- Machines (car for transportation of manure)	50	100%
- Animals for transportation (270 hours)	200	100%
- Tools (shovels, hoes, old inner tubes from car tires)	0	
Materials		
- Water	0	
- Scrap metal	0	
Agricultural		
- Fruit tree seedlings (local, 40)	40	100%
- Grape vines (local, 1,500)	1,500	100%
- Manure (1,500 kg)	300	100%
TOTAL	**2,690**	**100%**

Maintenance/recurrent activities
1. Repairs to the fence are carried out every year.
2. Vines and trees that fail are replaced.
3. Irrigation of new seedlings.
4. Grapes and trees pruned every year.
5. Harvesting of fruits and fodder: transport of the yield to the house by donkey.
6. Manuring, when replacing grapes or trees that had died: manure is transported from summer pastures to the village by cars and to the plot by donkeys (every year).

Maintenance/recurrent inputs and costs per ha per year

Inputs	Costs (US$)	% met by land user
Labour (390 person days)	180	100%
Equipment		
- Tools (hoes, scissors for pruning)	0	
- Animals for transportation (270 hours)	200	100%
Materials		
- Water	0	
Agricultural		
- Seedlings (around 20)	20	100%
- Vines (local, 150)	150	100%
- Manure (100 kg)	20	100%
TOTAL	**570**	**100%**

Remarks: Labour cost per day is US$ 2. The fence constructed by the farmer was free because he utilised scrap from a machinery depot. Note that the total length of fencing is relatively less for a larger plot. In the villages there is almost no money changes hands: there is a barter system between the farmers. Even salaries are often paid in terms of fruits, wood or free rent of land.

Assessment

Acceptance/adoption
- Out of 250 households 5 (2%) have currently fenced plots for fruit production.
- Adoption was spontaneous in all cases and there are signs of further spread.

Benefits/costs according to land user	Benefits compared with costs	short-term:	long-term:
	establishment	negative	positive
	maintenance/recurrent	negative	very positive

Impacts of the technology

Production and socio-economic benefits
- + + + increase in fruit production
- + + increase in production of high quality fodder
- + wood production increase
- + farm income increase (depending on the rainfall during the year)

Socio-cultural benefits
- + + + improved knowledge SWC/erosion
- + community institution strengthening (terrace construction requires collaboration of relatives and friends)

Ecological benefits
- + + + soil cover improvement
- + + + increase in soil moisture
- + + + efficiency of excess water drainage
- + + + increase in soil fertility
- + + + soil loss reduction
- + + biodiversity enhancement

Off-site benefits
- + + reduced transported sediments
- + reduced flooding of the road at the bottom of the slope (conserved area is too small to have significant impact)

Production and socio-economic disadvantages
- – – – labour constraints: high labour input needed for establishment and recurrent irrigation
- – increased input constraint (for manure application)

Socio-cultural disadvantages
- – – conflicts: in the beginning conflicts due to jealousy, loss of community grazing land and fear of landslides caused by water retention on sloping loess areas.

Ecological disadvantages
- – – poorly maintained terraces may lead to increased erosion

Off-site disadvantages
- – increased risk of landslides due to water harvesting

Concluding statements

Strengths and → how to sustain/improve	Weaknesses and → how to overcome
Rehabilitation of degraded areas: reduced soil erosion and increased productivity → Complement manure inputs by other fertilizers.	Bringing water for supplementary irrigation to the orchard is very labour intensive → An irrigation supply system could be installed (irrigation channels, water tank). But so far this is too expensive, and it is questionable whether irrigation could be installed and maintained sustainably on these steep slopes with loess deposits.
Production increase: good fruit yields → Introduce low input demanding and fast producing tree species and varieties.	Not all tree species can grow in these dry conditions (for example apple trees will not survive without regular irrigation or watering) → Additional irrigation water required (see above).
Diversification: different kinds of fruit trees growing on the plot → Other trees (nuts for example) and annual crops such as wheat might also be suitable for this area.	Difficulty in establishment of the young vines in the well developed grass → Remove or cut down grass and herbaceous plants around the vines at least until they have well established.
Income generation.	Generally high manual labour input → Difficult to reduce labour inputs.

Key reference(s): none.
Contact person(s): Sharif Aliev family, Khagatai Village, Rayon of Varzob, Tajikistan ■ Murod Ergashev, CAMP – Central Asian Mountain Partnership Program, 12, Istrafshan Str. Apt 5, 734025 Dushanbe, Tajikistan; phone: ++992 372 210227; murod@swiss.tojikiston.com

Farmer innovation and self-help group

Tajikistan – Шахсияти ихтироъкор ва Хашар

Overcoming administrative and technical problems, an innovative land user, assisted by a self-help group, has established a fruit garden within degraded communal grazing land.

Although in the 1980s the soviet government supported the establishment of private gardens in specified areas, the lack of irrigation water and suitable land often restricted this process. That was the case for Khagatai village, situated on the narrow valley floor of the Varzob River, below steep loess slopes. This marginal area is used for grazing and shows severe signs of water erosion; the hillsides are considered to be of little value.

In the early 1980s, widespread unemployment evidently had the effect of stimulating people to use their own initiative. In 1982, one innovative farmer started to fence-off an area of half a hectare to establish a private fruit garden on the degraded grazing land. Some say that the fencing of plots for private fruit and hay production is a traditional practice – abandoned after the 1950s – but taken up again recently to re-establish rights to individual plots. The practice is widespread in the higher villages of Varzob, where the farmer noted it and decided to set up his own plot. When it came to practical implementation, despite the land user having five sons, the labour-intensive terracing was only completed thanks to voluntary work of relatives and friends, a tradition locally termed *hashar*.

At first, when his initiative began to take shape – on land officially owned by a state farm – nobody reacted. However, the change in land management quickly showed positive productive results, and it may have been through jealousy that the people of Khagatai village then reported the case to the authorities. But the watering of the garden on the unstable loess slope in the immediate vicinity of the village, and the consequent risk of landslides, was put forward as the reason for the complaint. The authorities opened an investigation and a number of newspaper articles appeared. Since independent decision taking was not common in the soviet states, and furthermore rapid degradation of newly irrigated lands on the loess deposits was a burning issue, the case of this fruit garden attracted a lot of attention. However, convinced by the improved state of vegetation on the plot, the authorities finally allowed the farmer to continue.

In 1993 the prohibition on private cultivation of land was lifted in order to reduce problems of food shortage caused during the civil war that followed independence. It was during this time that four other land users from Khagatai village spontaneously began to imitate the practice.

left: The fenced plot 20 years after establishment: degraded grazing land on the steep and degraded slopes of Varzob Valley has been turned in a productive area. (Hanspeter Liniger)
right: The innovative farmer, Sharif Aliev, depended on the support of relatives and friends to establish the new land use system. (Gulniso Nekushoeva)

Location: Khagatai, Varzob, Tajikistan
Approach area: 0.15 km²
Land use: mixed: agro-silvopastoral (after)
Climate: subhumid
WOCAT database reference: QA TAJ04
Related technology: Conversion of grazing land to fruit and fodder plots, QT TAJ04
Compiled by: Ergashev M, Nekushoeva G and Wolfgramm B, Soil Science Institute, Dushanbe, Tajikistan
Date: July 2004, updated October 2004

Editors' comments: It was very unusual during the soviet times for a villager to take the initiative to establish a private plot on state land. However in this example, the success in establishing a vineyard on an overgrazed hill convinced the administration of its worth. Other land users have now followed this approach.

Problem, objectives and constraints

Problem
- the land in question is part of a communal grazing area and property rights are officially with Khagatai village (though in soviet times with a state farm)
- uncontrolled grazing on communal lands has resulted in overgrazing and thus to progressive water erosion on the steep loess deposits
- no attention was paid by the local authorities to soil and water conservation measures in areas considered of low agricultural potential

Objectives
- to establish an orchard with grape vines, fruit trees and fodder crops for private use

Constraints addressed		
Major	**Specification**	**Treatment**
Social/cultural/religious	Jealousy of other village members, who didn't like a land user fencing-off a plot in communal grazing land.	Others became convinced after the change in land use. Newspaper articles on the case also helped shape public opinion.
Institutional	Private initiatives on state land were not intended under the soviet system.	Activities tended to start on marginal land that was of little agronomic interest to state farms.
Financial	All inputs had to be provided by the land user himself.	Creative ways were developed to provide material for fencing, for transportation of irrigation water and for access to manure.
Technical	For the establishment of the orchard irrigation water was needed. This had to be brought 200 m up a steep slope.	Water in old inner tubes was transported to the orchard by donkey.
Availability of labour	Construction of terraces for tree planting is very labour intensive.	Voluntary work of relatives and friends: an approach locally called *hashar*.
Minor	**Specification**	**Treatment**
Legal	No individual property rights.	In soviet times the land belonged to a state farm. Today the land belongs to Khagatai village: efforts to achieve official individual ownership have not succeeded.

Participation and decision making

Target groups	Approach costs met by:	
	Land user, private	100%
		100%

Land users

Decisions on choice of the technology: Made by land user alone (bottom up).
Decisions on method of implementing the technology: Made by land user alone (bottom up).
Approach designed by: Land user.

Community involvement		
Phase	**Involvement**	**Activities**
Initiation	self-mobilisation	the initiative was initiated by an individual land user
Planning	self-mobilisation	the planning was done step by step: problems were addressed as they arose
Implementation	self-mobilisation	the project was implemented by the individual land user, relatives and neighbours participated voluntarily in terrace construction
Monitoring/evaluation	self-mobilisation	the project is monitored and evaluated by the individual land user
Research	interactive	post-implementation documentation (participatory)

Differences in participation of men and women: Mainly men participated: women are not usually expected to carry out field activities for cultural reasons. The coffee harvest is the only activity where men and women work together in the field.

left: The son of the innovator (centre, without hat) who manages the conserved area, discussing technical impact with researchers from the NCCR North-South Programme (see research). (Hanspeter Liniger)
right: Cutting grass in the fenced plot: land use was changed from open access grazing to cut and carry. (Hanspeter Liniger)

Extension and promotion

Training: The land user's own knowledge proved quite adequate when he started to plan and implement the SWC measures, despite the fact that he had not received formal training.
Extension: 'Extension' of the technology happened through observation and farmer-to-farmer exchange of ideas.
Research: There had been no research until the identification and documentation of this initiative through a Tajik-Swiss project under the framework of the National Centre of Competence in Research (NCCR) North-South (coordinated by the Centre for Development and Environment, Switzerland).
Importance of land use rights: In soviet times the land was owned by a state farm, today it belongs to Khagatai village and is used as communal grazing land. When the fruit garden was first established an investigation resulted in approval of the private land use on these marginal lands. Today, despite efforts to get an owner's certificate, the official ownership for the land where the fruit garden is situated is with Khagatai village. Under such circumstances the land user is not willing to invest any more in the expansion of area, because of this insecurity.

Incentives

Labour: All labour by land users was voluntary.
Inputs: All the inputs were fully financed by the land user himself. This includes hand tools, fruit tree seedlings, vines, manure, supplementary irrigation, water transport by donkey and by car.
Credit: No credit was provided.
Support to local institutions: None.
Long-term impact of incentives: No incentives were available.

Monitoring and evaluation

Monitored aspects	Methods and indicators
Bio-physical	ad hoc observations by the land user concerning the growth of seedlings
Economic/production	ad hoc comparison of yields between different years
No. of land users involved	ad hoc observations

Impacts of the approach

Changes as result of monitoring and evaluation: There were a few changes due to the observations made by the land user: he started to apply supplementary irrigation to the tree seedlings, as well as to apply manure each year.

Improved soil and water management: There has been a significant, though localised, improvement in soil and water management.

Adoption of the approach by other projects/land users: Other land users from Khagatai village have adopted the system on the same hillside. They started fencing-off plots in the 1990s during the civil war. At that time many people were unemployed, and labour was therefore available. Furthermore there was a shortage in food supplies and people relied on the production from the land.

Sustainability: Because this approach is based on local initiative there is no reason why it should not endure. The insecure land use rights are the only potential risk to the continuation of the activities.

Concluding statements

Strengths and ➜ how to sustain/improve	Weaknesses and ➜ how to overcome
Bottom-up approach: independent decision making by the individual land user based on dynamic and flexible response ➜ Give property rights to land users to motivate further investments in soil and water conservation/production.	Since it is an initiative of an individual land user, the SWC technology has not been documented so far, nor evaluated, and lessons learned have not been spread among the land users ➜ Documentation and spreading of lessons learned.
Rehabilitation of marginal land for production and generation of additional income ➜ Give property rights to land users to motivate further investments in soil and water conservation/production.	Only families with sufficient labour resources can establish such a garden by themselves ➜ Incentives from the state or other organisations are needed.
	Not all farmers can apply this technology since it is location specific ➜ Identify if fodder production (cut-and-carry) would be more attractive than open grazing; allocate land to the farmers.
	Current systems of land ownership (today the land belongs to Khagatai village) ➜ Provide land ownership to the farmers.

Key reference(s): none.
Contact person(s): Sharif Allev family, Khagatai Village, Rayon of Varzob, Tajikistan ▪ Murod Ergashev, CAMP – Central Asian Mountain Partnership Program, 12, Istrafshan Str. Apt 5, 734025 Dushanbe, Tajikistan; phone: ++992 372 210227; murod@swiss.tojikiston.com

Orchard-based agroforestry

Tajikistan – Хамбастагии богот ва зироат

An agroforestry system where legumes and cereals are planted in fruit orchards, giving simultaneous production and conservation benefits.

In Faizabad region, Tajikistan, an area which is characterised by hilly topography and deep but highly erodible loess soils, farmers traditionally cultivated beans and wheat in combination with fruit trees. This was a rather unsystematic agroforestry system, and during soviet times (in the 1980s) fruit production was intensified. Pure-stand orchards were established: the land was leveled and on slopes exceeding 20% terraces were constructed mechanically. The density of trees was increased, and the little space remaining between was used for hay production. Annual cropping was stopped.

After the soviet era, farmers reduced the number of trees, allowing room for intercropping. They also established new orchards according to this same pattern. The density of apples was reduced by expanding the spacing from approx 5 m to 10 m between rows and from 2 m to 4 m within rows. Along each row of trees a 2–3 m strip of grass was left to grow. Layout of fruit tree lines is a compromise between being along the contour and against the prevailing wind. After harvesting of fruit, between August and October, farmers sow their annual crops. Those who farm leased land merely intercrop wheat, whereas the few farmers who own their land, rotate crops with two years of wheat followed by one of legumes (beans or lucerne). Crops are grown both for home consumption and sale.

This agroforestry system provides protection against strong winds, heavy rains and flooding. Soil erosion (by water) has been reduced due to improved soil cover by the intercrop, and through leaf litter, which is left to decompose on the ground. Furthermore, after harvesting, about three quarters of the crop residues are left on the field as mulch. The remainder is used as fodder. Soil organic matter within the current agroforestry system is considerably higher than in the surrounding grazing areas. Soil fertility has improved also: beans can fix 60–80 kg/ha/year of nitrogen. Compared with other crops, wheat provides the best erosion protection. Since the lateral rooting system of the apple trees reaches only 1–1.5 m from the trunk, competition for nutrients is not a major problem. Neither is there a problem with shading, since during the crop establishment period the trees have dropped their leaves. In order to increase production, farmers plan to apply supplementary irrigation where possible.

Location: Faizabad, Tajikistan
Technology area: 45 km²
SWC measure: vegetative, agronomic and structural
Land use: cropland: orchards (before), mixed: agroforestry (after)
Climate: semi-arid
WOCAT database reference: QT TAJ03
Related approach: Transition from centralised regime to local initiative, QA TAJ03
Author: Sanginov Sanginboy and Bettina Wolfgramm, Soil Science Institute, Dushanbe, Tajikistan
Date: January 2004, updated December 2004

Editors' comments: The major advantage of agroforestry lies in the functional integration of different resources and farming techniques. In this way the productivity of the farm system can be increased, and soil and water resources simultaneously conserved. As fruit production is very important for income generation in Tajikistan, this agroforestry system is already popular and has potential for wider application.

Classification

Land use problems
Most of the rains fall in late autumn and early spring, and the rains coincide with very strong winds. The topsoil is therefore exposed to erosion during this period if left uncovered, and without a windbreak. A particular problem during the soviet period was that the intensive orchard system meant annual food crops were left out of the production system: soil cover was reduced and there was less food.

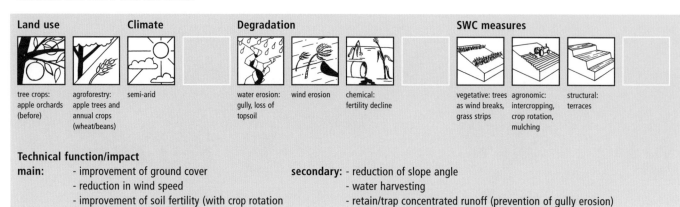

Land use		Climate		Degradation				SWC measures			

tree crops: apple orchards (before)

agroforestry: apple trees and annual crops (wheat/beans)

semi-arid

water erosion: gully, loss of topsoil

wind erosion

chemical: fertility decline

vegetative: trees as wind breaks, grass strips

agronomic: intercropping, crop rotation, mulching

structural: terraces

Technical function/impact
main:
- improvement of ground cover
- reduction in wind speed
- improvement of soil fertility (with crop rotation including beans and lucerne)

secondary:
- reduction of slope angle
- water harvesting
- retain/trap concentrated runoff (prevention of gully erosion)
- reduction of wind speed

Environment

Natural environment

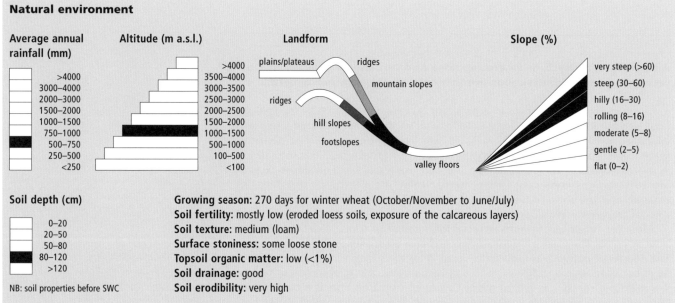

Average annual rainfall (mm)
>4000
3000–4000
2000–3000
1500–2000
1000–1500
750–1000
500–750
250–500
<250

Altitude (m a.s.l.)
>4000
3500–4000
3000–3500
2500–3000
2000–2500
1500–2000
1000–1500
500–1000
100–500
<100

Landform
plains/plateaus
ridges
mountain slopes
ridges
hill slopes
footslopes
valley floors

Slope (%)
very steep (>60)
steep (30–60)
hilly (16–30)
rolling (8–16)
moderate (5–8)
gentle (2–5)
flat (0–2)

Soil depth (cm)
0–20
20–50
50–80
80–120
>120

NB: soil properties before SWC

Growing season: 270 days for winter wheat (October/November to June/July)
Soil fertility: mostly low (eroded loess soils, exposure of the calcareous layers)
Soil texture: medium (loam)
Surface stoniness: some loose stone
Topsoil organic matter: low (<1%)
Soil drainage: good
Soil erodibility: very high

Human environment

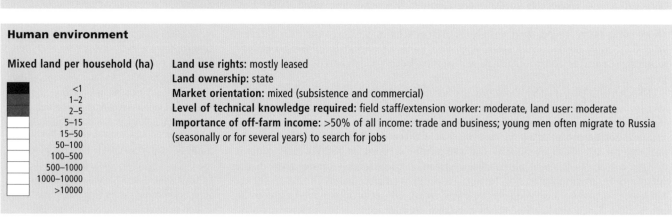

Mixed land per household (ha)
<1
1–2
2–5
5–15
15–50
50–100
100–500
500–1000
1000–10000
>10000

Land use rights: mostly leased
Land ownership: state
Market orientation: mixed (subsistence and commercial)
Level of technical knowledge required: field staff/extension worker: moderate, land user: moderate
Importance of off-farm income: >50% of all income: trade and business; young men often migrate to Russia (seasonally or for several years) to search for jobs

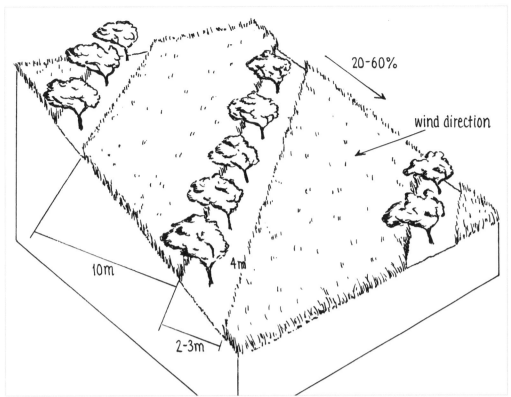

Technical drawing
Fruit trees intercropped with wheat (or beans): note the fruit trees are aligned on a 'compromise' between the direction of the prevailing wind and the slope.

20-60%

wind direction

10m

4m

2-3m

Implementation activities, inputs and costs

Establishment activities
1. Levelling of steep land into terraces with graders
2. Planting of fruit orchards
3. Thinning: doubling the spacing between trees (by farmers, after soviet era)

Note: these costs are not considered in the table

Establishment of new intercropped plots by farmers
1. Applying organic manure with machinery for crops and trees (November to March).
2. Ploughing with tractor to depth of 25–30 cm for annual crops (November to March).
3. Disc ploughing and harrowing with tractor (March).
4. Planting of fruit tree saplings by hand (March, April).
5. Chemical fertilizer application to crops (once during season).
6. Pest management with chemicals (two-three times where possible/affordable).

Duration of establishment: not specified

Establishment inputs and costs per ha

Inputs	Costs (US$)	% met by land user
Labour (around 20 person days)	60	100%
Equipment		
- Machines (30 hours)	120	100%
- Tools	10	100%
Agricultural		
- Fruit tree saplings (250)	250	100%
- Fertilizers (250 kg NPK)	50	100%
- Pesticides (6 kg)	30	100%
- Manure (15–20 tons)	30	100%
TOTAL	**550**	**100%**

Maintenance/recurrent activities
1. Ploughing of land and planting of crops.
2. Fertilisation and pest control.
3. Harvesting: wheat is the only crop that is harvested mechanically if tractors and fuel are available.
4. Mulching of trees.
5. Pest control for trees, three times a year (before and after flowering and after harvesting).
6. Pruning of trees.

Maintenance/recurrent inputs and costs per ha per year

Inputs	Costs (US$)	% met by land user
Labour (around 15 person days)	45	100%
Equipment		
- Animal traction (10 hours)	10	100%
- Tools	10	100%
Agricultural		
- Seeds (250 kg)	30	100%
- Fertilizers (250 kg)	50	100%
- Compost/manure (1 tons)	10	100%
- Pesticides (1 kg)	5	100%
Pruning	40	100%
Mulching	10	100%
TOTAL	**210**	**100%**

Remarks: Cost calculation refers to farmers who established new agroforestry plots (without receiving any incentives). These are farmers who have leased land from state farms. However, conversion of soviet orchards is more common than the establishment of new agroforestry plots (information on costs not available).

Assessment

Acceptance/adoption

Adoption rate is high: 3,500 households in the region, who leased the orchards, have converted them without any incentives. Marginal farmers received incentive support from NGOs (Care International, German Agro Action) or WFP (the UN's World Food Programme under their 'Food for Work' Programme).

Benefits/costs according to land user

Benefits compared with costs	short-term:	long-term:
establishment	positive	very positive
maintenance/recurrent	very positive	very positive

Impacts of the technology

Production and socio-economic benefits
+ + + crop yield increase
+ + + fodder production/quality increase
+ + wood production increase
+ + farm income increase

Production and socio-economic disadvantages
− trees hinder farm operations
− difficult to apply pesticides using machinery; furthermore pesticides are very expensive
− pruning is important, and farmers new to the system don't always have the skills required

Socio-cultural benefits
+ community institution strengthening
+ improved knowledge SWC/erosion

Socio-cultural disadvantages
− orchards managed by state farms are often not well looked after

Ecological benefits
+ + + soil cover improvement
+ + + increase in soil organic matter
+ + increase in soil fertility
+ + soil loss reduction
+ + biodiversity enhancement
+ + reduction of wind velocity
+ + increase water use efficiency
+ + increase nutrient use efficiency
+ increase in soil moisture
+ efficiency of excess water drainage

Ecological disadvantages
− up and down slope cultivation for supplementary irrigation promotes sheet and rill erosion

Off-site benefits
+ + reduced downstream flooding
+ + increased stream flow in dry season
+ + reduced river pollution
+ + reduced transported sediments
+ reduced downstream siltation

Off-site disadvantages
none

Concluding statements

Strengths and → how to sustain/improve

Easy to convert orchards → Land reform from state to private ownership would assist the process and strengthen farmers' associations.

Helps provide employment (mainly self-employment, partly employment of additional labourers) and increase self-sufficiency. With the cultivation of wheat, some farmers can solve their food problems and do not need an off-farm income.

Improvement of soil fertility and soil organic matter content → Use all the crop residue and leaves of trees as cover (mulch).

Considerable reduction of soil erosion → Adopt cover crop and rotation with other leguminous and minimum tillage system.

Wider spacing between the rows of trees (to 10 m) is best for the agro-forestry system to function well → Remaining orchards with the original (soviet) spacing of 5 m between the rows should be thinned.

Weaknesses and → how to overcome

The irrigation system established during soviet times required high maintenance inputs due to siltation of the canals. During the period of the civil war systems ceased to function, the canals filled up with sediments and finally overflowed during rain storms causing gully formation → Control of water flow within the orchard using cutoff drains and drainage ditches.

Lines of trees which are planted up and down the slope to provide wind protection are prone to water erosion → Compromise in layout design (see description).

Orchards managed by state farms are often not well looked after → leasing of land and awarding landholder certificates leads to improved orchard management.

Key reference(s): none
Contact person(s): Sanginov SR, Ergashev M, Akramov U, Mahamadkarimova S, Boturov U, Soil Science Institute, Rudaki aven 21A, Dushanbe, Tajikistan; soil2004@mail.ru; phone ++992-372-272979, fax ++992-372-213207

Transition from centralised regime to local initiative

Tajikistan – Ташаббуси дехконон ва хокимияти мутлак

left: Students documenting the technology; the farmer (brown hat) and a scientist from the Soils Institute (green hat) are the contributing specialists. (Peter Niederer)
right: The area around the orchards is used for grazing; note wind-swept trees in the background. (Hanspeter Liniger)

A land use system established during the authoritarian regime of the Soviet Union is being adapted to farmers' needs through their own initiative.

This case study compares two approaches which both contributed to the development of today's orchard-based agroforestry system: (1) Soviet approach: the previous state-run dictatorial system of the soviet times and (2) Farmers' initiative: the current bottom-up approach.

Farmers from the hilly Faizabad region with its deep and highly erodible loess soils had traditionally combined the cultivation of beans and wheat with fruit trees. In the 1980s the soviet administration decided to intensify apple production in this area and to establish orchards on a large scale, making use of the ideal natural environment. The system introduced comprised densely planted purestand orchards, mechanically constructed terraces (where the slopes required this), and an irrigation system. Establishment was conducted through a top-down/authoritarian approach, and all inputs for implementation and maintenance were provided by the state. Farmers worked as employees on the state farms and received cash wages.

After the collapse of the Soviet Union and the start of the civil war, Tajikistan suffered from acute food shortages. In 1993, the Tajik government lifted the prohibition on planting wheat in rainfed areas. Farmers leasing the land of the former state farms began to revert to intercropping annual crops – mainly wheat and beans – between thinned rows of apple trees. This was both for household use and for sale on the market. The initiative came from the farmers, and reflected the traditional system of production. However the pumping station and irrigation system have not been working for the last 10 years and therefore supplementary irrigation has not been available.

In contrast to former times, decision-making, management activities, and provision of inputs/finance are all carried out by the land users themselves. In some cases, marginal farmers received incentive support from NGOs or from the World Food Programme. Systematic assistance from extension services, financial support to purchase pesticides or fertilizers, and investment to restore the irrigation system would all help to improve the agroforestry system and thus raise yields.

Location: Faizabad, Tajikistan
Approach area: 45 km²
Land use: mixed: agroforestry
Climate: subhumid
WOCAT database reference: QA TAJ03
Related technology: Orchard-based agroforestry, QT TAJ03
Compiled by: Sanginboy Sanginov, Soil Science Institute, Dushanbe, Tajikistan
Date: May 2004, updated December 2005

Editors' comments: This case illustrates the challenges in the transition from state-run large-scale farming to individual management of smaller units. In this case, soviet Tajikistan had established pure-stand orchards. However, in response to acute food shortage during the civil war, farmers started to intercrop wheat and beans in their orchards: a better all-round production/conservation system.

Problem, objectives and constraints

Problem
- Soviet times: the original problems addressed by the authorities during the soviet era was how to increase agricultural production in a purely technocratic way, without consideration of the rural population.
- Post-soviet period: in 1993, when the soviet era ended and the prohibition on cultivation of wheat was lifted, the underlying problem was a shortage of food – and especially of wheat.

Objectives
- Soviet approach: increase apple production in a region with ideal biophysical conditions.
- Farmers' initiative: to make more intensive use of agricultural lands through an agroforestry system, and especially to provide food security by growing annual crops between the trees.

Constraints addressed

	Specification	Treatment
Soviet approach		
Financial	The establishment and maintenance of the irrigation system, terraces and the orchards themselves required high financial input.	Equipment, seedlings and salaries were all provided by the soviet state.
Farmers' initiative		
Financial	Lack of funds for fertilizers, manure (which is burned as fuel for heating) and pesticides.	Improved fertility management: farmers developed cost – effective practices such as crop rotation and fallow periods, etc.

Participation and decision making

Target groups

Land users (farmers)

Teachers/ students/ school children*

* only in soviet times

Approach costs met by:

	Soviet approach	Farmers' initiative
National government	100%	
Community/local		100%
	100%	100%

Decisions on choice of the technology: Soviet approach: made by the state and local authorities. Farmers' initiative: mainly by land users supported by specialists.

Decisions on method of implementing the technology: Soviet approach: made by technical specialists. Farmers' initiative: mainly by land users supported by agricultural extension service (technical assistance).

Approach designed by: National specialists designed the approach to establish the orchards in the 1980s (soviet approach). Since 1993 it was the land users who designed the approach.

Community involvement

Phase	Involvement	Activities
Soviet approach		
Initiation	none	
Planning	none	
Implementation	payment	casual labour
Monitoring/evaluation	interactive	observations, public meetings, workshops
Research	passive	technology development in the Faizabad Horticulture Institute
Farmers' initiative		
Initiation	self-mobilisation	farmers' innovation: increase crop production by intercropping in orchards
Planning	self-mobilisation	responsibility for all the steps
Implementation	self-mobilisation / interactive	responsibility for all the steps, technical assistance from extensionists
Monitoring/evaluation	self-mobilisation	observations
Research	none	

Differences in participation between men and women: During soviet times, decisions within the collective farms were mainly made by men, though both men and women worked in the field. Nowadays a large number of men migrate to other countries to raise household income. Therefore most of the work during the summer lies on the shoulders of women. During spring, and part of the autumn, men are present and active in fieldwork.

left: Farmer bringing fodder home from the field: grass is cut between the fruit trees. (Hanspeter Liniger)
right: The farmer and his agroforestry system: a combination of pear trees and wheat. (Hanspeter Liniger)

Extension and promotion

Training: When the establishment of pure-stand orchards started in the 1980s under the soviet regime, the knowledge of farmers in the area of orchard implementation and maintenance was inadequate. Training was provided on-the-job, by public meetings and through courses. Training focused on improving irrigation, tree planting practices and tree management. Training conducted during the establishment of the orchards was useful and adequate. No training was given (naturally) in intercropping of wheat and other cereals between the rows of apple trees – the farmers' initiative. However in order to manage and adjust the land use system to today's situation, more training is needed.
Extension: For the running of the orchards during the soviet times a top-down/authoritarian approach was used: specialists/instructors led implementation in the field. All inputs were provided by the state, and farmers were used as casual labour. The bottom-up approach based on farmers' initiative for establishment of orchard/wheat intercropping worked through farmer-to-farmer extension. Farmers were supported by extension staff.
Research: During the original establishment of the orchards, research was conducted. For the new system of intercropping with wheat, research contributed by providing support with respect to choice of varieties.
Importance of land use rights: Allowing cropping on the farms was the first move; then land use rights were shifted from state to individual farmers. While those orchards which are still managed as state farms are often not well looked after, leasing of land and issue of landholder certificates generally leads to improved orchard management. However, access to land belonging to state farms (through lease agreements) is limited to people who have previously been members of those state farms.

Incentives

Labour: When the orchard plantations were originally established, people worked on state farms for cash wages. Nowadays labour is voluntary.
Inputs: Soviet approach: State provision of all inputs needed; Farmers' initiative: no inputs provided. Marginal farmers are supported by NGOs (Care International, German Agro Action) or WFP (the UN's World Food Programme under their 'Food-for-Work' Programme).
Credit: For the original establishment of orchards credit was provided by the state at a very low interest rate. Currently, for cultivating cereals and legumes, farmers have access to credit, but the interest rate is very high.
Support to local institutions: No support to local institutions – now or before.
Long-term impact of incentives: The fruit trees were established under the soviet system through paid labour, and thus represent an asset that can be used profitably. With respect to the new initiatives, there are no incentives involved.

Monitoring and evaluation

Monitored aspects	Methods and indicators	
	Soviet system	Farmers' initiative
Bio-physical	regular measurements (not specified)	ad hoc observations of erosion and crop growth – sedimentation and plant development
Technical	regular measurements: quantity of water per ha – irrigation infrastructure	–
Economic/production	regular measurements of income and yields	regular calculation of farmers' yield and profit
Area treated	regular measurements	ad hoc calculation
No. of land users involved	regular measurements	ad hoc observation

Impacts of the approach

Changes as result of monitoring and evaluation: None under either.
Improved soil and water management: Currently: moderate positive impact on soil and water conservation through the agroforestry system.
Adoption of the approach by other projects/land users: None known.
Sustainability: The soviet approach of orchards managed through state farms effectively died with the collapse of the Soviet Union: the irrigation system ceased to function and inputs were not provided anymore by the state. Furthermore, the land use system was not adapted to the farmers needs. To improve productivity of the current system and thus stimulate the farmers' approach, further external support (with equipment, seed, gasoline, extension support etc) is needed.

Concluding statements

Strengths and ➜ how to sustain/improve	Weaknesses and ➜ how to overcome
Soviet approach	**Soviet approach**
Well managed and controlled land use system with efficient irrigation system, high production, ensured maintenance, provision of fertilizers and technical assistance.	No diversity, mono-cropping system aimed at maximised production; as soon as state support ceased, the system collapsed.
Farmers' initiative	**Farmers' initiative**
Farmers are themselves finding a way out of the poverty trap ➜ Land reform should go further and every farmer should be eligible for land certificates/titles.	Land use rights: as long as the land still belongs to the state, people have very little motivation to improve it ➜ Privatise the land.
Farmers get diversified and additional products (grain, apples, beans, hay, etc) ➜ The government should support the farmers' initiatives. The marketing system of the fruits should be developed.	Further extension of the agroforestry system is limited without support from the extension service ➜ The extension service should provide more inputs.

Key reference(s): none
Contact person(s): Tabarov Abdugaffor, Dekhan Farm Mehrobod, District Faizabad ▪ Ergashev M, Soil Science Institute, Rudaki aven 21A, Dushanbe, Tajikistan; murod@swiss.tojikiston.com

left: A series of dohs temporarily filled with runoff water before infiltration. (David Gandhi)
right: Harvesting chilli peppers from land brought under irrigation through the effect of dohs. (William Critchley)

Sunken streambed structure

India – *Doh*

Excavations in streambeds to provide temporary storage of runoff, increasing water yields from shallow wells for supplementary irrigation.

Dohs are rectangular excavations in seasonal streambeds, which are intended to capture and hold runoff to enhance groundwater recharge, thus increasing water for irrigation from nearby shallow wells. They also collect and impound sub-surface flow. *Dohs* are built in semi-arid areas where rainfall is low and seasonal.

The dimension of a typical *doh* is 1.0–1.5 m deep with variable length (up to 40 m) and width (up to 10 m) depending on streambed section, with an average capacity of 400 m³. The excavated material is deposited along the stream banks as a barrier against siltation from surrounding areas. The slopes of the excavation are gentle (an upstream slope of 1:6 or 17% and a downstream slope of 1:8 or 12%) so that water flows into it, and excess water out again, carrying silt rather than depositing it. The sides however are steep, to increase capacity – and would benefit from stone pitching to stabilise them. A silt trap comprising a line of loose boulders is constructed upstream across the streambed. *Dohs* are generally built in sequence. They may be as close as a few metres apart. Bends in the stream are avoided as these are susceptible to bank erosion.

The technology is used in conjunction with shallow wells *(odees)*, which enable farmers to harvest the increased groundwater for supplementary irrigation of annual crops – including vegetables such as chilli peppers. Water is pumped out of the wells. In the case study village, Mohanpada, each *doh* basically supplies an underground source of extra water to one well. Communities together with project staff carry out site selection, and then detailed design/estimates/layout is done with project technical assistance. As a supportive measure the catchment area is treated with gully plugs (small stone checks in gullies). A water harvesting tank (small reservoir or dam) may be excavated above the series of *dohs* where this is justified by a sufficiently large catchment area/suitable site. The capacity of the tank at Mohanpada is around 600 m³ and thus also has a positive impact on groundwater recharge.

Maintenance is agreed through meetings of user groups: manual desilting is planned and repairs of gully plugs also. In summary, *dohs* are low cost water recharge alternatives for poorer communities, and in this case study, the extra area brought under production has meant that all families that require it, now have access to some water for irrigation.

Location: Mohanpada, Ratlam, Madhya Pradesh, India
Technology area: 0.1 km²
SWC measure: structural
Land use: cropland and grazing land
Climate: semi-arid
WOCAT database reference: QT IND03
Related approach: Comprehensive watershed development, QA IND01
Compiled by: VK Agrawal and David Gandhi, Ratlam, Madhya Pradesh, India
Date: October 2002, updated June 2004

Editors' comments: Recharge structures for deep percolation of runoff and thus replenishment of groundwater for well-based irrigation are common features of Indian watershed management projects. The *doh* is innovative, being shallow, sited within a seasonally dry riverbed, and relatively cheap. This is a case study from a single village, Mohanpada, in Madhya Pradesh.

Classification

Land use problems
There are regular poor yields of agricultural crops on the degraded, rainfed fields. A further constraint is the limited amount of water in wells, restricting both the extent of irrigation, and the number of people with access to irrigation. There is an underlying problem of poverty, which in turn leads to seasonal out-migration to find work.

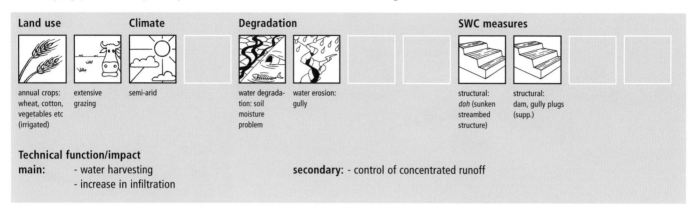

Land use

annual crops: wheat, cotton, vegetables etc (irrigated)

extensive grazing

Climate

semi-arid

Degradation

water degradation: soil moisture problem

water erosion: gully

SWC measures

structural: *doh* (sunken streambed structure)

structural: dam, gully plugs (supp.)

Technical function/impact
main: - water harvesting
- increase in infiltration

secondary: - control of concentrated runoff

Environment

Natural environment

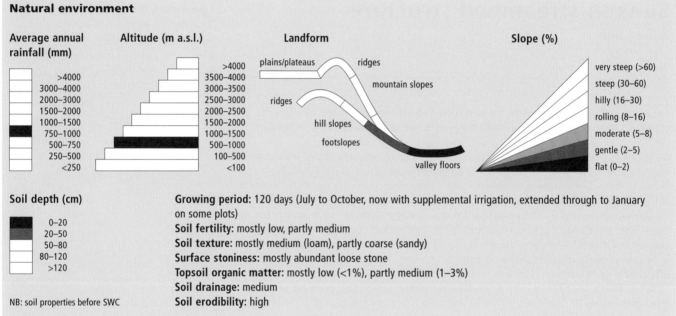

Average annual rainfall (mm)

>4000
3000–4000
2000–3000
1500–2000
1000–1500
750–1000
500–750
250–500
<250

Altitude (m a.s.l.)

>4000
3500–4000
3000–3500
2500–3000
2000–2500
1500–2000
1000–1500
500–1000
100–500
<100

Landform

plains/plateaus
ridges
mountain slopes
ridges
hill slopes
footslopes
valley floors

Slope (%)

very steep (>60)
steep (30–60)
hilly (16–30)
rolling (8–16)
moderate (5–8)
gentle (2–5)
flat (0–2)

Soil depth (cm)

0–20
20–50
50–80
80–120
>120

NB: soil properties before SWC

Growing period: 120 days (July to October, now with supplemental irrigation, extended through to January on some plots)
Soil fertility: mostly low, partly medium
Soil texture: mostly medium (loam), partly coarse (sandy)
Surface stoniness: mostly abundant loose stone
Topsoil organic matter: mostly low (<1%), partly medium (1–3%)
Soil drainage: medium
Soil erodibility: high

Human environment

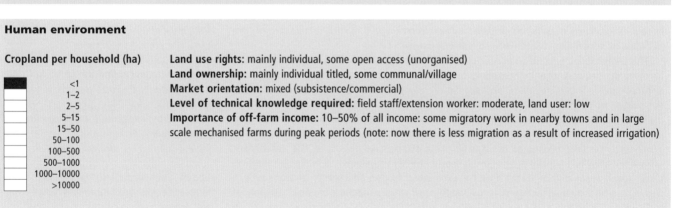

Cropland per household (ha)

<1
1–2
2–5
5–15
15–50
50–100
100–500
500–1000
1000–10000
>10000

Land use rights: mainly individual, some open access (unorganised)
Land ownership: mainly individual titled, some communal/village
Market orientation: mixed (subsistence/commercial)
Level of technical knowledge required: field staff/extension worker: moderate, land user: low
Importance of off-farm income: 10–50% of all income: some migratory work in nearby towns and in large scale mechanised farms during peak periods (note: now there is less migration as a result of increased irrigation)

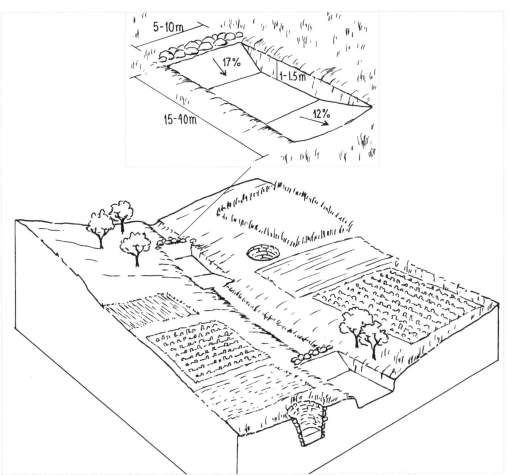

Technical drawing
Overview of sunken streambed structures *(doh)* with associated wells and irrigated plots. Note that several *dohs* are applied in series along the waterway.
Insert: Detail of a single sunken streambed structure. Gentle slopes in the direction of flow ensure minimal erosion of the structure, while lateral walls are steep to increase storage capacity (average 400 m³). Stone barriers help avoid siltation of *dohs*.

Implementation activities, inputs and costs

Establishment activities
1. Site selection with the community by eye.
2. Identification of the beneficiaries and user groups.
3. Design and estimations by project staff using surveying instruments ('dumpy levels') and measuring tapes.
4. Agreement of village committee.
5. Catchment treatment begins – using hand tools: including water harvesting tank (capacity in this case about 600 m³) and small gully plugs from earth or loose stone, as required.
6. Excavation of dohs (200–400 m³) as last action with silt traps upstream of each made from loose stone.
7. Wells *(odees)* may be deepened and pumps bought – though those costs are not included here.

Duration of establishment: 1 year

Establishment inputs and costs per ha

Inputs	Costs (US$)	% met by land user
Labour (225 person days)	225	25%
Equipment		
- Tools	15	100%
Materials		
- Stone (2 m³)	0	
TOTAL	**240**	**30%**

Maintenance/recurrent activities
1. Desilting of *dohs* in dry periods by hand.
2. Maintenance of catchment treatments (desilting of gully plugs etc) if required.

Maintenance/recurrent inputs and costs per ha per year

Inputs	Costs (US$)	% met by land user
Labour (5 person days)	5	100%
TOTAL	**5**	**100%**

Remarks: The construction of one *doh* costs between US$ 200–400, depending on the size of the *doh* (approximately one cubic metre can be excavated per person day at a cost of one US dollar). On a per hectare basis the costs are very variable, since they are related to the extra area brought under irrigation. In this case study there are four *dohs* within a total village area of 50 ha. Ten of the 50 ha have been brought into irrigated production (extra to the 5 ha already irrigated) due to the four *dohs* and the 'tank' and the costs outlined above are spread over those 10 ha. In this case half of the costs are directly attributable to *dohs* (average capacity 400 m³ each), and half to catchment treatment where the water-harvesting tank (a reservoir of approximately 600 m³) is the main cost. Where there is underlying rock, mechanical drills and blasting by dynamite may be required, which increases the costs. That was not the case in this village. The cost of deepening/widening the five wells *(odees)* has not been included here: that is carried out by the villagers themselves. While the project normally pays around 85% of labour costs, here at Mohanpada village the project only needs to pay 75%, due to a high level of commitment by the villagers.

Assessment

Acceptance/adoption
- All who implemented the technology did so with incentives – comprising wages from the project.
- Reasons for voluntary contributions (here representing 25% of costs) include visible production benefits.
- Spontaneous adoption is growing in neighbouring villages.

Benefits/costs according to land user	Benefits compared with costs	short-term:	long-term:
	establishment	positive	very positive
	maintenance/recurrent	positive	very positive

Impacts of the technology

Production and socio-economic benefits	Production and socio-economic disadvantages
+ + + crop yield increase	– increased economic inequity in some villages (between those with wells and those without)
+ farm income increase	
Socio-cultural benefits	**Socio-cultural disadvantages**
+ + + improved knowledge SWC/erosion	– socio-cultural conflicts (see above)
+ + community institution strengthening	– reduced amount of water to downstream users
Ecological benefits	**Ecological disadvantages**
+ + + groundwater increase	none
+ + + increase in soil moisture	
+ + soil cover improvement (where cultivated)	
+ + soil loss reduction (in catchment)	
Off-site benefits	**Off-site disadvantages**
+ + + reduced downstream flooding	– reduced peak flows so downstream users may be deprived of some water
+ + reduced downstream siltation	
+ reduced river pollution	
+ increased stream flow in dry season	

Concluding statements

Strengths and ➜ how to sustain/improve
Dohs are a low cost alternative method of increasing groundwater in a semi-arid area where production of high value legumes depends on irrigation – and *dohs* represent the best way in this situation of expanding the extent of irrigated land, and bringing irrigation to more families.

Small, multiple recharge points for replenishing groundwater for irrigation from wells ➜ Breaking hard pan in stream bed mechanically by drills or blasting to deepen *dohs* and thereby make them more effective.

No risk of breaches of bunds as the structures are sunken below ground.

Weaknesses and ➜ how to overcome
Group maintenance is required ➜ Form user groups.

Villagers are more used to (and may prefer) larger and deeper 'tanks' ➜ Establish more *dohs* to create more impact.

Dohs are limited in capacity and thus dry up quickly, as do the wells ➜ Establish more dohs to create more impact.

Key reference(s): none available – this is the first documentation

Contact person(s): Agrawal VK and Nayak T: danidain@mantrafreenet.com or pmdanida@sancharnet.in; Comprehensive Watershed Development Project, 22 Pratap Nagar, RATLAM – 457 001, MP, India ■ David Gandhi: david_gandhi@yahoo.com

left: A community assembles to discuss the formation of a village development plan. (David Gandhi)
right: At Mohanpada, the village development plan is brought out to be shown to visitors. (William Critchley)

Comprehensive watershed development

India

Participatory approach that includes a package of measures leading to empowerment of communities to implement and sustain watershed development.

The approach adopted under the Comprehensive Watershed Development Project (CWDP) is intended to ensure sustainability of development interventions. This can only be achieved through creating a sense of 'ownership' amongst users, which means involving the community in planning, implementation and management of the interventions. A further, specific objective is to benefit vulnerable sections of the community.

Various methods are employed to achieve these goals. There is, first of all, awareness generation within the community through exposure visits outside the area, street theatre and video shows. After this comes the formation and capacity building of village level institutions, in particular the Village Watershed Development Committees (VWDCs). Users' groups are also formed. Micro-planning (under a 'village development plan') using participatory rural appraisal (PRA) follows. There are arrangements to ensure participatory execution of the plan, specifying cost and benefit sharing (on average 75%–90% of the work is paid for in cash under this approach). Another important element is to ensure user rights to resources. This entails negotiation with government for rights to produce from common land. Eventually, after initial implementation, management becomes the task of the users' groups: this includes maintenance, distribution of benefits and conflict resolution.

The whole process involves NGOs along with government staff in order to achieve better communication all round. The participants have different roles. Government staff (at various levels) provides technical and financial support, as well as assistance towards gaining user rights over resources. NGOs are particularly important in awareness generation and mobilisation, capacity building of village level institutions, and in the process of negotiation with the Government. The village committee is central in planning and implementation of the village development plan, and in overseeing users' groups. Users' groups are involved in planning, implementation and then resource management. The village assembly helps to identify beneficiaries and users, and to give overall support to the VWDC. An external international donor, DANIDA of Denmark, supports the Comprehensive Watershed Development Project.

Location: three watersheds around Ratlam, Madhya Pradesh, India
Approach area: 260 km²
Land use: cropland and grazing land
Climate: semi-arid
WOCAT database reference: QA IND01
Related technology: Sunken streambed structure *(doh)*, QT IND03 – and other technologies
Compiled by: David Gandhi, DANIDA Advisor, Comprehensive Watershed Development Project, Ratlam, Madhya Pradesh, India
Date: September 2002, updated June 2004

Editors' comments: Participatory approaches to watershed development have been increasing in popularity over the last twenty years in India. There are many variations – depending on which organisation gives support. This is one example of a bilateral donor (DANIDA) working with a government agency.

Problem, objectives and constraints

Problem
- previous lack of consultation/involvement with the community in planning, implementation and management of watershed development interventions

Objectives
- create a sense of ownership amongst users
- ensure sustainability of technical and social interventions
- benefit more vulnerable sections of the community, including the poor and women
- involve the community in planning, implementation and management interventions

Constraints addressed		
Major	**Specification**	**Treatment**
Social/cultural/religious	Competition between villages for resources of land and water.	Negotiations facilitated by NGOs.
Social/cultural/religious	Lack of awareness and mobilisation on improvement of production systems.	Awareness generation programme.
Minor	**Specification**	**Treatment**
Institutional	Lack of effective village institutions.	Formation and capacity building of various institutions.
Legal	Uncertainty over rights to access to resources.	Negotiations facilitated by NGOs.
Technical	High cost water harvesting measures.	Demonstration of low cost alternatives such as the *doh* (sunken structure in dry riverbed to increase infiltration of runoff, which replenishes wells for irrigation: see 'related technology').

Participation and decision making

Target groups						Approach costs met by:	

Land users	
SWC specialists/ extensionists	
Teachers/school children/students	

Approach costs met by:	
International agency	85%
National government	5%
Community/local	10%
	100%

Decisions on choice of the technology: Mainly by SWC specialists with consultation of land users: 'exposure visits' to outside demonstration sites are used as a tool for sensitisation, motivation and awareness raising.
Decisions on method of implementing the technology: Mainly by land users – through village groups – supported by SWC specialists.
Approach designed by: National and international specialists.

Community involvement		
Phase	**Involvement**	**Activities**
Initiation	interactive	public meetings/awareness generation
Planning	interactive	PRA/discussion and negotiations
Implementation	interactive	responsibility for minor steps/land users provide labour
Monitoring/evaluation	interactive	measurements/observations by community with project staff
Research	passive	studies carried out by project staff

Differences in participation between men and women: Men traditionally make decisions. The project has worked towards involving women more, especially in self-help groups.

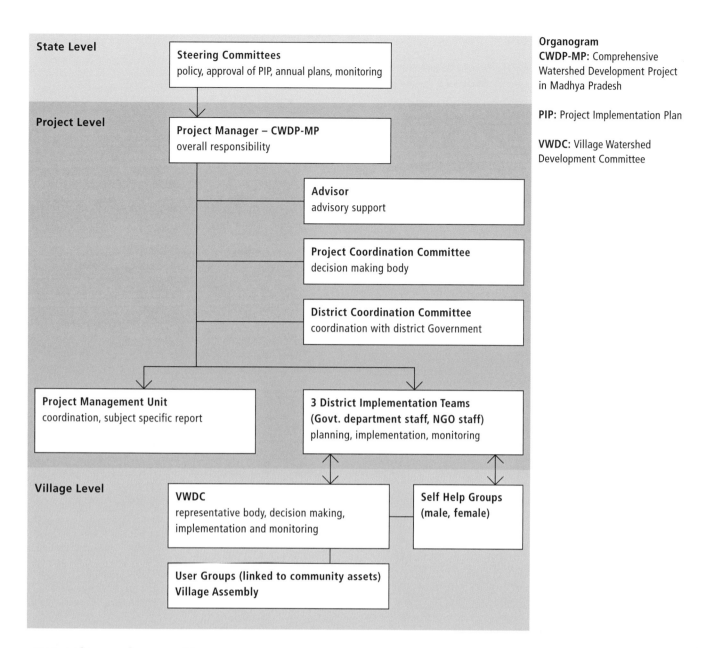

State Level	**Steering Committees** policy, approval of PIP, annual plans, monitoring	**Organogram** **CWDP-MP:** Comprehensive Watershed Development Project in Madhya Pradesh

Project Level

Project Manager – CWDP-MP
overall responsibility

PIP: Project Implementation Plan

VWDC: Village Watershed Development Committee

Advisor
advisory support

Project Coordination Committee
decision making body

District Coordination Committee
coordination with district Government

Project Management Unit
coordination, subject specific report

3 District Implementation Teams
(Govt. department staff, NGO staff)
planning, implementation, monitoring

Village Level

VWDC
representative body, decision making, implementation and monitoring

Self Help Groups
(male, female)

User Groups (linked to community assets)
Village Assembly

Extension and promotion

Training: There are courses, on the job training, and exposure visits. These are provided by government and NGO staff. Training concentrates on participatory approaches and low cost technologies. Capacity building for community groups and land users enables them to participate better in projects and to take ownership of assets. Effectiveness of the training has been fair.

Extension: National and State Government policies nowadays emphasise the 'participatory approach'. Extension has been delivered through multidisciplinary teams from Government departments, and village level workers through various NGOs. However Government – NGO cooperation needs now to be institutionalised. Effectiveness of extension has generally been good.

Research: Research has had little impact on the programme's effectiveness.

Importance of land use rights: Although ownership rights have generally not been a problem, people didn't want to carry out SWC on Government land, and weren't allowed to do so on Forest Department land. The NGOs involved however acted as intermediaries in negotiations and helped solve the problems, ensuring user rights in some cases.

Incentives

Labour: As is common in Indian watershed development initiatives, there is a substantial subsidy towards labour involved. Under this approach 75–90% of the labour input is paid for in terms of cash: the remainder is a voluntary contribution.

Inputs: Machinery is fully financed: hand-tools are not subsidised.

Credit: None is provided.

Support to local institutions: As noted in the introductory description, there is considerable help given to institutions – through finance and training provided by the project.

Long-term impact of incentives: There is dependency created in the short-term on wages, but this will decrease when higher yields of crops (partially because of increased irrigation) become apparent and when there is no need for further investment in infrastructure.

Monitoring and evaluation

Monitored aspects	Methods and indicators
Bio-physical	regular observations of general parameters
Technical	regular measurements of water levels in some wells
Socio-cultural	ad hoc measurements of (reduced) migration
Economic/production	regular measurements of yield
Area treated	ad hoc observations of hectares treated
No. of land users involved	regular measurements of attendance at meetings
Management of approach	none

Impact of the approach

Changes as result of monitoring and evaluation: Several technological changes have taken place as a result of a review: for example feedback on yield data led to crop variety recommendations. Levels of water in wells confirmed impact of the 'sunken structures' *(dohs)*.

Improved soil and water management: This was 'moderate'/fairly successful.

Adoption of the approach by other projects/land users: The approach has not yet been widely adopted, but the State Department of Agriculture has begun to expand this approach to other projects.

Sustainability: At this early stage outside support is still required before the villages can be left to manage and sustain the improvements.

Concluding statements

Strengths and ➔ how to sustain/improve	Weaknesses and ➔ how to overcome
Government system can be strengthened by co-operation with NGOs in watershed management projects ➔ Continue dialogue between partners at various levels.	Because of low literacy levels NGO support to village level institutions is required for more than just short-term ➔ Adult literacy classes of sufficient duration are needed.
Land users are developing a strong sense of ownership of the assets created (in terms of cost-sharing, a local contribution of up to 25% is high in Indian contexts) ➔ There needs to be continued support for 2–3 years after phasing out of bio-physical watershed development activities; also important to build up village funds through a 'community contribution' charge deducted from wages.	PRA brings out many social factors that are beyond the scope of the project to influence eg the feudal system ➔ NGOs need to have broad-based activity platforms that can address these issues as they arise.
Systematic approach to strengthen community participation ➔ Detailed 'process documentation' to be continued.	Shortage of female staff restricts contact with women ➔ Gender sensitisation training needed for project staff.
Leadership developed at village level ➔ NGOs should continue to advise/guide/monitor activities.	Women are not adequately involved in exposure visits ➔ Correct this imbalance/arrange separate visits for women.
Marginalised groups have been identified and given a 'say' ➔ NGOs should continue to advise/guide/monitor activities.	Project duration for planning and implementation too short ➔ Increase the timespan to 3 years or more.
Awareness has been raised about SWC through drama and exposure visits ➔ Continue, and include visits to successful income generating projects.	A 'community contribution' charge is currently deducted equally from all villagers by the project from wages paid ➔ Should be a greater voluntary contribution from the richer farmers.
Participatory planning has led to better understanding of resources and possibilities ➔ The entire village plan should be implemented in defined stages to allow impact to be noted/felt.	Segregation of responsibilities between Government and NGO staff ➔ Better integrated teamwork should be the goal.

Key reference(s): none

Contact person(s): Nayak T: danidain@mantrafreenet.com or pmdanida@sancharnet.in, Comprehensive Watershed Development Project, 22 Pratap Nagar, RATLAM – 457 001, MP India ■ David Gandhi: david_gandhi@yahoo.com

Planting pits and stone lines

Niger – *Tassa avec cordon pierreux*

left: Adding manure to the pits *(tassa)* before planting. (William Critchley)
right: Stone lines in combination with *tassa*: the two measures act together to capture runoff and improve plant performance. (Charles Bielders)

Rehabilitation of degraded land through manured planting pits, in combination with contour stone lines. The planting pits are used for millet and sorghum production on gentle slopes.

The combination of planting pits *(tassa)* with stone lines is used for the rehabilitation of degraded, crusted land. This technology is mainly applied in semi-arid areas on sandy/loamy plains, often covered with a hard pan, and with slopes below 5%. These denuded plains are brought into crop cultivation by the combination of *tassa* and stone lines. Planting pits are holes of 20–30 cm diameter and 20–25 cm depth, spaced about 1 m apart in each direction. The excavated earth is formed into a small ridge downslope of the pit. Manure is added to each pit, but its availability is sometimes a problem. At the start of the rainy season, millet or sorghum is sown in these pits. The overall aim of the system is to capture and hold rainfall and runoff, and thereby improve water infiltration, while increasing nutrient availability.

Stone lines are small structures, at most three stones wide and sometimes only one stone high. The distance between the lines is a function of the slope and availability of stone. Typically they are sited 25–50 m apart on 2–5% slopes. Stones are usually collected from nearby sites – though sometimes up to 5–10 km away – and brought to the fields by donkey carts or lorries (when a project is involved). They are positioned manually, along the contour. Stone lines are intended to slow down runoff. They thereby increase the rate of infiltration, while simultaneously protecting the planting pits from sedimentation.

Often grass establishes between the stones, which helps increase infiltration further and accelerates the accumulation of fertile sediment. Wind-blown particles may also build up along the stone lines due to a local reduction in wind velocity. The accumulation of sediment along the stone lines in turn favours water infiltration on the upslope side. This then improves plant growth, which further enhances the effect of the system. Construction does not require heavy machinery (unless the stones need to be brought from afar by lorry).

The technique is therefore favourable to spontaneous adoption. Stone lines may need to be repaired annually, especially if heavy rains have occurred. Manure is placed every second (or third) year into the previously dug pits and sand is removed annually: normally the highest plant production is during the second year after manure application.

Location: Tahoua, Niger
Technology area: 40 km²
SWC measure: structural
Land use: mixed (silvo-pastoral) and wasteland (before), cropland (after)
Climate: semi-arid
WOCAT database reference: QT NIG02
Related approach: Participatory land rehabilitation, QA NIG01
Compiled by: Oudou Noufou Adamou, Tahoua, Niger
Date: August 1999, updated June 2004

Editors' comments: The combination of planting pits and stone lines is becoming increasingly common throughout the West African Sahel. It is based on traditional methods, and was pioneered on the Central Plateau of Burkina Faso. It is best with application of manure or compost, and is thus most suitable to mixed farming systems. Stone lines are most appropriate when there is abundant loose stone close by: in flat stone-free areas planting pits may be used alone.

Classification

Land use problems
Soil fertility decline is the basic problem: this is due to degradation and nutrient mining. Loss of limited rainwater by runoff and loss of soil cover result in low crop production and food insufficiency. This occurs in combination with lack of pasture, resulting in shortage of manure.

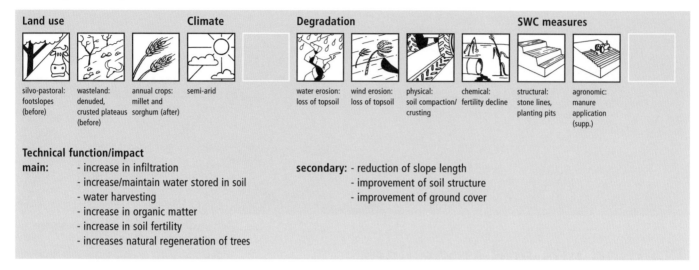

Land use
- silvo-pastoral: footslopes (before)
- wasteland: denuded, crusted plateaus (before)
- annual crops: millet and sorghum (after)

Climate
- semi-arid

Degradation
- water erosion: loss of topsoil
- wind erosion: loss of topsoil
- physical: soil compaction/ crusting
- chemical: fertility decline

SWC measures
- structural: stone lines, planting pits
- agronomic: manure application (supp.)

Technical function/impact
main:
- increase in infiltration
- increase/maintain water stored in soil
- water harvesting
- increase in organic matter
- increase in soil fertility
- increases natural regeneration of trees

secondary:
- reduction of slope length
- improvement of soil structure
- improvement of ground cover

Environment

Natural environment

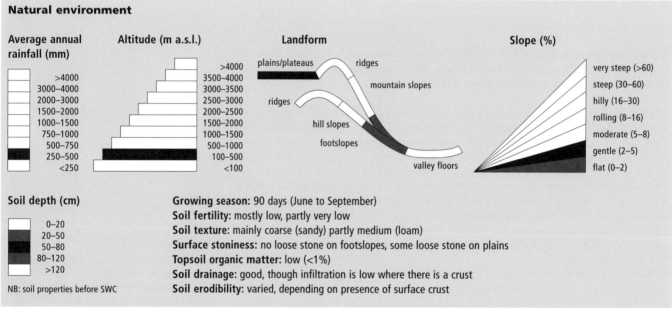

Average annual rainfall (mm)
- >4000
- 3000–4000
- 2000–3000
- 1500–2000
- 1000–1500
- 750–1000
- 500–750
- 250–500
- <250

Altitude (m a.s.l.)
- >4000
- 3500–4000
- 3000–3500
- 2500–3000
- 2000–2500
- 1500–2000
- 1000–1500
- 500–1000
- 100–500
- <100

Landform
- plains/plateaus
- ridges
- mountain slopes
- ridges
- hill slopes
- footslopes
- valley floors

Slope (%)
- very steep (>60)
- steep (30–60)
- hilly (16–30)
- rolling (8–16)
- moderate (5–8)
- gentle (2–5)
- flat (0–2)

Soil depth (cm)
- 0–20
- 20–50
- 50–80
- 80–120
- >120

NB: soil properties before SWC

Growing season: 90 days (June to September)
Soil fertility: mostly low, partly very low
Soil texture: mainly coarse (sandy) partly medium (loam)
Surface stoniness: no loose stone on footslopes, some loose stone on plains
Topsoil organic matter: low (<1%)
Soil drainage: good, though infiltration is low where there is a crust
Soil erodibility: varied, depending on presence of surface crust

Human environment

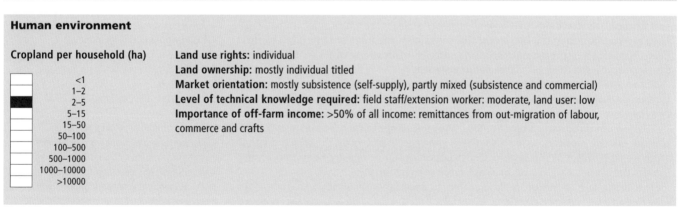

Cropland per household (ha)
- <1
- 1–2
- 2–5
- 5–15
- 15–50
- 50–100
- 100–500
- 500–1000
- 1000–10000
- >10000

Land use rights: individual
Land ownership: mostly individual titled
Market orientation: mostly subsistence (self-supply), partly mixed (subsistence and commercial)
Level of technical knowledge required: field staff/extension worker: moderate, land user: low
Importance of off-farm income: >50% of all income: remittances from out-migration of labour, commerce and crafts

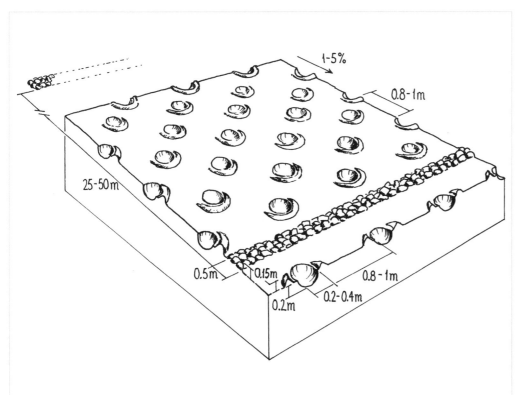

Technical drawing
Planting pits *(tassa)* capture rainfall runoff for cultivation of annual crops, and the stone lines – spaced at 25–50 metres apart – help hold back moisture and eroded soil.

Implementation activities, inputs and costs

Establishment activities

1. Digging pits *(tassa)* with a hoe in the dry season: the excavated earth forms ridges downslope of the hole. The pits are spaced about 1 m apart, giving approximately 10,000 pits/ha.
2. Digging out stones from nearby sites using a pick-axe and shovel.
3. Transporting stones with donkey cart or lorries.
4. Aligning the stones along the contour with the help of a 'water tube level': maximum of 3 stones wide.
5. Manuring the pits with approx 250 g per pit (2.5 t/ha).

All activities carried out in the dry season (November to May).
Duration of establishment: 1 year

Establishment inputs and costs per ha

Inputs	Costs (US$)	% met by land user
Labour for digging *tassa* (100 person days)	150	100%
Labour stone lines (25 person days)	40	100%
Equipment		
- Transporting stones with lorries 85–10 km)	40	0%
- Tools for *tassa*	5	100%
- Tools for stone lines	5	75%
Materials		
- Stone (50 m³)	0	
Agricultural		
- Compost/manure (2.5 t)	5	100%
TOTAL stone lines	85	52%
TOTAL *tassa*	160	100%
TOTAL stone lines and *tassa*	245	83%

Maintenance/recurrent activities

1. Removing sand from the *tassa* (annually, March–May).
2. Manuring the pits with about 250 g per pit (2.5 t/ha) every second year in October/November or March-May.
3. Check and repair stone lines annually and after heavy rains.

Maintenance/recurrent inputs and costs per ha per year

Inputs	Costs (US$)	% met by land user
Labour *tassa* (20 person days)	30	100%
Labour stone lines (1 person days)	1.5	100%
Equipment		
- Tools *tassa*	1	100%
Agricultural		
- Compost/manure (1.25 t)	2.5	100%
TOTAL	35	100%

Remarks: The costs are based on 300 m of stone lines per hectare (on a 3–4% slope). Maintenance costs refer to removing sand from the pits from the second year onwards, and to the application of manure every second year (costs are spread on an annual basis). If applicable, costs for transporting the manure need to be added. The general assumption in these calculations is that adequate manure is readily available close by. The availability of stones is the main factor in determining costs – though labour availability can affect prices also. If stones are not available in the field or nearby (from where they can be transported by donkey cart), they have to be carried by lorries, which is much more expensive. The costs here refer to fuel costs only, paid by a project: they do not include depreciation of lorries.

Assessment

Acceptance/adoption
All villagers accepted the technology with incentives of some hand tools and provision of transport for the collection of the stones (by lorries where necessary), which ensured a higher participation. There is moderate growing spontaneous adoption (for rehabilitation of the plains), but there are no estimates available regarding the extent.

Benefits/costs according to land user	Benefits compared with costs	short-term:	long-term:
	establishment	positive	very positive
	maintenance/recurrent	positive	very positive

Impacts of the technology

Production and socio-economic benefits	Production and socio-economic disadvantages
+ + + crop yield increase	– – increased labour constraints
+ + farm income increase	– – increased input constraints
Socio-cultural benefits	**Socio-cultural disadvantages**
+ + improved knowledge SWC/erosion	– land use rights conflicts of rehabilitated land
+ community institution strengthening through mutual aid in technology implementation	– conflicts between farmers and pastoralists because pasture land is being turned into cultivated fields
Ecological benefits	**Ecological disadvantages**
+ + long-term soil cover improvement	– waterlogging in planting pits after heavy rains
+ + increase in soil moisture	
+ + increase in soil fertility	
+ + increase in organic matter	
+ + soil loss reduction	
Off-site benefits	**Off-site disadvantages**
+ reduced downstream flooding	none
+ reduced downstream siltation	

Concluding statements

Strengths and → how to sustain/improve	Weaknesses and → how to overcome
Simple technology, individually applicable in the dry season, requiring only very little training/knowledge and no special equipment.	Labour demanding technology for implementation and maintenance → Mechanisation of tasks: transportation of stones and manure. However, this would raise the cost.
Making best use of manure, which is a limiting resource.	
Increase in agricultural production.	Instability of planting pits in loose soil, increased erosion on steeper slopes and with heavier rains → Avoid loose sandy soils and steep slopes.
Rehabilitation of degraded and denuded land: bringing back into production formerly uncultivated land; extension of farm land to the plateaus.	
	The effectiveness can be compromised if the various geo-morphological units (plateaus, slopes) are not treated simultaneously → Catchment area approach if downstream flooding is an issue.
	Possibility of land use conflicts concerning rehabilitated land, in particular with pastoralists → Better coordination/consultation before implementing the technology in an area.
	Implementation constraint: availability of manure and/or stones and transporting manure/stones to the plateaus and slopes → Subsidise transport means (or supply donkey carts) or/and apply stone lines only in areas where there are stones available close to the fields.

Key reference(s): Bety A, Boubacar A, Frölich W, Garba A, Kriegl M, Mabrouk A, Noufou O, Thienel M and Wincker H (1997): *Gestion durable des ressources naturelles. Leçons tirées du savoir des paysans de l'Adar.* Ministère de l'agriculture et de l'élevage, Niamey, 142 pp. ▪ Hassane A, Martin P and Reij C (2000) *Water harvesting, land rehabilitation and household food security in Niger: IFAD's Soil and Water Conservation Project in Illela District.* IFAD, Rome, 51 pp. ▪ Mabrouk A, Tielkes E and Kriegl M (1998) Conservation des eaux et des sols: Leçons des connaissances traditionnelles de la région de Tahoua, Niger. In: Renard, G., Neef, A,. Becker. K. and Von Oppen, M. (eds). *Soil fertility management in West African land use systems.* Proceedings of the Regional Workshop, 4-8 March 1997, Niamey, Niger. Margraf Verlag. Weikersheim/Germany. pp. 469–473.
Contact person(s): Charles Bielders, Dept. of Environ. Sciences and Land Use Planning – Agric. Engineering Unit, The Faculty of Bio-engineering, Agronomy and Environment, Université catholique de Louvain, Croix du Sud 2, boite 2, B-1348 Louvain-la-Neuve, Belgium, bielders@geru.ucl.ac.be ▪ Eric Tielkes, Centre for Agriculture in the Tropics and Subtropics, University of Hohenheim, 70593 Stuttgart, Germany, tielkes@uni-hohenheim.de

Participatory land rehabilitation

Niger – *Approche participative de récupération des terres individuelles et collectives*

left: A female extension worker showing the men of the village how to dig *tassa* – water harvesting planting pits. (Philippe Benguerel)
right: Harvested millet: production in the driest areas is possible through technologies promoted under projects with an appropriate approach. (William Critchley)

Planning and management of individual and village land, based on land users' participation, with simultaneous promotion of women's activities.

This approach is integral to the Tahoua Rural Development Project, PDRT *(Projet de Développement Rural de Tahoua),* a long-term project, which was initiated in 1988 and has been financed mainly through the German and Nigerien governments, but with voluntary participation and contributions from the local population.

The main goal of the approach is to plan and implement land management activities with villagers in such a way that sustainability is ensured. The specific objectives of the project are to: (1) increase the capacity of the villagers to design, implement and self-evaluate SWC activities; (2) develop and document management programmes for the village land; (3) restore and protect the agrosilvo-pastoral production potential; (4) develop and evaluate activities for the benefit of rural women; and (5) improve the capacity of government and private development agencies to coordinate and execute sustainable land rehabilitation. The technical focus of PDRT's approach is evident in its title. The project emphasises simple and cheap technologies that are replicable. Project extension work is carried out by facilitators and consists of awareness raising, demonstration and exchange trips.

Problem identification and planning of activities takes place in village meetings. The local land users are supported by project personnel who also provide technical assistance during the implementation of SWC measures.

Incentives are provided for the rehabilitation of marginal land for silvo-pastoral use, but nothing is given for individual agricultural land, other than the transport of stones using lorries – for those fields that do not have stones close by.

Through village groups and with the help of development agencies, the people of Tahoua district have succeeded in implementing measures to improve living conditions on a sustainable basis. However continuation of the approach is not ensured due to two major reasons: (1) land users do not have the means to carry on the activities on common land and (2) the government lacks the capacity and finance for extension. The project supported services stopped completely in 2003 – however a new programme began in 2004 with German cooperation and is currently attempting to use NGOs for extension work.

Location: Tahoua, Niger
Approach area: approx. 700 km²
Land use: mixed (silvo-pastoral) and wasteland (before), cropland (after)
Climate: semi-arid
WOCAT database reference: QA NIG01
Related technology: Planting pits and stone lines, QT NIG02
Compiled by: Oudou Noufou Adamou, Tahoua, Niger
Date: July 1998, updated June 2004

Editors' comments: Participatory approaches to SWC were developed by projects throughout the West African Sahel during the 1980s as a response to drought and land degradation. This particular approach is specific to the *Projet de Développement Rural de Tahoua,* in Niger and has been implemented over an area of approx. 700 km² since 1988. Together with improved rainfall over the last decade, such approach-technology combinations have been largely responsible for the recent widespread 'regreening' of many parts of the Sahel.

Problems, objectives and constraints

Problem
- previously the 'beneficiaries' of land rehabilitation programmes did not feel responsible/accountable and therefore were difficult to mobilise for voluntary participation in activities
- there had been no co-ordination and consultation between implementing agencies and organisations
- there was general degradation of the agrosilvo-pastoral ecosystem, and associated low returns from the land

Objectives
The general objective is to develop a participatory way of developing and implementing simple soil and water conservation measures – and ensuring sustainability by involving local people – with the overall goal of improving the status of the degraded ecosystem and uplifting the living conditions of the rural population.

Constraints addressed

Major	Specification	Treatment
Legal	Land ownership.	Application of the 'rural code', a legal instrument; however it does not sufficiently cover land access rights, therefore SWC technologies on common land can lead to exclusion of pastoralists who had former access to these sites.
Social	Missing (mainly male) labour due to seasonal out-migration.	Demonstrate technologies to improve the land and thus increase its profitability to reduce out-migration and search for less labour-intensive options.
Financial	Lack of financial resources of local groups for long term investments in SWC.	Create land users groups which can seek financial support together.

Minor	Specification	Treatment
Institutional	The government has neither the means nor the capacity to implement SWC everywhere.	Create decentralised bodies, eg farmer and pastoralist co-operatives.
Legal	Conflicts between various users of natural resources (eg farmers vs pastoralists).	Meetings and training on co-utilisation of certain resources, establishment of communally managed grazing schemes.
Social/cultural	Poor diffusion of information because of high illiteracy levels.	Adult literacy teaching, visual and/or oral extension forms (eg posters, theatre, radio).
Religious	Fatalism: 'God is responsible'.	Need to change mentality through training.
Institutional	Lack of coordination between projects.	Regional and national coordination.

Participation and decision making

Target groups

Land users   Planners   Politicians/decision makers

Approach costs met by:	
International agency	80%
National government	5%
Community/local	15%
	100%

Decision on choice of the technology: Made by land users supported by SWC specialist through village meetings, consultations, and participatory village assessments.
Decision on method of implementing the technology: Made by land users supported by SWC specialists during planning and training processes.
Approach designed by: National and international specialists.

Community involvement

Phase	Involvement	Activities
Initiation	self-mobilisation/interactive	problem identification in village meetings
Planning	interactive	self-evaluation of planning in village meetings
Implementation	self-mobilisation for individual land, payment/incentive for communal land	farmers supervised through project personnel
Monitoring/evaluation	interactive	through field observations (measurement of biomass development on certain sites) and self-evaluation in village meetings
Research	interactive	on-farm and on-station

Differences in participation between men and women: The participation of women is higher in community work (on common lands), partly because of seasonal out-migration of men. Work on individual fields is done mainly by men, but with a high participation of women during certain tasks – eg sowing and harvesting. Most women have small plots of land to cultivate by themselves.

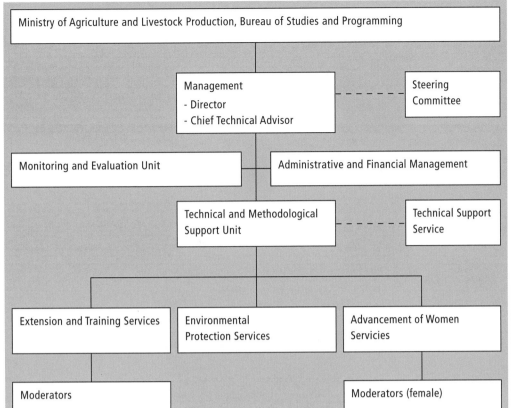

Ministry of Agriculture and Livestock Production, Bureau of Studies and Programming

Management
- Director
- Chief Technical Advisor

Steering Committee

Monitoring and Evaluation Unit

Administrative and Financial Management

Technical and Methodological Support Unit

Technical Support Service

Extension and Training Services

Environmental Protection Services

Advancement of Women Servicies

Moderators

Moderators (female)

Extension and promotion

Training: Training is carried out through public meetings, farm visits, courses, demonstration areas and hands-on practice. Target groups were first extensionists/trainers, then land users and also students. The training has generally been effective.
Extension: Project extension work is carried out by facilitators (extension staff) and consists of awareness raising, demonstration and exchange trips. The government extension service is unable to continue the work at the same level due to limited financial means. Effectiveness of extension on land users has been poor due to lack of coordination in planning and follow-up evaluation between project and extension services.
Research: On-farm research on technology and sociology is part of the approach. These include characterisation of SWC measures (with an emphasis on traditional technologies), and analysing problems of food-for-work, amongst other sociological studies. Some of this research was carried out by the project and some studies were carried out by local sociologists. No local research institutions were directly involved.
Importance of land use rights: At the outset, existing land ownership/land use rights were neglected and have therefore moderately hindered the implementation of the approach. The original objectives of SWC on common lands was to produce millet. However implementation took place without regard to existing land rights on these sites. As soon as people saw that it was possible to produce millet using this technology on these degraded lands, they brought forward historical claims and disputes developed as a result – though, more positively, in several areas a land market evolved. After these first experiences, PDRT stopped applying SWC technologies on common lands for crop production; instead the project changed focus towards silvo-pastoral production. Even this has provoked problems between agriculturalists and pastoralists.

Incentives

Labour: Labour is mostly voluntary, but partly rewarded with incentives. Food is provided for rehabilitation of marginal land for silvo-pastoral use, but nothing is given for individually owned agricultural land.
Inputs: The project has provided hand tools free of charge, occasionally subsidised seeds and tree nurseries, and furthermore has provided community infrastructure including roads and community buildings for meetings.
Credit: No credit was provided.
Support to local institutions: Local institutions received some support, essentially through training.
Long-term impact of incentives: A moderate negative impact is likely. In general, measures on individual fields are carried out and maintained well, without material incentives, but on communal land nothing is done without incentives (because of little interest, no direct profit, and the need for hard work). Local management structures for these rehabilitated sites will need to be developed by user groups.

Monitoring and evaluation

Monitored aspects	Methods and indicators
Bio-physical	regular measurements of area of improved land
Technical	regular measurements of area treated with various technologies
Economic/production	regular measurements of biomass production, yield of herbs, development of planted trees
Management of approach	regular measurements of finances, personnel, logistics, inputs used

Changes as result of monitoring and evaluation: There have been several changes since 1988. The project was reoriented from a focus merely on productivity towards a natural resources management approach. In 1990, anti-erosion technologies were introduced, and 1993/94 saw the start of a more comprehensive land management approach.

Improved soil and water management: There have been moderate improvements through establishment of the various SWC measures.

Adoption of the approach by other projects/land users: Various other projects in Niger – around six in total – have adopted the approach.

Sustainability: On common lands, land users will not be able to expand activities because they don't have the means (money, tools, lorries to transport stones, organisation) and they have no access to loans for implementation. However application of certain SWC technologies on individual fields – such as planting pits *(tassa)* or 'half moons' *(demi-lunes)* continues without any outside support.

Concluding statements

Strengths and ➜ how to sustain/improve	Weaknesses and ➜ how to overcome
Builds upon and improves indigenous knowledge of land users ➜ Self-evaluation is already sufficient to discuss weak points, successes and next steps.	The approach does not deal directly with out-migration of the young people ➜ Train young people (16–25 years): organise meetings and give ideas, for example: (1) rent cropland in small groups and grow vegetables during the dry season for sale; (2) train groups of SWC specialists.
Training and self-supervision of villagers ➜ Continue training, include all user groups, work out management schemes for reclaimed common lands.	Uncertain continuation: no formal decentralised body composed of villagers has been set up to take over functions currently under the project ➜ Provide sufficient training in terms of planning and also in skills to search for financial support.
Awareness creation about environmental issues and the importance of SWC technologies ➜ Continue this awareness creation.	
Increased production – most spectacularly on formerly abandoned areas ➜ Ensure maintenance of SWC technologies.	Disregarding existing land use rights led to conflicts between agriculturalists and pastoralists ➜ The project changed focus from crop production to silvo-pastoral production (see 'Importance of land use rights').
Improvement of village infrastructure: including roads and wells ➜ Continue with project/outside support as long as is possible.	

Key reference(s): Winckler H, Hertzler G (1996) *Préserver les coutumes, préparer l'avenir*. Présentation du PDRT, GTZ, Eschborn ■ Tielkes E (1998) Communally managed rotational grazing on reclaimed pastures in the northern Sahel. In: Lawrence P, Renard G and von Oppen M (eds) (1999) *Evaluation of technical and institutional options for small farmers in West Africa*. Margraf Verlag, Weikersheim/Germany. pp. 63–68 ■ Lycklama à Nijeholt R, Tielkes E and Bety A (2001) L'exploitation des pâturages aménagés : deux ans d'expériences au PDRT. In: Tielkes E, Schlecht E and Hiernaux P (eds). *Elevage et gestion de parcours, implications pour le développement*. Comptes-rendus d'un atelier régional ouest-africain sur 'La gestion des pâturages et les projets de développement: quelles perspectives?' October 2000, Niamey, Niger. Verlag Grauer, Beuren-Stuttgart/Allemagne. pp. 55–61.

Contact person(s): Charles Bielders, Dept. of Environ. Sciences and Land Use Planning – Agric. Engineering Unit, The Faculty of Bio-engineering, Agronomy and Environment, Université catholique de Louvain, Croix du Sud 2, boite 2, B-1348 Louvain-la-Neuve, Belgium, bielders@geru.ucl.ac.be ■ Eric Tielkes, Centre for Agriculture in the Tropics and Subtropics, University of Hohenheim, 70593 Stuttgart, Germany, tielkes@uni-hohenheim.de

Furrow-enhanced runoff harvesting for olives

إستغلال أثلام الفلاحة لحصاد المياه في بساتين الزيتون – Syria

Runoff harvesting through annually constructed V-shaped microcatchments, enhanced by downslope ploughing.

The Khanasser Valley in north-west Syria is a marginal agricultural area, with annual rainfall of about 220 mm/year. Soils are shallow and poor in productivity. The footslopes of degraded hills are traditionally used for extensive grazing or barley cultivation. However to achieve self-sufficiency in olive oil production, several farmers have developed orchards in this area – which is generally considered too dry for olives.

Trees are spaced at 8 m apart, within and between rows. Traditionally, farmers prefer to till their orchards by tractor in order to keep them weed-free (weeds may attract sheep, lead to fires and compete for water with the olive trees). As this tillage operation is usually practised up and down the slope, the resulting furrows stimulate runoff and erosion. However, when this is combined with V-shaped and/or fish-bone shaped microcatchments around individual trees, the furrows created can be used to harvest runoff water for improved production.

The V-shape earthen bunds (reinforced with some stones) are constructed manually, by hoe, around each tree. The furrows then divert runoff systematically to the microcatchments where it concentrates in basins around the trees. Each tree is effectively served by a catchment area of 60 m². The catchment: cultivated area ratio is thus approximately 60:1 (assuming the area exploited by the tree roots to be, initially at least, one square metre).

This technology saves irrigation water during the dry season, enhances soil moisture storage, and stimulates olive tree growth. Furthermore, fine particles of eroded soil are captured in the microcatchments. While these may be nutrient-rich, they also tend to seal the surface. The bunds need to be rebuilt every year. If the structures are damaged after a heavy storm, they need to be repaired. Labour input for establishment and maintenance is low, the technology is easy and cheap to maintain, and there is enough local skill to sustain and expand the system.

A supporting technology is to mulch the area around each tree with locally available stones (limestone and/or basalt) to reduce soil temperature during the summer, decrease surface evaporation and improve infiltration. The catchment areas between the trees are sometimes planted with low water-demanding winter annuals (lentils, vetch, barley, etc) especially when the trees are young. This helps to reduce surface erosion. Implementation of furrow-enhanced runoff water harvesting in olive orchards started in 2002, and adoption by farmers is growing gradually.

left: Runoff harvesting for olive trees by up-and-down tillage (by tractor) and V-shaped microcatchments (dug by hoe) in a semi-arid area, Khanasser Valley, Aleppo, Syria. (Francis Turkelboom)

right: Runoff is collected in micro-basins around each tree. The V-shaped bunds extend to the left. Stone mulching – as a supportive measure – further enhances moisture conservation by reducing evaporation (see picture in related approach). (Francis Turkelboom)

Location: Harbakiyeh and Habs, Khanasser Valley, Aleppo, NW Syria
Technology area: 0.05 km²
SWC measure: agronomic and structural
Land use: grazing land (before), cropland: orchard (after) and mixed: silvo-pastoral (after)
Climate: semi-arid
WOCAT database reference: QT SYR03
Related approach: Participatory technology development, QA SYR03
Compiled by: Francis Turkelboom, Ashraf Tubeileh, Roberto La Rovere, Adriana Bruggeman, ICARDA, Aleppo, Syria
Date: November 2004, updated April 2005

Editors' comments: Microcatchment runoff harvesting for tree planting in dry areas is a common practice worldwide. There are many traditional and project-introduced systems. This case study is an example developed jointly by researchers and farmers for olive trees in Syria.

Classification

Land use problems
There are a series of problems in this area, including: low and erratic rainfall, drought, low land productivity, poor water use efficiency, land degradation, limited ground water for irrigation, few agricultural options, and low income from agriculture.

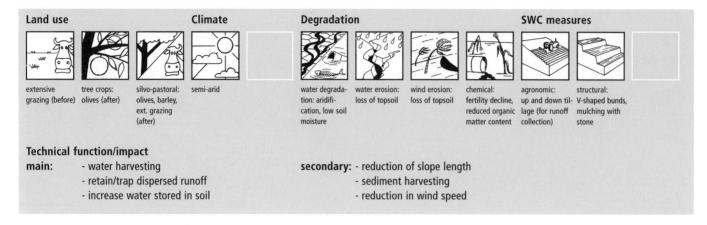

Land use
- extensive grazing (before)
- tree crops: olives (after)
- silvo-pastoral: olives, barley, ext. grazing (after)

Climate
- semi-arid

Degradation
- water degradation: aridification, low soil moisture
- water erosion: loss of topsoil
- wind erosion: loss of topsoil
- chemical: fertility decline, reduced organic matter content

SWC measures
- agronomic: up and down tillage (for runoff collection)
- structural: V-shaped bunds, mulching with stone

Technical function/impact
main:
- water harvesting
- retain/trap dispersed runoff
- increase water stored in soil

secondary:
- reduction of slope length
- sediment harvesting
- reduction in wind speed

Environment

Natural environment

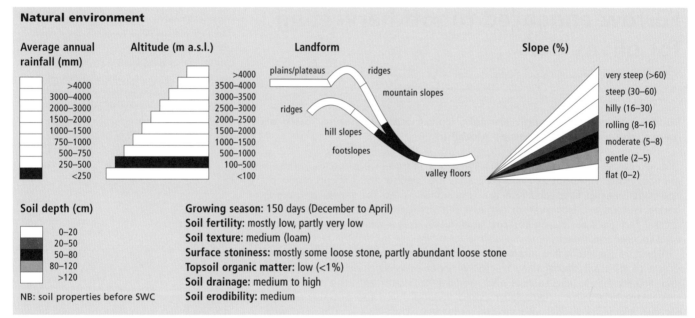

Average annual rainfall (mm)
- >4000
- 3000–4000
- 2000–3000
- 1500–2000
- 1000–1500
- 750–1000
- 500–750
- 250–500
- <250

Altitude (m a.s.l.)
- >4000
- 3500–4000
- 3000–3500
- 2500–3000
- 2000–2500
- 1500–2000
- 1000–1500
- 500–1000
- 100–500
- <100

Landform
- plains/plateaus
- ridges
- mountain slopes
- ridges
- hill slopes
- footslopes
- valley floors

Slope (%)
- very steep (>60)
- steep (30–60)
- hilly (16–30)
- rolling (8–16)
- moderate (5–8)
- gentle (2–5)
- flat (0–2)

Soil depth (cm)
- 0–20
- 20–50
- 50–80
- 80–120
- >120

NB: soil properties before SWC

Growing season: 150 days (December to April)
Soil fertility: mostly low, partly very low
Soil texture: medium (loam)
Surface stoniness: mostly some loose stone, partly abundant loose stone
Topsoil organic matter: low (<1%)
Soil drainage: medium to high
Soil erodibility: medium

Human environment

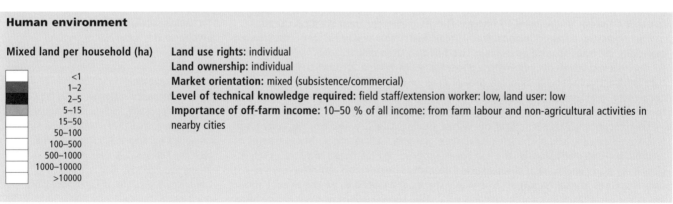

Mixed land per household (ha)
- <1
- 1–2
- 2–5
- 5–15
- 15–50
- 50–100
- 100–500
- 500–1000
- 1000–10000
- >10000

Land use rights: individual
Land ownership: individual
Market orientation: mixed (subsistence/commercial)
Level of technical knowledge required: field staff/extension worker: low, land user: low
Importance of off-farm income: 10–50 % of all income: from farm labour and non-agricultural activities in nearby cities

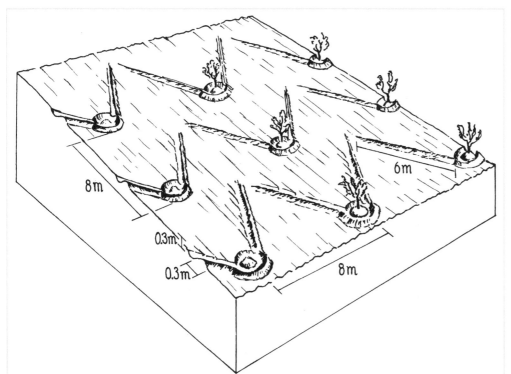

Implementation activities, inputs and costs

Establishment activities
V-shaped bunds are seasonal structures and thus established every year. Specifications are given under recurrent activities (see below).

Establishment inputs and costs per ha

Inputs	Costs (US$)	% met by land user
not applicable		

Maintenance/recurrent activities
1. Up-and-down tillage by tractor driven plough; in winter (November/December; beginning of rainy season).
2. Construction of runoff harvesting bunds and micro-basins, manually by hoe (November/December; beginning of rainy season).
3. Maintenance of bunds in winter/rainy season, after heavy rainfall; 1–3 times/year.

Labour for establishment of water harvesting structures: 10 person days; for repair: 5 person days.

Maintenance/recurrent inputs and costs per ha per year

Inputs	Costs (US$)	% met by land user
Labour		
- Construction (10 person days)	50	100%
- Repair (5 person days)	25	100%
Equipment		
- Machines (tractor rent)	10	100%
- Tools (hoe)	3	100%
Materials		
- Earth (in-situ available)	0	
TOTAL	**88**	**100%**

Remarks: The calculation covers the runoff harvesting technology alone – annual activities of ploughing and water harvesting structure establishment and maintenance. Planting of olive trees and their maintenance are not included here.

Assessment

Acceptance/adoption

- Generally moderate adoption: The technology is mainly applied by 'agriculturalists', that is households whose livelihoods mainly depend on agriculture. Farmers with more interest in off-farm labour or sheep rearing were less interested in adopting the technology.
- All of the land users who accepted the technology did so without receiving incentives – this was spontaneous adoption.
- The technology is expanding slowly but gradually.
- Reasons for adoption are, first, savings on the cost of irrigation water during the summer (fast returns); second, improved olive yield (long term benefit).

Benefits/costs according to land user

Benefits compared with costs	short-term:	long-term:
establishment	not applicable*	not applicable*
maintenance/recurrent	positive	not applicable**

* establishment is annual, see benefits compared to costs under maintenance/recurrent

** too early to define (olive trees still young)

Impacts of the technology

Production and socio-economic benefits
- + +   water saving
- + +   better tree growth
- +   crop yield increase

Production and socio-economic disadvantages
- – –   depends on availability of tractor
- –   hindered farm operations
- –   increased weed growth around trees
- –   increased labour constraints

Socio-cultural benefits
- + +   improved knowledge SWC/erosion
- +   improved landscape and environmental quality

Socio-cultural disadvantages
- none

Ecological benefits
- + + +   soil loss reduction
- + + +   reduced runoff
- + +   increase in soil moisture
- +   increase in soil fertility
- +   reduction of wind velocity
- +   biodiversity enhancement

Ecological disadvantages
- none

Off-site benefits
- +   reduced downstream flooding
- +   reduced downstream siltation

Off-site disadvantages
- –   reduced runoff for infiltration in valley bottom
- –   reduced sediment yields in valley bottom

Concluding statements

Strengths and ➜ how to sustain/improve

Increases soil moisture storage in low rainfall areas and allows expansion of olive plantation into drier areas ➜ Use organic amendments (mulch or manure), and more stone mulching.

Easy, low-cost and requires no extra external inputs.

Reduces soil erosion.

Reduces summer irrigation needs ➜ Use of localised (drip) irrigation will further reduce overall irrigation needs.

Improves olive productivity ➜ Rip land prior to planting to achieve further gains.

Weaknesses and ➜ how to overcome

Extra labour needed ➜ Construct during off-season.

Increases weed growth in the tree basin ➜ More stone mulching.

Trees will still need some irrigation in summer ➜ Make irrigation practices more efficient.

Key reference(s): Tubeileh A and Turkelboom F (2004) *Participatory research on water and soil management with olive growers in the Khanasser Valley.* KVIRS project, ICARDA, Aleppo, Syria ▪ Tubeileh A, Bruggeman A and Turkelboom F (2004) *Growing olive and other tree species in marginal dry environments.* ICARDA, Aleppo, Syria

Contact person(s): Francis Turkelboom – F.Turkelboom@cgiar.org ▪ Ashraf Tubeileh - A.Tubeileh@cgiar.org ▪ Adriana Bruggeman – A.Bruggeman@cgiar.org ▪ All from ICARDA, Aleppo, Syria; Fax: 00-963-(0)21-221.34.90; Tel: 00-963-(0)21-221.34.33; www.icarda.org

Participatory technology development

Syria – تطوير التقانات التشاركي

Participatory technology development, through close researcher-farmer interaction, for sustainable land management of olive orchards in dry marginal areas.

The purpose of participatory technology development is to gain from the synergy between indigenous knowledge and scientific expertise. The specific objective in this case was to develop and test water and land management techniques in order to sustainably improve olive production in a semi-arid area, while ensuring that the techniques were well adapted to local farming practices. The approach consists of group meetings, joint field trips, identification of local innovations, extension days, monitoring of farmer practices, and researcher-controlled experiments. The approach consists of a cycle with three major stages: a diagnostic phase, a testing phase, followed by monitoring and evaluation.

In this case study, farmers were invited based on their interest in growing olives. Participation throughout the learning cycle was completely voluntary: no material or financial incentives were used (although they expected them in the beginning of the process). The role of farmers was to identify priority problems and potential solutions, to test new technologies on their farms, and to evaluate their suitability.

Farmers observed the research experiment with water harvesting, and then adapted the technology to their needs. As shown, they built V-shaped bunds around their olive trees to capture rainwater runoff, but – contrary to the researchers' suggestion – they continued to plough the olive orchards, as this is their standard weed control practice. Weeds attract sheep, lead to fires and compete for water with the olives. This simple runoff harvesting system is well adapted to farmers' objectives, and their modification – the up-and-down slope furrows created through ploughing – actually serves to increase the efficiency of the water harvesting. The system is now being monitored by researchers to assess its technical and economic efficiency.

Improved farmer-researcher interaction helps farmers learn about a useful basic technique from researchers, while researchers learn in turn about potential improvements to the technology from local innovators. A community facilitator of ICARDA (International Centre for Agricultural Research in Dry Areas) facilitated the group discussions, and the researchers were asked to be open-minded to new approaches while conducting and monitoring field trials. The approach was tested by an interdisciplinary team of ICARDA as part of the 'Khanasser Valley Integrated Research Site'. This project aimed to develop local-adapted options for agriculture in dry marginal areas alongside a generally applicable integrated approach for sustainable land management in these zones.

left: Joint field visit including farmers and ICARDA researchers to a local innovator's field – Harbakiyah, Khanasser Valley, NW Syria. (Francis Turkelboom)
right: Priority ranking of problems for growing olives. The exercise took place at ICARDA's facilitation office at Harbakiyah, Khanasser Valley, and involves Khanasser farmers, a community facilitator, researchers from ICARDA, and development workers. (Francis Turkelboom)

Location: Khanasser Valley, NW Syria.
Approach area: 0.05 km²
Land use: grazing land (before), cropland: orchard (after) and mixed: silvo-pastoral (after)
Climate: semi-arid
WOCAT database reference: QA SYR03
Related technology: Furrow-enhanced runoff harvesting for olives, QT SYR03
Compiled by: Francis Turkelboom, Ashraf Tubeileh, Roberto La Rovere, Adriana Bruggeman, ICARDA, Aleppo, Syria
Date: April 2005

Editors' comments: Participatory technology development (PTD) has recently become accepted as a viable alternative to researchers acting independently from the land users. PTD implies a partnership between farmers and researchers, with the farmers' priorities put first. Joint experiments are carried out, and assessed together by both parties. This is a promising example from Syria. PTD is also a feature of the moroccan case study, 'Ecograze' from Australia and PFI from Uganda.

Classification

Problem
The lack of appropriate ways to develop sustainable technologies to remedy loss of runoff water and poor olive growth – in the context of low-input agriculture on gentle undulating land in water scarce areas with an absence of soil conservation measures.

Objectives
- design, test and disseminate alternative technologies adapted to local conditions
- strengthen local knowledge of SWC measures
- strengthen joint learning by farmers and researchers

Constraints addressed

Major	Specification	Treatment
Financial	Water harvesting is considered expensive due to labour cost.	Identification of a low-cost water harvesting measure, which can be implemented during the off-season. Cost-benefit analysis.
Technical	Difficulty in tilling the land when water harvesting structures are in place.	Integrating local innovations into the water harvesting system.

Minor	Specification	Treatment
Technical	Uncertainty about appropriate size of micro-catchment area.	Researcher-controlled research.
Technical	Uncertainty about the amount of water harvested.	Researcher-controlled research.
Technical	Lack of technical expertise for olive crop husbandry in dry areas.	Carry out farmer field days, disseminate and elaborate extension leaflets.

Participation and decision making

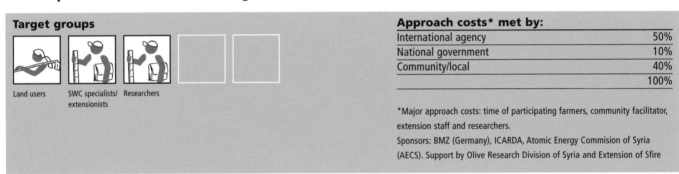

Target groups

Land users | SWC specialists/ extensionists | Researchers

Approach costs* met by:

International agency	50%
National government	10%
Community/local	40%
	100%

*Major approach costs: time of participating farmers, community facilitator, extension staff and researchers.

Sponsors: BMZ (Germany), ICARDA, Atomic Energy Commision of Syria (AECS). Support by Olive Research Division of Syria and Extension of Sfire

Decisions on choice of the technology: Mainly made by land users supported by SWC specialists.
Decisions on method of implementing the technology: By land users only.
Approach designed by: International specialists.

Community involvement

Phase	Involvement	Activities
Initiation	passive	public meetings
Planning	interactive	public meetings
Implementation	self-mobilisation	completely conducted by land-users
Monitoring/evaluation	passive/interactive	interviews and public meetings
Research	interactive	farmer experiments and controlled on-farm experiments

Differences in participation between men and women: Mainly men were involved, as most activities in olive orchards are managed by men. In addition, culturally bound gender segregation in public makes it difficult to organise gender-mixed meetings. Therefore, separate meetings were organised for women. In the case of one household, the de facto partner was a woman who takes most of the orchard-related decisions and does the work herself.

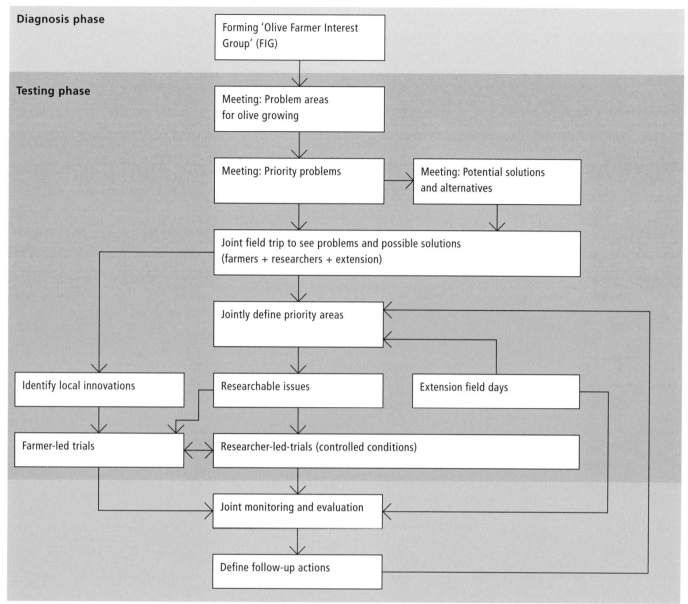

Diagnosis phase

Forming 'Olive Farmer Interest Group' (FIG)

Testing phase

Meeting: Problem areas for olive growing

Meeting: Priority problems

Meeting: Potential solutions and alternatives

Joint field trip to see problems and possible solutions (farmers + researchers + extension)

Jointly define priority areas

Identify local innovations

Researchable issues

Extension field days

Farmer-led trials

Researcher-led-trials (controlled conditions)

Joint monitoring and evaluation

Define follow-up actions

Approach process
Phases and methods of participatory technology development. (Francis Turkelboom)

Extension and promotion

Training: Demand-driven training of olive husbandry techniques (eg pruning, grafting, pest management) was conducted through public meetings, farm visits and on-the-job training. Training was reasonably effective.
Extension: Farmer-to-farmer extension was used: innovative farmers showed their technique to other olive farmers during farm visits. It was quite effective in spreading the idea among interested farmers. Extension in marginal agricultural areas is usually ill-equipped to facilitate such extension activities without outside support.
Research: Research was an important part of this approach. Technical and socio-economic topics were treated as follows: (1) Researcher-controlled on-farm experiments: this helped evaluate the impact of water harvesting design on the amount of water harvested and the olive crop response. (2) Monitoring of farmer-managed trials: to evaluate the performance of water harvesting under on-farm conditions. (3) Cost-benefit analysis: to check economic viability. (4) Analysis of perception of advantages and disadvantages of the technology.
Research was reasonably important for the effectiveness of the approach, as it provided better insights into constraining factors for water harvesting, and helped to clarify the potential amount of water saved.
Importance of land use rights: All water harvesting was done in private olive orchards. Secure land tenure was essential to invest in water harvesting structures.

Incentives

Labour: Labour was voluntary.
Inputs: No inputs were provided.
Credit: No credit was provided.
Support to local institutions: The approach facilitated technical interaction between interested olive growers in the area.
Long-term impact of incentives: Not applicable (the approach did not use any incentives).

Monitoring and evaluation

Monitored aspects	Methods and indicators
Bio-physical	regular observations and measurements (eg soil moisture)
Technical and management of approach	annual observation of water harvesting structures and management measures
Socio-cultural	ad hoc (twice) analysis of perceptions of the technology
Economic/production	ad hoc (once) analysis of cost and benefits
Area treated	annual field survey (using GPS)
No. of land users involved	annual farmer interview

Impact of the approach

Changes as a result of monitoring and evaluation: There were few changes: interest in the farmers' orchards and questions about the technology stimulated some other farmers to apply water harvesting.

Improved soil and water management: Adoption of the furrow-enhanced runoff-water harvesting technique resulted in a concentration of scarce rainwater and nutrients in the basins around the olive trees. The consequence is a significant reduction of soil loss and runoff at the field level.

Adoption of the approach by other projects/land users: This approach is now being applied in other ICARDA-coordinated projects in the region.

Sustainability: The complete PTD process/learning cycle needs outsider facilitation, but lack of outsiders will not stop farmers experimenting further by themselves. In terms of the technology itself, farmers can continue independently with water harvesting structures, as the system is very simple and relatively cheap.

Concluding statements

Strengths and → how to sustain/improve	Weaknesses and → how to overcome
Engagement of researchers with local innovators and thus interaction between scientific and indigenous knowledge → This approach can only be sustained if it is mainstreamed into national research and extension services.	Time demanding → Less time needed after the first experience.
Attitude changes by researchers about farmers' knowledge → Ditto.	Appropriate facilitating skills required → Mainstreaming facilitation skills.
Building on local knowledge → Ditto.	
Capacity building of both land users and researchers → Ditto.	
Demand-driven technologies → Ditto.	

Key reference(s): Tubeileh A and Turkelboom F (2004) *Participatory research on water and soil management with olive growers in the Khanasser Valley.* KVIRS project, ICARDA, Aleppo, Syria ■ van Veldhuizen L, Waters-Bayer A, Abd de Zeeuw H (1997) *Developing technology with farmers: a trainer's guide for participatory learning.* Zed Books, Londen, UK
Contact person(s): Francis Turkelboom – F.Turkelboom@cgiar.org ■ Ashraf Tubeileh – A.Tubeileh@cgiar.org ■ Adriana Bruggeman – A.Bruggeman@cgiar.org ■ All from ICARDA, Aleppo, Syria, fax 00-963-(0)21-221.34.90; tel 00-963-(0)21-221.34.33; www.icarda.org

left: A fully developed check dam: The stem cuttings – in this case associated with *Bromelia pinguin* – have grown to form a dense living barrier, and the area behind the dam has become level. (Mats Gurtner)
right: Check dams made of rooted tree stems reduce the speed of runoff water in the gully and trap sediment. (Mats Gurtner)

Check dams from stem cuttings

Nicaragua – *Diques de postes prendedizos*

Gully rehabilitation by check dams made of stem cuttings from trees. These living barriers retard concentrated runoff and fill up the gullies gradually with sediment.

Stem cuttings from specific tree species have the ability to strike roots and continue growing after being planted into the earth. In this case study local species have been used to create check dams in gullies: these include *jinocuebo (Simaroubaceaes bombacaceaes,* and also *jobo, tiguilote, pochote* from the same family). Other suitable species are *jocote (Spondias purpurea)* and *madero negro (Gliricidia sepium).* As an option the pinapple-like *piñuela (Bromelia pinguin)* can be planted in association with the stem cuttings to further reinforce the system.

Tree stems are cut into pieces 5–15 cm thick and 1.5–2.5 m long, depending on the depth of the gully. The cuttings are planted to half of their length, and formed into semi-circular barriers (see diagram). The dams retard runoff and thus retain eroded sediment. Spacing between dams depends on the gradient of the gully bed. For example on a 15% slope it is recommended to build a dam every 4 meters (see spacing under establishment activities). Between dams, the gully gradually fills up with eroded soil, the speed of the runoff is further reduced and agricultural land that has been divided by the gully is reconnected. Large and deep gullies may change over time into a sequence of narrow fertile terraces where crops can be grown.

However, the check dams should be seen as part of an integrated catchment management and protection plan, and thus be supported by other SWC measures on the lateral slopes, such as retention ditches and/or live barriers laid out along the contour. Erosion and runoff control on the sides of each gully is an essential part of the rehabilitation process. These check dams of rooted poles are more robust and durable than stone dams in soils of sandy/loamy texture. On moderate and steep slopes a combination of stem cutting and stone dams is recommended. After two to three years the barriers should be pruned – yielding wood and fodder. Dead poles should be replaced and the dam widened if necessary.

In this case study the dams are constructed in a semi-arid region with erratic rainfall where gullies are common on agricultural land, be it cropland or grazing land. The land users are mainly peasant farmers, growing crops for subsistence on smallholdings, and living in very poor conditions. This system of gully rehabilitation is promoted by an NGO entitled *'Asociación Tierra y Vida'* through farmer-to-farmer *(campesino a campesino)* extension.

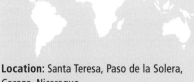

Location: Santa Teresa, Paso de la Solera, Carazo, Nicaragua
Technology area: 5 km²
SWC measure: structural
Land use: cropland, grazing land
Climate: semi-arid
WOCAT database reference: QT NIC04
Related approach: not documented
Compiled by: Reinerio Mongalo, *Asociación Tierra y Vida* (AT&V), Nicaragua
Date: April 2000, updated February 2004

Editors' comments: Various forms of vegetative control of gullies are widespread throughout the world. This particular form – the use of stem cuttings – has the advantage of establishing live barriers rapidly. One of the trees used in this case study, *madero negro (Gliricidia sepium),* is also known and utilised for the same purpose in various other countries.

Classification

Land use problems
There is a range of factors that limit agricultural production in the area: soil degradation, extensive gully formation on crop land, low soil fertility, lack of inputs for crop production, erratic precipitation. Also, lack of interest/knowledge and lack of resources hinder the implementation of SWC measures.

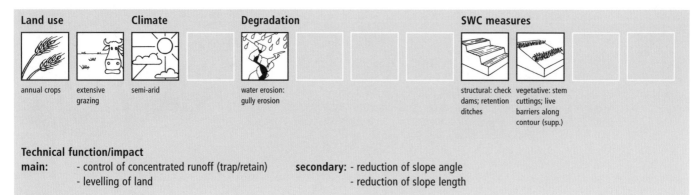

Land use
annual crops
extensive grazing

Climate
semi-arid

Degradation
water erosion: gully erosion

SWC measures
structural: check dams; retention ditches
vegetative: stem cuttings; live barriers along contour (supp.)

Technical function/impact
main:
- control of concentrated runoff (trap/retain)
- levelling of land

secondary:
- reduction of slope angle
- reduction of slope length

Environment

Natural environment

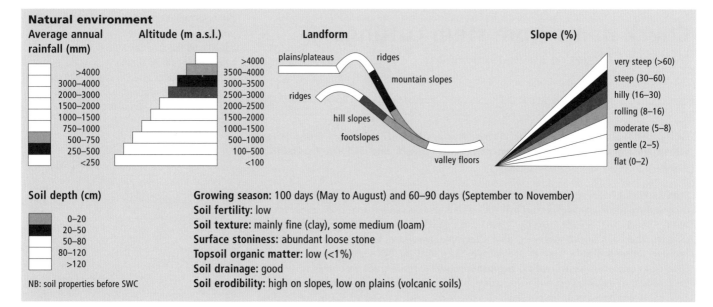

Average annual rainfall (mm)
>4000
3000–4000
2000–3000
1500–2000
1000–1500
750–1000
500–750
250–500
<250

Altitude (m a.s.l.)
>4000
3500–4000
3000–3500
2500–3000
2000–2500
1500–2000
1000–1500
500–1000
100–500
<100

Landform
plains/plateaus
ridges
mountain slopes
ridges
hill slopes
footslopes
valley floors

Slope (%)
very steep (>60)
steep (30–60)
hilly (16–30)
rolling (8–16)
moderate (5–8)
gentle (2–5)
flat (0–2)

Soil depth (cm)
0–20
20–50
50–80
80–120
>120

NB: soil properties before SWC

Growing season: 100 days (May to August) and 60–90 days (September to November)
Soil fertility: low
Soil texture: mainly fine (clay), some medium (loam)
Surface stoniness: abundant loose stone
Topsoil organic matter: low (<1%)
Soil drainage: good
Soil erodibility: high on slopes, low on plains (volcanic soils)

Human environment

Cropland per household (ha)
<1
1–2
2–5
5–15
15–50
50–100
100–500
500–1000
1000–10000
>10000

Land use rights: mainly individual, some leased
Land ownership: individual not titled, some individual titled
Market orientation: cropland: mainly subsistence (self-supply), some mixed (subsistence and commercial)
Level of technical knowledge required: field staff/extension worker: low, land user: moderate
Importance of off-farm income: 10–50% of all income: temporary or permanent migration, particularly young people

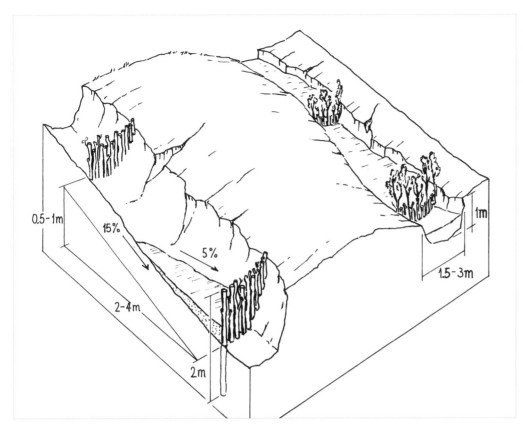

Technical drawing
Stem cuttings planted in gullies to form living check dams: recently planted (left) and cuttings that have begun to take root and sprout, resulting in the gully becoming filled with trapped sediment (right).

Implementation activities, inputs and costs

Establishment activities

1. Calculate and mark spacing between structures.
2. Cut poles out of selected local trees (diameter: 5–15 cm, length: 1.5–2.5 m depending on gully depth).
3. Dig small semi-circular ditches at the gully bottom (the depth of the ditch is half the length of the cuttings).
4. Plant the cuttings vertically into the ditch; put the thicker cuttings in the middle of the gully where runoff velocity is higher.
5. Fill ditch with excavated earth to fix the cuttings.
6. Water to encourage rooting.

Establishment activities carried out before rainy season (April/May).

Tools: 'line-level', tape measure, axe, machete, shovel, hoe.

Duration of establishment: 1–2 months

Establishment inputs and costs per ha

Inputs	Costs (US$)	% met by land user
Labour (50 person days)	100	100%
Equipment		
- Wheelbarrow	10	100%
- Tools	20	0%
Materials		
- Wood (300–500 poles)	60	100%
TOTAL	**190**	**90%**

Maintenance/recurrent activities

1. Biotrampas: pruning the trees every three years.
2. Cut-off drains: clearing of sediment, cutting bushes and grasses.
3. Stone check dams: pruning trees and bushes every three years. After full sedimentation, the dam may be increased in height.
4. Wooden check dams: pruning trees and bushes every three years.

All the maintenance activities can be made without machinery and require little labour and low-tech equipment.

Maintenance/recurrent inputs and costs per ha per year

Inputs	Costs (US$)	% met by land user
Labour (15 person days)	30	100%
Equipment		
- Tools	0	
Materials		
- Wood (<50 poles)	5	100%
TOTAL	**35**	**100%**

Remarks: Costs are calculated for a 100 m long, 2 m wide and 1 m deep gully with check dams every 4 m, on the basis of one gully per hectare. The wood (for poles) belongs to the land users themselves, thus the 'cost' does not involve purchase.

Assessment

Acceptance/adoption
- 30% of all farmers approached by the project (about 400 out of 1,200 land users) have built these check dams.
- 66% of those farmers accepted the technology with incentives; the remainder (34%) adopted check dams spontaneously without receiving any incentives other than training/technical assistance.
- Seeds, tools and credits were provided as incentives; the reasons for implementation included both the attraction of the incentives and perceived ecological benefits in terms of rehabilitation of degraded areas.
- There is a strong trend towards growing spontaneous adoption.
- Maintenance has been good.

Benefits/costs according to land user

Benefits compared with costs	short-term:	long-term:
establishment	negative	positive
maintenance/recurrent	neutral	very positive

Impacts of the technology

Production and socio-economic benefits
+ +	crop yield increase (where gullies planted)
+	fodder production (eg *madero negro = Gliricidium sepium*)
+	wood production increase (medium term)
+	farm income increase

Production and socio-economic disadvantages
–	labour constraints during establishment phase

Socio-cultural benefits
+ + +	improves relationships between land users
+ + +	improved knowledge SWC/erosion
+	community institution strengthening

Socio-cultural disadvantages
none

Ecological benefits
+ + +	increase in soil moisture
+ + +	soil loss reduction
+ +	increase in soil fertility

Ecological disadvantages
none

Off-site benefits
+ + +	reduced downstream siltation
+ +	reduced downstream flooding
+	reduced river pollution

Off-site disadvantages
none

Concluding statements

Strengths and → how to sustain/improve
Facilitated land management: area is no longer divided by gullies → Continue to construct and maintain.

Retards runoff speed: decreases erosion → Ditto.

Accumulation of fertile earth above the check dams, possibility of growing crops on 'terraces' between the structures → Ditto.

Increased soil moisture → Ditto.

Weaknesses and → how to overcome
The check dams used alone as SWC measure may not be adequate to withstand concentrated runoff → It is important to combine this technology with other SWC practices (eg retention ditches on slopes at both sides of gully, live fences, etc).

Only likely to be applied where land use rights are guaranteed.

Labour intensive.

Key reference(s): Gurdiel G (1993) *La construcción de diques.* Tierra Fresca, Simas-Enlace, Managua ■ PASOLAC (2000) *Guía Técnica de Conservación de Suelos y Agua.* PASOLAC, Managua ■ LUPE (1994) *Manual Práctico de Manejo de Suelos en Laderas.* Secretaría de Recursos Naturales, Tegucigalpa, Honduras

Contact person(s): Roger Rodriguez, PASOLAC, Apartado Postal No.6024, Managua, Nicaragua; pasolac@cablenet.com.ni; phone/fax: (505) 277-1175, 277-0451, 277-0850 ■ Reinerio Mongalo, *Asociación Tierra y Vida* (AT&V), Nicaragua; tvida@ibw.com.ni

Gully control and catchment protection

Bolivia – *Control de cárcavas*

Integrated gully treatment consisting of several simple practices including stone and wooden check dams, cut-off drains and reforestation in sediment traps (biotrampas).

The focus of the case study is a degraded catchment, located at high altitude (2,800–4,200 m a.s.l.), home to 37 households, which is characterised by severe gullies and landslides. Gullies are continuously expanding, and constitute a significant proportion of the catchment. These cause considerable loss of cropland as well as downstream damage to the city of Cochabamba.

A combination of structural and vegetative measures was designed and implemented with the purpose of: (1) preventing affected areas from further degradation by safely discharging runoff from the surrounding area through the main gullies down to the valley; (2) gradually stabilising the land through the regeneration of vegetative cover; (3) reducing downstream damage through floods and siltation; (4) ensuring accessibility to the mountainous agricultural area during the rainy season.

Cut-off drains at the heads of the gullies, reinforced with stones inside the channel and grassed bunds below, concentrate runoff and cascade it down over stone steps back into the waterways. Flow is controlled by stone and wooden check dams and discharged safely. Sediment is trapped behind these structures and terraces develop. Bushes or trees are planted above and below the check dams. Depending on availability of materials, wooden check dams are sometimes used and associated with tree planting (four trees above and four below each check dam).

These practices are complemented by SWC measures throughout the catchment: *biotrampas* are staggered sediment traps located on the steep lateral slopes. They comprise ditches behind wooden barriers where soil accumulates. *Biotrampas* create suitable sites for tree/bush planting while stabilising the hillsides, reducing erosion, increasing infiltration and slowing siltation of the check dams in the watercourses. Supporting technologies include fenced-off areas for reforestation of the lateral slopes/upper edge of the gully, and finally large gabion dams at the outlets of the gullies, usually 10–25 m in length, but exceptionally up to 200 m.

After a few years vegetation should have stabilised the system, and effectively replaced the wooden and stone constructions. The various practices enhance each other. Establishment is labour demanding, but other costs are low, as long as the material in question is locally obtainable. Maintenance costs are also low. The technology was implemented over a period of six years, starting in 1996, through the Programa de *Manejo Integral de Cuencas* (PROMIC).

left: Catchment gully control combines a variety of different SWC measures: the steep small gullies are protected by a series of wooden check dams, 8–12 m apart, whereas the larger gully (bottom right) is stabilised by stone check dams. After sedimentation, bushes and small trees will be planted. (Georg Heim)
right: Stabilisation of degraded hillsides: *biotrampas* are simple wooden barriers, with a staggered layout, which trap eroded sediment and create suitable sites for tree planting. (PROMIC)

Location: Pajcha Watershed, Cordillera del Tunari, Cochabamba District, Bolivia
Technology area: 6 km²
SWC measure: structural and vegetative
Land use: cropland and grazing land
Climate: semi-arid, subhumid
WOCAT database reference: QT BOL04 (combination); QT BOL05–09 (single components)
Related approach: Incentive-based catchment treatment, QA BOL02
Compiled by: Georg Heim, Langnau, Switzerland & Ivan Vargas, Cochabamba, Bolivia
Date: September 2003, updated June 2004

Editors' comments: Negative impacts of gullies may be felt on-site, but downstream also – as is the situation here. This case presents a combination of different technologies which enhance each others' impact. They are arranged systematically from the upper part of the catchment to the outlet of the gully. The overall cost is relatively low.

Classification

Land use problems

Deforestation, overgrazing and poorly managed channel irrigation in areas with steep slopes: poorly structured soils and extreme climatic variability causing erosion gullies, landslides, downstream flooding and sedimentation of agricultural land and settlements – including the city of Cochabamba.

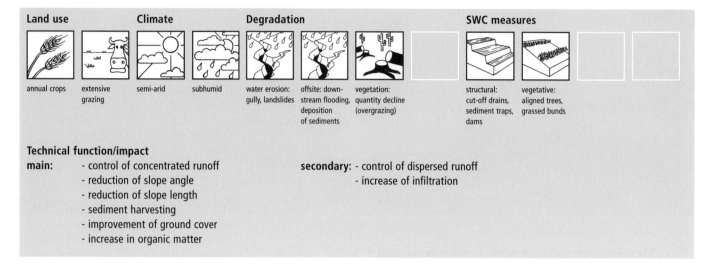

Land use		Climate		Degradation					SWC measures			
annual crops	extensive grazing	semi-arid	subhumid	water erosion: gully, landslides	offsite: down-stream flooding, deposition of sediments	vegetation: quantity decline (overgrazing)			structural: cut-off drains, sediment traps, dams	vegetative: aligned trees, grassed bunds		

Technical function/impact

main:
- control of concentrated runoff
- reduction of slope angle
- reduction of slope length
- sediment harvesting
- improvement of ground cover
- increase in organic matter

secondary:
- control of dispersed runoff
- increase of infiltration

Environment

Natural environment*

Average annual rainfall (mm) / Altitude (m a.s.l.) / Landform / Slope (%)

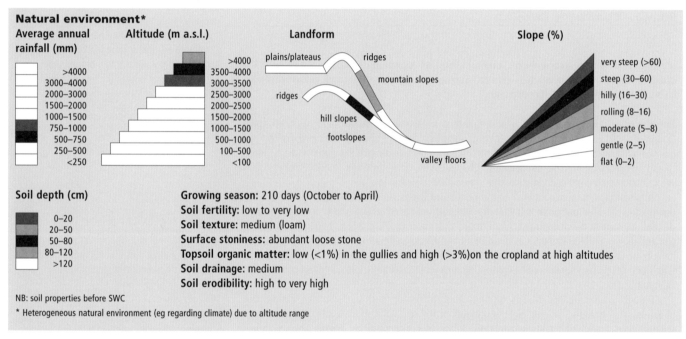

Soil depth (cm): 0–20, 20–50, 50–80, 80–120, >120

Growing season: 210 days (October to April)
Soil fertility: low to very low
Soil texture: medium (loam)
Surface stoniness: abundant loose stone
Topsoil organic matter: low (<1%) in the gullies and high (>3%)on the cropland at high altitudes
Soil drainage: medium
Soil erodibility: high to very high

NB: soil properties before SWC

* Heterogeneous natural environment (eg regarding climate) due to altitude range

Human environment

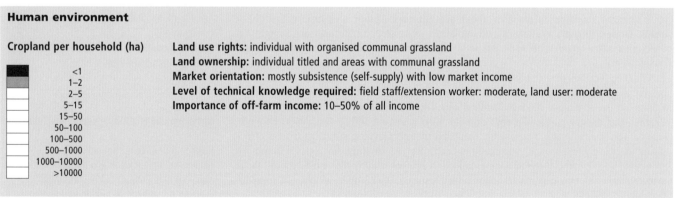

Cropland per household (ha): <1, 1–2, 2–5, 5–15, 15–50, 50–100, 100–500, 500–1000, 1000–10000, >10000

Land use rights: individual with organised communal grassland
Land ownership: individual titled and areas with communal grassland
Market orientation: mostly subsistence (self-supply) with low market income
Level of technical knowledge required: field staff/extension worker: moderate, land user: moderate
Importance of off-farm income: 10–50% of all income

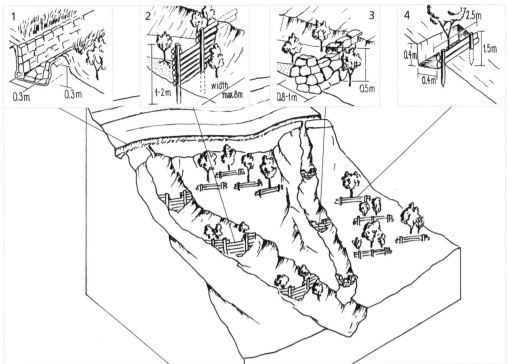

Technical drawing:
Gully control and catchment protection: an overview of the integrated measures.
Insert 1: Stone-lined cut-off drain with grass-covered bund and live barriers.
Insert 2: Wooden check dam: note that trees are established to further stabilise the gully (as for stone check dams).
Insert 3: Stone check dam.
Insert 4: *Biotrampa:* staggered structures which collect moisture and sediment for tree planting.

Implementation activities, inputs and costs

Establishment activities

- Cut-off drains: excavate channel above the gully. Lay stones in the bed and plant local bushes or grass on the bund below the ditch. The outlet of the ditch into the gully is stabilised by a few stone steps.
- Stone check dams: excavate a ditch perpendicular to the water channel during the dry season for a foundation. Build a dam wall with stones (length 2–3 m, width 0.8–1.0 m, height 0.5–1.0 m).
- Wooden check dams (up to 8 m long, 15–20 cm wide and 1 m high): soil excavation (see 2.). Fix logs with wire or nails to vertical poles. Position a bio-fibre fleece behind the dam to prevent sediment from flowing through.
- *Biotrampas:* excavate soil, hammer wooden posts into the soil and fix 2–3 horizontal logs with nails or wire to the wooden posts. (During dry season).
- Plant local bushes and trees in front and behind the *biotrampas* and the check dams (after sedimentation). Altitude acclimatisation (2 weeks) is required for the trees before planting.
- Establish fences to protect the plants.

Duration of establishment: not specified

Establishment inputs and costs per ha

Inputs	Costs (US$)	% met by land user
Labour (12 person days)	48	0%
Equipment		
- Tools	4	0%
Materials		
- Stone (56 m³)	0	
- Wood (5 m³)	33	0%
- Nails, wire, etc	2	0%
- Bio-fibre fleece	4	0%
Agricultural		
- Seedlings	19	0%
TOTAL	**110**	**0%**

Maintenance/recurrent activities

1. Biotrampas: pruning the trees every three years.
2. Cut-off drains: clearing of sediment, cutting bushes and grasses.
3. Stone check dams: pruning trees and bushes every three years. After full sedimentation, the dam may be increased in height.
4. Wooden check dams: pruning trees and bushes every three years.

All the maintenance activities can be made without machinery and require little labour and low-tech equipment.

Maintenance/recurrent inputs and costs per ha per year

Inputs	Costs (US$)	% met by land user
Labour (3 person days)	12	100%
Equipment		
- Tools	1	100%
Materials		
- Stone (0.5 m³)	0	
- Wood (0.04 m³)	1	100%
- Nails, wire, etc	1	100%
Agricultural		
- Seedlings	1	100%
TOTAL	**16**	**100%**

Remarks: Costs have been calculated for the whole catchment (6 km²) – including 100 m of cut-off drains, 6,750 m of stone check dams, 1,500 m of wooden check dams and 770 *biotrampas* – and then divided by the number of hectares. Wood is not locally available (because of national park laws) and needs to be brought into the area. Establishment and maintenance costs were paid by PROMIC during their intervention period of 6 years. The (high) costs of the gabion weirs further downstream are not included as these are not always required and vary considerably in size from site to site.

Assessment

Acceptance/adoption

During the project phase, all the farmers who implemented the technology did it with incentives (cash-for-work). Farmers initially maintained the structures because of PROMIC subsidies, and post-project, partially because of the benefits. However, only a few of them have built new structures post-project. This is due to different reasons: (1) PROMIC stopped its financial support; (2) the gullied areas are not used by farmers, therefore they have little reason to protect them; (3) the catchment is within a national park – and trees are protected, which means that wood for *biotrampas* construction is not available locally; (4) insufficient sensitisation regarding effects of erosion and SWC measures in the area.

Benefits/costs according to land use

Benefits compared with costs	short-term:	long-term:
establishment	very positive	very positive
maintenance/recurrent	very positive	very positive

Impacts of the technology

Production and socio-economic benefits	Production and socio-economic disadvantages
+ maintained crop and fodder production due to prevention of further land loss	– – high labour input for establishment (though paid in this instance)

Socio-cultural benefits	Socio-cultural disadvantages
+ + + improved knowledge SWC/erosion	– – – farmers implementing SWC are not those benefiting most from the impact in the short term
+ community institution strengthening	

Ecological benefits	Ecological disadvantages
+ + + soil loss reduction	none
+ + soil cover improvement	
+ increase in soil moisture	

Off-site benefits	Off-site disadvantages
+ + + reduced downstream flooding	none
+ + + reduced downstream siltation	

Concluding statements

Strengths and → how to sustain/improve	Weaknesses and → how to overcome
Reduction of landslips and flooding in the valley → New small gullies may originate inside an existing gully or around it. It is important to continue to maintain the current measures and construct new, even though the subsidies of PROMIC have been terminated.	The technology doesn't address the root cause of human induced gully erosion → Alongside the gully control technology it is necessary to apply complementary conservation measures on the cropland above the gully to prevent new gully development.
The technology could be implemented by the farmers themselves as materials (except for wood) and tools are locally available → Prolong the sensitisation work to convince the farmers of the necessity and benefits of the technology.	High labour input for establishment of SWC measures.
Reduction of soil loss in the watershed → Do not apply the mentioned practices in isolation but always in combination.	The technology partly depends on inputs that are not available locally: timber for establishment of wooden structures (which is a significant quantity) are brought in from outside (since the area is within a national park tree felling is not allowed) → An agreement on sustainable use of trees should be made with the national park authority.
Simple technology with high positive long-term impact, especially downstream.	

Key reference(s): Documentation of PROMIC (see address below)
Contact person(s): Georg Heim, Mooseggstrasse 9, 3550 Langnau, Switzerland; geoheim@bluewin.ch ■ PROMIC, *Programa de Manejo Integral de Cuencas*, Av. Atahuallpa final, Parque Tunari, casilla 4909, Cochabamba, Bolivia; promic@promic-bolivia.org; www.promic-bolivia.org

Incentive-based catchment treatment

Bolivia – *Manejo de áreas degradadas*

A project supported, incentive-based approach: farmers are sensitised about erosion, and involved in gully control and other measures to protect catchments.

The objective of the locally-based organisation *Programa de Manejo Integral de Cuencas* (PROMIC) is to involve land users in the control of soil erosion in the catchments above Cochabamba city. While erosion here is largely a natural process, it is aggravated by inappropriate agricultural practices. PROMIC receives funds from national and international governments, and works in an interactive manner. Together with local farmers, erosion processes in the context of the human environment were analysed to identify the needs of the agriculture population - and to plan a conservation and development programme. The aim was to convince farmers of the necessity to protect their agricultural land and stabilise the gullies below, and of the overall importance of implementing technologies to combat erosion.

The farmers were involved in the process through regular community meetings organised by PROMIC, in which they could adjust PROMIC's catchment intervention plans to their own requirements through an interactive process. PROMIC considered that the sensitisation work and the interactive process were essential to ensure long-term sustainable land use. In the short term, however, it will be mainly the city downstream – Cochabamba – that benefits from the implementation of the erosion control technologies. For that reason, the farmers were paid to carry out construction of the measures (through 'cash-for-work'). The farmers should, however, profit from the technologies in the long term. They were taught how to build and maintain check dams, cut-off drains and *biotrampas*. The implementation in the watershed started in 1996 and took six years: when the implementation phase was over, farmers no longer received financial subsidies. The long period of sensitisation should help to ensure that farmers incorporate erosion prevention technologies into their cropland above the gullies.

PROMIC still monitors the state of the structures from time to time, but most of the maintenance is left to the farmers themselves. PROMIC continues, however, to provide technical support and some transport of materials. Both internal and external evaluation followed the end of the implementation phase.

left: Individual planning (at farmer level) of activities to treat the large gully in the background: a PROMIC engineer and local people are involved. Note the city of Cochabamba in the distance. (Georg Heim)
right: The approach focuses on the regeneration and stabilisation of seriously degraded catchments by a combined package of structural and vegetative measures. (Georg Heim)

Location: Pajcha Watershed, Cordillera del Tunari, Cochabamba district, Bolivia
Approach area: 6 km²
Land use: cropland and grazing land
Climate: semi-arid, subhumid
WOCAT database reference: QA BOL02
Related technology: Gully control and catchment protection, QT BOL04 (description of combined technology); QT BOL05, BOL06, BOL07, BOL08 and BOL09 (description of single components)
Compiled by: Georg Heim, Langnau, Switzerland & Ivan Vargas, Cochabamba, Bolivia
Date: September 2003, updated June 2004

Editors' comments: SWC projects aimed primarily at achieving downstream benefits are faced with the difficult problem of how to achieve participation when production benefits do not immediately accrue to the land users on-site. Incentives of some form need to be used – at least in the establishment phase. A future option may be for city dwellers to pay for 'environmental services' provided by land users in the hills above.

Problem, objectives and constraints

Problem
- lack of knowledge about damage caused by erosion and benefits of various possible conservation technologies
- lack of financial resources: shortage of funds prevents farmers investing in technologies, even if these bring benefits to them (as well as to the downstream population)
- persistence of detrimental traditional agricultural practices, leading to accelerated degradation

Objectives
- teach farmers about sustainable land use
- build up skills amongst farmers to enable them to treat gullies without outside help
- reduce flooding and sedimentation in the valley of Cochabamba and general soil loss in the area through collaboration with farmers in the watershed
- improve traditional agriculture with a package of conservation-related practices
- indirectly support farmers by cash-for-work incentives which enables them to implement SWC technologies on their own fields

Constraints addressed

Major	Specification	Treatment
Financial	Few direct short-term profits from SWC technologies in gullies for the farmers in the watershed (the main beneficiary is the city of Cochabamba downstream).	Search for national and international subsidies to help the farmers to implement the technologies during the initial period.
Climate	Climatic extremes such as strong winds and excess or deficit of rain.	Plant trees at close spacing, and plant trees/ shrubs that can tolerate climatic extremes.

Minor	Specification	Treatment
Institutional	The local farmers' association is insufficiently organised to ensure the independent continuation of activities post-project.	Local farmers' association should be included in the sensitisation and implementation process.
Policy	The local administration/government doesn't subsidise and support SWC, except for a minor financial contribution to PROMIC.	Enhance awareness in the downstream city of Cochabamba to ensure policy and financial contributions from the city to the gully control technologies upstream: in other words payment for environmental services.
Policy	The location of the watershed in the National Park of Tunari means the farmers cannot cut wood for building structures.	Wood required has to be brought into the area from outside the park (this was paid for by the project).

Participation and decision making

Target groups

Land users/ local farmers association

Approach costs met by:

International agency	80%
National government	20%
	100%

Decisions on choice of the technology: Made by specialised engineers of PROMIC; farmers were involved by modifying initially proposed technologies.
Decisions on method of implementing the technology: Made by specialised engineers of PROMIC.
Approach designed by: National specialists with national university collaboration.

Community involvement

Phase	Involvement	Activities
Initiation	passive	interviews, information during regular meetings
Planning	interactive	results of the socio-economic diagnosis defined the planning; farmers were involved through regular meetings: interactive planning at individual and community level
Implementation	payment/incentives	all farmers had the opportunity to collaborate through paid labour
Monitoring/evaluation	passive	internal and external evaluations where farmers were interviewed
Research	passive	socio-economic diagnosis; collection and analysis of bio-physical baseline data

Differences in participation between men and women: There were no women working in the gully rehabilitation. The reason is a cultural taboo against women working with heavy materials; women are responsible for looking after cattle, and for the household.

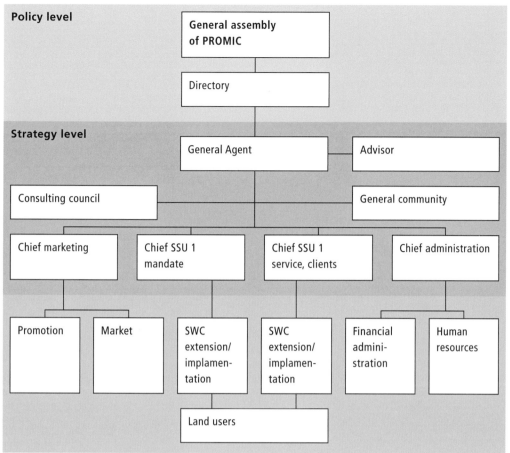

Organogram
- General assembly: National and international public and private institutions, members, foundation
- Directory: Prefecture, general agent, Swiss Agency for Development and Cooperation (SDC), Belgian Technical Cooperation (BTC), private enterpreneurs
- Consulting council: Munici-palities, projects, universities
- Advisors: General agent, marketing, SSU1, SSU2 (see below), administration
- SSU: Strategic service unit
- Services: Executive body for technology extension and implementation: PROMIC field technicians

Diagram labels:

Policy level:
- General assembly of PROMIC
- Directory

Strategy level:
- General Agent
- Advisor
- Consulting council
- General community
- Chief marketing
- Chief SSU 1 mandate
- Chief SSU 1 service, clients
- Chief administration
- Promotion
- Market
- SWC extension/ implamen- tation
- SWC extension/ implamen- tation
- Financial admini- stration
- Human resources
- Land users

Extension and promotion

Training: The approach included training on technical aspects and on long-term planning for sustainable land use. Some farmers were trained to become foremen – who in turn instructed other farmers. During the construction period PROMIC project staff trained farmers on the job in soil conservation practices. The visits of PROMIC project staff to individual farmer-families turned out to be the most effective method.

Extension: PROMIC carried out participatory planning of gully treatment: this included making farmers aware of the environmental and economic necessity for the technology. There was interactive planning of technology implementation at individual and community levels.

Research: Research was an important part of the approach, not only for planning (based on biophysical and socio-economic data), but also to stay in contact with the rural population and to obtain their confidence. Thanks to the research, the technology is well adapted to the biophysical conditions. Research topics included SWC (testing different measures), various soil parameters and a socio-economic survey.

Importance of land use rights: The gullied area is mainly common land in terms of use and ownership, but the fields above the gullies are mostly privately owned. At the beginning this played an important role, as the farmers were afraid to lose their land rights (due to bad experiences previously with similar projects). However, they collaborated during the implementation phase, as they recognised the programme's objectives and realised that there could be potential benefits for their own land, as well.

Incentives

Labour: 100% of the implementation was subsidised. Farmers were contracted to build the structures.

Inputs: Beside the labour for the rehabilitation of the gully area, PROMIC also paid for machinery, hand tools, transport of materials, seedlings and community infrastructure (roads). PROMIC also provided technical support and transport for further technology implementation on individual crop fields.

Credit: There was no credit facility for farmers.

Support to local institutions: Moderate training support for the local farmers' association was provided in terms of improvement of the association's organisation and reinforcement of their influence.

Long-term impact of incentives: Farmers now rarely treat any more gullies without payment – which implies a negative long-term impact. On the other hand, the incentives given (payment for construction work in the gullies) has had a positive short-term impact: the farmers now have more money for tools for soil conservation measures on their own cropland.

Monitoring and evaluation

Monitored aspects	Methods and indicators
Bio-physical	ad hoc measurements of erosion rate
Technical	regular observations (photo monitoring)
Socio-cultural	ad hoc interviews and visits
Economic/production	ad hoc interviews
Area treated	regular observation (visits and photo monitoring)
No. of land users involved	ad hoc surveys
Management of approach	ad hoc observations (external evaluation of impact)

Impacts of the approach

Changes as result of monitoring and evaluation: The approach was to initially target groups. Later, individuals were included (with individual farmer-family visits) to improve the effectiveness of the awareness raising and the implementation.
Improved soil and water management: The approach resulted in a considerable improvement in SWC. However, despite new knowledge about erosion, the farmers themselves hardly carry out any new gully conservation work without payment, and in the long term maintenance is not ensured.
Adoption of the approach by other projects/land users: Some other projects in Bolivia have copied parts of PROMIC's approach.
Sustainability: There is enough technical knowledge to continue with soil conservation in gullies. However the supportive technology of gabion dams (see related technology) can't be carried out by the farmers themselves, as there is a very high level of engineering knowledge and skill required. The other practices, such as stone and wooden check dams, cut-off drains and reforestation can be implemented by the farmers themselves. The problem is that off-site advantages outweigh the on-site benefits considerably. To achieve more long-term adoption by the farmers, the programme needs more time than just six years. Only a few farmers are able and willing to apply long-term sustainable land management in the gullies.

Concluding statements

Strengths and ➜ how to sustain/improve	Weaknesses and ➜ how to overcome
Integration of farmers in the process of implementation of soil conservation ➜ Farmers need to be even more integrated in the process of monitoring to guarantee the maintenance of the soil conservation achieved.	Sensitisation phase (for farmers and government) was too short to ensure sustained application of the technology without external support and supply. Established structures are often neglected and thus deteriorate ➜ Find new donors to continue the training/awareness raising on SWC technologies. Include the farmers in the monitoring visits and demonstrate examples of successful SWC (positive stimuli).
Transparent process during research, planning and implementation phases; incorporation of farmers' ideas (thus: good acceptance of PROMIC by the rural population).	Lack of money for replication and long-term maintenance of SWC measures ➜ Guarantee financial support in the threatened area, by the local government and international organisations.
Sensitisation of the farmers to erosion and degradation processes, and awareness creation about the impact and necessity of SWC in the hills to protect the valleys ➜ Continued sensitisation work after the implementation phase.	Farmers implementing SWC are not those benefiting most from the impact in the short term; even though the city of Cochabamba benefits considerably, financial support for implementation has stopped ➜ Seek financial support from Cochabamba; implement a system of payment for 'environmental services'
Good technical support during and after conclusion of the implementation phase ➜ Technical support not enough on its own – needs to be complemented by further sensitisation.	

Key reference(s): PROMIC documentation (see address below)
Contact person(s): Georg Heim, Mooseggstrasse 9, 3550 Langnau, Switzerland; geoheim@bluewin.ch ▪ PROMIC, *Programa de Manejo Integral de Cuencas*, Av. Atahuallpa final, Parque Tunari, casilla 4909, Cochabamba, Bolivia; promic@promic-bolivia.org; www.promic-bolivia.org

Landslip and stream bank stabilisation

Nepal – *Bans ko atta / Manra bandhi*

Integration of vegetative and structural measures for landslip, stream bank and gully stabilisation on hillsides.

A combination of measures, implemented by a group of neighbouring families, is used to address landslips, gully formation and stream bank erosion problems in the middle hills of Nepal. All these processes affect the stability of adjacent agricultural land and cause problems downstream. Small-scale farming is dominant in the area surrounding the treated land – which theoretically belongs to the government but is used by these families.

This pilot technological package is proving suitable in Nepal for steep/very steep slopes under subhumid climates within an altitudinal range of 1,000–1,500 m a.s.l. This type of intervention, combined with the active involvement of stakeholders (who contribute three quarters of the cost), was recently introduced to Nepal under a watershed management programme, co-funded by the European Commission (see related approach 'Integrated watershed management').

Initially, ditches with bunds on the lower side are constructed along the contour. Within the gullies and along the stream banks, cement bags (filled with cement, brick chips, sand and/or earth) are placed to avoid deepening of the channel. Wattle fences, made from woven bamboo are also used as checks in the gullies. These structures are complemented by vegetative measures: Nepalese alder *(Alnus nepalensis),* bamboo *(Dendrocalamus sp.),* cardamom *(Elettaria cardamomum),* and broom grass *(Thysanolaena maxima)* are planted. These species establish quickly in degraded sites and also control erosion, stabilise land and serve as cash crops, and for fodder, fuelwood and timber. Alder (locally called *utis)* is a nitrogen-fixing multipurpose tree which helps restore soil fertility.

Farmers can get economic benefits within a few years from these plants. Another advantage of this package is that the vegetative resources needed are locally available and cheap. Furthermore farmers already know how to propagate them. Maintenance costs are negligible. Once established, the stabilised and revegetated sites provide improved environments for birds and insects – thus favouring biodiversity – and they help protect natural springs. In this case study, the economic returns from the cash crops mainly go to one family. Another few families also utilise this site, extracting common products (fodder, litter, timber) for domestic use. Additionally, the location is regularly used as an unofficial demonstration site, being visited by various people (farmers, SWC specialists) interested in the technology. This represents an indirect benefit to a larger number of people and strengthens institutions at household and community levels.

left: Area three years after treatment (left of picture) and adjacent untreated area affected by steam bank erosion and land slips (right of picture). (Hanspeter Liniger)

right: Check dams made from cement bags filled with a mixture of sand, earth, cement and brick chips at Indrayani, Gagalphedi, Kathmandu District (top). Woven bamboo fences positioned in gullies near the Bajrayogrini Temple, Kathmandu District (bottom). Both sites are similar to the case study area. (P Mathema and I B Malla, respectively)

Location: Sakhintar, Kathmandu/Bagmati watershed, Kathmandu, Nepal
Technology area: 0.14 km²
SWC measure: structural and vegetative
Land use: wasteland (before), mixed: agro-silvopastoral (after)
Climate: subhumid
WOCAT database reference: QT NEP11
Related approach: Integrated watershed management, QA NEP11
Compiled by: Dileep K. Karna, Department of Soil Conservation and Watershed Management, District Conservation Office, Kathmandu, Nepal
Date: February 2003, updated August 2004

Editors' comments: This promising technology, new to Nepal, comprises a set of vegetative and structural measures for stabilisation of land where streams are cutting back into fields, or subsurface runoff causes landslips. Income is generated from various plants. The technology focuses on a problem common to the tropical/sub-tropical steeplands, and could be widely applicable both in Nepal and elsewhere.

Classification

Land use problems
- concentrated runoff from upstream agricultural areas
- landslides, gullies and stream bank erosion
- gullies backcutting into fertile agricultural land and also threatening irrigation canals and homesteads.

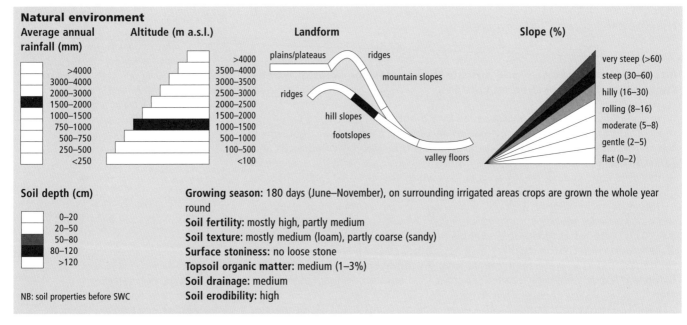

Land use	Climate	Degradation	SWC measures
wasteland: degraded shrubland (before) agro-silvopastoralism (after)	subhumid	water erosion: gully, mass movement, riverbank erosion chemical: fertility decline	structural: ditches/bunds, cement bags, wattle fences vegetative: tree/shrub cover, grasses (dispersed/aligned)

Technical function/impact
main:
- impede/retard concentrated runoff
- improvement of ground cover
- stabilisation of soil
- reduction of slope angle
- reduction of slope length

secondary:
- drain/divert concentrated runoff
- increase infiltration (due to improved ground cover)

Environment

Natural environment

Average annual rainfall (mm)
- >4000
- 3000–4000
- 2000–3000
- 1500–2000
- 1000–1500
- 750–1000
- 500–750
- 250–500
- <250

Altitude (m a.s.l.)
- >4000
- 3500–4000
- 3000–3500
- 2500–3000
- 2000–2500
- 1500–2000
- 1000–1500
- 500–1000
- 100–500
- <100

Landform
- plains/plateaus
- ridges
- mountain slopes
- ridges
- hill slopes
- footslopes
- valley floors

Slope (%)
- very steep (>60)
- steep (30–60)
- hilly (16–30)
- rolling (8–16)
- moderate (5–8)
- gentle (2–5)
- flat (0–2)

Soil depth (cm)
- 0–20
- 20–50
- 50–80
- 80–120
- >120

NB: soil properties before SWC

Growing season: 180 days (June–November), on surrounding irrigated areas crops are grown the whole year round
Soil fertility: mostly high, partly medium
Soil texture: mostly medium (loam), partly coarse (sandy)
Surface stoniness: no loose stone
Topsoil organic matter: medium (1–3%)
Soil drainage: medium
Soil erodibility: high

Human environment

Mixed land per household (ha)
- <1
- 1–2
- 2–5
- 5–15
- 15–50
- 50–100
- 100–500
- 500–1000
- 1000–10000
- >10000

Land use rights: open access
Land ownership: state
Market orientation: subsistence and mixed (subsistence and commercial)
Level of technical knowledge required: field staff/extension worker: high during establishment period, low to moderate during maintenance; land user: high for establishment, moderate to high during maintenance
Importance of off-farm income: <10% of all income: occasionally teaching at farmers' school; selling non-timber forest products in the local market; some people work in markets/shops/ on construction sites etc

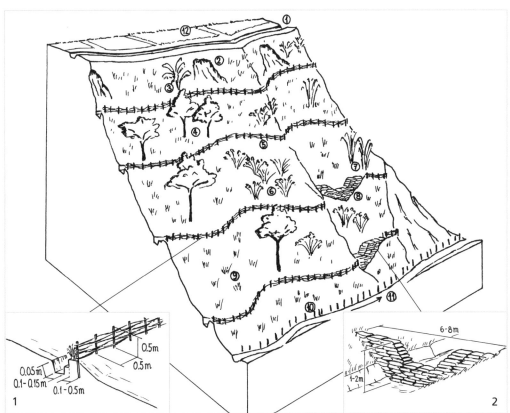

Landslip and stream bank protection: an overview of the multiple and integrated vegetative and structural measures: cut-off drain (1); land slip area (2); banana trees (3); alder trees (4); bamboo wattle fences (5); cardamom (6); bamboo planting (7); cement bag check dams (8); broom grass (9); bamboo cuttings (10); stream bank (11), agricultural fields in a flat area (12). Insert 1: Bamboo wattle fence combined with retention ditch and grassed bund to stabilise steep slopes and gullies. Insert 2: Old cement bags filled to form checks in gullies.

Implementation activities, inputs and costs

Establishment activities

1. Construction of contour bunds and ditches (January–April).
2. Stabilisation of slopes and gullies using bamboo wattle fences
3. Gully stabilisation with walls of cement bags placed across the gullies and along the stream banks (June).
4. Preparing the site for planting (June).
5. Planting of alder *(Alnus nepalensis,)*, cardamom *(Elettaria cardamomum)*, bamboo *(Dendrocalamus sp.)* and broom grass *(Thyosonaelana maxima)* (July–August).
6. Watering of plants using buckets (March–May, 1st year).
7. Application of farmyard manure at time of planting, and every December.
8. Weeding (January).
9. Earthing up (January).

All activities carried out manually.

Tools: local and traditional tools, A-frame, digging axe, hoe, pipe, water pump, baskets, shovel, hammer.

Duration of establishment: 1 year

Establishment inputs and costs per ha

Inputs	Costs (US$)	% met by land user
Labour (1,560 person days)	2,115	75%
Equipment		
- Tools	55	100%
- Empty cement bags (600)	10	0%
Materials		
- Cement bags (30) filled with earth/other material (50 kg each)	125	0%
- Bamboo	0	
Agricultural		
- Seeds (Alder: 50 g)	0	
- Seedlings (400 large cardamom slips)	5	0%
- Alder: saplings (2,500/ha)	40	100%
- Bamboo cuttings (600)	565	50%
- Manure (1 t/ha)	10	100%
TOTAL	**2,925**	**68%**

Maintenance/recurrent activities

1. Application of farmyard manure (January).
2. Weeding (January).
3. Preparing land for further planting of large cardamom and broom grass (March–April)
4. Thinning of cardamom, bamboo, alder, broom grass with a knife: *churi marna* (May, June).
5. Replanting of cardamom, broom grass, bamboo (June, July).
6. Earthing up (August–September and January).
7. Pruning of alders (December, January).

All activities done annually and by manual labour, no additional tools (see establishment).

Maintenance/recurrent inputs and costs per ha per year

Inputs	Costs (US$)	% met by land user
Labour (40 person days)	55	100%
Equipment		
- Tools	10	100%
Agricultural		
- Plant material (various)		
- Manure (500 kg)	5	100%
TOTAL	**70**	**100%**

Remarks: Labour costs: information based on oral information by farmer. Estimate was approx. 3 people per working day over 2 years.

Assessment

Acceptance/adoption
The technology was piloted in the case study area, but in the meantime, other farmers have taken it up outside the location.
- 18 families (47%) took up the technology with incentives: partly paid labour, seedlings, bamboo culms and cement bags.
- 20 relatively well resourced families (53 %), spontaneously adopted the technology because of its economic benefits on marginal land. This is a growing trend.
- Land users have adequately maintained what has been implemented.

Benefits/costs according to land user

Benefits compared with costs	short-term:	long-term:
establishment	negative	very positive
maintenance/recurrent	positive	very positive

Impacts of the technology

Production and socio-economic benefits
- + + + fodder production/quality increase
- + + wood production increase
- + + farm income increase: cash crop introduction

Production and socio-economic disadvantages
- – – – increased labour constraints during establishment
- – – – increased input constraints for establishment
- – labour constraints during maintenance
- – increased input constraints for maintenance

Socio-cultural benefits
- + + + community institution strengthening in a broad sense (eg as a result of common establishment activities; visits to the site by outsiders)
- + + + improved knowledge SWC/erosion
- + + improved health (due to cardamom's medicinal properties)
- + + national institution strengthening

Socio-cultural disadvantages
- – – socio-cultural conflicts
- – – might encourage other people to illegally extract the non-timber forest products (because of remoteness)

Ecological benefits
- + + + soil cover improvement
- + + + soil loss reduction from approx. 200 t/ha/year down to 10 t/ha/year
- + + + stabilisation of slope
- + + increase in soil fertility
- + + increase in soil moisture
- + + efficiency of excess water drainage
- + + spring protection (increase of water quantity/more steady flow)
- + biodiversity enhancement

Ecological disadvantages
- – – increased soil erosion and sediment transport (locally) during establishment of structural measures

Off-site benefits
- + + + stabilisation of off-site agricultural land
- + + reduced downstream siltation
- + + reduced runoff/transported sediments
- + reduced river pollution
- + increased stream flow in dry season
- + reduced downstream flooding

Off-site disadvantages
- – grazing pressure increase elsewhere because of SWC site being closed for grazing

Concluding statements

Strengths and ➜ how to sustain/improve

The technology requires resources which are largely locally available and of low cost ➜ Raising awareness that landslide threatened stream banks and steep slopes can be stabilised using local resources.

Technology addresses livelihood constraints ➜ Raising awareness that the technology is profitable.

Family members have learnt the technology. It is easy to replicate ➜ Provide training and schooling to farmers to spread this information to others (eg through village initiatives supported by government).

Better environment, increased biodiversity ➜ Ditto.

Soil and water conservation ➜ Ditto.

Fresh products, health benefits from cardamom ➜ Ditto.

Income generation through cash crop introduction (cardamom, bamboo, broom grass) ➜ Ditto.

Weaknesses and ➜ how to overcome

Establishment costs are high ➜ Subsidise the cost (extension service, projects). Reduce establishment costs by designing alternative structural measures without use of cement.

Socio-economic conflicts can arise when value of land is raised ➜ Take equity issues into account when implementing such a programme, and spread the benefits.

Establishment is very labour intensive.

The technology is adopted more by better resourced farmers ➜ Government programmes should involve poor farmers in land development with incentives for adoption of demonstrated technology.

Key reference(s): Bagmati Integrated Watershed Management Programme (2003): *Engineering Field Manual.* His Majesty's Government of Nepal, Ministry of Forest and Soil Conservation, Department of Soil Conservation and Watershed Management. Kathmandu, Nepal ■ Howell J (ed.) (1999): *Roadside Bio-engineering – reference manual.* Department of Roads, His Majesty's Government of Nepal

Contact person(s): Dileep K Karna and Indra Bahadur Malla, Department of Soil Conservation and Watershed Management, District Soil Conservation Office, Kathmandu Ward no. 29, Thamel, Kathmandu, Nepal; phone: 977 1 4410106; nfa@mail.com.np; dileep_karna@yahoo.com; indramalla@yahoo.com, dscoktm@mos.com.np; _ Sanjeev Bhuchar, ICIMOD, Kathmandu, Nepal; sbhuchar@icimod.org.np ■ see page 248

Integrated watershed management

Nepal – *Jan sahabhagita ma aadharit ekikrit jaladhar byabasthapan*

Integrated watershed management based on fostering a partnership between community institutions, line agencies, district authorities and consultants.

The Bagmati Integrated Watershed Management Programme (BIWMP) was based on fostering partnership among communities, district authorities, line agencies, and consultants. The main purpose was to ensure sustainable management of mountain watersheds. The means of addressing natural resource degradation problems were identified through participatory action research. These included options for better horticulture, agroforestry, irrigation, landslip stabilisation (see related technology), community forestry, vegetable cultivation, and wasteland development. The activities focussed on poverty reduction through sustained income generation, soil and water conservation in agriculture and forests, erosion hazard treatment and infrastructure improvement. All this took place in the context of equitable involvement of women and the socially disadvantaged with an emphasis on local ownership, institutional capacity building and sustainability.

The integrated watershed management programme included various participatory extension methods such as farmer-to-farmer exchange, training workshops and on-site demonstration. Under the programme, planning, implementation and monitoring of identified activities was done in a participatory manner. And the approach was deliberately flexible, adapting to new findings. Based on the priorities of the villagers, activities were implemented by individual households, farmers groups or village institutions.

BIWMP was initiated, coordinated and organised by the Department of Soil Conservation and Watershed Management (Ministry of Forest and Soil Conservation) with the active support of the European Commission. Within BIWMP there was cooperation with local institutions including VDCs (Village Development Committees), local NGOs (eg 'Friendship Sakhu', 'Helping Hands'), the CFUG (Community Forest User Group) – and individual households as in the case of the landslip and stream bank stabilisation initiate. It was considered essential that the approach would involve multiple stakeholders for SWC activities.

The first phase began implementation through user groups in 1986. In 1992 a European Commission mission evaluated the programme's activities and praised the technical packages, but suggested improvements to its implementation procedures, especially in terms of community organisation, extension, integration of activities and income generation activities. These were addressed in a second phase of the programme. Capacity building of community groups involved establishment of communication facilities, building up community networks, and empowering women and disadvantaged groups. BIWMP ended in 2003.

Location: Lalitpur, Kathmandu, Makwanpur, Bhaktapur, Sindhul; Bagmati river basin, Nepal.
Approach area: 570 km²
Land use: wasteland (before), mixed: agro-silvopastoral (after)
Climatic regime: subhumid
WOCAT database reference: QA NEP11
Related technology: Landslip and stream bank stabilisation, QT NEP11
Compiled by: Dileep Kumar Karna, Department of Soil Conservation and Watershed Management, District Soil Conservation Office, Kathmandu, Nepal
Date: December 2003, updated August 2004

Editors' comments: Watershed management through people's participation is common in Nepal. However, projects differ in specific approaches and in the technologies promoted. What marks this project's approach as unique in Nepal is the emphasis on people's participation, simultaneously stimulated by direct benefits accruing to the community from conservation-friendly plants.

Problem, objectives and constraints

Problem
BIWMP addressed problems related to institutional capacity for managing watershed resources.

Objectives
The overall objective was to overcome the constraints of effective implementation of a watershed management programme, through building synergies within a diversity of institutions. In case of the landslip and stream bank stabilisation work the specific objective was to come up with a technology that conserved soil and water but also provided direct benefits to the community through production.

Constraints addressed		
Major	**Specification**	**Treatment**
Institutional	Lack of inter-institutional collaboration.	Building and ensuring collaboration.
Technical	Lack of new options.	Training about new technologies.
Minor	**Specification**	**Treatment**
Social/cultural/religious	Following conventional top-down approaches.	Introduction of improved methods with more participation/ involvement of land users.

Participation and decision making

Target groups

Land users | SWC specialists/ extensionists | Planners | Politicians/ decision makers | Teachers/ students

Approach costs met by:	
International agency: European Commission	81%
Community/local: Bagmati watershed	15%
National government: His Majesty's Government (Nepal)	4%
	100%

Decisions on choice of the technology: Mainly made by SWC specialist with consultation of land users; the land users were not aware of the technologies.

Decisions on method of implementing the technology: Mainly made by SWC specialist with consultation of land users; measures implemented required acquiring technical know-how for starting the work.

Approach designed by: Mainly international and national specialists, partly land users. In case of the landslip and stream bank stabilisation technology, the approach was mainly designed by programme staff of the Kathmandu District Soil Conservation Office.

Community involvement		
Phase	**Involvement**	**Activities**
Initiation	interactive	rapid/participatory rural appraisal
Planning	interactive	rapid/participatory rural appraisal
Implementation	interactive	responsibility for major steps
Monitoring/evaluation	interactive	reporting, measurements/observations, public meetings, workshop/seminars
Research	interactive	on-farm trials

Differences in participation between men and women: The BIWMP in general had a bottom-up approach on planning and implementation and encouraged equitable involvement of women in activities. The decisions about implementing of the landslip and stream bank stabilisation technology were taken jointly by both men and women. However, contributions to the establishment and maintenance were made according to the traditional pattern of work allocation (for example digging mainly done by men, planting/watering mainly done by women).

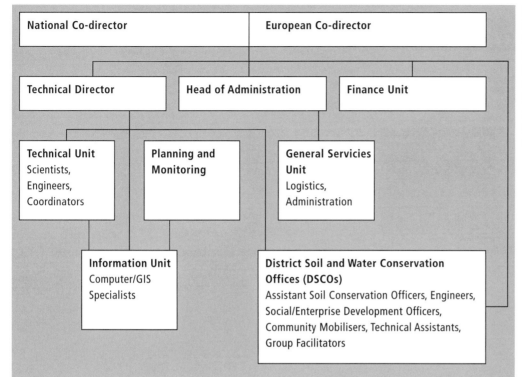

National Co-director	European Co-director

Technical Director	Head of Administration	Finance Unit

Technical Unit
Scientists,
Engineers,
Coordinators

Planning and Monitoring

General Services Unit
Logistics,
Administration

Information Unit
Computer/GIS
Specialists

District Soil and Water Conservation Offices (DSCOs)
Assistant Soil Conservation Officers, Engineers,
Social/Enterprise Development Officers,
Community Mobilisers, Technical Assistants,
Group Facilitators

Organogram
Organogram of the Bagmati Integrated Watershed Management Programme (BIWMP). The landslip and stream bank stabilisation work was implemented by the Kathmandu District Soil Conservation Office under the supervision of a ASCO (Assistant Soil Conservation Officer) Engineer.

Extension and promotion

Training: Training was provided on soil and water conservation in the form of visiting demonstration areas, farm visits and public meetings. The impact on land users and SWC specialists was excellent: after the training the land users and SWC specialists could easily implement horticultural, bioengineering, and agroforestry practices. The effectiveness of training on extension agents, planners and politicians was good, but only fair for teachers and students: there is still a lack of use of the outputs of the projects as educational materials.

Extension: The extension approach was Integrated Watershed Management with the following key elements: Participatory Rural Appraisal, trainings, farmer-to-farmer exchange, workshops, seminars and on-site demonstration. The impact of extension on land users was excellent. Extension focused on land users and SWC specialists together, and provided opportunities for them to test various technologies for watershed management. The involvement of village politicians, project decision makers and planners in monitoring the impact of extension, helped in the development of activities in watershed management for other areas.

Research: Research was a very important part of the approach. All research components (sociology, economics/marketing, ecology, technology) were covered (see key references) by various consultants and team staff members. Research activities were very efficient in contributing to the approach's effectiveness.

Importance of land use rights: Land use rights (including the security of traditional land use rights as in the case of the landslip and stream bank stabilisation technology) greatly helped the implementation of the approach.

Incentives

Labour: About 75% of the labour related to the landslip and stream bank stabilisation work was done voluntarily. The rest was paid in cash.

Inputs: Cement, bricks and stones for community infrastructure were fully financed by the programme, whereas seeds, seedlings, saplings were not (or only partly) financed.

Credit: No credit was provided.

Support to local institutions: The programme greatly supported local institutions by providing training and equipment.

Long-term impact of incentives: While there are clear positive environmental effects (because it ensures better management of a watershed and improved livelihood security for the families), there may be moderate negative impacts if the local communities are made dependant on external funds.

Monitoring and evaluation

Monitored aspects	Methods and indicators
Bio-physical	ad hoc measurements of land use changes
Technical	regular observations of technology effects
Socio-cultural	regular observations of status
Economic/production	regular observations of cash income
Area treated	ad hoc measurements: GIS mapping
No. of land users involved	regular observations of numbers
Management of approach	regular monitoring reports

Impacts of the approach

Changes as result of monitoring and evaluation: The described approach was designed on the basis of results from monitoring and evaluation of the first phase of the BIWMP (1986–1992). With the initiation of the second phase in 1992 changes were mainly focused on building the capacity of community groups to plan, implement and continue development activities after the initial input was completed. Capacity was built by (1) providing community-level training; (2) supporting the installation of communication facilities (telephone, radio etc.); (3) developing a strategy for empowering women and disadvantaged groups; (4) assisting the establishment of community networks.

Improved soil and water management: The approach greatly helped to improve soil and water management through the promotion of many activities related to agroforestry, water harvesting, landslip stabilisation and community forestry which were adopted by the land users.

Adoption of the approach by other projects/land users: There is lack of evidence whether this approach was chosen to address landslip and stream bank erosion problems in other areas by other projects.

Sustainability: Uncertain: whether land users can and will continue activities without external support has to be monitored at a later stage.

Concluding statements

Strengths and ➜ how to sustain/improve	Weaknesses and ➜ how to overcome
Involves all key actors in the field of watershed management ➜ Institutionalise such approaches.	It is 'project focussed' ➜ Needs to be institutionalised.
Has helped the land users in adopting improved livelihood options ➜ Effective government and community programmes needs to be promoted.	It does not focus on landless families ➜ Design activities for the landless in watershed management.
It encourages land users communities and local institutions to participate in the planning and decision making process ➜ Involve them in the planning and decision making process.	Some of the activities with high input requirements may not be spontaneously adopted by poor land users ➜ Further research on how to reduce inputs or provide specific incentives for such disadvantaged groups.
The implementation of technologies through the approach is cost-effective and socio-culturally accepted ➜ Take into account the local resources and knowledge.	

Key reference(s): Mallik DB (2000) Working with Community. *Jaladhar – quarterly newsletter of Bagmati Integrated Watershed Management Programme*. Issue 2, July – December ■ Bagmati Integrated Watershed Management Programme (1998, 1999, 2000, 2001) *Project Years 1–4, Annual Workplans July 1998–July 2002*. His Majesty's Government of Nepal, Ministry of Forest and Soil Conservation, Department of Soil Conservation and Watershed Management & Commission of European Communities. Kathmandu, Nepal

Contact person(s): Dileep K Karna and Indra Bahadur Malla, Department of Soil Conservation and Watershed Management, District Soil Conservation Office, Kathmandu Ward no. 29, Thamel, Kathmandu, Nepal; phone: 977 1 4410106; nfa@mail.com.np; dileep_karna@yahoo.com; indramalla@yahoo.com, dscoktm@mos.com.np ■ Sanjeev Bhuchar, ICIMOD, Kathmandu, Nepal; sbhuchar@icimod.org.np ■ additional contact persons: Bhupendra Singh Bisht, GBPIHEAD, Almora, India; bs_bisht@rediffmail.com; Madhav P. Dhakal, PARDYP – People and Resource Dynamics Project, ICIMOD, Kathmandu, Nepal; mdhakal@icimod.org.np; Basnet Druba, Farmer, Gagal Phedi VDC-4, Kathmandu; R. K. Gupta, CSKHPKV, Palampur, India; errkgupta@yahoo.com; Sudibya Kanti Khisa, Chittagong Hill Tracts Development Board, Khagradari, Bangladesh; khisask@bttb.net.bd; Bijendra K. Singh, Assistant Soil Conservation Office, Kavrepalanchok, Nepal; bijendra25@hotmail.com

Stone wall bench terraces
Syria – المدرجاتالحجرية

Ancient level bench terraces with stone walls, built to stabilise slopes, retain moisture, and create a suitable environment for horticulture.

Stone wall bench terraces in the hill ranges of western Syria comprise an ancient indigenous technology, introduced by the Romans and Byzantines about 2,000 years ago. Some new terraces are, however, still being built. The walls are constructed with limestone, largely found on site. The terraces are located in steep terrain (usually on slopes more than 25%) under low (and erratic) rainfall regimes of between 250 and 500 mm per annum. The terrace walls are 1–2.5 m high and the level beds 3–25 m wide, depending on slope.

Deep soil profiles (more than 2 m) have developed on steep slopes, where original soil depth was only shallow to medium. The terraces are very efficient in preventing soil erosion and in the retention of rainfall. They support trees and annual crops where they could not otherwise be grown.

These terraces are usually found near settlements. Construction is very labour intensive, considering how little land is effectively protected from erosion and brought into cultivation. High labour investment makes the construction process slow and retards further extension of the technology. However, if soundly constructed, maintenance requirements are low. Underlining this point, a large number of very ancient terraces can still be found intact, supporting a productive crop. Sometimes localised collapse of a terrace occurs due to concentrated runoff. In that case, the terrace in question may need to be rebuilt. To prevent such breaches, it is important to allow for discharge of excess runoff along drainage lines.

Currently, most terraces are used to grow fruit trees. These include olives, cherries, almonds, plums, pomegranates, apricots, and peaches. Husbandry practices are normally carried out by hand. Where space permits, however, draft animals are used for tillage. The curves of the terraces and access to the steep slopes make it very difficult/impossible to use tractors. Animal power is more versatile in this irregular landscape, but it is more expensive than tractor power, due to shortage of fodder.

left: Stone wall bench terrace with fruit trees in Tal Lata Village. (Michael Zöbisch)
right: Group of researchers and farmers discussing the technology at Tal Lata. (Hanspeter Liniger)

Location: Tal Lata Village, Ariha District, Idleb Province, Syria
Technology area: >5 km²
SWC measure: structural
Land use: cropland
Climate: semi-arid
WOCAT database reference: QT SYR01
Related approach: not documented
Compiled by: Zuhair Masri, ICARDA, Aleppo, Syria and Michael Zöbisch, Germany
Date: August 1999, updated May 2004

Editors' comments: Bench terraces with stone walls (risers) are a very common technology, with ancient origins. They are found, worldwide, on steep hillsides where erosion
is a problem and stone is available. Labour rates for initial construction are high, but the terraces are effective in multiple ways, and durable – given regular maintenance. Comparisons can be made with the examples from South Africa and Peru.

Classification

Land use problems
Before terracing, water erosion resulted in shallow to medium colluvial soils. Terracing made cultivation possible, but the beds tend to be very narrow and/or irregularly shaped, with large boulders set in them, making tractor cultivation (which is cheap) impossible.

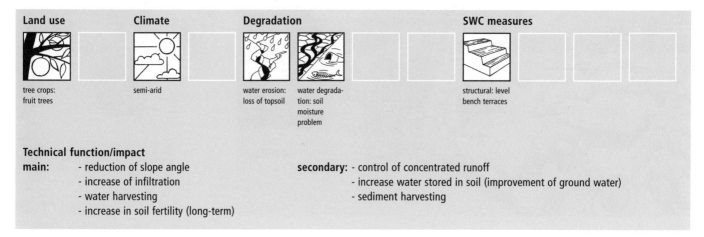

Land use	Climate	Degradation	SWC measures
tree crops: fruit trees	semi-arid	water erosion: loss of topsoil / water degradation: soil moisture problem	structural: level bench terraces

Technical function/impact
main:
- reduction of slope angle
- increase of infiltration
- water harvesting
- increase in soil fertility (long-term)

secondary:
- control of concentrated runoff
- increase water stored in soil (improvement of ground water)
- sediment harvesting

Environment

Natural environment

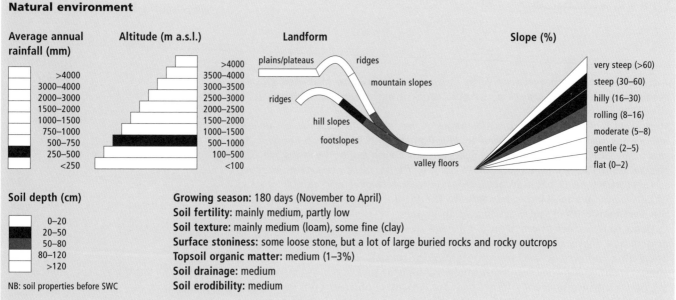

Average annual rainfall (mm): >4000, 3000–4000, 2000–3000, 1500–2000, 1000–1500, 750–1000, 500–750, 250–500, <250

Altitude (m a.s.l.): >4000, 3500–4000, 3000–3500, 2500–3000, 2000–2500, 1500–2000, 1000–1500, 500–1000, 100–500, <100

Landform: plains/plateaus, ridges, mountain slopes, ridges, hill slopes, footslopes, valley floors

Slope (%): very steep (>60), steep (30–60), hilly (16–30), rolling (8–16), moderate (5–8), gentle (2–5), flat (0–2)

Soil depth (cm): 0–20, 20–50, 50–80, 80–120, >120

NB: soil properties before SWC

Growing season: 180 days (November to April)
Soil fertility: mainly medium, partly low
Soil texture: mainly medium (loam), some fine (clay)
Surface stoniness: some loose stone, but a lot of large buried rocks and rocky outcrops
Topsoil organic matter: medium (1–3%)
Soil drainage: medium
Soil erodibility: medium

Human environment

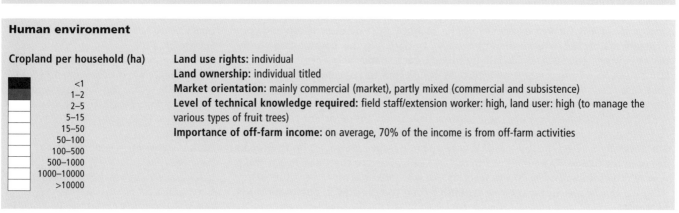

Cropland per household (ha): <1, 1–2, 2–5, 5–15, 15–50, 50–100, 100–500, 500–1000, 1000–10000, >10000

Land use rights: individual
Land ownership: individual titled
Market orientation: mainly commercial (market), partly mixed (commercial and subsistence)
Level of technical knowledge required: field staff/extension worker: high, land user: high (to manage the various types of fruit trees)
Importance of off-farm income: on average, 70% of the income is from off-farm activities

Technical drawing
Stone wall risers constructed in ancient times: these hold back the earth for production of fruit trees on the level benches.

Implementation activities, inputs and costs

Establishment activities

For terraces built currently:

1. Levelling the terrace bed by bulldozers where necessary.
2. Blasting rocks in the fields using drill and explosives (ammonium nitrate).
3. Collecting stones for wall building – which are available locally.
4. Building the stone walls with 1–2.5 m vertical interval (and therefore this height), a width of 60–80 cm and terrace beds 3–25 m wide.
5. Levelling land between stone walls.

Duration of establishment: 3–6 months (several persons)

Establishment inputs and costs per ha

Inputs	Costs (US$)	% met by land user
Labour (420 person days)	1,260	100%
Stone collection	50	100%
Equipment		
- Bulldozer (4 hours)	50	100%
- Hand Tools	50	100%
- Drill	5	100%
Materials		
- Ammonium nitrate (50–100 kg)	15	100%
- Detonators (50–100)	10	100%
- Fuses (25–50 m)	20	100%
- Stone (840 m³)	0	
TOTAL	**1,460**	**100%**

Maintenance/recurrent activities

Repairing terraces by hand requires an average of 5 person days every year.

Maintenance/recurrent inputs and costs per ha per year

Inputs	Costs (US$)	% met by land user
Labour (5 person days)	15	100%
Equipment		
- Hand tools	5	100%
Materials		
- Stone (small quality)	0	
TOTAL	**20**	**100%**

Remarks: Manual construction work requires 0.35–0.7 person days per metre length of terrace wall. Establishment costs were calculated for an average of 600 m length of stone wall (height 2 m, width 70 cm) per hectare on a 12% slope, with terrace beds therefore about 16–17 metres wide. Narrower terraces on steeper slopes are considerably more expensive to construct.

Analysis/assessment

Acceptance/adoption
- 95% of the land users (37 families) who have recently adopted the technology did so without incentives.
- The other 2 families received incentives ('soft' loans from the Agricultural Bank).
- Old and poor people needed incentive support – such as free soil levelling and rock blasting, transporting of stone, and construction. Cash-oriented, fruit growing, households build terraces themselves.
- The rate of spontaneous adoption is low because of the high costs.

Benefits/costs according to land user		Benefits compared with costs	short-term:	long-term:
		establishment	negative	positive
		maintenance/recurrent	positive	positive

Impacts of the technology

Production and socio-economic benefits	Production and socio-economic disadvantages
+ + + crop yield increase	– – high labour inputs in field operations (mechanisation is not possible)
+ farm income increase	
Socio-cultural benefits	**Socio-cultural disadvantages**
+ + + improved knowledge SWC/erosion	– potential socio-cultural conflicts (if the community refuses to participate in joint maintenance activities)
Ecological benefits	**Ecological disadvantages**
+ + + soil loss reduction	none
+ + increase in soil moisture	
+ increase in soil fertility	
+ biodiversity enhancement	
Off-site benefits	**Off-site disadvantages**
+ + reduced downstream flooding	none
+ + reduced downstream siltation	

Concluding statements

Strengths and → how to sustain/improve	Weaknesses and → how to overcome
The terraces make the cultivation of trees on hill slopes possible.	The establishment costs are high → Plant high value cash crops.
Soil and water is conserved and fruit crop yields are maintained/increased → Combine with soil fertility improvement (such as farm yard manure).	The mechanisation of farm operations is impossible because there is no access to the terraces for tractors, while animal power is constrained by high maintenance costs (fodder). Thus, field operations are limited to hand labour because → Subsidise mule ploughing.
The maintenance requirements are low. The terraces need little repair → Natural drainage lines must be prepared/maintained to prevent collapse during heavy rainfall.	

Key reference(s): Mushallah AB (2000) *The visible and the hidden in the country of olives.* Akrama Publ. Office. Damascus, Syria. pp 463
Contact person(s): Masri Zuhair, ICARDA, PO Box 5466, Aleppo, Syria; z.masri@cgiar.org, soilcons@scs-net.org

Rehabilitation of ancient terraces

Peru – *Andenes / Anchacas / Patapatas*

Repair of ancient stone wall bench terraces, and of an associated irrigation and drainage system.

The level bench terrace system in the Colca valley of Peru dates back to 600 years AD. Since then the terraces have been continuously used for crop production, but due to lack of maintenance they have deteriorated, and the population has lost its traditional knowledge of repair.

The rehabilitation of the terraces recreates their original structural design. Broken sections are cleared and the various materials – stones, topsoil, subsoil and weeds – are removed and separated. The foundation is re-established, followed by construction of the stone wall (the 'riser'). Backfilling with subsoil then takes place; this is consolidated and finally covered with topsoil. Simultaneously the complementary irrigation and drainage systems are reconstructed.

The rehabilitated terraces efficiently conserve soil and water on steep slopes, and they create a favourable microclimate for crops, reducing loss of stored heat at night by minimising air movement (preventing frosts) and mitigating dry conditions through moisture conservation. The main economic benefits are from increased yields and crop diversification.

Terraces are spaced and sized according to slope, eg on a 50% slope, terraces are 4 m wide with a 2 m high riser between terrace beds. Stones of ancient terraces had been widely used to build walls for boundary marking after privatisation of land, therefore a large amount of stone had to be provided by splitting rocks and transporting from other locations.

The area is characterised by steep slopes with loamy-sandy, moderately deep soils (on the terrace beds). Most of the annual precipitation (ca. 350 mm) falls within a period of 3 months, which makes irrigation necessary. The farmers in the area own, on average, 1.2 hectares of arable land, divided into around six plots in different agro-ecological zones. Production is mainly for subsistence.

Important supportive technologies include agronomic measures such as improved fallow, early tillage, ridging, and intercropping. Tree and shrub planting at the base of terrace walls is an optional measure with the aim of stabilising the walls, diversifying production and again ensuring a good microclimate. On average 250 trees/ha are planted; these are mainly native species such as *c'olle* (*Buddleia spp.*), *mutuy* (*Cassia sp.*), *molle* (*Schinus molle:* the 'pepper tree') and various fruit trees including *capuli* (*Prunus salicifolia*).

Location: Río Colca, Caylloma, Arequipa, Peru
Technology area: 100 km²
SWC measure: structural
Land use: cropland
Climate: semi-arid
WOCAT database reference: QT PER01
Related approach: Participatory catchment rehabilitation, QA PER01
Compiled by: Aquilino P. Mejia Marcacuzco, Center for Studies and Promotion of Development – DESCO, Arequipa, Peru
Date: July 2002, updated June 2004

Editors' comments: Terracing systems on hillsides date back to the beginning of agriculture. Often these feature walls ('risers') built of stone, and sometimes they are used for irrigation – as in this case from Peru. While many ancient systems have fallen into disrepair with out-migration of rural populations, this is an example of project-based rehabilitation.

Classification

Land use problems
- Loss of productive capacity: 30% of the agricultural land lost due to degraded terraces, severe deforestation (through cutting for fuelwood), overgrazing and burning of grazing areas.
- Inefficient irrigation practices (flooding) due to poor maintenance of irrigation system (and drainage system in poor condition), flood irrigation leads to deterioration of terraces.
- Loss of traditional knowledge of ancestral crop management practices (abandonment of appropriate rotation practices, lack of residue incorporation/recycling, unsystematic crop layout).

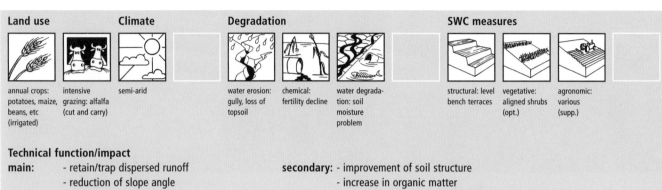

Land use	Climate	Degradation	SWC measures
annual crops: potatoes, maize, beans, etc (irrigated) — intensive grazing: alfalfa (cut and carry)	semi-arid	water erosion: gully, loss of topsoil — chemical: fertility decline — water degradation: soil moisture problem	structural: level bench terraces — vegetative: aligned shrubs (opt.) — agronomic: various (supp.)

Technical function/impact

main:
- retain/trap dispersed runoff
- reduction of slope angle
- reduction of slope length
- increase of infiltration
- water harvesting
- improvement of microclimate

secondary:
- improvement of soil structure
- increase in organic matter
- impede/retard concentrated runoff
- sediment harvesting
- increase/maintain water stored in soil
- impede/retard dispersed runoff

Environment

Natural environment

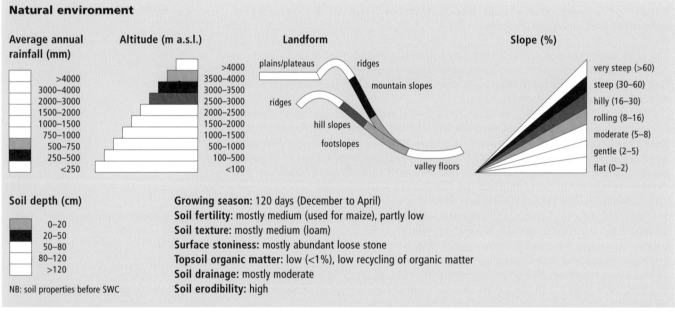

Average annual rainfall (mm)
- >4000
- 3000–4000
- 2000–3000
- 1500–2000
- 1000–1500
- 750–1000
- 500–750
- 250–500
- <250

Altitude (m a.s.l.)
- >4000
- 3500–4000
- 3000–3500
- 2500–3000
- 2000–2500
- 1500–2000
- 1000–1500
- 500–1000
- 100–500
- <100

Landform
- plains/plateaus
- ridges
- mountain slopes
- ridges
- hill slopes
- footslopes
- valley floors

Slope (%)
- very steep (>60)
- steep (30–60)
- hilly (16–30)
- rolling (8–16)
- moderate (5–8)
- gentle (2–5)
- flat (0–2)

Soil depth (cm)
- 0–20
- 20–50
- 50–80
- 80–120
- >120

NB: soil properties before SWC

Growing season: 120 days (December to April)
Soil fertility: mostly medium (used for maize), partly low
Soil texture: mostly medium (loam)
Surface stoniness: mostly abundant loose stone
Topsoil organic matter: low (<1%), low recycling of organic matter
Soil drainage: mostly moderate
Soil erodibility: high

Human environment

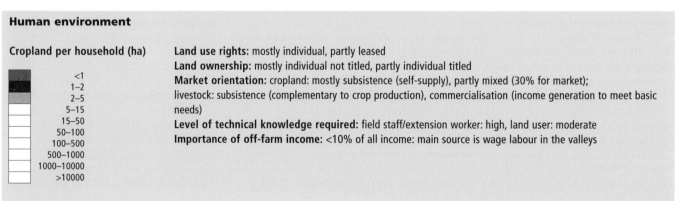

Cropland per household (ha)
- <1
- 1–2
- 2–5
- 5–15
- 15–50
- 50–100
- 100–500
- 500–1000
- 1000–10000
- >10000

Land use rights: mostly individual, partly leased
Land ownership: mostly individual not titled, partly individual titled
Market orientation: cropland: mostly subsistence (self-supply), partly mixed (30% for market); livestock: subsistence (complementary to crop production), commercialisation (income generation to meet basic needs)
Level of technical knowledge required: field staff/extension worker: high, land user: moderate
Importance of off-farm income: <10% of all income: main source is wage labour in the valleys

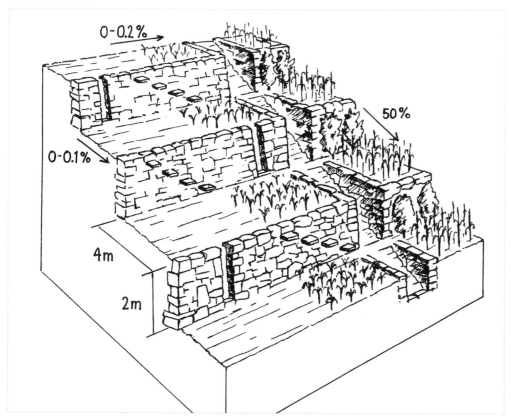

Technical drawing
Rehabilitated ancient terraces with high stone risers. Two options for irrigation and drainage of excess water are shown: outlets in the risers (left) and a broad water channel cutting perpendicularly through the terraces (right).

0–0.2%

0–0.1%

50%

4m

2m

Implementation activities, inputs and costs

Establishment activities
1. Separation of materials of collapsed wall: subsoil, topsoil, stone, weeds.
2. Cleaning and re-establishment of the foundation according to original structure.
3. Cutting stones from rocks (blasting and splitting); transporting.
4. Reconstruction of the stone wall, building on the basis of remaining intact structures of ancient terraces; simultaneous reconstruction of irrigation channels and complementary structures.
5. Backfilling with subsoil, moistening soil and consolidation with motor or manual compressor.
6. Covering with fertile topsoil.
7. Levelling of terrace bed and completion of riser edge (lip).
8. Planting of trees below terrace walls (optional).
9. Improved fallow, early tillage, ridging, and intercropping (supportive measures).

All activities carried out in dry period.

Used tools: A-frame, tape measure, motor drill, wheelbarrow, shovel, pick, steel bar, sledgehammer, hoe, hand compressor.

Duration of establishment: not specified

Establishment inputs and costs per ha

Inputs	Costs (US$)	% met by land user
Labour (130 person days)	560	40%
Equipment		
- Machines (compressor etc: 20 hours)	180	40%
- Tools (various: see description)	300	40%
Materials		
- Stone (450 m³)	200	40%
Agricultural		
- Seedlings (trees)	100	0%
Others		
- Construction supervisor (7 days)	60	0%
- Transport of inputs	0	
TOTAL	**1'400**	**35%**

Maintenance/recurrent activities
1. Irrigation system cleaning.
2. Clearing weeds from stone wall (dry season).
3. Inspection of the stone walls' stability (before sowing).
4. Repair structures (rainy season).
5. Tree and root pruning.

Maintenance/recurrent inputs and costs per ha per year

Inputs	Costs (US$)	% met by land user
Labour (6 person days)	25	100%
Equipment		
- Tools	100	100%
TOTAL	**125**	**100%**

Remarks: Person days needed for rehabilitation of 1 ha of ancient terrace system depend on degree of deterioration, the dimensions of the wall, slope angle (the steeper the more terraces) and availability of stones. In the case of the project, under a typical situation, for physical rehabilitation of 1 ha with 6 terraces, each ca 600 m long, 3–4 m wide and 2 m high, with one third of the main structures in disrepair, 18 men and 7 women work for 5 days; shrub planting is extra. Land users bear 35% of the overall costs: they also provide food for the group during work. The programme pays the rest. 450 m³ of additional stones are required to repair the broken parts, the cost includes blasting/splitting rocks and transport to the construction site. Supportive agronomic measures and agricultural inputs (seeds and manure) are not included. Maintenance costs vary considerably, depending on the specific situation: an average is taken here.

Assessment

Acceptance/adoption
- 90% of the land users (2,160 families) who applied the technology, did so with incentives.
- 10% land users (240 families) adopted the technology without incentives, on their own, aware of the need for SWC.
- 40% of terraces have been rehabilitated in 7 districts (8 micro-watersheds) of the Colca valley.
- The project provided incentives, through financing 65% of the overall implementation costs (labour, tools, explosives etc).
- There is a moderate trend towards spontaneous adoption.
- 95% of the repaired terraces have been well maintained, and land users are satisfied with the benefits; 5% of the terraces have been damaged again due to lack of maintenance, but land users continue using them for crop cultivation.

Benefits/costs according to land user

Benefits compared with costs	short-term:	long-term:
establishment	neutral/balanced	very positive
maintenance/recurrent	positive	very positive

Impacts of the technology

Production and socio-economic benefits
- + + + easier crop management (level bench, alignment of crops)
- + + + efficient use of irrigation water and fertilizers
- + + crop yield increase (average 30%)
- + + farm income increase

Socio-cultural benefits
none

Ecological benefits
- + + + soil loss reduction
- + + + efficiency of excess water drainage
- + + + regular crop growth and development
- + + biodiversity enhancement
- + + soil cover improvement
- + + increase in soil moisture
- + + increase in soil fertility
- + + improved microclimate (reduced wind; conserving heat)

Other benefits
none

Off-site benefits
- + + reduced downstream flooding
- + + increased stream flow in dry season
- + + reduced downstream siltation

Production and socio-economic disadvantages
- − − − increased input constraints (tools)
- − − increased labour constraints: heavy work (establishment), constant maintenance

Socio-cultural disadvantages
none

Ecological disadvantages
none

Other disadvantages
- − − careful management required (water and livestock)
- − − scarcity of stones (in some places)

Off-site disadvantages
- − reduced sediment yields (downstream)

Concluding statements

Strengths and ➜ how to sustain/improve
Traditional technology is of great value and adapted to local conditions➜ Awareness raising of the local population on maintenance of terraces.

Successful implementation is product of evaluation, analysis and documentation of experiences ➜ Further appraisal of the technology.

Soil maintained on steep slopes, no soil loss due to water erosion ➜ Continuous maintenance and appropriate management through training.

More efficient use of irrigation/rain water, longer storage of soil moisture ➜ Continuous maintenance of the system.

Maintenance of soil fertility ➜ Recycling of organic matter.

Facilitation of crop management activities (crop alignment, easier tillage with oxen plough, efficiency of pest control, etc) ➜ Appropriate crop management (see measures mentioned in description).

Improved microclimate facilitates crop growth and crop diversification ➜ Complete with improved agronomic practices and agroforestry.

Increased yields and food security ➜ Conserve crop diversity and genetic variety.

Cultural heritage ➜ Conservation of traditional practices.

Weaknesses and ➜ how to overcome
Specialised work, not easy to carry out – complex system of different structures ➜ Promote applied research and extension.

High rehabilitation costs; increased by loss of traditional forms of reciprocal work, and a trend towards individualism ➜ Reactivate and strengthen traditional labour systems based on reciprocity and mutual help.

Limited availability of stones impedes the rehabilitation process ➜ Carry stones from adjacent or remote places, give training in rock splitting.

Not appropriate for use of agricultural machines ➜ Awareness creation.

Private properties, but not titled ➜ Promote the legalisation of titles to facilitate the access to credit and technical assistance.

Vulnerability of terraces to damage by grazing animals ➜ Do not allow grazing on short terraces with high stone walls.

Land users are not skilled in repair of broken sections in the terrace system ➜ More training on maintenance and conservation.

Key reference(s): Mejia Marcacuzco AP (undated) *Folleto de divulgación: Andenes, construcción y mantenimiento* ■ Treacy, JM (undated) *Las Chacras de Coporaque: Andenes y riego en el valle del Colca.* Instituto de Estudios Peruanos. DESCO

Contact person(s): Rodolfo Marquina, Centro de Estudios y Promoción del Desarrollo – DESCO, Calle Málaga Grenet No. 678 Umacollo, Arequipa, Perú; descolca@terra.com.pe; www.desco.org.pe

Participatory catchment rehabilitation

Peru – *Participación comunitaria para la rehabilitación de cuencas*

Promoting the rehabilitation of ancient terrace systems based on a systematic watershed management approach.

The Center for Studies and Promotion of Development – DESCO, a Peruvian NGO, started the Terrace Rehabilitation Project in 1993 to re-establish ancient terracing and irrigation practices that had largely been lost. The project is part of a general integrated development programme. Its overall purpose is to restore the productive capacity of terraced cropland, and to generate better living standards in the Colca valley. The project has the following specific objectives: (1) to increase the productive infrastructure through soil conservation and better use and management of existing water resources; (2) to increase levels of production; (3) to stimulate people in soil conservation and land management; and (4) to encourage/promote relevant local institutions.

For implementation, a systematic watershed management approach was introduced. The catchment was considered the basic unit for development planning. Physical and socio-economic baseline studies were carried out. A strong community-based organisation, the catchment committee, was then founded. This consisted of representatives of major local grassroots organisations (irrigation committee, farmers' community, mothers' club etc). Responsibilities, commitments and rules were defined. Committee meetings and land user assemblies were the entities for planning, organisation and execution of project activities. DESCO initiated a process of 'concerted planning' in collaboration with other private and public institutions in Caylloma province.

In summary the project stages comprised: (1) project planning; (2) baseline studies; (3) catchment management plan; (4) constitution of the executive committee; (5) concerted planning of district development; and (6) organisation, execution, technical assistance and follow-up activities. Land users were required to participate in training courses and in fieldwork, to provide local materials and their own tools, and to fulfil duties within the organisations. Leaders and directors of grassroots organisations were responsible for planning and organisation of activities – implementation, training and follow-up – and for control and administration of project materials and inputs. The directors were also elected as representatives in the District Development Councils to participate in the evaluation and monitoring activities of the project.

Location: Río Colca, Arequipa, Peru
Approach area: 8,250 km²
Land use: cropland
Climate: semi-arid
WOCAT database reference: QA PER01
Related technology: Rehabilitation of ancient terraces, QT PER01
Compiled by: Aquilino P Mejia Marcacuzco, DESCO, Arequipa, Peru
Date: July 2002, updated June 2004

Editors' comments: The community action used under this terrace rehabilitation project is a form of a broader, integrated systematic approach. This latter approach is widespread in the whole Andean region, and a Latin American network of watershed management has been established. Within Peru, a broad range of NGO-driven development projects use this approach.

Problem, objectives and constraints

Problem
- lack of employment opportunities/depopulation of rural areas
- lack of planning and action in 'concerted development'
- little value associated with terrace rehabilitation
- low and unequal participation of women in field work
- general impoverishment of land users

Objectives
- to achieve higher levels of agricultural production and productivity through integrated development/management of soil and water resources
- to build capacity for planning, organisation and implementation of development activities

Constraints addressed

Major	Specification	Treatment
Social/cultural/religious	Women were treated unequally in terms of opportunities and salaries.	Equal treatment in salaries and better opportunities were ensured for women.
Financial	The poorest land users lacked the money to invest in terrace rehabilitation.	Manual labour and tools were subsidised.
Institutional	Coordination of planning and activities was lacking between different institutions and projects.	District Development Councils (CODDIS) were strengthened as entities for coordination and concerted action.
Minor	**Specification**	**Treatment**
Legal	There was a lack of legal (registered) institutions to coordinate planning and strategies for sustainable land use at community level.	An active effort was made to promote legalisation of, and give support to, grassroots organisations (eg Union of Land Users).
Economical	Investment in cash crops was a problem for poor small-holders.	Training/technical assistance was given for more profitable crops: eg potatoes, beans and peas.
Technical	Local specialists in terrace rehabilitation and for construction supervision were lacking.	Training and competitions were organised to develop skills and select the best.

Participation and decision making

Target groups

Land users | SWC specialists/ extensionists | Teachers/ students | Politicians/ decision makers

Approach costs met by:	
International NGO	60%
National government	20%
Community/local	20%
	100%

Decisions on choice of the technology: Mainly by SWC specialists with consultation of land users; the terraces were in an advanced stage of collapse and the local population did not have the means to reverse the process due to lack of economic resources.

Decisions on method of implementing the technology: Mainly by land users supported by SWC specialists; the technology is indigenous and adapted to the area. Evaluation workshops of, and activities permitting discussions on, the technology were carried out.

Approach designed by: National specialists.

Community involvement

Phase	Involvement	Activities
Initiation	interactive	rapid/participatory rural appraisal with public meetings, workshops, interviews
Planning	self-mobilisation	assemblies for decision making, workshops for local concerted planning
Implementation	interactive	casual labour, responsibility for minor steps (land users in general); responsibility for major steps (leaders)
Monitoring/evaluation	interactive	workshops, measurements/observations (directors of baseline organisations/leaders), reports (directors), interviews (directors/teachers), public meetings (land users)
Research	none	

Difference in participation between men and women: There were no differences in terms of salaries, but there were in terms of job opportunities: in a working group of 20 persons, typically only 5 women were contracted as terrace rehabilitation is very heavy work.

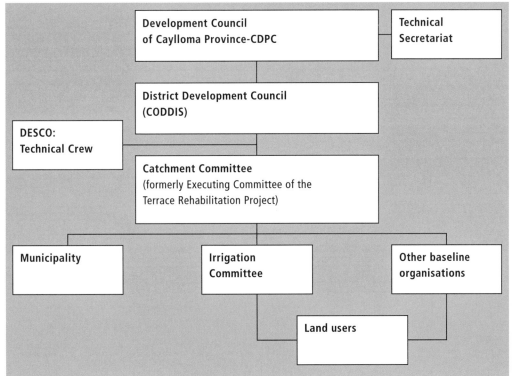

Organogram
District Development Council (CODDIS): social organisations, public and private institutions jointly prepare economic and social development plans in a partici- patory manner, and under the leadership of local government (prioritising development actions according to the needs of different stakeholders).

Development Council of Caylloma Province-CDPC

Technical Secretariat

District Development Council (CODDIS)

DESCO: Technical Crew

Catchment Committee (formerly Executing Committee of the Terrace Rehabilitation Project)

Municipality

Irrigation Committee

Other baseline organisations

Land users

Extension and promotion

Training: A training plan at three levels was drawn up, addressing the following target groups and topics: (1) Selected land users, leaders, supervisors: in-depth training on the interrelations between water, soil and plants; terrace and canal con- struction; institution/enterprise management; natural resource management, conservation practices, and crop production. (2) Directors of grassroots organisations and municipalities: treating organisational and administrative topics. (3) Farmers in general: treating topics of general interest and focussing on awareness raising. Training was carried out mainly on-the-job, but complemented by exchange of experiences and public meetings.

Extension: Key elements were technical assistance and sustained follow-up, supervision by specialised engineers, evaluation (reflection) and systematisation of gained know-how and developed practices with different stakeholders, and function testing of rehabilitated structures. Capacity for extension continuation has been built up within the catchment committee. However PRONAMACHS, a governmental SWC programme, is limited by lack of budget and through bureaucratic problems. The impact/effectiveness of training and extension on land users and SWC specialists was reported to be 'good', whereas the impact on extension workers, teachers and politicians/decision makers was only 'moderate' and on students and planners was given as 'poor'.

Research: Technology: research has been ongoing regarding functioning of the terrace and irrigation systems. Economy/ commercialisation: research regarding agronomic production, catchment appraisals and market studies have been carried out for the main products of the area. Research activities and studies carried out led to readjustment of the approach at catch- ment and field level.

Importance of land use rights: The fact that the land being rehabilitated is private property of the land users facilitated their commitment, as the project activities raised the value of the land.

Incentives

Labour: 60% of the labour costs were met by the project.

Inputs: Hand tools and equipment (A-frames, tape measures, motor drills, wheelbarrows, shovels, picks, steel bars, sledge- hammers, hoes, and compressors) were partly subsidised. Seedlings of tree species for establishment of the agroforestry com- ponent on terraces were produced in a project-owned nursery, and they were given free of charge to interested farmers. Fertilizers, biocides and seeds were not financed.

Credit: Credit was provided by FONDESURCO to land users who participated in the rehabilitation project (for seed supply) with a lower interest rate than on the market. FONDESURCO is an NGO (of which DESCO is a member) specialised in micro- finances in the rural sector.

Support to local institutions: Support was provided to existing institutions (in the form of training, organisation and financial inputs). But with the formation of a catchment committee, an important grassroots organisation was built up.

Long-term impact of incentives: A slight negative impact is expected in the long term: a few farmers do not maintain rehabilitated terraces (which leads to collapse of structures), however this is more due to negligence or carelessness than lack of awareness, or lack of ongoing incentives.

Monitoring and evaluation

Monitored aspects	Methods and indicators
Technical	regular measurements of improved structures, results of technology tests
Socio-cultural	ad hoc observations of land users changing attitudes of SWC
Economic/production	ad hoc measurements of crop production increase
Area treated	regular measurement of rehabilitated area
No. of land users involved	regular measurement of number of households that benefited directly
Management of approach	ad hoc observations of number of catchments rehabilitated with terraces and agroforestry

Impacts of the approach

Changes as result of monitoring and evaluation: There were various changes/readjustments of the approach: eg the concerted planning through the Local Development Councils was incorporated 5 years after the initiation of the project.
Improved soil and water management: There have been great improvements: introduction of high-value crops; 100% of the area cultivable; reduction of irrigation frequency by 20% due to higher efficiency of water storage by the terraces; various other SWC benefits.
Adoption of the approach by other projects/land users: A few other projects have adopted the approach: eg the project of the *Banco de Vivienda* PRATVIR in the Coporaque area; also 'Popular Cooperation' in Ichupampa (covering just 2 ha).
Sustainability: Land users can continue the activities without external support, using traditional systems of mutual help and new forms of local organisation (catchment committee). With increased income through integration of cash crops the maintenance of the structures can be sustained.

Concluding statements

Strengths and ➜ how to sustain/improve	Weaknesses and ➜ how to overcome
An effective systematic watershed management approach applied at catchment level ➜ Other projects/institutions should apply this approach.	Changes in leadership interrupt planned processes (of activities) ➜ Permanent training to encourage leadership qualities.
Soil conservation activities integrated in the plans of 'concerted development' ➜ Strengthening of the Local Development Councils (CODDIS).	Small holdings and land fragmentation are constraints for cost-effective agriculture ➜ Accelerate the process of land consolidation and entitlement.
Human capacity building: 60 specialists trained in rehabilitation technology ➜ Create opportunities to ensure continuation of their work.	The economic incentives provided by the project affected the existing reciprocal relationships (eg labour exchange) ➜ Cash for work incentives are sometimes useful to overcome labour constraints due to depopulation.
80% of land users have changed attitudes towards SWC, and are convinced of the benefits of terrace rehabilitation ➜ Promote SWC training and extension activities.	The generation of income encourages the purchase of industrialised products ➜ More training regarding consumption of local products.
Strengthened customs and traditions: rituals of offerings to the earth, to crops and animals; customs of mutual help in labour *(ayñi, minka)* and of exchanging food products *(treque)* ➜ Create spaces and mechanisms for daily practice of important cultural rituals/customs.	The approach requires the participation of all social and political stakeholders – which is practically impossible ➜ Strengthen the Local Development Councils (CODDIS).
Institutional capacity building: strengthening of organisations; increased participation ➜ Continue the training of leaders.	Labour overload in the family ➜ Better planning of work at the household level.
Complementary conservation practices have been integrated into the terraces system: agroforestry, improved fallow, etc ➜ Training of land users in the advantages and disadvantages of these practices.	Lack of a crop and irrigation plan for better water management ➜ Elaboration and application of a plan.

Key reference(s): none available
Contact person(s): Rodolfo Marquina, Centro de Estudios y Promoción del Desarrollo – DESCO, Calle Málaga Grenet No. 678 Umacollo, Arequipa, Perú; descolca@terra.com.pe; www.desco.org.pe

Traditional stone wall terraces

South Africa – *Mitsheto*

left: Field treated with traditional stone terrace walls, *mitsheto:* this is one of the best constructed series of walls in the area. (William Critchley)
right: Detail from the terraced field: behind the wall sediment has built up to a depth of approximately 50 cm over time. (William Critchley)

Stone walls built on sloping fields to create terraces for cultivation and conservation: both ancient and contemporary.

In this hilly, mixed farming area, stone terrace walls are a tradition. They are built across the slope when new land is cleared of loose stone and brought into crop cultivation. The dimensions of the terrace walls and the spacing between them depend on various factors, especially the slope and the amount of stone in the field. The walls may be up to 1.25 m high, from 1.0 to 1.5 m in base width, and between 20 and 50 m long. Spacing is from 3 to 10 m apart. Design of stone terrace walls varies. Some walls are very neatly built, others are merely piles of stone across the slope: this depends on the individual land user. The walls are built up each year with further stones: this may just be as more loose stone comes to the surface when ploughing, or also by digging out larger stones to deliberately build up the height of the walls as it silts up behind. Such terracing is generally confined to slopes between 20% and 50%. From 12% to 20% contour grass strips *(thambaladza)* are normally used, but below 12% land is rarely protected with structures or strips.

The purpose of terracing, apart from simultaneously clearing the land of stone, is to guard against loss of topsoil. Together with contour ploughing this helps to keep soil fertility in place on sloping cropland in a subhumid area. Rainfall is around 1,000 mm per annum and maize is the most common crop, but various other annuals (beans, pumpkins, sorghum etc) and perennials (peaches, avocadoes, oranges etc) are also grown.

This example of land conservation is probably unique in a former South African 'homeland'. In such areas, where the black population were concentrated at high population densities under the former *apartheid* regime, land degradation rather than soil conservation was the rule. These terraces continue to be built to this day as new land is opened up, despite the high amounts of labour (300–500 person days per hectare) involved in establishment. A study of the conservation systems used in the area and local attitudes to them, showed that the benefits of conservation were well understood by local farmers (see reference). Those questioned identified retention of soil – and of soil fertility in particular – as being of paramount importance. No mention was made of terraces being built simply to remove surface stone. The only downside mentioned (by a few) was the loss of cultivable land area. The key to the persistence of the terraces in this area is, therefore, that the land users understand and appreciate the place of terraces in maintaining soil fertility, and their considerable contribution to crop production.

Location: Thohoyandou District, Limpopo Province, South Africa
Technology area: 8 km²
SWC measure: structural
Land use: cropland
Climate: subhumid
WOCAT database reference: QT RSA03
Related approach: Community tradition, QA RSA03
Compiled by: William Critchley, Vrije Universiteit, Amsterdam, Netherlands
Date: May 1997, updated February 2004

Editors' comments: Traditional terraces with stone walls are common throughout Africa, and the rest of the world, wherever there is a combination of loose surface stone, sloping land and erosion. This is a good, living example from a former 'homeland' in South Africa, where many agricultural traditions had effectively been lost.

Classification

Land use problems
- decline in fertility of soils due to erosion and nutrient mining
- erosion from/caused by poor road drainage
- burning *veld* (rangeland) leading to runoff onto cropland

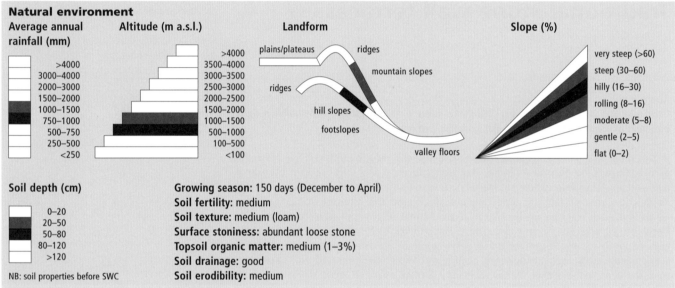

Land use

annual crops: maize, beans, sorghum, pumpkins

tree crops: peaches, oranges, avocados

Climate

subhumid

Degradation

water erosion: loss of topsoil

chemical: fertility decline

SWC measures

structural: stone wall terraces

agronomic: contour ploughing (supp.)

Technical function/impact

main:
- control dispersed runoff
- conserve/improve soil fertility

secondary:
- reduction of slope length
- reduction of slope angle

Environment

Natural environment

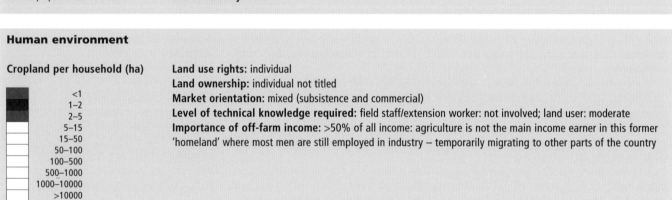

Average annual rainfall (mm)

>4000
3000–4000
2000–3000
1500–2000
1000–1500
750–1000
500–750
250–500
<250

Altitude (m a.s.l.)

>4000
3500–4000
3000–3500
2500–3000
2000–2500
1500–2000
1000–1500
500–1000
100–500
<100

Landform

plains/plateaus, ridges, mountain slopes, ridges, hill slopes, footslopes, valley floors

Slope (%)

very steep (>60)
steep (30–60)
hilly (16–30)
rolling (8–16)
moderate (5–8)
gentle (2–5)
flat (0–2)

Soil depth (cm)

0–20
20–50
50–80
80–120
>120

NB: soil properties before SWC

Growing season: 150 days (December to April)
Soil fertility: medium
Soil texture: medium (loam)
Surface stoniness: abundant loose stone
Topsoil organic matter: medium (1–3%)
Soil drainage: good
Soil erodibility: medium

Human environment

Cropland per household (ha)

<1
1–2
2–5
5–15
15–50
50–100
100–500
500–1000
1000–10000
>10000

Land use rights: individual
Land ownership: individual not titled
Market orientation: mixed (subsistence and commercial)
Level of technical knowledge required: field staff/extension worker: not involved; land user: moderate
Importance of off-farm income: >50% of all income: agriculture is not the main income earner in this former 'homeland' where most men are still employed in industry – temporarily migrating to other parts of the country

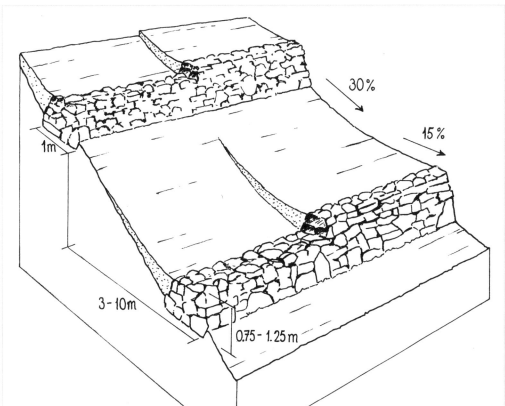

Technical drawing
Layout of stone wall terraces:
the walls are built up over time
(right) as soil accumulates behind
the barriers.

Implementation activities, inputs and costs

Establishment activities
1. Layout is by eye: no instruments used.
2. Construction of new stone walls begins with a shallow trench into which large foundation stones are laid (or rolled downhill with a 'crowbar' – a long steel lever – if very big).
3. Terrace walls are then built up with successively smaller stones: design depends on the individual.
4. Stiles (low points) are generally left in the walls to allow human passage, but these are 'staggered' (ie not all in a straight line up-and-down slope) to avoid gullies forming.
Construction is carried out during the dry/non-growing season.
Duration of establishment: usually spread over 2 years

Establishment inputs and costs per ha

Inputs	Costs (US$)	% met by land user
Labour (375 person days)	1,250	100%
Equipment		
- Tools (pick axe, crowbar)	20	100%
Materials		
- Stone (750 m³)	0	
Others		
TOTAL	**1,270**	**100%**

Maintenance/recurrent activities
1. The walls are increased in height each year as it silts up behind.

Maintenance/recurrent inputs and costs per ha per year

Inputs	Costs (US$)	% met by land user
Labour (50 person days)	160	100%
Materials		
- Stone (100 m³)	0	
TOTAL	**160**	**100%**

Remarks: Calculations are based on average-sized stone terrace walls (cross section 0.5 m²) spaced 6.5 metres apart on a typical slope of 30% (implying, in this case, a vertical interval of 2 metres). There is however a wide range of costs depending on amount of stone available and slope. Maximum establishment input may be as much as 550 person days per hectare on the steepest slopes, and may take 3 years to complete. While a small number of farmers have received subsidies, this calculation is based on the majority of cases where all inputs are met by the land user him/herself.

Assessment

Acceptance/adoption
- 95% of land users have built terraces without incentives; the remaining 5% received some ad hoc relief funds from government in drought years
- the knowledge of the SWC impact, plant growth benefits and need to cultivate stony land are the reasons behind acceptance of terracing
- there is a moderate trend to increase the amount of land terraced as people begin to cultivate the steeper slopes

Benefits/costs according to land user	Benefits compared with costs	short-term:	long-term:
	establishment	very negative	positive
	maintenance/recurrent	slightly positive	positive

Impacts of the technology

Production and socio-economic benefits	Production and socio-economic disadvantages
+ + crop yield increase	– – – increased labour constraints
+ + farm income increase	
Socio-cultural benefits	**Socio-cultural disadvantages**
+ + + improved knowledge SWC/erosion	none
+ + community institution strengthening	
Ecological benefits	**Ecological disadvantages**
+ + + soil loss reduction	none
+ + increase in soil fertility	
+ + increase in soil moisture	
Off-site benefits	**Off-site disadvantages**
+ + reduced downstream siltation	none
+ + reduced river pollution	

Concluding statements

Strengths and ➜ how to sustain/improve	Weaknesses and ➜ how to overcome
This is an important example of a thriving traditional technology in a country where most such ancient practices were ended by *apartheid* ➜ It has the potential to persist, if the Department of Agriculture acknowledges the importance of the system, encourages and gives training and organises exchange visits between farmers. Exchange of knowledge from farmer to farmer is facilitated by 'Landcare' and supported by the government.	High labour investment for establishment ➜ Hand tools, for example pickaxes and crowbars, could be supplied to the poorest families.
It makes use of abundant existing materials in the field (stone) and therefore input costs apart from labour are low: this is a win-win situation, clearing and building.	
Maintenance is simple – merely building up the walls gradually – and is effectively absorbed in everyday farming activities.	

Key reference(s): Critchley W and Netshikhovehla E (1998) Conventional views, changing paradigms and a tradition of soil conservation. *Development Southern Africa*, Vol 15, no 3, pp 449–469

Contact person(s): Rinda van der Merwe, Institute for Soil, Climate and Water, P/Bag x79, 0001 Pretoria, South Africa; rinda@arc.agric.za

Community tradition
South Africa

left: A retired miner, Elias, expanding his field and making new terrace walls as he proceeds: at this stage the stones are loosely arranged before construction of the walls takes place. (William Critchley)
right: Masonry skills are employed to build the houses (which are then plastered over) and to construct stone walls around the homesteads. (William Critchley)

Inherited, and still practiced, tradition of stone terracing – passed down from generation to generation.

The *VhaVenda* people of Limpopo Province in South Africa have a tradition of building with stone which has been passed down from generation to generation. They construct stone walls around their houses for example, taking a pride in the appearance of their homesteads. There is a historical monument nearby, the stone-built *kraal* at Dzata, the ruins of which are situated within a few kilometres of the study location. There may even be some evidence that the *VhaVenda* came originally from the area of the Great Zimbabwe (the famous stone-built fortress in Zimbabwe). It is not surprising therefore that the *VhaVenda* have used their masonry skills to build terraces in fields to counter erosion and simultaneously to make cultivation – along the contour by oxen – possible. This tradition has been passed down through the ages: it is institutionalised in the community and is practised together by men, women and children on a family basis. It is encouraged by community leaders: a particular example of this was in the 1960s when local chiefs were concerned at the sacred Lake Fundudzi 'turning red' – with sediment eroded from the land - and as a result they launched a conservation campaign to prevent soil wash into the lake. There has been modest and occasional support by the Department of Agriculture, in the form of ad hoc drought relief funds. There is quite a range of technical ability/care taken in terracing. Some walls are meticulously built; others are merely piles of stone across the slope. One of the reasons for this is that work tends to be done on an individual basis. Another result is that fields may take two years or more to be fully terraced. What is evident is that the land users – as well as being experienced masons – appreciate the benefits of the terraces they construct. An investigation of local environmental knowledge and conservation practices has demonstrated this clearly (see reference). The causes of erosion were explained by the interviewees as being part natural (rainfall, slope etc) and part anthropogenic (poor road building, up and down ploughing, burning of grassland etc). The main negative impact of erosion was considered to be loss of soil fertility: hence terracing for protection. This indigenous knowledge also extends to soils: eight local soil types and their differences in terms of texture, fertility and erodibility are recognised in the study area.

Location: Limpopo Province, South Africa
Approach area: 8 km²
Land use: cropland
Climate: subhumid
WOCAT database reference: QA RSA03
Related technology: Traditional stone wall terraces, QT RSA03
Compiled by: William Critchley, Vrije Universiteit, Amsterdam, Netherlands
Date: May 1997, updated February 2004

Editors' comments: Traditions of stone terracing are abundant all over Africa – as well as in Asia and Latin America, where they are better known and documented. This is a particularly good example of a conservation tradition embedded in a community, and probably unique in South Africa.

Problem, objectives and constraints

Problem
- the tradition presumably arose as a spontaneous local response to degradation: it remains well entrenched
- underlying problems of no flat land to cultivate, soil erosion/fertility decline on sloping fields, and loose stone and rocks impeding animal-draw ploughs

Objectives
The objective of the local people is simply to continue making cultivation possible and sustainable, through the local tradition of using stone walls to create terraces and to remove abundant stones from the field.

Constraints addressed

	Specification	Treatment
Labour	High labour demand to remove stone from inhibiting cultivation.	Traditional teaching that such stone can be used constructively to improve conservation and yield benefits.

Participation and decision making

Target groups

Land users

Approach costs met by:

National government	5%
Community/local	95%
	100%

Decisions on choice of the technology: Made by land users alone.
Decisions on method of implementing the technology: Made by land users alone.
Approach designed by: Land users alone.

Community involvement

Phase	Involvement	Activities
Initiation	self-mobilisation	passing on of knowledge from generation to generation
Planning	self-mobilisation	family-based (or individual) construction
Implementation	self-mobilisation	family-based (or individual) construction
Monitoring/evaluation	not applicable	
Research	not applicable	

Differences in participation between men and women: There are no differences. Women can be seen constructing stone walls as well as men.

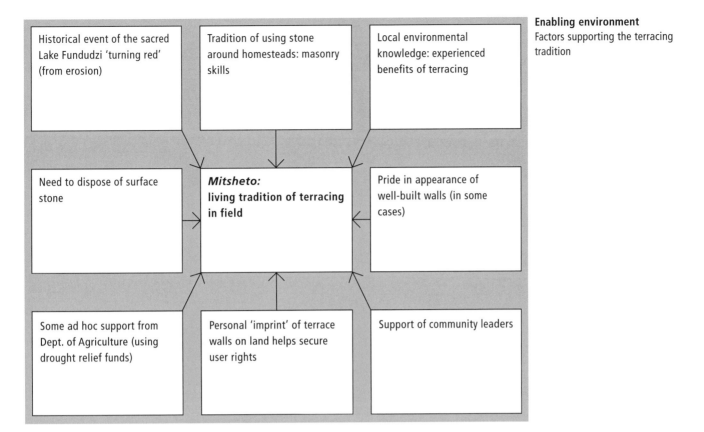

Historical event of the sacred Lake Fundudzi 'turning red' (from erosion)	Tradition of using stone around homesteads: masonry skills	Local environmental knowledge: experienced benefits of terracing
Need to dispose of surface stone	**Mitsheto:** living tradition of terracing in field	Pride in appearance of well-built walls (in some cases)
Some ad hoc support from Dept. of Agriculture (using drought relief funds)	Personal 'imprint' of terrace walls on land helps secure user rights	Support of community leaders

Extension and promotion

Training: There was/is no formal training – just father to son/mother to daughter.
Extension: Some encouragement from Department of Agriculture especially during soil and water conservation campaigns/ drought relief periods.
Research: None.
Importance of land use rights: Land is officially held, and allocated, by the chief. But building stone terraces on allocated land makes a personal 'imprint' and helps secure it.

Incentives

Labour: Almost entirely voluntary: some small support (approx 5% of the sample monitored) through Government during times of food scarcity with paid relief work.
Inputs: A (very) small amount of drought relief in recent years from Government (see above).
Credit: None.
Support to local institutions: Moderate support for SWC campaigns from local leaders (chiefs etc).
Long-term impact of incentives: There are no negative impacts as virtually no incentives have been used here.

Monitoring and evaluation

Monitored aspects	Methods and indicators
Biophysical	informal farmer observations only
Technical	informal farmer observations only
Economic/production	informal farmer observations only
Area treated	informal farmer observations only

Impacts of the approach

Changes as result of monitoring and evaluation: There have been no changes.

Improved soil and water management: Great: as part and parcel of the local tradition – for example contour ploughing is facilitated by the fact that the stone lines are on the contour, making this type of ploughing easier.

Adoption of the approach by other projects/land users: Only within this small pocket of Thohoyandou District (as far as known).

Sustainability: The *VhaVenda* have built terraces for generations so far, so no reason to think that things will change.

Concluding statements

Strengths and ➜ how to sustain/improve	Weaknesses and ➜ how to overcome
Traditional approaches have the potential to endure ➜ Acknowledgement and encouragement by the Government and/or NGOs will help this.	This tradition was largely unrecognised until recently: therefore an opportunity was lost to encourage people and help the approach spread ➜ Publicise widely and carry out farmer-to-farmer/community-to-community visits to further its spread and the spread of local SWC knowledge more generally.

Key reference(s): Critchley W and Netshikhovehla E (1998) Conventional views, changing paradigms and a tradition of soil conservation. *Development Southern Africa*, Vol 15, no 3, pp 449–469
Contact person(s): Rinda van der Merwe, Institute for Soil, Climate and Water, P/Bag x79, 0001 Pretoria, South Africa; rinda@arc.agric.za

Fanya juu terraces

Kenya

Terrace bund in association with a ditch, along the contour or on a gentle lateral gradient. Soil is thrown on the upper side of the ditch to form the bund, which is often stabilised by planting a fodder grass.

Fanya juu ('throw it upwards' in Kiswahili) terraces comprise embankments (bunds), which are constructed by digging ditches and heaping the soil on the upper sides to form the bunds. A small ledge or 'berm' is left between the ditch and the bund to prevent soil sliding back. In semi-arid areas, *fanya juu* terraces are normally constructed on the contour to hold rainfall where it falls, whereas in subhumid zones they are laterally graded to discharge excess runoff. Spacing is according to slope and soil depth (see technical drawing). For example, on a 15% slope with a moderately deep soil, the spacing is 12 m between structures and the vertical interval around 1.7 m. The typical dimensions for the ditches are 0.6 m deep and 0.6 m wide. The bund has a height of 0.4 m and a base width of 0.5–1 m. Construction by hand takes around 90 days per hectare on a typical 15% slope, though labour rates increase considerably on steeper hillsides because of closer spacing of structures.

The purpose of the *fanya juu* is to prevent loss of soil and water, and thereby to improve conditions for plant growth. The bund created is usually stabilised with strips of grass, often napier (*Pennisetum purpureum*), or makarikari (*Panicum coloratum var. makarikariensis*) in the drier zones. These grasses serve a further purpose, namely as fodder for livestock. As a supportive and supplementary agroforestry measure, fruit or multipurpose trees may be planted immediately above the embankment (eg citrus or *Grevillea robusta*), or in the ditch below in drier areas (eg bananas or pawpaws), where runoff tends to concentrate.

As a consequence of water and tillage erosion, sediment accumulates behind the bund, and in this way *fanya juu* terraces may eventually develop into slightly forward-sloping (or even level) bench terraces. Maintenance is important: the bunds need annual building-up from below, and the grass strips require trimming to keep them dense. *Fanya juu* terraces are associated with hand construction, and are well suited to small-scale farms where they have been used extensively in Kenya. They first came into prominence in the 1950s, but the period of rapid spread occurred during the 1970s and 1980s with the advent of the National Soil and Water Conservation Programme. *Fanya juu* terraces are spreading throughout Eastern African, and further afield also.

Location: Eastern Province, Kenya
Technology area: approx. 3,000 km²
SWC measure: structural
Land use: cropland
Climate: subhumid, semi-arid
WOCAT database reference: QT KEN05
Related approach: Catchment approach, QA KEN01
Compiled by: Donald Thomas; Kithinji Mutunga and Joseph Mburu, Ministry of Agriculture, Kenya
Date: January 1999, updated June 2004

Editors' comments: The *fanya juu* terrace is literally the structural mainstay behind Kenya's success story of soil and water conservation on small-scale farms. While similar terraces – with the bund above the ditch – can be found in many parts of the world, they are especially popular in Kenya. The area of focus here is Machakos District in Kenya's Eastern Province.

Classification

Land use problems
Low and erratic rainfall, soil erosion, surface sealing, water loss through runoff, low soil fertility as well as shortage of land and thus a need to conserve resources.

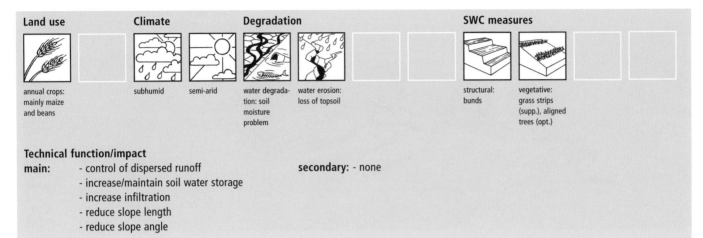

Land use

annual crops: mainly maize and beans

Climate

subhumid semi-arid

Degradation

water degradation: soil moisture problem

water erosion: loss of topsoil

SWC measures

structural: bunds

vegetative: grass strips (supp.), aligned trees (opt.)

Technical function/impact

main:
- control of dispersed runoff
- increase/maintain soil water storage
- increase infiltration
- reduce slope length
- reduce slope angle

secondary: - none

Environment

Natural environment

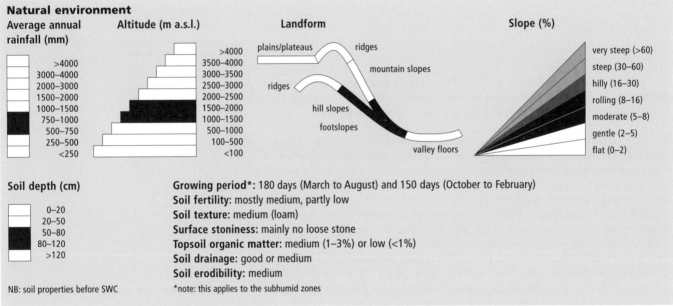

Average annual rainfall (mm)

>4000
3000–4000
2000–3000
1500–2000
1000–1500
750–1000
500–750
250–500
<250

Altitude (m a.s.l.)

>4000
3500–4000
3000–3500
2500–3000
2000–2500
1500–2000
1000–1500
500–1000
100–500
<100

Landform

plains/plateaus ridges
mountain slopes
ridges
hill slopes
footslopes
valley floors

Slope (%)

very steep (>60)
steep (30–60)
hilly (16–30)
rolling (8–16)
moderate (5–8)
gentle (2–5)
flat (0–2)

Soil depth (cm)

0–20
20–50
50–80
80–120
>120

NB: soil properties before SWC

Growing period*: 180 days (March to August) and 150 days (October to February)
Soil fertility: mostly medium, partly low
Soil texture: medium (loam)
Surface stoniness: mainly no loose stone
Topsoil organic matter: medium (1–3%) or low (<1%)
Soil drainage: good or medium
Soil erodibility: medium

*note: this applies to the subhumid zones

Human environment

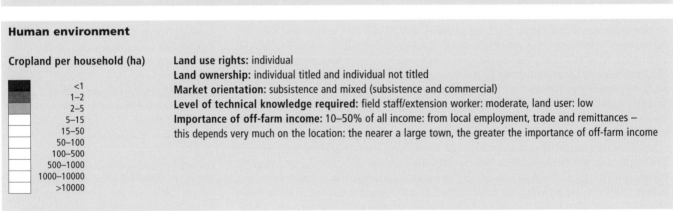

Cropland per household (ha)

<1
1–2
2–5
5–15
15–50
50–100
100–500
500–1000
1000–10000
>10000

Land use rights: individual
Land ownership: individual titled and individual not titled
Market orientation: subsistence and mixed (subsistence and commercial)
Level of technical knowledge required: field staff/extension worker: moderate, land user: low
Importance of off-farm income: 10–50% of all income: from local employment, trade and remittances – this depends very much on the location: the nearer a large town, the greater the importance of off-farm income

WOCAT ■ where the land is greener

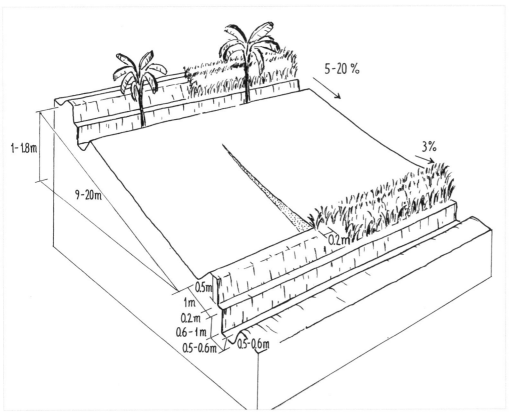

5-20 %

1-1.8m

9-20m

3%

0.2m

0.5m
1m
0.2m
0.6-1m
0.5-0.6m
0.5-0.6m

Technical drawing
Fanja juu terraces: newly constructed (left) and mature (right) with bananas planted below the bund and fodder grass on the riser: note leveling occurs over time (right).

Vertical interval and spacing for *fanya juu* terraces

| Slope | Terrace spacing | |
	Vertical Intervals	Horizontal Distance
(%)	(m)	(m)
5	1.00	20
10	1.35	14
15	1.73	12
20	1.80	9

Formula: Vertical Interval = (% slope / 4 + 2) x 0.3
max vertical interval = 1.8 m
(Source: Thomas 1997)

Implementation activities, inputs and costs

Establishment activities

1. Layout (alignment and spacing) of terraces either on the contour (dry areas) or on a slight grade (more humid areas) often using simple farmer operated 'line levels'.
2. Tilling soil to loosen for excavation (forked hoe, ox-drawn plough).
3. Digging ditch/trench and throwing the soil upwards to make the bund, using hoes and shovels.
4. Levelling and compacting bund.
5. Digging planting holes for grass.
6. Creating splits of planting materials (of vegetatively propagated species such as napier – *Pennisetum purpureum* and *P. makarikari* – *Panicum coloratum var. makarikariensis*).
7. Manuring (of napier grass and fruit trees)
8. Planting grasses.

All activities are done manually before the rainy seasons start (March and October) except planting of grasses (and trees where relevant), at the onset of rains.
Duration of establishment: usually within one year

Establishment inputs and costs per ha

Inputs	Costs (US$)	% met by land user
Labour (90 person days)	270	100%
Equipment		
- Animal traction (ox-drawn plough)	0	
- Tools (hoes, shovels, machete)	20	100%
Materials		
- Earth (275 m³)	0	
Agricultural		
- Compost/manure (1,000 kg)	10	100%
- Grass splits (20,000)	20	100%
TOTAL	**320**	**100%**

Maintenance/recurrent activities

1. Repairing breaches in structure where necessary.
2. Building up bund annually.
3. Cutting grass strips to keep low and non-competitive, and provide fodder for livestock.
4. Maintaining grass strips weed-free and dense.
5. Manuring of napier grass.

Maintenance/recurrent inputs and costs per ha per year

Inputs	Costs (US$)	% met by land user
Labour (10 person days)	30	100%
Equipment		
- Tools (hoes, shovels, machete)	5	100%
Agricultural		
- Compost/manure (250 kg)	3	100%
TOTAL	**38**	**100%**

Remarks: These calculations are based on a 15% slope (with 830 running metres of terraces per hectare) with typical dimensions and spacing: according to table and drawing above. In some areas tools are supplied free – but this is normally just for demonstration plots and is not included in this calculation.

Assessment

Acceptance/adoption
- 30% of those adopting have done so with incentives; the other 70% have done so without material incentives.
- The incentives referred to are tools – supplied by development programmes in some locations.
- There is some growing spontaneous adoption outside the area due to recognition of the benefits by farmers. This is especially so through women's groups. Within the area specified, Machakos District, almost all cropland is terraced.

Benefits/costs according to land user

Benefits compared with costs	short-term:	long-term:
establishment	slightly negative	positive
maintenance/recurrent	positive	very positive

Impacts of the technology

Production and socio-economic benefits	Production and socio-economic disadvantages
+ + crop yield increase	− − increased labour constraints
+ + fodder production/quality increase	− − loss of land (cropping area)
+ + farm income increase	− increased input constraints
+ wood production increase	− awkward to walk/carry burdens through the field
Socio-cultural benefits	**Socio-cultural disadvantages**
+ + improved knowledge SWC/erosion	none
+ + community institution strengthening	
+ national institution strengthening	
Ecological benefits	**Ecological disadvantages**
+ + increase in soil moisture (semi-arid)	none
+ + efficiency of excess water drainage (subhumid)	
+ + soil loss reduction	
Off-site benefits	**Off-site disadvantages**
+ + reduced downstream siltation	none
+ increased stream flow in dry season	
+ reduced downstream flooding	

Concluding statements

Strengths and → how to sustain/improve	Weaknesses and → how to overcome
Control runoff and soil loss → Ensure good design, maintenance of structures and adapt design to local conditions.	Loss of cropping area for terrace bund → Site-specific implementation: only where *fanya juu* terraces are absolutely needed, ie agronomic (eg mulching, contour ploughing) and vegetative measures are not sufficient in retaining/diverting runoff.
Storage of water in soil for crops → Ditto.	
Maintenance of soil fertility → Ditto.	High amounts of labour involved for initial construction → Spread labour over several years and work in groups.
Increased value of land → Ditto.	Risk of breakages and therefore increased erosion → Accurate layout and good compaction of bund.
	Competition between fodder grass and crop → Keep grass trimmed and harvest for livestock feed.

Key reference(s): Thomas D (editor) (1997) *Soil and water conservation manual for Kenya.* Soil and Water Conservation Branch, Nairobi
Contact person(s): Donald Thomas, Kithinji Mutunga and Joseph Mburu, Ministry of Agriculture, Nairobi, Kenya; Kithinji.Mutunga@fao.org

Catchment approach

Kenya

left: Catchment planning in action: local farmers and extension workers discuss technical interventions based on a participatory map. (Hanspeter Liniger)

right: Construction of *fanya juu* terraces is heavy work. The name *fanya juu* means 'throw it up' in Swahili and refers to the first step of establishment: ditches are excavated and the soil is thrown upslope to form an embankment. (Hanspeter Lingier)

A focused approach to integrated land and water management, including soil and water conservation, where the active participation of the villagers – often organised through common interest groups – is central.

The catchment approach promotes sustainable land management systems by conservation of a defined area (so-called 'micro-environments') through the active participation of the communities living there. It was launched in Kenya in 1988 to achieve greater technical and social impact – and at a more rapid pace – than the previous focus on individual farmers. This case focuses on a single 'catchment' in a subhumid area of Central Kenya. The emphasis is on structural measures – especially *fanya juu* terraces – but vegetative systems are promoted also. Other activities are supported such as spring protection, improved crop and animal husbandry, agroforestry, fodder production, fish ponds and others. The specific objectives are to stimulate the implementation of a variety of SWC measures leading simultaneously to improved production.

Each approach area is defined by cultural/administrative boundaries rather than strict hydrological watersheds or catchments (as its name confusingly implies). A conservation committee is elected from amongst the focal community before problem identification begins. Technical staff from relevant government and non-government agencies (NGOs) are co-opted onto the committee. The approach then involves participatory methods of appraisal and planning of solutions. Land users, together with the co-opted subject matter specialists, pool their knowledge and resources. Common Interest Groups (CIGs) are formed, with the aim of self-help promotion of specific farm enterprises. Training is given to the members of the CIGs by the Ministry of Agriculture. The farmers carry out the majority of the work themselves: monetary or other tangible incentives are few.

The end result is the micro-environment (catchment area) conserved for improved production, and left in the hands of the community to maintain and sustain. The catchment approach was developed under the National Soil and Water Conservation Programme – supported by (Swedish) Sida – and continues to be promoted as the Focal Area Approach (FAA) under the National Agricultural and Livestock Extension Programme (NALEP), which is again supported by Sida. However, under NALEP there is less emphasis on soil and water conservation than the previous programme, and more focus on promotion of productive enterprises.

Location: Muranga District, Kenya
Approach area: 1 km²
Land use: cropland
Climate: subhumid
WOCAT database reference: QA KEN01
Related technology: *Fanya juu* terraces, QT KEN05 and other technologies
Compiled by: James Njuki and Kithinji Mutunga, Ministry of Agriculture, Kenya
Date: August 2002; updated June 2004

Editors' comments: The catchment approach is linked to cultural or administrative boundaries, rather than to hydrological watersheds. This emphasis on social units and integrated land management is becoming more common worldwide. In Kenya the approach is constantly evolving and has recently been renamed the 'Focal Area Approach'.

Problem, objectives and constraints

Problem
- lack of tangible and assessable impact of SWC activities, technically or socially
- slow implementation of SWC
- underlying problems of poverty, declining soil fertility, soil erosion and fuelwood shortage

Objectives
Contribute to increased and sustained environmental conservation and improved agricultural production among communities, through participatory approaches to better land husbandry/SWC.

Constraints addressed		
Major	**Specification**	**Treatment**
Financial	Lack of capital hinders farmers from investing in structures.	Group work encouraged.
Technical	Lack of conservation knowledge.	Training through courses and field days.

Participation and decision making

Target groups

Land users | SWC specialists/ extensionists | Teachers/ students | Planners | Politicians/ decision makers

Approach costs met by:	
International agency	70%
National government	20%
Community/local	10%
	100%

Decisions on choice of the technology: Some by land users supported by SWC specialists, others initiated by SWC specialists.
Decisions on method of implementing the technology: Mainly by land users supported by SWC specialists.
Approach designed by: National specialists.

Community involvement		
Phase	**Involvement**	**Activities**
Initiation	interactive	public meetings
Planning	interactive	public meetings/Participatory Rural Appraisal etc
Implementation	self-mobilisation	implemented by community members
Monitoring/evaluation	passive	interviews
Research	none	none

Differences between participation of men and women: Many joint activities but men and women still stick to some traditional gender-related agricultural activities. For example women often concentrate on food crops, men on cash crops.

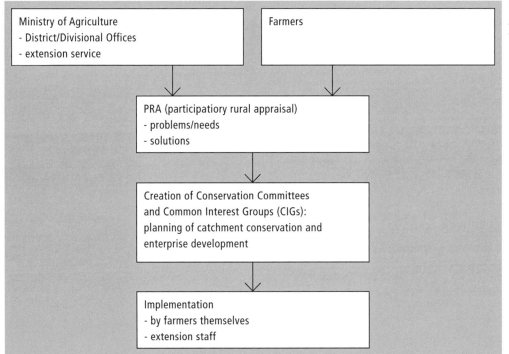

Ministry of Agriculture - District/Divisional Offices - extension service	Farmers

PRA (participatiory rural appraisal)
- problems/needs
- solutions

Creation of Conservation Committees and Common Interest Groups (CIGs): planning of catchment conservation and enterprise development

Implementation
- by farmers themselves
- extension staff

Extension and promotion

Training: Training is provided: including layout of measures; agroforestry; energy conservation; food preservation – as well as for specific farm enterprises. Carried out mainly through farm visits by Ministry of Agriculture agents. Impact is good both for farmers and extension workers.

Extension: Extension comprises farm visits, field demonstrations and field days. The extension service is said to be 'quite adequate' to take this process forward into the future. Impact is 'good' for farmers and teachers, and 'excellent' for technicians.

Research: Specific problems are researched as they arise. A strong research-extension linkage is being built up. Monitoring of the progress of the overall programme also takes place.

Importance of land use rights: Most land is individually owned, so there is no problem in that situation. Where land is rented, land users need to be persuaded to co-operate.

Incentives

Labour: All labour is provided on a voluntary basis.

Inputs: Seedlings and tools used to be partially financed through the catchment approach, though now the common interest groups are required to solicit help and assistance as need arises.

Credit: This is not provided directly, though a savings and credit 'stakeholder kitty' revolving fund is being promoted and developed.

Support to local institutions: This is moderate, and takes the form of training.

Long-term impact of incentives: Incentives (other than education and motivation) have been used at very low levels, and this now relates to the past. There is therefore little or no carry over of negative attitudes regarding activities currently undertaken. On the contrary, because people have seen the positive effects of conservation, they are motivated to continue.

Monitoring and evaluation

Monitored aspects	Methods and indicators
Bio-physical	ad hoc observations of production
Technical	ad hoc measurements of physical achievements and costs
Socio-cultural	ad hoc observations of CIG function
Economic/production	none
Area treated	regular observations
No. of land users involved	regular surveys
Management of approach	ad hoc observations

Impacts of the approach

Changes as a result of monitoring and evaluation: There have been few changes, but there is some enhanced collaboration between agencies, and – more income generating activities have been identified and implemented through common interest groups for crop production, marketing and livestock.

Improved soil and water management: The improvements to SWC are moderate: these have been mainly through *fanya juu* and level bench terraces.

Adoption of the approach by other projects/land users: Spread has been limited to one Non-Governmental Organisation in this particular case study area.

Sustainability: Interventions are likely to continue and be maintained, but this depends on common interest groups continuing to function actively.

Concluding statements

Strengths and ➜ how to sustain/improve	Weaknesses and ➜ how to overcome
Genuine community participation has been achieved under this approach ➜ Continue with participatory training.	Technologies tend to be implemented uniformly, not site-specifically ➜ SWC practices should be matched to each particular situation, eg structural measures such as *fanya juu* terraces should be promoted only where necessary, that is where agronomic and vegetative measures do not provide sufficient protection.
There is evidence of 'ownership' by the community which implies a feeling that what has been achieved is due to communal efforts and belongs to them ➜ Further training is more effective when benefits are appreciated in this way.	As yet uncertainty about continuation in specific areas if direct support stops after only one year ➜ Don't abruptly terminate this support after one year: continue approach for at least two or three years in each catchment (approach area).
Much improved extension/training – research linkages have been forged ➜ Continue focussed training/strengthen research-extension linkage.	Too small an area (of the country) is currently covered by NALEP ➜ More staff required: more effective use of staff.
New and productive farm enterprises have been promoted under the catchment approach alongside better SWC ➜ Continue to introduce/support where appropriate through Common Interest Groups.	In many places there is a lack of availability of inputs ➜ Provide better credit facilities for CIGs/farmers generally.

Key reference(s): Yeraswarq A (1992) *The catchment approach to soil conservation in Kenya.* Regional Soil Conservation Unit (now: Regional Land Management Unit, RELMA, a project under ICRAF, The World Agroforestry Centre, Nairobi) ■ Pretty JN, Thompson J and Kiara JK (1995) Agricultural regeneration in Kenya: The catchment approach to soil and water conservation. *Ambio* 24, no 1, pp 7–15
Contact person(s): James Njuki: njukig@yahoo.com (Ministry of Agriculture, Nairobi, Kenya) ■ Kithinji Mutunga: Kithinji.Mutunga@fao.org

Small level bench terraces
Thailand – ขั้นบันไดดินขนาดเล็ก

left: Establishment of small bench terraces, using hoes, in Chiang Mai Province, Thailand. The steep risers are compacted and a small drainage channel is formed on approximately every fourth terrace. (Samran Sombatpanit)
right: Well-established small bench terraces under horticultural crops, Chiang Mai Province, Thailand. (Samran Sombatpanit)

Terraces with narrow beds, used for growing tea, coffee, and horticultural crops on hillsides cleared from forests.

The terraces described in this case study from northern Thailand are found on hilly slopes with deep soils. The climate is humid and tropical, with 1,700–2,000 mm of rainfall annually. The main aim of the terraces is to facilitate cultivation of tea or coffee on sloping land: erosion control is secondary. Coffee and tea, as well as flowers and vegetables, are good alternatives to opium poppies – which it is government policy to eradicate.

After clearing natural and secondary forests by slash and burn, terraces are aligned by eye – and constructed by hoe. The width of the bed is 1.0–1.5 m depending on slope, though there are no specific technical guidelines. The length of each terrace can be up to 25 m. Down the slope, after every 3–4 terraces, there are lateral drainage channels, approximately 20–30 cm wide and 10 cm deep. Situated at the foot of a riser, each channel has a gradient of 0.5% or less. Excess water – some of which cascades over the terrace risers, with some draining through the soil – is discharged through these channels, generally to natural waterways. The risers are steep, with a slope of above 100%, and without a defined lip.

Natural grass cover develops on the risers: this is cut back by hand hoe or machete, or completely removed. The grass is often burned. After harvest (of annual crops), the land is left until immediately before the next rainy season. The terraces at this stage are covered by weeds and grasses. Land is then tilled by hoe. The weeds and grasses are removed and heaped in piles outside the cropped area. They are not composted or used for mulching – and here an opportunity is missed. Where soil fertility is a problem, chemical fertilizers are used. Maintenance includes building up/repairing of risers and levelling of terrace beds as required.

The technology was pioneered, and continues to be practiced, by refugee immigrants from China looking for new areas to start farming. These immigrants first came in the 1950s, and cultivated simply through slash and burn techniques. During the 1970s they visited relatives in Taiwan and brought back the idea of small terraces. Originally they settled illegally, but eventually they were given official permission to stay. However, official title deeds to their land have not yet been allocated.

Location: Amphur Mae Fa Luang, Chiang Mai, Thailand
Technology area: 5 km²
SWC measure: structural
Land use: forest land (before), cropland (after)
Climate: humid
WOCAT database reference: QT THA25
Related approach: not documented: immigrants own initiative
Compiled by: Prasong Suksom and Samran Sombatpanit, Bangkok, Thailand
Date: 2000, updated April 2004

Editors' comments: Small level bench terraces are found in various parts of the world. They are sometimes called 'step terraces' (or 'ladder terraces') because of their small size. They help in ease of cultivation as well as providing erosion control. This is a case study from northern Thailand, where immigrants introduced these terraces in the 1970s and 1980s.

Classification

Land use problems
- soil erosion on cultivated hillsides
- practical difficulties in tending tea, coffee, vegetables and flowers on sloping land: farming is much easier on levelled land

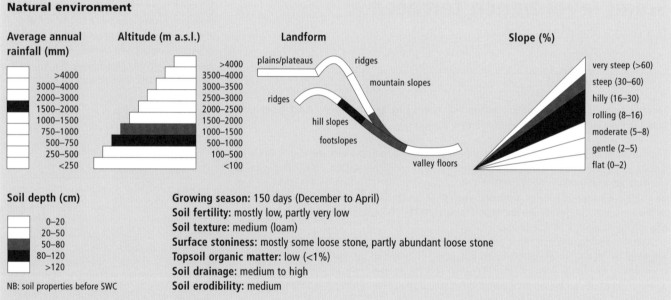

Land use

forest land (before)

perennial crops: tea and coffee (after)

annual crops: vegetables, flowers (after)

Climate

humid

Degradation

water erosion: loss of topsoil

chemical: soil fertility decline

water degradation: soil moisture problem (in dry periods)

SWC measures

structural: small bench terraces, drainage channels

vegetative: grass on risers (opt.)

Technical function/impact
main:
- reduction of slope length
- reduction of slope angle
- control of dispersed runoff

secondary:
- control of concentrated runoff
- increase of infiltration
- increase/maintain water stored in soil

Environment

Natural environment

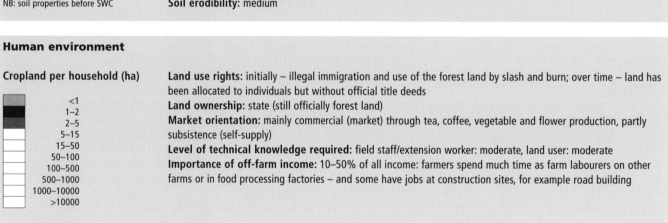

Average annual rainfall (mm)
- >4000
- 3000–4000
- 2000–3000
- 1500–2000
- 1000–1500
- 750–1000
- 500–750
- 250–500
- <250

Altitude (m a.s.l.)
- >4000
- 3500–4000
- 3000–3500
- 2500–3000
- 2000–2500
- 1500–2000
- 1000–1500
- 500–1000
- 100–500
- <100

Landform

plains/plateaus, ridges, mountain slopes, ridges, hill slopes, footslopes, valley floors

Slope (%)
- very steep (>60)
- steep (30–60)
- hilly (16–30)
- rolling (8–16)
- moderate (5–8)
- gentle (2–5)
- flat (0–2)

Soil depth (cm)
- 0–20
- 20–50
- 50–80
- 80–120
- >120

NB: soil properties before SWC

Growing season: 150 days (December to April)
Soil fertility: mostly low, partly very low
Soil texture: medium (loam)
Surface stoniness: mostly some loose stone, partly abundant loose stone
Topsoil organic matter: low (<1%)
Soil drainage: medium to high
Soil erodibility: medium

Human environment

Cropland per household (ha)
- <1
- 1–2
- 2–5
- 5–15
- 15–50
- 50–100
- 100–500
- 500–1000
- 1000–10000
- >10000

Land use rights: initially – illegal immigration and use of the forest land by slash and burn; over time – land has been allocated to individuals but without official title deeds
Land ownership: state (still officially forest land)
Market orientation: mainly commercial (market) through tea, coffee, vegetable and flower production, partly subsistence (self-supply)
Level of technical knowledge required: field staff/extension worker: moderate, land user: moderate
Importance of off-farm income: 10–50% of all income: farmers spend much time as farm labourers on other farms or in food processing factories – and some have jobs at construction sites, for example road building

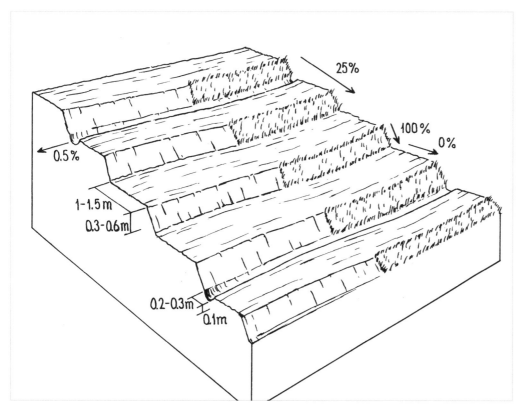

25%

0.5%

100%

0%

1–1.5 m

0.3–0.6 m

0.2–0.3 m

0.1m

Implementation activities, inputs and costs

Establishment activities

Clearing of forest is not included in the cost calculations.
1. Layout is simply by eye and best judgment.
2. Work begins on the lower part of the slope, and then progresses uphill.
3. Farmers cut into the hillside with hoes and drag the soil down to form the risers and level the terrace beds.
4. Risers are then stabilised/compacted by hoe.

Duration of establishment: one hectare of terraces can be constructed within a year by a family

Establishment inputs and costs per ha

Inputs	Costs (US$)	% met by land user
Labour (125 person days)	270	100%
Equipment		
- Tools (hand hoe)	5	100%
TOTAL	**275**	**100%**

Maintenance/recurrent activities

1. Land is prepared through tillage by hoe.
2. Weeds and grasses are removed and piled outside the cropping area.
3. Risers are built up/repaired where necessary.
4. Terrace beds may need levelling.

Maintenance/recurrent inputs and costs per ha per year

Inputs	Costs (US$)	% met by land user
Labour (20 person days)	45	100%
TOTAL	**45**	**100%**

Remarks: This calculation is based on a typical slope of approximately 20%, with risers of 0.2 m in height and beds 1.0 m wide. Maintenance costs include basic land preparation (for annual crops) or weeding etc for perennial crops.

Assessment

Acceptance/adoption

- 450 land users (90% of families who have adopted) took up the technology without incentives. These farmers grow various kinds of cash crops.
- 50 land users (10% of families who have adopted) accepted the technology with incentives: Doi Tung Crop Growers Group was supported by a private marketing company with cash to construct the terraces. The incentive helped farmers improve their farming systems, control erosion and make land management more sustainable – all in order to increase the amount of produce available to the company.
- There is a little growing spontaneous adoption: for example in the Mae Salong area farmers accept these terraces increasingly, but fruit growers tend to prefer intermittent 'orchard terraces' – terraces spaced apart, with 5 m or more of undisturbed land in-between. The benches in this case are backward sloping.

Benefits/costs according to land user	Benefits compared with costs	short-term:	long-term:
	establishment	slightly positive	positive
	maintenance/recurrent	slightly positive	positive

Impacts of the technology

Production and socio-economic benefits	Production and socio-economic disadvantages
+ + ease of cultivation	none
+ crop yield increase	
+ farm income increase	
Socio-cultural benefits	**Socio-cultural disadvantages**
+ + improved knowledge SWC/erosion	none
Ecological benefits	**Ecological disadvantages**
+ + + soil loss reduction	none
+ + increase in soil moisture during dry spells due to increased infiltration	
+ increase in soil fertility	
Other benefits	**Other disadvantages**
+ + can walk and work easier in the cropped area	none
Off-site benefits	**Off-site disadvantages**
+ + reduced downstream siltation	none
+ reduced transported sediments	
+ reduced river pollution	
+ reduced downstream flooding	
+ increased stream flow in dry season	

Concluding statements

Strengths and → how to sustain/improve	Weaknesses and → how to overcome
A relatively cheap method of terracing which makes cultivation easier and provides erosion control → Should be further promoted by extension agencies (in areas where cultivation is officially allowed). Allocation of official title deeds to land will speed up the adoption automatically.	Does not lend itself to mechanisation: the terrace beds are narrow and only suited to hand hoeing.
Compared with normal bench terraces, construction does not bring infertile subsoil to the surface.	In this situation grasses and weeds are merely piled and burned rather than being used to improve soil fertility → Teach farmers techniques of composting and/or mulching.

Key reference(s): none specified
Contact person(s): Prason Suksom, Samran Sombatpanit, 67/141 Amonphant 9, Soi Sena 1, Bangkok 10230, Thailand; phone/fax: ++66-25703641; sombatpanit@yahoo.com

left: Longan plantation on degraded hillsides. Bahia grass covers the terrace risers, the slopes between and partly the terrace beds to protect the soil from erosion. (Xinquan Huang)
right: The slope-separated orchard terraces are built along the contour. They help retain water and reduce soil erosion.
(Hanspeter Liniger)

Orchard terraces with bahia grass cover

China – 果园套种百喜草

Rehabilitation of degraded hillsides through the establishment of fruit trees on slope-separated orchard terraces, with bahia grass planted as protective groundcover.

In this case study orchards were established between 1991 and 1992 on degraded and unproductive hillsides (wasteland), with slopes of 12–45%. This was achieved by constructing level beds on the contour, mainly as continuous slope-separated orchard terraces, but in some cases as individual planting platforms. Terrace construction was generally undertaken by hand using hoes and shovels.

A typical terrace has a 4–5 m wide bed and a 1.0–1.5 m high riser. Commonly, a raised earth lip (0.3 m high) is constructed on the terrace edge to retain rainwater. The terrace riser walls are not protected. Even before terrace construction there was little topsoil and in some places the upper subsoil had been lost to erosion. The establishment of fruit trees (lychee, *Litchi chinensis* and longan, *Dimocarpus longan*) therefore required deep planting holes (1 m³), filled with organic matter/manure, into which seedlings were planted. In subsequent years additional large quantities of organic matter/manure were applied in circular trenches to the side of the trees, succeeding trenches being gradually further away as the trees grew. Bahia grass (*Paspalum notatum*) was planted for SWC purposes as a cover crop, to stabilise terrace risers and to improve soil fertility. It has not been used for fodder in this case. The germination rate of bahia grass seeds is comparatively low; therefore instead of direct seeding, nurseries were established to produce seedlings. The bahia grass seedlings were transplanted onto the terrace risers and beds (leaving a space around each fruit tree) and on the hillside slopes between the terraces. The grass grew and spread quickly, restoring a protective vegetative cover following terrace construction.

The primary overall purpose of the technology was to rehabilitate degraded hillsides through the planting of economically valuable fruit trees. Terracing reduces soil erosion while retaining most of the rainwater. The application of organic matter creates improved rooting conditions, while restoring and maintaining soil fertility. The bahia grass further provides protective groundcover preventing splash erosion, increasing surface roughness, and thereby slowing down runoff velocity, while contributing to the restoration of the soil's biological, chemical and physical properties. Irrigation ditches dug along the terraces help to reduce erosion further. This project was planned by SWC specialists: around 6,000 families were allocated orchard plots and provided with seedlings at a subsidised price.

Location: Gu Shan small watershed, Yongchun County, Fujian Province, Peoples' Republic of China
Technology area: 55 km²
SWC measure: structural, vegetative and agronomic
Land use: wasteland (before), cropland (after)
Climate: humid
Wocat database reference: QT CHN21
Related approach: not documented
Compiled by: Liu Zhengming, Soil Conservation Office, Yongchun County, Fujian, PR China
Date: June 2001, updated August 2004

Editors' comments: In China, large areas of degraded hillsides have been brought back into production by constructing terraces on which fruit trees are planted. In this example the technology has been further improved through planting of bahia grass, as a groundcover, to restore the structure and increase the soil organic matter. On a much smaller scale a case of degraded land conversion is presented from Tajikistan.

Classification

Land use problems
Degraded and unproductive hillside slopes (wasteland), with low and declining soil fertility, subject to severe soil erosion (sheet, rill, gully and mass movement) during periods of heavy and prolonged rainfall.

Land use	Climate	Degradation		SWC measures		
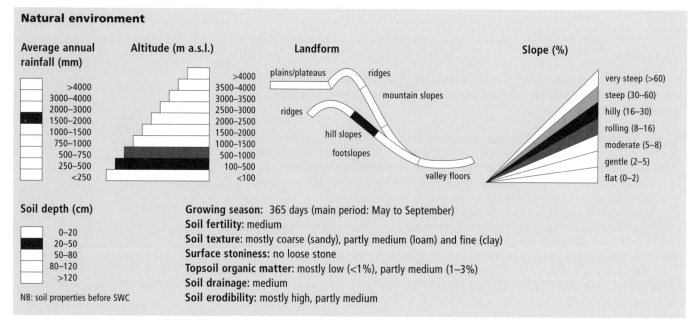						
wasteland (before)	humid	water erosion: loss of topsoil, gully, mass movement	chemical: fertility decline	structural: slope-separated terraces (forward sloping)	vegetative: dispersed grass, aligned trees	agronomic: organic matter application
fruit trees: lychee and longan (after)						

Technical function/impact
main:
- reduction of slope angle
- control of dispersed runoff
- control of raindrop splash
- improvement of ground cover
- increase in organic matter
- increase in soil fertility

secondary:
- increase of surface roughness
- improvement of soil structure
- increase/maintain water stored in the soil

Environment

Natural environment

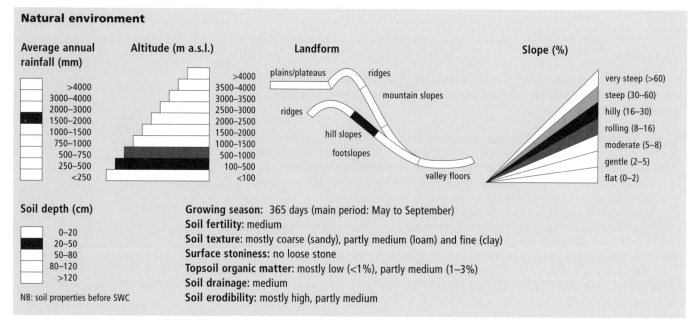

Average annual rainfall (mm)
- >4000
- 3000–4000
- 2000–3000
- 1500–2000
- 1000–1500
- 750–1000
- 500–750
- 250–500
- <250

Altitude (m a.s.l.)
- >4000
- 3500–4000
- 3000–3500
- 2500–3000
- 2000–2500
- 1500–2000
- 1000–1500
- 500–1000
- 100–500
- <100

Landform
- plains/plateaus
- ridges
- mountain slopes
- ridges
- hill slopes
- footslopes
- valley floors

Slope (%)
- very steep (>60)
- steep (30–60)
- hilly (16–30)
- rolling (8–16)
- moderate (5–8)
- gentle (2–5)
- flat (0–2)

Soil depth (cm)
- 0–20
- 20–50
- 50–80
- 80–120
- >120

NB: soil properties before SWC

Growing season: 365 days (main period: May to September)
Soil fertility: medium
Soil texture: mostly coarse (sandy), partly medium (loam) and fine (clay)
Surface stoniness: no loose stone
Topsoil organic matter: mostly low (<1%), partly medium (1–3%)
Soil drainage: medium
Soil erodibility: mostly high, partly medium

Human environment

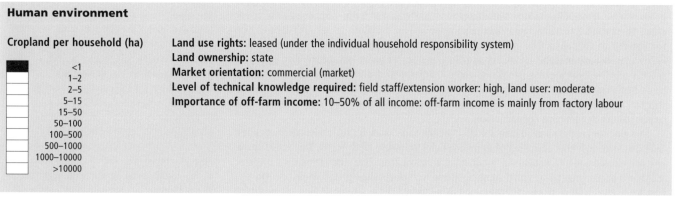

Cropland per household (ha)
- <1
- 1–2
- 2–5
- 5–15
- 15–50
- 50–100
- 100–500
- 500–1000
- 1000–10000
- >10000

Land use rights: leased (under the individual household responsibility system)
Land ownership: state
Market orientation: commercial (market)
Level of technical knowledge required: field staff/extension worker: high, land user: moderate
Importance of off-farm income: 10–50% of all income: off-farm income is mainly from factory labour

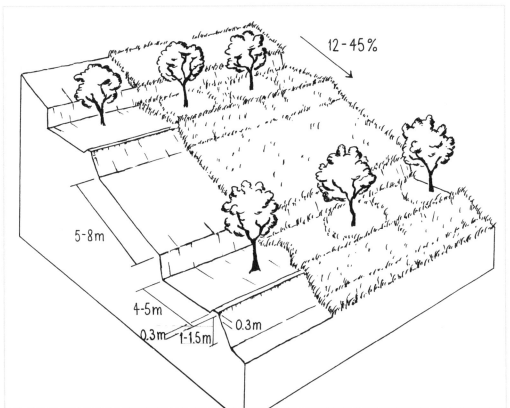

12 - 45%

5-8m

4-5m

0.3m 1-1.5m

0.3m

Technical drawing
Fruit trees on slope-separated terraces with a spacing of 5–8 metres between (dependent on slope). Terrace risers and beds are protected by the fast spreading bahia grass (right): note a grass-free space is maintained around each tree.

Implementation activities, inputs and costs

Establishment activities

1. Terraces were constructed by hand (during winter). Soil was excavated from the upper portion of the terrace and used to build up the lower portion behind the terrace riser wall to create a level platform (bed). Part of the excavated soil was used to build a terrace lip.
2. On each terrace one line of fruit trees was established. Deep planting holes (1 m³) were dug by hand and filled with organic matter/manure. Fruit tree seedlings were planted (in spring). Spacing between trees was approx. 6 m.
3. Bahia grass was transplanted onto the terraced hillside (in spring).

Duration of establishment: 2 years

Establishment inputs and costs per ha

Inputs	Costs (US$)	% met by land user
Labour (350 person days)	840	100%
Equipment		
- Tools (hoe, shovel)	0	
Materials		
- Earth	0	
Agricultural		
- Fruit tree seedlings (300)	350	60%
- Bahia transplants (60,000)	435	0%
- Fertilizers (1,000 kg)	145	100%
- Compost/manure (15,000 kg)	70	100%
TOTAL	**1,840**	**70%**

Maintenance/recurrent activities

1. Repairing terraces damaged by storms.
2. Digging trenches by the side of the fruit trees and filling with organic matter/manure.
3. Filling any gaps in the bahia grass.
4. In the first 1–2 years maintenance also involves replacing any fruit tree seedlings that do not survive.
5. Subsequently as the trees grow they require regular pruning, fertilization and pest control.
6. Weeding around the trees.

All maintenance activities through hand labour with simple tools.

Maintenance/recurrent inputs and costs per ha per year

Inputs	Costs (US$)	% met by land user
Labour (60 person days)	144	100%
Equipment		
- Tools (hoe, shovel)	0	
Agricultural		
- Fruit tree seedlings (30)	36	100%
- Bahia transplants (8,000)	58	100%
- Fertilizers (700 kg)	84	100%
- Biocides (20 kg)	10	100%
- Compost/manure (9,000 kg)	44	100%
TOTAL	**376**	**100%**

Remarks: For establishment: 200 person days for terrace construction, 100 for digging pits and planting trees, 50 for transplanting bahia grass. For maintenance: 15 person days for terrace maintenance, 40 for digging organic matter trenches, 5 for bahia grass gap filling. The SWC department produces bahia transplants in nurseries; these are then distributed to the farmers.

Assessment

Acceptance/adoption
All land users in the case study watershed applied the technology. 88% of them (5,755 families) accepted the technology with incentives. This project was planned by SWC specialists. Farmers were then allocated orchard plots. The government provided the fruit tree seedlings at 60% of the cost and the bahia transplants for free. Land users had to come up with 70% of the total costs (mainly their own labour). 12% of the land users (784 families) did not require incentives. There is a slow spontaneous adoption of the technology, based on the fact that bahia grass is remarkably helpful in controlling soil erosion.

Benefits/costs according to land user	Benefits compared with costs	short-term:	long-term:
	establishment	slightly positive	very positive
	maintenance/recurrent	slightly positive	very positive

Impacts of the technology

Production and socio-economic benefits	Production and socio-economic disadvantages
+ + + farm income increase	− − − increased input constraints (organic matter/manure)
+ + crop yield increase (fruit)	− − increased labour constraints
Socio-cultural benefits	**Socio-cultural disadvantages**
+ + + improved knowledge SWC/erosion	none
+ + national institution strengthening	
+ + community institution strengthening	
Ecological benefits	**Ecological disadvantages**
+ + + soil cover improvement	− − competition between fruit trees and bahia grass for water and nutrients
+ + + soil loss reduction	
+ + + rainwater retention	
+ + + decrease erosion due to raindrop splash	
+ + increase in soil fertility, organic matter content	
+ + increase in soil moisture	
Off-site benefits	**Off-site disadvantages**
+ + reduced downstream siltation	none
+ increased stream flow in dry season	
+ reduced downstream flooding	

Concluding statements

Strengths and → how to sustain/improve	Weaknesses and → how to overcome
An increase in vegetative cover reduces erosion, improves the ecological environment, increases soil fertility and organic matter content, improves water retention and thereby raises fruit tree yields → Control weeds and fertilize well.	Orchard development can extend too far up the slope, onto steep mountain sides → Reserve the upper slopes for forest, and restrict orchards to the lower slopes.
The combination of structural and vegetative measures has a quick impact on reducing soil erosion and preventing mass movement on hillside slopes → Increase the vegetative cover and improve soil properties through the addition of plenty of organic matter/manure.	Potential competition for water and nutrients between the bahia grass and the fruit trees → Clean weed (bahia grass included) in the area immediately around the fruit tree.
Improved land management practices bringing back degraded wasteland sites into economic production → Demonstration and extension while also improving the enabling legislative environment.	Increase in farm income becomes very positive only after fruit trees start producing → Consider replacing bahia grass with a more palatable perennial fodder plant to improve farm income in the short term.
	Low germination rate of bahia seeds → Expand experimental studies (seed treatments, cuttings, taking splits, etc).

Key reference(s): none
Contact person(s): Liu Zhengming, Soil Conservation Office of Yongchun County, No. 99 Liuan Road, Yongchun County 362600, Fujian Province, People's Republic of China ■ Nie Bijuan, Xuezhen Yang, Fujian Soil and Water Conservation Experimental Station, No. 6 Tong Pan Road, 350003 Fuzhou, People's Republic of China; fjswc@fjstbc.gov.cn ■ Zhangou Bai, ISRIC, PO Box 353, 6700 AJ Wageningen, The Netherlands; baizhanguo9910@hotmail.com, zhanguo.bai@wur.nl

Zhuanglang loess terraces
China – 庄浪水平梯田

left: Aerial view over Zhuanlang county where 90% of the hillsides are covered with terraces. Reducing runoff and erosion, maintaining soil fertility and making farming operations easier are key for rainfed agriculture in this semi-arid environment. (He Yu)

right: A 4 m high terrace riser, where the lower part is vertical and bare – demonstrating the stability of the loess soil at this depth. The upper part is sloping, and stabilised with grasses, bushes and trees. (Hanspeter Liniger)

Level bench terraces on the Loess Plateau, converting eroded and degraded sloping land into a series of steps suitable for cultivation.

The Loess Plateau in north-central China is characterised by very deep loess parent material (up to 200 m), that is highly erodible and the source of most of the sediment in the lower reaches of the Yellow River.

The plateau is highly dissected by deep gullied valleys and gorges. The steep slopes, occupying 30–40% of the plateau area, have been heavily degraded by severe top soil and gully erosion. Over the whole Loess Plateau approximately 73,350 km² of these erosion prone slopes have been conserved by terraces.

In the case study area (Zhuanglang County) the land that is suitable for terracing has been completely covered. The total terraced area is 1,088 km², accounting for 90% of the hillsides. The terraces were constructed manually, starting at the bottom of the slopes and proceeding from valley to the ridge. The terraces comprise a riser of earth, with vertical or steeply sloping sides and an approximately flat bed (level bench). Depending on farmers preference some terrace beds are edged by a raised lip (a small earth ridge) which retains rainwater, others remain without lip. The semi-arid climate does not require a drainage system. For typical hillside terraces on slopes of 25–35% the bed width is about 3.5–5 metres with a 1–2 metre riser, involving moving about 2,000–2,500 cubic metres of soil (see table of technical specifications). Generally the risers are not specifically protected, but there may be some natural grasses growing on the upper part. The lower part of the riser is cut vertically into the original soil surface, and has no grass cover, being dry and compact. However it is not erosion-prone since it has a stable structure.

Over most of the Loess Plateau, the soil is very deep and therefore well suited to terrace construction. In addition to downstream benefits, the purpose is to create a better environment for crop production through improved moisture conservation, and improved ease of farming operations. In an average rainfall year, crop yields on terraced land are more than three times higher than they used to be on unterraced, sloping land. The implication is that terrace construction – though labour intensive – pays back in only three to four years when combined with agronomic improvements (such as applying farm yard manure and planting green manure). Some farmers try to make the best use of the upper part of terrace risers by planting cash trees or forage crops – including *Hippophae rhamnoides* (seabuckthorn), *Caragana korshinskii* (peashrub) and some leguminous grass. This is locally termed 'terrace bund economy'. The plants stabilise the risers and at the same time provides extra benefits.

Location: Zhuanglang County, Gansu Province (Loess Plateau Region), PR China
Technology area: 1,080 km²
SWC measure: structural
Land use: cropland
Climate: semi-arid
WOCAT database reference: QT CHN45
Related approach: Terrace approach, QA CHN45
Compiled by: Wang Yaolin, Gansu GEF/OP12 Project Office, Lanzhou, PR China; Wen Meili, Department of Resources and Environmental Sciences, Beijing Normal University, PR China; Bai Zhanguo, World Soil Information, Wageningen, Netherlands.
Date: March 2006

Editors' comments: China has a history of terrace construction dating back thousands of years – for both rainfed crops and paddy rice. In the period since the 1950s, the Loess Plateau region has been extensively terraced to reduce off-site sediment levels in the Yellow River, and to create better conditions for crop production. The results are effective and spectacular covering an area of over 73,000 km².

Classification

Land use problems
Cultivation of unterraced hillside slopes leads to serious soil erosion and problems of downstream sedimentation. Loss of topsoil and rainwater in uncontrolled runoff has contributed to declining crop yields.

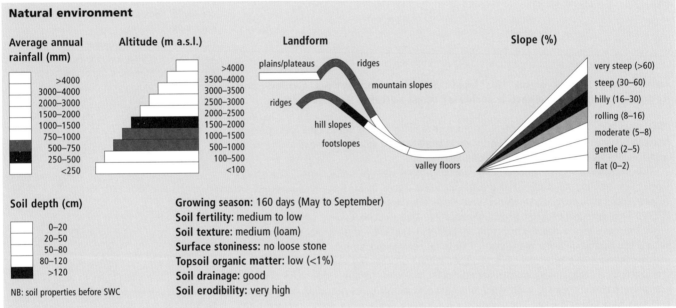

Land use

annual crops: wheat, maize, potato, peas, millet, sorghum

fruit trees: apple, pear and peach; walnut

Climate

semi-arid

Degradation

water erosion: loss of topsoil, gully

chemical: fertility decline

water degradation: soil moisture problem

off-site: downstream siltation of the Yellow River

SWC measures

structural: level bench terraces

Technical function/impact
main:
- reduction of slope angle/slope length
- retains runoff in-situ
- increases infiltration
- water harvesting/increases water stored in soil
- reduces downstream flooding and sediment deposition (a national/regional concern)

Environment

Natural environment

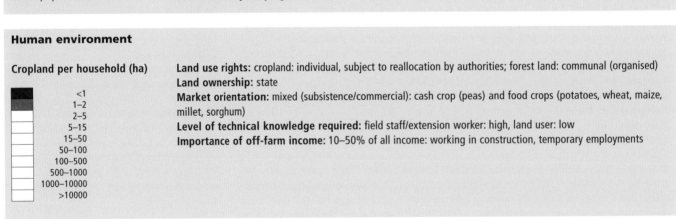

Average annual rainfall (mm)

>4000
3000–4000
2000–3000
1500–2000
1000–1500
750–1000
500–750
250–500
<250

Altitude (m a.s.l.)

>4000
3500–4000
3000–3500
2500–3000
2000–2500
1500–2000
1000–1500
500–1000
100–500
<100

Landform

plains/plateaus
ridges
mountain slopes
ridges
hill slopes
footslopes
valley floors

Slope (%)

very steep (>60)
steep (30–60)
hilly (16–30)
rolling (8–16)
moderate (5–8)
gentle (2–5)
flat (0–2)

Soil depth (cm)

0–20
20–50
50–80
80–120
>120

NB: soil properties before SWC

Growing season: 160 days (May to September)
Soil fertility: medium to low
Soil texture: medium (loam)
Surface stoniness: no loose stone
Topsoil organic matter: low (<1%)
Soil drainage: good
Soil erodibility: very high

Human environment

Cropland per household (ha)

<1
1–2
2–5
5–15
15–50
50–100
100–500
500–1000
1000–10000
>10000

Land use rights: cropland: individual, subject to reallocation by authorities; forest land: communal (organised)
Land ownership: state
Market orientation: mixed (subsistence/commercial): cash crop (peas) and food crops (potatoes, wheat, maize, millet, sorghum)
Level of technical knowledge required: field staff/extension worker: high, land user: low
Importance of off-farm income: 10–50% of all income: working in construction, temporary employments

25 – 35%

3.5 – 5 m

0.2 – 0.3 m

1 – 2 m

Original slope

1

Technical drawing
Layout of level bench terraces on the Loess Plateau: the lower, vertical section is cut into the compacted soil. Natural grasses – or planted grass/ shrub species – protect the more erodible and less steep upper part of the riser. The low 'lip' is optional.
Insert 1: Method of construction: the volume of soil to be excavated from the hillslope (see table below) equals the volume 'returned' to form the outer part of the terrace.
Insert 2: Chinese Bench Terrace Technical Specifications.

2 **Chinese Bench Terrace Technical Specifications**

Slope in %	Height of ridge (VI) in m	Bench width in m	Volume of soil to be dug (m³/ha)	Man days/ha (m³/man day)
~ 9 %	1.0	11.20	1,230	405
	2.0	22.30	2,670	885
~ 18 %	1.0	5.31	1,200	405
	1.5	7.80	1,830	600
	2.0	10.20	2,700	900
~ 27 %	1.0	3.37	1,305	435
	1.5	4.90	1,950	645
	2.0	6.30	2,670	885
~ 36 %	1.0	3.42	1,815	600
	2.0	4.34	2,445	810
	2.5	5.12	3,090	1,035
~ 47 %	2.0	3.80	2,475	825
	2.5	4.60	3,105	1,035
	3.5	6.30	4,320	1,440

Implementation activities, inputs and costs

Establishment activities
1. Contour lines are marked out using pegs to show the location for the base of each terrace wall (after harvest in September).
2. A trench is dug out along the marked line to serve as the foundation for the terrace wall.
3. The topsoil between the pegged lines is removed and put aside.
4. Alternative ways of constructing the wall/riser and bed: (a) Subsoil is placed in the trench and compacted to form the base of the terrace wall. Subsoil excavated from the upper portion of the terrace is then placed behind the wall. The wall is progressively built up (by compacting earth) with the excavated soil placed behind until a level terrace has been formed. (b) Terraces may be built without constructing an initial wall: soil excavated from the upper part of the (eventual) terrace bed is simply moved downslope to level the bed, while soil from the terrace below is thrown upwards to help build up the wall/ riser. This is done progressively.
5. The wall is raised slightly higher to form a lip to retain rainwater on the terrace bed (optional).
6. The set-aside topsoil is then spread over the terrace surface.
Duration of establishment: 3–4 months

Establishment inputs and costs per ha

Inputs	Costs (US$)	% met by land user
Labour		
- Construction: 600 m person days	1,200	97%
- Survey	60	0%
Equipment		
- Shovel, two-wheel carts	30	100%
Materials		
- Earth (2,000–2,500 m³)	0	
TOTAL	**1,290**	**93%**

Terrace construction (steps 2–6) usually begins just after harvest (in October) and continues over the winter months, being completed before the start of the next cropping season (January).Terraces were constructed entirely by hand, using shovels and 2-wheel carts to move soil from the back of the terrace to the front.

Maintenance/recurrent activities
1. Repairing any collapses in the terrace wall – often caused by heavy storms.
2. Re-levelling of the terraces where necessary.
This work is usually done by hand, using shovels and two-wheel carts.

Maintenance/recurrent inputs and costs per ha per year

Inputs	Costs (US$)	% met by land user
Labour (12 person days)	25	97%
Equipment		
- Tools (shovel, two-wheel carts)	10	100%
Materials		
- Earth (1–2 m³)	0	
TOTAL	**35**	**98%**

Remarks: Calculations above are based on the following situation: slopes of about 25–35%, bed width of 3.5–6 m, and a 1–2 m high riser, involving moving about 2,000–2,500 cubic metres of soil. Note: these calculations are based on several years experience in Zhuanglang: that is why they differ in some respects from the standardised table above.

Assessment

Acceptance/adoption
- The technology was implemented on a large scale through government initiated mass campaigns.
- The technology has generally not spontaneously spread beyond the areas developed through government intervention: the area that is suitable for terracing has been covered.
- Uncertainty over future land use rights limits the willingness of households to meet the costs of terrace construction.

Benefits/costs according to land user

Benefits compared with costs	short-term:	long-term:
establishment	negative	very positive
maintenance/recurrent	positive	very positive

Impacts of the technology

Production and socio-economic benefits
- + + + crop yield increase (wheat: from 750–900 kg/ha before terracing to 3,000–3,750 kg/ha within 3–4 years: includes agronomic improvements)
- + + + easier field operation
- + farm income increase

Production and socio-economic disadvantages
- – reduced production (first year only)

Socio-cultural benefits
- + + community institution strengthening
- + + improved knowledge SWC/erosion

Socio-cultural disadvantages
- none

Ecological benefits
- + + + soil loss reduction
- + + + increase in soil moisture

Ecological disadvantages
- none

Off-site benefits
- + + + reduced downstream siltation
- + + reduced downstream flooding
- + + reduced transported sediments

Off-site disadvantages
- – reduced river flows

Concluding statements

Strengths and ➔ how to sustain/improve

Reduced erosion, reduced loss of rainwater through runoff (increased in water use efficiency) and reduced fertility loss due to reduced slope angle and length ➔ Maintain the quality of terrace construction.

Increased soil moisture ➔ Construct/maintain a terrace lip to retain rainwater on the terrace.

Increased crop production (before 1983 hunger and starvation in the area) ➔ Combine with improved crop husbandry.

Easier field operations: the level terrace is easier to cultivate than the original hill slope.

Benefits pay back the investments after only three to four years; approx. calculated on the basis of US$ 450 extra income per annum per hectare (for wheat) vs US$ 1,200 labour investment per hectare.

Improvements of farmers' living standard and decline in poverty stricken population.

Diversification of production: terracing makes cultivation of new cash crops possible: flax (for linseed oil), pears, apples, apricots, water melon; all these give high returns and thus make terrace construction profitable.

Weaknesses and ➔ how to overcome

Decrease in production in first year ➔ Apply manure and fertilizer.

Terrace riser can be destroyed by storms – and, sometimes, rodent holes ➔ Good and timely repair and maintenance: planting upper parts of the risers with grass, bushes or even trees help to stabilise the risers but can lead to competition with the crop for water.

High cost/input for construction and establishment ➔ Given the high erodibility of the soil and the steep slopes there is no real alternatives to labour-intensive terracing.

High loss of soil moisture due to evaporation from the soil surface. Wind erosion due to tillage ➔ Protect soil surface for example by conservation agriculture – comprising permanent cover, crop rotation, reduced tillage – could be supplementary agronomic and vegetative options.

Key reference(s): *Terraces In China.* Published By Ministry Of Water Resources Beijing, PRC. 1989 ■ *Conservancy engineering budgetary estimate ration.* Issued by Ministry of water resources of PRC, Published by Yellow-river water conservancy publishing company, Zhengzhou, PRC, 2003 ■ *A Great Cause for Centuries – 50 Years in Water and Soil Conservation in China.* Published by Department of Soil and Water Conservation, Ministry of Water Resources Beijing, PRC, 2000 ■ Additional references: Dongyinglin, Changpiguang, Wangzhihua 1990: Discussion on several questions on increasing production of the terrace with two banks; *Soil and Water Conservation Science and Technology in Shanxi.* No. 1, p 36–37 ■ Liumingquan, Zhangaiqin, Liyouhua 1992. Pattern engineering of reconstruction the slope cropland; *Soil and Water Conservation Science and Technology in Shanxi,* No. 3, p 18–21 ■ Liangqichun, Changfushuang, Liming 2001. A study on drawing up budgetary estimate quota of terraced field; *Bulletin of Soil and Water Conservation,* Vol. 21, No. 5, p 41–44 ■ Lixuelian, Qiaojiping 1998. Synthetic technology of fertilizing and improving production on the new terrace. Terraces in China. *Soil and Water Conservation Science and Technology in Shanxi,* No. 3, p 13–14

Contact person(s): Wang Yaoling, GEF/OP12 Project Office, Gansu Desert Control Research Institute, Lanzhou 730030, People's Republic of China; phone ++86 13919467141; Gansu@gefop12.cn, yaolingw@gsdcri.com ■ Wen Meili, and Liu Baoyuan, Department of Resources and Environmental Sciences, Beijing Normal University, Beijing 100875, People's Republic of China; wmlyxj@163.com, baoyuan@bnu.edu.cn

Terrace approach
China – 庄浪梯田

Highly organised campaign to assist land users in creating terraces: support and planning from national down to local level

Before 1964, the slopes on China's Loess Plateau were cultivated up and down by machinery. Consequently soil and water were lost at high rates, and fertility and yields declined. Accessibility to cultivated land became more and more difficult due to dissection by gullies. The first terraces were established by self-mobilisation of the local land users. However there was no standard design. Furthermore, as the individual plots were very small and scattered all over the village land, terracing needed better coordination. Between 1964 and 1978, the local government at the county level took the initiative of organising farmers and planning terrace implementation according to specific technical design on a larger scale. At that time the land was still communally managed by production brigades. Through mass mobilisation campaigns people from several villages were organised to collectively terrace the land – village by village – covering around 2,000 hectares each year. Labour was unpaid.

The Yellow River Conservancy Commission (YRCC) came into being in 1948 – and the Upper and Middle Yellow River Bureau in 1977. This gave greater impetus to the implementation of SWC in the Loess Plateau. After 1978, land use rights were allocated to individuals (though official ownership was still vested in the state). SWC specialists and county level SWC bureaus started to work with groups of farmers who had land use rights within a given area. Survey and design were carried out. The farmers organised themselves, consolidated the parcels of land, and then after the conservation work was done they redistributed the terraced fields.

In the 1980s the government started to financially support land users involved in SWC projects. Subsidies ranged from (approx.) US$* 20/ha in projects at county level, to US$* 55/ha for national projects (eg through the Yellow River Commission), and up to US$* 935/ha when World Bank projects were involved – as in the recent past. Implements were provided by the farmers themselves. Then, in 1988 a nationwide project in SWC – which originally was proposed at county level – was approved by the national government. Furthermore, in 1991 a national law on SWC came into force. Protection of the Yellow River and associated dams became a priority at regional and national levels. In total, within Zhuanglang County, 60 SWC specialists/extensionists cover an area of 1,550 km², and most of the terraces were built with low levels of subsidies. Annual plans about implementation of new SWC measures were made during summer. Small areas were planned at village or township level, whereas bigger areas (> 7 hectares) were designed at county level. Implementation then took place during winter. Terracing was implemented first where access was easiest and closest to settlements, and only later, further away.

* exchange rate: 1 US$ = 8 Chinese Yuan (May 2006)

left: Mass mobilisation showing people from several villages helping each other. Initially, farmers were not paid but from the 1980s onwards farmers received cash and other support for their work. (Photo: from 'Terraces in China' Ministry of Agriculture)
right: Construction of terrace risers – following instructions given by a specialist. (Photo: from 'Terraces in China' Ministry of Agriculture)

Location: Zhuanlang County, Gansu Province, Loess Plateau Region, Northern China, People's Republic of China
Approach area: 1,555 km²
Land use: cropland
Climate: semi-arid
WOCAT database reference: QA CHN45
Related technology: Zhuanglang loess terraces, QT CHN45
Compiled by: Wang Yaolin, Gansu GEF/OP12 Project Office, Lanzhou, PR China; Wen Meili, Department of Resources and Environmental Sciences, Beijing Normal University, P R China; Bai Zhanguo, World Soil Information, Wageningen, Netherlands.
Date: May 2002, updated October 2005

Editors' comments: The terraces covering China's Loess Plateau are one of the most outstanding SWC achievements in the world. The evolution of this remarkable feat is worthy of note. It is an example of local initiative developing into an organised, structured campaign. The implementation process, through local government initially, and then taken up at national level, was supported by legislation and mass mobilisation.

Problem, objectives and constraints

Problem
- lack of organisation, capital and technical knowledge in farmer communities to counter the underlying problems of water loss, soil loss, fertility decline and downstream effects on the Yellow River (floods and sediment) at catchment level
- absence or poor maintenance of erosion control measures

Objectives
- water conservation (this is a semi-arid area)
- soil conservation: reduce soil loss on the sloping and erosion-prone land of loess plateau
- enhancing soil fertility, and consequently production
- improve people's living conditions

These primary objectives were to be achieved by building level bench terraces on a large scale through a structured and organised campaign. Finally at the national level, a fourth aim was added: the protection of the Yellow river (avoiding floods and reducing the sediment load).

Constraints addressed

Legal	Land users leased the land from the state and land users' rights were insecure in the long term. Investments in SWC were not encouraged.	National government persuaded land users to implement terraces by 'selling' the benefits (increased yield and easier workability of the land). After 1978, individual user rights motivated farmers to invest in SWC.
Technical	Poor knowledge of how to reduce water loss, soil loss and fertility loss. Technical solutions were needed at the catchment level, involving the whole population.	Enhanced guidance by SWC specialists.
Financial	Initially farmers were not paid and as they had no immediate benefit from, or security over, the use of the land. The investment in construction was a heavy burden on poor farmers.	After 1988, labour inputs by farmers started to be partly covered by subsidies provided by local and national government.

Participation and decision making

Target groups

Land users   Planners   Politicians/ decision makers

Approach costs met by:

Government	10%
Community/local	90%
	100%

Decisions on choice of the technology: Mainly made by SWC specialists with consultation of land users.
Decisions on method of implementing the technology: Decisions are made by politicians/SWC specialists; land users are consulted in the planning phase (experienced farmers may be involved initially).
Approach designed by: County level and national specialists.

Community involvement

Phase	Involvement	Activities
Initiation	self-mobilisation/interactive	Land users started implementing terraces but SWC specialists at the country level assisted in designing standards for terrace construction and township governments and production brigades organised whole villages and watersheds
Planning	passive	Being consulted in the planning phase. Experienced peasants may be involved in introducing the local situation.
Implementation	interactive	Major organisation done through the SWC bureau specialists with the village organisation including land users. Land users were actively involved in implementation.
Monitoring/evaluation	none	Reporting. No participation of land users
Research	none	On-station research. No participation of land users

Differences in participation of men and women: For manual labour, men can do more work and they have greater technical knowledge and skills related to terrace construction than women.

Left chain:
Ministry of Water Resources (MWR) → Yellow River Conservancy Commision (YRCC) → The Upper and Middle Yellow River Bureau → Provincial SWC Bureau → Municipal SWC Bureau → County Government / County SWC Bureau → Township Government → Villages → Production brigades → Land Users

Right chain:
Provincial Government → Provincial SWC Bureau → Municipal Government → Municipal SWC Station → County Government / County SWC Bureau → Township Government → Villages → Production brigades → Land Users

Extension and promotion

Training: Until 1978 the 'pyramid system' was used: the county level trained the township level, which trained the village level, which in turn trained the production brigades/farmers, who then trained other production brigades and farmers. Training was on-the-job, focussing on design and construction of terraces on sloping land (provided by the county level specialists and by land users from villages where implementation was already carried out; at a later stage national trainers were involved as well). With respect to courses, demonstration areas, and farm visits – these were effective for all target groups.

Extension: The pyramid system is also used for extension. At each government level (at the county, district and provincial levels) there is a SWC division which is in charge of SWC activities including extension (demonstration, farm visits, etc). Effectiveness with respect to land users has been good. With rural economic development, more and more land users plan to invest in the SWC activities, including terrace making. The extension system is quite adequate to ensure continuation of activities.

Research: Mostly on-station research; carried out at the provincial and national levels, mostly by technical staff. Land users have not been involved. Topics covered include economics/marketing, ecology, technology. Terrace building is based on scientific design, according to local conditions.

Importance of land use rights: The ownership of the land and its resources belongs to state and communities: land users can only lease the land for a period of time. Due to uncertainty over future user rights and possible reallocation of the land every few years (5, 10 or 20) by the village in response to changes in population and household needs, additional investments into land/SWC measures may be hindered. 1978 a first major change took place by allocating some individual land use rights.

Incentives

Labour: In the 1960s and 1970s farmers were not paid for their labour inputs. From the 1980s onwards the government started to reward the community for establishment of terraces with cash: projects paid on the basis of area treated, and at different rates.

Inputs: Shovels and carts were provided by land users.

Credit: Credit was available at interest rates (0.5–1% per year) lower than the market rates.

Support of local institutions: Financial support to local institutions was made available through SWC Bureaus.

Long-term impact of incentives: As more and more payment is currently being made to land users on the basis of the area treated, land users rely more and more on being paid for investments into SWC. The willingness to invest in SWC measures without receiving financial support has decreased. Thus the use of incentives in the current approach is considered to have a negative long-term impact.

Monitoring and evaluation

Monitored aspects	Methods and indicators
Bio-physical	regular measurements of runoff loss, sediment load, soil moisture
Technical	regular measurements of structure of terraced areas, slope of risers, levelness of terrace surface
Socio-cultural	ad hoc observations of land users' perceptions of terraces
Economic/production	regular measurements of yield, income of land users
Area treated	regular measurements of terraced area
No. of land users involved	ad hoc measurements of the numbers of farmers directly involved in terracing and farmers benefited directly
Management of approach	ad hoc observations of number of small watersheds terraced

Impacts of the approach

Changes as result of monitoring and evaluation: The approach changed fundamentally from self-mobilisation to organised mass movements guided by the government.

Improved soil and water management: Soil and water management have improved a lot: easier workability, intensified land use, in-situ water retention, top soil and fertilizer/manure are not washed away, etc.

Adoption of the approach by other projects/land users: As the Zhuanglang area was one of the pioneering areas for the Loess Plateau other regions were able to profit from the approach. But likewise, experiences gained in other counties helped improve the approach, and a basically similar approach has been applied over the whole Loess Plateau – though the level of subsidies for construction is much higher under World Bank projects.

Sustainability: Given the recent escalation in payments made to land users for implementation under certain projects it seems that the costs will be too high to sustain. Currently the Ministry of Finance is demanding that in-depth cost-benefit analyses are carried out involving environmental, social as well as economic assessments.

Concluding statements

Strengths and ➜ how to sustain/improve*	Weaknesses and ➜ how to overcome
Efficient organisation, planning to cover a large area, which is very susceptible to land degradation.	High costs: farmers depend on external support from the government, they are not willing to invest their labour without payments (as it used to be in communist times) ➜ New approach: give farmers loans for construction as now they use machines to do the work. In addition, search for cheaper SWC technologies and for improving the benefits.
Heavy investment made by the land users and local as well as national government to reduce land degradation.	
Many people involved and trained at different levels (pyramid system; see training/extension); commitment by all stakeholders.	
The collective activities/organisation strengthens the community and enhances social stability and coherence within villages; collective activities are expanded to other sectors, such as road construction, supply of agrochemical inputs, etc.	The steeper slopes which are also further away from the village, are now often not cultivated and maintained as they are too far and marginal in production ➜ Solutions need to be found for these areas, eg afforestation.
Farmers are getting direct benefits: marked increase in productivity, improved workability of the land, etc.	

* no recommendations provided on how to sustain/improve the strengths in this case study

Key Reference(s): Water and Soil Conservation Department of Yellow River Water Resources Committee of Ministry of Water Resources and Electric Power 1987: Corpus of economic benefits of water and soil measures, p77–102, 510–514 ■ Suide Water and Soil Conservation examination station of Yellow River Water Resources Committee, 1981. Corpus of Test Research of Water and Soil Conservation, p130–185 (the second volume) ■ Jiangdingsheng, ACTA CONSERVATIONIS SOLI ET AQUAE SINICA, 1987. Discussion on section design of the terrace on the Loess Plateau; Vol. 1, No. 2, p28–35

Contact person(s): Wang Yaolin, GEF/OP12 Project Office, Gansu Desert Control Research Institute, Lanzhou 730030, People's Republic of China; phone ++86 13919467141; Gansu@gefop12.cn, yaolingw@gsdcri.com ■ Bai Zhanguo, World Soil Information, Wageningen, The Netherlands ■ Liu Baoyuan, Department of Resource and Environmental Science, Beijing Normal University, Beijing 100875, PR China; phone ++086-10-62206955/9959; baoyuan@bnu.edu.cn ■ He Yu, Zhuanglang SWC Bureau, 744600, phone ++86 933 6621681; gszlheyu@163.com

Rainfed paddy rice terraces

Philippines – *Palayan*

left: Paddy fields on bench terraces are very effective in impounding water for rice cultivation, and in preventing soil erosion. Ifugao, Philippines. (Jose Rondal)
right: Close-up showing rice crop on the narrow benches. (William Critchley)

Terraces supporting rainfed paddy rice on steep mountain slopes: these have been in existence for more than a thousand years.

Terraced paddy rice on steep mountain slopes is the main method of rice cultivation in Cordillera Administrative Region (CAR) of the Philippines. This is a traditional technology: most of the terraces are at least a thousand years old. The terraces were constructed manually on steep hill slopes (30–60%) with small portions located in narrow valley bottoms. Farmers generally own one hectare or less of terraced land, and cultivation is intensive. The terraces ('paddies') curve along the contour, and are narrow, ranging from one to five meters in width, depending on the slope. The height of the riser is between one and two meters. Water supply for the rice crop depends on rainfall, and only one rice crop is grown per year.

The terraces impound rainwater – average rainfall is around 2,000 mm – and thus prevent soil erosion. Soil fertility is largely maintained because the impounded water and a zero rate of erosion preserve organic matter levels. Some nutrient loss occurs however with each harvest. The terraces are multi-functional: in addition to their agricultural use, they assist in environmental protection through flood mitigation, and they contribute to biodiversity. Furthermore they have become a tourist attraction.

Land preparation is mainly manual. Farmers puddle the soil with their bare feet. Excess water is drained to the terrace below by a small opening in the lip on top of the riser. Maintenance consists basically of repairing breached bunds/risers. Every planting season, a few centimetres of soil is added. To strengthen the bunds, some farmers plant grasses, which may be cut and carried for animal fodder: napier grass *(Pennisetum purpureum)* is an example. It is important not to disturb the soil of the bund, as this may encourage breaching.

The area where the technology is practiced is mostly between 2,000 and 2,500 m. Because of the cool climate caused by the high elevation, crop maturity takes longer than in the lowlands. In some cases, vegetables such as cabbages and sweet potatoes are grown after the rice is harvested. The farmers, indigenous to the area, have a distinct culture that is different to lowland rice farmers. Rituals connected with farming are widely practiced. There is an added economic benefit from tourism, as people from all over the Philippines – and beyond – travel there for the spectacular views and mild climate.

Location: Cordillera Region (Ifugao, Apayao, Kalinga, Mountain Province, Benguet), Philippines
Technology area: 15,000 km²
SWC measure: structural
Land use: cropland
Climate: humid
WOCAT database reference: QT PHI12
Related approach: not documented (traditional)
Compiled by: Jose Rondal, Bureau of Soils and Water Management, Quezon City, Philippines
Date: September 2003, updated May 2004

Editors' comments: Paddy rice terraces – irrigated or rainfed – have been used in many parts of Asia for thousands of years (see 'Traditional irrigated rice terraces' from Nepal with many similarities). The upland rural landscape is characterised by these traditional terraces, which not only provide the livelihoods for millions of people, but the beauty of the sculpted hillsides also attracts tourists.

Classification

Land use problems
The terraces allow crop cultivation in an area characterised by steep slopes and high rainfall. However, farming in this marginal areas is labour intensive, mechanisation is not an option on the narrow paddies, and even animal traction is rarely possible due to the steepness of the terrain and the high terrace risers. Non-terraced hill slopes are prone to very high runoff and soil erosion, production is zero.

Land use	Climate	Degradation			SWC measures	
annual crops: rice	humid	water erosion: loss of topsoil	chemical: fertility decline and reduced organic matter content		structural: level bench terrace	vegetative: grass on bunds/ risers (supp.)

Technical function/impact

main: - control of dispersed runoff (retain/trap)
            - increase/maintain water stored in soil

secondary: - reduction of slope angle
                 - reduction of slope length
                 - indirect maintenance of fertility

Environment

Natural environment

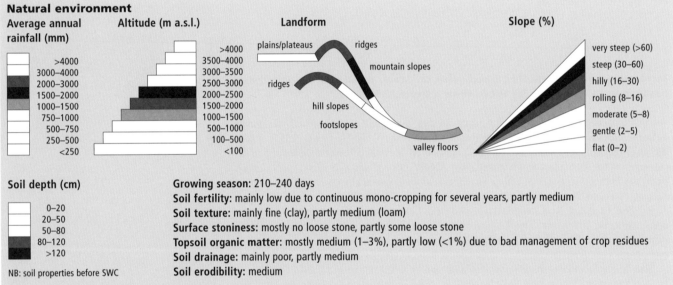

Average annual rainfall (mm)
>4000
3000–4000
2000–3000
1500–2000
1000–1500
750–1000
500–750
250–500
<250

Altitude (m a.s.l.)
>4000
3500–4000
3000–3500
2500–3000
2000–2500
1500–2000
1000–1500
500–1000
100–500
<100

Landform
plains/plateaus
ridges
mountain slopes
ridges
hill slopes
footslopes
valley floors

Slope (%)
very steep (>60)
steep (30–60)
hilly (16–30)
rolling (8–16)
moderate (5–8)
gentle (2–5)
flat (0–2)

Soil depth (cm)
0–20
20–50
50–80
80–120
>120

NB: soil properties before SWC

Growing season: 210–240 days
Soil fertility: mainly low due to continuous mono-cropping for several years, partly medium
Soil texture: mainly fine (clay), partly medium (loam)
Surface stoniness: mostly no loose stone, partly some loose stone
Topsoil organic matter: mostly medium (1–3%), partly low (<1%) due to bad management of crop residues
Soil drainage: mainly poor, partly medium
Soil erodibility: medium

Human environment

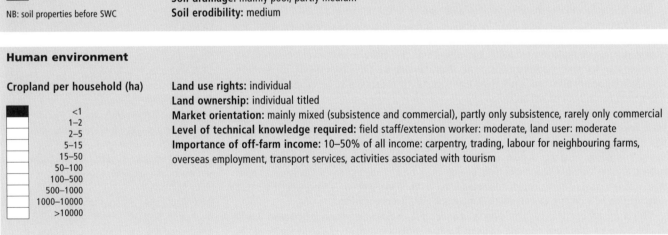

Cropland per household (ha)
<1
1–2
2–5
5–15
15–50
50–100
100–500
500–1000
1000–10000
>10000

Land use rights: individual
Land ownership: individual titled
Market orientation: mainly mixed (subsistence and commercial), partly only subsistence, rarely only commercial
Level of technical knowledge required: field staff/extension worker: moderate, land user: moderate
Importance of off-farm income: 10–50% of all income: carpentry, trading, labour for neighbouring farms, overseas employment, transport services, activities associated with tourism

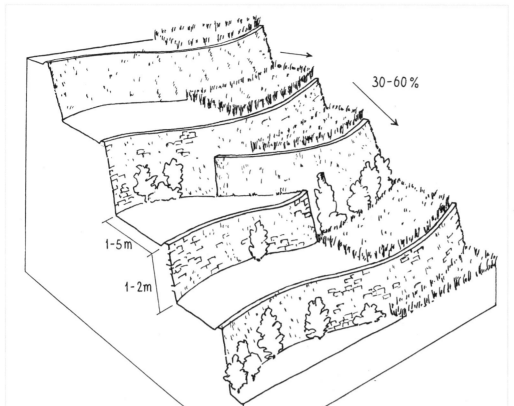

30-60 %

1-5 m

1-2 m

Implementation activities, inputs and costs

Establishment activities
1. Determination of contour lines by eye.
2. Levelling by moving soil from the upslope to the downslope part of the terrace.
3. Construction of bunds (lip at the terrace edge) of about 50-100 cm width and 30 to 40 cm height. Stones may be used if available on-site.

Only hand tools are used (hoe, spade, iron bars).
Duration of establishment: 1 year

Establishment inputs and costs per ha

Inputs	Costs (US$)	% met by land user
Labour (800 person days)	2,500	100%
Equipment		
- Hand tools	200	100%
TOTAL	**2,700**	**100%**

Maintenance/recurrent activities
1. Weeding by cutting grasses on the bund/riser using hand tools. Hoeing to remove weeds is not done as this will disturb the soil.
2. Repairing breached portion of the bunds. Adding a few centimetres of soil on top of the bund/riser for bigger storage volume.
3. Land preparation by puddling. In most cases, the use of animal traction is not possible because of the steepness of the slope and height of the risers.

Maintenance/recurrent inputs and costs per ha per year

Inputs	Costs (US$)	% met by land user
Labour (10 person days)	30	100%
Equipment		
- Hand tools	10	100%
TOTAL	**40**	**100%**

Remarks: The costs of establishment are estimates – as new terrace construction no longer takes place. The land has already been terraced for centuries. The 800 person days are for land levelling and bund construction, which comprises the main activity. The calculation was based on a land slope of 30–60%. The maintenance figure assumes regular light maintenance – and does not include major repairs to bunds.

Assessment

Acceptance/adoption

The technology is widely accepted. As the terraces were constructed hundreds of years ago and construction of new terraces is no longer done the question of 'adoption' is not relevant.

Benefits/costs according to land user		Benefits compared with costs	short-term:	long-term:
		establishment	not applicable	not applicable
		maintenance/recurrent	positive	very positive

Impacts of the technology

Production and socio-economic benefits
+ + + crop yield increase (compared with zero in the non-terraced scenario)
+ + + farm income increase
+ + fodder production/quality increase

Socio-cultural benefits
+ + community institution strengthening
+ + national institution strengthening
+ + improved knowledge SWC/erosion

Ecological benefits
+ + + increase in soil moisture
+ + + efficiency of excess water drainage
+ + + soil loss reduction
+ + biodiversity enhancement

Off-site benefits
+ + + reduced downstream siltation
+ + reduced downstream flooding

Production and socio-economic disadvantages
– – labour constraints conflicting with other income generating opportunities
– – inputs needed for fertility improvement

Socio-cultural disadvantages
none

Ecological disadvantages
none

Off-site disadvantages
none

Concluding statements

Strengths and ➜ how to sustain/improve

Low maintenance cost ➜ Regular maintenance.

Farmers are well versed (very familiar) with the rice production system – it is part of their culture ➜ Continuous 'Information Education Campaign' (IEC).

Terracing allows paddy rice production on very steep slopes, which are prone to very high erosion and water loss in such a monsoon area. It transforms steep unproductive slopes into productive land ➜ Incentives to encourage continuation of the use and maintenance of the terraces.

Weaknesses and ➜ how to overcome

Lack of moisture for about six months ➜ Moisture conservation (mulching): construction of water harvesting structures for supplementary irrigation.

Continuous mono-cropping ➜ Crop diversification. Other crops (such as sweet potato, cabbage, chilli) could be grown after rice towards the end of the rainy season through minimum or zero tillage.

Severe soil fertility decline in some locations – and therefore declining yields ➜ Fertility enhancement using organic and inorganic sources (manure, crop residues, compost, fertilizers etc).

Key reference(s): Breemen van N, Oldeman LR, Plantinga WJ and Wielemaker WG (1970) The Ifugao Rice Terraces. In: *Miscellaneous papers* (7) 1970, eds. N van Breemen et al Landbouwhogeschool, Wageningen, The Netherlands.
Contact person(s): Jose Rondal, Bureau of Soils and Water Management, Elliptical Road, Diliman, 1100 Quezon City, Philippines; joserondal@yahoo.com

Traditional irrigated rice terraces

Nepal – *Tari khet*

Level bench terraces with risers protected by fodder grasses, used for irrigated production of rice, potatoes and wheat.

The level bench terrace is a traditional technology that makes irrigated crop production possible on steep, erosion prone slopes. The majority of such terraces in Nepal were constructed by hand many generations ago, but some new land – mostly already under rainfed cultivation on forward sloping terraces – is still being converted into irrigated terraces. The initial costs for the construction of the terraces are extremely high – and annual maintenance costs are considerable also. The climate is humid subtropical, slopes are steep (30%–60%) and soils generally have a sandy loam texture. Terraces are cropped by small-scale farmers who have less than half a hectare of land each. Two to three annual crops are grown per year starting with paddy rice during the monsoon, followed by potatoes and/or wheat.

While terrace beds are usually 2–6 m in width, to save labour they are made as wide as they can be without increasing the danger of slips/land slides. Surveying was traditionally done by eye, but now a water-tube level may be used. Risers are 0.8–1.5 m high with a small lip (20–25 cm). The slope of the riser varies from 80 to 160%, depending on the initial gradient of the hill. Stones are incorporated in the risers if available, and grass species such as bermuda grass (*Cynodon dactylon*) and napier (*Pennisetum purpureum*) may be planted for stabilisation and as cattle fodder. The risers are compacted (with hoes) to improve ponding conditions for the paddy rice. Twice per year the risers are scraped with a special tool: (1) at the time of land preparation for paddy rice the lower part of riser is sliced, but the upper part is left protected with grasses against the monsoon rains; (2) at the time of wheat planting the whole riser (including the lip) is scraped and spread as green manure on the terrace.

Terraces are flooded with water for paddy rice cultivation: a smaller amount of water is diverted into the fields for other crops. Excess water is drained to the lower terrace by openings in the lip, which are filled with rice straw in order to filter out sediments. The depth of water for rice – when flooded completely – is normally between 10 and 15 cm. Fertility is maintained by addition of farmyard manure, spreading the scraped soil from the riser, and also through sediment carried in the irrigation water. Nowadays, mineral fertilizers are also applied.

Location: Sankhu Bhulbu, Manmata Subwatershed, Kathmandu Valley, Nepal
Technology area: 1 km²
SWC measure: structural, vegetative and agronomic
Land use: cropland
Climate: humid
WOCAT database reference: QT NEP10
Related approach: not documented (traditional technology)
Compiled by: Ramanand Bhattarai, District Soil Conservation Office, Lalitpur, Nepal
Date: November 2003, updated August 2004

Editors' comments: Irrigated bench terraces are a very common traditional technology, widespread in Nepal on footslopes and the middle hills of the Himalayas. There are close similarities with the paddy rice terraces of South East Asia: the Philippines (presented in this book), Indonesia and China. This is a case study from the Kathmandu valley.

Classification

Land use problems
- steep slopes, not suitable for agriculture in their original state (better for forestry, agroforestry, horticulture, and fruit trees)
- small and scattered plots of land
- land users find chemical fertilizers and water expensive
- there is water scarcity from September to May and too much rain in the monsoon period (June to August) with the danger of erosion and collapse of the terraces

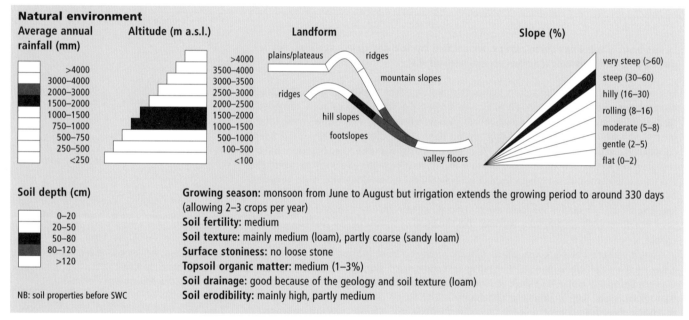

Land use

annual crops:
rice, potatoes,
wheat

Climate

humid

Degradation

water erosion:
gully, loss of
topsoil and
mass movement

SWC measures

structural:
level bench
terraces

vegetative:
fodder grass at
risers

agronomic:
green/farmyard
manure, inorganic fertilizers

Technical function/impact
main:
- control of dispersed and concentrated runoff
- reduction of slope angle and length
- increase/maintain water stored in soil
- increase in soil fertility

secondary:
- water harvesting
- water spreading
- improvement of ground cover

Environment

Natural environment

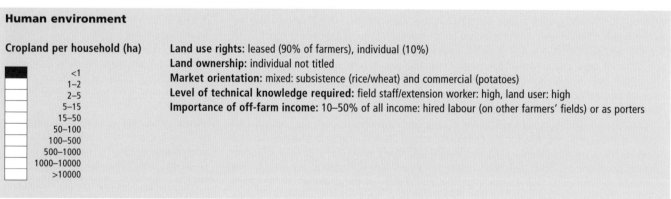

Average annual rainfall (mm)

>4000
3000–4000
2000–3000
1500–2000
1000–1500
750–1000
500–750
250–500
<250

Altitude (m a.s.l.)

>4000
3500–4000
3000–3500
2500–3000
2000–2500
1500–2000
1000–1500
500–1000
100–500
<100

Landform

plains/plateaus
ridges
mountain slopes
ridges
hill slopes
footslopes
valley floors

Slope (%)

very steep (>60)
steep (30–60)
hilly (16–30)
rolling (8–16)
moderate (5–8)
gentle (2–5)
flat (0–2)

Soil depth (cm)

0–20
20–50
50–80
80–120
>120

NB: soil properties before SWC

Growing season: monsoon from June to August but irrigation extends the growing period to around 330 days (allowing 2–3 crops per year)
Soil fertility: medium
Soil texture: mainly medium (loam), partly coarse (sandy loam)
Surface stoniness: no loose stone
Topsoil organic matter: medium (1–3%)
Soil drainage: good because of the geology and soil texture (loam)
Soil erodibility: mainly high, partly medium

Human environment

Cropland per household (ha)

<1
1–2
2–5
5–15
15–50
50–100
100–500
500–1000
1000–10000
>10000

Land use rights: leased (90% of farmers), individual (10%)
Land ownership: individual not titled
Market orientation: mixed: subsistence (rice/wheat) and commercial (potatoes)
Level of technical knowledge required: field staff/extension worker: high, land user: high
Importance of off-farm income: 10–50% of all income: hired labour (on other farmers' fields) or as porters

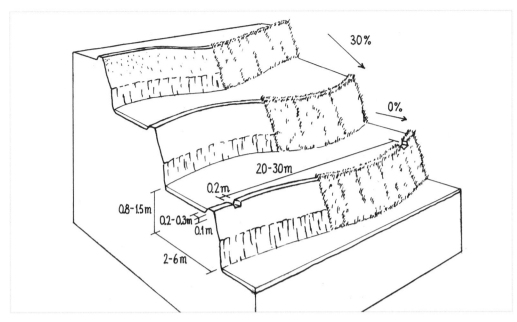

Technical drawing
Layout of irrigated terraces. Openings in the lips drain excess water. Grass cover stabilises lips and risers (right). After harvesting of rice, the grass is scraped off the lower part of the risers (left) and spread on the terrace beds.

Implementation activities, inputs and costs

Establishment activities

1. Construction of bund (riser) with soil from upper and lower sides (soil transported in jute bags).
2. Levelling terrace bed (soil moved from upper to lower part of terrace).
3. Making lips on edges of terraces.
4. Compacting risers.
5. Constructing irrigation canal.
6. Making openings in lips for excess water drainage.
7. Test-irrigating terrace for accurate levelling.
8. Planting grasses including bermuda grass *(Cynodon dactylon)*.
9. After 2–3 years: some narrow terraces may be merged to form a single, wider terrace.

All activities are done by hand: 1–6 before, 7–8 during the monsoon.
Duration of establishment phase: not specified

Establishment inputs and costs per ha

Inputs	Costs (US$)	% met by land user
Refer to remarks below		

Maintenance/recurrent activities

1. Harvesting of potato/wheat (January-March).
2. Transportation of cattle manure with *doko* (basket, carried on the back) to the field and leaving it in heaps (March).
3. Spreading the cattle manure (normally April).
4. Land preparation (ploughing/breaking compacted soil) for rice (April).
5. Flooding the paddy fields (June/July). Repeated 3–4 times during cultivation.
6. Slicing/scraping grass and soil on lower part of risers and spreading on terrace (when flooded, June/July).
7. Planting of rice. Application of mineral fertilizer (June/July).
8. Harvesting of rice (September/October).
9. Manuring (cattle manure), after harvest of rice (October).
10. Slicing/scraping grass and soil from whole of risers and spreading on terrace (October/November).
11. Repair of small collapses/slumps in risers (Oct./Nov.).
12. Land preparation (November).
13. Planting of potatoes, wheat. (November).
14. Application of mineral fertilizer (November/December).
15. Irrigation (Nov. repeated several times during cultivation).

All activities done by hand, except land preparation sometime done with small tractors or power tiller.

Maintenance/recurrent inputs and costs per ha per year

Inputs	Costs (US$)	% met by land user
Labour (125 person days)	350	100%
Equipment		
- Tools: hoe, spade, baskets *(doko)*	5	100%
Agricultural		
- Fertilizers (650 kg)	185	100%
- Compost/manure (30 t incl. transport)	300	100%
TOTAL	**840**	**100%**

Remarks: Current establishment costs are very difficult to determine since the majority of the traditional terraces were established a long time ago. Costs depend closely on the present status of the land (forward sloping terraces or uncultivated) and the need for irrigation canals. Farmers state that construction now could cost up to US$ 10,000 per ha if carried out by hand at full labour cost. Maintenance quoted above (approx. US$ 840 per ha) includes all associated annual crop production costs. In this case study 100% of the construction costs were borne by land users.

Assessment

Acceptance/adoption
- All the land users in the case study area who applied the technology did so without incentives, but in a nearby area 50% of costs have been met by the Bagmati Integrated Watershed Management Programme, when converting existing rainfed forward sloping terraces into level terraces (which can be irrigated).
- Maintenance has been continuously good over many generations.
- Main motivation: irrigation guarantees high returns from small areas.

Benefits/costs according to land user

Benefits compared with costs	short-term:	long-term:
establishment	very negative	positive
maintenance/recurrent	positive	very positive

Impacts of the technology*

Production and socio-economic benefits
+ + + crop yield increase
+ + + farm income increase
+ + + increase in livestock fodder
+ +   fodder production/quality increase

Socio-cultural benefits
+ + + improved knowledge SWC/erosion
+ +   community institution strengthening

Ecological benefits
+ + + increase in soil moisture
+ + + efficiency of excess water drainage
+ + + increase in soil fertility
+ + + soil loss reduction
+ +   biodiversity enhancement
+ +   soil cover improvement

Off-site benefits
+ + + reduced downstream flooding
+ + + reduced downstream siltation
+ + + increased groundwater recharge
+ + + increased soil moisture and nutrients downstream
+ +   reduced river pollution

Production and socio-economic disadvantages
– – – increased labour constraints (high labour inputs needed)
– –   increased economic inequity (not everyone has access to land for irrigation)
– –   increased input constraints
– –   loss of land due to terrace risers

Socio-cultural disadvantages
–   socio-cultural conflicts may arise when the agreed and scheduled water extraction amounts are exceeded
–   as part of a complex farming system the technology is vulnerable to changes in norms and traditions, (influence of the nearby city with possibilities of jobs)

Ecological disadvantages
–   crabs in irrigation water make holes in the terrace risers, which in turn can cause pipe erosion and collapse of risers

Off-site disadvantages
– –   reduced river flows (during dry season: river water is used upstream for terrace irrigation)
–   poor maintenance of terraces in the upper parts may cause landslides

* In this case: impacts of traditional paddy rice terraces in comparison to forward sloping rainfed terraces

Concluding statements

Strengths and ➜ how to sustain/improve	Weaknesses and ➜ how to overcome
Income and production increase ➜ Proper management of the terraces (including all maintenance activities).	Decreased grass production (grazing area reduced) ➜ Promote the planting of high value grass species on risers (such as bermuda grass).
Easier to cultivate flat terraces/less labour required (after establishment of the terraces).	In the opinion of the farmers terraces are still too narrow (for efficient use of tractors); they would like to have them even wider ➜ Investigate possibilities of constructing wider paddy rice terraces on steep slopes, which – according to present experience – is not possible.
Work sharing: the traditional terraces are part of a long tradition of work sharing within the community – no external labour is required ➜ Prevent loss of well established traditions and norms.	High labour costs for establishment.
Technology is easy to understand/apply.	
The irrigation element of this particular technology fosters social bonds within the community ➜ Prevent loss of well established norms and traditions.	
Increased opportunities for irrigation facilities: farmers without level terraces are not allowed (by the irrigation committee at village level) or do not make claims for irrigation water.	

Key reference(s): There is considerable literature on the construction and maintenance of irrigated terraces in general, but no references that specifically describe the traditional paddy rice terraces in Nepal
Contact person(s): Ramanand Bhattarai, District Soil Conservation Office, Lalitpur, Nepal; phone: +977 1 5520289; rnbhattarai@hotmail.com

left: Fence-line contrast between treatment paddocks with different utilisation rates: medium utilisation on the left and high utilisation paddock on the right. (CSIRO)
right: The impact of poor grazing land management: woodlands with a dense cover of '3P grasses' (top), degraded area with annual grasses, forbs and bare soil after heavy grazing (bottom). (CSIRO)

Ecograze

Australia

An ecologically sound and practical grazing management system, based on rotation and wet season resting.

Open eucalypt woodlands cover approximately 15 million hectares in the semi-arid plains of north-east Australia, and support about a million head of cattle. Keeping these grazing lands productive and healthy demands good management, and getting the right balance between stock numbers and the forage resource is a considerable challenge.

Land in good condition has a healthy coverage of so-called '3P grasses': native perennial, productive and palatable grasses, important to cattle and to the health of the landscape. Less palatable plants include annual grasses, native and exotic forbs and shrubs. The heterogeneity of the pasture resource results in uneven utilisation, and thus overgrazing in parts.

In order to prevent pastures in good condition from degrading, or to restore/improve deteriorated pastures, utilisation needs to be adjusted according to climate and the state of the '3P grasses'. In practice, the only means of manipulating pasture composition over large areas are grazing, resting from grazing, and burning.

The flexible Ecograze system includes wet season resting, and is based on the establishment of three paddocks with two herds within a rotational system. The key is that all paddocks get some wet season rest two years out of three. Wet season rests are divided into two phases: (1) the early wet season rest starts after the first rains in November/December and continues for 6–8 weeks, it is particularly good for perennial grass recovery; (2) the late wet season rest lasts until March/April and aids both seed set and vegetative recovery.

Average paddocks of around 3,000 ha in size are sub-divided into three relatively equal sizes, though some flexibility is required to balance variation in the productive capacity of different land types within the paddock. The paddocks are fenced and extra water points through polythene piping and additional water troughs, and where required, pumps are established. The return on investment can be realised within a few years.

The main management challenges are: (1) the timing and length of the early wet season rest, which depends on how effectively the early rains promote vegetative growth of perennial grasses, and (2) the movement of animals during the wet season. The number of stock movements are fixed – but the timing is flexible and should be responsive to the situation: the challenge is to learn to assess the pasture condition, read the situation, and schedule the timing and length of the rest period accordingly. The main criterion is the recovery state of perennial grasses.

Location: Lakeview/Allan Hills, Cardigan, Hillgrove/Eumara Springs, North-east Queensland, Australia
Technology area: 10 km²
SWC measure: management, vegetative
Land use: grazing land
Climate: semi-arid
WOCAT database reference: QT AUS01
Related approach: Development and promotion of Ecograze, QA AUS01
Compiled by: Andrew Ash, CSIRO, Queensland, Australia
Date: June 2001, updated December 2004

Editors' comments: Though degradation of rangelands is a global problem, there are few documented cases of successful management practices. Ecograze provides a flexible system that has been developed through collaborative research. Its principles of rotation and resting are relevant to most of northern Australia's tropical rangelands – and to other countries also.

Classification

Land use problems
Over the last 20 years there has been a decline in the condition of grazing lands in north-east Australia. The evidence is a decline of palatable, perennial, productive grasses ('3P grasses'), reduced ground cover and an increase in sediment and nutrient movement into streams. As a consequence of economic pressures and over-optimistic expectations of good rains, stocking rates have often been too high.

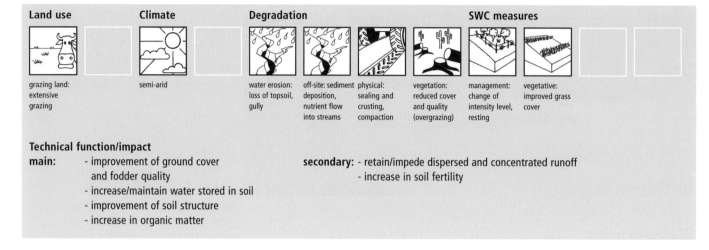

Land use	Climate	Degradation				SWC measures	
grazing land: extensive grazing	semi-arid	water erosion: loss of topsoil, gully	off-site: sediment deposition, nutrient flow into streams	physical: sealing and crusting, compaction	vegetation: reduced cover and quality (overgrazing)	management: change of intensity level, resting	vegetative: improved grass cover

Technical function/impact
main:
- improvement of ground cover and fodder quality
- increase/maintain water stored in soil
- improvement of soil structure
- increase in organic matter

secondary:
- retain/impede dispersed and concentrated runoff
- increase in soil fertility

Environment

Natural environment

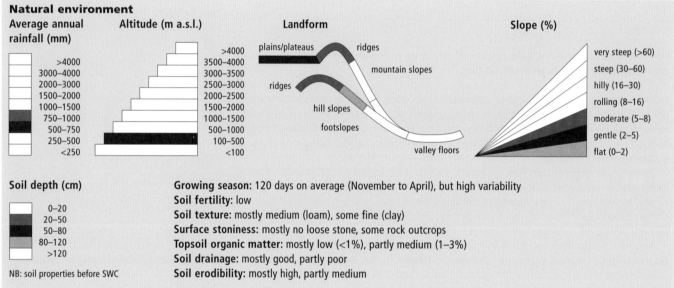

Average annual rainfall (mm)
- >4000
- 3000–4000
- 2000–3000
- 1500–2000
- 1000–1500
- 750–1000
- 500–750
- 250–500
- <250

Altitude (m a.s.l.)
- >4000
- 3500–4000
- 3000–3500
- 2500–3000
- 2000–2500
- 1500–2000
- 1000–1500
- 500–1000
- 100–500
- <100

Landform
plains/plateaus, ridges, mountain slopes, ridges, hill slopes, footslopes, valley floors

Slope (%)
- very steep (>60)
- steep (30–60)
- hilly (16–30)
- rolling (8–16)
- moderate (5–8)
- gentle (2–5)
- flat (0–2)

Soil depth (cm)
- 0–20
- 20–50
- 50–80
- 80–120
- >120

NB: soil properties before SWC

Growing season: 120 days on average (November to April), but high variability
Soil fertility: low
Soil texture: mostly medium (loam), some fine (clay)
Surface stoniness: mostly no loose stone, some rock outcrops
Topsoil organic matter: mostly low (<1%), partly medium (1–3%)
Soil drainage: mostly good, partly poor
Soil erodibility: mostly high, partly medium

Human environment

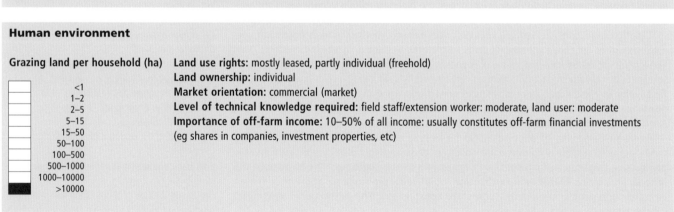

Grazing land per household (ha)
- <1
- 1–2
- 2–5
- 5–15
- 15–50
- 50–100
- 100–500
- 500–1000
- 1000–10000
- >10000

Land use rights: mostly leased, partly individual (freehold)
Land ownership: individual
Market orientation: commercial (market)
Level of technical knowledge required: field staff/extension worker: moderate, land user: moderate
Importance of off-farm income: 10–50% of all income: usually constitutes off-farm financial investments (eg shares in companies, investment properties, etc)

	Paddock A	Paddock B	Paddock C
Year 1 Early Wet	Rest	Graze	Graze
Late Wet	Graze	Rest	Graze
Dry	Graze	Graze	Rest
Year 2 Early Wet	Graze	Graze	Rest
Late Wet	Rest	Graze	Graze
Dry	Graze	Rest	Graze
Year 3 Early Wet	Graze	Rest	Graze
Late Wet	Graze	Graze	Rest
Dry	Rest	Graze	Graze

Layout of Ecograze system

The drawing refers to the 'two herd/three paddock Ecograze system'.
Paddock A is rested in the early wet season, while Paddocks B and C are grazed. Paddock B is then rested for the late wet season while Paddocks A and C are grazed. Paddock C is then rested for the dry season and the next early wet season while Paddocks A and B are grazed. Paddock A is then rested for the late wet season and the rotational cycle continues in this fashion for the three years of the full rotation.
Early wet season spelling should commence after the first significant rains in November/December and should continue for 6–8 weeks, depending on how effectively the early rains promote vegetative growth of perennial grasses.
Late wet season rest typically last until March/April, depending on length of growing season.

Implementation activities, inputs and costs

Establishment activities

1. Paddocks first need to be surveyed to understand the various plant communities and soils.
2. Based on the survey and location of water points, and the most practical location for fences, a paddock design is developed: paddocks are subdivided into relatively equal sizes.
3. Fencing the paddocks (2 person days per km); Material: barbed wire or plain wire for electric fences, steel fence posts, wooden or steel end assemblies to strain the fence, energisers (for electric fences).
4. Provision of extra water points through polythene piping and additional water troughs – and where required, pumps.

Duration of the establishment: 1 to 4 years

Establishment inputs and costs per ha

Inputs	Costs (US$)	% met by land user
Labour	4	100%
Equipment		
- Tools (various)	0	
Materials		
- for fencing: metal wire, wooden poles, etc	4	80%
- for extra water provision: PE pipes	2	80%
TOTAL	**10**	**90%**

Maintenance/recurrent activities

1. Mustering (gathering) and shifting (moving) livestock.
2. Monitoring pastures and soils.
3. Repair fences

Maintenance/recurrent inputs and costs per ha per year

Inputs	Costs (US$)	% met by land user
Labour	1	100%
Materials		
- wire, poles, etc (for repair)		
TOTAL	**1**	**100%**

Remarks: Current average paddock size is 3,000 ha – commonly 6 km x 5 km. To sub-divide the paddock into three requires two internal fences, each of 5.0 km. Costs of fencing and associated gates are about US$1,200 per km. Labour for fencing is also approximately US$1,200 per km (note: because of the large paddock size, on a per hectare basis this is equivalent to US$ 4.0 per hectare).

Assessment

Acceptance/adoption
There are indications that around 700 (of a total of 15,000) farmers across northern Australia have already adopted some aspects of Ecograze. Surveys indicate spontaneous adoption beyond the region as well. In time a large number of farmers are expected to adopt the technology. Three of the five farm families involved in the on-farm research/development of Ecograze have taken up some aspects of the research.

Benefits/costs according to land user

Benefits compared with costs	short-term:	long-term:
establishment	negative	positive
maintenance/recurrent	slightly negative	very positive

Impacts of the technology

Production and socio-economic benefits	Production and socio-economic disadvantages
+ + + fodder production/quality increase	− increased economic inequity
+ + + farm income increase	− increased labour constraints
Socio-cultural benefits	**Socio-cultural disadvantages**
+ + improved knowledge SWC/erosion	none
Ecological benefits	**Ecological disadvantages**
+ + + soil cover improvement	none
+ + + increase in soil moisture	
+ + soil loss reduction	
+ + biodiversity enhancement	
+ increase in soil fertility	
Off-site benefits	**Off-site disadvantages**
+ + + reduced downstream siltation	none
+ + + reduced transported sediments	
+ reduced downstream flooding	

Concluding statements

Strengths and → how to sustain/improve	Weaknesses and → how to overcome
Increased perennial grass cover, improved pasture productivity, increased animal carrying capacity and associated increased profit → Wide and long-term adoption of Ecograze system.	Adoption of technology needs long-term approach to accommodate for slow rate of change by ranchers → Continue to demonstrate the advantages of the technology.
Improved soil cover reduces erosion and sediment flow into streams and dams → Manage pasture condition through Ecograze to maintain '3P grasses'.	Implementing rotational grazing incurs (moderate) investment costs in the form of fencing and new water points → Investigate government subsidies and educate about long-term economic benefits.
Greater stability of forage supply leading to less problems and less stress in farm management → Wide and long-term adoption of Ecograze system.	
Soil carbon reserves maintained/improved → Wide and long-term adoption of Ecograze system.	
Plant biodiversity protected → Wide and long-term adoption of Ecograze system.	

Key reference(s): Ash A, Corfield J and Taoufik T (undated) *The ECOGRAZE Project: developing guidelines to better manage grazing country.* CSIRO, Meat and Livestock Commission and Queensland Government ■ Tothill JC and Gillies C (1992) *The pasture lands of northern Australia: their condition, productivity and sustainability* Occasional Publication No. 5, Tropical Grassland Society of Australia, Brisbane ■ Tothill J and Partridge I (1998) *Monitoring grazing lands in northern Australia* – edited by Occasional Publication No. 9, Tropical Grassland Society of Australia, Brisbane
Contact person(s): Dr Andrew Ash, CSIRO Sustainable Ecosystems, 306 Carmody Rd, St Lucia, Qld, 4067, Australia; andrew.ash@csiro.au; www.csiro.au

Development and promotion of Ecograze

Australia

Research-based development and promotion of Ecograze principles and practices through on-farm testing and demonstration.

In 1992, Meat and Livestock Australia (MLA), a producer-owned company that provides services to the entire Australian red meat industry, initiated the Ecograze project. Ecograze was intended to provide innovative management options for the pastures in the eucalyptus woodlands of north-east Queensland. It was an eight-year collaborative research project undertaken by staff of the CSIRO (Commonwealth Scientific and Industrial Research Organisation) Sustainable Ecosystems and Queensland Department of Primary Industries with input from Queensland Department of Natural Resources and Mines. It formally concluded in 2001. However, many of the analyses and extension activities have been ongoing since then.

Ecograze was conducted on five commercial grazing properties that spanned different conditions and consequently allowed extrapolation of results to a much wider area across northern Australia. Practical grazing management strategies have been developed. The Ecograze team assessed the economic implications of managing land in various states by linking a pasture production model, to a model of farm economics.

Research teams are currently testing the grazing management technology in commercial situations to understand the real costs and implications of implementing the research-derived Ecograze recommendations. The on-farm tests are supported by a number of new initiatives. These include a MLA funded project to specifically implement the Ecograze principles on farms as a means of reducing sediment and nutrients pollution of waterbodies. The National Action Plan for Salinity and Water Quality, through incentives, supports land management practices to reduce erosion, increase ground cover and minimise runoff. Funding is also provided by the Natural Heritage Trust to fence and sub-divide paddocks.

All of these initiatives are supported by State Government agencies, who have extension staff based in the regions to assist farmers with implementing new practices. In the case of Ecograze, there are extension officers in the NE Queensland region who are actively promoting its management principles and are assisting producers in planning new strategies. Many of the Ecograze principles are also included in a new Grazing Land Management (GLM) Education package, developed by MLA and research and development agencies. The GLM package, which is delivered via a three-day workshop, is being extended to producers across northern Australia.

Location: Northern Australia
Approach area: 1 000,000 km²
Land use: grazing land (extensive)
Climate: semi-arid
WOCAT database reference: QA AUS01
Related technology: Ecograze, QT AUS01
Compiled by: Andrew Ash, CSIRO, Queensland, Australia
Date: June 2002, updated December 2004

Editors' comments: This approach highlights the importance of active collaboration between researchers, farmers, the beef industry and the government – in this case to develop a system to improve the condition of grazing lands. Through the central involvement of research, management options have been identified to suit different land users' needs, climates, grazing pressures and pasture conditions.

Problem, objectives and constraints

Problem
- poor rangeland management leading to loss of productive palatable perennial grasses ('3 P' grasses) resulting in reduced ground cover, soil erosion, profit loss and in some cases irreversible land degradation
- lack of understanding of underlying problems regarding mismatch of animal numbers to forage supply (pressure on grazing land) in a highly variable climate
- no clear technical recommendations regarding resting and rotation of rangeland

Objectives
Development and promotion of Ecograze principles leading to adoption and thereby enhancing pasture productivity, soil condition and improved livelihoods for pastoralists.

Constraints addressed

	Specification	Treatment
Financial	Investment costs for fencing and water points can be burden on individual land holders.	There are various possible subsidies available (see 'Inputs', under 'Incentives').
Social	Many pastoralists are conservative and change their systems only slowly.	There are ongoing education programmes and demonstrations on target properties.

Participation and decision making

Target groups

Land users   Govt. agencies/ extensionists   Planners   Politicians/ decision makers

Approach costs met by:

National government	40%
Community/local	60%
	100%

Decisions on choice of the technology: Mainly made by land users in consultation with technology experts and government agencies; recognition that Ecograze principles can benefit land users and the environment due to research results of field trials.
Decisions on method of implementing the technology: Mainly made by land users.
Approach designed by: National and state specialists together with land users.

Community involvement

Phase	Involvement	Activities
Initiation	passive	field days, workshops
Planning	self-mobilisation	consultation with specialists
Implementation	self-mobilisation	fencing and water points
Monitoring/evaluation	self-mobilisation	field observations of pasture composition; economic assessments
Research	interactive	on-farm field trials and demonstration areas

Differences in participation between men and women: Traditionally, men undertake on-farm planning, implementation of activities and provide labour. Women play an important role in planning and management of finances, and tend to take a more strategic view on NRM issues than the men.

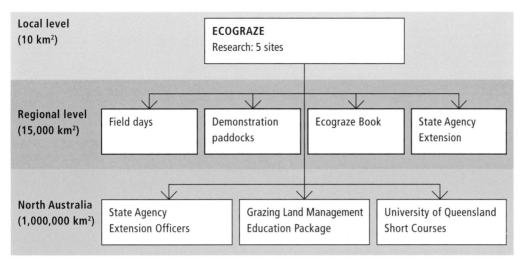

Local level (10 km²)	ECOGRAZE Research: 5 sites			
Regional level (15,000 km²)	Field days	Demonstration paddocks	Ecograze Book	State Agency Extension
North Australia (1,000,000 km²)	State Agency Extension Officers	Grazing Land Management Education Package	University of Queensland Short Courses	

Programme organization
Components and activities at different levels of the Ecograze programme.

Extension and promotion

Training: The Ecograze principles and findings have been incorporated into a training course entitled 'Grazing Land Management (GLM) Education Package'. To date (2005) over 100 farmers have participated in the course and it is anticipated that in the next three years this number will reach over 1,000 producers.

Extension: In on-going research trials in cooperation with land-users, government officers build up their knowledge and capacity to support farmers . Field days form part of the extension and education process. Government assistance with extension and training through free advice provided by extension officers is helpful. Subsidies to attend training courses like GLM Education also assist with the uptake and adoption of Ecograze. There is also a significant interaction between neighbouring properties in sharing of ideas and successes and failures. Commonly, these neighbouring properties are linked through catchment or 'Landcare' groups.

Research: The impact of the ongoing research on understanding and implementing the technology through the Ecograze project is significant, and continues to be so. Research into various technical aspects of grazing management has been recently supplemented by economic analyses of costs and benefits.

Importance of land use rights: In general, implementation of Ecograze principles is undertaken by an individual on private leasehold land. Ecograze is well suited to this individualised system.

Incentives

Labour: Labour inputs for implementation are voluntary.

Inputs: During the research phase of Ecograze, incentives were not available. However, since then, newly established Government initiatives such as the Natural Heritage Trust and the National Action Plan for Salinity and Water Quality, which commenced in 2003, have increased the number of incentives (eg support for on-ground works such as fencing, relocation of water points etc) available to implement management practices such as those recommended in Ecograze.

Credit: Credit was not, and will not be, provided as part of ongoing extension of the technology.

Support to local institutions: Local Landcare groups often request assistance, and this is provided either from the research agencies or from extension officers or through grant applications to the Natural Heritage Trust.

Long-term impact of incentives: This technology is focussed on changing attitudes to management rather than requiring on-going financial inputs or support. As a result, financial support is more through incentives to help with changing management practices rather than any provision of ongoing support in the form of stewardship payments.

Monitoring and evaluation

Monitored aspects	Methods and indicators
Bio-physical	regular measurements of pasture composition, forage supply and soil surface condition
Socio-cultural	ad hoc evaluation of farmers' observations and constraints
Economic/production	regular monitoring of real costs is carried out to be used in analyses
Area treated	ad hoc measurement of area being subject to new management practices
No. of land users involved	ad hoc surveys of landholders to assess uptake rates

Changes as result of monitoring and evaluation: Further research and testing, on-going monitoring and evaluation is underway after the initial project. It is too early to state what changes are likely other than obviously needing to adapt to individual land-users resources and available finances.

Improved soil and water management: Ecograze leads to retention of 3P grasses ('perennial, productive and palatable' grasses), and therefore better pasture coverage, soil retention and greater water use efficiency.

Adoption of the approach by other projects: Ecograze principles have been included in the new Grazing Land Management Education package – which is being used across northern Australia by Meat and Livestock Australia and other agencies also. It has also now been incorporated into university courses on grazing management.

Sustainability: Progress is continuing with further field trials and participation from land users. Those land users who have begun with the Ecograze system can continue without external support.

Concluding statements

Strengths and ➜ how to sustain/improve	Weaknesses and ➜ how to overcome
The approach is focussed on changing attitudes to management in the long term ➜ Continue with training and education programmes.	One-off training programs such as the Grazing Land Management Education package (a 3-day course) may not be enough to sustain initial commitment to testing new management options ➜ Create support network and supply follow-up training and/or support.
Adoption of the technology should result in financial reward ➜ Continue ongoing economic analysis as an indication of technology success.	
The system has been very well documented and adapted to the land users conditions through the involvement of research, the land users, primary industry, and extension ➜ Continued support for applied/on-farm research to adapt the system to the needs of the land users and the environment. Support for long-term monitoring.	
State government extension agencies have also readily accepted Ecograze and are actively promoting its principles with landholders.	

Key reference(s): Ash A, Corfield J and Taoufik T (undated) *The ECOGRAZE Project: developing guidelines to better manage grazing country.* CSIRO, Meat and Livestock Commission and Queensland Government
Contact person(s): Dr Andrew Ash, CSIRO Sustainable Ecosystems, 306 Carmody Rd, St Lucia, Qld, 4067, Australia; andrew.ash@csiro.au; www.csiro.au

left: Rehabilitation of degraded rangeland in its initial stages: stone lines are established after the area has been cleared of invasive tree species: the branches are used for 'brush packing' and fencing. (Anuschka Barac)
right: Oversowing with grass seeds, manuring with cattle dung and application of lime speeds up regeneration of the grass cover. (Anuschka Barac)

Restoration of degraded rangeland
South Africa

Eradication of invasive species and revegetation of degraded rangelands by different treatments, including oversowing with grass seed mixture, supplementing with lime, cattle dung, and 'brush packing' (laid out branches).

A research investigation was undertaken in an area of degraded communal rangeland, which had been invaded by an alien tree species *(Acacia mearnsii* – black wattle). Competition from the water-demanding *A. mearnsii,* combined with overgrazing, had resulted in an almost total absence of palatable grasses. All that was left were a few patches of star grass (or bermuda grass: *Cynodon dactylon).* Prior to the research, discussions were held between personnel of the 'Working for Water' programme of the South African government and community members.

The purpose of the trials was to determine how best to eradicate the invasive trees and revegetate the rangeland. The restoration area was not fenced off and was thus open to grazing. The trials comprised five treatments, with three replicates each, on plots of 10 m by 20 m. In all treatments the *A. mearnsii* was eradicated manually, and chemical biocide applied to the stumps to prevent regrowth. Lime and grass seed (of palatable species) were applied to the loosened surface and covered with soil. The five treatments were:
(A) oversowing with grass seed mixture, supplementing of dolomitic lime, cattle dung, and 'brush packing' (see below for explanation of term);
(B) oversowing with grass seed mixture and supplementing with cattle dung;
(C) oversowing with grass seed mixture and supplementing with dolomitic lime;
(D) oversowing with grass seed mixture and brush packing;
(E) oversowing with grass seed mixture only.

In addition stone lines were laid out along the contour, between plots. The 'brush packing', referred to in treatments A and D comprised branches laid out in strips across the slope to retard runoff, trap soil, improve the micro-climate for establishing grass seedlings and protect the young plants from browsing by animals. The results showed treatment A to be the most effective in restoring the productive and protective function of the rangeland. From the trials, the estimated costs of applying the best technology would be US$ 230 per hectare. The key constraints for successful adoption however are not just technical, but include: (1) the need to protect the area from grazing and trampling by animals during the establishment period; (2) stopping removal of brushwood for firewood; and (3) the need for community agreement on initial protection and subsequent sustainable utilisation of the restored range.

Location: Elandsfontein, Johannesburg, Gauteng Province, South Africa
Technology area: 9 km²
SWC measure: vegetative, structural and agronomic
Land use: grazing land
Climate: subhumid
WOCAT database reference: QT RSA42
Related approach: not documented
Compiled by: Anuschka Barac, Potchefstroom, South Africa
Date: July 2001, updated May 2004

Editors' comments: Attempts to restore degraded rangeland have long been on the agenda in Africa. There are three basic variations: (1) excluding livestock (2) treatment with vegetative and other interventions or (3) a combination. The experimental treatments here were of type (2). Long-term success, however, depends on management of livestock to sustain improved cover.

Classification

Land use problems
Lack of grazing for livestock as the rangeland has become unproductive due to the invasion of an alien woody species (*Acacia mearnsii*), and unrestricted open access grazing due to a lack of community control.

Land use	Climate	Degradation				SWC measures		
extensive grazing: open access to cattle and goats.	subhumid	vegetation: reduced cover, quality and quantity decline	chemical: soil fertility decline	physical: compaction of soil surface, crusting	water erosion: loss of topsoil	vegetative: oversowing grass seed mixture	agronomic: manuring, lime, 'brush packing' (trash lines)	structural: stone lines

Technical function/impact
main:
- improvement of ground cover
- control of raindrop splash
- retards dispersed runoff
- increase in organic matter
- increase in soil fertility

secondary:
- improved soil structure
- increased infiltration
- sediment harvesting
- reduced slope length (due to stone lines)

Environment

Natural environment

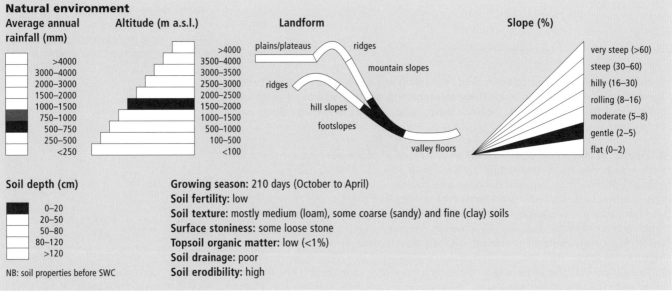

Average annual rainfall (mm): >4000, 3000–4000, 2000–3000, 1500–2000, 1000–1500, 750–1000, 500–750, 250–500, <250

Altitude (m a.s.l.): >4000, 3500–4000, 3000–3500, 2500–3000, 2000–2500, 1500–2000, 1000–1500, 500–1000, 100–500, <100

Landform: plains/plateaus, ridges, mountain slopes, ridges, hill slopes, footslopes, valley floors

Slope (%): very steep (>60), steep (30–60), hilly (16–30), rolling (8–16), moderate (5–8), gentle (2–5), flat (0–2)

Soil depth (cm): 0–20, 20–50, 50–80, 80–120, >120

NB: soil properties before SWC

Growing season: 210 days (October to April)
Soil fertility: low
Soil texture: mostly medium (loam), some coarse (sandy) and fine (clay) soils
Surface stoniness: some loose stone
Topsoil organic matter: low (<1%)
Soil drainage: poor
Soil erodibility: high

Human environment

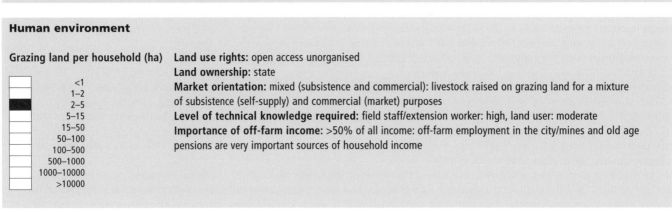

Grazing land per household (ha): <1, 1–2, 2–5, 5–15, 15–50, 50–100, 100–500, 500–1000, 1000–10000, >10000

Land use rights: open access unorganised
Land ownership: state
Market orientation: mixed (subsistence and commercial): livestock raised on grazing land for a mixture of subsistence (self-supply) and commercial (market) purposes
Level of technical knowledge required: field staff/extension worker: high, land user: moderate
Importance of off-farm income: >50% of all income: off-farm employment in the city/mines and old age pensions are very important sources of household income

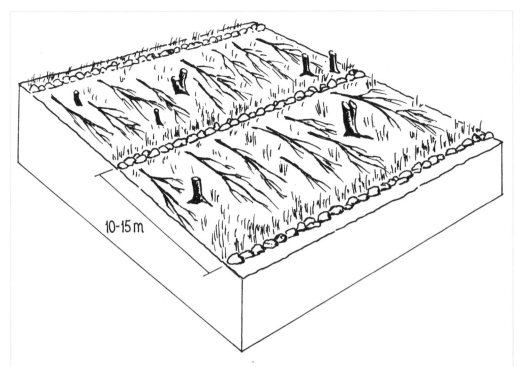

Technical drawing
Trees of invasive acacia species cut and branches spread as 'brush packing' for protection of degraded rangeland: note also stone lines and regenerating grass.

10-15 m

Implementation activities, inputs and costs

Establishment activities
Note: all activities described here as for treatment A: not all relevant to each treatment (see details in description)
1. Manual eradication of trees with chain saw and axe.
2. Application of chemical biocide to the stumps to prevent any regrowth.
3. Ripping of soil surface to a depth of 5 cm using a three tined hand implement.
4. Application of dolomitic lime and raking it into soil.
5. Application of organic material (cattle dung).
6. Oversowing with grass seed mixture.
7. Brush packing along contour and construction of rock contours across the slope.

All the branches and stones were collected from the restoration area.
Total duration of restoration: 3 years, from removal of trees until revegetation trials were laid out and technology was established

Establishment inputs and costs per ha

Inputs	Costs (US$)	% met by land user
Labour (10 person days)	35	0%
Equipment		
- Machines (chain saw)	65	0%
- Tools (rake, shovels, axe 3-tined hand hoe)	5	0%
Agricultural		
- Seeds (16 kg/ha)	70	0%
- Fertilizers (4 t/ha)	25	0%
- Biocides (1.5–2 kg/ha)	30	0%
- Compost/manure (whatever available)	0	
TOTAL	**230**	**0%**

Maintenance/recurrent activities
Following initial establishment maintenance was limited to two follow up applications of herbicide (after 3 and 5 months). Maintenance of contour lines was not carried out after restoration. The total maintenance period was for one year.

Maintenance/recurrent inputs and costs per ha per year

Inputs	Costs (US$)	% met by land user
Labour (2 person days)	7	0%
Equipment		
- Tools	5	0%
Agricultural		
- Biocides (1.5–2 kg/ha)	20	0%
TOTAL	**32**	**0%**

Remarks: These costs were calculated by upscaling to one hectare from the test plots – and treatment A is the one detailed here (oversowing with grass seed mixture, supplementing of dolomitic lime, cattle dung, and 'brush packing') which is the most successful and most expensive. Note that the whole period including establishment and maintenance was four years.

Assessment

Acceptance/adoption

The research investigation formed part of a Government scheme for poverty alleviation of rural poor communities ('Working for Water' under the Department of Water Affairs and Forestry: this programme focuses on removal of invasive alien species which threaten water supplies), but has been purely a research activity. The need for community agreement on the initial protection and subsequent sustainable utilisation of the restored range is a key constraints for acceptance of the technology.

Benefits/costs according to land user

Benefits compared with costs*	short-term:	long-term**:
establishment	negative	positive
maintenance/recurrent	slightly negative	positive

* costs not met by community

** long term refers to the period of the experiment

Impacts of the technology

Production and socio-economic benefits	Production and socio-economic disadvantages
+ + + fodder production/quality increase	– – – brushwood needed for firewood
+ + + farm income increase	– increased labour constraints
Socio-cultural benefits	**Socio-cultural disadvantages**
+ + + community institution strengthening (research was done in a communal area)	none
+ + + improved knowledge SWC/erosion	
+ + + job creation	
Ecological benefits	**Ecological disadvantages**
+ + + soil loss reduction	none
+ + + biodiversity enhancement	
+ + + reduction of wind velocity	
+ + + soil cover improvement	
+ + increase in soil moisture	
+ increase in soil fertility	
Off-site benefits	**Off-site disadvantages**
+ reduced downstream flooding	none
+ reduced downstream siltation	

Concluding statements

Strengths and ➜ how to sustain/improve	Weaknesses and ➜ how to overcome
Improvement of grazing resources ➜ Fencing rehabilitated areas to keep cattle out until the grasses are sufficiently established, should be part of the technology in future.	The question of controlling 'open access' grazing by the community is the key to long-term success of rehabilitation ➜ It is incumbent on the local municipal council to negotiate with communities regarding grazing control and community-based natural resource management more generally.
Improved soil moisture availability by removing an alien species with a high water demand ➜ Use of a biocide on the cut stems to prevent any regrowth of the alien species.	Removal of brushwood for firewood by community members and other aspects of long-term maintenance ➜ See above: perhaps also seeking funds to pay labourers and buy biocides.
Reduced erosion by controlling runoff ➜ Regular maintenance of the contour stone lines.	

Key reference(s): Harris JA, Birch P and Palmer J P (1996) *Land restoration and reclamation – Principles and Practices.* Addison Wesley Longman, England. 230 pp.
Contact person(s): Ms. Anuschka Barac, Principle Nature Conservation Scientist (Botanist), North West Province DACE – Mafikeng, South Africa; phone: ++27-18-389-5201, fax: ++27-18-389-5640; abarac@nwpg.gov.za

left: *Desho* grass *(Pennisetum pedicellatum)* and multipurpose trees established to increase productivity of grazing lands. (Daniel Danano)
right: Cut and carry of grass for stall-feeding from improved pasture. (Daniel Danano)

Improved grazing land management

Ethiopia – *Gitosh masheshal*

Rehabilitation of communal grazing lands, through planting of improved grass and fodder trees and land subdivision, to improve fodder and consequently livestock production.

This case study focuses on the highly populated, humid highland regions of Ethiopia that experience serious shortages of pasture. Due to rapid population growth, communal grazing areas are increasingly being converted into cropland. This has led to enormous pressure on the little remaining grazing land, through overstocking of dairy cows and oxen, and thus overgrazing, resulting in considerably decreased productivity.

Improved grazing land management is vital to increase food security and alleviate poverty, as well as to bring environmental rewards. To address these problems, the national SWC programme in Ethiopia initiated a grazing land management project over a decade ago. Implementation of the technology includes the initial delineating of the grazing land, and then fencing to exclude open access. This is followed by land preparation, application of compost (and, if necessary, inorganic fertilizers) to improve soil fertility, then planting of improved local and exotic fodder species, including multipurpose shrubs/trees such as *Leucaena sp.* and *Sesbania sp.* and the local *desho* grass *(Pennisetum sp.). Desho* has a high nutritive value and regular cuts are ensured. It is planted by splits, which have high survival rates and establish better than grasses which are seeded. Other grass seeds, as well as legumes, including alfalfa (lucerne: *Medicago sativa)* and clovers in some cases, are mixed with fodder tree seeds and then broadcast.

Maintenance activities such as weeding, manuring and replanting ensure proper establishment and persistence. Fodder is cut and carried to stall-fed livestock. Once a year, grass is cut for hay, which is stored to feed animals during the dry season. Experience shows that such grazing land is best managed when individually owned and used. In the study area, the community has distributed small plots (<0.5 ha) of communal grazing land to individual users to develop, manage and use.

The overall purpose of the intervention is to improve the productivity of grazing land and control land degradation through the introduction of productive techniques and improved fodder species, which consequently improve livestock production. Commercialisation of animals and marketing of their products increases the income of farmers. The government provides technical assistance, close follow-up, and some inputs for initial establishment. Land users are trained in compost/manure application, planting of seeds, splits and seedlings, and general maintenance.

Location: Chencha, Ethiopia
Technology area: 20 km²
SWC measure: agronomic, vegetative and management
Land use: grazing land (before), mixed: silvo-pastoralism (after)
Climate: humid
WOCAT database reference: QT ETH26
Related approach: Local level participatory planning approach (LLPPA), QA ETH25 (p 321)
Compiled by: Daniel Danano, Addis Abeba, Ethiopia
Date: July 2003, updated October 2004

Editors' comments: Rehabilitation of communal grazing lands is both a technical and social challenge. Here is a promising example from Ethiopia that is spreading quickly. The key is subdivision of land into individual plots where cut-and-carry of grass and stall-feeding of livestock is practiced. This is only a possible option, however, where rainfall is favourable.

Classification

Land use problems

Population growth has resulted in a substantial reduction in land holdings (<0.5 ha per family) and this in turn has led inevitably to encroachment onto communal grazing lands for cultivation. Livestock numbers on the other hand have remained unchanged, and this has led to overstocking of the few areas left. Livestock production, which accounts for 40% of the average household income, is thus reduced and farmers' income declines correspondingly.

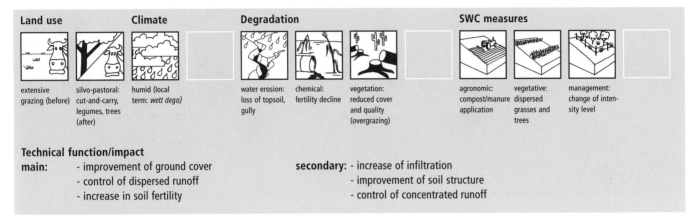

Land use	Climate	Degradation	SWC measures
extensive grazing (before)	silvo-pastoral: cut-and-carry, legumes, trees (after)	humid (local term: *wett dega*)	water erosion: loss of topsoil, gully / chemical: fertility decline / vegetation: reduced cover and quality (overgrazing)	agronomic: compost/manure application / vegetative: dispersed grasses and trees / management: change of intensity level

Technical function/impact

main:
- improvement of ground cover
- control of dispersed runoff
- increase in soil fertility

secondary:
- increase of infiltration
- improvement of soil structure
- control of concentrated runoff

Environment

Natural environment

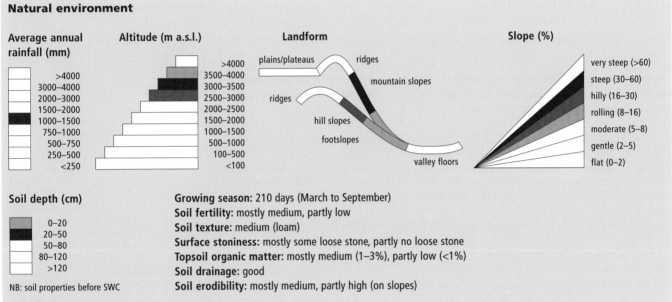

Average annual rainfall (mm)
- >4000
- 3000–4000
- 2000–3000
- 1500–2000
- 1000–1500
- 750–1000
- 500–750
- 250–500
- <250

Altitude (m a.s.l.)
- >4000
- 3500–4000
- 3000–3500
- 2500–3000
- 2000–2500
- 1500–2000
- 1000–1500
- 500–1000
- 100–500
- <100

Landform
- plains/plateaus
- ridges
- ridges
- mountain slopes
- hill slopes
- footslopes
- valley floors

Slope (%)
- very steep (>60)
- steep (30–60)
- hilly (16–30)
- rolling (8–16)
- moderate (5–8)
- gentle (2–5)
- flat (0–2)

Soil depth (cm)
- 0–20
- 20–50
- 50–80
- 80–120
- >120

NB: soil properties before SWC

Growing season: 210 days (March to September)
Soil fertility: mostly medium, partly low
Soil texture: medium (loam)
Surface stoniness: mostly some loose stone, partly no loose stone
Topsoil organic matter: mostly medium (1–3%), partly low (<1%)
Soil drainage: good
Soil erodibility: mostly medium, partly high (on slopes)

Human environment

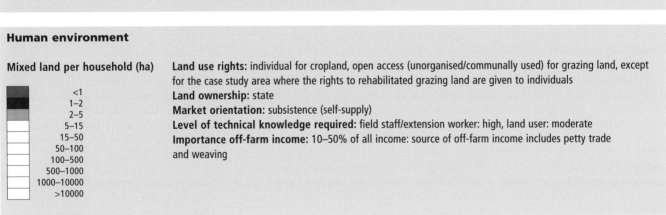

Mixed land per household (ha)
- <1
- 1–2
- 2–5
- 5–15
- 15–50
- 50–100
- 100–500
- 500–1000
- 1000–10000
- >10000

Land use rights: individual for cropland, open access (unorganised/communally used) for grazing land, except for the case study area where the rights to rehabilitated grazing land are given to individuals
Land ownership: state
Market orientation: subsistence (self-supply)
Level of technical knowledge required: field staff/extension worker: high, land user: moderate
Importance off-farm income: 10–50% of all income: source of off-farm income includes petty trade and weaving

Technical specifications for grazing land improvement:
Splits of *desho* grass *(Pennisetum pedecillatum)* are planted in lines, using a hand hoe, after good seed-bed preparation. Spacing between grass splits is 10 x 10 cm. The white line is a boundary between two households' plots (width of plot: 15–20 m). Trees are planted at irregular spacing (around 5 m apart), layout is not specified.
(Daniel Danano)

Implementation activities, inputs and costs

Establishment activities

1. Delineation of the area to be conserved and establishment of a fence (mostly of deadwood, available before the onset of rains).
2. Subdivision of communal land into individual plots of 0.3–0.5 ha.
3. Planting material preparation in nurseries: grass splits *(desho: Pennisetum pedecillatum)* and tree seedlings (multipurpose trees, eg *Leucaena sp.* and *Sesbania sp.*).
4. Good seedbed preparation with a hand hoe, sometimes with oxen plough depending on plot size (at the onset of the rains).
5. Compost/manure preparation. Material used includes animal manure, leaf litter, wood ash, soil and water.
6. Planting of grass splits and tree/shrub species in lines; sowing of grass seed by broadcasting (early in the rainy season).
7. Compost application (one month after planting).
8. Weeding.

Duration of establishment: 1 year

Establishment inputs and costs per ha

Inputs	Costs (US$)	% met by land user
Labour (450 person days)	320	100%
Equipment		
- Tools (hand hoe)	5	50%
- Animal traction (1 pair of oxen, 4 days)	17	100%
Materials		
- Fencing with dead wood	55	100%
Agricultural		
- Grass splits (240,000 tillers)	450	0%
- Tree seedlings (1,000)	5	0%
- Fertilizers if applied (100 kg)*	60	100%
- Compost/manure (4,500 kg)	140	100%
TOTAL	**1035**	**56%**

*Farmers usually cannot afford fertilizers

Maintenance/recurrent activities

1. Cut-and-carry, to stall-fed animals, begins when fodder is ready (after 2–3 months growth). A sickle is used for cutting. In good seasons two to four cuts are possible (in April, June, August and October).
2. A final cut for hay is taken early in the dry season (end of October) when the grass has matured well.
3. Weeding each year.
4. Compost/manure application, mixed with soil, during seedbed preparation (only where plants have died and need replacement and fertilisation).
5. Enrichment planting and gap filling after a year, repeated each year.

Maintenance/recurrent inputs and costs per ha per year

Inputs	Costs (US$)	% met by land user
Labour (50 person days)	35	100%
Equipment		
- Tools (hand hoe, sickle)	4	100%
Materials		
- Fencing with dead wood	5	100%
Agricultural		
- Seeds (25 kg of *desho*)	30	100%
- Tree seedlings (250)	2	100%
- Fertilizers (25 kg)	15	100%
- Compost/manure (1,000 kg)	35	100%
TOTAL	**126**	**100%**

Remarks: Seedlings are given by the government for initial establishment. For further extension of area and replanting, the land users set up their own nurseries. After 2–3 years maintenance costs decrease substantially as the grass cover closes up and maintenance activities such as replanting/enrichment planting and compost application are reduced or cease. The local daily wage is about US$ 0.70 a day, but varies depending on the intensity of the work. In this calculation the standard rate has been applied.

Assessment

Acceptance/adoption
The 50 households who accepted the technology in the initial phase, did so with incentives. They were provided with planting materials (seeds, seedlings, grass splits) and hand tools.
The rate of spontaneous adoption is very high. At present over 500 households have taken up the technology and the total area covered is about 20 km².

Benefits/costs according to land user

Benefits compared with costs	short-term:	long-term:
establishment	slightly positive*	very positive
maintenance/recurrent	positive	very positive

*Milk production compensates for some of the high investment costs (previously, production was low).

Impacts of the technology

Production and socio-economic benefits
- + + + increase in livestock production
- + + + increase in fodder production
- + + increase in fodder quality
- + + Increase in income (selling animals and their products)
- + wood production increase

Socio-cultural benefits
- + + + community institution strengthening
- + + + national institution strengthening (increased willingness of the national institution to assist and support organised farmers groups, ie community institutions)
- + + + improved knowledge SWC/erosion

Ecological benefits
- + + + soil cover improvement
- + + + increase in soil fertility
- + + + soil loss reduction
- + + increase in soil moisture
- + + biodiversity enhancement

Other benefits
- + + + improvement in household diets (milk), improve health
- + + increase in the availability of livestock products on the market lowers prices to the consumer

Off-site benefits
- + + + reduced transported sediments
- + + increase in stream flow in dry season
- + + reduced downstream siltation
- + + reduced downstream flooding

Production and socio-economic disadvantages
- – – – initial dependence on incentives such as free seeds, seedlings, tools
- – – decrease in size of grazing plots due to land fragmentation
- – – labour constraints

Socio-cultural disadvantages
- none

Ecological disadvantages
- none

Other disadvantages
- none

Off-site disadvantages
- – – grazing pressure has increased on remaining open access grazing land

Concluding statements

Strengths and → how to sustain/improve
Availability of fodder (grass, hay, shrubs) in sufficient quantities, and all year round → Increase the area under such development.

Reduction in soil loss and land degradation → Maintain adequate cover by planting more grass.

Introduction of high yielding species as well as increase in land productivity and livestock production → Introduce bigger variability of quality species and improve maintenance activities such as weeding and cultivation.

Improved diet: livestock by-products such as milk, butter and cheese are essential food items required by the households → Keep on increasing/improving quantity/quality of livestock feed.

Increased income through commercialisation and marketing of animals and their by-products. Meets financial needs for paying taxes, school fees, clothes etc.

Increased national income due to export of animals and their products.

Weaknesses and → how to overcome
At the initial stage of establishment it is very labour intensive → Use of improved land preparation methods such as oxen ploughing.

Substantial cash for inputs, particularly seedlings, is required → Produce seedlings of improved species and making compost in backyards.

Needs high fertilizer application → Focus more on organic fertilizers.

High pressure on remaining grazing areas → Keep animals in stall (stable) or park, at least part of the day and during the night, and introduce cut-and-carry more widely.

Key reference(s): Adane Dinku, *Chencha Wereda, Natural Resources Management Annual Report,* 2001 and 2002
Contact person(s): Daniel Danano, Ministry of Agriculture, PO Box 62758, Addis Ababa, Ethiopia; ethiocat@ethionet.et

Area closure for rehabilitation

Ethiopia – *Meret mekelel*

Enclosing and protecting an area of degraded land from human use and animal interference, to permit natural rehabilitation, enhanced by additional vegetative and structural conservation measures.

Area closure involves the protection and resting of severely degraded land to restore its productive capacity. There are two major types of area enclosures practised in Ethiopia: (1) the most common type involves closing of an area from livestock and people so that natural regeneration of the vegetation can take place; (2) the second option comprises closing off degraded land while simultaneously implementing additional measures such as planting of seedlings, mulching and establishing water harvesting structures to enhance and speed up the regeneration process. The focus of this case study is on this second type.

The selection of measures chosen for rehabilitation depends mainly on the land use type, and to a lesser extent on climate, topography and soil type. Degraded croplands with individual land use rights are normally treated with additional structural measures to retain soil moisture and trap sediment, and with agronomic measures to restore soil fertility. Open access grazing lands are closed for natural regeneration while partly treated with additional measures, and open access woodlands are simply closed. In the case study area 60% of the enclosed area is under treatment with additional conservation measures and 40% is under natural regeneration. First, the area to be closed is demarcated and protected with fencing, usually live fences, and a site guard may be assigned to further ensure protection. Structural measures such as micro-basins, trenches, and bunds that enhance water infiltration and soil moisture may be constructed to increase survival rate of vegetative material planted. Hillside terraces, spaced at a 1 m vertical interval with a width of 1 m are constructed on steep slopes (exceeding 20%). Nitrogen-fixing and multipurpose shrubs/trees (for fodder, fuel) such as *Acacia saligna, Sesbania sesban, Leucaena leucocephala* as well as local grass species such as napier *(Pennisetum purpureum)* and rhodes *(Chloris gayana)* are planted as additional measures for conservation.

The maintenance of area enclosures involves activities such as replanting, maintaining of fences, pruning of trees and weeding. After one year, cut-and-carry of grass for stall-feeding can be partly practiced – which is of economic benefit to the farmers. Rehabilitation normally takes about 7–10 years depending on the level of degradation and intensity of management. Land use is limited to selective cutting of trees, collection of dead wood and cut-and-carry of grass for livestock fodder. On individually owned enclosures land users start cutting trees after three years (for eucalyptus) and after 7–8 years (for other trees), while on communal land farmers are allowed to collect dead wood after 3–4 years, and the community decides about the use of trees.

left: Structural measures in the enclosed area, such as stone and earth bunds, speed up the rehabilitation process: they improve soil moisture and thus facilitate growth of natural vegetation or planted seedlings. (Daniel Danano)
right: Women planting local grass species on a severely degraded hillside in a recently closed area. (Daniel Danano)

Location: Bilate River Catchment (Rift Valley Lakes Basin), Alaba, South Ethiopia
Technology area: 20 km²
SWC measure: management, vegetative, agronomic and structural
Land use: cropland and grazing land (before), mixed: silvo-pastoral (after)
Climate: subhumid, partly semi-arid
WOCAT database reference: QT ETH25
Related approach: Local level participatory planning approach (LLPPA), QA ETH25
Compiled by: Daniel Danano, Addis Abeba, Ethiopia
Date: July 2003, updated June 2004

Editors' comments: Protecting degraded land against grazing is a common practice worldwide. In Ethiopia it is the second most important SWC practice after structural conservation measures. About 1.2 million hectares of degraded lands have been closed for rehabilitation in Ethiopia during the past three decades. As this case study shows, results are encouraging both in terms of effective protection and enhanced production.

Classification

Land use problems
Over 30% of the land in the study area is degraded, resulting in low crop yields and poor livestock production. Severe water erosion is the main cause of land degradation on all slopes, followed by fertility depletion due to intensive cultivation practices and overgrazing. Serious gully formation and a high sediment load in the Bilate River threaten Lake Abaya. Communal grazing lands, woodlands with open access, and cultivated lands on steep slopes without conservation measures are particularly affected. By tradition, land users in rural Ethiopia can own as many livestock as they wish, which encourages overstocking.

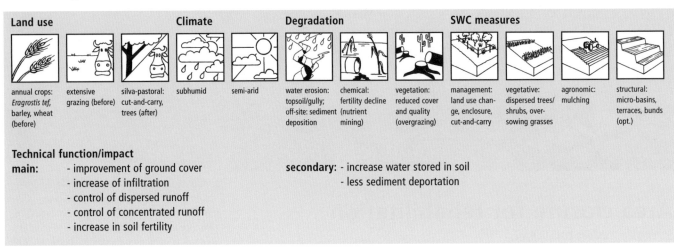

Land use
annual crops: *Eragrostis tef*, barley, wheat (before) | extensive grazing (before) | silva-pastoral: cut-and-carry, trees (after)

Climate
subhumid | semi-arid

Degradation
water erosion: topsoil/gully; off-site: sediment deposition | chemical: fertility decline (nutrient mining) | vegetation: reduced cover and quality (overgrazing)

SWC measures
management: land use change, enclosure, cut-and-carry | vegetative: dispersed trees/ shrubs, over-sowing grasses | agronomic: mulching | structural: micro-basins, terraces, bunds (opt.)

Technical function/impact
main:
- improvement of ground cover
- increase of infiltration
- control of dispersed runoff
- control of concentrated runoff
- increase in soil fertility

secondary:
- increase water stored in soil
- less sediment deportation

Environment

Natural environment

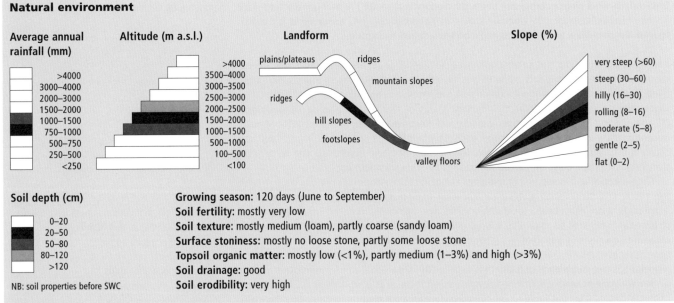

Average annual rainfall (mm)
>4000
3000–4000
2000–3000
1500–2000
1000–1500
750–1000
500–750
250–500
<250

Altitude (m a.s.l.)
>4000
3500–4000
3000–3500
2500–3000
2000–2500
1500–2000
1000–1500
500–1000
100–500
<100

Landform
plains/plateaus | ridges | mountain slopes | ridges | hill slopes | footslopes | valley floors

Slope (%)
very steep (>60)
steep (30–60)
hilly (16–30)
rolling (8–16)
moderate (5–8)
gentle (2–5)
flat (0–2)

Soil depth (cm)
0–20
20–50
50–80
80–120
>120

NB: soil properties before SWC

Growing season: 120 days (June to September)
Soil fertility: mostly very low
Soil texture: mostly medium (loam), partly coarse (sandy loam)
Surface stoniness: mostly no loose stone, partly some loose stone
Topsoil organic matter: mostly low (<1%), partly medium (1–3%) and high (>3%)
Soil drainage: good
Soil erodibility: very high

Human environment

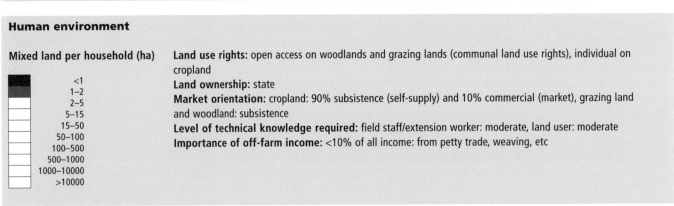

Mixed land per household (ha)
<1
1–2
2–5
5–15
15–50
50–100
100–500
500–1000
1000–10000
>10000

Land use rights: open access on woodlands and grazing lands (communal land use rights), individual on cropland
Land ownership: state
Market orientation: cropland: 90% subsistence (self-supply) and 10% commercial (market), grazing land and woodland: subsistence
Level of technical knowledge required: field staff/extension worker: moderate, land user: moderate
Importance of off-farm income: <10% of all income: from petty trade, weaving, etc

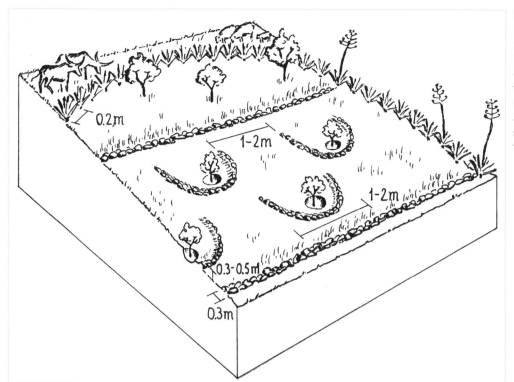

Technical drawing
Rehabilitation of degraded land based on enclosure with live fence. Natural regeneration of vegetative cover is supported by water harvesting structures and planting of nitrogen-fixing/multipurpose shrubs and trees as well as local grass species. On steeper slopes hillside terraces may be established.

Implementation activities, inputs and costs

Establishment activities

1. Marking the boundary and establishment of live fences: digging pits and planting sisal *(Agave sisalana)*, early rainy season (before June).
2. Construction of structural measures such as micro- basins, trenches, bunds or hillside terraces before rains.
3. Planting of trees *(Eucalyptus spp., Grevillea robusta)* as well as nitrogen fixing shrubs: *Acacia saligna, Sesbania sesban, Leucaena leucocephala* (early rainy season).
4. Oversowing/interplanting with local grass species: napier grass *(Pennisetum purpureum)*, rhodes grass *(Chloris gayana)* (early rainy season).
5. Mulching with tree leaves/grass around newly planted trees, before rains when there is less vegetative cover.

Duration of establishment: 2 months

Establishment inputs and costs per ha

Inputs	Costs (US$)	% met by land user
Labour (250 person days)	175	50%
Equipment		
- Tools (local digging hoe, spade, shovel)	25	100%
Materials		
- Earth	0	
- Stones	0	
Agricultural		
- Seeds (grass, 100 kg)	40	0%
- Seedlings (2,000 trees)	150	0%
Others		
- Site guard (3kg grain/ha/year)	1	100%
TOTAL	**390**	**30%**

Maintenance/recurrent activities

1. Repairing breaks in structures before rains.
2. Replanting/gapping up live fence and trees during rains in the early establishment period.
3. Harvesting grass during rainy season.
4. Pruning of trees in the dry season.
5. Weeding after rains.

Maintenance/recurrent inputs and costs per ha per year

Inputs	Costs (US$)	% met by land user
Labour (50 person days)	35	100%
Equipment		
- Tools (local digging hoe, spade, shovel)	5	100%
Agricultural		
- Seeds (grass, 25 kg)	10	0%
- Seedlings (500 trees)	40	0%
Others		
- Site guard (3kg grain/ha/year)	1	100%
TOTAL	**90**	**45%**

Remarks: Labour for establishment activities: 250 person days per ha for structural measures and planting of trees, plus guarding. Labour for maintenance: 50 person days for replanting/weeding. A common daily wage is US$ 0.70 (= 6 Ethiopian Birr), however in this case the site guards were given 3 kg of grains per ha per year. They can control over 200 ha.

Assessment

Acceptance/adoption
- In the early stages of area closure implementation all land users accepted the technology with incentives (work tools and food). In the study area there were around 300 families.
- After a year, more than 90% of them continued activities without food-for-work support. At present almost all the beneficiary households accept the technology due to its benefits: fodder (grass, cut-and-carry), wood for fuel/construction.
- Food-for-work incentives were provided by the project for people participating in the initial establishment of structural measures (trenches, micro-basins), pitting and planting activities.
- Adoption rate has considerably increased owing to improved ownership feeling and immense benefits obtained through the practice. However, if labour-intensive structural measures are required people rely on food-for-work incentives.

Benefits/costs according to land user

*cut-and-carry

Benefits compared with costs	short-term:	long-term:
establishment	positive*	very positive
maintenance/recurrent	positive	very positive

Impacts of the technology

Production and socio-economic benefits	Production and socio-economic disadvantages
+ + + fodder production/quality increase (cut-and-carry of grass)	– – – reduced grazing area/high pressure on remaining grazing areas
+ + wood production increase	– – increased labour constraints
+ + farm income increase (selling grass/wood)	– increased input constraints
Socio-cultural benefits	**Socio-cultural disadvantages**
+ + + community institution strengthening	– unequal share of benefits (some illegal cutting of vegetation
+ + + improved knowledge SWC	is involved)
Ecological benefits	**Ecological disadvantages**
+ + + soil cover improvement (>80%)	– soil erosion increase (locally)
+ + + increase in soil moisture (>50%)	– waterlogging
+ + + increase in soil fertility (increased organic matter, nitrogen fixing shrubs)	– competition between naturally regenerating and oversown (grass) species
+ + + soil loss reduction (initially 50% reduction, after 2–3 years >90% reduction)	
+ + + biodiversity enhancement (recovering disappearing local species)	
Off-site benefits	**Off-site disadvantages**
+ + + ground water recharge and increased stream flow in dry season	– – – increased pressure on other grazing lands which are not closed
+ + + reduced river pollution	
+ + + reduced transported sediments and downstream siltation	
+ + + reduced flood risk downslope	

Concluding statements

Strengths and ➜ how to sustain/improve	Weaknesses and ➜ how to overcome
Reduction of on-site and off-site land degradation, reclamation of degraded non-productive land (regenerating fertility) ➜ Strengthen maintenance and protection to increase biomass production of enclosure.	On highly eroded areas and in areas with low rainfall the survival rate of trees and shrubs is low and as a result the benefits only come after a very long period. This situation becomes unacceptable to the land users ➜ Select suitable local and exotic multipurpose tree/shrub species adapted to the local conditions (*Acacia spp.*, *Eucalyptus spp.*, *Grevillea robusta* etc). Construct water-harvesting structures (trenches, micro-basins). Raise awareness among land users through meetings and training.
Fodder shortage is reduced through cut-and-carry of grass in enclosures (after 1 year) ➜ Introduce more productive and nutritious grass/legume species.	
Collection of dead wood from enclosures (after 3–4 years) mitigates fuelwood shortage ➜ Introduce alternative fast growing multi-purpose tree species such as *Grevillea robusta* (fodder for smallstock in very dry periods).	Investment costs are rather high for land users ➜ Credits, loans, cooperatives.
Cutting wood for construction of houses and wooden farm implements (after 7–8 years) ➜ Continue planting of multipurpose trees.	Inequitable share of benefits ➜ Awareness should be increased through enhancing the LLPP approach (see related approach on the following pages).
Increased honey production through increased bee activity in enclosures ➜ Improve beehives, 'bee feed' (bee-friendly plants), and access to market.	
Emergence of springs, which have disappeared due to deforestation/land degradation ➜ Maintain proper ground cover to improve infiltration and percolation of rainwater.	
Income generation: farmers sell grass/wood collected from area enclosures; they make profit despite seven years enclosure ➜ Better management of planted grass, making of hay, improve market systems.	

Key reference(s): Chadokar PA (1985) *Multipurpose Plant Species for Soil and Water Conservation. Assistance to Soil and Water Conservation Programme.* ETH/81/003 ■ Betru Nedassa (1995) *Biological Soil Conservation Measures.* Land Rehabilitation and Reforestation Project. Project 2488 MOA/WFP

Contact Person(s): Daniel Danano, Ministry of Agriculture, PO Box 62758, Addis Ababa, Ethiopia; ethiocat@ethionet.et

Local level participatory planning approach

Ethiopia

left: Participatory planning meeting underway in the community of Alaba, involving farmers and field technicians. (Daniel Danano)
right: Field activities for area closure in Alaba: women's participation in the implementation phase is more than 50%, however decisions are principally taken by men. (Daniel Danano)

An approach used by field staff to implement conservation activities, involving farmers in all stages of planning, implementation and evaluation.

The Local Level Participatory Planning Approach (LLPPA) starts with the selection of communities based on needs and problem assessment. Then development committees are formed, consisting of one or two technical staff and seven to eight farmers. They are elected by the community through a general assembly of land users.

The development committees plan and coordinate development activities. They first conduct a survey of the biophysical and socio-economic conditions of the area. Then problems are identified and prioritised with the community members through participatory rural appraisal (PRA). Land use analysis, followed by the definition of objectives, identification of development options and selection of appropriate SWC interventions, is carried out on a consultative basis. Targets for achievements are established, and resources and inputs are determined. Finally the development committee prepares a work plan. The plan for SWC activities is then submitted to the community leaders, and the approval of the plan is made by the general assembly of land users, in consultation with the technical field staff.

The development committee is given the responsibility for organising implementation. The beneficiaries actively participate in this implementation, in maintenance and in utilisation of the assets created, by contributing their labour and resources. Whenever required technical field staff give technical advice during implementation of development activities – area closure for rehabilitation in this case. Participatory monitoring and evaluation of activities is another important element of the approach.

The main purpose of LLPPA is to enhance farmers' involvement in all steps of the development process, from the initial stages of planning, to implementation of the activities, and in the evaluation of the achievements. A good relationship between land users and field workers, and acceptance as well as support of the development activities by the land users are fundamental prerequisites for fruitful implementation and maintenance of SWC measures.

Location: Alaba, South Ethiopia, Ethiopia
Approach area: 20 km²
Land use: cropland, grazing land, forest
Climate: subhumid, partly semi-arid
WOCAT database reference: QA ETH25
Related technology: Area closure for rehabilitation QT ETH25, Improved grazing land management QT ETH26
Compiled by: Daniel Danano, Addis Ababa, Ethiopia
Date: December 2002, updated June 2004

Editors' comments: Having learned from past mistakes, where solutions were imposed, a participatory approach to conservation has emerged in Ethiopia and is supported by the Ministry of Agriculture in collaboration with the World Food Programme. The LLPPA is the planning tool used in the entire country – and is popular with both communities and development agents.

Problem, objectives and constraints

Problem
Difficulties in attaining sustainable development through area closures for rehabilitation are due to:
- lacking sense of ownership: land users feel that development attained in enclosures belongs to the government
- lack of awareness about land degradation problems, and the values of conservation measures
- reluctance to maintain activities and protect assets created
- shortage of livestock feed, fuelwood and construction material
- increasing land degradation problems (on- and off-site) due to improper land use and poor farming practices
- food insecurity and poverty

Objectives
- encourage the involvement of the beneficiary population and the technical personnel in the whole development process (ie initial planning, implementation, monitoring/evaluation) so that sustainable development, leading to improved living conditions is attained
- reduce land degradation (gully formation and landslides, sediment flow into downstream water harvesting and storage tanks) and enhance natural regeneration and fertility of soils in order to increase the productivity of degraded areas: provide livestock feed, fuel and construction wood, and higher crop yields

Constraints addressed

Major	Specification	Treatment
Lack of awareness	Lack of awareness about soil degradation and appropriate management practices.	Awareness raising through training and awareness creation seminars.
Technical	Cultivating steep slopes due to overpopulation and land subdivision (holdings of 0.25–0.5 ha/household).	Apply appropriate land use practices according to land potential and apply SWC practices. Alternative income generation.
Technical	Deforestation: illegal cutting of trees due to lack of fuel/construction wood, letting livestock into closed areas. Lack of management plans for planted trees.	Training and awareness raising on how to assume responsibilities to protect the assets developed. Plant trees in woodlots and provide alternative energy sources (eg kerosene).
Technical	Overgrazing of sloping lands resulting in severe gullies (on >50% of the land) and landslides. No controlled grazing.	Practice zero grazing, cut-and-carry and/or controlled grazing.

Minor	Specification	Treatment
Financial	Lack of financial resources: >90% of the community members are poor.	Provision of hand tools by the project. Provide training to raise awareness about benefits.
Policy	Land tenure (land is state and public property).	Assure land user rights and provide certificates.

Participation and decision making

Target groups

Land users | SWC specialists/extensionists | Planners regional/national | Politicians/decision makers

Approach costs met by:

International agency (World Food Programme, WFP)	40%
National government	10%
Community/local	50%
	100%

Decisions on choice of the technology: Made by the community/land users in consultation with SWC specialists/extension workers.
Decisions on method of implementing the technology: Made by the community members based on the plan of action prepared by the development committee (comprising farmers and technical staff).
Approach designed by: National and international experts.

Community involvement

Phase	Involvement	Activities
Initiation	interactive	self-motivation: few farmers take the initiative
Planning	interactive	initiated by technical staff, motivated by the development committee: identify problems, prioritise them and seek solutions
Implementation	interactive and payment/incentives	community is responsible for implementation, some incentives are given for motivation: farmers are organised into working teams
Monitoring/evaluation	passive	initiated by extension agents, annual evaluation during community meeting
Research	none	none

Differences in participation of men and women: In the approach area women's participation is more than 50% (and this is increasing) in the implementation of SWC measures. However, women are still not playing a sufficient role in decision making, due to cultural norms/values.

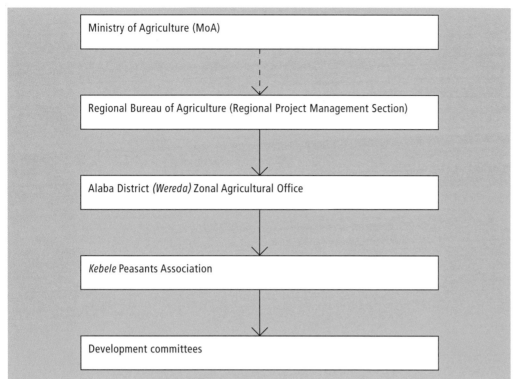

Extension and promotion

Training: Extension workers and *Wereda* district soil conservation specialists are given regular training on LLPPA and area closure management. Community leaders and the development committee are trained every year on the various techniques of soil conservation. Two to three day awareness creation seminars are held for the community in general. The awareness creation programme played a significant role in convincing beneficiaries to actively participate in the SWC programme. Training for community leaders has helped them to improve their leadership and coordinating capacities. The training given to field staff has improved their skills and hence enabled them to effectively implement the programme.

Extension: Key elements of the extension approach are: training, demonstration of the technology and provision of the necessary inputs for application. The extension has been very efficient, farmers have accepted the technology and the impact is visible. The extension service has been adequate, due to support by MoA and donor agencies such as the World Food Programme.

Research: Very little work is done with regard to research in area closure and LLPPA.

Importance of land use rights: Area closures would provide better opportunities and advantages to the beneficiaries if hillsides were distributed to individual farmers, and if they were provided with user right certificates for the plots developed by them. In that case each farmer would give more attention to the protection and maintenance of assets developed.

Incentives

Labour: Since farmers participating in the construction of structural measures are poor and the activities are labour intensive, they are given 3 kg of grain/person day as an incentive (food-for-work). Site guards protect large areas (from 200 ha to 1,000 ha They are often landless and hence are also rewarded with 3 kg of grain/ha/year. Nevertheless, voluntary labour contribution by the community for activities such as planting, weeding and other management activities is more than 50%.

Inputs: Seed and seedlings are provided free of charge.

Credit: No credit is provided.

Support to local institutions: There is considerable support to local institutions: they get more money through selling trees and grass from enclosures, which in turn strengthens the institutions financially and socially. The development committee continues to exist after the project phases out. The same committee could take up other development issues.

Long-term impact of incentives: Long-term impacts are uncertain. The beneficiaries need to be made better aware of the fact that incentives are merely to encourage their initial participation. Only then can dependency be avoided.

Monitoring and evaluation

Monitored aspects	Methods* and indicators
Bio-physical	change in slope, sediment trapped in ditch (behind the structures), soil depth, ground cover, amount of biomass, rate of regeneration of local trees and shrubs, productivity of livestock, spring water discharge, soil loss, runoff
Technical	quality of structural measures (determined by frequency of maintenance required), survival rate of planted trees
Socio-cultural	community participation in planning and implementation, trends in (a) the participation of poor and rich farmers, (b) women's participation, (c) decision making between men and women
Economic/production	amount of grass produced, household income from enclosures, availability and production of wood for fuel, increase in soil fertility
Area treated	area treated by structural and vegetative measures
No. of land users involved	land users participating in planning, implementation, decision making
Management of approach	number of land users participating in the implementation, land users participating in maintenance activities, type of activities undertaken on voluntary basis

* All indicators are measured once a year by the technical staff assigned to the sites in consultation with the farmers. The project undertakes such observations in order to evaluate the impact of the project interventions.

Impacts of the approach

Changes as result of monitoring and evaluation: As a result of monitoring and evaluation improvements in quality of micro-basins and/or trenches, for example, led to better attaining the standards of technology design initially proposed.
Improved soil and water management: Applied conservation measures in areas under closure considerably improve soil and water management, resulting in an increase in soil depth, ground cover, biomass, and in survival rates of planted trees and forage shrubs.
Adoption of the approach by other projects/land users: There has been a high adoption rate (both with and without project support) of the approach as well as the technology – as can be observed in nearby communities.
Sustainability: Land users can continue without support – and are actually doing so where the support for area closure has already stopped.

Concluding statements

Strengths and ➜ how to sustain/improve	Weaknesses and ➜ how to overcome
Involvement of land users in decision making ➜ More work on empowerment/land use rights.	Dependence on incentives ➜ Improve the methods of using incentives: incentives should be understood as a means for promoting participation rather than as a payment.
Encourages working in a team ➜ Further strengthen team organisation.	Low sense of ownership ➜ Distribute the enclosures to individual land users.
Application of appropriate land use practices contributing to sustainable development ➜ Further improvement of productivity by encouraging land users to make maximum use of development achievements.	The involvement of rich members of the community in the development committee is low ➜ Development committee needs to be represented by different target groups.
Rapid benefits obtained: provision of livestock fodder (through cut-and-carry), fuel wood and construction material ➜ Expand use of improved planting materials.	Site guards are given incentives by the project ➜ The community will have to assume this responsibility in future.

Key reference(s): Escobedo et al (1990) *The minimum planning procedures for soil and water conservation in Ethiopia. Assistance to Soil Conservation Project.* ETH016, FAO ▪ Voli C et al (1999) *The Local Level Participatory Planning Approach for the soil and water conservation programme in Ethiopia.* MOA/WFP
Contact person(s): Daniel Danano, Ministry of Agriculture, PO Box 62758, Addis Ababa, Ethiopia; ethiocat@ethionet.et

left: Drip irrigation systems considerably improve water use efficiency: The improved black *pepsee* pipes deliver water directly to the chilli pepper plants. (Shilp Verma)
right: Components of *pepsee* mirco-irrigation system: pipes and joints. (IDEI)

Pepsee micro-irrigation system

India – *Pepsee*

A grassroots innovation that offers most of the advantages of conventional micro-irrigation at a much lower establishment cost.

The continued expansion of irrigation in India is causing increasing water shortages. This may be compounded by the potential effects of climate change. Drip irrigation – delivering small amounts of water directly to the plants through pipes – is a technology that could help farmers deal with water constraints. It is considerably more efficient in terms of water use than the usual open furrows or flood irrigation.

In West Nimar, Madhya Pradesh, droughts, diminishing groundwater, limited and erratic power supply coupled with poverty, compelled farmers to look for a technology that would enable them to irrigate their crops (mainly cotton) within these constraints. They tried out several cost-saving options such as using old bicycle tubes instead of the conventional drip irrigation pipes. But nothing caught on – until about five years ago – when a local farmer experimented with thin poly-tubing normally used for frozen fruit-flavoured 'lollypops' called *pepsee*. It spread to neighbouring cotton farmers, and its popularity has meant that today pepsee has become widespread in the region. *Pepsee* micro-irrigation systems slowly and regularly apply water directly to the root zone of plants through a network of economically designed plastic pipes and low-discharge emitters. Technically speaking *pepsee* systems use low density polythene (65–130 microns) tubes which are locally assembled. Being a low pressure system the water source can be an overhead tank or a manually operated water pump to lift water from a shallow water table.

Such a system costs less than US$ 40 per hectare for establishment. But the tubes have a short life span of one (or two) year(s); an equivalent standard buried strip drip irrigation system amounts to between five and ten times the initial cost. The latter would, however, last for five to ten years. The critical factor is the low entry cost. *Pepsee* systems thus act as 'stepping stones' for poor farmers who are facing water stress but are short of capital and cannot afford to risk relatively large investment in a technology which is new to them, and whose returns are uncertain. The technology is today available in two variants: the original white *pepsee* and a recently introduced black *pepsee* which is of slightly better quality. Recently, a more durable and standardised version of *pepsee,* given the brand name 'Easy Drip', has been developed and promoted by a local NGO, IDEI (see corresponding approach). Easy Drip is one product within a set of affordable micro-irrigation technologies (AMIT) promoted by IDEI.

Location: West Nimar, Madhya Pradesh, India
Technology area: no information
SWC measure: structural and management
Land use: cropland
Climate: semi-arid
WOCAT database reference: QT IND15
Related approach: Market development and support, QA IND15
Compiled by: Shilp Verma, Vallabh Vidyanagar, Gujarat, India
Date: January 2005, updated March 2006

Editors' comments: In India, around a third of all cropland is irrigated, and water shortages threaten production. Here is a case of a low cost innovation which increases efficiency of water use. Irrigation is generally not covered by WOCAT, but this case study demonstrates that (a) water use efficiency and cost are crucial elements in irrigated systems and (b) irrigation can be described and evaluated in a similar way to rainfed systems through WOCAT.

Classification

Land use problems
Acute groundwater stress associated with lowering of the groundwater table limits water for irrigation, coupled with poverty and reluctance to risk investing in relatively expensive – but efficient – drip irrigation systems.

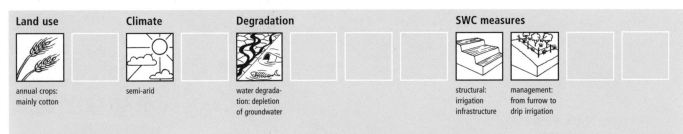

Land use	Climate	Degradation			SWC measures	
annual crops: mainly cotton	semi-arid	water degradation: depletion of groundwater			structural: irrigation infrastructure	management: from furrow to drip irrigation

Technical function/impact
main:
- water supply
- improved water-use efficiency (reduced loss through evaporation), well directed, selective and targeted irrigation

secondary:
- ensures constant water supply in the crucial phase of germination, higher germination and establishment rate
- improvement of ground cover: better crop growth and greater area under irrigation

Environment

Natural environment

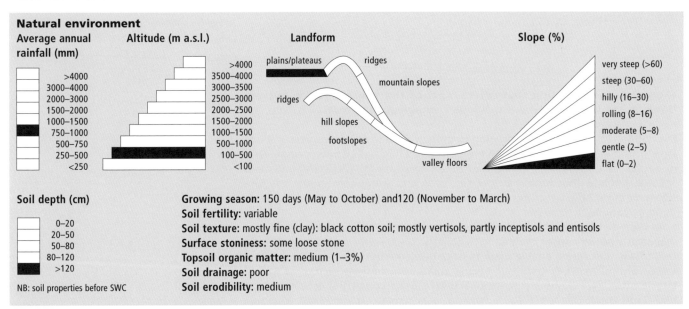

Average annual rainfall (mm)
- >4000
- 3000–4000
- 2000–3000
- 1500–2000
- 1000–1500
- 750–1000
- 500–750
- 250–500
- <250

Altitude (m a.s.l.)
- >4000
- 3500–4000
- 3000–3500
- 2500–3000
- 2000–2500
- 1500–2000
- 1000–1500
- 500–1000
- 100–500
- <100

Landform
- plains/plateaus
- ridges
- mountain slopes
- ridges
- hill slopes
- footslopes
- valley floors

Slope (%)
- very steep (>60)
- steep (30–60)
- hilly (16–30)
- rolling (8–16)
- moderate (5–8)
- gentle (2–5)
- flat (0–2)

Soil depth (cm)
- 0–20
- 20–50
- 50–80
- 80–120
- >120

NB: soil properties before SWC

Growing season: 150 days (May to October) and 120 (November to March)
Soil fertility: variable
Soil texture: mostly fine (clay): black cotton soil; mostly vertisols, partly inceptisols and entisols
Surface stoniness: some loose stone
Topsoil organic matter: medium (1–3%)
Soil drainage: poor
Soil erodibility: medium

Human environment

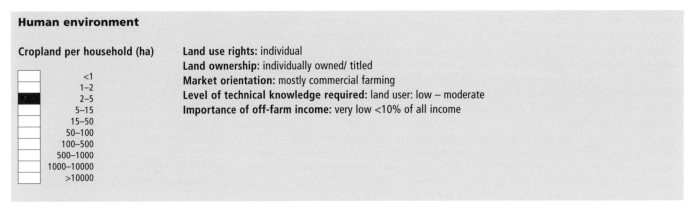

Cropland per household (ha)
- <1
- 1–2
- 2–5
- 5–15
- 15–50
- 50–100
- 100–500
- 500–1000
- 1000–10000
- >10000

Land use rights: individual
Land ownership: individually owned/ titled
Market orientation: mostly commercial farming
Level of technical knowledge required: land user: low – moderate
Importance of off-farm income: very low <10% of all income

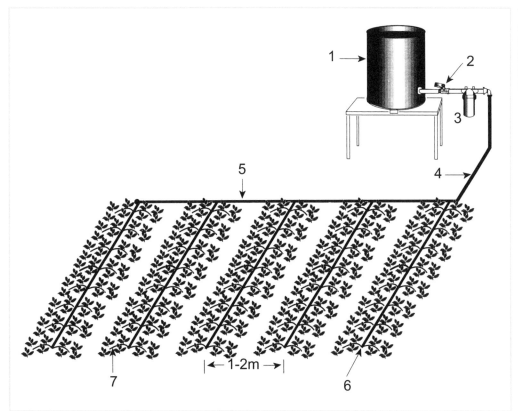

Technical drawing
Components of *pepsee*/'Easy Drip' irrigation systems are described below.
Source: Sijali IV 2001, Drip irrigation, RELMA, Nairobi

|← 1-2m →|

1) Water source: For *pepsee*, commonly a water pump (in most cases electric) is used to lift water from a well and directly feed the irrigation system. Alternatively, an overhead tank (minimum of 1 m above ground level) can be used for smaller systems up to 400 m² area.
2) Control valve: valve made of plastic or metal to regulate pressure and flow of water into the system
3) Filter: Strainer filter to ensure that clean water enters into the system (optional in *pepsee* systems).
4) Mainline: 50 mm PVC (Polyvinyl chloride) or PE (Polyethylene) pipe to convey water from source to the sub-main.
5) Sub-main: PVC/PE pipe to supply water to the lateral pipes which are connected to the sub-main at regular intervals.
6) Lateral: PE pipes along the rows of the crops on which emitters are connected directly. Pipe size is 12–16 mm.
7) Emitters/micro-tubes: Device through which water is emitted at the root zone of the plant with required discharge. In *pepsee* farmers simply make pin holes in the plastic tube for water to pass. Easy Drip has inbuilt drippers/outlets along the lateral line which give a continuous wetting strip. It is mainly used for row crops.

Pepsee uses cheap, recycled plastic tubes instead of the rubber pipes used in conventional drip irrigation kits. Space between emitters is variable, for cotton cultivation it is commonly 1.2 m (between plants, within and between rows). There is (usually) one emitter for each plant. Different sizes of valves, mainlines, etc, are available, depending on flow rate of water in the system. Additional components are joints (connectors) and pegs (used to hold the lateral and micro-pipes in place).

Implementation activities, inputs and costs

Establishment activities

1. Installation of water pump, control valve, filter (optional) and PVC piping (main/sub-main and lateral pipes).

For details see technical drawing above.

All activities are carried during the dry season.

Duration of establishment: a few weeks

Establishment inputs and costs per ha

Inputs	Costs (US$)	% met by land user
Labour (4 person days)	4	100%
Materials		
- Lateral piping (*Pepsee* tube)	17	100%
- Main/sub-main PVC piping	34	100%
- Other parts (valves, joints etc)	40	100%
TOTAL	**95**	**100%**

Maintenance/recurrent activities

1. Re-installation of lateral *pepsee* tubes (every 1–2 years).

Maintenance/recurrent inputs and costs per ha per year

Inputs	Costs (US$)	% met by land user
Labour (4 person days)	4	100%
Materials		
- Lateral piping (*Pepsee* tube)	17	100%
TOTAL	**21**	**100%**

Assessment

Acceptance/adoption
No detailed information available regarding spread – though this is estimated to be several thousand farmers within West Nimar. All adoption has been spontaneous, without incentives, and the group which has adopted best comprises those who were previously using furrow irrigation. A large number of *pepsee* adopters are the resource poor farmers but rich farmers have also adopted *pepsee*.

Benefits/costs according to land user

Benefits compared with costs	short-term:	long-term:
establishment	positive	positive
maintenance/recurrent	positive	positive

Impacts of the technology
Note: compared with standard flood irrigation

Production and socio-economic benefits
- + + + greater irrigated area with same amount of water
- + + higher yields

Socio-cultural benefits
- + + poverty reduction
- + + more farmers able to irrigate their land
- + drip irrigation confers the image of a progressive farmer

Ecological benefits
- + + + improved water use efficiency

Off-site benefits
- none

Production and socio-economic disadvantages
- – – higher labour requirement

Socio-cultural disadvantages
- none

Ecological disadvantages
- – – more land brought under irrigation

Off-site disadvantages
- none

Concluding statements

Strengths and → how to sustain/improve
Low initial investment and recurrent costs: risk in adopting new system limited → Keep costs of new variations of pepsee low.

There are significant benefits in terms of reduced water use per unit of land, and in terms of yield per unit land area as well.

Few extra skills required to implement and operate the system.

An eventual shift to conventional drip system is feasible: pepsee acts as a 'stepping stone' → Promote improved drip systems where pepsee has taken off.

Higher yields, better quality, higher germination rate, lower incidence of pest attack; facilitates pre-monsoon sowing.

Weaknesses and → how to overcome
Pepsee is based on drip pipes which have a limited life: delicate and cannot withstand high pressure → Develop/use stronger piping materials such as 'Easy Drip'.

The increased water use efficiency has allowed an expansion in the area irrigated – which has used up the water 'saved'.

Pepsee systems require replacement of lateral pipes each year and thus incur recurrent input and labour costs → Develop/use stronger piping materials such as 'Easy Drip'.

Key reference(s): Verma S, Tsephal S. and Jose T (2004) *Pepsee* Systems: grassroots innovation under groundwater stress. *Water Policy*, 6, pp. 303–318. ■ http://www.iwaponline.com/wp/00604/wp006040303.htm
Contact person(s): Shilp Verma, IWMI-Tata Water Policy Program, International Water Management Institute, Elecon Complex, Anand Sojitra Road, Vallabh Vidyanagar, Gujarat 388120, India; s.verma@cgiar.org ■ Amitabha Sadangi, International Development Enterprises – India, C 5/43, Safdurjang Development Area (1st & 2nd Floor), New Delhi 110016, India; amitabha@ide-india.org

Market support and branding for input quality

India – *Krishak Bandhu*

left: Demonstrating the technology: 'A satisfied customer is the best spokesperson for generating demand'. This is the basic philosophy of IDEI. (IDEI)
right: The assembler procures components from different manufacturers/suppliers and prepares a final product. (IDEI)

Market development and support through use of a brand name – *Krishak Bandhu* ('the farmer's friend') – to help ensure quality amongst manufacturers and suppliers of drip irrigation equipment.

Poor smallholder farmers are generally slow in adopting new technologies, especially when such decisions require relatively large initial investments which only yield returns over a long period of time. Even when subsidies are made available, the high transaction costs act as a hindrance. After more than three decades of promotion by government, and despite subsidies as high as 90%, conventional drip irrigation technology remains exclusively popular amongst 'gentlemen' (better-off) farmers in India. Since it was first introduced in the 1970s, the total area under drip irrigation expanded sluggishly from 1,500 ha in 1985 to 225,000 ha in 1998, which is tiny compared to an estimated national potential of 10.5 million hectares.

IDE, India (IDEI) is an NGO dedicated to troubleshooting such problems through a unique market development approach. IDEI promotes simple, affordable, appropriate and environmentally sound technologies for poor smallholder farmers through private marketing channels, under the brand name *Krishak Bandhu*. Donor resources are accessed by IDEI to stimulate markets by creating demand for such technologies and by ensuring an efficient supply chain for the equipment. The key to the IDEI approach lies in its adoption and application of commercial business principles as well as in its path of socio-economic development as a tool to sustainability of programmes. IDEI seeks to create a strong and continuing demand by motivating and nurturing an effective supply chain (including manufacturers, dealers and assemblers of micro irrigation equipment). In West Nimar, Madhya Pradesh (as in the whole of India) IDEI supports the marketing of cheap, good quality equipment for so-called 'Affordable Micro-Irrigation Technologies' (AMIT) such as *pepsee* (see associated technology). The promoted technology in this case is based on a farmer's innovation, which then was promoted and spread by IDEI. IDEI has intervened in four major ways: (1) technically it has further developed the local innovation, *pepsee*, and come up with an improvement, aptly named 'Easy Drip'; (2) it has promoted small manufacturers of drip irrigation equipment and associated them with a brand name; (3) it has trained and supported private sector 'service providers' to assist farmers to install and adopt the systems; (4) on an *ad hoc* basis, IDEI commissions and supports studies on up-take and impact. Technologies promoted by IDEI provide returns on investment of at least 100% in one year which is crucial in explaining the success of *pepsee*. Within five years the projects supported by IDEI should become self-sustaining.

Location: West Nimar, Madhya Pradesh, India
Approach area: not specified
Land use: cropland
Climate: semi-arid
WOCAT database reference: QA IND15
Related technology: Pepsee micro-irrigation system, QT IND15
Compiled by: Shilp Verma, Vallabh Vidyanagar, Gujarat, India
Date: January 2005, updated March 2006

Editors' comments: Smallholder farmers in India, as elsewhere, are reluctant to invest in technologies that only repay their outlay over the long term. However, where they can be assured of good quality and low price, these misgivings can be allayed. Here is an example of the further technical development and market assistance, by an NGO, of a local technological innovation – low cost drip irrigation. This highlights the benefits of market support for pro-poor technologies that suit specific needs of smallholders.

Problem, objectives and constraints

Problem
An underlying problem of increasing growing groundwater scarcity combined with the high investment costs of conventional drip irrigation equipment. On top of this is the reluctance of smallholder farmers to take government subsidies because of the high transaction costs (not easy to access; long delays and the reluctance to adopt new technologies). Local and cheap technological options are available, but quality and marketing channels are not assured.

Objectives
To bring affordable and appropriate water saving technologies to the rural poor through creating effective supply chains and developing markets, under a brand name associated with reliability.

Constraints addressed

Major	Specification	Treatment
Financial	Private business decisions are based on profit margins and volumes and the often fragmented and cash-starved customers do not constitute an attractive market on their own.	IDEI develops and nurtures the market for low-cost smallholder friendly technologies; thereby providing incentives to private businesses by encouraging growth in the size of the market.
Socio-cultural	Poor consumers are averse to risk and prefer to emulate the success of early-adopters. Hence, there's often a lag period between the introduction of the technology and its poverty impact.	Every project should become self-sustaining within five years. IDEI therefore establishes the supply chain for manufacturing, distributing and local network of components. It also undertakes mass marketing to create a sufficient demand for the supply chain to be viable and profitable.
Economic	Poor consumers cannot make large investments and may even be willing to pay a higher per unit price as long as the one-time investment is lowered.	IDEI identifies and develops appropriate technologies that have high poverty-alleviation potential, are produced locally; are environment friendly; and provide return on investment of at least 100% in one year.

Minor	Specification	Treatment
Socio-cultural	Certain technologies face socio-cultural barriers to adoption.	IDEI deals with such aspects at the design stage of the product itself thereby eliminating them. Additionally, it uses communication packages to facilitate adoption.

Participation and decision making

Target groups

Smallholder farmers

Approach costs met by:

Donor agencies (international)	100%
	100%

Decisions on choice of the technology: Made by land users alone; on the basis of their specific requirements.
Decisions on method of implementing the technology: Mainly by land users supported by specialists/'service providers' (IDEI, the supporting NGO)
Approach designed by: national/international specialists

Community involvement

Phase	Involvement	Activities
Initiation	active	innovative development of *pepsee* technology, experimentation (farmers initiative)
Planning	passive	IDEI carrying out awareness creation etc
Implementation	passive	dealers, retailers marketing produce: technical backstopping provided by IDEI
Monitoring/evaluation	passive	market surveys, studies, assessments initiated and carried out by IDEI
Research	passive	planned and carried out by IDEI

Difference in participation between men and women: Traditionally, irrigation investments in particular, and farming in general, has been male-dominated. However, recent studies indicate that women play a critical role in the decision-making process, as these investments often compete with other household requirements.

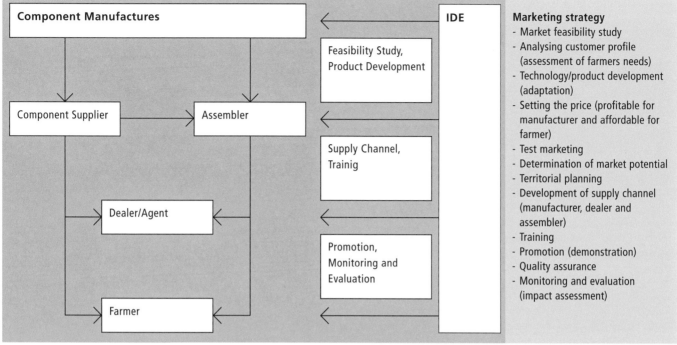

left: Supply channels of AMIT (Affordable Micro-Irrigation Technologies) systems and the role of IDEI (IDEI)
right: Key elements of the AMIT marketing strategy (IDEI)

Extension and promotion

Training: Training and extension are combined: while there are no dedicated training courses, through the network of service providers (who have been trained by IDEI), know-how on drip irrigation is spread among adopter and potential adopter farmers. Brochures and pamphlets (several in the local language) are circulated and there is an informative website.
Extension: (see training)
Research: Apart from research carried out by scientists (published in journals etc) IDEI has its own series of research reports which present the results of various studies on promotion and impact of low cost water saving technologies conducted (see references).
Importance of land use rights: Land is owned privately, thus there is no hindrance to investment in irrigation infrastructure.

Incentives

Labour: No incentives to support labour are given to land users.
Inputs: There are no material incentives given out to stimulate adoption. The necessary inputs are cheap and are fully paid for by the farmers.
Credit: No credit facility is provided.
Support to local institutions: Very important: this is the core of the approach. IDEI supports the whole chain from manufacturers and dealers to assemblers.
Long-term impact of incentives: Not applicable since there are no material incentives.

Monitoring and evaluation

Monitored aspects	Methods and indicators
Bio-physical	regular measurement of the improvement in water-use efficiency
Technical	regular measurement of the appropriateness of the technology to different crops and locations; also trying out technologies with new crops
Socio-cultural	regular assessments of impact on women and on the poor
Economic/production	regular measurements of returns vis-à-vis investments
Area treated	regular assessment of total scale of adoption; IDEI's estimates suggest that their technologies have so far reached 30,000 families

Impacts of the approach

Changes as a result of monitoring and evaluation: IDEI carries out a number of studies to investigate the impact of their technologies and the scale and dynamics of adoption. The results of these studies feed into their strategic and operational plans. For example, IDEI was the first to introduce drips in mulberry cultivation in Kolar. That became a huge success story.
Improved soil and water management: The widespread adoption of the *pepsee* and Easy Drip irrigation infrastructure has greatly improved water use efficiency
Adoption of the approach by other projects/land users: Several grassroots NGOs have recognised the potential of IDEI's low cost technologies and are promoting them in their respective regions. For instance, IWMI's own action research initiative in north Gujarat (called the North Gujarat Sustainable Groundwater Initiative) is actively partnering with IDEI (and other drip manufacturers) to try out various water saving technologies in Banaskantha District.
Sustainability: The entire approach relies on creation of markets which are initially promoted and supported by IDEI. It is perhaps too early to say whether the market would be sustained after IDEI withdraws but because of the fact that *pepsee* was a grassroots innovation and emerged spontaneously, there is a good chance of this happening. IDEI keeps a five year horizon for its intervention, and targets that the market should become self-sustaining by the end of this period.

Concluding statements

Strengths and → how to sustain/improve	Weaknesses and → how to overcome
IDEI believes in the essential dignity of people and their capacity to overcome social and economic pressures, problems and exploitations. It therefore treats poor farmers as customers and not recipients of charity. It applies business models to achieve development by tapping and developing small enterprises in the rural economy and creating markets.	IDEI's reach is dependent on its ability to access donor funds. This might become a limitation at some stage.
It applies business models to achieve development by tapping and developing small enterprises in the rural economy and creating markets → Further promote market creation and then let the market forces take off on their own.	IDEI needs to work more closely with the government agencies. While market creation seems to be a very useful model, it needs to tap the government resources which are pumped every year in the business of promotion of drip irrigation.
The IDEI market creation approach to development ensures that there is awareness and availability of low-cost products that will have a high poverty alleviation impact → Ditto.	
Growth in this approach will take place if the supply chain is performing and profitable. The early adopters may not be the poorest but if the product meets the needs of the farmers, the rural poor will follow suit and considerable market growth could result, creating a sustainable supply channel → Ditto.	

Key reference(s): IDEI *Affordable Micro Irrigation Technologies: Marketing Manual.* International Development Enterprises, USA. ■ Phansalkar, S.J. (2003). *Appropriate Drip Irrigation Technologies Promoted by IDEI: A Socio-Economic Assessment.* International Development Enterprises, India (IDEI), New Delhi. ■ Shah, T. and Keller, J. (2002). Micro-irrigation and the poor: A marketing challenge in smallholder irrigation development. In Sally, H.; Abernethy, C. L. (Eds.), *Private irrigation in Sub-Saharan Africa: Regional Seminar on Private Sector Participation and Irrigation Expansion in Sub-Saharan Africa,* Accra, Ghana, 22–26 October 2001. Colombo, Sri Lanka: IWMI; FAO; ACP-EU Technical Centre for Agricultural and Rural Cooperation. pp.165–183. ■ Verma, S., Tsephal, S. and Jose, T. (2004). *Pepsee Systems: Grassroots Innovation under Groundwater Stress. Water Policy,* 6, pp. 303–318.
Contact person(s): Amitabha Sadangi, International Development Enterprises – India, C 5/43, Safdurjang Development Area (1ˢᵗ & 2ⁿᵈ Floor), New Delhi 110016, India; amitabha@ide-india.org ■ Shilp Verma, IWMI-Tata Water Policy Program, International Water Management Institute, Elecon Complex, Anand Sojitra Road, Vallabh Vidyanagar, Gujarat 388120, India; s.verma@cgiar.org; www.iwmi.org/iwmi-tata

left: Windbreak of millet stalks help stop dune encroachment. (Philippe Benguerel)
right: Bird's eye view of a stabilised sand dune. Clearly distinguishable is the enclosed area with improved vegetation cover and the chequerboard pattern of the millet stalk palisades. (Andreas Buerkert)

Sand dune stabilisation

Niger – *Fixation des dunes*

A combination of three measures to stabilise dunes: area closure, the use of palisades, and vegetative fixation through natural regeneration as well as planting.

In the Sahelian zone of Niger, sand dune encroachment can lead to loss of agricultural and pastoral land, and threatens villages. These dunes may form as a result of an increase in wind erosion, but more frequently originate from formerly stabilised dunes that have become mobile again following the disappearance of vegetation. Vegetation loss may occur through a combination of unfavourable climatic conditions and overexploitation by grazing and fuelwood gathering.

Sustainable dune fixation requires the regeneration of vegetation on the mobile parts of the dunes. For plants to establish, the dunes need to be protected by mechanical measures while being defended against any kind of use. Hence, the technique of dune stabilisation consists of a combination of three measures. These are as follows: (1) Area closure by wire fencing and guarding to prevent exploitation of the area during the rehabilitation phase until vegetation is sufficiently established (2–3 years). (2) Construction of millet stalk palisades arranged ideally in 'checker-board' squares, which act as windbreaks. These physical structures are a barrier to sand transport by wind, and thus are a prerequisite for revegetation. After two years the palisades fall apart and decompose – and the vegetation takes over the dune fixation function. Small erosion gullies can be controlled by check dams made from stone or millet stalks. (3) Natural regeneration, planting and seeding of annual and perennial plants (including *Acacia spp.* and *Prosopis spp.)* for soil stabilisation.

As soon as vegetation cover is established on the denuded surfaces the dunes can be used for grazing or for harvesting of herbs and fuelwood. Period and frequency of use should be determined in common agreement with all actors involved. In addition the pasture on the dune can be used as a 'reserve' for late dry-season grazing, depending on vegetation development and herd size. Between 1991 and 1995, just over 250 ha of sand dunes were stabilised in the case study area. Incentives were provided by the 'Projet de Développement Rural de Tahoua' (PDRT, see also 'Participatory land rehabilitation' approach). After 1995 no further dunes were stabilised due to the high cost of the wire fencing, which local communities simply could not afford themselves. However, as the objective of the fence is to keep out humans and animals during critical periods (the rainy season), the same effect could be obtained at no financial cost through 'social fencing', that is agreement between stakeholders on where there should be no grazing. Furthermore the technology itself – which works well – could be relevant to situations where higher investment can be justified for specific reasons.

Location: Niger, district of Tahoua
Technology area: 2 km²
SWC measure: management, structural and vegetative
Land use: grazing land
Climate: semi-arid
WOCAT database reference: QT NIG15
Related approach: Participatory land rehabilitation, QA NIG01 (p 217)
Compiled by: Oudou Noufou Adamou, Tahoua, Niger; Eric Tielkes, Germany; Charles Bielders, Belgium
Date: August 1999, updated June 2004

Editors' comments: In the Sahelian zone of Niger, wind erosion constitutes one of the major causes of land degradation. Measures to combat wind erosion and sand encroachment were developed through a rural development project. However in this case the cost was too high to justify continuation: nevertheless the technology itself may be applicable in other situations.

Classification

Land use problems
The area suffers from an imbalance between availability of natural resources (constrained by soil fertility and rainfall) and the rapid growth of the human and livestock populations. As a result, there is chronic food insufficiency and an associated overexploitation of the natural resource base. Accelerated wind and water erosion further enhance the degradation of the soil resources. From the farmers' perspective, the main problems are lack of grazing land, wood and drinking water (due to sinking water tables), insufficient and unevenly distributed rainfall. Sand dunes are fragile: when overexploited, they soon remain with only unpalatable plant species, eg *Panicum turgidum*. When the vegetation cover on dunes decreases even further, dunes start moving again, threatening fields, villages or depressions used for fruit and vegetable cropping.

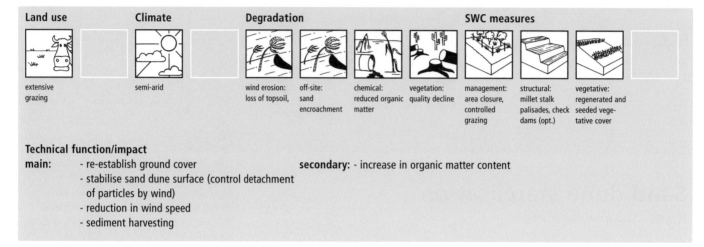

Land use	Climate	Degradation				SWC measures		
extensive grazing	semi-arid	wind erosion: loss of topsoil,	off-site: sand encroachment	chemical: reduced organic matter	vegetation: quality decline	management: area closure, controlled grazing	structural: millet stalk palisades, check dams (opt.)	vegetative: regenerated and seeded vegetative cover

Technical function/impact
main:
- re-establish ground cover
- stabilise sand dune surface (control detachment of particles by wind)
- reduction in wind speed
- sediment harvesting

secondary: - increase in organic matter content

Environment

Natural environment

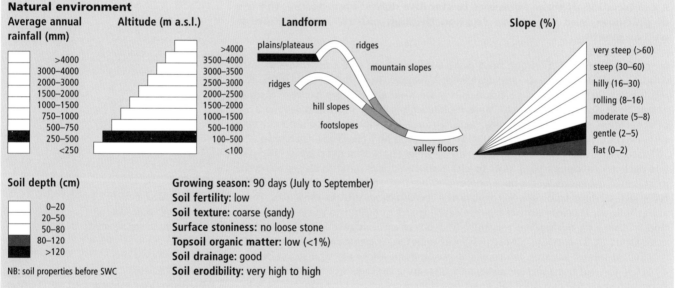

Average annual rainfall (mm)
- >4000
- 3000–4000
- 2000–3000
- 1500–2000
- 1000–1500
- 750–1000
- 500–750
- 250–500
- <250

Altitude (m a.s.l.)
- >4000
- 3500–4000
- 3000–3500
- 2500–3000
- 2000–2500
- 1500–2000
- 1000–1500
- 500–1000
- 100–500
- <100

Landform: plains/plateaus, ridges, mountain slopes, ridges, hill slopes, footslopes, valley floors

Slope (%)
- very steep (>60)
- steep (30–60)
- hilly (16–30)
- rolling (8–16)
- moderate (5–8)
- gentle (2–5)
- flat (0–2)

Soil depth (cm)
- 0–20
- 20–50
- 50–80
- 80–120
- >120

NB: soil properties before SWC

Growing season: 90 days (July to September)
Soil fertility: low
Soil texture: coarse (sandy)
Surface stoniness: no loose stone
Topsoil organic matter: low (<1%)
Soil drainage: good
Soil erodibility: very high to high

Human environment

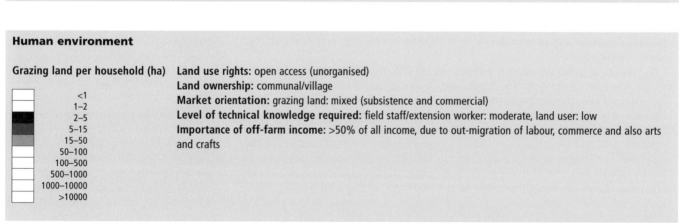

Grazing land per household (ha)
- <1
- 1–2
- 2–5
- 5–15
- 15–50
- 50–100
- 100–500
- 500–1000
- 1000–10000
- >10000

Land use rights: open access (unorganised)
Land ownership: communal/village
Market orientation: grazing land: mixed (subsistence and commercial)
Level of technical knowledge required: field staff/extension worker: moderate, land user: low
Importance of off-farm income: >50% of all income, due to out-migration of labour, commerce and also arts and crafts

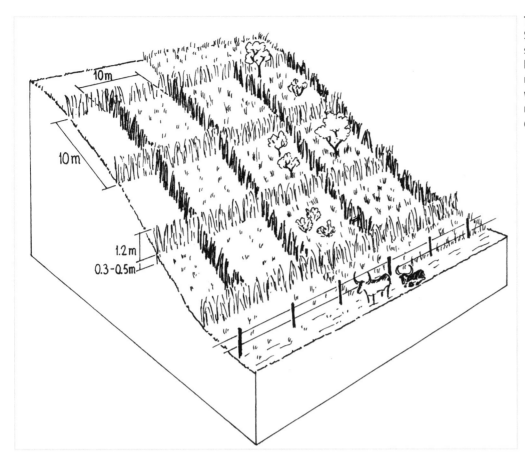

Technical drawing
Sand dunes in the process of stabilisation: millet stalk palisades hinder detachment and displacement of sand particles through wind, and help vegetative cover to re-establish. Fences exclude animals during the restoration process.

Implementation activities, inputs and costs

Establishment activities

1. Construction of wire fence around the dune (December to June).
2. Harvesting of millet stalks (October to February), 2,000 bundles/ha (1 bundle = 6–10 kg).
3. Palisade construction (December to June), 2000 m/ha.
4. Seeding of herbaceous plants (May, just before rainy season).
5. Transplanting of locally available trees reared in a tree nursery (June to July, early rainy season). Compost was mixed with soil for the planting bags. No fertilizers or biocides were used.
6. Guarding the fenced area (all year around).

Duration of establishment: 2–3 years (site specific)

Establishment inputs and costs per ha

Inputs	Costs (US$)	% met by land user
Labour (200 person days)	300	100%
Equipment		
- Tools (hoe, donkey cart, machete)	10	0%
Materials		
- Wire fence	1,120	0%
- Millet stalks	0	
Agricultural		
- Herbaceous seeds (harvested by population)	0	
- Tree seedlings (300)	20	0%
- Compost/manure (farm yard manure)	0	
TOTAL	**1,450**	**20%**

Maintenance/recurrent activities

1. Guarding the area closure (all year around).
2. Replanting of dead tree/shrub seedlings (June to July, 20% replanting).
3. Controlled grazing once the dune has been stabilised: for periods of between 1 day and a week every 2 to 3 weeks – as determined by site and rainfall.

Maintenance/recurrent inputs and costs per ha per year

Inputs	Costs (US$)	% met by land user
Labour (30 person days)	45	100%
Equipment		
- Tools	0	
Agricultural		
- Seedlings (60 plants)	5	0%
- Compost/manure (farm yard manure)	0	
TOTAL	**50**	**90%**

Remarks: Labour (per ha, for establishment) includes installing wire fence (16 person days), collecting and transporting millet stalks and installing palisades (175 person days), sowing of herbaceous plants (2 person days), planting tree/shrub species (6 person days). Seedlings: under PDRT the tree nursery was financed by the project and the plants delivered to the 'village' – planting was done by the local population.

Assessment

Acceptance/adoption
All the families that accepted the technology did so with incentives: the whole village was involved. There is no spontaneous adoption as the technology is too expensive, labour intensive, and implemented on communal land.

Benefits/costs according to land user	Benefits compared with costs	short-term:	long-term:
	establishment	very negative	negative
	maintenance/recurrent	negative	negative

Remark: off-site benefits are difficult to assess and do not necessarily accrue to the local land users

Impacts of the technology

Production and socio-economic benefits
+ +   fodder production/quality increase
+   wood production increase

Production and socio-economic disadvantages
– – –   cost
– –   increased labour constraints
– –   increased input constraints (millet stalks are taken from the fields where they have a function as mulch and fodder)
–   temporary loss of land, reduced access to pastures

Socio-cultural benefits
+ + +   improved knowledge SWC/erosion
+ +   community institution strengthening

Socio-cultural disadvantages
– – –   requires concerted action from all land users during, but even more after, rehabilitation
–   socio-cultural conflicts between agriculturalists and pastoralists

Ecological benefits
+ + +   soil cover improvement
+ + +   soil loss reduction
+ + +   reduction of wind velocity
+ +   biodiversity enhancement
+   increase in soil moisture
+   increase in soil fertility

Ecological disadvantages
–   soil erosion increase (locally)

Off-site benefits
+ + +   reduction in transported sediments
+ + +   land or village protected from sand encroachment

Off-site disadvantages
none

Concluding statements

Strengths and → how to sustain/improve
Technically it is feasible to prevent dune encroachment and hence reduce the danger it exerts on arable/pastoral land and villages → Prevent overexploitation, apply SWC measures that are technically and financially feasible (eg use cheaper fencing material or 'social fencing').

Decrease loss of arable/pastoral land → Prevent overexploitation.

Additional income to the land user → Planting multipurpose tree/shrub species on the protected dunes, encourage pasture management systems eg rotational grazing.

Weaknesses and → how to overcome
Soil cover is very sensitive to overexploitation → In order to increase acceptance, involve the whole community in the planning and management processes of the stabilised dune.

Social conflicts between farmers and herders due to area closure → In order to increase acceptance, involve all actors, including pastoralists or their representatives, in the planning and management process of the stabilised dune.

Use materials for the palisades that do not have an alternative use as fodder (as millet stalks do) for example twigs of *Leptadenia pyrotechnica*). Plastic nets exist for making palisades, but these are very expensive. Labour requirements difficult to circumvent.

Area closure to prevent exploitation of stabilised dunes means restricted access to potential grazing areas → Initiate the establishment of sustainable management systems eg communally managed rotational grazing systems.

High costs for fencing → Involved actors can agree upon a local convention that prohibits access during rehabilitation – 'social fencing' – and restricted exploitation after this phase. PDRT started to plant *Euphorbia balsamifera* within the fence with the idea of eventually removing and using it on another site.

Key reference(s): none.
Contact person(s): Charles L Bielders, Dept. of Environ. Sciences and Land Use Planning – Agric. Engineering Unit, The Faculty of Bio-engineering, Agronomy and Environment, Université catholique de Louvain, Croix du Sud 2, boite 2, B-1348 Louvain-la-Neuve, Belgium, bielders@geru.ucl.ac.be ■ Eric Tielkes, Centre for Agriculture in the Tropics and Subtropics, University of Hohenheim (790), 70593 Stuttgart, Germany; tielkes@uni-hohenheim.de; www.troz.de

Forest catchment treatment

India

left: A dam supplying irrigation water to a village, sited within a treated forest catchment. (William Critchley)
right: Enrichment planting of grasses and trees within the degraded forest land: note also contour trenches for infiltration. (Gudrun Schwilch)

Catchment treatment of degraded forest land including social fencing, infiltration trenches and enrichment planting with trees and grasses for production and dam protection.

Forest catchment treatment aims to achieve production and environmental benefits through a combination of structural, vegetative and management measures in badly degraded catchments above villages. These efforts are concentrated in the highly erodible Shiwalik Hills at the foot of the Himalayan range where soil erosion has ravaged the landscape, and the original forest has almost disappeared.

The purpose of forest catchment treatment is first to rehabilitate the forest through protection of the area by 'social fencing' (villagers agreeing amongst themselves to exclude livestock without using physical barriers), then construction of soil conservation measures (staggered contour trenches, check dams, graded stabilisation channels etc; see establishment activities), and 'enrichment planting' of trees and grasses within the existing forest stand to improve composition and cover. These species usually include trees such as *Acacia catechu* and *Dalbergia sissoo,* and fodder grasses – as well as *bhabbar* grass *(Eulaliopsis binata),* which is used for rope making. The combined measures are aimed at re-establishing the forest canopy, understorey and floor, thereby restoring the forest ecosystem together with its functions and services. Biodiversity is simultaneously enhanced.

The second main objective is to provide supplementary irrigation water to the village below through construction of one, or more, earth dams. The village community – organised into a Hill Resource Management Society – is the source of highly subsidised labour for forest catchment treatment. After catchment protection around the proposed dam site(s), the dam(s) and pipeline(s) are constructed. The dams are generally between 20,000 and 200,000 m³ in capacity, and the pipelines usually one kilometre or less in length.

Apart from irrigation, the villagers benefit from communal use of non-timber forest resources. Forest catchment treatment (associated with the approach termed 'joint forest management' – JFM) has been developed from a pilot initiative in Sukhomajri village in 1976, and has spread very widely throughout India. This description focuses on Ambala and Yamunanagar Districts in Haryana State.

Location: Ambala and Yamunanagar Districts, Haryana State, India
Technology area: 198 km²
SWC measure: structural, management and vegetative
Land use: forest
Climate: subhumid
WOCAT database reference: QT IND14
Related approach: Joint forest management, QA IND14
Compiled by: Chetan Kumar, TERI, Delhi, India
Date: September 2002, updated June 2004

Editors' comments: This integrated catchment treatment associated with 'joint forest management' is a well-known success story, especially in the degraded Shiwalik foothills of the Indian Himalayas. Forest land is rehabilitated and its ecological function restored through a series of conservation measures. It is often associated with dams for downstream irrigation.

Classification

Land use problems
The Shiwalik Hills are extremely prone to both surface erosion and landslides, and general degradation of vegetation due to over-exploitation. Some areas have become completely denuded because of overgrazing and woodcutting. Furthermore there is no, or inadequate, water for irrigation of crops.

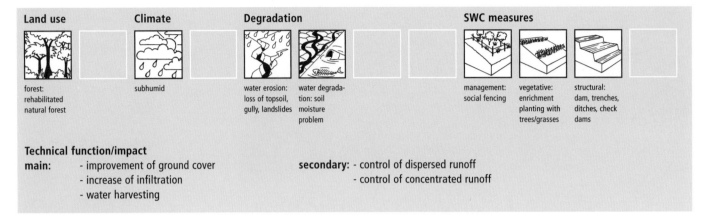

Land use	Climate	Degradation		SWC measures		
forest: rehabilitated natural forest	subhumid	water erosion: loss of topsoil, gully, landslides	water degradation: soil moisture problem	management: social fencing	vegetative: enrichment planting with trees/grasses	structural: dam, trenches, ditches, check dams

Technical function/impact
main:
- improvement of ground cover
- increase of infiltration
- water harvesting

secondary:
- control of dispersed runoff
- control of concentrated runoff

Environment

Natural environment

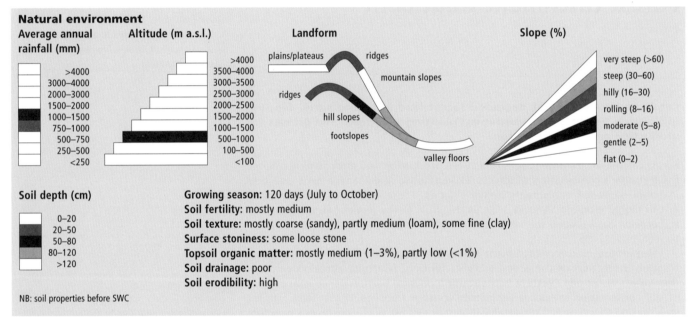

Average annual rainfall (mm)
- >4000
- 3000–4000
- 2000–3000
- 1500–2000
- 1000–1500
- 750–1000
- 500–750
- 250–500
- <250

Altitude (m a.s.l.)
- >4000
- 3500–4000
- 3000–3500
- 2500–3000
- 2000–2500
- 1500–2000
- 1000–1500
- 500–1000
- 100–500
- <100

Landform
- plains/plateaus
- ridges
- mountain slopes
- hill slopes
- footslopes
- valley floors

Slope (%)
- very steep (>60)
- steep (30–60)
- hilly (16–30)
- rolling (8–16)
- moderate (5–8)
- gentle (2–5)
- flat (0–2)

Soil depth (cm)
- 0–20
- 20–50
- 50–80
- 80–120
- >120

Growing season: 120 days (July to October)
Soil fertility: mostly medium
Soil texture: mostly coarse (sandy), partly medium (loam), some fine (clay)
Surface stoniness: some loose stone
Topsoil organic matter: mostly medium (1–3%), partly low (<1%)
Soil drainage: poor
Soil erodibility: high

NB: soil properties before SWC

Human environment

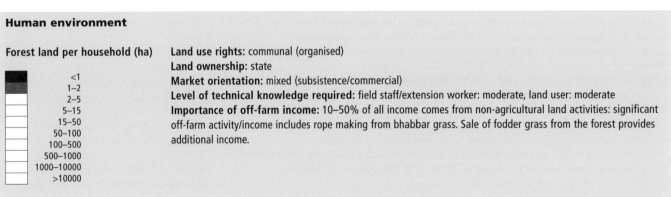

Forest land per household (ha)
- <1
- 1–2
- 2–5
- 5–15
- 15–50
- 50–100
- 100–500
- 500–1000
- 1000–10000
- >10000

Land use rights: communal (organised)
Land ownership: state
Market orientation: mixed (subsistence/commercial)
Level of technical knowledge required: field staff/extension worker: moderate, land user: moderate
Importance of off-farm income: 10–50% of all income comes from non-agricultural land activities: significant off-farm activity/income includes rope making from bhabbar grass. Sale of fodder grass from the forest provides additional income.

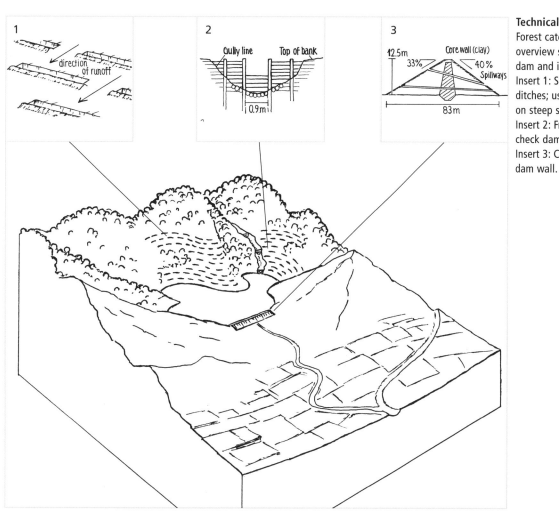

Forest catchment treatment: an overview showing protected forest, dam and irrigated cropland below.
Insert 1: Staggered infiltration ditches; used for erosion control on steep slopes.
Insert 2: Front view of wooden check dam; used for gully control.
Insert 3: Cross-section of earth dam wall.

Implementation activities, inputs and costs

Establishment activities
1. Introduction of social fencing system through Hill Resource Management Societies.
2. Construction of a series of staggered contour trenches on slopes.
3. Construction of stone/earth/wood check dams in gullies.
4. Construction of graded stabilisation channels which capture runoff and discharge it safely.
5. Enrichment planting of tree seedlings (*Acacia catechu*, *Dalbergia sissoo* etc), grasses *(bhabbar* grass: *Eulaliopsis binata)* on bunds of earth and hill slopes, and Ipomea cornea in channels.
6. Construction of earth dam wall for water harvesting and concrete pipelines for irrigation.

All activities are carried out pre-monsoon, in the first six (dry) months of the year – except enrichment planting which takes place at the beginning of the monsoon rains.
Duration of establishment: 2 to 3 years

Establishment inputs and costs per ha

Inputs	Costs (US$)	% met by land user
Labour (125 person days)	250	5%
Machines (bulldozer hours)	75	0%
Materials		
- for dam wall	25	0%
Agricultural		
- Seedlings	50	0%
TOTAL	**400**	**3%**

Maintenance/recurrent activities
Miscellaneous, including:
1. Desilting of water harvesting structures.
2. Repair of channels.
3. Maintenance of structures.

Maintenance/recurrent inputs and costs per ha per year

Inputs	Costs (US$)	% met by land user
Labour (25 person days)	50	95%
TOTAL	**50**	**95%**

Remarks: This information is indicative and is based on calculations derived from Thaska village (Yamunanagar District) where there are 3 dams – collecting the runoff from the total forest catchment of 75 ha. The cost range of treatments per hectare of rehabilitated forest is generally US$ 200–700 (where the main cost is that of the dam construction) and typically the area of supplementary irrigation (command area) is twice as large as the forest catchment treated (in this case the irrigated area is 150 ha).
Cost per unit: the treatment of a 25 ha unit of catchment including construction of a dam costs around US$ 10,000.

Assessment

Acceptance/adoption
- All land users in the 60 villages of the two districts accepted the technology with incentives.
- Incentives comprise an initial government/donor subsidy paying 95% of the labour and supplying machinery (bulldozers), dam wall materials/pipelines and planting materials.
- The spread of such forest treatment within Haryana (and outside) is happening steadily.
- Maintenance of the systems is increasingly left to the people themselves.

Benefits/costs according to land user

Benefits compared with costs	short-term:	long-term:
establishment	very positive	very positive
maintenance/recurrent	very positive	very positive

Impacts of the technology

Production and socio-economic benefits
+ + + fodder production/quality increase
+ + + wood production increase
+ + + farm income increase

Socio-cultural benefits
+ + + community institution strengthening
+ + + improved knowledge SWC/erosion

Ecological benefits
+ + + soil cover improvement
+ + + soil loss reduction
+ + efficiency of excess water drainage
+ + increase in soil moisture
+ + biodiversity enhancement

Other benefits
+ + + increased tree cover
+ + + increased grass
+ + + increased non-timber forest products

Off-site benefits
+ + + crop yield increases (from new irrigation water)
+ + reduced downstream siltation
+ increased stream flow in dry season
+ reduced downstream flooding

Production and socio-economic disadvantages
− increased economic inequity (those with irrigation vs those without)

Socio-cultural disadvantages
− socio-cultural conflicts (see above)

Ecological disadvantages
none

Other disadvantages
none

Off-site disadvantages
− − reduced runoff for filling dam (in some cases)

Concluding statements

Strengths and → how to sustain/improve
Increased surface and groundwater help to fill the dam rather than running off and causing flooding and erosion lower down (but not always: see first off-site disadvantage) → Ensure continuous protection/regular maintenance.

Increased fodder and fuel from the renewed forest resources → Ditto.

Reduction of runoff and erosion in the previously degraded catchment → Ditto.

Improved forest conditions – both canopy and understorey delivering general ecosystem benefits → Ditto.

Increased crop yield from irrigation made possible through irrigation from the dam → Ditto.

Increased household income → Ditto.

Increased community institution strength → Strengthen Hill Resource Management Societies.

Weaknesses and → how to overcome
In some cases reduction in runoff (because of increased vegetation) causes less water for irrigation → Manipulate vegetative cover as required (selective cutting).

Conflicts in water distribution → Conflict resolution may need to be carried out through Hill Resource Management Societies.

High labour input.

Key reference(s): Singh TP and Varalakshmi V (1998) *The Decade and Beyond: Evolving community-state partnership.* TERI, New Delhi ▪ Poffenberger M and McGean B (eds) (1996) *Village Voices, Forest Choices. Joint Forest Management in India.* Oxford University Press, Delhi
Contact person(s): Chetan Kumar, TERI, Habitat Place, Lodhi Road, New Delhi 110 003, India; c.kumar@cgiar.org; www.teriin.org

Joint forest management

India

left: Villagers at Thaska (in Yamunagar District) discuss their plans and problems with staff of TERI. (William Critchley)
right: The chair of the Hill Resource Management Society at Thaska Village, below the village dam. (William Critchley)

Government and NGO supported community protection of forested catchments, through village-based Hill Resource Management Societies.

Joint forest management (JFM) in India emerged in the 1980s from community initiatives in forest protection. At that time, less than half of the official forest land had good tree cover. Forest protection groups took action, based on 'social fencing' of degraded forest land. JFM was adopted by support agencies – NGOs and Government (State Forest Department) – when its full potential was realised. It is an approach that leads to environmental and production benefits through community co-operation in natural resource management. State-supported JFM in Haryana began on a pilot basis in Sukhomajri village in 1976, and has built on the success of that initiative, spreading to a total of nearly 200 km², covering 60 villages in Ambala and Yamunagar Districts. The National Joint Forest Management Resolution of 1990 supported the rights of forest communities country-wide. In the same year, the Haryana State Government signed an agreement with The Energy and Resources Institute (formerly TERI: Tata Energy Research Institute) – underpinned by financial support from the Ford Foundation – to help establish Hill Resource Management Societies (HRMS). These state-sponsored, village level societies are key to the success of JFM, and their links to the State Forest Department are crucial. The founding principles of HRMS include appropriate social composition, accountability and conflict resolution. They are open to all members of the village communities – regardless of gender or caste – who pay membership fees, and are then officially registered. Management committees are elected, and each must include at least two women. The HRMS oversee forest catchment management activities by villagers, arrange distribution of irrigation water (where applicable) and liase with the State Forest Department and TERI. Hill Resource Management Societies derive income from non-timber forest products – particularly from sales of bhabbar grass (used for rope making) – and from water use charges. This income is managed by the HRMS and used for village development and community welfare. The HRMS plan activities together with the State Forest Department. Under the guidance of the HRMS, communities provide labour (for physical works in the catchment etc), which is partly paid, implement social fencing and share the multiple benefits. Where there is a water harvesting dam all members have the right to claim an equal share of the water, irrespective of whether they have land to irrigate or not.

Location: Ambala and Yamunanagar Districts, Haryana State, India
Approach area: 198 km²
Land use: forest
Climate: subhumid
WOCAT database reference: QA IND14
Related technology: Forest catchment treatment, QT IND14
Compiled by: Sumana Datta, TERI, Delhi, India
Date: June 2002, updated June 2004

Editors' comments: Joint forest management (JFM) is one of the new community based participatory approaches to common property resources: up to 14 million hectares in India are cared for in this way. The Shiwalik hills in the northern part of Haryana State are home to some of the most successful JFM experiences in the world.

Problem, objectives and constraints

Problem
- the main basic problem to be confronted was lack of control over the degradation of forest in the Shiwalik Hills which was leading to erosion and siltation of water bodies, and a lack of forest products/grazing
- there was no community organisation established to address these issues on land that was handed over to the village for management by the Forest Department

Objectives
- develop democratic and powerful Hill Resource Management Societies
- protect the forest land, by means of local participatory governance, and thereby improve the flow of forest products
- boost agricultural productivity through irrigation in village fields from dams in the protected catchments

Constraints addressed

Major	Specification	Treatment
Social	Lack of local institution for natural resource management.	Set up Hill Resource Management Societies.
Financial	Inadequate budget from Forest Department for implementation.	Water charges help to provide finance – but the State Government should assist more.
Minor	**Specification**	**Treatment**
Technical	Inadequate appreciation/understanding of integrated soil and water conservation/production approach within Forest Department.	Build awareness in Forest Department.

Participation and decision making

Target groups

Land users: forest dependent families, users of irrigated land

Approach costs met by:

International NGO	50%
State government	25%
Community/local	25%
	100%

Decisions on choice of the technology: Mainly made by SWC specialists with consultation of land users.
Decisions on method of implementing the technology: Mainly made by SWC specialists with consultation of land users in the initial pilot scheme at Sukhomajri, but in other villages, later, land users have taken the lead role with SWC specialists' support.
Approach designed by: National specialists.

Community involvement

Phase	Involvement	Activities
Initiation	interactive	public meetings/Participatory Rural Appraisals
Planning	interactive	Participatory Rural Appraisals/meetings/workshops
Implementation	interactive	taking responsibility for organisation of casual labour
Monitoring/evaluation	interactive	public meetings/interviews/questionnaires
Research	interactive	trials with various varieties of crop seed

Differences in participation between men and women: There were moderate differences due to social and cultural practices. Women are active in only a few Hill Resource Management Societies, but at least two women must be on each management committee.

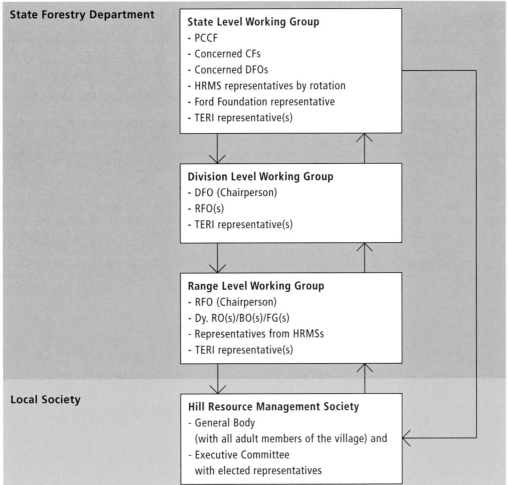

State Forestry Department

State Level Working Group
- PCCF
- Concerned CFs
- Concerned DFOs
- HRMS representatives by rotation
- Ford Foundation representative
- TERI representative(s)

Division Level Working Group
- DFO (Chairperson)
- RFO(s)
- TERI representative(s)

Range Level Working Group
- RFO (Chairperson)
- Dy. RO(s)/BO(s)/FG(s)
- Representatives from HRMSs
- TERI representative(s)

Local Society

Hill Resource Management Society
- General Body
  (with all adult members of the village) and
- Executive Committee
  with elected representatives

PCCF: Principal Chief Conservator of Forests
CF: Conservator of Forests
DFO: Divisional Forest Officer
RFO: Range Forest Officer
HRMS: Hill Resources Management Societies
Dy. RO(s): Deputy Range Officer
Dy. BO(s): Deputy Block Officer
FG(s): Forest Guard

Extension and promotion

Training: Training is given to land users by the Forest Department in conjunction with TERI on water harvesting structures and their maintenance. There are also workshops and meetings to evolve and maintain a water distribution system. Generally training is effective.

Extension: Extension, through the Forest Department's agents, covering forest management and irrigation is given to certain groups amongst the HRMS, but is not yet adequate. More is required from Government.

Research: Research is carried out by TERI, and covers various aspects (including both technical and social issues). Results are published in handbooks as well as having been compiled in 'The Decade and Beyond' (see references).

Importance of land use rights: Ownership rights affected the approach to a great extent and in a positive way: user rights to forest land are made available equally to all, to reduce potential conflict between unequal 'land owners'.

Incentives

Labour: For establishment of dams and infrastructure, labour is rewarded (up to 95%) with cash wages. Over the last few years there have been some contributions from HRMS funds (derived from water user charges etc), which go towards maintenance work.

Inputs: Machinery (bulldozers are used to construct dams etc), hand-tools (various), and some basic community infrastructure (buildings) are financed and provided.

Credit: No credit is provided.

Support to local institutions: The establishment and training of Hill Resource Management Societies is an important part of the approach.

Long-term impact of incentives: The impact is moderately negative: the prevailing culture of wages given for major works like dams makes it unlikely that these would ever be done by voluntary labour. However some general maintenance tasks are beginning to be carried out by the people themselves.

Monitoring and evaluation

Monitored aspects	Methods and indicators
Bio-physical	ad hoc measurements of change in vegetation
Technical	ad hoc observations of erosion status/siltation of water bodies
Socio-cultural	regular observations and measurements of level of participation
Economic/production	regular observations and measurements of change in income
Area treated	ad hoc observations
No. of land users involved	regular observations and measurements
Management of approach	regular observations

Impacts of the approach

Changes as result of monitoring and evaluation: Internal reviews are carried out every one or two years: there have been several changes proposed and carried out as a result. These changes were in aspects of sharing water irrigation, and in methods of utilising income derived from forest products – especially *bhabbar* grass *(Eulaliopsis binata)*.

Improved soil and water management: There has been a huge improvement in soil and water management – the forest canopy and its understorey have been restored with all associated benefits. Additionally, in fields below the forest area, levelling of land for irrigation reduces its vulnerability to erosion.

Adoption of the approach by other projects/land users: The original experiment in Sukhomajri has been replicated in 60 other villages within Ambala and Yamunagar Districts – and further afield in Haryana and India generally.

Sustainability: Land users can continue to maintain what infrastructure has been put in place (dams, irrigation pipelines etc) but technical guidance is required – and at least some budget from the Forestry Department. In terms of managing the forest resources itself, the existence of the HRMS should ensure that this will continue.

Concluding statements

Strengths and ➜ how to sustain/improve	Weaknesses and ➜ how to overcome
Creation of strong people's self-help institutions – the Hill Resource Management Societies ➜ Create more awareness among women.	Sustainability of SWC is dependent on regular maintenance ➜ Increased budgetary allocation through Forest Department required.
Cost-effective rehabilitation technologies ➜ Build more capacity amongst land users to implement and manage sustainably.	Weak market linkage ➜ Strengthen market linkages for agricultural, livestock and forest products.
Emphasis on training and managerial capacity building ➜ Continue emphasis on/targeting of women.	Moderate participation of women ➜ Build better awareness among women.
Integrated approach of natural resource regeneration ➜ Policy required for encouraging interdepartmental development activities.	Lack of credit for investment in agriculture and business ➜ Popularise micro-credit concept under women's self-help groups.
Equitable access to benefits ➜ New rules and by-laws needed to sustain this.	Lack of opportunity/knowledge for value addition to forest products ➜ Training programmes for micro-enterprise development are needed.
Opportunity to earn more from agriculture through irrigation ➜ Better access to improved seed and technology required.	
Opportunity to earn more from livestock ➜ Better access to market, and thus value addition, needed.	
The creation and efficient operation of Hill Resource Management Societies ➜ Continued outside support for HRMS required.	

Key reference(s): Singh TP and Varalakshmi V (1998) *The decade and beyond: evolving community and state partnership.* The Energy and Resources Institute, Delhi, India

Contact person(s): Sumana Datta, Varghese Paul, TERI, Habitat Place, Lodhi Road, New Delhi 110 003, India; sumana@winrockindia.org, vpaul@teri.res.in; www.teriin.org

Strip mine rehabilitation

South Africa

Rehabilitation of areas degraded by strip mining, through returning stockpiled topsoil and transplanting of indigenous species, to promote revegetation.

In contrast to the land degradation commonly caused when 'strip mining' is carried out, a land rehabilitation technology, which was first developed experimentally, is now routinely applied by mining companies on the west coast of South Africa. Indeed it is now a legal requirement in South Africa for mining companies to rehabilitate mined areas to a condition and productivity equivalent to the pre-mining situation.

The primary purpose of the technology described here is to achieve this result – thus allowing the site to be used again for extensive grazing by sheep and wild animals. Revegetation also reduces wind erosion. The technology further contributes to increasing biodiversity, as particular attention is given to planting a range of locally endemic and other indigenous species.

The sequence of operations is as follows: during strip mining operations the topsoil is pushed to one side by bulldozer, and stockpiled. The substrata is then excavated mechanically, removed by tipper truck, and processed to extract the heavy metals. The tailings (waste materials) are returned by tipper truck to the area from which they were mined, and then levelled by bulldozer. The stockpiled topsoil is returned and spread by bulldozer over the levelled tailings. Indigenous succulents and other plant species are dug out by hand, with a spade, from either the surrounding areas of natural vegetation, or from the piles of topsoil (where plants may have naturally established) and transplanted manually into the newly spread topsoil. The planted areas are protected from wind erosion by erecting fine mesh nylon netting as windbreaks. These are 0.8 metre high and 5 metres apart. The nets are usually installed for a period of up to 2–3 years. Subsequently they are removed, once the vegetation has successfully become re-established, and they may be re-used at the next rehabilitation site. Maintenance activities continue for a few years – until the site is rehabilitated. An individual mine strip is usually about 1 km long and some 100 m wide.

This form of strip mine rehabilitation has been in operation since 1990, and costs on average just over US$ 200 per hectare, with all expenses met by the mining company. This particular approach was developed for the Anglo-American subsidiary – 'Namaqua Sands'. A similar approach was adopted by 'PBGypsum Mines' located further inland, where rehabilitation is also conducted on several hundreds hectares of mined land. Not all mining companies use the same technology, however.

left: Post-rehabilitation phase: between the wind break nets a variety of indigenous succulents and other plants is growing. (Kirsten Mahood)
right: Large-scale strip mine rehabilitation at the establishment stage in 2000: topsoil is returned and spread by bulldozers (top); two years later dense vegetation cover protects the area (bottom). (Kirsten Mahood)

Location: Brand-se-Baai, Western Cape, South Africa
Technology area: <10 km²
SWC measure: vegetative and structural
Land use: mining (before), grazing land (after)
Climate: arid
WOCAT database reference: QT RSA47
Related approach: not documented
Compiled by: Kirsten Mahood, Stellenbosch, South Africa
Date: October 2001, updated June 2004

Editors' comments: In most parts of the world, industrial activities have – historically - resulted in significant land degradation through direct surface disturbance or dumping of waste. This is an example where a technology has been developed for the rehabilitation of areas degraded through mining, and then returned to productivity.

Classification

Land use problems
Land degraded and unproductive due to strip mining activities.

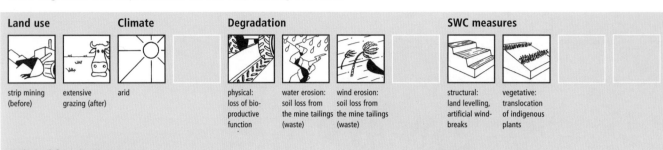

Land use	Climate		Degradation			SWC measures	
strip mining (before)	extensive grazing (after)	arid	physical: loss of bio-productive function	water erosion: soil loss from the mine tailings (waste)	wind erosion: soil loss from the mine tailings (waste)	structural: land levelling, artificial wind-breaks	vegetative: translocation of indigenous plants

Technical function/impact
main:
- restoration of the bio-productive function of the land
- reduction in wind speed
- improved ground cover

secondary:
- increase in organic matter
- increase in soil fertility
- improvement of soil structure
- increased infiltration

Environment

Natural environment

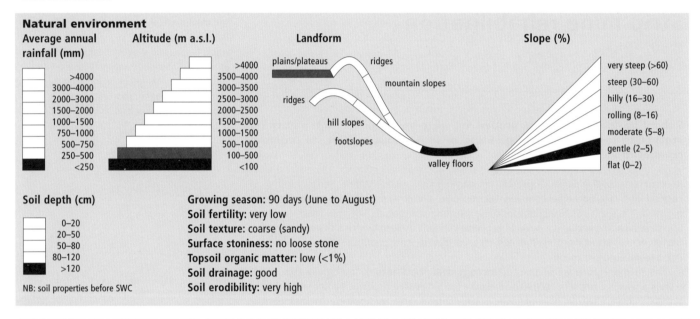

Average annual rainfall (mm)
- >4000
- 3000–4000
- 2000–3000
- 1500–2000
- 1000–1500
- 750–1000
- 500–750
- 250–500
- <250

Altitude (m a.s.l.)
- >4000
- 3500–4000
- 3000–3500
- 2500–3000
- 2000–2500
- 1500–2000
- 1000–1500
- 500–1000
- 100–500
- <100

Landform
- plains/plateaus
- ridges
- ridges
- mountain slopes
- hill slopes
- footslopes
- valley floors

Slope (%)
- very steep (>60)
- steep (30–60)
- hilly (16–30)
- rolling (8–16)
- moderate (5–8)
- gentle (2–5)
- flat (0–2)

Soil depth (cm)
- 0–20
- 20–50
- 50–80
- 80–120
- >120

NB: soil properties before SWC

Growing season: 90 days (June to August)
Soil fertility: very low
Soil texture: coarse (sandy)
Surface stoniness: no loose stone
Topsoil organic matter: low (<1%)
Soil drainage: good
Soil erodibility: very high

Human environment

Grazing land per household (ha)
not applicable

Land use rights: mining concession, after rehabilitation the land rights fall back to the previous owners (herders).
Land ownership: state
Market orientation: commercial mining operation
Level of technical knowledge required: field staff/extension worker: moderate, land user/employee: moderate
Importance of off-farm income: not applicable

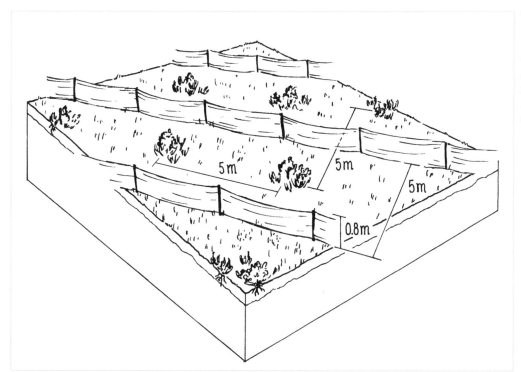

Implementation activities, inputs and costs

Establishment activities

1. Removal and stockpiling of topsoil.
2. Excavation, removal and processing of substrata to extract heavy minerals.
3. Return and levelling of the mine tailings.
4. Return and spreading of topsoil (20–50 cm thick layer, 2000–5000 m³; not massive earth moving).
5. Minimum tillage/land preparation
6. Collecting/digging up of indigenous plants and transplanting into returned topsoil (manually, transport by tractor/trailer).
7. Erection of fine mesh nylon net windbreaks (manually, transport by tractor/trailer).

Activities 1–4 are a continuous process associated with mining activities, using heavy earth moving machinery (bulldozers, front end loaders, tipper trucks). Activities 5 & 6 take place immediately prior to the onset of the rainy season. Activity 7 can take place at any time of the year.
Duration of establishment: 1 year

Establishment inputs and costs per ha

Inputs	Costs (US$)	% met by land user
Labour (6 person days)	75	100%
Equipment		
- Machines (50 hours)	67	100%
Materials		
- Nylon netting	70	100%
Agricultural		
- Seedlings ('wildlings'; 2,000)	0	
TOTAL	**212**	**100%**

Maintenance/recurrent activities

Maintenance activities restricted to:
1. Ensuring the nylon nets remain upright.
2. Supplementary watering during the winter months, when rainfall inadequate, to support plant growth.

Maintenance/recurrent inputs and costs per ha per year

Inputs	Costs (US$)	% met by land user
Labour (3 person days)	37	100%
TOTAL	**37**	**100%**

Remarks: Removal, stockpiling and returning topsoil (as well as processing substrata and returning mine tailings) are part of mining activities and thus not included in the calculation of rehabilitation costs. Rehabilitation costs include only spreading of topsoil, land preparation and collecting/transplanting native vegetation and installing nylon nets. The costs of the nets will be less than the amount quoted if they are re-used. Calculation of costs is difficult since mining companies do not keep separate accounts for rehabilitation work.

Assessment

Acceptance/adoption

It is a legal requirement for companies to rehabilitate areas they mine to a condition and productivity equivalent to pre-mining.

Benefits/costs according to land user	Benefits compared with costs	short-term:	long-term:
	establishment	slightly positive	very positive
	maintenance/recurrent	positive	very positive

Impacts of the technology

Production and socio-economic benefits	Production and socio-economic disadvantages
+ + + fodder production/quality increase	– – extra costs of rehabilitation
+ + + land rehabilitation	
Socio-cultural benefits	**Socio-cultural disadvantages**
+ + + improved knowledge of SWC/erosion	none
Ecological benefits	**Ecological disadvantages**
+ + + reduction of wind velocity	– – incomplete biodiversity restoration on site
+ + + restoration of bio-productive function	
+ + soil cover improvement	
+ + biodiversity enhancement	
Other benefits	**Other disadvantages**
+ + land can be used again for extensive grazing after mining	– – success of transplanting depends on rainfall which is unreliable and low
Off-site benefits	**Off-site disadvantages**
+ + reduced wind transported sediments	none

Concluding statements

Strengths and ➜ how to sustain/improve	Weaknesses and ➜ how to overcome
Low establishment costs and very low maintenance costs ➜ Make use of whatever resources and potentials are naturally available (such as micro-catchments to trap rainwater and improve soil moisture conditions for plants) to lower establishment costs.	Rehabilitation is an extra cost for the mining company ➜ Ensure mining company meets the costs through enforcing legislation.
Costs are met by the mining company – no costs are transferred to those who subsequently use the land for grazing ➜ Regular monitoring of soil and vegetation conditions.	
Land productivity is restored and biodiversity increased ➜ Seeding as well as transplanting.	
Wind erosion minimised.	

Key reference(s): none available

Contact person(s): Andrei Rozanov, University of Stellenbosch, P/Bag XI Matieland, Stellenbosch 7602 Western Cape, Republic of South Africa; dar@sun.ac.za ■ Kirsten Mahood, Principal Technical Officer (Outreach), Centre for Invation Biology, Private Bax X1, Matieland 7602, South Africa; phone: ++27-21-8082833; fax: ++27-21-8082995; cell: ++27-82-7112154; kmahood@sun.ac.za

Annex

Dummy explanation pages of case studies: SWC technologies

QT: refers to Questionnaire on Technologies and its related database

Two photographs are included here to provide – ideally – an overview and detail of the technology: from QT 2.1.3 or from the WOCAT photographic database

Name of Technology (QT 1.2.1)

left: The rehabilitat
with integrated irrig
leads to considerab
in semi-arid Andear
from 8–60%. (DESC
right: Abandoned t
clearly contrast wit
tated. The agrofores
along the terrace walls) is an optional supportive measure. (DESCO)

left: Photo caption and name of photographer(s)

right: Photo caption and name of photographer(s)

Rehabilitation of ancient terraces
Peru – *Andenes / Anchacas / Patapatas*

Country – local name of technology (QT 1.2.2)

Repair of ancient stone wall bench terraces, and of an associated irrigation and drainage system.

A summarised definition of the technology in one sentence: from/based on QT 2.1.1

the Colca valley of Peru dates back to 600 years
been continuously used for crop production, but
y have deteriorated, and the population has lost
ir.
The rehabilitation of the terraces recreates their original structural design.
the various materials – stones, topsoil, subsoil and
ated. The foundation is re-established, followed
ll (the 'riser'). Backfilling with subsoil then takes
finally covered with topsoil. Simultaneously the
rainage systems are reconstructed.
iciently conserve soil and water on steep slopes,
croclimate for crops, reducing loss of stored heat
vement (preventing frosts) and mitigating dry
nservation. The main economic benefits are from
fication.
according to slope, eg on a 50% slope, terraces
er between terrace beds. Stones of ancient terra-
ld walls for boundary marking after privatisation
nt of stone had to be provided by splitting rocks
ations.
steep slopes with loamy-sandy, moderately deep
t of the annual precipitation (ca. 350 mm) falls
ich makes irrigation necessary. The farmers in the
es of arable land, divided into around six plots in
Production is mainly for subsistence.
ogies include agronomic measures such as impro-
, and intercropping. Tree and shrub planting at
ptional measure with the aim of stabilising the

A concise description of the technology, based on QT 2.1.2, standardised by editors, usually including information on:
- the overall purpose
- establishment and maintenance procedures
- natural and human environment including land use, and land degradation problems
- costs (from QT 2.7)
- how long the technology has been practised
- 'supportive technologies/measures' – those that add extra effectiveness or value to the main technology (where relevant; QT 2.8).
This section should give the reader a descriptive overview of the technology, which is then supplemented by data in the rest of the case study.

walls, diversifying production and again ensuring a good microclimate. On average 250 trees/ha are planted; these are mainly native species such as *c'olle*
(*Buddleia spp.*), *mutuy* (*Cassia sp.*), *molle* (*Schinus molle:* the 'pepper tree') and
various fruit trees including *capuli* (*Prunus salicifolia*).

Location: Río Colc
Technology area:
SWC measure: str
Land use: cropland
Climate: semi-arid
WOCAT database
Related approach
rehabilitation, QA F
Compiled by: Aqu
Center for Studies a
Development – DES
Date: July 2002, up

Location: location, district, country: from QT 1.3.1
Technology area: in km² indicating the particular site studied; from QT 1.3.1
SWC measure: agronomic/vegetative/ structural/management or combi- nation: from QT 2.2.2.2
Land use: cropland/grazing land/ forest/woodlands/mixed/other: from QT 2.2.2.1
Climate: humid/subhumid/semi-arid/ arid: from QT 2.5.2
WOCAT database reference: QT code
Related approach: name and code of approach: from QT 1.2.5
Compiled by: for original and up- dated versions (if these differ) name and address of main author QT 1.1
Date: of original data collection and update – month and year

Editors' comment
hillsides date back
culture. Often these
built of stone, and s
for irrigation – as in
many ancient syste
repair with out-mig
this is an example o
tation.

Editors' comments: a short piece of text giving some information on the spread/ importance/ status/ repre- sentativeness of the technology. The idea is to put the technology into global context. This text is added by the editors.

SWC Technology: Rehabilitation of anc

263

Land use problems: This brief description of the major land use problems – without SWC – in the area is derived from the specialists' and the land users opinions combined, both of which questions fall under QT 2.2.1

Classification

Land use problems
- Loss of productive capacity: 3 cutting for fuelwood), overgr
- Inefficient irrigation practice; condition), flood irrigation lea
- Loss of traditional knowledge lack of residue incorporation/(

Land use: Here there is a choice between cropland/ grazing land/ forest or woodland/ mixed and 'other' with various subcategories
Climate: The choice here is between humid/ subhumid/ semi-arid/ arid: taken from QT 2.5.2
Degradation: The types of soil degradation addressed by the technology are given here: water erosion/ wind erosion/ chemical deterioration/ physical deterioration/ water degradation/ vegetation degradation – with further specification where relevant: from QT 2.2.2.4
SWC measures: The relevant SWC category/ies is/are given; the choice is between agronomic/ vegetative/ structural/ management with possible combinations: from QT 2.2.2.2. There should be further specification of measures according to the SWC categorisation system given in Annex T4
Supportive measures **(supp.)** are desirable but not essential measures for the functioning of SWC. Optional measures **(opt.)** indicate additional choices.
For definition of **pictograms** refer to page 359.

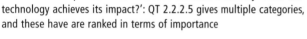

Land use	Climate
annual crops: potatoes, maize, beans, etc (irrigated)	intensive grazing: alfalfa (cut and carry)	semi-arid

Technical function/impact
main: - retain/trap dispersed runoff
- reduction of slope angle

secondary: - improvement of soil structure
- increase in organic matter

main: here the question was 'what are the main means by which the technology achieves its impact?': QT 2.2.2.5 gives multiple categories, and these have are ranked in terms of importance

secondary: from the same question (QT 2.2.2.5); those appearing lower down the rank are listed here

Environment

Natural environment

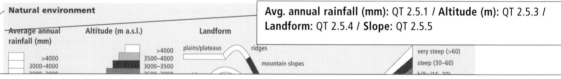

Average annual rainfall (mm) | Altitude (m a.s.l.) | Landform

>4000, 3500–4000, 3000–3500 — plains/plateaus, ridges, mountain slopes — very steep (>60), steep (30–60)

Avg. annual rainfall (mm): QT 2.5.1 / **Altitude (m):** QT 2.5.3 / **Landform:** QT 2.5.4 / **Slope:** QT 2.5.5

Natural environment ranked in the charts below: ■ very important/most common; ■ important; ■ less important. Note that within the technology area there can be a range of environments. In some cases, even where the area is small, the annual rainfall (for example) may be on the boundary between two categories – or not exactly known – thus both categories may be given a rank in that situation.

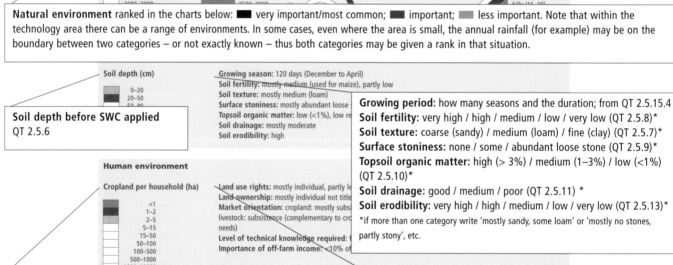

Soil depth (cm): 0–20, 20–50, 50–80

Growing season: 120 days (December to April)
Soil fertility: mostly medium (used for maize), partly low
Soil texture: mostly medium (loam)
Surface stoniness: mostly abundant loose
Topsoil organic matter: low (<1%), low re
Soil drainage: mostly moderate
Soil erodibility: high

Soil depth before SWC applied
QT 2.5.6

Growing period: how many seasons and the duration; from QT 2.5.15.4
Soil fertility: very high / high / medium / low / very low (QT 2.5.8)*
Soil texture: coarse (sandy) / medium (loam) / fine (clay) (QT 2.5.7)*
Surface stoniness: none / some / abundant loose stone (QT 2.5.9)*
Topsoil organic matter: high (> 3%) / medium (1–3%) / low (<1%) (QT 2.5.10)*
Soil drainage: good / medium / poor (QT 2.5.11) *
Soil erodibility: very high / high / medium / low / very low (QT 2.5.13)*
*if more than one category write 'mostly sandy, some loam' or 'mostly no stones, partly stony', etc.

Human environment

Cropland per household (ha): <1, 1–2, 2–5, 5–15, 15–50, 50–100, 100–500, 500–1000

Land use rights: mostly individual, partly title
Land ownership: mostly individual not title
Market orientation: cropland: mostly subsi
livestock: subsistence (complementary to cr needs)
Level of technical knowledge required: f
Importance of off-farm income: <10% of

Cropland (or grazing land, mixed land, forest land) per household*
Table (size of land per household in hectares): ranked ■ (very important/ most common): ■ (important): ■ (less important); dependent on what form of land use where the SWC is implemented: whether QT 2.6.13.6 (cropland);
2.6.14.13 (grazing land);
2.6.15.6 (forest/ woodland)

*Note: title of this box will change depending on land use

Land use rights: open access (unorganised) / communal (organised) / leased / individual; QT 2.6.4
Land ownership: state / company / communal/village / group / individual – not titled / individual – titled; QT 2.6.4
Market orientation: QT 2.6.13.1/ QT 2.6.14.1/ QT 2.6.15.1 (answer chosen from list below depends on land use system) subsistence (self-supply) / mixed / commercial (market)
Level of technical knowledge required: both from QT 2.6.11
field staff / extension worker: low / moderate / high
land user: low / moderate / high
Importance of off-farm income: from QT 2.6.10: <10% / 10–50% / >50% of all income
Comment regarding off-farm income: especially source of that income

352   WOCAT ■ where the land is greener

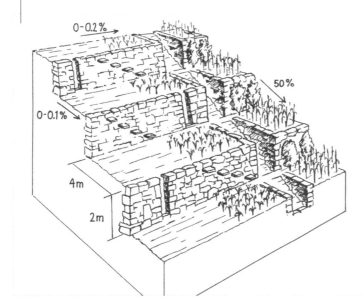

0-0.2%

50%

0-0.1%

4m

2m

Implementation activities, inputs and costs

Establishment activities
1. Separation of materials of collapsed wall: subsoil, topsoil, stone, weeds.
   e foundation according to original

   nd splitting); transporting.
   lding on the basis of remaining
   simultaneous reconstruction
   ntary structures.
   soil and consolidation with motor

   ion of riser edge (lip).
   (optional).
   g, and intercropping (supportive

   or drill, wheelbarrow, shovel, pick,
   pressor.

Establishment inputs and costs per ha

Inputs	Costs (US$)	% met by
Labour (130 person days)		
Equipment		
- Machines (compressor etc: 20 hours)		
- Tools (various: see description)		
Materials		
- Stone (450 m³)		
Agricultural		
- Seedlings (trees)		
Others		
- Construction supervisor (7 days)		
- Transport of inputs		
TOTAL		

Maintenance/recurrent activities
1. Irrigation system cleaning.

   season).
   y (before sowing).

Maintenance/recurrent inputs and costs per ha per year

Inputs	Costs (US$)	% met by
Labour (6 person days)		
Equipment		
- Tools		
TOTAL		

or rehabilitation of 1 ha of ancient terrace system depend on degre
gle (the steeper the more terraces) and availability of stones. In the cas
ehabilitation of 1 ha with 6 terraces, each ca 600 m long, 3–4 m wide a
srepair, 18 men and 7 women work for 5 days; shrub planting is extra
ovide food for the group during work. The programme pays the res
broken parts, the cost includes blasting/splitting rocks and transport t
and agricultural inputs (seeds and manure) are not included. Mainte
ic situation: an average is taken here.

ent terraces, Peru ■ WOCAT 2007
265

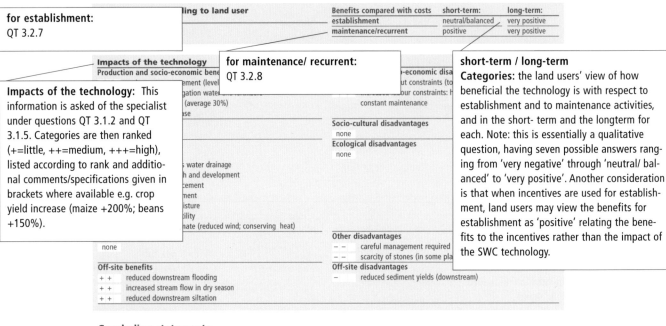

Acceptance / Adoption

The information below relates to the spread of the technology. Within the area covered by the case study (the 'technology area': see box on page one) we are considering only those people who have applied the technology (though often this means all/ nearly all the households). The infomation below refers to how the spread has occured/ is still occuring – with a special focus on the role of incentives. The following details are given:

- % land users / number of families who accepted the technology with incentives; from QT 3.4.1.1
- % land users / number of families who accepted the technology without incentives (spontaneous adoption); from QT 3.4.2.1
- which groups accepted with/ without incentives? What were these incentives and what were their reasons for adoption? From QT 3.4.1.2 and QT 3.4.2.2
- is there a trend towards growing spontaneous adoption? comments here from QT 3.4.2.4

Assessment

Acceptance/adoption
- 90% of the land users (2,160 f
- 10% land users (240 families)
- 40% of terraces have been rel
- The project provided incentive
- There is a moderate trend tov
- 95% of the repaired terraces
  terraces have been damaged

---

for establishment:
QT 3.2.7

...ling to land user

Benefits compared with costs	short-term:	long-term:
establishment	neutral/balanced	very positive
maintenance/recurrent	positive	very positive

Impacts of the technology
Production and socio-economic bene...

Impacts of the technology: This information is asked of the specialist under questions QT 3.1.2 and QT 3.1.5. Categories are then ranked (+=little, ++=medium, +++=high), listed according to rank and additional comments/specifications given in brackets where available e.g. crop yield increase (maize +200%; beans +150%).

for maintenance/ recurrent:
QT 3.2.8

...o-economic disa
...ut constraints (to
...our constraints: h
constant maintenance

Socio-cultural disadvantages
none
Ecological disadvantages
none

short-term / long-term
Categories: the land users' view of how beneficial the technology is with respect to establishment and to maintenance activities, and in the short- term and the longterm for each. Note: this is essentially a qualitative question, having seven possible answers ranging from 'very negative' through 'neutral/ balanced' to 'very positive'. Another consideration is that when incentives are used for establishment, land users may view the benefits for establishment as 'positive' relating the benefits to the incentives rather than the impact of the SWC technology.

...s water drainage
...h and development
...cement
...ment
...isture
...tility
...nate (reduced wind; conserving heat)

Other disadvantages
– – careful management required
– – scarcity of stones (in some pla...

Off-site benefits
+ + reduced downstream flooding
+ + increased stream flow in dry season
+ + reduced downstream siltation

Off-site disadvantages
– reduced sediment yields (downstream)

Concluding statements

Strengths and → how to sustain/improve
...great value and adapted to local conditions→
...al population on maintenance of terraces.
...s product of evaluation, analysis and docu-
Further appraisal of the technology.
...pes, no soil loss due to water erosion →
...d appropriate management through training.
...on/rain water, longer storage of soil moisture
...of the system.
→ Recycling of organic matter.
...nent activities (crop alignment, easier tillage
...of pest control, etc) → Appropriate crop
...mentioned in description).
...tates crop growth and crop diversification →
...ronomic practices and agroforestry.
...ecurity → Conserve crop diversity and genetic
...vation of traditional practices.

Weaknesses and → how to overcome
Specialised work, not easy to carry out – complex system of different structures → Promote applied research and extension.
High rehabilitation costs; increased by loss of traditional forms of recipro-cal work, and a trend towards individualism → Reactivate and strengthen traditional labour systems based on reciprocity and mutual help.
Limited availability of stones impedes the rehabilitation process → Carry stones from adjacent or remote places, give training in rock splitting.
Not appropriate for use of agricultural machines → Awareness creation.
Private properties, but not titled → Promote the legalisation of titles to facilitate the access to credit and technical assistance.
Vulnerability of terraces to damage by grazing animals → Do not allow grazing on short terraces with high stone walls.
Land users are not skilled in repair of broken sections in the terrace system → More training on maintenance and conservation.

Concluding statements
The answers to QT 3.5.1 and 3.5.2 summarise the technology's strong and weak points and how these could be, respectively, sustained/ improved or overcome. The questions were divided into two: the author's opinion and the land user's' viewpoints. The answers (which often coincided and were seldom contradictory) have been combined in this table.

Key reference(s): Mejia Marcacuzco AP (undated) *Folleto de divulgación: Andenes, construcción y mantenimiento* ■ Treacy, JM (undated) *Las Chacras de Coporaque: Andenes y riego en el valle del Colca.* Instituto de Estudios Peruanos. DESCO
Contact person(s): Rodolfo Marquina, Centro de Estudios y Promoción del Desarrollo – DESCO, Calle Málaga Grenet No. 678 Umacollo, Arequipa, Perú; descolca@terra.com.pe; www.desco.org.pe

Key reference(s)
References to literature are specified here: not just taken from the questionnaire annex T1, but in some cases added to by the editors. Many technologies have not been documented before.

Contact person(s)
The name and contacts of the author(s) so that specific interests/ question from readers can be followed up, taken from annex T1.

Dummy explanation pages of case studies: SWC approaches

QA: refers to Questionnaire on Approaches and its related database

Two photographs of approach activities are included here: from QA 1.3.4 or from the WOCAT photographic database

Name of Approach (QA 1.2.1)

Participatory catchment rehabilitation
Peru – *Participación comunitaria para la rehabilitación de cuencas*

Country – local name of approach

left: Initial labour i[...] activities is high. In[...] equipment was par[...] the participation of[...] **right:** Women parti[...] tation of ancient te[...] was involved in pla[...] evaluation of the SWC activities. (DESCO)

left: Photo caption and name of photographer(s)
right: Photo caption and name of photographer(s)

Promoting the rehabilitation of ancient terrace systems based on a systematic watershed management approach.

A summarised definition of the approach in one sentence: from/ based on QA 2.1.1.1

[...]otion of Development – DESCO, a Peruvian NGO,
[...]n Project in 1993 to re-establish ancient terracing
[...]largely been lost. The project is part of a general
[...]mme. Its overall purpose is to restore the produc-
tive capacity of terraced cropland, and to generate better living standards in the
[...] following specific objectives: (1) to increase the
[...]h soil conservation and better use and manage-
[...]; (2) to increase levels of production; (3) to stimu-
[...] and land management; and (4) to encourage/
[...]ns.

This body of text constitutes a concise description of the approach, usually including the overall purpose, specific objectives, methods (including incentives), stages of implementation, role of participants, project description, donors, project dates (where relevant). It is based on the answer to QA 2.1.1.2: 'summary of approach with main characteristics'. The intention is that this section should give the reader a descriptive overview of the approach, which is then supplemented by data in the rest of the case study.

[...]atic watershed management approach was intro-
[...]idered the basic unit for development planning.
[...]eline studies were carried out. A strong communi-
[...]ment committee, was then founded. This consi-
[...]local grassroots organisations (irrigation commit-
[...]rs' club etc). Responsibilities, commitments and
[...]meetings and land user assemblies were the ent-
[...]and execution of project activities. DESCO initia-
[...]nning' in collaboration with other private and
[...]rovince.

[...]comprised: (1) project planning; (2) baseline stu-
[...]t plan; (4) constitution of the executive commit-
tee; (5) concerted planning of district development; and (6) organisation, execution, technical assistance and follow-up activities. Land users were required to participate in training courses and in fieldwork, to provide local materials and their own tools, and to fulfil duties within the organisations. Leaders and directors of grassroots organisations were responsible for planning and organisation of activities – implementation, training and follow-up – and for control and administration of project materials and inputs. The directors were also elected as representatives in the District Development Councils to participate in the evaluation and monitoring activities of the project.

Location: Rio Colc[...]
Approach area: 8,[...]
Land use: cropland[...]
Climate: semi-arid[...]
WOCAT database[...]
Related technolo[...] terraces, QT PER01[...]
Compiled by: Aqui[...] DESCO, Arequipa, P[...]
Date: July 2002, up[...]

Editors' comment[...] used under this terr[...] is a form of a broa[...] approach. This latte[...] in the whole Andea[...] American network [...] has been establishe[...] range of NGO-drive[...] this approach.

Location: location, district, country: from QA 1.3.1
Approach area: in km² indicating the particular site studied; from QA 1.3.1
Land use: same as in related QT
Climate: same as in related QT
WOCAT database reference: QA code
Related technology: name of related technology given in related QT
Compiled by: for original and updated versions (if these differ) name and address of main author
Date: of original data collection and update – month and year

Editors' Comments: here is a short piece of text giving some information on the spread/ importance/ status/ representativeness of the approach. The idea is to put the approach into global context. This text is added by the editors.

SWC Approach: Participatory catchment[...]

267

Problem, objectives and

Problem
- lack of employment opportun
- lack of planning and action i
- little value associated with te
- low and unequal participation
- general impoverishment of land users

Objectives
- to achieve higher levels of agr
  and water resources
- to build capacity for planning

Problem
A list of the main problems addressed by the approach, in order of importance: from QA 2.1.3.1, intended to indicate what gaps the approach was intended to fill, so that the associated technologies could be effectively implemented.

Objectives
Description of the main objectives of the approach: text taken directly or summarised from QA 2.1.4.1

Constraints addressed

Major	Specification	Treatment
Social/cultural/religious	Women were treated unequally in terms of opportunities and salaries.	Equal treatment in salaries and better opportunities were ensured for women.
		...re subsidised.
		...s (CODDIS) were strengthened ...nd concerted action.
		...o promote legalisation of, ...ts organisations (eg Union
		...was given for more profitable ...d peas.
Technical	Local specialists in terrace rehabilitation and for construction supervision were lacking.	Training and competitions were organised to develop skills and select the best.

Constraints addressed
This is a list of the specific constraints 'hindering the implementation of the SWC technology' and an indication of 'the treatment offered by the approach' to overcome these. These are grouped under 'major' and 'minor' categories, such as 'social', 'financial' and 'legal': from QA 2.1.3.3. The intention here was to highlight those problems that arose, especially after the approach was put into practice, and how these were tackled.

Participation and decision making

Target groups

Approach costs met by:

International NGO	
National government	
Community/local	

Approach costs met by
The various donors/ contributors listed in QA 2.3.1.1, based on figures or estimates

Target groups
Meaning those identified to be addressed through the approach – from QA 2.2.1.1.
For definition of **pictograms** refer to page 360.

...nd users; the terraces were
...the process due to lack of
economic resources.

Decisions on method of im
technology is indigenous and ac
technology were carried out.
Approach designed by: Nation

Decisions on choice of the technology: Categories here are specified in QA 2.1.5.1, and comments allowed
Decisions on method of implementing the technology: Categories here are specified in QA 2.1.5.2, and comments allowed
Approach designed by: Taken from QA 2.1.7.1: where the four options of 'national specialists', 'international specialist', 'land users' and 'others' are specified

Community involvement

Phase	Involvement
Initiation	interactive
...f-mobilisatic	
	eractive
	eractive
	ne

...major steps (leaders)
workshops, measurements/observations (directors of baseline organisations/leaders),
reports (directors), interviews (directors/teachers), public meetings (land users)
trial plots

Community involvement
This table below is based on a mix of answers to questions QA 2.2.3.1 and QA 2.2.3.2
phase / Involvement* / activities
* either 'none' 'passive' 'payment/ incentives' 'interactive' or 'self-mobilisation'

...pation between men and women:** There were no differences in terms of salaries, but there were
...unities: in a working group of 20 persons, typically only 5 women were contracted as terrace rehabili-
...rk.

Differences in participation between men and women: Taken from question QA 2.2.3.3 this is a summary of the different roles played by women and men under the approach, with reasons for these differences explained where possible.

268

Here appears an organogram – if available from the answer to QA 2.1.2.6: where this is not the case, for example in an approach which is basically a tradition, a drawing or a photograph is included in its place

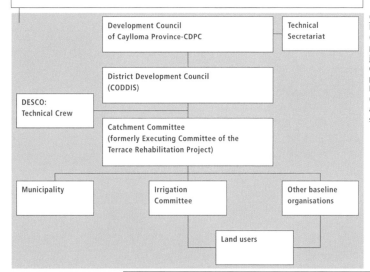

| Development Council of Caylloma Province-CDPC | | Technical Secretariat |

DESCO: Technical Crew

District Development Council (CODDIS)

Catchment Committee (formerly Executing Committee of the Terrace Rehabilitation Project)

Municipality

Irrigation Committee

Other baseline organisations

Land users

Organo... Caption
District [
(CODDIS): social organisations, public and private institutions jointly prepare economic and social development plans in a partici-patory manner, and under the leadership of local government (prioritising development actions according to the needs of different stakeholders).

Extension and promotion

Training: A training plan at ...
users, leaders, supervisors: i...
struction; institution/enterpr...
(2) Directors of grassroots or...
general: treating topics of g...
but complemented by excha...
Extension: Key elements we...
(reflection) and systematisa...
testing of rehabilitated stru...
However PRONAMACHS, a g...
The impact/effectiveness of t...
impact on extension workers...
given as 'poor'.
Research: Technology: rese...
commercialisation: research ...
for the main products of the...
ment and field level.
Importance of land use ri...
their commitment, as the pr...

Extension and promotion
Training: A short piece of text, formulated from the answers to QA 2.4.1.2 and QA 2.4.1.3 (the subjects and form/ method of training) and from QA 3.2.4.1 where the effectiveness of training ('poor', 'fair', 'good' 'excellent') on different specified target groups is rated.
Extension: A similar piece of text here, formulated from QA 2.4.2.1 which asks for the 'name of extension approach' and its 'key elements' and a description of the adequacy of extension services to continue SWC activities in the future (QA 2.4.2.5) supplemented by a rating of effectiveness of extension ('poor', 'fair', 'good' 'excellent') on different target groups with an explanation – from QA 3.2.4.2
Research: Was applied research part of approach? QA 2.4.3.2 asks this basic question and requires an overall rating of 'not', 'low', 'moderate' or 'great'. It further asks for a list of topics researched. The text here goes on to describe and explain impact of the applied research on the effectiveness of the approach – taken from QA 3.2.4.3
Importance of land use rights: Did ownership rights affect (help/hinder) the implementation of SWC (QA 3.2.5.1)

Incentives

Labour: 60% of the labour costs were met by the project.
Inputs: Hand tools and equipment (A-frames, tape measures, motor drills, wheelbarrows, shovels, picks, steel bars, sledge-hammers, hoes, and compres... ...
ponent on terraces were pr...
Fertilizers, biocides and seed...
Credit: Credit was provided...
with a lower interest rate th...
finances in the rural sector.
Support to local instituti...
financial inputs). But with t...
Long-term impact of ince...
rehabilitated terraces (which...
of awareness, or lack of ong...

SWC Approach: Participatory catch...

Incentives
Labour: This section answers the question of whether labour for implementation was voluntary, or rewarded with incentives. If it was rewarded, specifications of those incentives for land user's labour input are given. It is taken from QA 2.5.1.1
Inputs: Under this heading there is the answer to QA 2.5.1.2 which seeks to find out whether inputs were provided, and if so, what inputs and whether financed. And if financed, under what conditions and what terms?
Credit: The answer to QA 2.5.2.1 forms the basis for this information: whether credit was provided for activities under the approach, and if so whether the interest rate was equal to, or lower than, the commercial market rate.
Support to local institutions: Here is a sentence or two, taken from the answer from QA 2.5.1.3 which asks whether local institutions were specifically supported under the approach, to what extent and in what way. Naturally some projects or programmes focus strongly on institution-building, other not so.
Long-term impact of incentives: QA 3.2.6.3 asks the question of whether incentives – if used under the approach – were likely to have (or have had already) a long-term impact, whether negative or positive. The answer should be graded 'none', 'low', 'moderate' or 'great' and an expla-nation given.

Monitoring and Evaluation
Monitored aspects: Taken from QA 3.1.1.1 with aspects that had been monitored under the approach, including methods and indicators.

Monitoring and evaluation

Monitored aspects	Methods and indicators
Technical	regular measurements of improved structures, results of technology tests
Socio-cultural	ad hoc observations of land users changing attitudes of SWC
Economic/production	ad hoc measurements of crop production increase
Area treated	regular measurement of rehabilitated area
No. of land users involved	regular measurement of number of households that benefited directly
Management of approach	ad

Impacts of the approach

Changes as result of monitor concerted planning through the
Improved soil and water man the area cultivable; reduction o various other SWC benefits.
Adoption of the approach by ject of the *Banco de Vivienda* PR
Sustainability: Land users can c new forms of local organisation tenance of the structures can be

Concluding statements

Impact of the approach
Changes as result of monitoring and evaluation: Any changes – to the approach or to the associated technology – should be described here, and a basic grading of whether these changes (if any) were 'few' 'several' or 'many'. Taken from the answer to QA 3.1.3.1.
Improved soil and water management: A very brief assessment and grading of what improvements to SWC, if any, were adopted by land users as a result of the approach. Taken from QA 3.2.1.1.
Adoption of the approach by other projects/land users: Taken from question QA 3.2.3.3: whether the approach had spread to other projects or been institutionalised.
Sustainability: A basic question is whether the land users can continue to implement / maintain SWC technologies without continued support (QA 3.3.1.1). This is especially relevant where the approach is associated with a project, and most particularly where incentives have been provided.

Strengths and → how to sustain/improve	Weaknesses and → how to overcome
An effective systematic watershed management approach applied at ... ojects/institutions should apply this approach. ... integrated in the plans of 'concerted ... ing of the Local Development Councils	Changes in leadership interrupt planned processes (of activities) → Permanent training to encourage leadership qualities.
	Small holdings and land fragmentation are constraints for cost-effective agriculture → Accelerate the process of land consolidation and entitlement.
) specialists trained in rehabilitation ... tunities to ensure continuation of their work. ... nged attitudes towards SWC, and are ... terrace rehabilitation → Promote SWC ... ities.	The economic incentives provided by the project affected the existing reciprocal relationships (eg labour exchange) → Cash for work incentives are sometimes useful to overcome labour constraints due to depopulation.
raditions: rituals of offerings to the earth, ... ms of mutual help in labour *(ayñi, minka)* and ... s *(treque)* → Create spaces and mechanisms ... nt cultural rituals/customs.	The generation of income encourages the purchase of industrialised products → More training regarding consumption of local products.
g: strengthening of organisations; increased ... e training of leaders.	The approach requires the participation of all social and political stakeholders – which is practically impossible → Strengthen the Local Development Councils (CODDIS).
n practices have been integrated into the ... y, improved fallow, etc → Training of land users in the advantages and disadvantages of these practices.	Labour overload in the family → Better planning of work at the household level.
	Lack of a crop and irrigation plan for better water management → Elaboration and application of a plan.

Concluding statements
The answers to QA 3.3.2.1 and QA 3.3.3.1 summarise the approach's strong and weak points and how these could be sustained/improved or overcome. The questions were divided into two: the author's opinion and the land users' viewpoints. The answers (which often coincided and were seldom contradictory) have been combined in this table.

Key reference(s): none available
Contact person(s): Rodolfo Marquina, Centro de Estudios y Promoción del Desarrollo – DESCO, Calle Málaga Grenet No. 678 Umacollo, Arequipa, Perú; descolca@terra.com.pe; www.desco.org.pe

Key reference(s)
References to literature are specified here: not just taken from the questionnaire annex A1, but in some cases added to by the editors. Many approaches have not been documented before.

Contact person(s)
The name and contacts of the author(s) so that specific interests/ question from readers can be followed up, taken from annex A1.

Pictograms SWC technology

Land use types

 Annual cropping: land under temporary/ annual crops usually harvested within one, maximally within two years (eg maize, rice, wheat, vegetables)

 Perennial (non-woody) cropping: land under permanent (not woody) crops that may be harvested after 2 or more years, or only part of the plants are harvested (eg sugar cane, banana, sisal, pineapple)

 Tree and shrub cropping: permanent woody plants with crops harvested more than once after planting and usually lasting for more than 5 years (eg coffee, tea, grapevines, oil palm, cacao, coconut, fodder trees, fruit trees)

 Extensive grazing land: grazing on natural or semi-natural grasslands, grasslands with trees/ shrubs (savannah vegetation) or open woodlands for livestock and wildlife

 Intensive grazing land: grass production on improved or planted pastures, including cutting for fodder materials (for livestock production)

 Natural forests: forests composed of indigenous trees, not planted by man

 Plantations, afforestations: forest stands established by planting or/and seeding in the process of afforestation or reforestation

 Agroforestry: crops and trees (mixed)

 Agropastoral: cropland and grazing land (mixed)

 Agrosilvopastoral: cropland, grazing land and forest (mixed)

 Silvopastoral: forest and grazing land (mixed)

 Mines and extractive industries

 Settlements, infrastructure networks: roads, railways, pipe lines, power lines

 Wastelands, deserts, glaciers, swamps, etc

Climate

 Arid: length of growing period (LGP) 0–74 days

 Semi-arid: LGP 75–179 days

 Subhumid: LGP 180–269 days

  Humid: LGP >270 days

The length of growing period (LGP) is defined as the period when precipitation exceeds 50% of the potential evapotranspiration and the temperature is higher than 6.5° C.

Degradation

 Water erosion: loss of topsoil by water; gully erosion; mass movements; riverbank erosion / coastal erosion; offsite effects: deposition of sediments, downstream flooding, siltation of reservoirs and waterways, etc

 Wind erosion: loss of topsoil by wind; deflation and deposition; offsite effects of wind erosion: Covering of the terrain with windborne sand particles from distant sources ('overblowing')

 Chemical deterioration: fertility decline and reduced organic matter content; acidification; lowering of the soil pH; soil pollution; salinisation/alkalinisation

 Physical deterioration: soil compaction; sealing and crusting; waterlogging; subsidence of organic soils; loss of bio-productive function due to other activities (eg construction, mining)

 Water degradation: aridification/soil moisture problem; water quality decline (pollution of water bodies by chemicals and eroded sediments); water quantity decline (groundwater, surface water).

 Vegetation degradation: reduction of vegetation cover; quality and species composition decline; quantity decline (loss of vegetative production)

Pictograms SWC technology continued

Pictograms SWC approach

SWC measures

 Agronomic measures: measures that improve soil cover (eg green cover, mulch); measures that enhance organic matter/ soil fertility (eg manuring); soil surface treatment (eg conservation tillage); subsurface treatment (eg deep ripping)

 Vegetative measures: plantation/reseeding of tree and shrub species (eg live fences; tree rows), grasses and perennial herbaceous plants (eg grass strips)

 Structural measures: terraces (bench, forward/ backward sloping); bunds, banks (level, graded); dams, pans; ditches (level, graded); walls, barriers, palisades

 Management measures: change of land use type (eg area enclosure); change of management/intensity level: (eg from grazing to cut-and-carry); major change in timing of activities; control/ change of species composition

Targed groups

 Land users

 SWC specialists/extensionists

 Planners

 Teachers/students

 Politicians/decision makers

WOCAT ■ where the land is greener

WOCAT categorisation system

A hierarchical system is proposed to categorise SWC technologies. The hierarchical system combines 3 basic sets of information: first, on the land use where the technology is applied, secondly on the degradation type addressed and thirdly on the conservation measure. Each of these sets is subdivided into additional hierarchical levels. Each item on each hierarchical level has a predefined abbreviation. The combination of these letters makes up the code that fully describes a SWC technology, eg CaWtS1 for annual crops on bench terraces addressing loss of topsoil. See also www.wocat.net.

a) Land use
C: Cropland
- Ca: annual cropping
- Cp: perennial cropping
- Ct: tree and shrub cropping

G: Grazing land
- Ge: extensive grazing
- Gi: intensive grazing

F: Forest/woodland
- Fn: natural
- Fp: plantations, afforestation
- Fo: other (eg selective cutting of natural forests and incorporating planted species)

M: Mixed land
- Mf: agroforestry (cropland and forest)
- Mp: agro-pastoral (cropland and grazing land)
- Ma: agro-silvopastoral (cropland, grazing land and forest)
- Ms: silvo-pastoral (forest and grazing land)
- Mo: other

O: Other land
- Oi: mines and extractive industries
- Os: settlements, roads, infrastructure network
- Oo: others (wastelands, deserts, glaciers)

b) Degradation type addressed
W: Water erosion
- Wt: loss of topsoil (surface erosion)
- Wg: gullying (gully erosion)
- Wm: mass movement
- Wr: riverbank erosion
- Wc: coastal erosion
- Wo: off-site degradation (deposition of sediments, downstream flooding, siltation of reservoirs and waterways, and pollution of water bodies with eroded sediments)

E: Wind erosion
- Et: loss of topsoil (surface erosion)
- Ed: deflation and deposition
- Eo: off-site effects (covering of the terrain with windborne sand particles from distant sources ('overblowing'))

C: Chemical deterioration
- Cn: fertility decline and reduced organic matter content (not caused by erosion, eg leaching, fertility mining)
- Ca: acidification (lowering of the soil pH)
- Cp: soil pollution (contamination of the soil with toxic materials)
- Cs: salinisation/alkalinisation (a net increase of the salt content of the (top)soil leading to productivity decline)

P: Physical deterioration
- Pc: compaction (deterioration of soil structure by trampling or the weight and/or frequent use of machinery)
- Pk: sealing and crusting (clogging of pores with fine soil material and development of a thin impervious layer on the soil surface obstructing the infiltration of rainwater)
- Pw: waterlogging (effects of human induced hydromorphism)
- Ps: subsidence of organic soils, settling of soil
- Pu: loss of bio-productive function due to other activities (eg construction, mining)

V: Vegetation degradation
- Vr: reduction of vegetation cover
- Vs: quality and species composition decline
- Vq: quantity decline (loss of vegetative production)

H: Water degradation
- Ha: aridification/soil moisture problem
- Hp: water quality decline (pollution)
- Hq: water quantity decline (groundwater, surface water)

The degradation type that is mainly addressed by the SWC measure must be indicated under this system. In the case of several degradation types being more or less equally addressed by the same technology, this should be indicated as a combination of (two or more) categories eg CaWtV1+ CaCnV1, which means that the vegetative measure V1 (trees and shrubs cover) addresses both sheet erosion (Wt) and fertility decline (Cn). If subcategories are not specified, a '–' should be added instead of a letter.

c) Conservation measure
M: Overall management
- M1: Change of land use type:
  - enclosure/resting
  - protection
  - change from crop to grazing land, from forest to agroforestry, from grazing land to cropland, etc
- M2: Change of management/intensity level:
  - from grazing to cutting (for stall feeding)
  - farm enterprise selection: degree of mechanisation, inputs, commercialisation
  - from mono-cropping to rotational cropping
  - from continuous cropping to managed fallow
  - from 'laissez-faire' (unmanaged) to managed, from random (open access) to controlled access, from herding to fencing
  - adjusting stocking rates
  - staged use to minimise exposure (eg staged excavation)
- M3: Layout according to natural and human environment:
  - exclusion of natural waterways and hazardous areas
  - separation of grazing types
  - distribution of water points, salt-licks, livestock pens, dips (grazing land)
- M4: Major change in timing of activities:
  - land preparation

- planting
- cutting of vegetation
- M5: Control/change of species composition
  (if annually or in a rotational sequence done eg on cropland -> A1)
- reduce invasive species
- selective clearing
- encourage desired species
- controlled burning/residue burning

A: Agronomic/soil management

- A1: Vegetation/soil cover
  - better soil cover by vegetation (selection of species, higher plant density)
  - early planting (cropland)
  - relay cropping
  - mixed cropping/intercropping,
  - contour planting/strip cropping
  - cover cropping
  - retaining more vegetation cover (removing less vegetation cover)
  - mulching (actively adding vegetative/non-vegetative material or leaving it on the surface)
  - temporary trash lines (and in A2 as 'mobile compost strips')
  - others
- A2: Organic matter/soil fertility
  - legume inter-planting (crop and grazing land; induced fertility)
  - green manure (cropland)
  - applying manure/compost/residues (organic fertilizers), including 'mobile compost strips' (trash lines)
  - applying mineral fertilizers (inorganic fertilizers)
  - applying soil conditioners (eg use of lime or gypsum)
  - rotations/fallows (associated with management measures)
  - others
- A3: Soil surface treatment
  - conservation tillage: zero tillage, minimum tillage and other tillage with reduced disturbance of the top soil
  - contour tillage
  - contour ridging (crop and grazing land), done annually or in rotational sequence
  - breaking compacted top soil: ripping, hoeing, ploughing, harrowing
  - pits, redone annually or in rotational sequence
  - others
- A4: Subsurface treatment
  - breaking compacted subsoil (hard pans): deep ripping, 'subsoiling'
  - deep tillage/double digging
  - others

V: Vegetative

- V1: Tree and shrub cover
  - dispersed (in annual crops or grazing land): eg *Faidherbia albida, Grevillea robusta, Sesbania sesban*
  - aligned (in annual crops or grazing land): eg live fences, hedges, barrier hedgerows, alley cropping
    Subcategories:
    - on contour
    - graded
    - along boundary
    - linear

- against wind
- in blocks
  Subcategories:
  - woodlots
  - perennial crops (tea, sugar cane, coffee, bananas)
  - perennial fodder and browse species
    Further subcategories for dispersed, aligned and in blocks:
    - natural reseeding
    - reseeding
    - planting
- V2: Grasses and perennial herbaceous plants
  - dispersed
  - aligned (grass strips)
    Subcategories:
    - on contour
    - graded
    - along boundary
    - linear
    - against wind
  - in blocks
    Further subcategories for dispersed, aligned and in blocks:
    - natural reseeding
    - reseeding
    - planting

S: Structural

Structures constructed with soil or soil enforced with other materials (S1–S7) or entirely from other materials eg stone, wood, cement, others (S8)
- S1: bench terraces (bed <6%):
  - level (incl. rice paddies)
  - forward sloping/outward sloping
  - backward sloping/back-sloping / reverse
- S2: forward sloping terraces (bed >6%)
- S3: bunds/banks
  - level (tied/non-tied)
  - graded (tied/non-tied)
  - semi-circular
  - v-shaped
  - trapezoidal
  - others
- S4: graded ditches/waterways (to drain and convey water)
  - cut-off drains,
  - waterways
- S5: level ditches/pits
  - infiltration, retention
  - sediment/sand traps
- S6: dams/pans: store excessive water
- S7: reshaping surface (reducing slope, etc)/top soil retention (eg in mining storing top soil and re-spreading)
- S8: walls/barriers/palisades (constructed from wood, stone concrete, others, not combined with earth)
- S9: others

Note: Often there are combinations: list them according to priorities: eg Ge/Wt/A3V2

Combinations

The measures described above are often combined where they are complementary and thus enhance each other eg: structural (terrace) with vegetative (grass and trees) with agronomic (ridges). Therefore the measures should be listed according to priorities eg GeWtA3 + GeWtV2 + ...

ACT	African Conservation Tillage Network, Harare, Zimbabwe
ACW	Agroscope Changins-Wädenswil Research Station, Federal Department of Economic Affairs, Switzerland
ADB	Asian Development Bank, Manila, Philippines
ADDAC	Asociación para la Diversificación y Desarrollo Agrícola Comunal, Matagalpa, Nicaragua
AFZ	Association des Femmes Pag-La-Yiri de Zabré, Ouagadougou, Burkina Faso
AGRIDEA	Swiss Association for Agricultural Extension, Lindau, Switzerland
ARET	Allerton Research and Educational Trust, Loddington, Leicestershire, UK
ASC-UPLB	Agricultural Systems Cluster, University of the Philippines, Los Baños, Philippines
ASOCON	Asia Soil Conservation Network, Jakarta, Indonesia
AT&V	Asociación Tierra y Vida (AT&V), Nicaragua
BNU	Beijing Normal University, Department of Resources and Environmental Sciences, Bejing, PR China
BSWM	Bureau of Soils and Water Management, Department of Agriculture, Quezon City, Philippines
CAMP	Central Asia Mountain Programme, Bishkek, Kyrgyzstan
CDE	Centre for Development and Environment, University of Bern, Switzerland
CEAS	Centre Ecologique Albert Schweitzer, Neuchâtel, Switzerland
CETRAD	Centre for Training and Integrated Research in ASAL Development, Nanyuki, Kenya
CHTDB	Chittagong Hill Tracts Development Board, Bangladesh
CIB	Centre of Excellence of Invasion Biology, University of Stellenbosch, Matieland, South Africa
CIS	Centre for International Cooperation, Vrije Universiteit Amsterdam, The Netherlands
CISEC	Centro de Investigaciones y Servicios Comunitarios, Cali, Colombia
CSIRO	Commonwealth Scientific and Industrial Research Organisation, Australia
DANIDA	Danish International Development Assistance, Copenhagen, Denmark
DANWADEP	Danida's Watershed Development Programme, New Delhi, India
DEC	Dept. for Erosion Control, Faculty of Forestry, Belgrade University, Serbia & Montenegro
DED	Deutscher Entwicklungsdienst, Bonn, Germany
DESCO	Centro de Estudios y Promoción del Desarrollo, Lima, Peru
DoA	Department of Agriculture, Pretoria, South Africa
DSCOKTM	Department of Soil Conservation and Watershed Management, District Soil Conservation Office, Kathmandu, Nepal
DSCO	District Soil Conservation Office, Lalitpur, Nepal
FAO	Food and Agriculture Organisation of the United Nations, Rome, Italy
FAO-RAP	FAO Regional Office for Asia and the Pacific - (RAP), Bangkok, Thailand
FAO-SNEA	FAO Sub-Regional Office for North Africa - (SNEA), Tunis, Tunisia
FSWCC	Fujian Soil and Water Conservation Centre, Fuzhou, PR China
GDCRI	Gansu Desert Control Research Institute, PR China
GREAD	Group of Research, Studies and Actions for Development, Niamey, Niger
GTZ-CCD	Deutsche Gesellschaft für Technische Zusammenarbeit - UN Convention to Combat Desertification, Bonn, Germany
IAEA	International Atomic Energy Agency, Joint FAO / IAEA Division, Vienna, Austria
ICARDA	International Centre for Agricultural Research in the Dry Areas, Aleppo, Syria
ICIMOD	International Centre for Integrated Mountain Development, Kathmandu, Nepal
ICRAF	International Centre for Research in Agroforestry, Nairobi, Kenya
ICRAF-Claveria	ICRAF Claveria Research Site, MOSCAT Campus, Claveria, Misamis Oriental, Philippines
ICRISAT	International Crops Research Institute for the Semi-Arid Tropics, Niamey, Niger
IDEI	International Development Enterprises India, New Delhi, India
IFAD-GM	International Fund for Agricultural Development - Global Mechanism, Rome, Italy
IMNU	Inner Mongolia Normal University, College of Geographical Sciences, Inner Mongolia, PR China
INERA	Institut de l'Environnement et de Recherches Agricoles, Ouagadougou, Burkina Faso
InGeo	Institute of Geography, Ministry of Science, Almaty, Kazakhstan
INRA	Institut National de la Recherche Agronomique, Centre Aridoculture, Settat, Morocco
INSAH	Institut du Sahel, Bamako, Mali
IRHA	International Rainwater Harvesting Alliance, Geneva, Switzerland
ISCW/ARC	Institute for Soil, Climate and Water of the Agricultural Research Council, Pretoria, South Africa
ISRIC	World Soil Information, Wageningen, The Netherlands
IWMI	International Water Management Institute, Pretoria, South Africa (Headquarters: Colombo, Sri Lanka)
IWMI-TATA	IMWI-Tata Water Policy Research Program, Gujarat, India
KAU	Kyrgyz Agrarian University, Bishkek, Kyrgyzstan
KVL	The Royal Veterinary and Agricultural University, Denmark
LDD	Land Development Department, Ministry of Agriculture and Cooperatives, Bangkok, Thailand

MADRPM	Ministère de l'Agriculture du Développement Rural et des Pêches Maritime, Morocco
MAAIF	Ministry of Agriculture, Animal Industries and Fisheries, Entebbe, Uganda
MAFS-SCLUPU	Ministry of Agriculture and Food Security, Soil Conservation and Land Use Planning Unit, Dar el Salaam, Tanzania
MAG	Ministerio de Agricultura y Ganadería, Puriscal, Costa Rica
MoA-Ethiopia	Ministry of Agriculture, Addis Abeba, Ethiopia
MoA-Kenya	Ministry of Agriculture, Nairobi, Kenya
NCCR N-S	National Centre of Competence in Research North-South, Bern, Switzerland
NRW	Natural Resources and Water, Queensland Government, Brisbane, Australia
OSS	Observatoire du Sahara et du Sahel, Tunis, Tunisia
PARDYP	People and Resource Dynamics in Mountain Watersheds of the Hindu Kush-Himalayas
PASOLAC	Programa de Agricultura Sostenible en Laderas de América Central, Managua, Nicaragua
PRC-GEF	Gansu Project Management Office, PRC-GEF Partnership on Land Degradation in Dryland Ecosystems, PR China
PROMIC	Programa Manejo Integral de Cuencas, Cochabamba Bolivia
RELMA	Regional Land Management Unit, SIDA, Nairobi, Kenya
SDC	Swiss Agency for Development and Cooperation, Bern, Switzerland
SEARNET	Southern and Eastern Africa Rainwater Network
SOWAP	Soil and Water Protection project and its organisations, Europe
SWCB	Soil & Water Conservation Branch, Ministry of Agriculture, Nairobi, Kenya
SWCMC	Soil and Water Conservation Monitoring Centre, MWR, Beijing, PR China
SYNGENTA	Environmental Safety Assessments and Contracts, Jealott's Hill International Research Centre, Berks, UK
SYNGENTA FOUNDATION	Syngenta Foundation for Sustainable Agriculture, Basel, Switzerland
TERI	The Energy and Resources Institute, New Delhi, India
TROZ	Tropenzentrum – Centre for Agriculture in the Tropics and Subtropics, University of Hohenheim, Stuttgart, Germany
TSSRI	Tajik Soil Science Research Institute, Dushanbe, Tajikistan
TVN	The Vetiver Network, Maryland, USA
UCL	Université Catholique de Louvain, Agricultural Engineering Unit, Soil and Water Conservation, Louvain-la-Neuve, Belgium
UK-SMI	UK Soil Management Initiative, Loddington, Leicester, UK
UNEP	United Nations Environment Programme, Nairobi, Kenya
WASWC	World Association of Soil and Water Conservation, Beijing, PR China
WDCU	Watershed Development Coordination Unit, New Delhi, India
WORLP	Western Orissa Rural Livelihood Project, Bhubaneswar, India

Acronyms

GLASOD	Global Assessment of Soil Degradation
LADA	Land Degradation Assessment in Drylands
M&E	Monitoring and Evaluation
NGO	Non-Governmental Organisation
SLM	Sustainable Land Management
SWC	Soil and Water Conservation
UNCCD	United Nations Convention to Combat Desertification
WOCAT	World Overview of Conservation Approaches and Technologies